"While the phrase, 'integrating faith and learning,' has become the overarching end for many Christian colleges and universities, what does this mean and how is it to be implemented? According to David Dockery, president of Union University and a visionary and thoughtful leader in Christian higher education, a helpful translation is helping students to learn 'to think Christianly.' His introduction in this volume provides an illuminating and edifying framework, which also sets the stage for the 23 essays that follow. These essays provide insightful reflections on the foundational commitments that ought to guide our efforts as well as useful guidance on how these commitments are to be achieved in the disciplines and various practices that constitute our Christian liberal arts universities."

Michael Beaty
Professor of Philosophy, Baylor University

"Time and again, David Dockery assembles a first-rate team of scholars to grapple with the important and timeless issues of biblical integration. Once more he has not disappointed. As the entirety of creation declares God's glory, so does every field of study bear his fingerprints. The centrality of God to all knowledge is why the integration of faith and learning in Christian higher education is so critical. This book calls us back to the Christian intellectual tradition with a firm theological foundation, offering a discipline-by-discipline illumination of all truth as God's truth."

Barry Corey
President, Biola University

"*Faith and Learning* speaks clearly and with great insight to what I believe is the preferred future of Christian higher education. David Dockery and 24 contributing authors have created a road map to a thriving and effective Christian university built on the foundation of our historic Christian intellectual tradition. This seminal book gives both depth and breadth to the idea that a Christian university can be in the future what it was in the past: a confessional community where Christ-centered truth illuminates our scholarship and transforms our character."

Jon Wallace
President, Azusa Pacific University

FAITH AND LEARNING

A HANDBOOK FOR CHRISTIAN HIGHER EDUCATION

DAVID S. DOCKERY

EDITOR

B&H ACADEMIC

NASHVILLE, TENNESSEE

Faith and Learning: A Handbook for Christian Higher Education

ISBN: 978-1-4336-7311-5

Published by B&H Publishing Group
Nashville, Tennessee

Dewey Decimal Classification: 260
Subject Heading: CHURCH AND EDUCATION \ FAITH \ LEARNING AND SCHOLARSHIP

Printed in the United States of America

1 2 3 4 5 6 7 8 9 10 • 17 16 15 14 13 12

SB

Contents

Concluding Applications

Dedicated

to

Bill and Carol Latimer

With deepest admiration and genuine gratitude for their faithful and gracious support for the work of Christian higher education

Contributors

David S. Dockery serves as President and University Professor of Christian Thought at Union University. He is the author or editor of more than 30 books, including *Renewing Minds: Serving Church and Society through Christian Higher Education.*

Gene C. Fant Jr. serves as Vice President for Academic Administration and Dean of the College of Arts and Sciences at Union University. In addition to his work on *God as Author*, Fant is a frequent contributor to the *Chronicle of Higher Education.*

Kenneth Magnuson holds the Ph.D. from Cambridge University. He currently serves as Professor of Christian Ethics at Southern Baptist Theological Seminary.

Harry Lee Poe is the Charles Colson Professor of Faith and Culture at Union University. Poe is the author of numerous articles, chapters, and books, including *The Gospel and Its Meaning.*

Klaus Issler holds degrees in education, theology, and philosophy. He serves as Professor of Christian Education and Theology at Biola University. Among his many publications, Issler is author of *How We Learn: A Christian Teacher's Guide to Educational Psychology* and *Teaching for Reconciliation: Foundations and Practice of Christian Educational Ministry.*

Gregory Alan Thornbury is the coeditor of *Shaping a Christian Worldview* and an editor for the online publication, *Kairos Journal.* Thornbury is Professor of Christian Thought and Dean of the School of Theology and Missions at Union University.

Taylor Worley serves as the Associate Dean of Spiritual Life at Union University, where he also teaches in the School of Theology and Missions. Worley holds the Ph.D. from St. Andrews University.

John T. Netland holds the Ph.D. from UCLA. A respected voice in the field of Christian Higher Education, Netland is Professor of English and Chair of the English Department at Union University.

Scott Huelin holds the Ph.D. from the University of Chicago. Formerly a member of the faculty at Valparaiso University, Huelin currently serves as Director of the Honors Community and Associate Professor of English at Union University.

James A. Patterson, Ph.D., Princeton, serves as Associate Dean of the School of Theology and Missions at Union University, where he also serves as University Professor of Christian Thought and Tradition.

Hunter Baker is the 2010 Novak Award recipient and author of *The End of Secularism.* A frequent contributor to a variety of periodicals, Baker holds the Ph.D. from Baylor University and serves as Associate Dean of the College of Arts and Science and Associate Professor of Political Science at Union University.

Roman R. Williams holds the Ph.D. from Boston University and currently serves as Assistant Professor of Sociology at Union University.

Steve Halla is Associate Professor of Art at Union University. Halla previously served at Southern Baptist Theological Seminary and holds the Ph.D. from the University of Texas system.

Christopher W. Mathews is the Chair of the Department of Music at Union University. He previously taught at Clemson University.

Kevin S. Trowbridge is Lecturer in Public Relations and Student Media Advisor at Lee University. He previously served as Vice President for Communication for the Council for Christian Colleges and Universities.

Mark Bolyard holds the Ph.D. from the University of North Carolina. He currently serves as Chair of the Department of Biology at Union University.

Jimmy H. Davis serves as the Hammons Chair of Pre-medical Studies, and University Professor of Chemistry at Union

University. He is co-author (with Harry Lee Poe) of *Chance or Dance: An Evaluation of Design*.

Jeannette Russ holds the Ph.D. from Vanderbilt University. She currently serves on the faculty in the Department of Engineering at Union University.

E. Blake Watkins holds the Ph.D. from the University of Georgia. Prior to joining the Union University faculty in the School of Pharmacy, he served on the faculty at the University of Mississippi.

Mary Anne Poe is the Director of the Center for Just and Caring Communities and Associate Professor of Social Work at Union University.

Emily Lean holds the Ph.D. from the Walton College of Business at the University of Arkansas. She currently serves as Assistant Professor of Business at Union University.

Thomas Rosebrough holds the Ph.D. from Ohio State University. He currently serves as Executive Dean of the College of Education and Human Studies at Union University.

Ralph Leverett, Ph.D. Vanderbilt University, is Professor of Education at Union University. Rosebrough and Leverett are co-authors of *Transformational Teaching in the Information Age*.

Kimberly C. Thornbury serves as Vice President for Student Life and Dean of Students at Union University. She has contributed to *Shaping a Christian Worldview* and *Christian Leadership Essentials*.

C. Ben Mitchell is the Graves Professor of Moral Philosophy at Union University. A prolific author, Mitchell is the editor of the forthcoming *Dictionary of Christian Bioethics*. He also serves as editor of the *Journal of Ethics and Medicine*. Before coming to Union he taught at Trinity Evangelical Divinity School where he served as Director of the Center for Bioethics and Human Dignity.

PREFACE

Faith and learning, scholarship and piety, Christian tradition and intellectual inquiry, head and hearts: How do we bring these things together in an informative, enriching, and interdependent way? It is to this question that this volume is dedicated. Even as the authors in this book have worked hard to explore this challenge in general, most have wrestled with the particulars of what these issues mean for the various departments and disciplines represented on the campus of a twenty-first-century Christian university.

The authors in this book recognize that the practical outworkings of an educational model, which is informed by the Christian intellectual tradition and which is committed to bringing faith and learning together, may have a different look or methodology in one subject when compared with another. We all agree that our choices are not limited to an unquestioning acceptance of either the Christian tradition on the one hand or open-ended inquiry on the other. We are aware that the unquestioning acceptance of tradition can degenerate into a cold and rigid traditionalism. We are also attuned to the reality that in higher education at-large, free inquiry, unanchored to faith and tradition, often results in unbelieving skepticism, advancing the directionless state that characterizes aspects of twenty-first-century culture. Such an open-ended approach cannot and will not sustain the Christian faith or its truth claims.

Our vision for the Christian university represents something other than this "either/or" option. We believe that the calling of Christian higher education is to reflect the life of Christ and to shine the light of truth. Our distinctive mission must not be forced into inappropriate either/or choices. We have chosen another course: the calling to be "both/and." We reject those who call for us to create false dichotomies or to join together unrelated ideas in an irrationalistic pluralistic fashion. Instead, we offer this volume as a representation of our commitment to the "divine and" grounded in Jesus Christ himself, who is both fully God *and* fully human and who is for us both light *and* life.

This multi-authored volume, which includes the contributions of both entry-level faculty members and seasoned scholars, is designed primarily with Christian college, university, and seminary students in mind. We believe that this resource can also provide insightful and helpful guidance for faculty and staff members, trustees, parents, and pastors. The chapters explore the question of the place of the Christian faith on the university campus, whether in administrative matters, the broader academic world, or in student life. Many of the chapters explore how significant Christian thinkers have addressed the various subjects, and their related issues, throughout the history of the church. The historical, theological, and biblical framework is designed to help students interact with and engage contemporary challenges to the Christian faith in the various fields of study and inquiry.

I want to offer my deep gratitude to the contributors of this volume. I have learned much from each one and trust that our readers will likewise value their contributions. I also wish to offer appreciation to Chris Cowan, Dean Richardson, and Jim Baird at B&H for their oversight of the project. For the dedicated efforts of Melanie Rickman, Cindy Meredith, Mike Garrett, and Hunter Bragg for this book, I am thankful beyond expression. I also want to thank many others who offered encouragement and help along the way. A work of this kind could not have been done without the loving and prayerful support of Lanese, Jon, Sarah, Ben, Julie, Tim, and Andrea. May God's blessings rest upon each one of them. We dedicate the book to the glory of God and pray that it might somehow be used to extend the work of his kingdom.

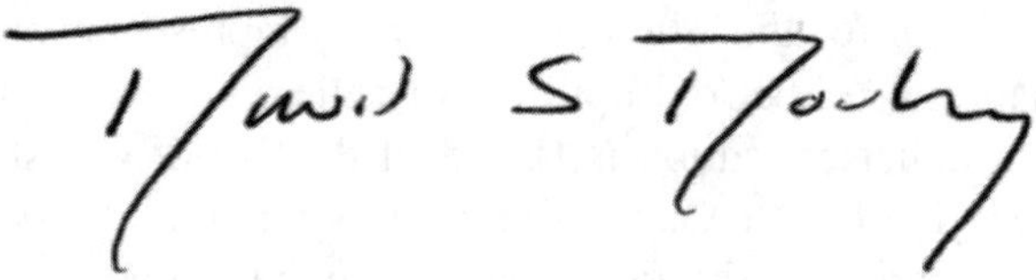

Soli Deo Gloria
David S. Dockery

Foundational Commitments

1

Introduction—Faith and Learning: Foundational Commitments

David S. Dockery

Some seek knowledge for
The sake of knowledge:
That is curiosity;

Others seek knowledge so that
They themselves may be known:
That is vanity;

But there are still others
Who seek knowledge in
Order to serve and edify others:
And that is charity.

These famous words from Bernard of Clairvaux (1090–1153) provide an illuminating framework for Christian educators who desire to bring the Christian faith to bear on the learning process.[1] Students and educators, who are committed to a faith and learning paradigm, seek knowledge in order to serve and edify others, which provides a distinctive way and motivation for thinking about the work of higher education.

Our starting point in thinking about the role of the Christian faith in the work of higher education can be found in the words of Jesus called the Great Commandment (Matt 22:36–40). Here we are told to love God with our hearts, our minds, and our souls—and to love others completely. Jesus' words refer to a whole-hearted devotion to God with every aspect of our being, from whatever angle we choose to consider it—emotionally, volitionally, or cognitively. This kind of love for God will then result in obedience to all He has commanded. These words of Jesus serve as the framework for our initial considerations regarding our calling as Christian educators.

1. Faith and Learning: A Call to Love God with Our Minds

The first and greatest commandment makes plain that we are to love God with our minds. As T. S. Eliot so appropriately expressed:

> Our purpose is not merely "to make men and women pious Christians:
> a system which aimed too rigidly at this end alone would become only obscurantist.
> We must primarily teach people to be able to think in Christian categories."[2]

We want to love God with our hearts. We should love God with our souls. But we must love God with our minds as well. Learning to think Christianly, or, to express it differently, to be a thoughtful Christian, will shape the way we think about schools, businesses, health care agencies, governments, social structures, recreation, and, yes, our homes and churches, too. To love God with our minds means that we think differently about the way we live and love, the way we worship and serve, the way we work to earn our livelihood, the way we learn and teach.

We need more than just new ideas and enhanced programs for our churches and our institutions; we need distinctively Christian thinking, the kind of tough-minded thinking that results in culture-engaging living. To achieve this end, we need to hear afresh the significance of Jesus' words for us. For as Eliot said so fittingly, to love God with our minds suggests the ability "to be able to think in Christian categories." Such thinking means being able to define and hold to a world and life view grounded in the truth of God's revelation to us. It means seeing life and learning from a Christian vantage point; it means thinking with the mind of Christ.

This perspective involves the whole of our human personality. Our mind is to be renewed, our emotions purified, our conscience kept clear, and our will surrendered to God's will. Living out the significance of the Great Commandment entails all that we know of ourselves being committed to all that we know of God.[3]

2. Faith, Learning, and the Unity of Knowledge

Our initial step in thinking about Christian higher education is to meditate on the unity of knowledge as a seamless whole, because all true knowledge flows from the One Creator to His one creation. Thus specific bodies of knowledge relate to each other not just because scholars and students work together in community, not just because interdisciplinary work broadens our knowledge, but because all truth has its source in God, composing a single universe of knowledge.

Consequently, education involves much more than the passing on of content to our students. It also means the shaping of character, and it moves toward the development and construction of a convictional way of seeing the world by which we can see, learn, and interpret life from the vantage point of God's revelation to us. We want to see the development of men and women who are intellectually curious and who are growing in their understanding and appreciation of God, of His creation and grace, and of humanity's place of privilege and responsibility in God's world.

Our minds must be renewed by God's Spirit. We must become persons whose thinking is shaped by God's revelation to us as we think about God and His world. We need to learn to approach subject matter with more than what is often called "neutrality." We need an effective response to secularized thinking, one that questions the Enlightenment ideal of autonomous reason and recalls Augustine's model of faith seeking understanding, recognizing that wherever we may find truth, it is the Lord's, even as we struggle with issues and carry on debate in the pursuit of truth.[4] In doing so, following the admonition of the apostle Paul, we will seek to "take captive every thought to make it obedient to Christ" (2 Cor 10:5 NIV). Such a lofty calling can only take place across our learning communities as our minds are renewed by God's Spirit (Rom 12:2).

A serious commitment to the renewing of minds values exploration and genuine intellectual struggle while wrestling with the great ideas of history and the significant issues of our day. We do so with faith commitments, seeking to discover and expound God's truth wherever it is found. Likewise, we bring to this calling an accompanying humility that acknowledges that God, the source of all truth, knows all things and we do not.

3. Faith, Learning, and the Disciplines

Christians called to the academy are also called to think deeply about the things of God in relation to our disciplines. This task will be intellectually challenging, with great implications for all aspects of life, for we now see the reshaping of geopolitical alignments, the altering of the human genome, and the shaking of capitalist foundations, among numerous other challenges. The work will not be easy, but it certainly will be faithful to the calling upon Christ-followers. We will never be prepared to engage these matters if we adopt the anti-intellectualism sometimes found in the churches. We are to have the mind of Christ, a concept which certainly requires us to think and wrestle with the challenging ideas of history and the issues of our day. To do otherwise would result in another generation of God's people becoming ill equipped for faithful thinking and service in this century. Serious Christian thinking is needed to help interpret an ever-changing culture. This means being able to see life and learning from a Christian vantage point; it means thinking with the mind of Christ.

Christian thinking calls for us to bring the Christian faith to bear upon our study and our research within our various disciplines. Drawing on the long Christian tradition to help us in this task, we can begin to restore coherence to learning. This will help move us toward the development and construction of a convictional approach to education by which we can see, learn, and interpret the world from the perspective of God's revelation to us.

A call to serious Christian thinking simultaneously affirms our love for God and our love for study, the place of devotion and the place of research, the priority of affirming and passing on the great Christian traditions and the significance of honest exploration, reflection, and intellectual inquiry. These matters are in tension, but not in contradiction when they are framed by a faith-informed commitment.

Some of our friends in the academy may regard such a notion as a medieval remnant at best or, in the words of Kris Kristofferson when he sang, "a walking contradiction, partly truth and partly fiction." Yet among an increasingly large number of intellectuals, there has arisen a deep suspicion of today's thoroughly secularized academy, so that there is indeed a renewed appreciation for and openness to what George Marsden calls "the outrageous idea of Christian scholarship."[5] As Mark Schwehn of Valparaiso University has suggested, it is time to acknowledge that the thorough secularization of the academy is at the least unfruitful.[6]

Might we summarize some key points of this intentional Christian thinking in the academy for which we are calling?

- Intentional Christian thinking is derived from the unifying principle that God is Creator and Redeemer.
- It seeks answers through curious exploration and serious wrestling with the fundamental questions of human existence.
- It aspires to be internally consistent and flows from a coherent and comprehensive way of seeing the world.
- It recognizes the need to be aware of contemporary cultural, social, and religious trends.
- Serious Christian thinking lives with the recognition that we will at times reflect an engagement mind-set while at other times we need to take on an antithetical perspective from the avenues of thought pursued by others in the academy. This approach will not entirely please those who see truth as a battle in which it is perfectly clear who stands with the forces of light or darkness. Sometimes the issues with which we wrestle are filled with ambiguities. Even with the help of Scripture and Christian tradition, we recognize that we are finite humans who see as through a glass darkly.
- Ultimately, Christian thinking grows out of a commitment to "sphere-sovereignty," whether in the arts, science, humanities, education, business, healthcare, or social areas.

Thus, prioritizing Christian thinking means subordinating other endeavors to the improvement of the mind in pursuit of truth, taking every thought captive to Jesus Christ. At three places in the book of 2 Corinthians, Paul reminds us that Christians cannot presume that their thinking is Christ-centered. In 2 Cor 3:14 we learn from the example of the Israelites that their minds were hardened. Then in 4:4 Paul says that the unregenerate mind is blinded by the god of this world. In 11:3 the apostle announces that Satan has ensnared the Corinthians' thoughts. So, as we have previously seen, the apostle in 2 Cor 10:5 has called for all of our thinking to be liberated by coming under the lordship of Christ. As in the days of the Corinthian correspondence, our minds and our thinking are likewise ensnared by the many challenges and opposing perspectives in today's academy. Certainly, this is a high calling for us as we seek to live faithfully in the twenty-first century. Not only can we learn from the apostle Paul and Bernard of Clairvaux, but we have much to learn from the entire Christian intellectual tradition.

4. Faith, Learning, and the Influence of the Christian Intellectual Tradition

It is not just the apostles who give us guidance on the subject of Christian thinking, for we also learn from the postapostolic period. We can learn to think deeply about the things of God from those who have gone before us. Justin Martyr and Irenaeus were probably among the first in postapostolic times to articulate the need for faith-informed thinking and scholarship. In Alexandria in the third century, both Clement and Origen instructed their converts not only in doctrine, but in science, literature, and philosophy. Augustine in the fifth century, in *On Christian Doctrine*, penned the thought that every true and good Christian should understand that wherever we may find truth it is the Lord's.

This legacy may be found in almost every culture, for wherever the gospel has been received, the academy and Christian scholarship have generally followed. This legacy can be traced through Bernard, Erasmus, Luther, Calvin, Melanchthon, Pascal, Kepler, Edwards, Washington, Lewis, Sayers, and numerous others.

Within this Christian intellectual tradition we find what Anglican scholar H. E. W. Turner calls "the pattern of Christian truth."[7] Of course some scholars, such as the German scholar Walter Bauer in his work *Orthodoxy and Heresy in Earliest Christianity*, have challenged the continuity of this tradition. Today Bauer's argument is articulated by scholars like Elaine Pagels in the academy and popularized in such works as Dan Brown's *The DaVinci Code*. These modern-day skeptics would seek to drive a wedge between the Jesus of history and the classical theological confession.

Today we would suggest that the pattern of Christian truth, drawn from the teachings of Christ and the apostles, lies at the heart of the Christian intellectual tradition. This pattern is both shaped by and informed by our confession of the Christian faith. Timothy George makes a helpful distinction in noting that when we call for faith to inform and shape our thinking it is *fides quae*, the faith which is believed, more so than *fides qua*, the faith by which we believe. Imbedded in Scripture and made known throughout history is this pattern of the faith once for all delivered to God's people (Jude 3), which provides guidance in our search for understanding. With George, we choose to prioritize pattern over pastiche.[8]

Certainly we all learn apart from the great Christian intellectual tradition, apart from the vantage point of faith. But we cannot connect various aspects of knowledge into a unified whole, we cannot fully understand the grand metanarrative, we cannot truly grasp how to explore and engage the issues in history and science, business and healthcare, apart from an integrated approach to learning. We recognize that it will require hard work to understand what such an affirmation means for all aspects of life.

We gladly acknowledge that there is no corner of the universe to which the Christian faith is indifferent. Echoing Abraham Kuyper, we recognize that not one inch in terms of space, not one second in terms of time, does not belong to Christ, and thus a call to apply the Christian intellectual tradition is a recognition of the fullness of the incarnation and the intemporization of Jesus Christ. It is in this way that the Christian faith has significance for all spheres of life.[9]

We would not want to be interpreted as implying that the intellectual aspect of the faith is all there is to Christianity, no, not at all. Yet those called to serve as Christian educators have been given responsibility on our campuses and as members of the academy at large to think deeply about how the Christian faith influences life and culture, for right thinking lays the foundation for right living.

5. Faith, Learning, and the Place of Theological Commitments

Thinking deeply about the things of God involves theological commitments. Following John Stott, J. I. Packer, Alister McGrath, Thomas Oden, and others, we would suggest that our thinking needs to be framed by confessional essentials related to the trinitarian God. These essentials include the authority of God in and through Scripture, the majesty of Jesus Christ in and through the cross, and the lordship of the Holy Spirit in and through His manifold life-giving ministries. Thus a thoughtful Christian will focus on the trinitarian shape of the Christian faith: (1) in the initiative of the creator God in *revealing* Himself, (2) in the love of

Christ in *redeeming* us from our sins, and (3) in the Holy Spirit in *regenerating* us and facilitating every aspect of thinking and living Christianly.[10]

Theology can render service to thoughtful Christians in many ways. It satisfies the mind so that we can know God, so that we can know the living Christ. Theology is vitally important for both the teaching and culture-engaging task. Theology is necessary as a touchstone for understanding what we believe and for recognizing the principles by which our lives are to be shaped. Such beliefs and practices come from serious theological reflection.

We need to cultivate a holistic orthodoxy, based on a high view of Scripture and congruent with the trinitarian and Christological consensus of the early church. We must ground our efforts not only in the biblical confession that Jesus is Lord, but in the great tradition flowing from the Apostles' Creed to the confessions of Nicea in AD 325 and Chalcedon in AD 451. Likewise, we must claim the best of the Christian confessional heritage as well. Such historic confessions, though neither infallible nor completely sufficient for all contemporary challenges, can provide guidance in seeking to balance the mandates for right Christian thinking, right Christian believing, and right Christian living.

Such historically grounded confessions can also help us think rightly about faith and about how we relate to one another in love, pointing out for us the important differences between primary, secondary, and tertiary issues in Christian theology and practice. For example, a bedrock primary doctrine essential for us to confess is that salvation is by grace alone, but the different Calvinistic or Arminian expressions of that truth are secondary, not primary. Confessing that Christ will return is a primary doctrine, but defining the nature of the millennium is a secondary or probably even a tertiary matter. The great confessional tradition, though not the final authoritative word, can serve as a tremendously helpful resource for us in distinguishing primary issues from second- and third-order doctrines.[11]

All Christians need to grow and mature in thinking deeply about the things of God. Some at this time might be asking, "Does this mean that all involved Christians are to be theologians in the sense of being uniquely summoned to the task of leading in theological thought?" Certainly we would like to encourage all Christ-followers to be theologians, but not necessarily theologians in the technical sense of that term. What is needed today is for believers to think lofty thoughts about God and to live accordingly, that is, to live according to God's way revealed in Holy Scripture. Some theologians suggest that theology essentially is thinking about God. If they are right, and we believe they basically are, then to abdicate the theological domain to specialists alone either because of a lack of interest or because of the technicalities involved is not only harmful to the development of thoughtful Christians, but we believe also that it is displeasing to God. The truth is that every believer is in some sense a theologian, for all believers who know God have the responsibility to see and understand the revelation of God for their foundational beliefs, while integrating these beliefs into their life and work.[12] Theology is certainly not the whole of life; but there must be a place for the true intellectual love of God, for Jesus has told us to love God with our heart, soul, strength, and mind, and also to love our neighbor as ourselves. This should not lead to some cold intellectual approach to the faith unaccompanied by affection. For too many, theology is a kind of intellectual aloofness or uncommitted intellectual curiosity. Theology is more than interpreting God's revelation for me as an individual; theology represents our interpretation of God and His world for the community of faith. It is vitally important that we understand theology not merely in individualistic terms. We need to move toward a corporate and confessional understanding of these ideas.

The responsibility of making theology helpful to and for Christ-followers rests both with professional theologians and with other thinkers across the disciplines as well. Theology must be made understandable to nonprofessional theologians. Too often what theologians write is unintelligible for many outside the discipline. Lest anyone misunderstand, we think that serious theological research and investigation must continue, but that cannot be the end of the theological enterprise.

In the past, theologians of the church wrote so that literate people could understand, and it must be acknowledged that Augustine, Aquinas, Luther, Calvin, and Wesley are often much easier to read and understand than many contemporary theologians. Today we need theologians who can write in ways that are understandable, powerful, and effective. In this vein the Reformers frequently commended the biblical writers for their clarity, simplicity, and brevity, and sought to emulate them in their own writings. If theology is to impact the Church and inform the work of Christian higher education, theologians must learn to communicate in understandable ways.

We must admit that some theologians have unduly complicated the Christian faith or distracted us from aspects of helpful Christian thinking and living. Rightly understood, theology can enable all of us to recover a true understanding of human life, regaining a sense of the greatness of the soul. Theology can help us reclaim the awareness that God is more important than we are, that the future life is more important than this one, and that a right view of God gives genuine significance to life, work, and ministry.[13]

Thus, understanding theology in the context of the great Christian intellectual tradition of the church at large and within the stream of various denominational traditions can provide insight for today and guidance for the future. In this way theology can help us engage the wrong-headed thinking often evident in today's academy. Knowledge of the past keeps us from confusing what is merely a contemporary expression from that which is enduringly relevant. Theology helps present to the church and the academy a valuable accumulation of enduring insights along with numerous lessons and warnings, both positive and negative. Theology that is done with the focus on the church and done for the good of those serving in society will always have one eye on the historical past of the Christian tradition.

Do these theological commitments stifle honest intellectual exploration? We do not think so. Our challenge is to preserve faithfully and pass on the Christian tradition while encouraging honest intellectual inquiry. We believe these two things can coexist, even if in tension, in an enriching dialectical dependence. Guidance and balance in these matters will come as we are faithful in integrating an informed theological foundation with all areas of learning. For Christian thinkers to address these matters we must hear afresh the words of Jesus in the Great Commandment to love God with all that we are (Matt 22:36–40). This kind of love for God will guide us toward a whole-hearted devotion to distinctively Christian thinking. Students and professors will be able to see life from a Christian vantage point, learning to think Christianly about all of life.

What we are calling for is certainly intellectually challenging. It is not the easiest road for us to travel, but it is the one faithful to the best of our Christian heritage, and it provides no room for mere anti-intellectual piety, much less some vague spirituality. We are to have the mind of Christ; this certainly requires us to think and wrestle with the challenging ideas of history and the issues of our day. The loss of theological verve weakens churches, Christian institutions and organizations, and ultimately hampers the *Missio Dei*. Christian thinking is needed to engage the world. Instead of allowing our thoughts to be captive to culture, we must take every thought captive to Jesus Christ. What is needed is a bedrock, nonnegotiable commitment to a belief in a triune God—in one mediator between God and humanity, the man Christ Jesus, who was God incarnate.

This commitment represents a belief in a totally truthful and authoritative Bible and in the message of God's justifying work by grace through faith revealed in its pages. It is rooted in a focus on the Church and lives in hope of the return of Christ, resulting in a commitment to a life of prayer, holiness, obedience, and growth in Christ. These truths are not culturally confined, nor are they easily expunged without great peril. What is needed for this time is an ancient kind of orthodoxy, a primitive but passionate core of theological truths that nurtured persecuted believers in the past and will be the only thing to comfort once the flames of suffering are stoked again. If persecution looms on the horizon, then our orthodox commitments must give us a firm rock on which to stand—commitments that are firm but loving, clear but gracious, ready to respond to issues and challenges that the culture and world present to Christ-followers, but not necessarily responding to every contextual skirmish or intramural squabble.

It is often heard that theology is divisive and thus should be de-emphasized in the context of Christian higher education. We, however, want to affirm that theology is foundational for the development of mature, thoughtful followers of Christ. The apostle Paul says that believers with an immature faith will be "tossed back and forth by the waves, and blown here and there by every wind of teaching" (Eph 4:14 NIV).

Healthy theology that matures the head and heart not only enables believers to move toward maturity, but it results in the worship and exaltation of God, for good theology leads to doxology.

Following his exposition regarding sin, justification, sanctification, and the future of Israel, the apostle Paul concludes this section of the Epistle to the Romans with these words:

> Oh, the depth of the riches of the wisdom and knowledge of God!
> How unsearchable his judgments, and his paths beyond tracing out!
> "Who has known the mind of the Lord?
> Or who has been his counselor?"
> "Who has ever given to God, that God should repay him?"
> For from him and through him and to him are all things.
> To him be the glory forever! Amen. (Rom 11:33–36 NIV)

While it may be true, as previously noted, that the writings of a few Christian thinkers unduly complicate the Christian faith, sound theology lays the foundation for the sound practice of Christian life. Ministry and service based on unsound theology will not only be unhealthy, but could even be dangerous. Worship that does not see God as He has revealed Himself does not rightly glorify God. Theology can enable thoughtful believers to understand better the faith we desire to share in our missional efforts and, moreover, can help lead us to an awareness of the grandeur, greatness, and goodness of the God we worship.

Our primary source for learning to think about God is Holy Scripture. Though we learn much from God's revelation in nature and through our own experience, these matters must be tested by God's Word in Scripture. It is important for us to recognize what others have thought about such things, for in many ways we stand on their shoulders as we seek to communicate the meaning of the Christian faith that has been passed down to us over the past 2,000 years. We believe, therefore, that theological reflection equips and encourages thoughtful believers in their relationship with and service to God.

One might well ask: "How do we know that our theology is true and sound?" This question is an important one in light of the challenges that Christians face at this time, including rampant unbelief, the growth of various cults, the expanding perspectives on religious pluralism, and the rise of secularism.

We would like to suggest that we can do theology with a level of confidence because God has made Himself known to His people (1 Cor 2:10). Humans, who have been created in the image of God, can think God's thoughts after Him and organize these thoughts. Believers can know and experience God because both our hearts and minds have been made new by God's regenerating grace, enabling us to interpret and apply God's self-manifestation of Himself made known in Holy Scripture. This ability to perceive spiritual truth is made possible by the illuminating work of the Holy Spirit (Ps 119:18; 1 Cor 2:14–15).

Thoughtful Christians, informed by Scripture, can recover a true understanding of human life, a sense of the greatness of the soul. It helps us recover the much-needed awareness that God is more important than we are and that the future life takes priority over this one. A right view of God provides significance and security for thoughtful Christ-followers. We thus understand that happiness is the promise of heaven and that holiness is our calling while in this world.

Theologically informed believers will be better able to understand what we believe and why we believe it. We can appreciate our heritage and enliven our future hope. The truth content of the faith can be preserved. It is the express calling of thoughtful believers to seek to understand and expound the whole counsel of God (Acts 20:7).

Without the foundation of solid theology, the church will see a lack of effective long-term preaching, evangelism, or missionary outreach. Thoughtful believers will recognize that a "what you don't know can't hurt you" attitude is anything but helpful, especially if such an approach is taken toward ultimate matters like heaven and hell. On the other hand, sound, reliable theology, based squarely on God's Word, offers reassurance and hope. We need to hear what God has said and rest our case there.[14]

6. Faith and Learning: Engaging the Ideas and Issues of Our Day

A commitment to faith and learning will help us develop a way of seeing and engaging God's world that is joyously able to contemplate a wide range of ideas. This approach to education also holds out hope for restoring the endangered virtues of kindness, humility, love, grace, truth, beauty, goodness, honor, justice, and purity (Phil 2:1–4; 4:8). A Christian way of thinking about life is not just one's personal faith expression, nor is it simply a theory. It is an all-consuming way of life, applicable to all spheres of life.

James Orr, in *The Christian View of God and the World*, maintains that there is a definite Christian view of things that has a character, coherence, and unity of its own, and stands in sharp contrast with counter theories and speculation offered by those opposed to biblical revelation. A Christian worldview has the stamp of reason and reality and can stand the tests of both history and experience. Such a holistic approach offers a stability of thought, a unity of comprehensive insight that bears not only on the religious sphere but on the whole of thought. A Christian worldview is not built on various types of truth (religious and philosophical or scientific), but on a universal principle and all-embracing system that shapes religion, natural and social sciences, law, history, healthcare, the arts, the humanities, and all disciplines of study with application for all of life.[15]

James Orr in 1891 and Abraham Kuyper in 1898 brilliantly articulated the meaning and implications of such a Christian worldview at the turn of the nineteenth century. Over the past 50 years, James Sire, C. S. Lewis, Carl F. H. Henry, J. P. Moreland, William Lane Craig, Arthur Holmes, David Naugle, and Charles Colson, among others, have articulated well the essence of a Christian worldview. Thoughtful Christians in our time must seek to build upon their work to articulate a coherent and purposeful way of seeing the world around us for the twenty-first century—a time of tremendous challenges and changes—and to show how such Christian thinking is applicable across the educational and cocurricular activities on campus.

We recognize that truth, morality, and interpretive frameworks are being ignored, if not rejected in our world. Throughout modern culture, the very existence of normative truth is being challenged. We observe these challenges in the poststructuralism of Jean-Francois Lyotard, the deconstructionism of Jacques Derrida, the radical subjectivism of Michael Foucault, and the reader-focused hermeneutic of Stanley Fish. A normative view of truth has been devalued if not lost in our contemporary culture.

Thoughtful Christians will need to begin to address these things in a fresh way. Such thinking will seek to connect the church's tradition, by framing these things in light of a foundational confession of our belief in God the Father, Maker of heaven and earth (the Apostles' Creed). This confessional framework will help us wrestle with life's big questions:

Where did we come from?
Who are we?
What has gone wrong with the world?
What solution can be offered to deal with these challenges?

In addition, we must seek to answer the key questions of life and their general implications or specific applications such as: Why do we exist? What is the purpose of life? Central to our framework is the good news of the resurrection of Jesus Christ (see 1 Cor 15:3–4). The resurrection establishes Jesus' lordship and deity, as well as guarantees the salvation of sinners (see Rom 1:3–4; 4:24–25). Jesus' resurrection enables believers to see, think, and live anew.

7. Faith and Learning: Influenced by a Confessional Framework

This confessional framework becomes an influencing aspect for our understanding of Christian higher education, giving us a sense of God's plan and purpose for this world, helping to inform and shape our identity as believers. We no longer see ourselves as alienated sinners. This way of thinking is not escapism, but an energizing motivation for godly and faithful living in the here and now. It also gives us confidence and hope for the future. In the midst of life's challenges and struggles, this framework or worldview helps to stabilize life, serving as an anchor to link us to God's faithfulness and steadfastness.

A Christian way of thinking about the world has implications for understanding history. We see that history is not cyclical or random. Rather, we see history as linear, a meaningful sequence of events leading to the fulfillment of God's purposes for humanity (see Ephesians 1). Human history will climax where it began—on the earth. This truth is another distinctive of Christian thinking, for Christianity is historical at its heart. According to its essential teaching, God has acted decisively in history, revealing Himself in specific acts and events. Moreover, God will act to bring history to its providential destiny and planned conclusion.

God who has acted in history in past events will also act in the future to consummate this age. So when we ask, "How will it end?" we do not simply or suddenly pass out of the realm of history into a never-never land. We pass to that which is never-the-less certain of occurring because God is behind it and is Himself the One who tells us it will come to pass.

Developing a worldview is an ever-advancing process for us in which Christian convictions more and more shape our participation in culture. This disciplined, vigorous, and unending process will help shape how we assess culture and our place in it. Otherwise, culture will shape us and our thinking. Thus thoughtful Christians not only have a different way of thinking, but a distinctive way of seeing and doing, based on a new way of being.

A Christian worldview provides a coherent way of seeing life. It is a perspective distinct from such philosophies and approaches as deism, naturalism, and materialism (whether Darwinian, humanist, or Marxist forms), existentialism, polytheism, pantheism, mysticism, or deconstructionist postmodernism. The theistic emphasis of Christianity provides bearings and direction when confronted with New Age spirituality or secularist and pluralist approaches to truth and morality. Fear about the future, suffering, disease, and poverty are informed by a Christian worldview grounded in the redemptive work of Christ and the grandeur of God. As opposed to meaningless and purposeless nihilistic perspectives, a Christian way of thinking offers meaning and purpose for all aspects of life.[16]

8. Faith, Learning, and Character Formation

To the extent we succeed in putting these things into practice and in guiding students in these important matters, we will succeed in the development of the intellectual, moral, and character formation across our campuses. Thus, at the heart of our Christ-centered approach to education is the belief that God has revealed Himself to us in creation, in history, in our conscience, and ultimately in Christ, and that this revelation is now primarily available to us in Holy Scripture. It is here we find the words of Jesus Himself, claiming that He alone is the way to God, claiming that He is not only the way and the life, but He is also the Truth.

This revealed truth is the foundation of all we believe, teach, and do. We believe that this God-revealed truth is the framework in which we understand and interpret our world, the events of human history as well as our responsibilities toward God and one another in this world. This is what it means for us to become thoughtful followers of the Lord Jesus Christ and to love God with our hearts, our strength, and our minds.[17]

9. Faith and Learning: Toward a Model of Christian Thinking for a Post-Christian Context

The essence of the Christian faith is that God is Savior, but we fail to understand the comprehensiveness of the Christian faith unless we also see God as Creator, Sustainer, Ruler, Father, and Judge. These foundational blocks are essential for framing a Christian worldview.

We want our commitments to be informed by the whole of nature and of history, as well as philosophy and literature, those elements that we believe to be at the heart of a liberal arts curriculum. We can emphasize the greatness of God, who is not only the beginning and ending of all things, but the One to whom we ultimately will give account. The apostle Paul claimed that these things are known by and in God's creation (see Acts 17; Romans 1).

Many people today are rejecting the Christian faith not because they perceive it to be false, but because they believe it is superficial or trivial. People are looking for an integrated way of seeing life that brings coherence to all learning and helps make sense of life's experiences—some of which are quite confusing.

In many, many ways, our post-Christian Western culture in general—and American culture in particular—resembles the pre-Christian Athens of Paul's day, particularly in the focus on the new, the novel, and the world of chance as emphasized by the Epicureans. Our culture is similarly enthralled by novelty. C. S. Lewis, in his famous collection of essays, *God in the Dock,* in which he highlights the value of classic works, maintains that we are obsessed with the new and the novel. Truth and values in our culture of novelty seem to be of little concern or consequence. Paul models for us and thereby invites us to integrate Christian truth in culturally relevant ways and to communicate and live this truth in the midst of an incredibly superficial world.[18]

We recognize that piety alone will not sustain the high ideal of the Christian intellectual tradition. Serious engagement with issues will be needed. Thus, our goal as Christians must be to engage the issues of our day in the various areas of learning, while recognizing that God, the source of all truth, is central in every academic discipline and every sphere of life. Bringing the Christian faith to influence our learning is the most distinctive task of Christian thinking—always was, is now, always will be. This ideal involves not only the study itself, but also the motivation for the study. We can see God behind it all and over it all, whether in math, art, science, literature, or other fields of study. Beyond academic disciplines, this practice also influences the way we see life and the way we live. This does not, as some opponents of Christian thinking have argued, transform all learning into religion studies. Rather, as Charles Wesley penned in his hymn, we are uniting "the pair so long disjointed—knowledge and vital piety."

As we move toward the conclusion of this chapter, we offer eight implications for thoughtful Christians, which can be offered based on our previous observations. Piety is essential but not enough by itself to bring about mature thoughtful believers.

- We recognize that the Christian intellectual tradition calls for rigorous Christian thinking in all spheres of education.
- We acknowledge the sovereignty of the triune God over the whole cosmos, and thus sovereign not only over all aspects of theology but over all aspects of the learning enterprise.
- We acknowledge that all truth, both revealed and discovered, has its source in God.
- We believe that the pursuit of truth is best undertaken within a community of learning that also attends to the moral, spiritual, and social development of teachers and learners.
- We acknowledge that the unity of knowledge shaped by love informs and shapes all scholarship, teaching, and learning.
- We recognize that the goal for the development of thoughtful Christians is not merely a deeper sense of piety, as important as that may be. We desire to help people think in Christian categories. What ultimately is needed is both the renewal of the mind and the renewal of the heart.
- We recognize that approaching the learning process from the vantage of faith means more than approaching learning from one's personal experience. Faith includes a full commitment of the whole person to the Lord Jesus, a commitment that involves knowledge, trust, and obedience. Though faith is more than doctrinal assent, it must include

an understanding of the truth content of the Christian faith. Approaching learning from the perspective of faith includes not only the faith by which we trust in Christ, but also the faith that we believe.

- Even as we seek to bring faith to bear upon our learning and to encourage other Christians to think about life in Christian categories, we recognize that we still look through a glass darkly, meaning that we need a sanctified humility about our own beliefs and conclusions and a sanctified tolerance regarding the beliefs and conclusions of other Christ-followers.[19]

10. Faith and Living: Implications for Faithful Living

A person who thinks deeply about the things of God and applies theological reflection to the critical issues of our day will be equipped to live well in relation to others in the world. Thus, this approach to life provides a framework for ethical thinking because humans, who are made in God's image, are essentially moral beings. We also recognize that the fullest embodiment of good, love, holiness, grace, and truth is found in Jesus Christ (see John 1:14–18).

Right thinking is not all there is to the Christian faith; we must also apply the Christian faith, for we are to be "doers of the Word" (James 1:22). We are to love our neighbor and care for orphans and widows. We are to be agents of reconciliation in the church and in society. We are to build bridges where there are walls, particularly with reference to the racial divide that has haunted our country since its inception.

This is what it means to love our neighbor, to be doers of the Word. If we stop and think upon that last phrase, it is shocking. We normally are hearers of the Word, thinkers about the Word. We can spell a word and reflect upon a word, but to do the Word puts a different shape on what it means for us to apply the Christian intellectual tradition to all of life.

Careful Christian thinking therefore also points to ethics. Certainly it is possible to act one way and to think another, but it is not possible for us to do so for long, for even the biblical writer has admonished us, "As [a person] thinks in his heart, so is he" (Prov 23:7 NKJV). Since one of the goals for helping Christ-followers become thoughtful Christians involves helping students live in the world with a lifestyle that issues in glory to God, then we must think—and think deeply—not only of personal ethics, but also of the implications of the biblical faith for social, economic, and political ethics.

We need to seek God's guidance in how we can best contribute to constructive exercises that will help us honor, respect, and love one another. We want to model the love and forgiveness of Christ in the workplace. We desire to be quick to offer forgiveness when we have been wronged. At the same time we want to claim responsibility and seek forgiveness when we have wronged others. We will ask God to help us be agents of reconciliation to a broken and hurting world, which remains in disorder as a result of the fall. We pray that God would give us grace to be agents of redemption in this broken world and to embrace one another regardless of national, ethnic, or racial background. In order to do so, it will be vital for us to understand how to think about and interpret the ideas and issues of our day.

Humility, gentleness, love, and kindness are virtues of thoughtful believers. In our speech we are to use our words for good and positive purposes. We demonstrate thoughtfulness for and consideration to others by speaking what is helpful in building them up. In our actions we are to be kind and loving, reflecting the character of God who has forgiven us in Christ (Eph 4:32). Thoughtful believers reflect the love of Christ, resulting in lives that encourage harmony in relationships and sensitivity to the needs of others.

On this foundational framework can be built authentic Christian educational institutions characterized by love, joy, peace, patience, kindness, goodness, faithfulness, gentleness, and self-control (Gal 5:22–23). To see students at these institutions develop, spiritual formation must be intentional, which includes caring mentors. This noble goal will lead us to meet each student as the person he or she is in Christ's eyes, which leads us back around to our starting point in Christ's Great Commandment.

Jesus taught us to apply our love for God with mind, heart, and soul by loving others. Divine love issues in interpersonal love, influencing even the most basic elements of life. Being a thoughtful Christian should lead to a life of thoughtfulness, for thinking must be accompanied by action. If we do not show love to one another the world has a right to question whether Christianity is true.

At the heart of an application of the Great Commandment is the visible demonstration of valuing one another. We will seek to model the love of Christ in all our communication and relationships, whether in the workplace, the classroom, the meeting room, or the home. Ultimately the love and grace that has been lavished upon us will lead us to lives of dependence on God and thoughtfulness toward others.

Faithful Christ-centered institutions of higher education are needed today as never before. Let us pray that a new generation of thoughtful believers will step forward with a desire to learn more about God and His world, His purposes, and His activities as they impact our various spheres of life. Thoughtful believers will have a different purpose and motivation for learning and living. We need educators to ask for fresh eyes to see the potential role that developing a generation of engaged students has as the means for establishing a Christian presence in the world. Let us, with wisdom, humility, and confidence, recognize the unique calling that is ours, ready to provide an answer for the hope that is ours through Jesus Christ the Lord (1 Pet 3:15).

We pray that God will renew Christ-centered educational institutions as we seek to develop a new generation of thoughtful Christians, even as we pray for all involved in this important enterprise. May these commitments not be easily lost or forgotten, but may they remain firmly rooted in our minds and hearts for years and decades to come for the glory of God.

Questions for Further Reflection

1. How will the process of learning to think in Christian categories result in a unity of thought across the academic disciplines of study? Is the process itself important? Why or why not?
2. Identify several key linkages between your formal academic discipline and at least three other rubrics of study in the academy. Describe the way you reason and apply revealed truth to the questions raised when seeking these critical linkages.

3. Will a love for God and a love for study ever produce dissonance of the thought? If so, how do you go about reconciling the apparent contradictions?
4. May faculty of the Christian university rigorously study and teach perspectives that are opposite to the teaching of the Bible and the traditions of the Church? Should opposing viewpoints be allowed in classroom instruction? Why or why not?
5. Is the incarnation of Jesus Christ only salvific in scope and application? How might the truth of the incarnation of Christ apply and/or answer specific challenges encountered in formal academic study?

Resources for Further Study

Burtchaell, James T. *The Dying of the Light: The Disengagement of Colleges and Universities from Their Christian Churches*. Grand Rapids: Eerdmans, 1998.

Carter, Stephen L. *The Culture of Disbelief*. New York: Basic, 1993.

Dockery, David S. *Renewing Minds: Serving Church and Society through Christian Higher Education*. Nashville: B&H, 2008.

Eaton, Philip. *Engaging the Culture, Changing the World*. Downers Grove, IL: InterVarsity, 2011.

Hauerwas, Stanley. *The State of the University: Academic Knowledge and the Knowledge of God*. Oxford: Blackwell, 2007.

Henry, Douglas V., and Michael D. Beaty, eds. *Christianity and the Soul of the University*. Grand Rapids: Baker, 2006.

Holmes, Arthur. *The Making of a Christian Mind*. Downers Grove, IL: InterVarsity, 1985.

Hunter, James Davison. *The Death of Character: Moral Education in an Age without Good or Evil*. New York: Basic, 2000.

———. *To Change the World*. New York: Oxford University Press, 2010.

Knonman, Anthony T. *Education's End: Why Our Colleges and Universities Have Given Up on the Meaning of Life*. New Haven, CT: Yale University Press, 2007.

Litfin, Duane. *Conceiving the Christian College*. Grand Rapids: Eerdmans, 2004.

Marsden, George M. *The Outrageous Idea of Christian Scholarship*. New York: Oxford University Press, 1997.

———. *The Soul of the American University: From Protestant Establishment to Established Unbelief*. New York: Oxford University Press, 1994.

Moreland, J. P. *Love God with All Your Mind*. Colorado Springs: NavPress, 1997.

Newman, John Henry. *The Idea of a University*. Notre Dame, IN: University of Notre Dame Press, reprint 1967.
Noll, Mark. *The Scandal of the Evangelical Mind*. Grand Rapids: Eerdmans, 1994.
Packer, J. I., and Thomas Oden. *One Faith*. Downers Grove, IL: InterVarsity, 2004.
Pelikan, Jaroslav. *The Idea of a University: A Reexamination*. New Haven, CT: Yale University Press, 1992.
Pope John Paul II. *Ex Corde Ecclesiae. On Catholic Universities*. Encyclical Letter, 1990.
Schwehn, Mark. *Exiles from Eden: Religion and the Academic Vocation in America*. Oxford: Oxford University Press, 1993.
Sommerville, C. John. *The Decline of the Secular University*. Oxford: Oxford University Press, 2006.
Taylor, Charles. *A Secular Age*. Cambridge: Belknap, 2007.
Turner, H. E. W. *The Pattern of Christian Truth*. London: Mowbray, 1954.
Weigel, George. *The Cube and the Cathedral*. New York: Basic, 2005.

Endnotes

[1] See F. R. Evans, *Bernard of Clairvaux: Selected Works* (Mahwah, NJ: Paulist, 1987).

[2] T. S. Eliot, *Christianity and Culture* (New York: Harcourt Brace, 1940), 22.

[3] See J. P. Moreland, *Love God with All Your Mind* (Colorado Springs: NavPress, 1997); Millard J. Erickson, *The Evangelical Heart and Mind* (Grand Rapids: Baker, 1993).

[4] See Augustine, *On Christian Doctrine,* trans. D. W. Robertson Jr., in *Library of Liberal Arts* 80 (New York's Liberal Arts, 1958).

[5] See George M. Marsden, *The Outrageous Idea of Christian Scholarship* (New York: Oxford University Press, 1997).

[6] See Mark Schwehn, *Exiles from Eden: Religion and the Academic Vocation in America* (New York: Oxford University Press, 1993).

[7] See H. E. W. Turner, *The Pattern of Christian Truth: A Study of the Relations Between Orthodoxy and Heresy in the Early Church* (London: Mowbray, 1954).

[8] See Timothy George, "The Pattern of Christian Truth," *First Things* 154 (2005): 21–25.

[9] See Abraham Kuyper, "1898 Stone Lectures, Princeton University," in *Creating a Christian Worldview: Abraham Kuyper's Lectures on Calvinism*, comp. Peter S. Heslam (Grand Rapids: Eerdmans, 1998).

[10] See J. I. Packer and Thomas C. Oden, *One Faith* (Downers Grove, IL: InterVarsity, 2004).

[11] See Jaroslav Pelikan, *The Christian Tradition: A History of the Development of Doctrine,* 5 volumes (Chicago: University of Chicago, 1971–91).

[12] See Millard J. Erickson, *Christian Theology* (Grand Rapids: Baker, 1985); John Jefferson Davis, ed., *The Necessity of Systematic Theology* (Grand Rapids: Baker, 1978); John Frame, "Studying Theology as a Servant of Jesus,"

Reformation & Revival 11:1 (2002): 45–69; and John Hannah, "The Place of Theology in the Postmodern World," *Reformation & Revival* 11:1 (2002): 11–32.
[13] See Robert Saucy, "Doing Theology for the Church," in Davis, *The Necessity of Systematic Theology*, 61–74; David S. Dockery, "A Theology for the Church," *Midwestern Journal of Theology* 1:1 (2003): 10–20.
[14] See David F. Wells, *No Place for Truth; or Whatever Happened to Evangelical Theology?* (Grand Rapids: Eerdmans, 1995).
[15] See James Orr, *The Christian View of God and the World* (1891; repr., Grand Rapids: Eerdmans, 1954).
[16] See J. P. Moreland and William Lane Craig, *Philosophical Foundations for a Christian Worldview* (Downers Grove, IL: InterVarsity, 2003); David Naugle, *Worldview: The History of a Concept* (Grand Rapids: Eerdmans, 2002).
[17] See Arthur Holmes, *The Making of a Christian Mind* (Downers Grove, IL: InterVarsity, 1985); Holmes, *Shaping Character* (Grand Rapids: Eerdmans, 1990).
[18] See C. S. Lewis, *God in the Dock* (Grand Rapids: Eerdmans, reprint 1994).
[19] These implications, as well as other points in this article, are amplified in David S. Dockery, *Renewing Minds: Serving Church and Society through Christian Higher Education* (Nashville: B&H, 2008). Also, see David S. Dockery and Timothy George, *The Great Tradition of Christian Thinking* (Wheaton: Crossway, 2012).

2

The Heartbeat of Christian Higher Education: The Core Curriculum

Gene C. Fant Jr.

Apples symbolized education long before records, computers, and smartphones came along. We know of the so-called apple polisher, the wiseacre student who tried to curry favor with a teacher through a simple gift, but perhaps the image has deeper roots. This kind of fruit is a worthy symbol, as it contains not only the meat that may be consumed in the present but it also contains seeds that may be planted to ensure a distant harvest in another time. In this way, education is represented as a continuous stream between the past (the tree), the present (the fruit's flesh), and the future (the seeds), all bound up in a single image. Education embodies past discoveries, present-day explorations, and future applications yet to come.

Perhaps this symbolism was not lost on former generations who were farmers and gardeners. Because few of us still cultivate our own orchards, we no longer value an apple's core. It is a scrap to be thrown away, its seeds worthless to us. We cut away the core of most fruits so as not to spoil the flavor and texture of the flesh, tossing it aside into the garbage.

Like apples, education also easily detaches from its rightful context, and people forget its primary purpose. This is particularly easy when we look at the "core curriculum," the set of courses that together make up the general education program at most colleges. For many students, the core curriculum has become a set of impediments standing in the way of "real" courses. For some university budget managers, the core curriculum is the cash generator that pays for smaller upper-division courses by matching large course sections with entry-level faculty. For faculty members, the core curriculum easily becomes a final turf battle to prevent the total elimination of the liberal arts basis of higher education. All of these views ignore the opportunity that a rigorous core curriculum provides. At religious institutions in particular, the distinctiveness of the mission of Christ-centered higher education should be the general education program as a primary site of implementation, coherence, and community, all of which underscore the simultaneous, coequal importance of both *orthodoxy* ("right thinking" about God) and *orthopraxy* ("right action" toward fellow persons).

One of the current misunderstandings about higher education is that it is a self-guided intellectual buffet. In this view, universities provide a range of courses, consumed according to student tastes and preferences, with only a few cohesive requirements in the chosen major's subject providing substance. The goal of post-secondary work, thus, is the completion of a degree, typically one that prepares students for gainful employment; certain majors are "pre-rich" (pre-med, pre-law, engineering, and business), and the rest are "pre-service" (religion, social work, education, and psychology)—or "pre-figuring out what to do with one's life."

For millennia, though, education was thought of as a formative process, the goal of which was *education for the sake of education.* The fruit of such labor was the students themselves: thinking persons in possession of high-level skill sets. Education produced abilities, not merely credentials for professional fields or the workforce. This process conveyed a moral force, which included soul formation. Developing students' minds was never detached from the development of character or the cultivation of the spirit. Even pre-Christian Western education underscored the idea that heads, hands, and hearts were somehow united in the living out of the worthwhile life. Christianity articulated this afresh, asserting the rationality of faith itself and the importance of leading lives that are cogent outgrowths of one's very faith. This explains why Christian principles have been so closely associated with the intellectual achievements of Western civilization.[1]

Approaches to education that aim at practicality without regard for intellectual formation risk the creation of "men without chests," to use C. S. Lewis's term.[2] Martin Luther King Jr. put an even finer point on this: "The function of education, therefore, is to teach one to think intensively and to think critically. But education which stops with efficiency may prove the greatest menace to society. The most dangerous criminal may be the man gifted with reason, but with no morals."[3] In an age where the news is filled with indictments of many brilliant criminals who have bilked fortunes or abused power for selfish purposes, the need for a model of education that includes ethics and spiritual development is abundantly clear.[4] Christian colleges in particular have a unique opportunity to engage in an approach to education that employs a specific worldview rooted in both Scripture and the extensive Christian intellectual tradition.[5]

The Core Curriculum

The vast majority of American colleges include some sort of core curriculum. Indeed, the regional accrediting bodies governing most institutions require a general education program as a part of the basic requirements for a degree.[6] Institutions retain great latitude in the construction of their own core curricula, but general education is a substantial part of the work completed by students. These courses are not preprofessional but rather provide foundational thinking skills for further study. Core courses are taken by all students, regardless of degree focus or postgraduation plans. This portion of the curriculum may be small (nontraditional institutions tend to have few requirements) or quite large (traditional liberal arts institutions have extensive requirements). These courses are usually undertaken during the first two years of study, with many institutions mandating completion of a large portion of these courses prior to the pursuit of the academic major or minor.

At one time, general education courses were somewhat similar among institutions, but during the second half of the twentieth century these courses began to lose their uniformity. At many institutions, the core curriculum faces deep-seated challenges:

- At large research-oriented universities, general education courses are taught primarily by graduate students, part-time faculty, or instructors without terminal degrees, rather than by permanent (sometimes called "tenure-track") faculty. Indeed, only rarely does a freshman at a large university take one of these courses with a tenured professor. One result of this development has been the loss of "ownership" of the core curriculum; permanent faculty members feel little personal investment in those courses, which tend to be viewed as being of secondary or even tertiary importance.

- Class sizes in general education courses have grown significantly at many institutions. Because many of these courses are taught in large sections, several hundred students often are packed into large lecture halls, with testing performed through the use of computers and few, if any, writing assignments. The lack of personal interaction with faculty members has likewise impacted the sense of investment some students feel about such courses. With only minimal feedback on assignments, many students feel that they are merely "punching the clock" in these courses, marking time to complete graduation requirements.
- General education courses as a whole may lack an overall sense of philosophical coherence. Students rarely understand the rationale for the courses and since the classes are taught with few connections made between the concepts in one area and those in another, a pastiche develops that never quite makes sense. This reinforces the idea that the core curriculum represents a checklist that must be completed prior to taking "real" courses in the academic major. Adding to this lack of internal coherence among the courses is the rising loss of coherence for general education itself due to the advent of student choice among courses. At many institutions, students are able to take a wide range of classes selected from a fairly expansive list of options. When this happens, the program becomes so fragmented that it may lose any sense of real substance.

Christian higher education, with very few exceptions, operates through institutions that value teaching over research, so the contact with full-time, permanent professors tends to be much more significant at all levels. Indeed, one of the best markers of such institutions for prospective students may be identified during an on-campus visit: classroom size.[7] While the first two challenges cited above do not affect many religious institutions, the last one certainly does. Religious higher education is not immune from the silo mentality that views everything as independent and disparate, even as it is not immune from the loss of coherence in the general education program itself.

For Christian colleges, the stakes related to the full integration of all coursework into a coherent framework is of the highest order. A Christian understanding of truth (or Truth) is rooted in the idea of the essential lordship of Christ over all of creation, including the world of ideas.[8] As core courses explore their various disciplines and approaches to the world of knowledge, students have a unique opportunity to see both the expansiveness of the Christian intellectual tradition and the ways that biblical and historical principles have influenced culture and life as a whole. Such a foundational understanding of the faith that was delivered once for all (Jude 3) is lived out through the glorification of God through our hearts, souls, and minds (Matt 22:37). This allows the cultivation of the mind in unison with the formation of the soul, with the ultimate attenuation of the heart to the utter glorification of God through our lives.

The *Liberal Arts*-Based Core Curriculum

The rich history of the core curriculum is rooted in the whole expanse of Western education. While the etymology of the word "core" is a bit unclear, the term does seem related in some ways to the French *coeur* or "heart," which derived from the Latin *cor* and the Greek *cardia.* Rightly understood, the core curriculum should be the very heartbeat of an institution, distilling the central essence of its mission and vision. Further, the core curriculum should seek to change or refine students' hearts as a metonymy for their entire lives, including their minds. The general education program, thus, contains the intellectual seed-corn that will provide students with lifelong learning and satisfaction.

Before modern times, education was effected through the home. Sons were taught some skills by their mothers before being initiated into the world of men and the professions, just as daughters were taught the domestic arts by their mothers. At some point, the system advanced into a more formal system, where professional educators or tutors taught the children of the wealthy or assembled children in small schools that were comprised of, typically, extended family groups. The Greeks termed these tutors *pedagogues* (meaning "to lead or guide a child"), the word that has become the technical term in English for education, *pedagogy.*

Interestingly, pedagogues often were slaves who were attached to households with children.

Most educated persons, apart from the slave-pedagogues, were expected to apply their learning in professions or in their roles as citizens. The trades were given particular knowledge that might advance one's career as a butcher, a weaver, or a baker, but for a select few, a more elaborate education was viewed as necessary to prepare for public service in particular. This breadth of learning developed into what became termed the liberal arts, which were fairly well codified by the time the Romans had established themselves as the cultural successors of the Greeks.

The connection between liberal arts education and citizenship is quite strong; indeed, the "liberal" part of the term comes from the Latin term for "free" (*liber*), as the skills in thinking, communication, and leadership skills acquired through such an education were thought best for "free" men, not slaves. Through extensive readings, memorization, and dialogues, these sons of freemen were prepared for duties as citizen-leaders. Foremost among these skills were those of critical thinking and rational analysis, with an emphasis on the kinds of application that might be communicated to others. Further, a life of active reflection was encouraged, where one would not merely react to the events of the day but would learn from them through rigorous pondering and hindsight analysis. Learning was, then, a steady stream from the past to the future, with citizen-scholars standing in the midst of the flow, at once receiving the best thoughts of those who had gone before them and also transmitting those thoughts to present circumstances that would shape the future. This passing on of knowledge between generations and the compendious nature of the knowledge that was available was summed up in a term that the Greeks often employed, *enkuklios paideia*, "general education," the expression from which the English word *encyclopedia* derives its name.

As the Roman Empire passed into the Christian Middle Ages, the liberal arts formed a mature set of educational concepts. By this time, seven "arts" or skills dominated the commonly taught core for education, which set the pattern for virtually all higher education in the West. The liberal arts were conceived of as a carefully wrought pattern that progressed deliberately toward the goal of producing rigorous thinkers. The first level of work was called the *Trivium* (the "three roads" or "paths"), which included grammar, rhetoric, and logic; the second level was the *Quadrivium* (the "four roads"), which explored arithmetic, astronomy, music, and geometry.

These two levels were both sequential *and* intentional, the goal being the advancement of higher-level abilities in analysis and thinking. In the Trivium, grammar sought to prepare students to understand how language works; logic (also called "dialectic") helped students learn to think in disciplined ("rational") ways; and rhetoric sought to combine the two skills in the communication of thought from one person to another. As those skills were mastered, the Quadrivium refined how students understood the larger world, using mathematics as the primary tool for ordering and analyzing the universe. The roads, however, did not stop with the Quadrivium, as students who mastered both paths to learning were then allowed to pursue the highest aims for thinkers (at least until the Enlightenment): philosophy and theology (which was sometimes called "the queen of the sciences").

The Enlightenment (post-Descartes, c. 1637) began to detach theology from the liberal arts, viewing it as unworthy of rational inquiry in comparison to the empirical pursuits of modern science, but the Industrial Revolution and the rising pragmatism that resulted from the advent of new technologies began the final process of undermining liberal arts education. The Enlightenment removed the first term from the idea of "Christian liberal arts education" while the more narrow demands of technical education stripped away the second term, leaving us with specialized professional education standing as the dominant form of education in the third millennium of the Christian era. Rampant empirical skepticism undermined liberal arts education in Europe, while the American love of practicality has circumscribed its dominance in the United States.

Most American institutions, however, have retained some of the nomenclature of the liberal arts in two of the primary undergraduate degrees conferred by most universities, the "bachelor of arts," which emphasizes languages, arts, or humanities, and the "bachelor of science," emphasizing mathematics or science. Both of these are general degrees that prepare students for more specialized study in graduate or professional schools.

As specialized education became more common in American colleges (study in business, education, engineering, nursing, and other fields where entrance into the profession is achieved with an undergraduate degree), the liberal arts were retained in the general education program, where breadth was instilled in students. The idea that the core prepares students for more specialized learning reflects the liberal arts' own tradition of using the Trivium to build toward the Quadrivium and finally philosophy and theology.[9]

A *Christian* Liberal Arts-Based Core Curriculum

For Greco-Roman students, the goal of the liberal arts was tied to citizenship in the state. As the liberal arts were modified with the advent of Christianity, the goal became the production of Christian thinkers of significant rigor—citizens of a heavenly kingdom fit to produce helpful works in this world. Some pre-Christian forms of liberal arts education sought to explore theology as its ultimate goal, believing (in general) that theology was the great unifier of knowledge. As Christian thinkers reshaped this element of liberal arts education, the ultimate goal of theological exploration was strengthened and further exalted as a worthy undertaking.[10]

The transition from a pagan educational approach to one that was distinctively Christian was not, however, without difficulties. Many early church fathers felt that pagan culture was too corrupt to be adapted into Christian culture. One of the chief casualties of this tension was drama, which was exterminated by writers such as Tertullian (d. c. 220) and Cyprian (d. 258) who believed that it was irredeemable.[11] The scriptural record, however, actually includes references to, and quotations from, pagan writers. For example, when Paul speaks before the Areopagus in Acts 17, he quotes from pagan poets Epimenedes and Aratus in his address, indicating that he saw at least some value even in pagan writers. Augustine of Hippo (354–430) picked up on this notion and extended it in specific ways, helping to redeem the Greco-Roman tradition for later generations of scholars. Augustine was an adult convert, in the midst of a successful career as a public intellectual. His conversion began a reformulation of his pagan training, with his understanding of the world measured against biblical revelation and the emerging traditions of the church. In his monumental works *On Christian Doctrine* and *Confessions*, he urged believers to reject falsehood wherever it might lie, but to likewise embrace all truth that comported with Scripture no matter where it might be found. To provide evidence for his point, he turned to the Exodus of the Israelites from Egypt and their looting of gold and silver from their oppressors. These objects were later melted down to form the furnishings for God's temple. In this way, the precious metals were restored to their "proper use," redeemed from their pagan service.[12]

In doing this, Augustine established the principle that considered pagan discoveries about the world in the light of the Incarnation and biblical revelation. This principle helped to extend the emerging doctrine of general revelation, the idea that the Creator had embedded evidence of His character and identity throughout the created world so that nonbelievers might anticipate the coming of the Incarnation and the fulsome revelation of Scripture.[13] This approach to learning that preceded the advent of Christianity became known as "the spoils of Egypt," which provided generations of educators with a coherent reason for incorporating elements of non-Christian thought within the context of biblically faithful learning.

A rigorous core curriculum, then, will include a full spectrum of thinkers and subject matter, including both Christian and non-Christian thinkers, all of whom are examined by the rubric of scriptural revelation and Christian tradition. Indeed, the harvest of "the spoils of Egypt" has been the expansive Christian intellectual tradition that formed the foundations of the Western tradition in every academic discipline undertaken in general education courses. The Christian intellectual tradition is the application of a Christian worldview to the various academic pursuits that help us to understand the world and humankind's place in it. For example, George Washington Carver was deeply convinced that God's providence extended throughout all of creation, so he set out to find uses for plants that he believed were underused. As Carver wrote, "I indulge in very little lip service but to ask the Great Creator silently, daily, and often many times a day to permit me to speak to Him through the three great kingdoms of the world which He created—the animal, mineral, and vegetable kingdoms—to understand their relations to each other, and our relations to them and to the Great God who made all of us."[14] This was his motivation for scrutinizing the lowly sweet potato and the peanut, finding dozens of uses for each and advancing the study of horticulture in the process.[15]

Stories like Carver's fill the history of every academic discipline, and core courses that introduce students to the foundational concepts of these disciplines would be well served to include some kind of overview of the great thinkers who influenced the disciplines and how their faith generated their philosophies. A proper consideration of the Christian intellectual tradition is not, however, a form of hagiography or hero worship; a more appropriate approach is the examination of the principles that underlie the discoveries, rather than merely focusing on the discoverers. Inordinate discussion of the thinkers rather than their principles may result in an accidental barrier to seeing precisely how extensive the impacts of those principles may be.[16] For example, it would be wise to consider Martin Luther King Jr.'s influence on the twentieth-century civil rights movement, but if we only consider his life, without examining the biblical principles on which he built his thoughts, then we have missed the true power of his legacy.

Just as Augustine used an event from Scripture to consider the relationship between Christian and non-Christian thought, a further example from history provides a complementary idea. In AD 70, Roman troops destroyed the city of Jerusalem, razing the temple and looting its wares as plunder. According to tradition, the gold and silver of the temple provided the funds that paid for the construction of the Arch of Titus in Rome in AD 82.[17] This fascinating reversal of the Israelite's plunder of Egypt allowed the Roman plunder of another temple to be changed to an "improper use" of God's gold. These "spoils of Jerusalem" provide us with another pattern: identifying how Christian principles have been co-opted and adapted by non-Christian thinkers, meaning that these ideas lie downstream from a Christian worldview. Part of the work of Christian scholarship is the identification of these ideas, ensuring that the legacy of Christian thought is not obscured by post-Christian use.

The tensions between Christian and secular thought have created misunderstandings of the Christian liberal arts tradition. The Fundamentalist–Modernist conflict of the 1920s and its echoes across the subsequent century have created suspicion regarding liberal arts-based education among some. A dichotomy between the terms "fundamentalist" and "liberal" has been fostered in many circles, including those of orthodox Christianity: if to be "liberal" is to be heterodox then by transference the "liberal" arts must be antireligious. This transference is unfortunate and is rooted in a genuine struggle over the very definition of the term *liberal.*

In its original sense, the liberal arts were "liberal" in that they sought to free individuals from their own selfish desires and delusions.[18] Fully educated persons, then, were liberated from the delusion of viewing themselves as the centers of the world and the ultimate arbiters of right and wrong. One of the reasons that early Christian educators embraced the liberal arts (and still do) is the resonance of this concept with Paul's writings about the struggles between the old, sinful self and the new, redeemed self (Rom 6:5–7; Eph 4:22; Col 3:9) as well as Peter's words about the same struggle with the sinful self: "Therefore, get your minds ready for action; be self-disciplined, and set your hope completely on the grace to be brought to you at the revelation of Jesus Christ. As obedient children, do not be conformed to the desires of your former ignorance but, as the One who called you is holy, you also are to be holy in all your conduct; for it is written: 'Be holy, because I am holy'" (1 Pet 1:13–16 HCSB).[19] Post-Enlightenment views of religion and other institutions or schools of thought inverted the goal of liberation to one of the individual rebelling against external forces and exalting internal sufficiency. For these thinkers, to be liberal was to be free from the superstitions of outdated forms of thought and repressive forces. In the Christian view, then, one is liberated from the self to the exaltation of God; in the post-Enlightenment view, the individual is liberated from religion (or any other form of power over the individual), to live as one sees fit within one's own understanding and reckoning.[20] Rightly understood, a Christian glorification of God over the self is tied more closely with the historical basis of the liberal arts than is the exaltation of the self over and against God. In some ways, then, Christian institutions have a specific role as conservators of the original goal of the liberal arts.

In the United States, almost all institutions of higher learning prior to the Civil War were established to be Christian colleges built on the liberal arts. From Harvard (whose original motto was not the familiar "Veritas" now preserved in its logo but rather was *Veritas Christo et Ecclesiae*, "Truth for Christ and Church") and

Princeton to most of the smaller colleges that dotted the American frontier, the history of American higher education is impossible to write without noting the enablement of Christian sects and churches. Indeed, Brown University and the University of Chicago both began their days as Baptist colleges.[21]

A *Distinctively* Christian Liberal Arts-Based Core Curriculum

From the variety of denominations and congregations to the seemingly infinite approaches to worship that are employed around the world, no two Christian entities are exactly alike.[22] Indeed, identifying what lies at the core of the Christian faith seems daunting. The various schisms that have rent the corporate church throughout history are proof of the difficulties associated with precise articulations of the faith that lie beyond the basic declaration of the New Testament: "Jesus is Lord" (Rom 10:9).

Just as Christ and Paul warned believers to be wary of feeling ashamed because of the gospel (e.g., Mark 3:38; Rom 1:16), Christian institutions must eschew any sense of bashfulness in taking on themselves the name of Christ. Our current intellectual climate avoids strict definitions and rules, viewing them as burdensome and restrictive, but the clear reality is that a dividing line must distinguish between "Christian" and "non-Christian." Often we will run ahead of such a dividing line, using a set of doctrinal distinctives to articulate a stricter sense than merely "Christian." In other cases, though, institutions may avoid distinctives to a degree that risks the slippery slope toward institutional apostasy. For our purposes, perhaps the simplest dividing line is the Great Commandment: "'Love the Lord your God with all your heart, with all your soul and with all your mind.' This is the greatest and most important command. The second is like it: 'Love your neighbor as yourself.' All the Law and the Prophets depend on these two commands'" (Matt 22:37–40). In this passage lies the brilliance of Christ's declaration that true faith is the union of two equally important elements: orthodoxy (right belief) and orthopraxy (right practice). Any form of Christianity that emphasizes one element to the exclusion of the other is, by Christ's own declaration, outside the boundaries of the true faith. To some extent, Christ was drawing out a "Way" (Acts 9:2 and other passages) that would avoid the path of a grace-free legalism on the right and a Christ-free gospel on the left.

For a Christian liberal arts-based core curriculum to be faithful to the Great Commandment, it must find coherent ways to inculcate a love for God and for others. This does not mean watering down the academic coursework or content, but rather shifting the goal from the exaltation of the self to the exaltation of God. One of the best ways to do this is by creating a sense of a communal commitment to viewing learning itself as a devotional activity. Study is one means through which we may learn about God and His ways. This was, in fact, the primary methodology of Christian higher education for the past thousand years. The liberal arts were viewed as critical to building a foundation to proper thinking about God (theology). The Christian humanism of Desiderius Erasmus (1466–1536), Roger Ascham (c. 1515–68), Edmund Spenser (c. 1552–99), Francis Bacon (1561–1626), Isaac Newton (1643–1727), and so many others viewed all education as pointing to the divine order built into the universe. All truth, in this view, is God's truth because He is the Author of all that is true; thus, the pursuit of truth is the pursuit of God. The fullest fruit of this view toward education is the expansive Christian intellectual tradition, which may be broadly examined throughout the core curriculum.

Similarly, a coherent core curriculum must provide students with a passion for loving their neighbors. This does not mean watering down academic coursework, but rather employing fully integrative service learning and other kinds of applied learning in support of other assessments of student learning. Christian learning communities, then, will emphasize a sense of connection among persons.

One way to understand our connectedness is through intellectual empathy. This concept means that the core will allow students to learn how to think like a variety of practitioners of different academic fields. For example, when someone studies a controversial topic, it is helpful to be able to think through the issues relevant to that topic utilizing the methods of different academic disciplines. Thus, a student may examine the facts like a scientist to understand those facts as empirical data, like an economist to understand the costs of the proposed solutions, like a political scientist to learn how the solutions might play out in the realm of governments (including local, regional, national, and international considerations), like a sociologist to ponder the human effects of the solutions on culture, and like an ethicist to scrutinize their larger-picture ramifications on creation as a whole.

The value of empathy is that it yields a strong sense of shared humanity. Certainly empathy is not a characteristic reserved exclusively for Christians,[23] but when it is combined with the gospel's clarion call to care for the lost, the oppressed, and the downtrodden, it results in a special sensitivity to the world.

The successful combination of orthodoxy and orthopraxy in a core curriculum will yield several benefits for the institution. First, it will provide a sense of purpose and cohesion to the program, in that courses will fit together (and even overlap) in complementary ways. This clarity of purpose can likewise produce a core curriculum that emphasizes shared experiences among the learning community. By having a strong overriding content in the general education program, both professors and students will be able to have common experiences over the course of the core, providing effective points of reference and teachable moments for their discussions. Finally, a strong core curriculum will allow students the opportunity to pursue a sense of calling for their lives. As students come under the intellectual mentorship of professors and are exposed to a variety of thinkers and academic disciplines, they will be able to learn about opportunities for service and employment that had not heretofore been known.

Challenges to a Christian Liberal Arts-Based Core Curriculum

One of the primary challenges to the idea of a Christian liberal arts-based core curriculum is the notion that anything "Christian" is automatically irrational because it is rooted in faith. This view is particularly popular among secular critics of Christianity, many of whom follow the thoughts of either Karl Marx, who viewed religion as "the opiate of the people," or Sigmund Freud, who viewed religious fervor as a form of mental illness. The influences of Marx and Freud are manifold in the academy, and the ramifications of this kind of thought are felt even within some Christian college faculty members, who feel ashamed to be labeled as believers because of the disapprobation of the larger profession. Likewise, some critics deem religious orthodoxy to be a barrier to free thought and expression, believing that any hegemony (authority structure) that lies outside of the individual thinker is automatically corrupt and corrosive. For these reasons and others, there is a strong sense in many circles that to be "religious" is to be "lesser" because religious thought, particularly religious orthodoxy, is intellectually defective.

The antidote to these criticisms is the recovery and extension of the vast Christian intellectual tradition. In every academic discipline, it is impossible to create an honest survey of the discipline's history without an examination of the influence of Christian thought and worldview. In literature, for example, the entire practice of literary criticism would be impossible without the work of Augustine, Dante, Chaucer, Spenser, Shakespeare, Milton, Johnson, Eliot, and an almost endless stream of devout believers whose creative works and hermeneutical discourses have built Western literary thought.

Another challenge to a rigorous Christian liberal arts core curriculum comes in the form of degree compression, the threefold challenge of alternative credit completion, reduced hours for undergraduate degree completion, and the increased hours for professional academic majors.

The second half of the twentieth century saw an explosion of methods by which college credits could be earned outside of the traditional college classroom. Some approaches allowed high school students to "double-dip" their coursework, earning college credit for their high school courses; others allowed standardized examinations to provide credit; and still others allow unparalleled mobility of credit hours, taking courses at a variety of institutions (including online institutions) and transferring them to their "primary" institution. Rare is the student who completes every single college credit through the traditional offerings of a campus. These options mean that students are increasingly bypassing the traditional general education program. For Christian colleges this is particularly challenging because it also means that these students are missing out on the very courses that are often the institutions' most distinctive courses in terms of mission and content.

Not only are students bypassing the traditional core, degree requirements have been eliminating the space once held by general education classes. The number of credit hours required for the completion of undergraduate degrees has been declining for the past few decades. Not long ago, it was common for degrees to require 128 semester hours of work, but the threshold now is moving to 120 hours. Additionally, many legislators are pressing for "three-year" baccalaureate degrees. While three-year degrees are nothing new, current proposals often have students completing a portion of their college courses during their high school career and heading to college with most if not all of their freshman year courses completed.[24] To ensure this possibility, these legislators have strongly encouraged institutions either to trim their degree hour counts or to find ways to credential other experiences as course-bearing.

Finally, the expansion of the technical content of many fields has increased the number of credits required for the completion of the major requirements for the degree. This stands, in many cases, at odds with the previous issue of degree compression. Demanding fields such as engineering, nursing, business, and even the fine arts have ramped up the rigor of their programs' contents, particularly in fields that require a licensure examination.

Christian colleges must be proactive in dealing with these three challenges to the core curriculum. The marketplace of higher education carries with it very real forces that must be met. Certainly realities must be recognized; the forbearance of all alternative credit is, for most institutions, unrealistic; it is difficult to maintain degree completion totals that are out of step with other universities in the same market; likewise, it is impossible to resist accreditor mandates that enlarge academic major requirements. Campus leaders must find ways to protect the essential elements of the general education program as well as the cocurricular activities that undergird the first year of college for traditional students. Additionally, institutions must ensure that a vigorous general education program is intact for nontraditional programming, ensuring that those programs, especially degree-completion programs, include mission-specific content that reflects the Christian mission of the university.

Practicalities

The bulk of this chapter has been spent exploring the ideals associated with the core curriculum. Perhaps it would be best to conclude with a few practicalities, for all ideals are empty if they do not find application in the real world.

- *For students:* The core curriculum is a once-in-a-lifetime opportunity to study under professors whose expertise they would not otherwise learn. Such an opportunity should not be squandered. Students must learn how to study devotionally in their courses: consider every course assignment as an opportunity to learn about God and His creation. Students should pray that He will use all of their courses, starting with the core courses, to prepare them for their specific, unique calling in life. Such an approach allows students to fall in love with study itself, knowing that its ultimate goal is formative and is a means to discoveries that will continue to unfold over a lifetime.

  Similarly, students should view core courses as opportunities to explore career and service options that they had not previously known. Most students enter college with a very limited understanding of the various options about employment and career paths. Bright students in particular may have been told that pre-medicine or pre-law are the only truly worthwhile pursuits, while other students who have sensed a calling to full-time Christian service may think that God only calls people to be missionaries, pastors, or ministers of music. All vocations are holy callings, even as those who serve the church full time are set apart in some ways. Career exploration through core course experiences can help a student gain valuable skills in business or education or any other field that God may use to open doors for ministry, whether in full-time service to the church or as uniquely prepared volunteers for kingdom work.
- *For parents:* Parents sometimes wonder why their students are paying tuition for courses that "never" will be used. Parents need to encourage their students to find ways to take full advantage of the opportunities afforded by core courses. Many parents will, perhaps, be able to reflect on their own college experiences and remember that the professors who taught their own core courses are among those who are remembered the most fondly. Professors who teach core courses have great influence on the lives and futures of students, and parents should pray for faculty frequently. Parents also should ask their students about the core courses and listen to hear any new emerging

intellectual passions that might emerge from such classes. Such queries will provide food for many future conversations. Finally, parents should not be overly anxious about the kinds of new career interests that core courses may yield. Some of these interests will pass, but most students will change majors and career objectives as they learn more about life, the world, and God's calling in their classes.

- *For faculty:* At many larger institutions, faculty members view the teaching of core courses as being fit only for entry-level or part-time faculty members. Such a view is less common at most Christian universities, where teaching of all kinds is a high priority. Even in these settings, however, it is easy for faculty members to teach core courses so commonly that they move into a kind of "cruise control" mode that leaves the courses gasping for fresh air. Faculty members have a responsibility to view general education courses as a unique privilege that should not be underappreciated. Academic departments that are represented in the core should commit themselves to frequent reviews of the course content and teaching methodologies.

  Likewise, faculty members who teach core sections should look for ways to collaborate where overlaps and interfaces between courses may exist. A world literature professor and a world history professor could find ways to link their syllabi assignments. A New Testament professor could work with an art appreciation professor to match up particular images and passages that inform each other. In the same way, alternative approaches to collaboration may produce refreshing opportunities for instruction, such as special study abroad sections or unique service learning integrations.
- *For administrators:* Academic administrators bear a particular responsibility to the core curriculum through their responsibilities to the intellectual and spiritual lives of their campuses. Foremost among these responsibilities is the need for institutional coherence about the university mission and program goals. Administrators should be fierce guardians of a rigorous core curriculum precisely because of the importance of such work to the formation of students. A campus must have a clear sense of its identity and

its direction, or the core curriculum will spin away from having any sort of unified sense or meaning. This is more critical for Christian colleges than, perhaps, any other sector of higher education, for when Christian institutions lose a strong sense of mission, they lose the very defining adjective that distinguishes them from other institutions.

Maintaining the link between the core curriculum and the mission is not enough, however, as the way that general education is treated relative to other academic programs makes a difference as well. At many institutions, general education courses are housed in the largest classrooms on campus, meaning that they easily come to be viewed as cash generators rather than as critical mission-underpinnings. This affects not only class sizes but also impacts the way that these courses are staffed. Because core courses may be taught by faculty who lack doctorates or other high-level degrees, there is often a temptation to use mostly adjunct (part-time) and junior (inexperienced) faculty members to teach those courses. In cases where an institution does not pursue a rigorous approach to faculty development, these faculty members can be overwhelmed by the thought of including elements that deal with the theological or philosophical aspects of their discipline. In worst-case scenarios, institutions end up allowing the vast bulk of core courses to be taught by part-timers who, while capable teachers, have little commitment to the Christian mission of the university. This can be a deadly combination in terms of how effective the core is: large classes taught by inexpensive faculty members. Judged by mere pragmatism, such an arrangement seems to make financial sense, but such a view is short-sighted in that it can create an atmosphere that treats the core as though it were unimportant apart from the financial considerations. A vigorous core curriculum will be taught in classrooms (including those that are virtual) that allow for maximum interaction between students and faculty and that include instructors who are deeply committed to the mission and philosophical foundations of the institution.

Conclusion

When the Spanish conquistadors encountered the Aztec civilization (c. 1520), they stumbled across a religious system that was built on human sacrifice. During festivals, sacrificial victims were lined up, taken to the tops of the stepped pyramids that anchored cities, and priests with obsidian knives cut out the hearts of the still-living persons. The hearts beat on for a bit, even as the excoriated victims lived long enough to behold their own hearts in the bloody hands of the priests. Excoriated bodies cannot, of course, live for long. They die quickly and begin the process of decay.

Challenges to the general education program threaten to excoriate higher education, leaving it without a heart and heading toward eventual decay. Christian institutions should be about the business of intellectual encouragement, the development of students' hearts, souls, and minds. Rightly conceived, the core curriculum should reflect the very heartbeat of the institution: a vision for how we might love God and love others with every aspect of our beings.

Questions for Further Reflection

1. What is the danger of an education that ignores the whole person (heart, soul, and mind)?
2. What are some challenges to general education programs?
3. When did the liberal arts become so linked with core curricula?
4. What are the two approaches to defining "liberal," and what are the effects of these two definitions?
5. What are the two parts of the Great Commandment that must be combined in order to create a distinctively Christian approach to education?

Resources for Further Study

Dockery, David S. *Renewing Minds: Serving Church and Society through Christian Higher Education.* Nashville: Broadman & Holman, 2007.

Holmes, Arthur F. *The Idea of a Christian College.* Rev. ed. Grand Rapids: Eerdmans, 1987.

Lewis, C. S. *The Abolition of Man*, or *Reflections on Education with Special Reference to the Teaching of English in the Upper Forms of Schools.* San Francisco: Harper San Francisco, 1974 reprint.

Litfin, Duane. *Conceiving the Christian College*. Grand Rapids: Eerdmans, 2004.

Poe, Harry Lee. "The Religious Spectrum in Higher Education." In *Christianity in the Academy: Teaching at the Intersection of Faith and Learning*, 31–52. Grand Rapids: Baker, 2004.

Riesen, Richard A. *Piety and Philosophy: A Primer for Christian Schools*. Ozark, AL: ACW Press, 2002.

Ringenberg, William C. *The Christian College: A History of Protestant Higher Education in America*. 2nd ed. Grand Rapids: Baker, 2006.

Endnotes

[1] This view of the West has been outlined clearly in works such as Philip J. Samson's *6 Modern Myths about Christianity and Western Civilization* (Downers Grove, IL: InterVarsity, 2001). Indeed, even secularists admit this debt to Christianity; for two examples see John D. Steinrucken, "Secularism's Ongoing Debt to Christianity," *American Thinker*, July 30, 2010 (http://www.americanthinker.com/2010/03/secularisms_ongoing_debt_to_ch.html), and Camille Paglia, "Religion and the Arts in America," *Arion* 15.1 (Spring/Summer 2007): 1–20 (http://arts.ccpblogs.com/files/2008/08/paglia-religion-and-the-art.pdf).

[2] C. S. Lewis, *The Abolition of Man, or Reflections on Education with Special Reference to the Teaching of English in the Upper Forms of Schools* (San Francisco: HarperSanFrancisco, 1974 repr.).

[3] Martin Luther King Jr., "The Purpose of Education," *Maroon Tiger* (January–February 1947), 10. Reprinted at http://mlk-kpp01.stanford.edu/index.php/encyclopedia/documentsentry/doc_470200_000/.

[4] For an excellent collection of essays on this topic, see Douglas V. Henry and Michael D. Beaty, eds., *The Schooled Heart: Moral Formation in American Higher Education* (Waco, TX: Baylor University Press, 2007).

[5] While I do not have space in this chapter to address the role of student life in the core curriculum, I am of the opinion that general education should have a clear, strong partnership with the cocurricular elements of the university, especially in a traditional, residential setting. Wise campus leaders will find ways to interleaf the work of residence life, student leadership development, and other units on campus with the work of the academic classroom curriculum. This is, of course, an extension of the view that a Christian university should be a learning community that considers all of its members as partners in the educational enterprise.

[6] The Southern Association for Colleges and Schools includes Standard 2.7.3 on general education requirements: "In each undergraduate degree program, the institution requires the successful completion of a general education component at the collegiate level that (1) is a substantial component of each undergraduate degree, (2) ensures breadth of knowledge, and (3) is based on a coherent rationale. . . . [The baccalaureate requirement] constitutes . . . a minimum of 30 semester hours or the equivalent. These credit hours are to be drawn from and include at least one course from each of the following areas: humanities/fine arts, social/behavioral sciences, and natural science/ mathematics. The courses do not narrowly focus on those skills, techniques, and procedures specific to a particular

occupation or profession." *The Principles for Accreditation: Foundations for Quality Enhancement* (2010): 17.

[7] Classroom size is not the same as student to faculty ratio; because a variety of formulas may be used to generate this ratio, the best indication of true class size is the number of classrooms that seat 25 or fewer.

[8] This concept is rooted in, among other Scriptures, Col 1:19–21, "For God was pleased [to have] all His fullness dwell in [Christ], and through Him to reconcile everything to Himself by making peace through the blood of His cross—whether things on earth or things in heaven. Once you were alienated and hostile in your mind because of your evil actions."

[9] Perhaps the most famous liberal arts-based core curriculum is the "Common Core" implemented by Robert Maynard Hutchins and Mortimer Adler at the University of Chicago in the 1940s. This program generated the Great Books study adopted by many other institutions.

[10] Richard A. Riesen, *Piety and Philosophy: A Primer for Christian Schools* (Ozark, AL: ACW Press 2002), is a most useful resource for the overlap between the liberal arts and the Christian faith; see particularly pages 61ff.

[11] Interestingly, a few "closet" dramatists such as Terrence remained in circulation. Closet dramas were written for private edification in one's study or closet and were not intended for production on stage. For most of the Fathers, apparently, performances were more corrupting than the mere reading of the texts.

[12] Augustine, *Confessions,* trans. F. J. Sheed (New York: Sheed and Ward 1944), 113.

[13] See Rom 1:18–23 for part of the rationale for this doctrine.

[14] *George Washington Carver in His Own Words*, ed. Gary R. Kremer (Columbia, MO: University of Missouri Press, 1991), 141.

[15] Carver's open discussions of the role of faith in guiding his research were criticized by the *New York Times* in a famous editorial "Men of Science Never Talk That Way," published Nov. 20, 1924. This set off a fairly controversial series of exchanges between religious leaders and secular critics of openly religious intellectuals.

[16] Another effect of considering principle over personality is the avoidance of distracting arguments over the status of a thinker's orthodoxy or sinful nature. Almost anyone who lifts up the name of Christ will have beliefs that are heterodox in the eyes of some, including luminaries such as C. S. Lewis and John Milton. In the same way, all believers struggle with their sinful natures, and we should not be surprised to learn of moral failings, sometimes significant ones, in leading thinkers. When we focus on the principles that these persons use in their works, we are minimizing these persons and maximizing the impetus for their works: the glorification of God, which may be emulated in our academic work.

[17] The carvings on the arch include the only known contemporary depictions of the furnishings of the temple in Jerusalem.

[18] Marcus Aurelius, the Stoic philosopher, battled the idea of the selfish, pleasure-seeking ego in his influential treatise *Meditations*, trans. George Long (repr., Mineola, NY: Dover 1997), which became standard reading for young scholars for two millennia. More recently, in 1946, José Ortega y Gasset wrote, "General education means the whole development of an individual, apart from his occupational training. It includes the civilizing of his life purposes, the refinishing of

his emotional reaction, and the maturing of his understanding about the nature of things according to the best knowledge of our time." *Mission of the University*, trans. Howard Lee Nostrand (London: Kegan Paul, 1946), quoted in Henry Rosovsky, *The University: An Owner's Manual* (New York: Norton, 1990), 100. Rosovsky himself spends a great deal of time exploring the value of humility, humanity, and humor in liberal education, traits which he learned from John Buchan (101).

[19] All Scripture quotations are taken from the Holman Christian Standard Bible.

[20] This contrast seems to echo hauntingly the words of Satan in Gen 3:4–5: "'No! You will not die,' the serpent said to the woman. 'In fact, God knows that when you eat it your eyes will be opened and you will be like God, knowing good and evil.'" This same thought underlies the sentiment that Isaiah once offered: "We all went astray like sheep; we all have turned to our own way " (53:6 HCSB).

[21] For a helpful survey of Christian education in the United States, see William C. Ringenberg, *The Christian College: A History of Protestant Higher Education in America*, 2nd ed. (Grand Rapids: Baker, 2006).

[22] For a dazzling survey of the breadth of Christian higher education, see Harry Lee Poe's "The Religious Spectrum in Higher Education," in *Christianity in the Academy: Teaching at the Intersection of Faith and Learning* (Grand Rapids: Baker 2004), 31–52.

[23] Indeed, empathy is often cited as one of the primary results of a liberal arts education. See, for example, Howard W. Figler, Carol Carter, Joyce Bishop, and Sarah Lyman Kravitz, *Keys to Liberal Arts Success* (Upper Saddle River, NJ: Prentice Hall, 2002), 10ff.

[24] I have written about my own experiences in graduating with my undergraduate degree in 1984, after only three years of coursework, at *The Chronicle of Higher Education*, "Confessions of a 3-Year Degree Student," Nov. 4, 2009 (http://chronicle.com/article/Confessions-of-a-3-Year-Deg/49001/).

3

ETHICAL AND MORAL REASONING

Kenneth Magnuson

There is a distinctive ethical and moral dimension at the center of Christian higher education. This chapter will explore ethical and moral reasoning issues from that vantage point. Moral reasoning is not primarily about how to work our way through complex moral dilemmas, nor is it concerned first with what position to take on controversial issues such as war or euthanasia or abortion, nor even with how to make the next ethical decision that we face. We may be tempted to think that moral reasoning, or ethics itself, can be reduced to one or another of these things. When books on ethics suggest this, at least implicitly, by their focus and content, they offer a truncated view of moral reasoning and of ethics. Moral reasoning may include these things, but it cannot be reduced to them. But if it is not these things, then what is it? Put simply, Christian moral reasoning is the task of discerning who we ought to be, what we ought to pursue, and how we ought to think and act, individually and collectively as human beings. With these questions in mind, the aim of this chapter is to explore some of the contours of Christian moral reasoning.

The Will of God and Christian Moral Reasoning

Christian moral reasoning may also be described as discerning the purposes and will of God as revealed in Scripture, especially in the person and work of Jesus Christ. Several aspects of God's will may shed light on Christian moral reasoning. God's will is universal. In one sense, this means that it applies to all people. God as Creator bids all people to do His will, not just those who "opt in" or acknowledge Him. In another sense, it means that His will is general, which may and must be expressed in specific ways (for example, we are called to love our neighbor, which may be conveyed by caring for someone who is sick, or in some other way). Further, it means that God's will is expressed in generic commands, which must be applied to particular cases; for example, the command "do not steal" is generic, and it must be perceived that shoplifting or illegally downloading software or underpaying taxes are particular instances of stealing.[1]

God's will is not only universal but also comprehensive, involving every area of our lives, and relating to individual, community, and global concerns. It has to do with who we are and ought to be, including our character and the virtues that we nurture. It has to do with what we do and how we think about such things as education, work, worship, marriage, and children, as well as issues like war, stem cell research, abortion, sexual ethics, the environment, immigration, poverty, and many other moral concerns. Further, it has to do with life's purposes, including ultimately how to glorify God in all that we do.

Often God's will is clear and moral reasoning is fairly simple and straightforward. God commands plainly, for example, that we should not murder, commit adultery, bear false witness, or steal. Even when it is more difficult to perceive (should we lie to protect human life? when is civil disobedience necessary?), discerning God's will requires not so much that we learn a complex formula but that we develop the skill to apply knowledge wisely. So, the apostle Paul prays that the Colossians would be filled with the knowledge of God's will "in all wisdom and spiritual understanding" (Col 1:9 HCSB). Further, Paul indicates that the purpose of knowing God's will is to "walk worthy of the Lord" (v. 10 HCSB). This expression shows a deep concern for how people conduct their whole lives. Moral reasoning involves thinking about a "walk" that is pleasing to God, which suggests not only a particular action or even a series of actions, but a manner of life that includes a person's disposition and direction in life. To live in such a way, Paul indicates, is to grow in the knowledge of God (Col 1:10). Thus moral reasoning is not simply an abstract discipline or rational exercise, but it is something that is done before and in relation to God. By knowing God we come to know how we ought to live, and by living as we ought to we come to know God more fully.

In his letter to the Romans, Paul urges, "Do not be conformed to this age, but be transformed by the renewing of your mind," in order that we may know and do the will of God (Rom 12:2 HCSB). Christian moral reasoning involves a distinct way of thinking. As Michael Banner contends, for moral reasoning to be Christian it must "proceed from a fully theological description and interpretation of the world" or its prescriptions will be "a simple reflection of governing secular norms."[2] He adds, "Human life is truly understood and rightly ordered only as it is understood and ordered in the light of this knowledge of God and humankind."[3] Similarly, Oliver O'Donovan says, "the foundation of Christian ethics must be evangelical foundations; or, to put it more simply, Christian ethics must arise from the gospel of Jesus Christ. Otherwise it could not be *Christian* ethics."[4] Christian moral reasoning is structured by the gospel of Jesus Christ. So it is in view of "the mercies of God" that Paul makes his appeal to live holy lives (Rom 12:1 HCSB). The gospel sets the agenda and framework for Christian ethics as it discloses the truth about God and humankind, as it transforms the heart and mind through faith, shapes character, and calls for and enables true obedience.

Christian Moral Reasoning and the Public Square

Before proceeding we may anticipate an objection to *Christian* moral reasoning, at least as it pertains to public dialogue. It claims that to engage in public discourse Christians must not speak from a distinctly Christian perspective, but rather must exclude religious truth-claims and restrict their arguments to presuppositions and conclusions that are accepted by the majority. How might this claim be answered?

One response appeals to *natural law* as the most promising way for Christians to engage publicly.[5] It may be said briefly that natural law refers to "moral principles that are both right and knowable to everybody by the ordinary exercise of human reason."[6] It is not possible to offer an adequate description or examination of natural law here, but a few comments are in order. While it has much to commend it, a natural law approach cannot hope to satisfy those who would exclude all matters of faith from public debate. This is in part because moral arguments from natural law are dependent on a worldview that includes beliefs about God. Thus, it encounters a serious problem in public debate, for natural law moral arguments are difficult to sustain apart from certain beliefs about God, but disallowed if its arguments are connected to those beliefs.

Further, if the claims of natural law are knowable to any reasonable person, why are such arguments not sufficient to reach a significant degree of consensus on moral truth? Michael Banner offers an explanation, suggesting that "the claims of natural law are, where uncontroversial, uninteresting and where interesting, controversial."[7] For instance, if natural law claims that killing innocent human beings is wrong, it will be uncontroversial. Yet little will have been achieved, for natural law will be challenged precisely where its claims are controversial, such as areas of disagreement over that which constitutes wrongful killing. If, for example, natural law arguments are used to claim that euthanasia and abortion are examples of wrongful killing and are never or rarely justified, but that killing in war and capital punishment are justified in some cases, there will be many who reject its claims. Given the interminable debate on such issues, it is difficult to maintain that arguments from reason alone are "knowable to everybody"—or that they will produce the same conclusions. Accordingly, while J. Budziszewski affirms the use of natural law, he asserts that it "is best grounded not in the study of nature independent of God's Word but in the Word of God itself."[8] So grounded, it must be recognized that it faces the challenge brought against distinctly Christian thinking.

If Christian moral reasoning cannot be sustained apart from theological knowledge grounded in the Bible, may Christians speak *distinctly as Christians* only to each other? Or may they speak in public only when invited to do so by those who perhaps anticipate an answer that they welcome? Put simply, no, and not merely because Christians, too, are citizens with a right to speak. The simplest argument against excluding a Christian perspective in public debate, in the name of neutrality, is provided by critics of Christianity such as Marx, Nietzsche, and Freud. They contended that there is no neutral perspective from which Christianity is able to make a case for its truth claims. But then, it can be said that there is no neutral position from which anyone is able to speak, including critics of a Christian perspective.[9] If a neutral perspective were demanded in order for anyone to speak publicly, significant public discourse would cease.

In any case, forsaking a distinctly Christian perspective in an attempt to be heard in public dialogue may imply that it is neither true nor persuasive, and often leads to theological and biblical compromise, generating arguments that accommodate whatever views are fashionable. Conversely, making a case from a distinctly Christian perspective, while others contend for their own perspective, is not to forsake dialogue. Indeed, as Banner maintains, "Far from making dialogue impossible we might even say that such an understanding of our engagement with the public realm is a precondition of it, since where one partner in a conversation allows his or her contribution to be decisively shaped by the need to avoid disagreement, what results is not dialogue at all but the absurd (and finally rather patronizing) attempt to echo in advance the views of the other."[10] Rather than agreeing to be silent or accommodating secular critics, there are strategies that Christians can employ in public discourse. One might challenge the presuppositions and conclusions of other views, expose inconsistencies in their arguments, encourage others to consider alternative conclusions that are consistent with their own presuppositions, or simply offer a different set of presuppositions, arguments and conclusions in the hope that they will be received by some despite the initial rejection of the perspective from which they come.[11]

It will, of course, be necessary for Christians to find areas of agreement with others in order to develop a workable public policy on many issues. Yet Christians do not need to give up what is distinctly Christian in the task of moral reasoning in order to engage with other views. Indeed, it would be pointless to do so. And, of course, Christians should not expect others to give up their distinctive views, for the same reasons.

At this point we may sketch out two main aspects of moral reasoning. Once we have done that, we will consider broad ethical frameworks within which moral reasoning takes place before offering a theological proposal that includes both the ethical framework for and certain specific details of Christian moral reasoning.

Two Main Aspects of Moral Reasoning: Reflection and Deliberation

Oliver O'Donovan asserts that "Christian moral reasoning involves the exercise of two kinds of thought together: 1. reflection; and 2. deliberation. Reflection is thought *about* something; when we reflect, we ask 'What is the truth?' Deliberation is thought *towards action*; when we deliberate, we ask, 'What are we to do?'"[12]

In seeking to know the truth about something, moral reflection is concerned with understanding a situation and its context rightly. For moral theology, according to Bernard Haring, the basic task is "to gain the right vision, to assess the main perspectives, and to present those truths and values which should bear upon decisions to be made before God."[13] The Bible describes an order to reality that must be received and perceived in order to make proper sense of human action and of the facts or details that we process in making a moral decision. Some acts, like murder, do not require prolonged reflection to discern what is true and to form a moral judgment. We have a clear conviction (and a command!) that murder is wrong. That judgment makes sense because it is part of a worldview in which human life is understood to be worthy of protection. In a Christian perspective, murder is wrong because the victim's life is sacred, for all human beings are created in the image of God, and God has prohibited any unauthorized taking of human life.

The prohibition of murder is straightforward enough, but what about a different case, such as torture? It may be argued that torture is wrong for the same reason that murder is wrong, i.e., that God has created human beings in His own image and has deemed human life to be sacred, so that the abuse of any human being is an attack upon God and is therefore wrong. Yet someone might defend torture—even if wrongly so—on the basis that they do not believe human life is sacred, or because they think that the person who would be tortured may be treated inhumanely because that is the way he has treated others. Or they may believe that there is an exception to the general prohibition against torture when certain conditions apply, such as when it is known that a terrorist involved in a plot to kill thousands of innocent people has information that can save lives, and it seems the information can only be attained through torture.

These examples illustrate the relationship between reflection and deliberation. First, it can be seen that moral deliberation is grounded in moral reflection. Indeed, according to O'Donovan, "deliberation cannot happen at all without reflection" for it "depends on a reflective grasp of some truth."[14] Deliberation is concerned with possible alternatives for action that are available to us, which are clarified and limited through moral reflection. Deliberation may follow immediately on a period of reflection. Or, it may flow from reflection that has taken place long before, or from beliefs that are held not because of extended reflection but because they are revealed (by God or another authority) and accepted as such or because there is a large degree of consensus on the matter.

Another point that underscores the significance of moral reflection is this. If deliberation depends upon a grasp of some truth, then where truth is grasped inadequately—or not at all—the deliberation that follows will be lacking, often leading to immoral action. In the above example, for instance, someone might defend torture based on faulty moral reflection. Perhaps the fault is in failing to understand that human beings bear God's image. Or the fault may be a failure to grasp that even suspected terrorists are human beings who must be treated with dignity—even though they may have denied others of their dignity—otherwise the would-be torturer may commit the very evil that he is fighting against. Another insight of reflection may be to note that torture is often ineffective for gaining reliable information.

In some cases, deliberation may be problematic because little or no moral reflection has preceded it. Consider a case in which Susan, a single woman, finds herself in a crisis pregnancy, and without reflecting significantly on her situation, she thinks about how to deal with her crisis. She contemplates all the options, which include: (1) having the baby, marrying the father, and raising the baby together; (2) having the baby and raising the baby by herself; (3) having the baby and raising the baby with help from her family; (4) having the baby and placing the baby with an adoptive family; (5) having an abortion. The very nature of a crisis is that there typically are no easy solutions. Perhaps before becoming pregnant, Susan considered abortion unthinkable, but now, because she is in this crisis, it is a real option and she may consider it, not because she defends abortion in principle, but because it may seem to be the "lesser of two evils." Her doubts about that choice may be alleviated by arguments that the fetus is merely a potential human being, not a human being in its own right.

It is possible to understand the deliberation in this example to be faulty at least in part because Susan has not attended adequately to moral reflection. We may, for instance, ask what it means to say that she "found" herself in a crisis pregnancy, and whether thinking in such terms is a subtle way of evading moral responsibility for her actions. The way we articulate a situation shapes our understanding, for it may reveal or conceal what is true. Often we first need to articulate better—more truthfully—the situation, and that is part of the task of moral reflection. In this respect, we might also question whether we ought to think of this crisis merely as *her* crisis. For there is, or was, a man involved, David, who bears responsibility as the father of the child, so that if there is a crisis, it is his crisis too. It may also be understood as a crisis for the families of Susan and David, and even for the community to which they belong, which also bears responsibility.[15]

Another and more obvious impact that moral reflection will have on this case has to do with the child in Susan's womb. For if it is perceived that the child is a human being, who must therefore be treated with dignity, then the options for deliberation will not include abortion. Abortion will not be considered the *lesser of two evils*, giving it a certain degree of credibility, for other options available, though they may be difficult or inconvenient, are *not* evil. Again, it is the work of reflection both to grasp and to articulate things truthfully. For that reason, we might seek to clarify one or two other things. We might ask, for example, whether the use of the term "fetus" is sometimes a way of obscuring the identity of the child, and point out that the term is simply Latin for "offspring," used in medical terminology to denote the stage, not the status, of the human being. Finally, our reflection might clarify what it means to refer to the unborn child as a potential human being. Such language conceals the reality that the unborn child is not merely a *potential* human being, but an *actual* human being in an early stage of development in comparison to the newborn or the child in school or the adult human being whom the unborn child has the potential to become.

Some of these points need to be developed if they are to stand up to scrutiny, and, from a Christian perspective, they need to be tested biblically and theologically. Here the purpose is simply to demonstrate the significance of adequate reflection, and to show how moral deliberation depends upon reflection, for better or for worse. Moral reasoning is a skill that involves learning to grasp what is true about the world and to understand how moral decisions relate to and flow from the truth that has been grasped. Whether and how that skill is developed, and just how reflection and deliberation are understood and related, depends upon the way that ethics in general is conceived.

Of the many perspectives for ethics that could be discussed, we will focus on three that are widely adopted. After sketching briefly a few salient features of each perspective, it will be possible to offer a proposal for a biblical/theological framework for ethics, and how moral reasoning operates within that framework.

Three Frameworks for Ethics: Deontology, Consequentialism, and Virtue Ethics

Deontology

One major ethical framework, *deontology*, from the Greek *deon* for obligation or duty, emphasizes moral principles or duties as central to understanding ethics. The binding character of universal moral norms forms the basis of moral obligation. Immanuel Kant offers a paradigmatic statement of the deontological perspective in what he calls a categorical imperative: "Act only on that maxim whereby thou canst at the same time will that it should become a universal law."[16] Moral reasoning in this view seeks to discover and apply universal moral norms, such as the mandate that we ought to value every human life. Closely related to such norms are moral principles, which may be articulated as a statement ("murder is wrong" or "every human life has dignity") or command ("do not murder"). Such principles may be applied and stated more precisely at the level of moral rules or acts, either in prohibitions (e.g., against euthanasia, which ends human life, or drunk driving, which endangers human life) or in mandates (e.g., "Good Samaritan" laws or the requirement to build a fence around a swimming pool, which may save lives). A moral norm is understood to be universal, i.e., it applies to all people at all times, while a moral rule is not, since it is adapted to different contexts.[17]

For a deontologist, moral obligation is not determined by the consequences of an act. A morally right act may sometimes produce undesirable results, but that does not make it a wrong act, and a morally wrong act may sometimes produce desirable results, but that does not justify the act. A deontologist need not ignore or have no regard for consequences. They may be important, but they simply are not considered primary for determining moral action. In other words, good ends cannot justify immoral means.

Consequentialism

In contrast to deontology, *consequentialism* considers the morality of acts in terms of whether or not they produce desirable results. Indeed, the necessity of producing desirable results forms the basis of moral obligation. Acts or rules are not thought to have *intrinsic* moral value, that is, they are not understood to be intrinsically good or evil. Rather, they have *instrumental* value in relation to intended or achieved consequences. One of the primary formulators of this view, John Stuart Mill, put it this way: "Acts are right in proportion as they tend to promote happiness, wrong as they tend to produce the reverse of happiness."[18] Happiness, in this view, is what human beings rightly pursue. It is not necessarily measured in terms of immediate pleasure, but often in a broader sense of human flourishing, which may take into account both intensity and duration of pleasure.

Consequentialism denotes a variety of views in ethics in which the morality of an act is judged solely or primarily in terms of the consequences of the act. The concern may be with the greatest good for the greatest number of people, as in classic forms of utilitarianism (perhaps the most widely defended form of consequentialism in principle), or with the moral agent's own happiness, as in ethical egoism (perhaps the most widely followed form in practice). Moral reasoning operates on the principle of utility, or what works best to produce a desired result. This view is often summarized by the slogan, "the end justifies the means," which is a fair summary, though only to a point. Few would argue that a good end justifies *any* means, but rather that acts which on balance promote greater happiness are justified while acts that on balance do not produce happiness are not justified. Consequentialism is sometimes referred to as a *teleological* perspective (from the Greek *telos*, for "end" or "goal"), though the two terms are not properly interchangeable for, as we shall see, teleology refers to broader concerns than the consequences or results of our acts.

Virtue Ethics

A third perspective for ethics is not primarily concerned with evaluating the morality of actions on the basis of universal moral norms *or* consequences. In fact, it is not primarily concerned with evaluating the morality of *actions* at all. Rather, *virtue* ethics has to do first and foremost with *who we are* and not simply *what we do*. Virtue ethicists are often critical of views that focus on acts and the tendency to portray ethics in terms of moral dilemmas that must be negotiated through moral reasoning, sometimes referred to as "quandary ethics."[19] From this perspective, to focus on moral dilemmas is to distort what ethics is truly about. The problem for ethics is not so much a matter of the *intellect*—learning how to discern the right thing to do when facing life's moral dilemmas—as it is a matter of the *will*—learning to do what we know we ought to do. Stanley Hauerwas has addressed these concerns repeatedly in his writings. In *The Peaceable Kingdom*, for instance, he states, "in matters of significance even involving the 'hardest choices' there was no 'decision' to be made. Rather, the decision makes itself if we know who we are and what is required of us."[20]

Thus, virtue ethics is oriented to the moral agent, rather than the moral act, and to the character of the agent and the community to which the agent belongs. Moral reasoning tends to be centered on reflection—considering the virtues that are to be pursued and which shape our lives—though questions of deliberation inevitably must be asked. Indeed, if moral obligation is derived from the nature and demands of virtue, it is nonetheless true that there must be concrete acts that correspond to and express the virtues and ideals and expectations of the community to which we belong. Yet, as Hauerwas suggests, those acts flow from the character of the moral agent rather than from an abstract decision-making process. Since virtuous character is required to make good decisions consistently, virtue ethics focuses on forming character. This in turn highlights the importance of the relationships and role models found in family and community, where virtue is formed.

A Biblical and Theological Assessment and Proposal

In assessing these perspectives, it is necessary to indicate how the task of Christian ethics is conceived in relation to the Bible. Oliver O'Donovan acknowledges a variety of sources that contribute to Christian moral thought, but rightly insists that "it derives its substance predominantly from the reading of the Bible."[21] Yet there are different perspectives on just how that substance is derived from the Bible.[22] A deontologist will often focus on its commands and how they express universal moral norms. Indeed, it is difficult to ignore deontological features in the Bible. God reveals Himself as the Creator and Lord whose commands call for glad obedience to live in right relationship with Him and with one another. A central task of Christian moral reasoning is to hear the commands of God in Scripture and apply them in the contemporary context. Yet it would be a truncated reading of the Bible to see it, as a deontologist might be tempted to do, mainly as a rule book, for the Bible provides Christian ethics with much more than "a series of naked commands."[23] Michael Banner points out that one of the problems with viewing the Bible as a rule book is that it does not take the Bible seriously enough, for like an instruction manual for an appliance, once we think that we have learned what is required, it may be set aside for later reference, if needed to solve a problem.[24]

We might press this further, and question the very notion of *using* the Bible in Christian ethics at all. This is not to question the relevance and authority of the Bible, but rather to suggest that talk about how to *use* the Bible in Christian ethics is misguided. A contribution of virtue ethics is the reminder that, rather than *the reader using the Bible*, perhaps to mine it for its commands, *the Bible shapes the reader*. It sets the agenda for moral reasoning, rather than answering to an agenda set by the reader. As we read and meditate upon the Bible, it penetrates the heart and mind, transforming our worldview and shaping not merely our actions but our motives, desires, and character. In other words, we are shaped not only by the commands of God that we encounter in the Bible, but also by its message and the reality behind the narrative—especially the metanarrative wherein the gospel of Jesus Christ is the central focus of the history of redemption—that may be missed by those who simply search for commands.

The Bible, then, includes elements of both deontology and virtue ethics. Consequentialism, on the other hand, doesn't fare so well. It is not that it is unbiblical to assert the importance of consequences, or to regard the end or goal to be an important consideration for choosing a course of action, or even to view human happiness—properly understood—as a central concern of ethics. However, consequentialism overstates the case, making consequences the *ultimate* criterion by which acts are judged, which effectively denies the morality of *acts* altogether. Further, its understanding of the ends of human action, particularly of happiness, is subjective and arbitrary, depending on human reason without regard for a normative biblical perspective or, for that matter, any normative perspective at all. The legitimate concerns of consequentialists may in fact be met by a more robust form of teleology than consequentialism is able to offer.

As indicated earlier, to the extent that consequentialism understands morality to be related to the goals or ends of acts, it may be understood as a *teleological* perspective. However, teleology has to do with much more than consequences, so that a teleological perspective need not be consequentialist. For instance, the Westminster Shorter Catechism begins with the teleological question, "What is the chief end of man?" and answers, "Man's chief end is to glorify God, and to enjoy him forever."[25] Indeed, a biblical account of ethics is teleological, concerned as it is with the end or goal of human acts—even the most benign acts, so that "whether you eat or drink, or whatever you do, do everything for God's glory" (1 Cor 10:31 HCSB). Yet in the ethical framework of the Bible, the teleological perspective is not at odds with universal moral norms, as it tends to be in consequentialism. Rather, moral norms are integral to such a perspective, for the Bible affirms that God creates the world with purpose, and His commands are ordered to His purposes. The purposes or ends of life are given by God and are objective, to be perceived and received, not chosen by human beings who order means and ends as they see fit. The work of moral reasoning is to perceive how human aims, behavior, and character align with God's purposes, will and character, rather than seeking to produce certain consequences. Oliver O'Donovan defends and expounds a view of Christian ethics that is robustly teleological in *Resurrection and Moral Order*. "The order of things that God has made is there. It is objective, and mankind has a place within it. Christian ethics, therefore, has an objective reference because it is concerned with man's life in accordance with this order."[26]

In such an account of Christian ethics, happiness has its place, even a central place, as consequentialists recognize. Yet the happiness that is properly a concern of Christian ethics is one that is not discovered by unaided human reason, which is guided by selfish desires, satisfied by short-term gratification, and suspicious of and resistant to external commands. It is Jesus, and not human reason, for instance, who reveals that those who mourn, and are even persecuted, are blessed, i.e., profoundly happy (Matt 5:3–10). They are blessed because they will inherit God's kingdom, yet their joy is not merely future, but is experienced in this age through an abundance of things that matter most and fulfill God's intentions for our lives (Mark 10:30; John 10:10). True happiness is found in God's will, and ultimately in God Himself, as Augustine declared, "you have made us for yourself, and our hearts are restless until they find their rest in you."[27] As such, the problem is not that human beings pursue happiness, but that they settle for things that will not ultimately satisfy. So C. S. Lewis writes, "We are half-hearted creatures, fooling about with drink and sex and ambition when infinite joy is offered us, like an ignorant child who wants to go on making mud pies in a slum because he cannot imagine what is meant by the offer of a holiday at the sea. We are far too easily pleased."[28] Christian ethics contemplates a happiness that is not sought in consequentialist perspectives.

The above discussion reveals that deontology, teleology, and virtue ethics are not mutually exclusive but are complementary dimensions of Christian ethics.[29] Moral norms are expressed in commands that are ordered to God's purposes in creation and redemption, for God's glory and for human good, because they restrain sin and protect a community from "disintegration through self-interest, force, and violence."[30] In this way, biblical prohibitions, or restraints on sinful action, are neither oppressive nor suppressive of human good, but rather are given for the sake of relationships within a community. They promote human flourishing in the enjoyment of God's gifts of life, sex and marriage, property and commerce, communication, and so on. The prohibition of sex outside of marriage, for instance, is protective of the integrity of marriage, an individual's sexuality, and the deepest pleasure of sex, i.e., the purposes for which sex and marriage are given by God.[31] By willing obedience to God's commands, human beings are able to live individually and in community without the disintegration that occurs when we pursue actions and ends contrary to that for which we have been made. God's commands are teleologically ordered to God's glory and human good.

Like moral norms (and commands that are related to them), virtues are also ordered to God's purposes in creation. They are complementary to and indeed necessary for a proper deontology, for virtue is correlated to action. Virtue is necessary to be able consistently to act rightly, for acts are not performed in a moral vacuum, but flow from one's character, whether good or bad. At the same time, virtue is known by habits formed through the repetition of acts that characterize the virtues, measured by commands that indicate or delimit what the particular virtue does. Ultimately, virtue and virtuous acts are a work of God by the gift of His Spirit, "for it is God who is working in you, enabling you both to desire and to work out His good purpose" (Phil 2:13 HCSB).

Christian moral reasoning, then, is a matter of moral reflection and deliberation, which flows from a Christian worldview perspective that is derived from the Bible. In particular, it operates within a Christian ethical framework that integrates deontology and virtue ethics with a teleological perspective. What remains is to sketch briefly how these things come together in making moral decisions.

A Model for Moral Decision-Making

In *Moral Choices*, Scott Rae provides a model for making ethical decisions, which he applies to several case studies to show how it works. He lists, explains, and applies seven elements in his model:[32]

1. Gather the Facts.
2. Determine the Ethical Issues.
3. Determine What Virtues/Principles Have a Bearing on the Case.
4. List the Alternatives.
5. Compare the Alternatives with the Virtues/Principles.
6. Consider the Consequences.
7. Make a Decision.

My purpose here is not to examine Rae's work, though his discussion of case studies nicely demonstrates examples of moral reasoning. Rather, I will propose a model that seeks to integrate the above discussion of moral reasoning. While it is similar in substance, it attempts to avoid certain features of models that present a step-by-step approach, which tend to be a problem not of the model itself, but of its users, such as the tendency to think that simply moving through each step will produce a morally good act. The elements in the model that I propose are as follows:

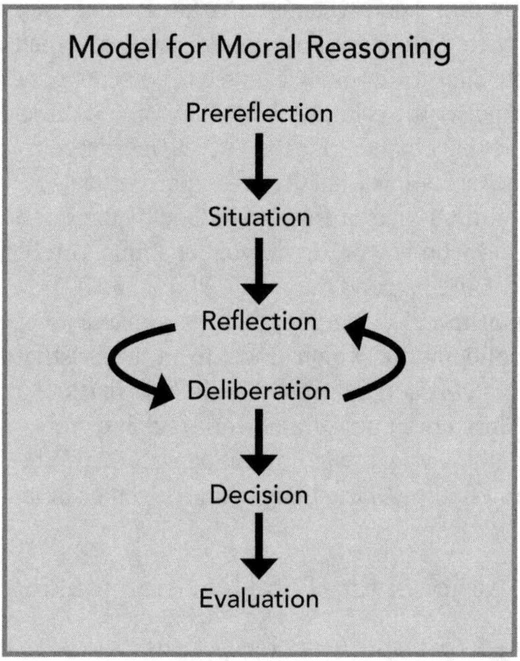

Prereflection signifies that even prior to our reflection on a particular case we have a worldview through which we interpret what we see, just as we speak in hermeneutics of presuppositions that we bring to a reading of any text that affect our understanding of the text. Prereflection involves who we are and how we think, shaped by our upbringing and education. Virtue and teleological dimensions are central here, for how we interpret a situation is particularly affected by the virtues that we possess or lack and by the purposes that we perceive in the world. Ultimately, in a biblical perspective, prereflection is determined by our relation to God, for we are either enlightened or darkened in our understanding, depending upon whether we acknowledge God or turn away from Him (e.g., Rom 12:1–2; Eph 4:17–24). Of course, inasmuch as the deontological perspective is closely related to the other two, it will operate in our prereflection as well, though it may not be as pronounced.

To place the *situation* in this model is simply to recognize that moral decision-making takes place in relation to some situation, real or hypothetical. The central task of moral reasoning, as discussed earlier, involves *reflection* and *deliberation*. We need only make a few comments here to place these elements in the decision-making process. It is significant to note, first, that while deliberation follows on and is shaped by reflection, it does not stand apart from it, or follow on reflection in a strict chronological sense, as if it is a task performed only after reflection has been completed. There is influence in both directions, as indicated by the arrows in the diagram. Second, this model may be related to the one presented by Rae as follows. The first three elements of Rae's model are part of reflection (gathering facts, determining ethical issues, and discerning what virtues and principles relate to the case), while the next three elements are part of deliberation (listing alternatives, comparing the alternatives with virtues and principles, and considering the consequences), followed by actually making a decision.

Third, in both reflection and deliberation, while we may consider a situation distinctly from the perspective of teleology, virtue, or deontology, yet they belong together and influence each other. In reflection, our understanding of moral norms arises from and is shaped by our understanding of purpose and virtue. For example, if we discern God's purpose for speech and communication and what is entailed by the virtue of truthfulness, we may better grasp what is demanded by the prohibition of false witness. At the same time, attention to moral norms helps to shape our understanding of virtue and purpose, as when the prohibition of false witness informs us as to what is entailed by the virtue of truthfulness and of the purpose of speech and communication. This shows how difficult it is to separate the three aspects of ethics. In deliberation, the three aspects influence each other as well. As we consider alternatives, we may ask how the alternatives relate to ultimate purposes, how they flow from and shape our character, and to what extent the best alternative is determined by a particular moral norm. Finally, while considering the alternatives, it is important to take into account anticipated consequences, which will play a role in narrowing the options, other things being equal.

At some point, a *decision* is made, even if the decision is not to act at all. Yet moral reasoning does not end even when the decision has been made, for it is then open to *evaluation* by the moral agent and others, which is critical to maintain perspective and to sharpen our skills. This is a particularly important aspect of the process because moral decisions are made frequently without opportunity to engage in sustained reflection and deliberation, and it is then left to the task of evaluation to sharpen the mind and will for the ongoing process of moral reasoning. Finally, it should be recognized that as we engage in moral reasoning, whether spontaneously or with a great deal of thought, we are shaped so that we arrive at a new place of prereflection, which is a product, for better or worse in both our will and intellect, of our cumulative moral decisions. As C. S. Lewis wrote, "Every time you make a choice, you are turning the central part of you, the part of you that chooses, into something a little different from what it was before. And taking your life as a whole, with all your innumerable choices . . . all your life long you are slowly turning this central thing into a Heavenly creature or into a hellish creature."[33] Moral reasoning matters.

Questions for Further Reflection

1. Should distinctly Christian moral reasoning have a place in the public square? Why or why not?
2. What are the main features of moral reasoning?
3. How is moral reasoning shaped by the Bible?
4. How does moral reflection affect our decision-making?
5. Which framework(s) for ethics best fit(s) the ethical framework of the Bible?

Resources for Further Study

Banner, Michael. *Christian Ethics: A Brief History*. Oxford: Wiley-Blackwell, 2009.

———. *Christian Ethics and Contemporary Moral Problems*. Cambridge: Cambridge University Press, 1999.

———. "Introductory Remarks: Christian Ethical Reasoning." *Transformation* 15 (April 1998): 15–17.

Bonhoeffer, Dietrich. *Ethics*. Translated by Neville Horton Smith; edited by Eberhard Bethge. New York: Macmillan, 1955.

Brock, Brian. *Singing the Ethos of God: On the Place of Christian Ethics in Scripture*. Grand Rapids: Eerdmans, 2007.

Bromiley, Geoffrey W. *God and Marriage*. Grand Rapids: Eerdmans, 1980.

Budziszewski, J. *What We Can't Not Know*. Dallas: Spence Publishing Company, 2003.

———. *Written on the Heart: The Case for Natural Law*. Downers Grove, IL: InterVarsity Press, 1997.

Haring, Bernard. *Free and Faithful in Christ*. 3 vols. New York: Seabury, 1978–81.

Hauerwas, Stanley. *The Peaceable Kingdom: A Primer in Christian Ethics*. Notre Dame, IN: University of Notre Dame Press, 1983.

Kant, Immanuel. *Fundamental Principles of the Metaphysics of Ethics*. Translated by Thomas Abbott. 10th ed. New York: Longmans, Green, 1937.

Lewis, C. S. *Mere Christianity*. New York: Touchstone, 1996 reprint.

———. *The Weight of Glory: And Other Addresses*. San Francisco: HarperCollins, 2001 reprint.

MacIntyre, Alasdair. *After Virtue: A Study in Moral Theory*. 2nd ed. Notre Dame, IN: University of Notre Dame Press, 1984.

———. *Three Rival Versions of Moral Enquiry: Encyclopaedia, Genealogy, and Tradition*. Notre Dame: University of Notre Dame Press, 1990.

Mill, John Stuart. *Utilitarianism*. London: Longman, Green, Longman, Roberts, and Green, 1864.

O'Donovan, Oliver. "Christian Moral Reasoning." In *New Dictionary of Christian Ethics and Pastoral Theology*, edited by David J. Atkinson, David F. Field, Arthur Holmes, and Oliver O'Donovan. Downers Grove, IL: InterVarsity Press, 1995.

———. *Resurrection and Moral Order: An Outline for Evangelical Ethics*. 2nd ed. Grand Rapids: Eerdmans, 1994.

Ogletree, Thomas W. *The Use of the Bible in Christian Ethics*. Philadelphia: Fortress Press, 1983.

Porter, Jean. *Natural and Divine Law: Reclaiming the Tradition for Christian Ethics*. Grand Rapids: Eerdmans, 1999.

Rae, Scott B. *Moral Choices: An Introduction to Ethics*. 3rd ed. Grand Rapids: Zondervan, 2009.

Endnotes

[1] On distinguishing "universal," "generic," and "general," see Oliver O'Donovan, "Christian Moral Reasoning," in *New Dictionary of Christian Ethics and Pastoral Theology*, ed. David J. Atkinson, David F. Field, Arthur Holmes, and Oliver O'Donovan (Downers Grove: InterVarsity, 1995), 125.

[2] Michael Banner, "Introductory Remarks: Christian Ethical Reasoning," *Transformation* 15 (April 1998): 15.
[3] Ibid.
[4] Oliver O'Donovan, *Resurrection and Moral Order: An Outline for Evangelical Ethics*, 2nd ed. (Grand Rapids: Eerdmans, 1994), 11.
[5] For a defense of natural law from a Protestant perspective, see the work of J. Budziszewski, including *Written on the Heart: The Case for Natural Law* (Downers Grove, IL: InterVarsity, 1997) and *What We Can't Not Know* (Dallas: Spence Publishing Company, 2003). From a Roman Catholic perspective, see Jean Porter, *Natural and Divine Law: Reclaiming the Tradition for Christian Ethics* (Grand Rapids: Eerdmans, 1999).
[6] Budziszewski, *Written on the Heart*, 109.
[7] Michael Banner, *Christian Ethics: A Brief History* (Oxford: Wiley-Blackwell, 2009), 51.
[8] Budziszewski, *Written on the Heart*, 183–84.
[9] See Banner, *Christian Ethics: A Brief History*, especially chap. 6. See also the work of Alasdair MacIntyre, especially *Three Rival Versions of Moral Enquiry: Encyclopaedia, Genealogy, and Tradition* (Notre Dame: University of Notre Dame Press, 1990) and *After Virtue: A Study in Moral Theory*, 2nd ed. (Notre Dame: University of Notre Dame Press, 1984).
[10] Banner, "Introductory Remarks," 16.
[11] Ibid., 15. See also Michael Banner, *Christian Ethics and Contemporary Moral Problems* (Cambridge: Cambridge University Press, 1999), chap. 1.
[12] O'Donovan, "Christian Moral Reasoning," 122.
[13] Bernard Haring, *Free and Faithful in Christ* (New York: Seabury, 1978–81), 1:6.
[14] O'Donovan, "Christian Moral Reasoning," in Atkinson et al., *New Dictionary*, 122.
[15] This is a point made by Dietrich Bonhoeffer, *Ethics*, trans. Neville Horton Smith, ed. Eberhard Bethge (New York: Macmillan, 1955), 175–76.
[16] This was one of several formulations of categorical imperatives, and it is repeated in slightly different ways in Immanuel Kant, *Fundamental Principles of the Metaphysics of Ethics*, trans. Thomas Abbott, 10th ed. (New York: Longmans, Green, 1937), section 2; see, for example, in this edition, p. 46.
[17] So, for instance, the command in Deut 22:8 to build a parapet around the roof of a house is not a universal moral norm, but an application of the norm to value and protect human life. The parapet is a wall around a flat roof, to protect people from falling when they gather on the roof. It does not pertain to a sloped roof where people do not gather.
[18] John Stuart Mill, *Utilitarianism* (London: Longman, Green, Longman, Roberts, and Green, 1864), 9–10.
[19] Stanley Hauerwas, *The Peaceable Kingdom: A Primer in Christian Ethics* (Notre Dame, IN: University of Notre Dame Press, 1983), 4.
[20] Ibid., 129.
[21] O'Donovan, *Resurrection and Moral Order*, 18.
[22] For a discussion of the Bible and Christian ethics, see Brian Brock, *Singing the Ethos of God: On the Place of Christian Ethics in Scripture* (Grand Rapids: Eerdmans, 2007).

[23] O'Donovan, *Resurrection and Moral Order*, 18.
[24] Banner, *Christian Ethics: A Brief History*, 20–21.
[25] *The Westminster Confession of Faith, The Shorter Catechism* (Glasgow: Free Presbyterian Publications, 1958), question 1.
[26] O'Donovan, *Resurrection and Moral Order*, 17.
[27] Augustine, *Confessions*, trans. Henry Chadwick (New York: Oxford University Press, 1991), 1.1.
[28] C. S. Lewis, *The Weight of Glory: And Other Addresses* (San Francisco: HarperCollins, 2001 reprint), 26.
[29] C. S. Lewis nicely describes these dimensions in *Mere Christianity*, book 3, chap. 1 (repr., New York: Touchstone, 1996), 71–73.
[30] The expression used by Geoffrey W. Bromiley, *God and Marriage* (Grand Rapids: Eerdmans, 1980), 19.
[31] Studies have consistently indicated greater satisfaction, pleasure, and frequency of sex among married couples. See, for instance, Linda J. Waite and Maggie Gallagher, *The Case for Marriage: Why Married People Are Happier, Healthier, and Better Off Financially* (New York: Broadway, 2000); Edward Laumann, *The Social Organization of Sexuality: Sexual Practices in the United States* (Chicago: University of Chicago Press, 1994), 363–65; William Mattox Jr., "What's Marriage Got to Do with It?" *Family Policy* 6:6 (February 1994): 3.
[32] Scott B. Rae, *Moral Choices: An Introduction to Ethics*, 3rd ed. (Grand Rapids: Zondervan, 2009), 106–8. Rae, in turn, indicates that he has adapted his model from a course taught by William W. May at the University of Southern California.
[33] Lewis, *Mere Christianity*, 87.

4

The Gospel, Worldview, and Christian Higher Education

Harry Lee Poe

What makes a Christian approach to higher education unique is Jesus Christ. With the high value placed on individualism and personal liberty in American culture, however, many American Christians in higher education have difficulty understanding what Jesus Christ could possibly have to do with the modern academic disciplines. We might also wonder what He could possibly have to do with banking, government, or any other sphere of life.

During the past hundred years, American Christians have tended to think of the Christian faith in a fragmented fashion depending upon an individual's personal interests. For some, Christianity means that Jesus died for our sins and we can go to heaven when we die. For some, Jesus provides an ethical basis for social behavior. For some, faith is a personal, private matter that involves an individual's private relationship with Jesus Christ. For some, Christianity means the organized religion of the West together with its rules and traditions. This fragmented approach to faith as an individual choice represents a vast departure from New Testament faith and the stream of faith in Christ over the past nineteen centuries in all parts of the world.

In order to teach from a Christian faith perspective, a person must understand the Christian faith. First of all, the Christian faith refers to faith in Jesus Christ. Christians believe that their faith in Jesus Christ forms the basis for their relationship with God. It matters what they think and believe about Jesus in order for them to have faith in Jesus to provide access to God. Access to God is dependent on faith in Jesus. Any partial glimpse at Jesus inhibits the possibility of access to God. When the New Testament speaks of "faith," it does not mean a general idea of a cheery disposition. It does not mean the oft-quoted modern aphorism, "It doesn't matter what you believe; it only matters that you believe." How people understand their faith will influence, if not determine, how they approach every other issue in life, including higher education.

With the growth of a secular, materialistic view of the world in the late nineteenth century, some streams of modern Western Christianity ceased to believe aspects of the Christian faith that had been normative since the resurrection. Elements of the life of Christ were regarded as folk tales, such as the Virgin Birth and the bodily resurrection of Christ. Other ideas were rejected as merely cultural tradition, such as the revelation of God to His people by the prophets. Miracles lost credence as a violation of the laws of nature. God's role in creation ceased to be acceptable in the face of naturalistic assumptions of causality. Liberalism drained the faith of its supernatural dimension in an effort to explain the phenomenon of religion in purely natural terms.

Conservative Christianity developed a functional liberalism from an entirely different path. Driven by a pragmatic, utilitarian concern that ran through American culture by the middle of the twentieth century, evangelicals sought to reduce the faith down to a simple, concise statement that would aid in evangelism. The "gospel in a nutshell" identified the gospel, or the Christian faith, with the death and resurrection of Jesus. A theological approach described the Christian faith as "creation, fall, redemption." These reductions of the faith accomplished the same end as a hundred years of liberalism. People raised in "Bible believing" churches no longer understood the faith. It is impossible for a teacher to teach from a faith perspective if they do not understand their faith and its implications.

The Gospel

The summation of faith in Jesus Christ is referred to as the *gospel*. Paul declared, "Believe on the Lord Jesus Christ, and you will be saved" (Acts 16:31 NKJV). What is it about Jesus that one must believe?[1] Paul told the Corinthians that it is by the gospel that we are saved (1 Cor 15:2). He told the Romans that the gospel is "God's power for salvation to everyone who believes" (Rom 1:16 HCSB).

The gospel, also called the apostles' teaching, also called the preaching, is the content of what Christians believe about Jesus Christ. The gospel explains who Jesus is and why it matters. Jesus once asked his disciples, "who do you say that I am?" (Matt 16:15). The gospel answers this question. What is more, the gospel provides a basis for answering all the deepest questions of every culture. God has placed a question in every heart and culture that only the gospel answers. Our task is to listen for the question. Every academic discipline asks a different set of questions, and different aspects of the gospel address different kinds of issues with which disciplines and cultures are concerned. Knowing the gospel and its implications, and listening for the question, form the heart of teaching from a Christian faith perspective.

What It Is Not

When we reduce the gospel to an easily manageable idea like "Jesus died for your sins and you can go to heaven when you die," we are left with a reductionistic expression of the Christian faith. Such clichés do not answer the question, "Who is Jesus?" Redemption can be so emphasized that other biblical elements, which flow from it, can be practically ignored. Consider just a few of these:

- Forgiveness
- Justification
- Regeneration
- Adoption
- Sanctification
- Freedom
- Cleansing
- Reconciliation
- Healing
- Empowerment
- Peace
- Ransomed
- Immortality
- Glorification
- Endurance

- Meaning and Purpose
- Identity
- Hope
- Love
- Immediate Access to God

None of these ideas has any significant meaning for faith unless we put it in the context of the person and work of Jesus Christ as revealed in the gospel.[2] One feature of our modern Western worldview is that Americans like to reduce complex ideas into simple slogans, jingles, and sound bites. We run our political campaigns in this fashion, having been trained by the advertising industry for over half a century to keep it simple. Such an approach rarely leads to truth, but it aids quick decisions. American Christian evangelism after the 1950s aimed at quick decisions.

For 1,900 years, Christians understood the gospel based on the teaching of Jesus and His apostles. The gospel tells the story of Jesus from eternity to eternity, from the creation of the world through the new creation at the end of time. It is not necessary to impose the Christian faith on the modern academy because the Western university and higher education as we know it are products of the Christian faith as Christians explored the implications of the gospel. What then is the gospel?

What It Is

The clichés give us partial answers. The gospel does involve the death of Jesus and creation, but it involves much more. Part of the confusion stems from the modern evangelical tendency to read the Bible as isolated, free-standing verses. When they read in 1 Cor 15:3–4 that the *death* and *resurrection* are part of the gospel that Paul preached, they tend to think that the death and resurrection exhaust the gospel. In this reduction, however, they leave out Paul's insistence in the same passage that the *fulfillment of the Scriptures* is also part of the gospel, for Christ Himself validated Himself as the One who fulfills the promises of God. Paul had a lot more to say about the matter, however, than just these three points. For instance, he also said that the gospel includes the *return of Christ at the Second Coming* (Rom 2:16). It also includes the *humanity of Jesus* who was a descendent of David (Rom 1:3; 2 Tim 2:8) and the *deity of Jesus* as Son of God (Rom 1:4; Col

1:15,19). It also includes an understanding of what kind of God exists: the *Creator God* who made the heavens and the earth (Col 1:16). Paul also insisted that the gospel is not only about who Jesus was, but about who He is as the *Exalted Lord* who hears our prayers, governs the universe, heads the church, and draws us into Himself (Phil 2:9–11; Col 1:17–18). Finally, Paul and all the other apostles taught that the gospel includes the *gift of the Holy Spirit* to all who believe (Gal 3:2–3,23–29). He wrote all of his letters to people who were Christians and had believed the gospel. Whenever he gave a teaching, he based it on a particular aspect of the gospel. In 1 Corinthians 15 Paul is teaching about the resurrection, so he only mentions those aspects of the gospel necessary to explain the resurrection.

We can see the elements of the gospel in a gospel sermon, such as the one Peter preached in Jerusalem to the Jews on the Day of Pentecost. In that sermon, he assumes what kind of God exists, and he assumes that his audience, which has come from all over the world to worship at the temple, also knows what kind of God exists. A worldview assumes what everybody knows and is surprised to find people who think differently.

Peter's sermon makes seven major points about faith in Jesus:

1. The Scriptures have been fulfilled (2:16,25,30–31,34).
2. The Holy Spirit has come because of Jesus (2:17–21,33).
3. Jesus is fully human and fully God, both Christ and Lord (2:22–23,34–36).
4. Jesus died for our sins (2:23).
5. Jesus rose from the dead (2:24–32).
6. Jesus is exalted to the right hand of God (2:33–36).
7. Judgment day is coming and Jesus is the Lord who will deliver those who call upon His name (2:20).

The fundamental assumption of the Jewish worldview forms the eighth aspect, the one not mentioned by Peter:

8. God is the one who made the world and all things.

When Paul, John, and the other apostles told the gospel to Gentiles who did not know what kind of God exists, they always began at the beginning, by explaining that God is the one who made the heavens, the earth, the seas, and everything in them

(John 1:1–5; Acts 14:15–17; 17:24–28). The sharing of the gospel was normally accompanied by an invitation for people to respond to Jesus in faith and receive the blessings of relationship with Him (Acts 2:38; 13:38–41; 26:24–29).

These basic ideas, expressed in different words for different audiences, form the sole content of the New Testament. The four Gospels and the Epistles, taken together, both tell the story and theologically interpret who Jesus was, what He came to do, and what the implications are for His followers. This gospel became the measuring stick, or canon, for determining which documents to include in the New Testament. Documents that did not "measure up," such as the Gnostics writings of the second, third, and fourth centuries, were easily seen for the forgeries they were.

In the century following the death of the apostles, the Gentile church summarized the gospel to affirm what Christians believe. The summaries of Ignatius and Irenaeus became the basis for the Apostles' Creed, the standard statement of the Christian faith for over 1,500 years:

> I believe in God the Father Almighty, Maker of heaven and earth;
> and in Jesus Christ his only Son, our Lord; Who was conceived by the Holy Ghost; born of the Virgin Mary, suffered under Pontius Pilate,
> was crucified, dead and buried; He descended into hell;
> the third day he rose again from the dead;
> he ascended into heaven and sitteth on the right hand of God the Father Almighty;
> from thence he shall come to judge the quick and the dead.
> I believe in the Holy Spirit,
> the holy catholic church; the communion of saints;
> the forgiveness of sins;
> the resurrection of the body; and the life everlasting. Amen.

Notice that the Apostles' Creed affirms faith in God as Father, Son, and Holy Spirit. Notice also that the creed elaborates who the Lord Jesus Christ is and what He does, as well as elaborating that the Holy Spirit applies salvation, or the benefits of relationship to Christ.

All Christian theology simply elaborates the implications of this gospel, the story of who Jesus is and what He has done to effect our salvation. Christian theology explores the ramifications of salvation for all of life. Higher education as it developed in the West arose within the church as an institutional expression of the desire to explore the implications of the gospel. As such, the approach to education in the West departed from the classical education of ancient Greece and Rome in several particulars. The distinctive features and disciplines of the curriculum of the Western university arose because of the particular affirmations of the gospel.

The Gospel and the Curriculum

When Christians teach from a Christian perspective, their faith in Jesus Christ as He reveals Himself through the gospel informs that teaching. If we think that the gospel only involves the death of Jesus for our sins or the theme of redemption, then our faith has little, if anything, to say about most of higher education or any other vocation or sphere of life. The gospel, however, involves much more. The various families of disciplines within the Western university curriculum relate in a primary way to one of the elements of the gospel, and different issues that arise within particular disciplines may relate to other aspects of the gospel.[3] The families of disciplines within the Western university include the sciences and mathematics, the fine arts, the humanities, the social sciences, and the professions.

The Sciences

The modern sciences relate to several aspects of the gospel. First of all, as they developed, the modern sciences assumed a real world produced by a *Creator God*. This assumption automatically separates Western thought from Eastern thought. Though Eastern cultures had a vast head start over the West in the establishment of civilization, their conception of the world and of deity precluded the kind of attitude toward the physical world that allows science to develop. Second, the *resurrection* affirms the physical world in a continuing way. Unlike the traditions of the Greeks, Buddhists, and Hindus that regard the physical world as vile and polluted, to be discarded and escaped, Christianity affirms the transformation of the physical world as a continuing reality. The physical world has permanent significance for God and is worthy of study. Third, the sciences assume an orderly world that follows orderly laws yesterday, today, and tomorrow according to the laws laid down by God. The universe is not capricious. The *exalted Christ* reigns and upholds the universe by His word of power (Heb 1:3). This understanding of the universe as a rational, orderly, purposive, knowable creation of God that God cares about provided a basis for Christians to seek to know the laws of God for His creation.

The Fine Arts

Like the sciences, the fine arts relate to the gospel through the *Creator God* but in a different way. God not only makes people; He makes people in His own image, the *imago dei*. The Creator God makes people to be creative. Poetry, music, painting, sculpture, drama, fiction, and the breadth of artistic expression emerge from the transcendent nature of people. Art points to something else beyond the experience of physical survival needs. In the modern world, we have driven a wedge between the disciplines, but we do well to recall that arts and sciences were originally together in the academy for a reason. The same creativity that allows for art also allows for scientific discovery and technological invention. This same creativity leads to new innovations in business and educational practices.

The Humanities

Like the sciences and the arts, the humanities as they developed in the West assume a *Creator God*. Like the fine arts, the humanities assume that people are made in the image of God. While being made in the image of God represents the glory of humanity, having fallen from the glory of God represents the tragedy of humanity. Language and the ability to communicate reflect the image of God, but the need to study the mechanics of grammar, linguistics, and communication theory reflect the tragedy of the fall. Humans have the capacity to communicate like the God in whose image we are made, yet we fail to communicate. The humanities deal with the understanding of communication, or interpretation. Modern critical hermeneutics began with the interpretation of the Bible. Critical theory began with the assumption that communication has an intended meaning, even if that meaning is not clear to the receiver. The *fulfillment of Scripture* provides the basis for the Christian understanding of the nature of revelation as objective truth with cognitive meaning intended for the receiver. Whereas the objective of the classical study of grammar and rhetoric was to win the argument, the objective of Christian hermeneutics is to arrive at the truth and to communicate meaningfully.

The Social Sciences

The social sciences as disciplines within the modern curriculum emerged in the latter part of the nineteenth century as part of a broader project to understand the world in terms of exclusively naturalistic explanations. For this reason, the social sciences relate to the gospel in a contrary way than the *Creator God* as an effort to deal with the problem of humanity without reference to a spiritual condition, such as sin. Sociology, psychology, economics, anthropology, political science, international relations, and related disciplines explore specific aspects of human life in social context to account for what is wrong with the human race and to suggest possible remedies. In the twentieth century philosophy and history began to be understood more as social sciences than as humanities. Nonetheless, the social sciences address the human phenomenon that the Bible calls sin. At all levels of personal and social interaction, the social sciences study how humans work and how they fail to work correctly.

The Professions

Not surprisingly, the professions also relate to the gospel in terms of the *Creator God* who made humans in His image and intends for them to have meaningful work. The professions represent the point at which people integrate their education. The professions are not disciplines like the other disciplines of the university. Instead, they are super-disciplines that require the integration and interaction of multiple disciplines. For instance, the healing professions combine biology, chemistry, math, psychology, nutrition, and other disciplines in order to provide care to a patient. Engineering combines math, physics, chemistry, art, and other disciplines to conceive and construct solutions to a variety of problems touching every aspect of life.

The Disciplines and the Gospel

Not surprisingly, all of the families of disciplines in the Western university curriculum relate in some way to the question of what kind of God, and therefore what kind of universe, exists. Each family of disciplines explores different questions; therefore the implications of the existence of a Creator God take the curriculum in different directions. Though the curriculum begins at the same fundamental starting point, individual disciplines involve questions and issues that relate to other aspects of the gospel (see fig. 1).

The Gospel and Christian Doctrine

Faith Affirmation	*Doctrines*	*Implication Examples*
Creator God	God, Providence, Creation, Humanity, Sin	Possibility for objective truth and value, possibility of knowledge of the external world, understanding the problem with humanity
Fulfillment of Scripture	Inspiration, Revelation	Theory of knowledge beyond empiricism and rationalism necessary for new knowledge
Fully Human/Fully God	Incarnation, Christology	Ethical and moral values
Death for Sins	Atonement, Justification, Redemption	The high cost of love
Raised from the Dead	Resurrection	Value of the individual and of the physical world, hope
Exaltation	Lordship, Ecclesiology, Kingdom	God's involvement in human affairs
Gift of the Holy Spirit	Pneumatology (Holy Spirit), Regeneration, Adoption, Sanctification	Transformation, empowerment
Second Coming	Eschatology, Theodicy	A goal or purpose to the universe and human history

Figure 1

For instance, the Western understanding of history until the second half of the twentieth century was that history has a direction. Even Marxism was influenced by this deeply held conviction.

History has a beginning with the Creation, and it has an ending with the Second Coming of Christ. The healing professions as practiced in the West assume the value of human life based on the Creator God who made people in His image. They assume the affirmation of human life by God who stepped into time and space as fully human and fully divine, who touched and healed people, and who affirmed human flesh by His resurrection from the dead. The healing professions also assume the divine purpose of healing for human beings by the continuing experience of prayer to the Exalted Christ by whom Christians have experienced healing and on account of the present power of the Holy Spirit through whom healing occurs.

All disciplines have ethical issues that face them. The ethical value system of the West emerged from the teachings of the incarnate Christ during His teaching ministry on Earth and through His apostles who wrote the New Testament, in which all ethical teaching is based upon one of the aspects of the gospel. For instance, Paul cites the self-giving of Christ in taking on flesh and dying for our sins as the reason to show consideration for others (Phil 2:3–11).

Worldview

A worldview is the core beliefs and values of a culture. While every individual in a culture has their own *point of view* unique to them, a worldview represents the common core beliefs and values shared by the overwhelming majority of a culture.[4] A culture's worldview involves commonly held core beliefs and values about religion, philosophy, science, government, economics, human relationships, and anything else of concern to a culture. Not all cultures necessarily have commonly held beliefs and values about the same things. For instance, late Greek culture of the classical period had no common philosophy, but medieval Western culture did. A culture's worldview works much the same as a recipe for a cake. If you change one ingredient, you change the cake. If you change several ingredients, you have a vastly different cake. The Christian faith represents one such element of a worldview that may dramatically change a culture.[5]

One of the most important distinctions between the Western and Eastern worldviews concerns the conception of time. Cultures influenced by Buddhism, Hinduism, Shintoism, and traditional nature religion have a cyclical view of time corresponding to the perpetual repetition of the seasons and represented by the belief in the endless cycle of birth, death, and rebirth. In the West, however, we have a linear view of time that stretches from the creation of the world to the return of Christ. The gospel changed the culture's concept of time and the nature of the universe which helped make modern science possible.

A culture's worldview manifests itself in the learned customs, behaviors, products, and practices of people in the culture. A culture develops institutions responsible for teaching, enforcing, and protecting the worldview of a culture. We may think of the family, government, judicial system, armed forces, police, educational system, and religious establishment as the institutions that preserve, protect, and defend the culture. Every culture develops its own educational system which may be as simple as parents teaching their children how to fish and weave baskets, or it may be as complex as the Western educational systems of graded schools and the university system. Thus, we may think of a culture as an integrated system of learned beliefs and values, customs, and institutions which express these beliefs, values, and customs, which binds a society together and gives it a sense of identity, dignity, security, and continuity[6] (see fig. 2).

Ancient Rome

Jesus was born into the Roman Empire, a vast territory ruled by military dictatorship embracing many cultures and languages without a strong worldview to hold the empire together. Like most empires that overreach their ability to assimilate people and create a common culture, the Roman Empire was held together by its armies and the desire for "peace."

The first Christians were social deviants in every culture of the Empire because they held beliefs and values at odds with every culture. When Paul visited Athens, he found Stoic philosophers with one *point of view* and Epicurean philosophers with another *point of view*, but both groups shared the same *worldview*. The philosophers held a common point of view about the value of philosophy and the old-fashioned pagans who still worshipped the pantheon of deities had another point of view about the gods. Both groups, however, shared the same worldview about society, the role of women, the important virtues, fate, rules for the household,

Culture and Worldview

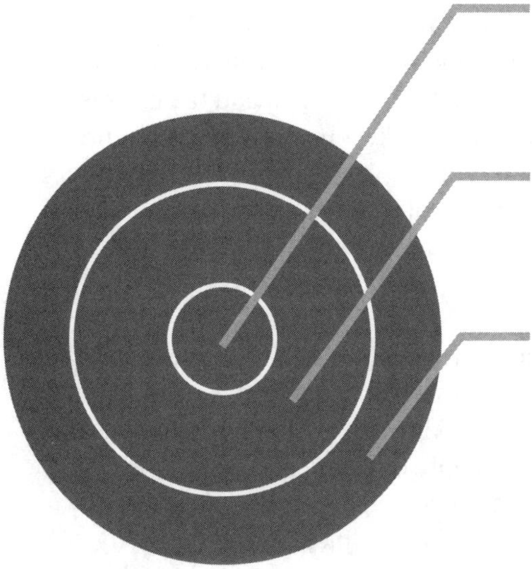

Figure 2

and dozens of other matters that defined Greek culture. Paul had a different worldview because he was a Jewish Pharisee who believed Jesus was both the Messiah and the Son of Man.

In Jewish culture of the first century, the first essential of the gospel on which all others depended was that the Scriptures had been fulfilled. The Pharisees had been studying the prophecies about the Messiah, a descendant of David who would establish a never-ending throne, and the prophecy that God Himself would appear in the form of a Son of Man during the time of the fourth great world empire. With the Babylonian, Persian, and Greek empires behind them, the Pharisees were in a fever pitch of excitement during the reign of Augustus Caesar, for the fourth world empire had come and the beginning of the end must be near. Jesus made clear that He fulfilled the prophecies (Matt 5:17–18; 26:54–56; Luke 4:16–21; 24:25–27,44–49). Among the Gentiles, however, the rest of the gospel made no sense without an understanding of what kind of God exists. The Gentiles knew nothing of the ancient prophecies or the law of Moses.

The pluralistic Roman Empire had no single, dominant question arising from a unified worldview, so we find that in different places, different aspects of the gospel provided the bridge for a culture to receive the knowledge of Jesus Christ. In some situations, the Holy Spirit was the key. In other situations, the Exalted Christ who has authority over demons and evil spirits was the key. In some cases, the certainty of the Last Judgment and the promise of deliverance from judgment was the key. In our modern culture, forgiveness through the atoning death of Jesus has been the key since the Reformation, but with a collapsing worldview no single spiritual question still unites Western culture.

From Ancient to Medieval Worldview

Some cultures remain stable for centuries and experience very slow change, such as the cultures of China and India and ancient Egypt. Western culture has gone through three dramatic phases since the time of Christ. The collapse of classical culture took centuries from the time of Socrates, who taught his disciples that only one God exists, until the time of Constantine, who acknowledged over 700 years later that Jesus Christ is that one God. Still, the transformation from ancient to medieval culture took several more centuries. A number of changes to the ingredients of the Western worldview led to the collapse of ancient institutions and the creation of new ones.

As Christianity spread and became the dominant religion in the West, the old pluralism of many religions faded away. When Augustine (d. 430) adopted the philosophy of Plato or Neo-Platonism to organize his theology, he provided the West with a general philosophical framework. These two changes in religious belief and philosophical conviction had a dramatic impact on the nature of Western institutions. Plato's philosophy included the idea of a hierarchy of being from lowest life forms, such as slaves and women, up the levels of the celestial spirits to the Great Oversoul. Adapted to civil government, Plato's hierarchy placed the emperor at the top of the social hierarchy, beneath which in descending order came kings, dukes, counts, barons, knights, and peasants. The church during the Middle Ages developed a similar hierarchy with the Pope at the top, followed by cardinals, archbishops, bishops and abbots, deans and archdeacons, and priests and monks. The wedding of the Christian faith to Platonic philosophy led to the feudal system and the culture known as Christendom of the Middle Ages.

Platonic philosophy also influenced the direction taken by art. The West did not simply forget how to paint and how to sculpt. The other-worldly atmosphere of medieval theology and art manifested itself throughout the culture. Plato's revulsion over the physical world and the human body affected the attitude of the Western church toward marriage and sex, leading to a celibate priesthood in the West, while priests in the East continued to marry and have children.

The medieval culture lasted for approximately a thousand years. It perpetuated the science of the Roman period that had not been lost or destroyed in the warfare of the waves of invasion from the East. The medieval worldview included the best science of the ancient world and the understanding of the Greeks that the stars and planets were identified with celestial beings.

The Roman Empire stretched across Western Europe to the Fertile Crescent, but it had very little in the way of a common worldview to hold it together in times of crisis. Christendom stretched across Western Europe, but it had no central government or identity as an empire, yet it had a commonly held worldview. To the extent that the people of the West affirmed the Apostles' Creed and worshipped Jesus Christ, they had a Christian worldview. Their institutions were not biblical in the sense that Scripture instructed Christians to create such a society, but their worldview was Christian to the extent that their faith in Christ was one of their core beliefs and values that gradually altered other beliefs and institutions.

At the same time that feudal Christendom developed in the West, the Christian Empire of the East developed in an entirely different way. For the thousand-year period of the medieval world following the death of Augustine in 430, the Roman Empire continued in Constantinople. Instead of the military dictator of ancient Rome, the Christian emperor ruled absolutely as a hereditary monarch. As God's chosen instrument on earth, as God's will on earth, the emperor no longer had need of the Roman Senate, which was abolished. No hereditary nobility with its hierarchy of feudal responsibility existed in what came to be called the Byzantine Empire. The Eastern Church was not influenced by Plato in the same manner as that of those in the West. A pluralism of the ancient philosophical schools continued to flourish in Constantinople. Unlike the new schismatic church of Rome, the Eastern Church had no single supreme head. The Patriarch of Constantinople was one of a group of patriarchs within the Eastern Empire that included the Patriarchs of Jerusalem, Alexandria, and Antioch. Yet, the worldview of Byzantine culture also was a Christian worldview. Even though the two cultures disagreed about some core beliefs and values, they shared a common faith expressed by the Apostles' Creed until 1453, when Constantinople fell to the Sultan of the Turks and the Roman Empire finally came to an end.

From Medieval to Modern Worldview

Two hundred years before the fall of Constantinople, an Italian monk who taught at a monastery in Paris invented the modern world by substituting a new ingredient in the medieval worldview. He exchanged the philosophy of Plato for that of Aristotle. Thomas Aquinas (d. 1274) came to be regarded as the greatest theologian of the medieval period. Over a period of the next 300 years, his theology circulated throughout Europe, and its implications were enormous.

While Plato placed his emphasis on the other world, the world of ideas, Aristotle placed his emphasis on this world, the world of experience. While Plato said that we know what a chair is because the idea of a chair was planted in us prior to our birth from the world of ideas, Aristotle said that we know what a chair is because we learn about chairs by encountering individual chairs. Plato began with the great universal ideas which had their independent existence as the "real" things beyond the material world. Aristotle began with individual occurrences. After 400 years, this simple change in the ingredients of the worldview resulted in the birth of modern science and modern democracy in the seventeenth century. Without the core Platonic philosophical belief that had created the feudal system, that world could not continue. In China, where the philosophy of Confucius went without rival for 2,000 years, the culture remained virtually suspended in spite of conquests and upheavals. A stable worldview enables a culture to survive enormous catastrophes.

Death for Sins. The core beliefs and values of a culture do not exist in isolation from each other. The worldview of a culture represents an integrated whole in which all the elements influence one another. One of the implications of the death of Christ is the forgiveness of sins. This implication was Martin Luther's big issue, and it has tended to become the exclusive concern of the modern evangelical understanding of the gospel. Each element of the gospel has many implications, and another implication of the death of Jesus Christ besides forgiveness is freedom. Freedom is a radical idea that had no home in any culture until Christ said, "Then you will know the truth, and the truth will set you free. . . . So if the Son sets you free, you will be free indeed" (John 8:32,36 NIV). In the first book ever written in the New Testament, Paul explored the idea of freedom that comes through Christ. He explained, "It is for freedom that Christ has set you free" (Gal 5:1 NIV).

Gift of the Holy Spirit. The idea of the equality of people does not arise from the philosophers of ancient Greece, since they believed in the essential inequality of people. In Galatians, Paul explained the implication of being baptized into Christ Jesus by the coming of the Holy Spirit. All believers in Jesus Christ live within Him, and Paul could hardly write a paragraph without speaking of the mystical relationship a believer has of being "in Christ." He explained that in Christ, "There is no Jew or Greek, slave or free, male or female" (Gal 3:28 HCSB).

Fulfillment of Scripture. One of the most cataclysmic events that fell in the hinge between the medieval world and the modern world was the Reformation. Reformation ideas began long before Luther nailed his Ninety-five Theses to the church door in Wittenberg in 1517. In the face of the abuses of the hierarchical system of the Church of Rome and several rival Popes, John Wycliffe turned to the Bible as the final religious authority on Earth in the late fourteenth century. Evangelicals tend to assume the authority of Scripture but also tend to forget the basis for its authority. Every religion has its holy books. Why should the Bible have any more authority than the Qur'an or the Bhagavad Gita? The Bible not only claims to be revelation from God; it also provides a test for its reliability. God told Moses that His prophets would be known because what they said would come to pass (Deut 18:17–22). Hinduism and Buddhism have no prophecies because they have no self-conscious God to reveal anything, and their holy books make no claim to be revelation from God. The Qur'an was delivered by the Prophet Mohammed, but it contains no specific fulfilled prophecies (beyond the general predictions of victory in battle).

The reliability of the Bible as a final authority in matters of religion led John Wycliffe to argue that the accumulated traditions of the church which had grown up in the thousand years since Augustine should be cast aside. His method was to go back to the source of religious knowledge: the Bible.

Modern science developed along the same path. When Francis Bacon proposed the scientific method in the early seventeenth century, a hundred years after Luther, he proposed doing what the Reformers had done. Hardly any significant scientific knowledge had been acquired since the time of the ancient Greeks. Bacon argued it was because science had been held captive by the tradition of Greek philosophy, and especially the philosophy of Aristotle. Though Aristotle placed emphasis on knowledge through sensory observation, he also had elaborate, logical explanations for most physical phenomena from gravity to the nature of the planets to the basis for life forms. As the Reformers jettisoned tradition and went back to the source for religious knowledge, Bacon proposed abandoning the Greek philosophical tradition and going to the source of scientific knowledge: the physical world as we find it.

Creator God. The fundamental presupposition of the gospel faith is belief in a Creator God who has established a rational, good world. God established His laws for the governance of the universe and they continue inviolate. The universe does not operate capriciously but according to the laws of God. Science could not emerge and prosper without such a rational, orderly universe. Islam believes in a Creator God but not one who established laws to rule the universe. The God of Islam rules the universe by his will, and all things that occur are the result of the will of God, not of God's laws. Some Muslims have adapted to a broader understanding of the will of God, but others see a fundamental conflict between modern Western science and Islam.

Fully Human / Fully Divine. During His incarnation upon the earth as Jesus of Nazareth, God demonstrated a basis for human behavior that forms and undergirds the Western understanding of ethics. The core values that animate Western culture in terms of the value of life, care for the needy, and regard for others come from the teachings of Jesus. These values have grown so deeply entrenched in the Western worldview that their origin is forgotten by most secular people. The gospel has been so effective in influencing the core values of the West that they are taken for granted, but they have not come from a naturalistic or materialistic understanding of the universe. It is admittedly possible to hold the values of the Western worldview without holding to the Christian faith from which those values came. In his Cambridge lectures on Thomas Hardy, Lord David Cecil observed, "Hardy's very pessimism is of a kind only possible to one indissolubly wedded to Christian standards of value. Christian teachers have always said that there was no alternative to Christianity but pessimism, that if Christian doctrine was not true, life was a tragedy. Hardy quite agreed with them. But he could not think the doctrine true, all the same. He found it impossible to believe the Christian hope. He may have been mistaken in this. Myself, I think he was."[7] Without that faith in Christ, however, those values cannot long endure. Substitute one ingredient in a culture, and the culture will change, just as ancient Rome did.

The Second Coming. It is not enough for the world to have a beginning in order to have science. The world must also have a direction. Things happen in a certain sequence in our world. Time came into being when the world came into being. Up close over the course of only a hundred generations, time may appear to move in a circle. The ancient nature religions saw the seasons come around again, year after year. Nothing changed. The sun rises and the sun sets, and there is nothing new under the sun, or so Solomon mocked his neighbors. Without the direction of the universe toward something, scientific experimentation could not happen. Things change over time. The universe grows more complex at every level. Human knowledge grows. The gospel tells us that God is weaving a story that has a direction and it has an ending.

These basic gospel affirmations shaped the worldview of Western culture into the modern age, but their affirmation has all but disappeared as aspects of the Western worldview. Like Hardy, the West clings to the implications of the gospel, but without faith in Jesus Christ revealed by the gospel story, the core Western values cannot long survive.

The Next Cultural Age

As we have seen, the gospel had a profound influence on the development of Western culture from the medieval to the modern period. The ingredient that changed, however, was the primary philosophical belief from the Platonism of the medieval period to the Aristotelianism of the early modern period. As science attempted to operate free of the domination of Aristotle's philosophical system in the seventeenth and eighteenth centuries, the West entered a new age of philosophical pluralism the likes of which it had not seen since the old Roman Empire. A variety of philosophical schemes emerged in the eighteenth and nineteenth centuries to fill the gap left by the decline of Aristotle. Major philosophical beliefs that have an impact on the concept of what can be known and how one should behave include pragmatism, utilitarianism, existentialism, materialism, and naturalism, among others. This pluralism of philosophical thought produced new ideologies that rivaled Christianity as a belief system. Grand narratives based on economics, politics, biology, and psychology arose that left the core beliefs of the Western worldview fragmented and without consensus.

By the beginning of the eighteenth century, the gospel itself came under direct fire. Deism emerged as an alternative approach to religion that denied God's involvement in the world once it had been set in motion, the laws of nature established, and the moral law instilled. Deism left no room for revelation from God, for an incarnation of God in the flesh, for an atoning death which seemed impossible for God to experience, or for a resurrection. Deists could accept, however, some sort of view of the Holy Spirit as the divine spark that animates all people. A deistic attitude prevailed in the nineteenth century during which the universities experienced the first major reforms in a thousand years. The classical education based on the medieval curriculum was transformed to include the new learning.

Professional education like law, medicine, and engineering once involved apprenticeship, but in the late modern period, they moved into the academy. New disciplines came into being at the same time that we call the social sciences: sociology, political science, economics, and psychology. By the end of the nineteenth century, universities had even begun to study literature written in English as English departments began to be accepted and the study of modern fiction was accepted as more than simple popular entertainment. After the Crimean War and the Civil War, nursing came to be accepted as a profession with standards. Schools of nursing attached to hospitals soon moved into the universities. Social work moved from the churches into the universities where it was usually combined with sociology.

A general euphoria over the inevitable progress of civilization and the eventual achievement of a utopian society pervaded popular Western culture on the eve of World War I. The perfectibility of humanity through education and industry had become the new creed of a growing influential section of the population. It would prove to be an ill-founded dream.

The Canary in the Mine

In the twentieth century, Western culture began to collapse as the core beliefs and values of the culture eroded. Major crises may provide the occasion for the reconsideration of old beliefs and values. The 20 million deaths of World War I followed by 20 million more deaths in the influenza epidemic of 1918 led many Europeans to question the existence or the goodness of God. Alternative belief systems in the forms of fascism and communism provided the basis for new cultural experiments that led to more conflict and mass death.

When World War I began, the world was ruled by a handful of European cousins. Monarchy had been the model for government since the dawn of recorded history. By the end of the war, the nature of government and its basis had changed with the collapse of the Austrian, German, Ottoman, and Russian empires. On the eve of the war, the Chinese throne had been abolished. Following World War II, the French and British empires were dissolved. It took centuries for the Roman Empire to collapse, but these great modern empires that were all the size of ancient Rome all collapsed in a matter of a few years. With the end of World War II, the Japanese faced an even greater cultural challenge than the loss of the emperor. Hirohito was allowed to remain as emperor, but he was forced to resign as God.

The arts reflect the collapse of the worldview of Western culture. The art forms of a culture reflect and express the worldview of the culture. Byzantine art manifests the beliefs and values and Byzantine culture. The paintings of China reflect and manifest the beliefs and values of Chinese culture. The art of the West in the twentieth century reflect the collapse of a coherent worldview. Art had no sure touchstone. Poetry went from being a popular form of entertainment for the masses to a specialized art form for a small intellectual audience. Formal orchestral music and opera went from being a popular art form for the masses to being a highly intellectual form of entertainment for a small elite group. The experiments of James Joyce and others took the form of the novel in a different direction, but the culture refused to give up stories. The arts function like the canary in the mine for a culture in trouble. (In earlier times, miners took canaries in the mines because they would collapse first if any toxic gas had infiltrated the mine.) On the other hand, the twentieth century saw the beginning of new artistic vitality. The motion picture became the great new art form of the twentieth century. The movie score and sound track replaced the symphony as the most popular orchestral musical form.

The conflict that so many people perceive between the gospel and the modern academy does not arise because of the nature of the academic disciplines or the truth claims of the gospel. Usually the conflict arises because of philosophical beliefs or cultural values that have gradually become associated with a discipline, but have no innate relationship to the discipline. Part of the task of Christians in the academy is to remind members of their respective guilds of the nature and methodology of their disciplines.

A Christian Response

In the face of the collapse of Western culture in the wake of a century of devastating wars, philosophical and ideological turmoil, artistic confusion, moral decay, and spiritual infirmity, one might have cause for despair had Christians not faced the same problems several times before. The gospel has not merely survived the collapse of Western culture twice before; it has provided the spiritual and intellectual basis for the renewal of Western culture twice before. In both cases, the old culture did not revive. Instead, culture was transformed.

If the gospel is true, it is of infinite importance for higher education. If it is not true, it does not matter at all.

Questions for Further Reflection

1. In what ways, if at all, does the whole gospel inform your point of view in different areas of life?

2. What kinds of questions about the world does your discipline ask?
3. What philosophical ideas currently influence how members of your discipline approach their work, and to what extent are these ideas compatible or incompatible with the gospel?
4. Does your discipline have a stable methodology that has not undergone significant change in the last century, or is your discipline's methodology a matter of continuing debate? If it is a matter of continuing debate, how do the options relate to the gospel?
5. What core values of our culture, if lost, would threaten the nature of learning in your discipline?
6. How does a faith perspective provide you with greater insight, a broader range of questions, or a different set of questions in your discipline?

Resources for Further Study

Dockery, David S., and Gregory A. Thornbury. *Shaping a Christian Worldview*. Nashville: B&H, 2002.

Poe, Harry L. *Christianity in the Academy*. Grand Rapids: Baker, 2004.

———. *Christian Witness in a Postmodern World*. Nashville: Abingdon, 2001.

———. *The Gospel and Its Meaning*. Grand Rapids: Zondervan, 1996.

———. *See No Evil*. Grand Rapids: Kregel, 2004.

Endnotes

[1] For an extended discussion of this issue, see Harry L. Poe, *The Gospel and Its Meaning* (Grand Rapids: Zondervan, 1996).

[2] For a discussion of the meaning of the death of Christ beyond redemption and forgiveness, see Harry Lee Poe, *See No Evil* (Grand Rapids: Kregel, 2004), 171–89.

[3] For a more expansive discussion of the relationship between the gospel and the academic disciplines, see Harry Lee Poe, *Christianity in the Academy* (Grand Rapids: Baker, 2004), 93–175.

[4] In describing how William Lamb, second son of the first Viscount Melbourne, matured into a leading figure of British political life in the early nineteenth century, Lord David Cecil draws the distinction between a person's worldview within a culture and their point of view particular to themselves: "Life and books alike started him thinking, questioning, drawing conclusions. Gradually his scattered reflections fused with the inclinations of his temperament to compose themselves into a considered philosophy of life. It was an odd and individual one. So also was the man of which it was the expression. The mature William presented to

the world a personality and point of view curiously unlike those of other people." See Lord David Cecil, *Lord M.; or the Later Life of Lord Melbourne* (London: Constable, 1954), 3.

[5] For a discussion of the role of the Christian faith in the change of Western culture since classical times and how the gospel may continue to influence ongoing change, see Harry Lee Poe, *Christian Witness in a Postmodern World* (Nashville: Abingdon, 2001).

[6] This definition is based on "The Willowbank Report," in *Perspectives on the World Christian Movement: A Reader,* ed. Ralph D. Winter and Steven C. Hawthorne (Pasadena, CA: William Carey Library, 1981), 509. This report came from a consultation on "Gospel and Culture" sponsored by the Lausanne Committee for World Evangelization in 1978. Most definitions of culture focus on the social and corporate nature of culture and its worldview. Ruth Benedict defines culture as "total social heritage." Eugene Nida defines it as "all learned behavior that is socially acquired, including its meaning." John Honigman defines it as "the sum total of artifacts, activities, thoughts, and feelings that are socially standardized and transmitted along with their interrelationships and organizational structure."

[7] Lord David Cecil, *Hardy the Novelist: An Essay in Criticism*, The Clark Lectures given at Cambridge in 1942 (London: Constable and Co., 1943), 156.

5

Philosophy of Education

Klaus Issler

The teaching-learning process encompasses an intentional, dynamic encounter between teachers and students—often within a group setting—involving complex, multidimensional interactions, with the intent to facilitate greater progress to wholeness and maturity. God's nature and attributes are unchanging and God is infinitely omniscient, needing no instruction (Isa 40:13–14; Rom 11:33–34). Humanity, on the other hand, was created in the image of God (Gen 1:26) as finite persons who must learn to come to maturity. Humans begin life as immature creatures designed to change through the means of (a) supernatural transformation, (b) human development, and (c) human learning—and for this final means we as teachers have the most influence.

Although learning can take place without purposeful instruction—and at times without any awareness (e.g., acquiring our first language as a child)—the focus here will be on learning associated with teaching. Complete learning is not possible without God's mysterious work, yet God has ordained that human teachers have a legitimate (and lesser) role to play. The chapter offers an orientation, informed by a Christian perspective, regarding the main components of the teaching-learning process, then clarifying a framework for the development of a philosophy of education, and finally offering a few suggestions for improved practice.

The Teaching-Learning Process

A Distinctive Christian Perspective

What is distinctive about the teaching-learning process that is uniquely Christian? At one level of analysis, the process of teaching and learning is a common human experience regardless of Christian beliefs and commitments since all are created in God's image. On this level to do it well, teachers must attend to the study and practice of normal development and teaching-learning processes shared by all humans. Even studying the Bible by itself cannot guarantee any *unique* effects—nonbelievers can make sense of much of the Bible.

The distinctively Christian factor relates to the transformational encounter with God in regeneration and God's subsequent dynamic participation in the lives of each Christian. Along these lines, then, Christian teaching is an intentional interaction superintended by God the Holy Spirit (Rom 8:12; 1 Pet 1:2) who indwells (John 14:16) and empowers (Eph 3:16) both Christian teachers and Christian learners, with the broader goal of transformation into Christlikeness (Rom 8:29; Gal 5:22–23; Eph 4:13–16). When teachers and learners are genuinely walking with the Spirit of God, His divine, transforming power makes it possible to exceed what is normally expected of our human capacities (Gal 3:3; Eph 3:16). This divine enablement permits a greater flourishing among those with the spiritual gift of teaching (Rom 12:6–7; 1 Cor 12:28–29; 1 Pet 4:11).

Regarding the study of the Bible, Christian learners must listen to the Spirit who enlivens the Scripture to become living and active in their hearts and minds (1 Cor 2:10–16; Heb 4:12). Thus, along with the normal process of learning, and to the extent learners are *filled*—not just indwelt—by the Spirit and sustaining a dynamic spiritual relationship, a distinctively Christian teaching and learning experience can unfold. Thankfully, the teaching-learning process is carried out under the authority of God,[1] and with God's commitment to supervise the process (Rom 8:28; 1 Cor 10:13), He ultimately will see the process through to completion (Eph 4:11–16).

Christians are called to be lifelong learners, as evidenced in our Lord Jesus Christ's invitation: "Come to me, all of you who are laboring and bearing burdens, and I will give you rest. Take my yoke upon you and learn from me, because I am meek and humble in heart, and you will find rest for yourselves. For my yoke is kind and my burden is light" (Matt 11:28–30).[2] The heart of the Great Commission is to "make disciples" (Matt 28:19). The word *disciple* means to be a "learner" or "student." New Testament professor Michael Wilkins explains, "In the Christian sense, a disciple of Jesus is one who has come to him for eternal life, has claimed him as Savior and God, and has embarked upon the life of following him."[3]

Following Jesus is a lifelong process, for there is much to learn. If being renewed in our minds (Rom 12:2) is an essential aspect of growing toward maturity, how do we go about that? The apostle Paul explains that we may fill our minds with truth in all of its varied manifestations: "Whatever is true, whatever is honorable, whatever is just, whatever is pure, whatever is lovely, whatever is commendable—if there is any moral excellence and if there is any praise—dwell on these things" (Phil 4:8 HCSB). In one address to Athenian philosophers Paul—educated as a Pharisee under the rabbi Gamaliel (Acts 22:3) and trained also as a tent-maker (Acts 18:3)—was sufficiently acquainted with philosophical writings to quote one of their own to make a point (Acts 17:28). Furthermore, King Solomon studied diverse subjects to the degree that many from the surrounding nations came to learn from his distinctive wisdom (1 Kgs 4:29,32–33).

Scripture teaches that we can learn much by observing nature: "Go to the ant, you slacker! Observe its ways and become wise. Without leader, administrator, or ruler, it prepares its provisions in summer; it gathers its food during harvest" (Prov 6:6–8 HCSB). From nature we can also discern something of the character of God himself: "For His invisible attributes, that is, His eternal power and divine nature, have been clearly seen since the creation of the world, being understood through what He has made" (Rom 1:20 HCSB). Dallas Willard explains, "The biblical and the classical sources . . . *take the physical universe to be the conclusive evidence for the existence of God*."[4] Because there is much to learn in life, one of our educational aims as teachers will be to help our students sustain the motivation and skills to continue as lifelong learners—and disciples of Jesus Christ.

Jesus' calling on this earth also included a teaching mission, the most common title ascribed to Him was "teacher" ("rabbi," "master" KJV, John 13:14). As mentioned above, in His Great Commission, Jesus commanded the church to "make disciples of all nations . . . *teaching them to observe everything I have commanded you*" (Matt 28:19–20 HCSB, emphasis added; cf. Col 3:16). Consequently, in some sense all Christians are called to be teachers. Yet some teachers have greater accountability in light of roles related to two primary instructional contexts: (a) parents in the home (Deut 6:4–9; Prov 6:22; Eph 6:4) and (b) teachers in the local church (2 Tim 2:2; office of teacher, Acts 13:11; Eph 4:11; 1 Tim 5:17; Heb 13:7,17). Furthermore, some of us employ our spiritual gift of teaching (Rom 12:7; 1 Cor 12:28–29) in a full-time capacity as faculty in Christian higher education. Although our intent is to do good, we must be aware of potential harm in which we can hinder student learning (e.g., Luke 11:52).

The Paradox of the Teaching and Learning Process

Clarifying the interaction between teaching and learning is complicated. Should it be comparable to coaching athletes or machining a tool on a lathe? Is the relationship directly causal—so that a specific method always yields a specific result? Such a causal model fits more appropriately to research within the natural sciences involving investigations of physical entities—bombarding atoms and chemical reactions, for example. Human beings are much more than such material objects. The term "correlational" may fit, but this label offers little insight. At the heart of the teaching-learning process is a relationship among willing persons with a common purpose, that is, a relationship of consensus—if you will, a relationship among causal agents—implying some expression of free will.

As with any relationship involving persons, no specific action by one person ("teaching") can automatically guarantee a predetermined response by another person ("learning"). If such guarantees were possible, inquiry into education would adopt an educational engineering approach, with little place for genuine student participation. Rather, let us value both teachers and students and propose that teaching is typically what teachers do, and learning is typically what students do. Each student is ultimately responsible for his or her own learning, according to D. Bob Gowin, "Learners are viewed as the efficient cause of learning; therefore, they can be held responsible for learning."[5] This explains why learning can occur without teaching (students learn on their own), and teaching can take place without learning (students fail to understand; cf. Mark 8:14–21).

How can we make some sense of this paradox—that students are primarily in the driver's seat of their learning, yet teachers are responsible to bring about student learning and are often effective? John Dewey (1933) suggested an analogy from retail sales to help explain this paradox of the teaching-learning process: "There is the same exact equation between teaching and learning that there is between selling and buying."[6] Teachers engage in plans and activities to offer students opportunities for learning. Students expend their effort to learn, under the care of teachers, with the prospect of becoming, in some way, better persons. Ultimately, human flourishing—in which learning is a factor—thrives best where truth is valued and welcomed (John 8:31–32) and where genuine love displaces fear (1 John 4:18).

Yet, despite no direct causal relationship, teachers are not without any idea of how best to facilitate learning. Due to knowledge gleaned from research and reflective experience about patterns of teacher-student interactions and their results, teachers can plan for instruction that will likely or probably facilitate student learning, given students who are willing and able. Teachers are accountable for faithfully carrying through with good intentions in their teaching, and for some measure of positive results in students. If a good number of students are not "buying," we may wonder if what we are selling is legitimate.

In his work *The Teacher*, philosopher, theologian, and pastor Augustine (354–430) touched on two points mentioned above, offering a distinctively Christian view on learning. The teacher cannot cause understanding in students; this is something students must do themselves. Furthermore, God Himself is involved in this learning process.

> Do teachers hold that it is their thoughts that are perceived and grasped rather than the very disciplines they take themselves to pass on by speaking? . . . When the teachers have explained by means of words all the disciplines they profess to teach, even the disciplines of virtue and of wisdom, then those who are called "students" consider within themselves whether truths have been stated. They do so by looking

> upon the inner Truth, according to their abilities. That is therefore the point at which they learn. . . . [T]hey inwardly discover that truths have been stated. . . . Men are mistaken in calling persons "teachers" who are not, which they do because generally there is no delay between the time of speaking and the time of knowing; and since they are quick to learn internally after the prompting of the lecturer, they suppose that they have learned externally from the one who prompted them.[7]

Prior to these comments, Augustine said,

> When we deal with things that we perceive by the mind, namely by the intellect and reason, we're speaking of things that we look upon immediately in the inner light of Truth, in virtue of which the so-called inner man is illuminated and rejoices. Under these conditions our listener, if he likewise sees these things with his inward and undivided eye, knows what I'm saying from his own contemplating, not from my words. Therefore, when I'm stating truths, I don't even teach the person who is looking upon these truths. He's taught not by my words but by the things themselves made manifest within when God discloses them.[8]
>
> Regarding each of the things we understand, however, we don't consult a speaker who makes sounds outside us, but the Truth that presides within over the mind itself, though perhaps [the teacher's] words prompt us to consult Him. What is more, He Who is consulted, He Who is said to *dwell in the inner man* [Eph 3:16–17], does teach: Christ—that is, *the unchangeable power and everlasting wisdom of God* [1 Cor 1:24], which every rational soul does consult, but is disclosed to anyone, to the extent that he can apprehend it, according to his good or evil will.[9]

According to Augustine, although the human teacher has a role to play, the Inner Divine Teacher is more important. In *On Christian Teaching*, Augustine exhorts lecturers to pray to God for themselves and for their listeners, employing a pun with the Latin word *orator* which could mean either orator (one who speaks) or pray-er (one who prays).

> [T]he aim, as I say, that [our orator] pursues to the best of his ability when he speaks of these things [that are just and holy and good] to be listened to with understanding, with pleasure, and with obedience. He should be in no doubt that any ability he has and however much he has derives more from his devotion to prayer than his dedication to oratory; and so, by praying for himself and for those he is about to address, he must become a man of prayer before becoming a man of words. As the hour of his address approaches, before he opens his thrusting lips he should lift his thirsting soul to God so that he may utter what he has drunk in and pour out what has filled him.[10]

Thus, for the fullest teaching and learning to occur, both teachers and students must cultivate a sensitive and responsive mind and heart to attend to this essential divine interaction within.

Seven Components of the Teaching-Learning Encounter

Having clarified the interaction between teaching and learning, let us consider the main components of a teaching-learning encounter. Every teaching-learning situation in some way involves the following seven aspects: Teacher, Student, Subject Matter, Setting, Aim (Intention), Method, and Outcome/Result.[11] These seven components can be clustered further into three groups:

Persons:	*Boundaries:*	*Process:*
1. Teacher 2. Student	3. Subject Matter 4. Setting	5. Aim 6. Method 7. Outcome

For example, when teaching goes awry we can begin to check off potential problem areas for improvement by working through the list. To illustrate these seven components, consider a simple teaching episode in the life of Jesus (as *Teacher*) and His disciples (as *Students*) (Mark 8:14–21). Table 1 provides a summary of the analysis. The *Setting* of the lesson is on a boat, and the text also notes that the disciples had forgotten to take some bread along. They had just left a brief dispute with the religious leaders (vv. 11–13), which will become the *Subject Matter* of His lesson. Jesus warns them (*Method*: mini lecture), "Watch out! Beware of the yeast of the Pharisees and the yeast of Herod" (v. 15 HCSB). We can infer Jesus' *Aim*, that He wanted them to be wary of the false teaching of the Pharisees and Herodians. Yet the disciples were tripped up by the metaphor ("yeast") and thought Jesus was rebuking them for their forgetfulness about literal "yeast"—no bread in the boat (student *Outcome*).

Table 5.1
Seven-Component Analysis of a Gospel Teaching Episode—Mark 8:14–21

Components	*Analysis*
1. Teacher:	Jesus
2. Students:	12 Disciples
3. Subject Matter:	1. The doctrine of the Pharisees 2. Faith in God's provision of food
4. Setting:	In a boat on the Sea of Galilee Episode follows a situation in which the Pharisees were arguing with Jesus (8:11–13) and, earlier, the feeding of the 4,000 (8:1–10). Disciples did not bring any food on the boat.
5. Aim:	1-Initial Aim: 1. To demonstrate an awareness/understanding of the danger of Pharisee teaching (cf. Matt 16:12) 2-Spontaneous Aim 2a. To demonstrate an awareness of God's recent miraculous provision of food by identifying facts from recent miracles in which food was provided; and 2b. To demonstrate an attitude of faith in God's provision of food/material needs by not expressing concern about the lack of bread in the boat

6. (Teacher) Method:	*7. (Student) Outcome:*
M1. Jesus' warning with metaphor (15)	O1. Misunderstood discussion about bread (16)
M2a. Recitation question & answer (17–20)	O2a-1. Correct responses given regarding miraculous feeding of 5,000/4,000; (19–20) O2a-2 (No indication given regarding expressing an attitude of faith)
M2b. Concluding challenge/ question (21)	O2b. (No response)
[M3. Follow-up comment cf. Matt 16:11–12]	

In light of their response (*Teacher* evaluation of student *Outcome*), Jesus then moves to a second lesson about the faithfulness of God's provision through Him (*Subject Matter*-2) and for the need of the apostles to have faith in Him (*Aim*-2). He employs a recitation question-answer format (*Method*-2) regarding the recent miracles of feeding the 5,000 (Mark 6:30–44) and the 4,000 (Mark 8:1–10). They answer His two questions correctly (*Outcome*-2), yet it would still take time for their confidence in Jesus to grow (which is perhaps Jesus' long-term *Aim*).[12] The Markan episode concludes with Jesus expressing His disappointment about their lack of faith in His power—they really do not know who He is and have been taken in by the skepticism of the Pharisees—"Do you still not understand?" (*Teacher* evaluation of student *Outcome*).[13] This historical account of Jesus' teaching illustrates a fundamental teaching-learning encounter, but it does not provide all the details of the process.

For our own teaching, we have better access to much of what transpires, and this framework can become a great aid for improving the teaching-learning process. For example, consider these categories, based on this framework, to use when you are asked to observe a colleague, or for evaluating your own teaching:

1. Competence in [3] Subject Matter (including integration of faith and learning)
2. Organization of the Session related to [5] Aims, goals, teaching plan and [7] Outcomes: what Aims you deem were accomplished and how well
3. Teaching [6] Method(s) and any educational interaction with students (including any comment on Facilities/ [4] Setting and resources used in teaching)
4. [2] Student-[1] Teacher relationships, Class Atmosphere (including person, character of the [1] Teacher)
5. Recommendations for Improvement (if not included in the above)

Frankena's Framework for Analyzing a Philosophy of Education

Beyond a focus on teaching-learning encounters, another helpful model provides more attention to foundational matters regarding the development of a philosophy of education. William

Frankena (1908–94; a professor of philosophy at the University of Michigan and also a Christian) suggested that a philosophy of education should answer three fundamental questions:

1. *What* particular competencies should we cultivate in students?
2. *Why* should we cultivate these particular competencies in students?
3. *How* should we cultivate these particular competencies in students?

To help articulate responses to these questions, Frankena proposed a five-component model of "boxes" (Boxes A–E) for analyzing and articulating any educational philosophy.[14] Each box is related to certain kinds of information for educational theorizing and practice—but does not dictate the content. Each box must be filled in with particular contents supplied by educators in light of their conception of education. Figure 1 depicts the relation of the five boxes (my adaptation turns the model from a vertical alignment to a horizontal one, so that Box B is depicted as foundational to all the other Boxes).

The model includes issues related to *theory* (Boxes A, B, and C)—focusing on elements usually ignored or assumed by educators—and to practice (Boxes C, D, and E)—identifying the more familiar aspects of education. Note that Box C acts as a hinge between theory and practice. A brief overview of the model is offered below, using a simplified example of educating a concert pianist and becoming fluent in a foreign language to illustrate the contents of each box, and to suggest the idea that "lifestyle" components are entailed by each discipline.

The Applied Boxes C, D, and E

To understand the five Boxes, it may be easier to begin with Box C, as the pivotal link between theory and practice. The content of Box C (*Competencies to Be Learned*) encompasses the varied responses to *Question #1*: *What* particular competencies should we cultivate in students? "Competencies" include a wide spectrum of learning: particular knowledge, reasoning, attitudes, skills, habits, and dispositions (e.g., intellectual, emotional, volitional, social, and moral competencies), that students must acquire in order to do *well* in the discipline under study. Including a few broader items related to living a good life is perhaps appropriate

Figure 1. Adaptation of William Frankena's Framework for Analyzing a Philosophy of Education © Klaus Issler 12/10 rev

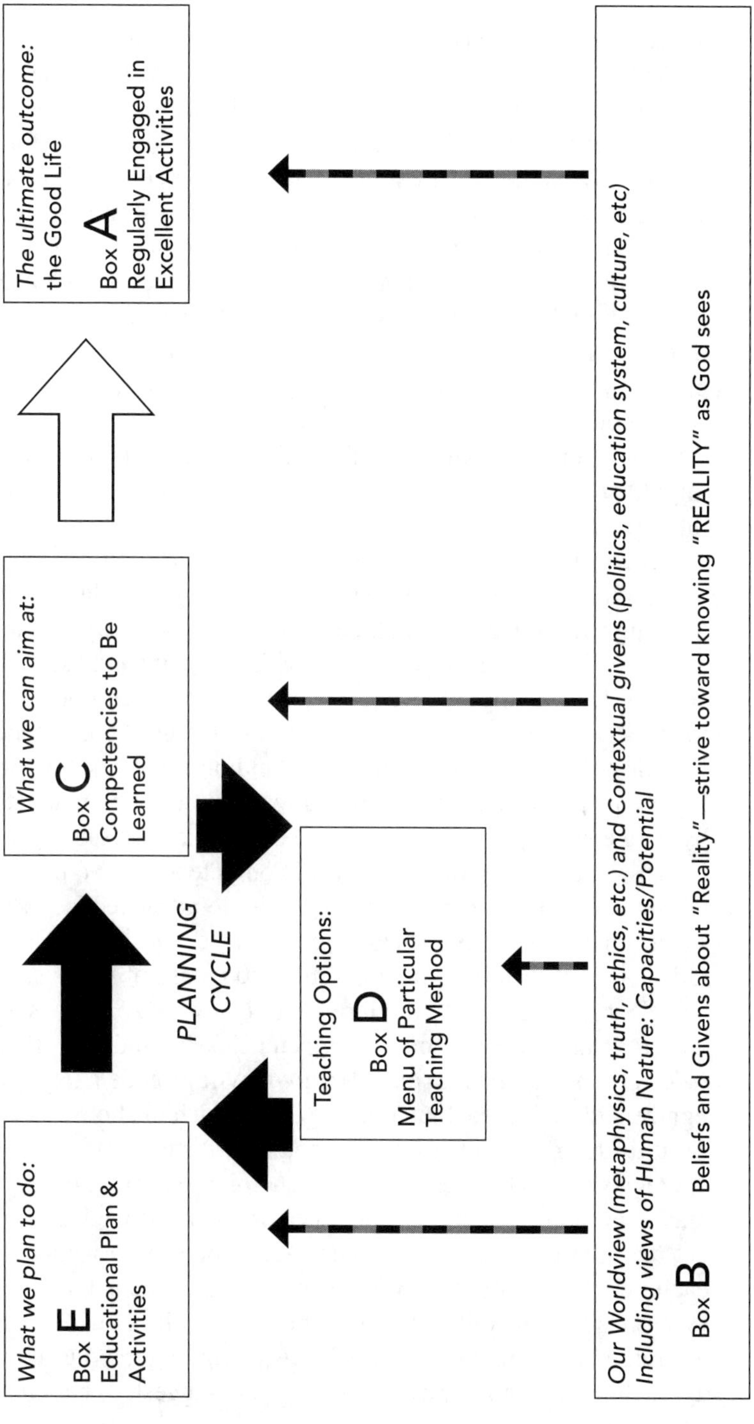

as well. Here teachers identify the kind of person they wish the student to become as a result of instruction in the particular field of study. For example, regardless of discipline, we want our students to develop their in-depth, conceptual thinking skills further and to grow in their desire to be lifelong readers of the discipline. That means we would focus on both the "want to's" along with the "how to's," helping students acquire the desire to think at deeper levels and to become avid readers. Content in Box C could include a list of broader educational goals of the whole college/university, or focus on a particular school or department, a particular degree program, a series of related courses involving prerequisites, or a single course.

For example, if we think of learning to excel at the piano, we might list basic competencies (e.g., practicing scales and chords), intermediate competencies (reading or improvising a worship song or Broadway tune), and advanced competencies (mastering classic sonatas and concertos, or performing in a modern Jazz trio). In learning a foreign language, there would be basic competencies in each of the key areas of reading, listening, writing, and speaking, such as recognizing a hundred vocabulary words and being able to use the major rules of grammar. Intermediate competencies include correct pronunciation, understanding a conversation, writing a paper, and making a presentation that could be understood by native speakers. Box C lists the educational outcomes toward which we teach, identifying areas of competencies, and the range within each competency from very basic to advanced, across the spectrum of categories such as cognitive, affective, skills sets, attitudes, and dispositions, in observable and measurable ways.

Next, Boxes D and E both relate to *Question #3*: *How* should we cultivate these particular competencies in students? Box D (*Menu of Particular Teaching Methods*) will provide a list of recognized, effective teaching options from which to choose in order to cultivate one or more of the competencies listed in Box C. These strategies of teaching can be based on common sense, one's own teaching experience or the experience of others, as well as empirical research on teaching and learning.[15] For Box D we ask: For each item listed in Box C, what is an effective means for students to learn? One cannot learn to play the piano well or learn to speak a foreign language fluently only by listening to good music or by a watching a foreign movie. As Aristotle suggested, habituation is one helpful method of learning for all disciplines—practice, practice, practice.[16] Students can improve piano performance and language fluency through persistent supervised practice with constructive feedback.

Finally in Box E (*Educational Plan and Activities*) we develop the specific, logistical plan for teaching all of the items in Box C, based on the options of teaching methods from Box D, given our situation (e.g., ability of the student, available resources, competencies of the teacher), and then we carry them out and teach our students. Which factors are included in the plan depends on the scope. Are we planning one course, or a particular sequence of courses within a major, or all the courses within a degree program? From an institutional perspective, additional factors include, for example, matters related to time and location of the course, budget of teaching resources and teaching assistants, and maintenance of the facilities (e.g., classrooms, faculty/staff offices, restrooms). Regarding practice for piano and language learning, as part of their planning teachers may need to coordinate regular availability of practice rooms and language laboratory for all students with a master weekly schedule—if these resources are available.

So in Box C we list the competencies to be cultivated in students, from Box D we select for teaching from this list of recognized teaching methods that are matched with and can cultivate each particular competency, and then in Box E we identify the educational plan, and then carry it out.

The Theoretical Boxes—A and B

Boxes A and B both relate to *Question #2*: *Why* should we cultivate these particular competencies in students? At the head of the Frankena model is Box A (*Regularly Engaging in Excellent Activities*), toward which all planning and effort is directed. As teachers, we recognize that our Box C goals—what can be measured or observed within a formal educational setting—are necessarily limited. But whatever the limitations, our ultimate hope is that a synergy of these varied discrete competencies will become united in the students' characters, so they are able to transition toward a flourishing lifestyle related to the discipline, regularly engaging in relevant excellent activities of the discipline with fluency. When our graduates develop into the kind of persons matching the craft of the discipline, they are able regularly to engage in discipline-related activities, and do them well. For example our piano student becoming a concert pianist or our language student becoming one who can easily translate a speech into another language illustrate the attainment of these goals.

Aristotle claimed *eudaimonia* (translated as "happiness") was the highest human good; living the good life, "living well" or "doing well."[17] Although contemporary usage of the word *happiness* has reduced the term to signify simply a feeling of satisfaction or pleasure, Aristotle and others argued that *eudaimonia* was something sought for its own sake alone. David Naugle explains,

> Classically among the great Western philosophers and theologians, happiness denoted the state of the genuine fulfillment of human nature that resulted from being properly related as a person to the truth of reality. Educating the soul to conform it to reality, rather than conforming reality to the dictates of the individual soul, was the secret to the happy life. But those days of defining happiness and the good life, and what it means to be truly human, are long gone.[18]

For Christians, God is the ultimate source of happiness, as John Calvin clarifies: "If God contains the fullness of all good things in himself like an inexhaustible fountain, nothing beyond him is to be sought by those who strive after the highest good and all the elements of happiness."[19] Naugle proposes that the Old Testament word *shalom* may be the biblical concept most closely aligned with this classical meaning signifying well-being, wholeness, fulfillment, prosperity, and absence of strife (translated in the LXX as *sōzō*, "save"; *eirēnē*, "peace"; and *teleios*, "complete").[20] *Shalom* "was influential in broadening the Greek idea of *eirēnē* [peace] to include the Semitic ideas of growth and prosperity."[21] The key phrase for Box A is "doing X well and fluently" usually as second nature. It is a phrase that normally cannot yet apply to our students still in training, or sadly to some graduates who never acquire the appropriate desires and dispositions of the discipline. Furthermore, we have aspirations that in some way our teaching will also nurture them in living well the good life. For Box A we ask, what kind of routine lifestyle or pattern of living do we wish our students to engage in regarding our field of study? And, what is our conception of maximal human flourishing for our students? We do our best to help students acquire Box C competencies and dispositions, while we also model as best we can our particular version of a Box A lifestyle in the discipline and the good life.

In Box B (*Beliefs and Givens about Reality*) we articulate our worldview—our main beliefs regarding ultimate reality (metaphysics) and what we know to be true about God, the world, and human persons and their capacities, particularly as it relates to our discipline and the learning of that discipline within the regional community. We identify what is the nature of truth (epistemology), and what is moral and ethical, and what we understand about beauty (aesthetics). Also in Box B we include empirical statements about the *givens of life,* such as the various systems in place (e.g., type of government, economic system, and educational system) and specific cultural mores, religious values, and opportunities within our living situation that impact learning and living in our part of the world. These may also influence which particular dispositions can or should be cultivated and listed in Box C. In Box B, we include the theological, philosophical, and empirical statements that justify or give a rationale for the particular competencies listed in Box C and those of the good life related to our discipline in Box A.

For example, a Christian worldview acknowledges two realms of reality, coexisting simultaneously: (a) the visible, physical, "natural" realm, and (b) the invisible, immaterial, supernatural realm, in which God exists as do angels and demons. Furthermore, there are two grand kingdoms vying for everyone's allegiance: the kingdom of God (Matt 12:28) and the kingdom of Satan (Matt 12:26). God "has rescued us from the domain of darkness and transferred us into the kingdom of the Son He loves" (Col 1:13 HCSB). As a result of these truths we recognize that all people are engaged in a spiritual conflict about which kingdom to serve (Eph 6:10–13).

Regarding our illustration, we would draw on conceptions of human capabilities, for example, that in general all humans have the capacity for appreciating aesthetics and playing a musical instrument well, or for learning a foreign language fluently, although some may have disabilities preventing the full development of these potentialities. We would also identify the ethical principles that actually govern how we teach and interact with our students.

More will be developed on the important topic of worldview below. Using this Frankena five-box framework can help teachers and educational leaders keep in mind the foundational claims and ideas that undergird the particular education plan that is designed, and that distinctly Christian values are kept in focus. The model is a helpful means to provide answers to these basic educational questions: What particular competencies should we cultivate in students? (Box C) Why? (Boxes A and B) How? (Boxes D and E).[22]

Worldview Matters

Regarding worldview, today we engage in an uphill struggle as we attempt to nurture our students' confidence in God within a distinctively Christian perspective. Currently, competing worldviews vie for our loyalties and our students' allegiance. J. P. Moreland proposes that "a three-way worldview struggle rages in our culture: between ethical monotheism (especially Christianity), [philosophical] postmodernism, and scientific naturalism."[23] Our basic Christian conception of what counts as knowledge and truth is being assaulted by both of these non-Christian worldviews. That is, religious claims have no standing in the public square—they are regarded as mere opinion, matters of "faith" not knowledge, where faith is believing something that has no scientific or reasonable basis—or they are merely one particular community's story of faith that has no greater value than that of any other community.

At the Heart of the Matter

> A worldview, then, is a semiotic system of narrative signs that creates the definitive symbolic universe which is responsible in the main for the shape of a variety of life-determining, human practices. It creates the channels in which the waters of reason flow. It establishes the horizons of an interpreter's point of view by which texts of all types are understood. It is that mental medium by which the world is known. The human heart is its home, and it provides a home for the human heart. At the end of the day it is hard to conceive of a more important human or cultural reality, theoretically or practically, than the semiotic system of narrative signs that makes up a worldview.[24]

For each of us our worldview is central to the core of our being and living.

Jesus Himself taught this same point, speaking in terms of the "heart." In Luke 6:45 He said, "A good man produces good out of the good storeroom of his heart. An evil man produces evil out of the evil storeroom, for his mouth speaks from the overflow of the heart." This teaching about the centrality of inner heart formation is really not new information. It is an amplification of what was taught much earlier in the Old Testament Scriptures. According to Bruce Waltke, "'Heart' (*leb/lebab*) is the most important anthropological term in the Old Testament . . . but the English language has no equivalent. It occurs 46 times in Proverbs and 858 times in the Old Testament."[25] In his comment on Prov 4:23: "Guard your heart above all else, for it is the source of life," Waltke notes, "This direction or bent of the heart [wise, pure, or perverse] determines its decisions and thus the persons' actions. . . . Since the heart is the center of all of a person's emotional-intellectual-religious-moral activity, it must be safeguarded above all things (4:23)."[26]

Why should we be concerned about competing worldviews out there? Because within, our worldview—whatever beliefs we have about reality—almost always guides how we live. We can discern our actual values and worldview by our actions and lifestyles. It is possible then to profess to believe something, but that particular professed belief may not actually be embedded within one's worldview and evident in one's lifestyle. In fact the opposite belief might actually be held in one's worldview. So, it is probably the case that we profess to believe more Christian truths than we actually live and practice. As Dallas Willard suggests, "our souls, accordingly, are soaked in secularity."[27] Various tenets of these competing worldviews probably have a greater hold on our personal worldviews than we prefer to admit or than we realize.[28]

Excellence in Teaching and Teacher Character

In this final section of the chapter, we return to a focus on the teacher and suggest some ideas for practice. How can we best improve our teaching? An initial response might focus on our instructional methods and how we could use modified or additional teaching strategies, and while that can be a helpful exercise Scripture directs our attention elsewhere: "Students are not above their teacher, but all who are fully trained will be like their teacher" (Luke 6:40 TNIV). Jesus presents here (vv. 39–49) "the kind of inward character which produces the type of behaviour outlined in the earlier sections."[29] He alerts his disciples not to follow in the wayward trail of the Pharisees in v. 39 (cf. Matt 15:14; 23:16), particularly not to judge others (cf. vv. 37 and 41). So, in v. 40, He refers to their own situation: they will become like Him when they are fully trained. Since He does not practice such criticism (v. 37), they ought not to do it either. Then, as mentioned earlier, in v. 45 our Lord points to the inward source of outward conduct, either from the good or evil stored up in one's heart.

Thus the character of the teacher will largely influence what kind of student outcomes are accomplished, and this reinforces the importance of teachers modeling Box A ideals, as mentioned above. This seems to be a missing element in discussions of the pursuit of educational excellence, improving the practice of teaching through a focus on teachers cultivating certain "habits" or "dispositions." The connection between character and excellence was made long ago by Aristotle: "human excellence will be the disposition that makes a good man and causes him to perform his function well."[30]

Two contrasts may help us unpack his point and get a better handle on the concept of excellence. First, within our understanding of "excellence" we usually include a qualitative distinction of exemplifying high standards worthy of our praise, "to perform his function well" in the words of Aristotle. For example, we do not praise a veteran teacher who still uses the very same notes and lesson plans as the first year of teaching. The pursuit of excellence for a teacher will at least involve incremental innovations and added insights and creativity over the years. Second, the excellent teacher is one who typically goes beyond the call of the routine, especially accomplishing that which takes extra effort, to do what is best for students. We usually do not praise a teacher for simply preparing to teach a lesson, unless special circumstances apply (e.g., developing it when he or she is very sick or in other circumstances that create extra hurdles to overcome). At least two factors, then, characterize the excellent teacher: (a) reaching for higher standards, and (b) regularly going beyond the routine. These are matters of the heart, not just the head; of character, not just technique.[31] Teaching involves more than performing educational skills; it involves a life influencing a life.

One further matter requires clarification. Some may wish to equate "effective teacher" with "excellent teacher." The concept of "effective teacher" draws our focus to means-end concerns, the consequences of teaching as evidenced in student outcomes. These indicators are largely identified with short-term outcomes: within the scope of a unit, a semester or a year of study. But by such a limited criterion, Jesus must be regarded as an ineffective teacher on occasion during His earthly ministry.[32] The Gospel writers seem to go out of their way to underscore how dull the disciples were, as was evident in the Mark 8:14–21 passage studied earlier in the chapter (also see Mark 8:31–33; Luke 22:24–27; John 14:8–9). But, when we think about the excellent teacher, we must use a broader set of criteria and look at both short- and long-term effects.

Furthermore, the term *effective* seems to be associated primarily with what can be validated exclusively through empirical research. But there are other sources of knowledge from which we can glean truths about excellent teachers and teaching (e.g., the Bible, or our conceptual analysis of the topic as exemplified in this chapter). Effectiveness is an important aspect of excellence, but there is more to excellence than empirical research can tell us.[33] As an example of such habits of excellence that can undergird our teaching ministry, two nontypical dispositions are presented below to stimulate our thinking. Readers may wish to ponder these matters further and expand the list as a follow-up exercise.[34]

The Teacher as a Fellow Learner

Even though we may be experts and mentors, our theology reminds us that we are fellow learners in the grace of life. The humble posture of fellow learner invites our students to come to us freely and without fear. Are students willing to risk sharing their ignorance by asking questions or by expressing new thoughts? How much effort do we expend to identify with our students, to look at the issue from their point of view? On occasion can we share a bit of our own learning trajectory, the new areas of study we have been pursuing with a brief report in progress? What questions are we pursuing for which we do not yet have complete answers?

How do we come to empathize with our students' life situations? Since Jesus, very God, took on human form to identify with us, we have an example to follow. First, we realize that no task is too menial; nothing is beneath our dignity. Remember how Jesus washed the disciples' dirty feet? Secondly, there may be times when we can be with our students in a nonteacher capacity, where we relate as members of the family of God. Since we may need to break through cultural perceptions of the teacher-student roles, we may need to take the initiative here. In addition to grander ways of doing this, let us keep in mind simple means such as cleaning up after class or receiving a student's criticism without defensiveness. Until this comes naturally, we may need to look for menial tasks to do—not for show of course—but as a school for learning humility and being with our students as fellow followers of Jesus.

The Teacher as a Partner

As teachers, we must ask some fundamental questions: What right do we have to teach, to attempt to bring about changes in another? In bringing about these changes, who determines the ultimate ends toward which we strive in our teaching? Within a Christian perspective, only God has such ultimate authority to determine such ends. As Jesus was appointed for His ministry on this earth, so we have been appointed for ours (Matt 28:18–20; John 17:8). Our ultimate authority does not come from a local church, a denomination, an educational institution, or the state; it comes from our Lord Jesus Christ Himself.

Yet we do stand under various degrees of delegated authority, and we are called into a spirit of cooperation and coordination with these partners. There is no room for lone rangers or prima donnas. We must hold hands and work together to accomplish the task. We stand on the shoulders of our forebears who have taught us. And we stand side by side with fellow teachers who share this grand project.

An honest recognition of our ultimate commission and our necessary partnership can nurture a posture of humility before our students. Since we are not God's sole gift to humanity, we can urge our students to take classes from other teachers to round out their education fully. We may wish to invite fellow teachers to share their expertise in our classroom so students are not hindered by our own foibles and whims. We pursue the best for our students by not claiming exclusive rights to them. And they will rise up to new heights through the labors of many human teachers, not just one. Furthermore, as Augustine exhorted us, we are partners with God in the teaching of our students. We pray for ourselves and for them for responsive hearts and minds to the Inner Teacher so the truth can set us free.

A century ago, American public educators were required to have "exhibited testimonials of Good Moral Character" as an essential qualification.[35] We with kingdom priorities must be concerned about more than mastery and techniques. We should keep our standards high, for "everyone who is fully trained will be like his teacher" (Luke 6:40 HCSB), for this privilege also bears a grave responsibility, for teachers "will receive a stricter judgment" (Jas 3:1 HCSB).

Summary

Although Christian teachers have an important role in student learning, students are primarily in the driver's seat. Furthermore, God mysteriously enables an enriched learning process when both teacher and student are receptive and attentive to such divine inner teaching. One model for analyzing a teaching-learning encounter suggests seven distinctive components: teacher, student, subject matter, setting, aim, method, and outcome. On a grander scale, Frankena proposed a five-factor model for analyzing a philosophy of education (these labels are mine): A: regularly engaging in excellent activities; B: beliefs and givens about reality; C: competencies to be learned; D: menu of particular teaching methods; and E: educational plan and activities. One implication of this model is that it is important for teachers to attend to the particular worldview that grounds our teaching (Box B). Finally, it was suggested that an excellent teacher is one who increasingly embodies certain dispositions, exemplifying high standards and regularly going beyond the routine. Which particular dispositions are we increasingly developing as we attempt to model the Box A ideals of our discipline?

Questions for Further Reflection

1. The author suggests three persons involved in the teaching-learning process: teacher, student, and God. Do you agree or disagree? Explain. Clarify in your own words and with as much detail as you can your understanding of the role of each person in the teaching-learning process. In specific ways does your explanation include a distinctly Christian element?
2. Do you think that the proposed Seven Components of Teaching are comprehensive? What additional factor would you include? Use either the seven-factor model, or your adapted model, and analyze a gospel teaching episode of Jesus, similar to what was done in the chapter.

Some passages for analysis:

a. Mark 9:14–29 (with parallels in Matt 17:14–20 and Luke 9:37–43)
b. Mark 10:17–31 (with parallels in Matt 19:16–30 and Luke 18:18–30)
c. Mark 10:35–45 (with parallels in Matt 20:20–28)
d. Mark 11:12–14,20–25 (with parallels in Matt 21:18–22)
e. Luke 7:36–50
f. John 21:1–25

3. Draw a diagram of the five boxes of Frankena's Framework. Explain the contents of each of and how they relate to each other. Then think of a recent course you have taught or taken as a student, and use the five boxes to analyze that course. Provide as much detail as you can and fill in the data for each box. Now consider one or two ways for improving the course.
4. What counts as "knowledge" today? Why is Christian teaching often regarded as outside of the domain of knowledge? Did Jesus regard His teachings as outside of the domain of knowledge? How can one verify knowledge? Is knowledge solely verifiable through empirical investigation, or solely through consensus of the community?
5. Is there a genuine difference between excellent and effective teaching? Explain.
6. What kinds of dispositions or character traits do you think would be important for Christian faculty to develop? Why are these important? What kinds of dispositions or character traits do you think would be important for Christian students to develop? Why are these important?

Resources for Further Study

Craig, William Lane, and Paul M. Gould, eds. *The Two Tasks of the Christian Scholar: Redeeming the Soul, Redeeming the Mind.* Wheaton: Crossway, 2007.

Frankena, William. *Three Historical Philosophies of Education.* Glenview, IL: Scott, Foresman, 1965.

Lockerbie, D. Bruce, ed. *A Passion for Learning: The History of Christian Thought on Education*. Chicago: Moody, 1994.

Peterson, Michael L. *With All Your Mind: A Christian Philosophy of Education.* Notre Dame, IN: University of Notre Dame, 2001.
Rorty, Amelie Oksenberg, ed. *Philosophers on Education: New Historical Perspectives*. London: Routledge, 1998.
Spears, Paul, and Steven Loomis. *Education for Human Flourishing: A Christian Perspective*. Downers Grove, IL: InterVarsity, 2009.
Willard, Dallas. *Knowing Christ Today: Why We Can Trust Spiritual Knowledge*. New York: HarperOne, 2009.

Endnotes

1 Robert W. Pazmino, *By What Authority Do We Teach? Sources for Empowering Christian Educators* (Grand Rapids: Baker, 1994).
2 Alternate translation by Donald Hagner, *Matthew 1–8*, Word Biblical Commentary 33A (Dallas, TX: Word, 1993), 322.
3 Michael Wilkins, *Following the Master: Discipleship in the Steps of Jesus* (Grand Rapids: Zondervan, 1992), 40–41.
4 Dallas Willard, *Knowing Christ Today: Why We Can Trust Spiritual Knowledge* (New York: HarperOne, 2009), 99, italics in original.
5 D. Bob Gowin, *Educating* (Ithaca, NY: Cornell University, 1981), 152.
6 John Dewey, *How We Think* (Chicago: Henry Regnery, 1933), 36.
7 Augustine, *The Teacher* (*De magistro*), in *Against the Academicians and the Teacher*, trans. Peter King (Indianapolis, IN: Hackett, 1995), [14.45], 145.
8 Ibid., [12.40], 141.
9 Ibid., [11.38], 139.
10 Augustine, *On Christian Teaching*, trans. R. P. H. Green (Oxford: Oxford University Press, 1997), [15.32], 121.
11 I was introduced to this seven-part framework during my master's degree at the University of California, Riverside, by Prof. J. T. Dillon in the early 1980s. It appears in his *Questioning and Teaching: A Manual of Practice* (New York: Teacher's College, 1988), an outstanding book on the use of questions in teaching. A six-part framework is used by Harold Burgess in *Models of Religious Education* (1975 [repr., Nappanee, IN: Evangel Publishing, 1996, 2001], 9): Aim, [Subject-matter] Content, Teacher, Learner, Environment, and Evaluation. "Method" is included within "Content." I prefer to keep these two distinct.
12 For further reading on nurturing confidence in God, see J. P. Moreland and Klaus Issler, *In Search of a Confident Faith: Overcoming Barriers to Trusting in God* (Downers Grove, IL: InterVarsity, 2008).
13 The parallel passage in Matt 16:5–12 provides more details about this event.
14 For further reading, see William Frankena, "A Model for Analyzing a Philosophy of Education," *High School Journal* 2/1 (1966): 8–13; and *Three Historical Philosophies of Education* (Glenview, IL: Scott, Foresman, 1965) in which, after explaining the model in chapter 1, in succeeding chapters Frankena uses the model to analyze the educational philosophies of Aristotle, Immanuel Kant, and John Dewey.
15 For suggestions on effective teaching strategies see table 22–6 in T. J. Shuell, "Teaching and Learning in a Classroom Context" (chap. 22), in *Handbook of*

Educational Psychology, ed. David Berliner and Robert C. Calfee (New York: Simon & Schuster/Macmillan, 1996).

[16] For further reading in practice and habitation, see J. P. Moreland and Klaus Issler, *The Lost Virtue of Happiness: Discovering the Disciplines of the Good Life* (Colorado Springs, CO: NavPress, 2006).

[17] Aristotle, *The Ethics of Aristotle: The Nicomachean Ethics*, trans. J. A. K. Thomson (New York: Penguin, 1986), [1095a 15–22] 66 (original trans. published 1953).

[18] David K. Naugle, *Reordered Love, Reordered Lives: Learning the Deep Meaning of Happiness* (Grand Rapids: Eerdmans, 2008), 10.

[19] John Calvin, *Institutes of the Christian Religion*, trans. Ford Lewis Battles, ed. John T. McNeill, Library of Christian Classics (Philadelphia: Westminster Press, 1960), 1005 [3.25.10].

[20] Naugle, *Reordered Love*, 23.

[21] G. L. Carney, "Shalom," in *Theological Wordbook of the Old Testament*, ed. R. Laird Harris (Chicago: Moody, 1980), 2:931. See my article on "Happiness" in *Dictionary of Christian Spirituality*, ed. Glen Scorgie (Grand Rapids: Zondervan, 2010).

[22] Notice that each question includes a normative task, what "should" be the case. Frankena clarified that the contents of Boxes A, C and E are specifically normative in nature, in that the contents of these boxes are based on decisions (what *ought* to be the case). Boxes B and D are specifically descriptive in nature, articulating relevant reality (what *is* the case).

[23] J .P. Moreland, *Kingdom Triangle: Recover the Christian Mind, Renovate the Soul, Restore the Spirit's Power* (Grand Rapids: Zondervan, 2007), 22.

[24] David K. Naugle, *Worldview: The History of a Concept* (Grand Rapids: Eerdmans, 2002), 329–30.

[25] Bruce K. Waltke, *The Book of Proverbs: Chapters 1–15*, New International Commentary on the Old Testament (Grand Rapids: Zondervan, 2004), 90.

[26] Ibid., 91–92.

[27] Dallas Willard, *The Divine Conspiracy: Rediscovering Our Hidden Life in God* (San Francisco: HarperSan Francisco, 1998), 71.

[28] For further reading regarding the difference between professed beliefs and actual beliefs, see my *Living into the Life of Jesus: The Formation of Christian Character* (Downers Grove, IL: InterVarsity, 2012).

[29] I. Howard Marshall, *The Gospel of Luke: A Commentary on the Greek Text*, New International Greek Testament Commentary (Carlisle, UK: Paternoster, 1978), 267.

[30] Aristotle, *Ethics,* 100 [1106a20].

[31] Even though we may perform certain techniques effortlessly (i.e., "routinely" for us) at a high standard, we are still worthy of praise since these actions flow from the habits we formed in the crucible of painstaking effort. For a more nuanced and detailed discussion of praiseworthy actions, see Richard Swinburne, *Responsibility and Atonement* (Oxford: Clarendon, 1989), chap. 2: "Moral Responsibility and Weakness of Will."

[32] "Jesus was an accomplished yet ineffective teacher. He taught well, even masterfully in respects, yet the learning that came about did not correspond to the quality of the teacher." J. T. Dillon, *Jesus as a Teacher: A Multidisciplinary Case*

Study (Bethesda, MD: International Scholars, 1995), 161. Dillon draws this conclusion based on the response (or lack of response) from all Jesus' listeners, including the religious leaders, and without consideration of the long-term learning outcomes in the lives of His followers in the book of Acts.

[33] Research related to short-term learning outcomes can help us improve our teaching for certain kinds of effects, such as cognitive outcomes. Yet consideration of a longer scope is necessary for assessing teaching for dispositional and attitude formation.

[34] For additional suggested habits see my "Habits of the Excellent Teacher," in *With an Eye on the Future: Development and Mission in the 21st Century* [Festschrift for Ted Ward], ed. D. Elmer and L. McKinney (Monrovia, CA: MARC, 1996), 215–22; "A Conception of Excellence in Teaching," *Education*, 103 (1983): 338–43; and *How We Learn: A Christian Teacher's Guide to Educational Psychology* (Eugene, OR: Wipf & Stock, 1994).

[35] From "Teacher's Certificate" of 1882, cited in Laura Ingalls Wilder, *Little Town on the Prairie* (New York: Harper & Row, 1941), 306.

Christian Faith and the Disciplines

6

Biblical and Theological Studies in the Christian University

Gregory Alan Thornbury

Introduction: The Bible's Radical Claim about Knowledge

Toward the close of the first millennium, the people of England faced the constant threat of Viking invaders. Things looked grim until the vulnerable island of Britain united behind a great warrior from the House of Wessex, a king who is known to history as Alfred the Great. As Alfred's story tells, great leaders are not usually mere warriors, and they never achieve greatness alone. By Alfred's side during this great period of conflict with the Vikings stood his trusted advisor, Asser, a Welsh priest who served as the king's spiritual guide. Alfred knew, however, that it was not enough merely to have access to someone who knew the Scriptures. He wanted Asser to teach him biblical and theological studies in the midst of fending off foreign invaders. To this end, the priest taught the monarch Latin, and Alfred soon became able to read the Vulgate, the Latin translation of the Bible. He did not stop there. Alfred proceeded to compile his own commentary on Scripture, which he took with him into battle. Further, he understood that a nation would not be prepared for a time of crisis without a strong church, so the king proceeded to translate for his bishops theological works from Augustine, Gregory the Great, and Boethius into his native Anglo-Saxon language. Alfred the Great held a belief that no society could rise above its collective knowledge of Scripture and theology. It is an axiom that is abandoned at a culture's peril.[1]

What follows in these next few pages is a sort of invitation to a new generation of Alfreds and Assers, who realize the threats and opportunities of the days in which we live, and turn to the faith once for all delivered to the saints for its rescue. The context in which most young men and women will have the best opportunity to steep themselves in biblical and theological studies will be in colleges and universities, specifically those who dedicate themselves to the proposition and promise of Christian higher education. For it is in these contexts where students will encounter the kind of scholars who not only have the highest degree of academic preparation available, but also have a heart for godliness and the discipleship of young Christ-followers.

If you are reading this and you are a student thinking about a call to serve the kingdom of God in building up His church, you need to know this: a call to follow Christ is a summons to prepare. That preparation must be done in the Scriptures and the soul-enlivening truths that flow from the heart of God. If you are a parent considering whether or not it is worth it to send your child to a Christian university, you know that the decision is not a trivial matter, for it involves with whom your child will be spend four of the most formative years of a crucial phase of his life. In this connection, the words of John Adams to his beloved Abigail during his service in the Continental Congress come to mind. Addressing the subject of their children's education, he wrote: "Fix their ambition upon great and solid objects, and their contempt upon little, frivolous, and useless ones. . . . Every decency, grace, and honesty should be inculcated upon them."[2] Every student and parent owes to himself or herself a period of self-examination to answer the challenge posed by President Adams. What are the truly "great and solid objects" upon which to fix our attention and affix our affections? Elsewhere in this volume, we have read appeals to the importance of a panoply of disciplines that reside at the heart of the core of a great Christian liberal arts education. With deference to all these, we are reminded of the words of the prophet Isaiah: "The grass withers, the flowers fade, but the word of our God remains forever" (Isa 40:8 HCSB). If we consecrate ourselves to honor and study the body of divinity that flows from God's revelation to us, we will never be disappointed with the result.

How does this commitment to the Word of God play itself out in a university education? Much discussion has been afforded in this volume and many others like it around the catchphrase "the integration of faith and learning." But this concept will become little more than a shibboleth if it does not mean "the integration of the Faith with learning." In other words, you cannot apply something into your education that you cannot readily identify and talk about rigorously, rationally, and comprehensively. The Bible is not some loose-knit pastiche of take-it-or-leave-it spiritual principles, but rather bedrock for all sorts of learning. It is our job to see whether or not we actually believe that proposition or not.

Though the German philosopher Immanuel Kant was no Christian, he was right on the mark when he said that as "supreme being" God "is an ideal without a flaw, a concept which completes and crowns the whole of human knowledge."[3] Even a skeptic like Kant had to admit the truth: only an eternal and transcendent Creator God can explain the richness and diversity of human knowledge. Without God, the world ultimately cannot make sense.

The Bible makes a radical claim about the nature of ultimate reality. It asserts that apart from the acknowledgment of its divine origin, the universe remains an unsolvable puzzle. As theologian Carl Henry has put it, "All merely human affirmations about God curl into a question mark."[4] Solomon—an impressive philosopher in his own right—boiled the issue down to the following proposition: "The fear of the LORD is the beginning of knowledge" (Prov 1:7a). This reverent recognition of the Creator (note: "fear" in this passage does not equal fright) provides the necessary foundation for education (Ps 2:11; Eccl 12:13; Isa 11:2–3).

Attentive readers will note that the "fear of the Lord" is not just the starting point for spiritual axioms. The proverb states that it is the beginning of all knowledge. The Hebrew word used for knowledge here covers the entire scope of human inquiry. Presupposing the God of the biblical type offers the only sensible way to begin uncovering the true and unified meaning of things. (Certainly, such scientific patriarchs as Kepler, Newton, Pasteur, and Mendel understood this.) Paul explained why: "For everything was created by Him [i.e., Christ], in heaven and on earth, the visible [e.g., planets, plants, animals, material things] and the invisible [e.g., numbers, laws, aesthetic and economic principles]. . . ."

Reinforcing the point, he concluded, "All the treasures of wisdom and knowledge are hidden in Him" (Col 1:16; 2:3).

"All," of course, means all. *All* is an audacious word for the apostle to use and Solomon to imply. The claim, however, does not mean that pagans never get anything right. After all, Solomon admired the king of Tyre's expertise with architecture and construction (2 Chr 2:3). Paul appreciated the writings of the Greek philosopher-poets (Acts 17:28). Nonbelievers will continue to make singular advances in their individual modes of expertise, whether that is in mathematics, medicine, or other disciplines. But until they come to terms with the transcendent Ruler, they will never understand the "uni" in the word "universe."

Only the biblical account of the creation of every aspect of existence, the fall into sin and disorder, and redemption through the gospel of Jesus Christ provides a satisfactory "big picture." Critics of Christianity say that God's people are anti-intellectual. Quite to the contrary, the church is the only earthly institution poised to pose the toughest question of all: how does one explain the beautiful but baffling complexity of the world without reference to God—the "ideal without a flaw"? The answer to that question must be as bold as the Bible's claim about knowledge itself.

Theological Preparation in a Technological Age

If we can agree that biblical and theological studies form an essential foundation for a student's university years, we must then consider what sort of education might best equip them for service in the diffuse and rapidly changing cultural environment in which we currently live. Much research has been done on the characteristics of this generation of students, but of special interest to those who would teach theology is the influence of technology on those who would commit themselves to studying holy or transcendent things.[5] Education theorist Marc Prensky coined the term "digital native" in 2001 for learners who have grown up accustomed to technology being their primary interface for education.[6] Ever since Nicholas Carr penned his famous *Atlantic Monthly* essay entitled, "Is Google Making Us Stupid?" the debate has raged over the relative merits that technology brings with it to the learning process.[7] In the essay, he argues that people who use the Internet regularly—today's students and teachers included—tend to have a drastically reduced ability to pay attention to and comprehend a longer work (like books). Further, instead of reading thoroughly, we skim or "power-browse" through the text, looking for "the right answer," placing immediacy and efficiency in a more cherished place than deep reading and comprehension. As other researchers have argued, the ability to think critically about the authority and reliability of various different kinds of texts is in decline.[8] We are less likely to distinguish between the relative weights of a magazine article versus an academic dissertation, a website as compared to an academic monograph. In such an environment, Thomas Aquinas's dictum has never been more apt: "What you read, set about to understand, verifying what is doubtful."[9]

Perhaps of even greater concern are the fears that our dependence on technology and social media actually undermine the personal relationships that they are supposed to support. No more sobering account of this set of conditions has been offered than the one provided by psychologist Sherry Turkle in *Alone Together: Why We Expect More from Technology and Less from Each Other*. In her compelling investigation in the subject, Turkle concludes that "we seem determined to give human qualities to objects and content to treat each other as things."[10] The remainder of Turkle's book explores the ways in which technology makes us feel vulnerable and protected simultaneously—a seeming impossibility.

In the midst of the debate over how technology is changing education, we need to be reminded that this concern has been on the minds of many generations before ours. For example, in the *Phaedrus*, Plato portrays Socrates as worrying to one of his interlocutors that the innovation of writing will displace the need for memorization and books as a depository of data without reliable teachers to come beside them and offer wisdom about how to interpret what has just been read.[11] No one today worries that the legacy of the book has been deleterious to the soul of humanity. But Plato does point to the difference between sheer information transfer and a discerning kind of intelligence. From the perspective of Christian thought, wisdom comes from the Scriptures and from the gathered *consensus fidei* of the church that has accumulated over two millennia of its history. It is upon this conviction that a Christian university can build the sort of biblical and theological studies program that will train the next generation of worthy and wise guides through the intellectual landscape of a postmodern world.

The *Telos* of Biblical and Theological Studies

Today's generation of incoming college students lives in one of the environments least conducive to education in recent memory. Parents, friends, and even teachers all too often send young people the message that what really matters in life is your career, how much money you make, and how "competitive" you are in the global marketplace because Tiger Moms are reading Amy Chua and No-bones Dads are reading Thomas Friedman's *The World Is Flat.* Certainly, we all have a vested interest in there being enough science, technology, and engineering folks to keep the global economy afloat. But no society has ever flourished without its spiritual guides, priests, and prophets—which makes the task of training up a new generation of pastors and church leaders as important as it has ever been. What raises the stakes even more toward this end is that the urgency to take up the study of biblical languages, philosophy, and theology has also never been greater. The truth of the matter is that the best time to become prepared for ministry is during those magical, never-to-be-repeated special four years of undergraduate study at a university, when your attention and focus can be riveted toward the pursuit of the "great objects" of which John Adams wrote to Abigail. Speaking from personal experience, I can recount anecdote after anecdote of someone delaying preparation for ministry until a later, more opportune time, only never to return to their call to serving the church, taking the gospel to the nations, or fulfilling their passion to serve directly Christ's kingdom. Indeed, the most miserable person you will ever meet is the one who "puts his hand to the plow and looks back." Such a person, Jesus said, is not fit for service in the kingdom of God (Luke 9:62).

Even assuming that someone is motivated toward a life of service, that still does not address the question of why a university education is necessary preparation. After all, undertaking a serious academic study has been given a bad reputation by some in the academy who do more than their fair share to contribute to the stereotype that scholarship and research are so esoteric and "ivory tower" that they hold little practical value for the actual world in which we live. But as the French philosopher and spiritual writer Antonin Sertillanges once wrote, "The source of our knowledge is not in books, it is in reality, and in our thought. Books are signposts; the road is older, and no one can make the journey for us."[12] Thus, scholarship becomes a portal to another world—a world of both allies and enemies. We must read things with which we both agree and disagree, for, as Francis Schaeffer used to say, it is in the antithesis that we come to appreciate the truth. We should be eager to engage in the great ideas that have shaped the hearts of men and women over the centuries, and be no respecter of persons as we read. For, as Thomas Aquinas once averred, "Do not heed by whom a thing is said, but rather what is said you should commit to your memory."[13]

Even with this said, a skeptical person still might not be convinced that the world of academe is relevant in an age in which there are so many other pressing battles to be fought, and in a world in which so many people just need to hear the good news of the gospel. C. S. Lewis raised this question to his own students at Oxford University, while the Second World War was being waged all around them, at St. Mary the Virgin Church on Sunday, October 22, 1939. In his sermon, "Learning in War-Time," Lewis queried "how it is right, or even psychologically possible, for creatures who are at every moment advancing either to heaven or to hell to spend any fraction of the little time allowed them in this world on such comparative trivialities as literature or art, mathematics or biology,"[14] and "How can you be so frivolous and selfish as to think about anything but the salvation of human souls?"[15] Lewis countered that we always must live in light of the highest expressions of human flourishing. What is more, he argued that only people who have drunk deeply from the well of the reservoir of the faith that has sustained the church during its history would be prepared to lead a nation after the bloody conflict with Hitler. We fight in wartime because we believe that there are really real, really true, and really good things about our world to discover. Such realities shame our pragmatist pretensions and our self-imposed urgencies.

The liberal arts, however, are not the only subjects to suffer during wartime. As numerous studies have shown, biblical and theological literacy are at historic lows. Insofar as people know the Word at all, it is largely scattershot. People have picked up a smattering of teachings along the way from sermons or books that they have read, but they have not really grasped the Bible as an enthralling, captivating revelation that places our fingers on the pulse of the grand sweep of the history of redemption. As B. B.

Warfield exhorted his students, "Nothing will suffice [for a 'well-done ministry'] but to know; to know the Book; to know it at first hand; and to know it through and through. A comprehensive and thorough theological training is the condition of a really qualified ministry. When we satisfy ourselves with a less comprehensive and thorough theological training, we are only condemning ourselves to a less qualified ministry."[16]

Some parents might be under the impression that sending their child to study theology at a university is an exercise in little more than esoteric intellectual adventures. The purpose of receiving a first-rate biblical and theological studies education, however, is not to mow a student's brain. It is to conform them to the image of Christ through the rigorous study of the languages in which the Bible was originally written and through introducing them to the *consensus fidei* of the church throughout the ages. Such a preparation is a not only a safeguard against heresy, although it most certainly is that; it is also insurance against harming the souls of the people of God, the church for whom Christ died. For millennia, the way that servants of the church have been educated is in a one-on-one situation of discipleship with a mentor. And in a world fascinated with the fantasy that face-to-face classroom teaching can be supplanted by online education, I would point people back to the doctrines of creation and incarnation, and remind our generation that the church did not receive a virtual Messiah or a substitutionary atonement by proxy. There is no substitute for living in the same town as your Rabbi, eating a meal with him, following him as he teaches you the mystery of the gospel. Indeed, as Paul R. House exhorted his fellow theological educators in the Association of Theological Schools:

> God sent his son, not just his word. Moses, Elijah, Huldah, Jesus, Barnabas, Paul, Aquila, and Priscilla mentored future servants of God. They did so face-to-face in community settings. They did so individually and in groups. They ate together. They prayed and worshipped God together. They suffered and shared together. They did use the medium of writing to advance their mission, but it was always to supplement synchronous education conducted in the same location as the learners. Jesus was able to send twelve disciples and then seventy disciples through such personal means. The early church multiplied disciples and ministers in this fashion.[17]

Whatever one's view of distance education ultimately is, no one can gainsay the importance of personal presence—of knowing that your mentor is available to say to you what the apostle Paul bluntly was able to say to a struggling Corinthian church: "Imitate me, as I also imitate Christ" (1 Cor 11:1). Regardless of the delivery system, everyone can agree that the outcome of a good theological education is biblical fidelity and an adherence to the faith once for all delivered to the saints.

The Foundations of Knowledge: Reading Old Books

Now that we have established the purpose of and need for a theological education, we turn to the tools for the trade. It is very simple: reading old books. Everyone who loves truth loves those dusty, precious volumes that not only adorn shelves but beckon to be read. The Puritan divine Samuel Davies memorably wrote of the consolation of his bibliotheca: "The venerable dead await me in my library to entertain me and relieve me from the nonsense of surviving mortals." Indeed, when we steep ourselves in the wisdom of the ages, we are reminded that our modern age is not automatically smarter than our forebears. By reaching back into the past, we gain primary knowledge. This, of course, raises the matter of the tyranny of the novel, the feeling that we must be up-to-date on all the latest arguments or controversies before we can revisit the past. Nothing could be a more wrongheaded notion than this, for as Thomas Aquinas advised students, "Choose to enter, not straightway into the ocean, but by way of the little streams; for difficult things ought to be reached by way of easy ones."[18] The easiest and most profitable starting place for grounding students in preparation for ministry, then, is the study of classic works of theology. This means that a student will have to read both defenders of the faith and the heretics that provoked them, the orthodox worthies and the provocateurs that bedeviled them. In order to recognize error in our time, you must read the great debates from previous times: Augustine versus Pelagius, Luther versus Erasmus, Calvin versus Pighius, Nettleton versus Finney, and others.

One objection might be that the life of the mind might decrease passion for ministry and hurt efforts to reach the lost with the gospel. But this has never been true of the great men of God in the past who possessed both keen minds and warm hearts. A rich, active, and vital relationship with Christ is an absolutely necessary companion to academic study. George Whitefield exhorted those under his charge in a similar manner when he remarked, "Learning without piety, will only make you more capable of promoting the kingdom of Satan. Henceforward, therefore, I hope you will enter into your studies not to get a parish, nor to be polite preachers, but to be great saints."[19] The temptation to become puffed up with pride because of our knowledge is a characteristic drummed out of us if we would only read the book of Proverbs. As C. S. Lewis reminds us in "Learning in War-Time," there is a crucial difference between loving the truth and being obsessed with the extent of our *own* knowledge and how educated we are. This is a great peril and will deaden the effectiveness of anyone preparing for the ministry. If we become too puffed up with pride, Lewis warns, "The time for plucking out the right eye has occurred."[20] In other words, intellectual arrogance can be just as harmful to our soul as lust, jealousy, and greed. For as the apostle John warned the early church, it is the lust, the flesh, the eyes, and *the pride of life* that drain the life from our ministries, either current or future. And as Sertillanges rightly notes, "Purity of thought requires purity of soul; that is a general and undeniable truth."[21]

One of the best aspects of a proper undergraduate theological education is the thrill of sitting at the feet of godly professors, pastors, and missionaries in the classroom. Philosopher and theologian Nicholas Wolterstorff explains that it is in the classroom where the delight of learning is experienced and where a devotional gratitude toward God, the author of knowledge, is cultivated. Christian higher education, he goes on to explain, should be a place of *shalom*, an environment that focuses on the restoration of our relationships with God, with society, with nature, and one another.[22] Such a forum sets the stage for what ministry will be like on the mission field or within the local church. The classroom should thus not be a million miles away from these practical realities, but rather right next door.

Shortly after his retirement, Karl Barth visited the United States to deliver a series of lectures. A number of evangelical theologians met with him to discuss differences in their respective theological positions. The issues were substantive and among them was the weighty matter of the nature of biblical inspiration and the epistemological delivery of divine revelation. Amongst the evangelicals who interacted with Barth was Edward John Carnell, then the president of Fuller Theological Seminary in Pasadena, California, but a great philosopher and theologian in his own right. The campus of seminarians was abuzz when they learned that Carnell would address the student body upon his return. No doubt some of them thought they might hear a great theological war story from their hero pitted against the neo-orthodox Barth. But Carnell would have none of it. As he stood before the crowd assembled, he outlined the substance of his conversation with the author of *Church Dogmatics* and the most notable theologian of the twentieth century. He pointed to the aspects of disagreement but was struck by Barth's deportment, his kindness and generosity in the argument. He remarked that Barth reminded him of the description of the Lord Himself in the prologue to John's Gospel. Eyeing up the group of future Christian ministers, Carnell concluded: "Jesus came as one from God the Father, full of grace and truth. Remember to never get the order wrong."[23]

We will never be good ministers of the gospel unless we speak the truth in love. Therefore, when we are young, it is imperative for us to be surrounded by mentors who will show us how to behave, teach, and live in community. If you are preparing for a life of service to the kingdom of God, do not attend any university where you are unsure the faculty will pour their life into you and pour into these never-to-be-repeated invaluable years of your life. Choose wisely.

The Curriculum for Biblical and Theological Studies

Having established now the need for a university education in theology, its purpose, and its environment, we turn to the nuts and bolts of the program: the curriculum. These are, however, no *mere* nuts and bolts, for the foundation of any preparation for teaching, preaching, or service in Christ's kingdom are the Scriptures themselves. The starting point, of course, is the study of the original languages themselves: Greek and Hebrew. Although some college and seminary programs downplay the importance of the languages mostly for practical reasons, those who cherish the English translations we now possess must recognize that behind every single one of them is an army of translators who never cease the important work of making the Word of God understandable in the common language of everyday people. This was certainly the task of the 72 scholars who composed the Greek translation of the Old Testament—the Septuagint—a cause that was likewise taken up by Jerome who produced the first Latin translation of the Scriptures, called the Vulgate. Later, the availability of the Bible in the vernacular stood at the heart of the movement that produced the Protestant Reformation. The recovery of the authority of the Bible, coupled with its availability, pointed Christians back to the source of the gospel. Writing in a letter to Martin Dorp in May 1515, Erasmus remarked regarding Greek and Hebrew acquisition: "These [original] tongues are so valuable for the study of holy scriptures that it seems to me only a grossly impudent man could set up for a professor of theology without knowing them."[24] Martin Luther understood that a central aspect to his project of recovery was biblical translation, and that there is no translation without knowledge of the original tongues of the text of the Bible. In an address to school officials in his day, Luther offered the following reflections that today seem oddly prophetic for our own times:

> For the devil smelled a rat, and perceived that if the languages were revived a hole would be knocked in his kingdom which he could not easily stop up again.
>
> In proportion then as we value the gospel, let us zealously hold to the languages. And let us be sure of this we will not long preserve the gospel without the languages. The languages are the sheath in which this sword of the Spirit is contained; they are the casket in which this jewel is enshrined; they are the vessel in which this wine is held; they are the larder in which this food is stored; and, as the gospel itself points out, they are the baskets in which are kept these loaves and fishes and fragments. If through our neglect we let the languages go (which God forbid!), we shall not only lose the gospel, but the time will come when we shall be unable either to speak or write a correct Latin or German. As proof and warning of this, let us take the deplorable and dreadful example of the universities and monasteries, in which men have not only unlearned the gospel, but have in addition so corrupted the Latin and German languages that the miserable folk have been fairly turned into beasts, unable to speak or write a correct German or Latin, and have well-nigh lost their natural reason to boot.
>
> It is inevitable that unless the languages remain, the gospel must finally perish.[25]

Luther's words are a powerful reminder of the responsibility that we have to know the Word of God inside and out, from original languages to the vast array of tools and commentaries now at our disposal to understand what God requires of us in our studies, congregations, and missional endeavors. But talk is cheap. If you want to understand what any school of theology or ministry values, just look at their catalog. Any program needs to root its students in foundations: biblical hermeneutics, church history, theology, ethics, philosophy, and spiritual disciplines. Upon that base should be added a rich mixture of bricks made out of other specialized theology, ministry, and missions courses. Practical courses such as internships and semester abroad experiences should readily be on offer. At the end of their studies, as B. B. Warfield concluded, students should be the following:

a. Sound biblical critics and able interpreters
b. Defenders of the Christian faith
c. Able and sound divines
d. Useful preachers and faithful pastors
e. Qualified to exercise discipline and to take part in the government of the church in all its judicatures[26]

Every few months, or so it seems, evangelicalism is rocked by another book by a prominent Christian pastor or scholar who has deviated from the established canons of orthodoxy. Some of these departures are more serious than others, but the only way to really know what is a serious heresy, and what is not, is to devote oneself to the suite of theological disciplines: biblical theology, historical theology, and systematic theology. Here is what distinguishes each:

(a) *Biblical theology* attempts to show the progression of divine revelation in the context of the grand sweep of the history of redemption. It focuses on the narrative arc of Genesis to Revelation and shows how all of the Bible, both Old and New Testaments, are in fact Christian Scripture.

(b) *Historical theology* maps the rise, growth, and maturation of the faith of the church throughout the ages. Each era reveals situations in which some error in biblical interpretation confronts God's people. During the first few centuries of church history, when the error was grave enough, bishops gathered together in synods and councils to determine what the baseline was for orthodoxy, and to distinguish truth from heresy. All aspiring ministers need to learn dicta of the Councils of Nicea, Constantinople, Chalcedon, and Orange so that they might be able to know what primrose paths have led away from the gospel before and will once again, should we allow it to do so.

(c) *Systematic theology* analyzes and synthesizes the biblical materials and develops propositional statements from Scripture that accurately, if not exhaustively, bear witness to God, His created order, the sinfulness of human beings, the person and work of Christ, and the ongoing witness of the Holy Spirit in the world. Once regarded as "Queen of the Disciplines," that estimation of systematic theology has suffered from the rise of philosophical skepticism and scientism—the view that reality can ultimately best be understand through the modes of biology or chemistry. Such a turn of historical events is unfortunate because it signals an ominous turn for the church away from the epistemological weight of the biblical revelatory data that can alone be the basis of our confidence. Systematic theologians use rational thought to give a doctrinal shape to the biblical text, which helps believers understand how to understand difficult biblical passages in light of everything else in the Scriptures.

Without theology to guide them—universities being a primary example—the church or the institutions that flow from her will be like castaways adrift at sea. We can tell ourselves that we can survive without rooting ourselves in the ancient words of Scripture or the sturdy creeds and confessions that flow from God's Word, but we would be only offering ourselves an empty consolation. As the great Baptist leader E. Y. Mullins once opined: "A creed is like a ladder. On it you may climb up to a lofty outlook, a purer spiritual atmosphere, or you may climb down to the low platform of a barren orthodoxy."[27] Unless we can convince ourselves once again that our faith is precious, that it should be taught broadly and deeply from the original sources, our colleges, universities, and seminaries rightly deserve only one fate: oblivion.

Conclusion

We live in times in which the study of the Bible and theology may seem risky at best or irrelevant at worst. So be it. The church has stared down worse enemies than the low opinion of comfortable *bourgeois* Western evangelicals and fearlessly taken the gospel to the nations. It began with the apostles and martyrs who did not think more highly of themselves than they did of Christ, who died for the church. It continued with the church fathers, men like Jerome and Augustine, Chrysostom and the Cappadocians, who were not only great men of God but some of the greatest scholars the world has ever known. It continued with intellectual giants like Jonathan Edwards, whose titanic intellect still singles him out as one of the great philosophical and theological geniuses in American history. It advanced through fearless individuals like William Carey, who, though he lacked the educational opportunities available to other ministers of his day, sparked the modern missions movement by winning the lost because he had a passion to translate the Bible into the Bengali language of the people in India to whom he gave his life. The call to serve came to flourishing in the work of Lottie Moon, who took the gospel to China and refused to leave her fellow Christians behind when certain starvation and death was her only reward in this life.

The question for anyone thinking about formal biblical and theological studies as a preparation for ministry is not whether it is a good "career" move. The question is whether you are ready to join such august company, the great cloud of witnesses who "by faith conquered kingdoms, administered justice, obtained promises, shut the mouths of lions, quenched the raging of fire, escaped the edge of the sword, gained strength after being weak, became mighty in battle, and put foreign armies to flight. . . . The world was not worthy of them" (Heb 11:33–34,38 HCSB). It still is not. But their memory is honored every time a candidate for ministry takes seriously his or her calling, and agrees with the heart of Sandhu Sundar Singh when he wrote the gospel hymn: "The world behind me, the cross before me. No turning back. No turning back."

Questions for Further Reflection

1. What advantage does study at a Christian university bring to a student?
2. When interacting with the thoughts and discoveries of non-Christians, is it safe to assume that only Christians will be able to fully understand how all knowledge fits together and is useable in the universe? Why or why not?
3. Is there a danger of the phrase "the integration of faith and learning" becoming a "catchphrase" that is really void of meaning? Why or why not?

4. How has technology changed the modern learning landscape both academically and spiritually? Have such changes happened previously in history? What can be learned from the changes about the presence and pursuit of knowledge?
5. Can any society flourish without spiritual guides who are careful students of the Bible? Why or why not?
6. Is theological education a necessity? If so, should it be part of a university's curriculum?
7. How does the life of the mind impact a passion for the ministry?

Resources for Further Study

Henry, Carl F. H. *God, Revelation, and Authority*. 6 vols. Waco, TX: Word, 1976–83.

Schmeltekopf, Donald, and Dianna Vitarza. *The Future of Baptist Higher Education*. Waco, TX: Baylor University Press, 2006.

Sertillanges, A. G. *The Intellectual Life*. Translated by Mary Ryan. Washington, DC: Catholic University of America Press, 1998.

Wolterstorff, Nicholas. *Educating for Life: Reflections on Christian Teaching and Learning*. Edited by Gloria Goris Stranks and Clarence W. Joldersma. Grand Rapids: Baker, 2002.

Endnotes

[1] Justin Pollard, *Alfred the Great: The Man Who Made England* (London: John Murray, 2005), 232–51.

[2] John Adams to Abigail Adams, 28 August 1774, in *The Letters of John and Abigail Adams,* ed. Frank Shuffelton (New York: Penguin, 2004), 26.

[3] Immanuel Kant, *Critique of Pure Reason*, trans. N. K. Smith (New York: St. Martin's, 1965), B 669.

[4] Carl F. H. Henry, *God, Revelation, and Authority* (Dallas: Word, 1976), 2:8.

[5] Cf. Tim Elmore, *Generation iY: Our Last Chance to Save Their Future* (Poet Gardener, 2010); Richard Franklin, "Who Will Our Students Be in a Postmodern, Postdenominational, and Materialistic Age?" in *The Future of Baptist Higher Education*, ed. Donald D. Schmeltekopf and Dianna M. Vitanza (Waco, TX: Baylor University Press, 2006), 101–12.

[6] Marc Prensky, "Digital Natives, Digital Immigrants," *On the Horizon* 9 (2001): 1–6.

[7] Nicholas Carr, "Is Google Making Us Stupid?" *The Atlantic Magazine* (July/August 2008), http://www.theatlantic.com/magazine/archive/2008/07/is-google-making-us-stupid/6868/.

[8] Ian Rowlands et al., "The Google Generation: Information Behaviour of the Researcher of the Future," *Aslib Proceedings* 60 (2008): 303.

[9] Thomas Aquinas, *How to Study*, trans. Victor White (Oxford: Blackfriars, 1949), 6.
[10] Sherry Turkle, *Alone Together* (Kindle edition; New York: Basic, 2011), location 187 of 7517.
[11] Plato, *Phaedrus and Letters VII and VIII*, trans. Walter Hamilton (London: Penguin Classics, 1973), 96–97.
[12] A. G. Sertillanges, *The Intellectual Life: Its Spirit, Conditions, Methods*, trans. Mary Ryan (Washington, DC: Catholic University of America Press, 1998), 169–70.
[13] Aquinas, *How to Study*, 6.
[14] C. S. Lewis, "Learning in War-Time," in *The Weight of Glory: And Other Addresses* (New York: HarperCollins, 2001), 48–49.
[15] Ibid., 50.
[16] B. B. Warfield, "Our Seminary Curriculum: What Ought It to Be?" *The Bible Student and Teacher* 9 (1909): 184.
[17] Paul R. House, "Hewing to Scripture's Pattern: A Plea for Personal Theological Education," *Colloquy* (Spring 2010): 4.
[18] Aquinas, *How to Study*, 5.
[19] George Whitefield, "To the Students, etc., Under Conviction at the Colleges of Cambridge [Harvard] and New Haven [Yale], in New England and Connecticut," in *The Revived Puritan: The Spirituality of George Whitefield*, ed. Michael A. G. Haykin (Dundas, Ontario: Joshua, 2000), 143.
[20] Lewis, "Learning in War-Time," 57.
[21] Sertillanges, *Intellectual Life*, 22.
[22] Nicholas P. Wolterstorff, *Educating for Life: Reflections on Christian Teaching and Learning*, ed. Gloria Goris Stronks and Clarence W. Joldersma (Grand Rapids: Baker, 2002), 256, 261–62.
[23] See George M. Marsden, *Reforming Fundamentalism: Fuller Seminary and the New Evangelicalism* (Grand Rapids: Eerdmans, 1987), 195.
[24] Erasmus, "A Defense of Folly," 244.
[25] Martin Luther, "To the Councilmen of All Cities in Germany That They Establish and Maintain Christian Schools," in *The Christian in Society,* vol. 2, trans. Albert T. W. Steinhaeuser and Walther I. Brandt, *Luther's Works: American Edition* 45, ed. Walther I. Brandt (Philadelphia: Fortress, 1962), 358–59.
[26] Warfield, "Seminary Curriculum," 184.
[27] E. Y. Mullins, *Baptist Beliefs* (Valley Forge, PA: Judson Press, 1925), 10.

7

The Study of Philosophy

Taylor Worley

For the past several years, Dave Edmonds and Nigel Warburton have hosted an extensive series of interviews with some of the most prestigious philosophers in the world. These interviews were offered as a free podcast called "Philosophy Bites," and recently published in a book with the same title.[1] Not only do these interviews appear in bite-size sessions; they address the most biting aspects of philosophy today. In one particularly helpful session, they edited together dozens of responses to the simple question: "What is philosophy?" Each time they refrained from telling the person interviewed that they would be asked this question, and on several occasions those interviewed found themselves at a loss for an intelligible response. Most rambled, many gave a quick retort, and some just laughed and moved on.[2]

Readers may be happy to learn that even among elite philosophers opinions differ greatly on the question of what philosophy is. This disparity, however, serves to highlight the passion with which we answer such a question. Beneath these technical debates, I think we will find that philosophy still means what it has always meant for human civilization. As Studs Terkel said in his foreword to *This I Believe*—a collection of personal philosophies from remarkable people—philosophy is the pursuit of truth, and, "The pursuit is all."[3] Such a pursuit can never be too far away from the interests of Christians—people who claim to have encountered not only the Truth but the Way and the Life as well. Therefore, when such pursuits of truth find a place in a Christian liberal arts education, the discipline of philosophy represents immense possibilities for the future of faith and learning. In this way, I wish to demonstrate that philosophy always has and hopefully will continue to be an invaluable aid to the intellectual life of Christianity and the faith of the church. I plan to do this by reviewing the most significant pictures of philosophy we have, grasping the nature of the relationship between faith and philosophy, and identifying those points on the horizon for philosophy that will most benefit Christian faith and learning.

Pictures of Philosophy: Old and New

I would like to identify a few common perspectives on the discipline that exist in popular culture and the modern academy. While some of these characterizations share ancient origins, each reflects contemporary sentiments that still hold sway in the court of public opinion. Not surprisingly, any discussion of the relationship between philosophy and Christian faith and learning must begin by addressing the old and sometimes prevailing view of the discipline in *conflict* with the faith.

Alternately ancient and contemporary, this primarily negative assessment of philosophy understands the discipline to be, at best, irreconcilable to the nature of Christian belief and, at worst, unremittingly antagonistic to the faith. Viewing philosophy with deep suspicion is not at all a recent development. The origins of this view reach back to the earliest generations of Christianity and can perhaps be traced to a certain reading of Paul's admonitions to the church at Colossae:

> Therefore, as you have received Christ Jesus the Lord, walk in Him, rooted and built up in Him and established in the faith, just as you were taught, overflowing with gratitude. Be careful that no one takes you captive through philosophy and empty deceit based on human tradition, based on the elemental forces of the world, and not based on Christ. (Col 2:6–8 HCSB)

Tertullian and the Church Fathers

The reservation and caution communicated in Paul's words to the church at Colossae reach a state of entrenched opposition toward philosophy among some influential theological voices by the time of the late second century. At that time the Christian apologist Tertullian (c. AD 160–c. 220) forcefully questioned the validity of Christian engagement with pagan philosophy. Famously reflecting on Paul's words to the Colossians, he posited in his work *De Praescriptione Haereticorum* ("On the prescription of heretics"): "What indeed has Athens to do with Jerusalem? What concord is there between the Academy and the Church?"[4] Tertullian asserts the fundamentally irreconcilable nature of pagan philosophy as represented by Plato's Academy and the teachings of Christ as represented by the Porch of Solomon in Jerusalem.[5] Christianity and philosophy seemed two separate worlds that should not be brought together. For Tertullian, engagement with pagan philosophy necessarily led to unfortunate contaminations of the pure gospel of Christianity. While Tertullian's famous quip has remained a battle cry for Christians with similar suspicions about philosophy, such straightforward opposition cannot tell the whole story of Christianity's relationship with philosophy.

It should be noted that Tertullian's context was a particularly difficult one. The young Christian movement was beset by multiple heresies and challenges, and Christian apologists like Justin Martyr, Athenagoras, Irenaeus, and later Clement of Alexandria and Origen did a great service to protect the faith from falling prey to new forms of Gnosticism or admixtures of pagan belief. There was no naïveté about the dangers of pagan philosophy, but perspectives diverged on how helpful philosophy could be in articulating the Christian message. Although with much greater reserve than his contemporaries, Tertullian utilized philosophy in his efforts as a Christian apologist.[6] His reliance on philosophy manifests itself in different ways. In particular, his discourse on the soul (*De Anima*) follows a Stoic method of dialogue and strategically incorporates Stoic terms and concepts to persuade his pagan interlocutor Hermogenes. After alluding to the demonic origins of pagan philosophy in his first chapter, Tertullian goes on to claim that some philosophers have indeed glimpsed truth by thinking the same thoughts as Christians, and later in the same work he acknowledges one such corroborating voice in the Roman Stoic Seneca. In general, however, Tertullian uses philosophy in a much broader way than simply identifying sympathetic notes in pagan texts. As an influential apologist of the second and third century, Tertullian will be forever remembered for his envisioned divorce between Athens and Jerusalem but more importantly for his development of several key theological terms, which included *persona* ("person") and *substantia* ("substance"). These terms, along with the other Latin terms he introduced in his theological writings, would prove invaluable for articulating apostolic Christian doctrine in the extremely pivotal debates of the fourth and fifth centuries with trinitarian and Christological heresies. Tertullian's use of these important terms did not happen in an historical vacuum but in negotiation with contemporary paradigms of thought. This necessarily meant engaging with and appropriating an intellectual vocabulary that previously belonged only to the philosophers. While Tertullian never advocated the common-ground approach of some of his fellow apologists, it is clear from his legacy that a dialogue between philosophy and theology is somewhat inevitable.

That Tertullian's sentiments about Athens and Jerusalem have received something of a popular rebirth among Christians in the last century is due in no small part to the unabashed hostility of academic philosophers in the English-speaking world toward religion in general and Christian theism in particular. Surely, we are all familiar by now with the enduring stereotype of an atheistic professor of philosophy who wantonly challenges young Christians in their vulnerable first years of college. Although this stereotype has legitimate origins in the actual experiences of many people, there is reason to believe that the tide is turning. Philosophers who are committed Christians are making serious contributions to the discipline. Alongside the notable achievements that will be discussed below, two important volumes have emerged in recent decades announcing a renaissance in Christian philosophy and surveying many of the influential voices in the movement. Kelly James Clark's *Philosophers Who Believe* and Thomas Morris's *God and the Philosophers* allow a variety of Christian philosophers to tell the story of how Christians have made significant advances at restoring the historically strained relationship of faith and reason.[7] This reconciling movement has allowed Christians once again to see a complementary relationship between the faith and philosophy.

Augustine to Aquinas

Although it may seem quite foreign to our modern sensibilities, Christians in both the East and the West have held a generally positive view of philosophy. In the West, the Christian tradition considered philosophy the "handmaiden of theology" because of the indispensable aid it provided the historic teachers of the church. This perspective on the relationship between faith and philosophy was made possible through the eloquent wisdom of Augustine of Hippo (AD 354–430). Having taught rhetoric in Rome and Milan and spent time alongside a gnostic sect called the Manicheans, Augustine was quite familiar with inappropriate unions of pagan philosophy with the Christian gospel. Rather than adopt a position of simple compromise or rigid conflict, Augustine came to see how the Neoplatonic philosophy he enjoyed so much could actually bolster his faith. Reflecting on philosophy's value in his work *De Doctrina Christiana* ("On Christian doctrine"), Augustine likens the Christian use of philosophy to the treasures of Egypt that the children of God took with them in the Exodus, that is, the treasures of learning Moses received (cf. Acts 7:22) and the silver and gold used to furnish the Tabernacle.[8]

Augustine's view on the "spoils of the Egyptians" established a new and generative paradigm for Christian thought, and the flowering of theology in the Middle Ages would have been impossible without it. In many ways, the scholarly motto of Anselm of Canterbury (1033–1109), *fides quaerens intellectum* ("faith seeking understanding"), which he derived from Augustine, comes as a fulfillment of this new trajectory for faith and learning.[9] While some perspectives along the way have privileged one over the other, Anselm sought a healthy balance of the two, for, as Thomas Williams explains, *fides quaerens intellectum* more fully connotes "an active love of God seeking a deeper knowledge of God."[10] Following Anselm in this tradition, Thomas Aquinas (1225–74) emerged as one of the greatest philosophers of Western civilization, and he too builds upon the Augustinian legacy in profound ways. Like Augustine's use of Neoplatonic thought, Aquinas utilized the recently recovered treasures of Aristotle to help inform and articulate Christian doctrine in his day. Though a theologian and a Dominican in holy orders, much of Aquinas's work reads like classic philosophical discourse. His monumental treatises the *Summa Theologica* and the *Summa Contra Gentiles* build their arguments with architectonic grace. While the method of harmonizing faith and reason differs in Augustine and Aquinas, the desire to put philosophy into the service of divine truth does not waver in either scholar's work. So it is that the greatest achievements *in philosophy* throughout the Middle Ages issue from Augustine's conciliatory respect for the place of philosophy in Christian reflection. As a result of this rich legacy in Augustine, Anselm, and Aquinas, philosophy and theology were bound together until the modern period. While the deep rift between philosophy and theology that characterizes the very nature of modernism has not been fully mended, Christian philosophers and theologians have not been discouraged by this unfortunate divorce. Their efforts are now gaining significant momentum in restoring philosophy as a natural complement to theology, in particular, and helpful for Christian reflection in all disciplines more generally. As Thomas Morris explains, "after a long and fitful process of separation" it seems that God and the philosophers are finally on speaking terms again.[11]

Modern Apathy

Today, the greatest threat to the future of philosophy is simply indifference to the discipline itself. Perhaps you have heard the following joke: "What's the word for philosophy major in Italian? *Barista.*" The joke relates a common opinion of philosophy that circulates in popular culture and, most likely, many evangelical contingents too. For too many, philosophy amounts to little more than intellectual cosmetics. Images of navel-gazing undergrads engaging in useless argumentation and endless studying fill out this tragically popular caricature of philosophy. Unfortunately, the contemporary disregard for philosophy motivated by such a caricature is based not on strong opinions of the discipline as a course of study but rather a growing pragmatism. Such educational pragmatism concentrates its intense focus quite narrowly on clear career tracks in higher education and tends to devalue the traditional liberal arts. This trend can be easily confirmed by the U.S. Department of Education's record of the top 10 college majors of the last few decades. The data shows overwhelming growth in professional programs like business, healthcare, and information technologies.[12] Unsurprisingly, philosophy does not show up on any of these top-10 lists of popular undergraduate majors.

Having identified a few important pictures of philosophy and explored some of the baggage each view represents, let us now turn to an explication of principles. At this point, it makes sense to lay out the best reasons for maintaining an integrationist approach to the study and application of philosophy in Christian higher education. If the terminology of integration seems at all unclear, it will hopefully come into focus just below.

Faith and Philosophy: An Undeniable Bond

In essence, the question of philosophy's relationship to the faith is really a matter of consequence for Christian discipleship. All Christian traditions can agree that the gospel and its call for a response imply what we might call Jesus' "discipleship principle." By that phrase, we mean that in conversion Jesus calls believers to bring the entirety of their life under His lordship and authority. Like Jesus' teaching on the widow and her mite or the rich young ruler, this means leveraging everything in one's life for Christ and His kingdom. While the forms of submission—the avenues of discipleship—have changed considerably since the time of the New Testament and the forms of life in society have evolved even more, the discipleship principle has been an enduring fixture in all Christian traditions. As unlikely as it may seem, philosophy has played a vital role in helping Christians throughout the ages discern the shape of their discipleship. To see the continuing significance of philosophy for faith and learning, let me explain what I mean here.

Paul and Philosophy

If we return to the cautionary words of the apostle Paul from the letter to the Colossians, we can find the root of what we need to make the important distinction between philosophy and the gospel. The immediate context of the situation that Paul is addressing with the term "philosophy" in Col 2:8 does not relate directly to the larger philosophical landscape of Greco-Roman antiquity but rather to the specific claims of false teachers plaguing the young church. The false teachers are likely promoting their rivals' claims about Christ under the guise of wisdom with the unoriginal title *tēs philosophia* ("the philosophy").[13] So that we should read "false teaching" in place of "philosophy" in this verse, Paul's warning here provides additional insight. He not only identifies this false teaching as conceptually contrary to the gospel he planted, but he also seems to indicate that the methods of understanding utilized by this rival teaching run counter to the way in which this church learned the gospel (i.e., how they were "rooted," "built up," and "established in the faith"). In this way, Paul warns them to avoid these heresies by recognizing that the reasoning employed by the false teachers also represents a threat to the establishing of their young faith. Paul makes an important distinction here because in that day things as diverse as political theory, poetry, theoretical accounts of the universe's origin, religious superstitions, and magical incantations all came under the umbrella term "philosophy." This distinction in the nature of philosophy, however, helps us understand another instance of Pauline teaching better. In the Mars Hill discourse of Acts 17, Paul addresses an elite group of Epicurean and Stoic philosophers and strategically quotes two poets from their own intellectual literature, Epimenides of Crete and Aratus.[14] In this instance, Paul is willing to accept the reasoning of these poets while he surely intends to redirect the conclusions of that reasoning toward an understanding of Christ. More than simply drawing an illustration from his context, Paul simultaneously commends the efforts of their philosophical questioning *and* challenges them to consider the claims of his message as the answer to those questions.[15]

Contextualization and Philosophy

From the witness of Paul's ministry, we can safely conclude that in its essence philosophy includes both methods of inquiry *and* principles of intellectual conviction. Therefore, even though philosophy *can* transport counterfeit gospels and instill forms of learning antithetical to Christian discipleship, the discipline should not be excluded from the project of Christian reflection outright. Principally, this position rests on the fact that the Christian gospel is not itself a philosophy. As evident from the New Testament witness, the gospel is much larger and more comprehensive and at the same time more profoundly simple than the formulations of any human reason.[16] As contrasted with the typically abstract and ahistorical claims of philosophers, the gospel remains *trans*historical, articulated in the perfect tense. In other words, the gospel affirms specific historical events—the culmination of salvation history in the life, death, and resurrection of Jesus Christ, and the advent of his Church at the coming of the Holy Spirit—that have effects to this very day. As the effects of these historical events continue to go out, the gospel message infiltrates new times and places perpetually.

Infiltration is actually contextualization, the process by which the "faith once for all delivered to the saints" (Jude 3) is lived out in the faithful witness of true disciples in particular places at particular times. Contextualization describes the task of embodying the *fides quae* ("the faith that") in the *fides qua* ("the faith by which"). In this way, the transhistorical faith—the essential deposit of Christian belief that all Christians have believed at all times in all places—becomes incarnated in the living, breathing forms of discipleship available to the Church in each age of her history. As you can imagine, this description simplifies the very complex negotiations that are involved in such a process of contextualization. How can we be sure that the forms of life available to us in the here and now can actually sustain forms that preserve a fidelity to the biblical principles of discipleship? Philosophy can help us with these questions. Under the right conditions and through sober-minded Christian influence, philosophy can greatly aid both the Church's self-understanding and her witness in the world. Such possibilities, however, are only available to us when philosophy is rightly construed. In other words, what understanding of philosophy seems most conducive to the purposes of faith and learning?

Starting Points

Let us return to that properly philosophical question: what is philosophy? Trying to answer that question might resemble trying to explain the nature of water to a fish, but try we shall. Based on the simple etymology of the term, *philosophy* means "love of wisdom." The connotation of the term today, however, carries much more baggage than that simple definition. Of all the available characterizations of the discipline, few evidence more wisdom than Roger Scruton's. In his book *An Intelligent Person's Guide to Philosophy*, Scruton rejects the monopoly modern science claims to have on truth and argues for a vision of philosophy as a spiritual discipline, which depends to a great extent on the soul of the person doing it. He explains that "philosophical questions arise at the periphery of ordinary thinking, when words fail, and we address the unknown with an invented discourse."[17] To his understanding, philosophy occupies a uniquely valuable place in higher learning because it seeks to engage "deep and serious questions to which science has no answer."[18] In this way, what distinguishes philosophy initially from other disciplines emerges from the distinct subjects of its inquiry. Philosopher and historian of ideas Leszek Kołakowski offers a sweeping survey of Western philosophers that traces the defining questions that shaped each of their careers.[19] Kołakowski considers, for example:

- What is the good life? (Socrates)
- What is the source of truth? (Plato)
- What is evil? (Augustine of Hippo)
- Could God not exist? (Anselm of Canterbury)
- How can we achieve certainty? (René Descartes)
- Do we have free will? (Benedict Spinoza)
- What can we know? (David Hume)
- How is knowledge possible? (Immanuel Kant)
- Is there good and evil? (Friedrich Nietzsche)

Just in this short list of perennial questions in philosophy, we encounter inquiries about truth, knowledge, being, perception, ethics, religion, and fate. In Scruton's account, philosophy is founded on the question "why?" and is sustained by the quest for the greater "why" behind each layer of questioning. Like an annoying relative at a family reunion, philosophy has the bad habit of bringing up all the questions that you should never address in polite conversation. The courage to ask tough questions, however, does not fully commend philosophy for our purposes.

For this reason, we must establish a sense of how philosophy works—in particular, the methods of its inquiry. Throughout the history of the discipline, philosophy has relied on the timeless tools of critical dialectic, logic, and rational discourse. *Dialectic* is the practice by which contested viewpoints and their premises are interrogated by thoughtful conversation partners and debated back and forth until the interlocutors reach either consensus or impasse.[20] Plato's records of the dialogues of Socrates are classic examples of this practice.[21] Secondly, *logic* provides the ground rules for such debate, and it reasons on the basis of certain first principles. Aristotle's discussions of logic remain some of the earliest and most influential explorations into formal logic. His influence stems from his elucidation of a helpful set of first principles that include the law of identity (P = P), the law of noncontradiction

(P ≠ non-P), and the law of excluded middle (either P or non-P). In addition to providing these basic principles of argumentation, logic also helps to dispel fallacious or invalid claims through rigorous consideration of their reasoning. Thirdly, philosophers have sought to maintain clarity and eloquence in argumentation and keep their language as rational as possible. In other words, anything that can be said should be said simply and clearly. *Rational discourse* preserves the opportunity for a philosopher's audience to grapple with the concepts articulated in debate and not to get distracted by the argument's rhetoric. While some philosophical traditions have esteemed rational language in philosophy above everything and made it the sole objective of philosophy (e.g., the ordinary language philosophers of Oxford University), the rational orientation of philosophy's discourse over the millennia has surely served to protect its unique goals. Dialectic, logic, and rationality represent only the basic tools that philosophers employ for their reflective task. We will look more closely at a particular class of services that philosophy might render to the faith.

William Abraham, a contemporary analytic philosopher who happens also to be a Christian, has described philosophy's merits in terms of aiding Christians in fulfilling their intellectual responsibilities to society. Abraham acknowledges that the contemporary return of philosophers of faith is not an altogether novel occurrence. Instead, he affirms that "down through history, mature believers have made use of all sorts of concepts and arguments drawn from philosophy in order to give a reason for the hope that is within them."[22] While recognizing philosophy's immense value, Abraham is also quick to point out that philosophy is no substitute for the gospel or the work of the Holy Spirit in the lives of believers. Philosophy cannot guarantee the flourishing of the faith, but it can surely be an aid to the faith. Abraham describes in detail the ways in which philosophy can serve the faith.

> Philosophy has a more modest role in the life of faith. It can clear away obstacles, clarify crucial concepts and options, lay bare the process of relevant justification, make manifest hidden assumptions, bring to light unforeseen consequences of belief, open up to view contradictions and paradoxes, and the like. These are intrinsically important to creatures endowed with reason, and they have their own place in the fostering of the intellectual love of our great God and Savior.[23]

Abraham's endorsement begs the question: how might Christians discern their faith in these ways without the aid of philosophy? Indeed, the history of Christianity demonstrates that when Christians have seized upon these opportunities great acts of service have been rendered to both church and society. The legacy of *fides quaerens intellectum* in the Christian intellectual tradition is a heritage of learning that all modern disciplines have received and utilized. In this way, the formation of the university in the late medieval period as cathedral schools gave way to burgeoning faculties of various subjects should be seen as a gospel-advancing effort to unify all ways of learning in service to God and humankind.

While it seems entirely acceptable to follow Abraham's lead and claim these same benefits, let me offer a few distinct examples of how philosophy played and continues to play this complementary role in the history of the church. I will draw out a case from late antiquity and highlight an example from late modernity.

The ancient example comes from the second-century work *The Epistle to Diognetus*, in which we find one of the earliest examples of Christian apologetic.[24] The unnamed author provides a defense of Christianity that in essence explains *how* the believers can be "in the world but not of the world":[25]

> For Christians are not distinguished from the rest of humanity by country, language, or custom. For nowhere do they live in cities of their own, nor do they speak some unusual dialect, nor do they practice an eccentric way of life. . . . But while they live in both Greek and barbarian cities, as each one's lot was cast, and follow the local customs in dress and food and other aspects of life, at the same time they demonstrate the remarkable and admittedly unusual character of their own citizenship. They live in their own countries, but only as nonresidents; they participate in everything as citizens, and endure everything as foreigners. . . . In a word, what the soul is to the body, Christians are to the world.[26]

Here, we learn that what distinguished the witness of early Christianity was not the *means* of her discipleship (i.e., identity markers like nationality, speech, or cultural customs) but rather the *mode* of discipleship (i.e., "the remarkable and admittedly unusual character of their own citizenship"). The church was surely in the world but not living their lives according to the ways of the world. Obviously, the author does not wish to say that the church participated in all aspects of the society in which they found themselves; all sorts of civic participation are ruled out by the New Testament for the unfortunate connections to idol worship or immorality. *The Epistle to Diognetus* demonstrates that Christians have the ability to restore the world like the soul exists to redeem the body.[27]

By the phrase the "unusual character of their own citizenship," the apologist indicates that the church has this redemptive presence in society not by accident but rather through intentional action shaped and informed by their own conviction and critical reason.[28] In this case, critical reason affords them the discernment to judge between what can be redeemed and what must be avoided in a religiously antagonistic environment. Clearly, cultivating this critical reason and implementing it remains a much more difficult task than simply withdrawing from society and culture altogether or accommodating the beliefs and practices of the faith to more acceptable forms of life in that hostile environment. The apostolic witness of the faith, however, will not allow such defeatist options and rather calls all Christians to "discern what is pleasing to the Lord" and "test the spirits."[29] I want to affirm that such a calling requires, at the very least, an exposure to philosophy as a means of understanding the conceptual vocabulary and thought structures that undergird a society and culture. Let me offer a timelier example to further my challenge.

The last few decades have witnessed the encounter of Christianity with the postmodern turn in philosophy. By *postmodern turn*, historians of philosophy point to the way in which philosophy has turned away from some of its traditional preoccupations to a more intense examination of language and the limits of speech. Adding to these complicated developments, this turn in postmodernity has also seen a *re*-turn to the philosophy of religion. Such developments have not surprisingly been met with a great deal of intellectual hostility by Christian and non-Christian philosophers alike.

Unfortunately, opinions of postmodernism and its theories tend toward the extremes of either complete renunciation or wholesale accommodation, but neither extreme represents a faithful way forward. These ongoing debates and disputes serve to shield evangelicals from a problem much larger and more important than simply the resolution of these differences of opinion. As

Myron Penner points out in the introduction to the edited volume *Christianity and the Postmodern Turn*, there is, in fact, something larger at stake.

> How does my language, my culture, and my social environment affect the (Christian) categories I use to understand God, the world, and others? A theology that does not significantly address this question hardly seems fit for the twenty-first century—at the very least it will not deal well with the postmodern turn and those who make it.[30]

We will explore below how Christian philosophers are seizing the opportunities of this period in the history of philosophy not only to respond to these challenges but also to advance the intellectual fortunes of Christian faith and learning. Here, however, Penner uncovers a somewhat uncomfortable implication of the contextualization project, namely, that in order to contextualize the faith successfully believers must listen to the various readings that the world offers of the Church. At the very least, these readings, and the challenge of postmodernism in particular, force us to evaluate the reasons we have for believing the faith and practicing it the way that we do. Serious self-evaluation will always involve some painful tests, but it is ultimately necessary to preserve a faithful witness to Christ in every time and every place.

In the final section, I will introduce some exciting developments in the discipline of philosophy for the future of faith and learning, but before relating those trajectories, let us review what has been offered here in understanding the relationship of Christianity and philosophy. The challenges of living the Christian life faithfully in one's particular context demand that our discipleship be informed by critical reason and thoughtful discernment. Philosophy with its age-old tools of reasoning and critical imagination provides us a discipline that has pursued the great questions of human civilization and served the Christian intellectual tradition of *fides quaerens intellectum.* On this understanding, the Christian faith stands to benefit greatly from philosophy when we firmly establish the primacy of the gospel and maintain the view of philosophy as a handmaiden to Christian belief and practice. By God's good providence, the tradition of "faith seeking understanding" is alive and well today in many institutions of Christian higher education and philosophy has a sure future in that fertile environment.

Fresh Opportunities for Faith and Learning in Philosophy

If it is not already clear, let me say that this is an exciting and rewarding time to study philosophy. But that was not always the case for Christians. While anti-religious and anti-Christian bias cannot be fully expunged from the academy, Christian philosophers such as Alvin Plantinga, Basil Mitchell, and Richard Swinburne in the analytic tradition and Merold Westphal and John Caputo in the continental tradition have made great strides in restoring viable options for a faith and learning approach to philosophy.[31] However, these brave Christian philosophers have not stormed the secular stronghold just to impose a moratorium on bold and provocative projects in philosophical questioning. Rather, they wish to make genuine contributions to both the academy and the church. The bold and generative projects of those philosophers have made possible a host of fascinating options for intellectual exploration, but I would like to survey only two important streams here. First, Christian philosophers today have utilized the discipline for the enrichment of Christian wisdom. Secondly, the contours of the discipline today allow for a use of philosophy in almost every subject or discipline, and the transfer of philosophy's methods of inquiry to diverse fields means that nearly any study can be improved to benefit a faith and learning approach. Let us take these developments in turn.

Analytic Philosophy and Christian Thought

Following the path of these modern Christian philosophers, successive generations are opening up new fields of exploration and collaboration between philosophy and theology. Remarkably, these explorations are taking place in both the analytic and continental traditions. As Oliver Crisp has indicated, within the philosophy of religion we are observing what is best described as a "metaphysical turn."[32] For analytic philosophy of religion, this has meant a flood of new interest in philosophical theology—the accommodation of rigorous philosophical inquiry in the uniquely theological domain.[33] For continental philosophy of religion, we have seen a "turn to religion" such that both Christians and non-Christians have been provoked into new ways of considering religion.[34]

As numerous commentators have noted, there has been a returning interest in metaphysics within analytic philosophy since the 1960s and '70s, and this renaissance of philosophical theology has come about through such influential figures as Alasdair MacIntyre and Antony Flew. Their edited volume *New Essays in Philosophical Theology* introduced into the analytic discourse once more a constructive approach to the philosophy of religion, and their groundbreaking work created the conditions for successive generations to extend such projects in even more creative ways.[35] Charles Taliaferro describes the transformation of the discipline in this way:

> With comprehensive, religious skepticism in recession since the 1960s, the floodgates in philosophy of religion have opened. Projects in the field are up and running on such topics as God's nature, comparative reports of religious experience, religious ethics, diverse theories about the origin of evil, and religious teachings about divine incarnations. We are now in an era that is more friendly to philosophical experimentation and conjecture on such matters. Earlier a principal goal of a respectable project in philosophy of religion would be to assess whether religious beliefs made any sense at all. Now a proper philosophical project may be focused on a far more specific question such as: Is divine foreknowledge compatible with free will?[36]

Alternately working under the labels *philosophical theology* and *Christian philosophy of religion*, philosophical theologians have sought to apply the rigorous methods of the analytic tradition to Christian doctrine in order to clarify and lay bare difficult theological concepts.[37] Harriet Harris and Christopher Insole explain the rationale of the analytic tradition: "The focus on language and meaning comes from a conviction that the best way of understanding ourselves and the world is to look at what we think, and the best way of getting at what we think is to analyse what we say."[38] Fresh and exciting scholarship in philosophical theology continues to surface at an astounding rate.[39] Consideration of the core doctrines of Christianity has been the focus of multiple publications now such as the Oxford Readings in Philosophical Theology series, and the conversation is still expanding.[40]

In recent years, this trajectory has led to the formation of a new hybrid discipline called analytic theology. In a collection of essays published under that new heading, Oliver Crisp and Michael Rea explore the ways in which analytic philosophy could be more fully integrated into the project of systematic theology. Without calling for collapsing distinctions between the two, these philosophers and their colleagues see a bright future for theology strategically enhanced by the rigor and clarity of expression of analytic philosophy. Examples of these efforts can now be found in conversation with almost every vital Christian doctrine, with a consistent and thorough methodology. For instance, rather than asking how we might verify the biblical witness concerning the virgin birth by means of philosophy, an analytic theology approach simply asks how we might make plain the conceptual elements of that claim and its subsequent theological implications.[41] In one sense, the work of these philosophers bears striking resemblance to the way in which the ancient doctors of the church utilized philosophy as a tool for working out a defense of the faith. These philosophers believe that since the tradition of analytic philosophy has over time developed conceptual tools toward an increasingly rigorous analysis of language, these tools should now be put to use in studying theological language as well. Rather than imposing a foreign logic upon the discipline of theology, these efforts aim to demonstrate the internal logic within the historic claims of Christian doctrine. In this way, philosophy can be utilized toward greater self-understanding within Christianity.

Continental Philosophy and Christian Thought

While the "metaphysical turn" in philosophy of religion has meant a more rigorous analysis of theological language for Christian analytic philosophers, the continental tradition has inspired very different trajectories. If the analytic tradition sought greater clarity through philosophical discourse, the continental tradition probed the enduring mysteries of philosophy and addressed itself to the profundity that remains after philosophical questioning expires. Much like the analytic tradition, these trajectories of exploration have developed in the wake of Immanuel Kant's (1724–1804) challenge to metaphysics, *Critique of Pure Reason*.[42] The Kantian critique established firm limits to human reason and effectively severed any hope for a transcendent knowledge of the world through human rationality. To state it bluntly, reason—it's all in your head. While the analytic tradition (after the failure of logical positivism) invested itself in clarifying the claims of philosophy and understanding as much as possible what the imminent philosopher of language Ludwig Wittgenstein (1889–1951) called "language games," the continental tradition has pursued the mysteries of human experience through encounter with the self and the "other."[43] In other words, while the analytic tradition pretends that Kant's critique never happened, the continental tradition is searching for a light switch in the darkened room of human existence.[44] These continental explorations have followed the paths of phenomenology, hermeneutics, psychology, and ethics and religion, but as philosophers revisit these questions through the lens of their own biography, fresh and provocative expressions emerge. Such expressions become rich resources from which Christian philosophers continue to pursue their own explorations.

In the edited volume *Postmodern Philosophy and Christian Thought,* Merold Westphal explores the conjunction in the book's title and determines that the word *and* there can imply a healthy sense of appropriation on the part of Christian thinkers. He explains, however, that "any Christian appropriation of postmodern philosophy will be both a yes and a no."[45] By this qualification, he means that Christians can incorporate the best insights and suggestions from postmodern thinkers without necessarily adopting their atheological or anti-Christian biases.[46] Perhaps more importantly, Westphal sees how postmodernism's consistent critique of religious traditions and institutions can make possible a helpful criticality for Christians that would not otherwise be available to them.[47]

Indeed, many of the most influential philosophers of the continental tradition have developed their thought as a form of resistance to authoritarian traditions in theology or philosophy and have passed on a tradition of questioning that has manifested itself in the postmodern moment as a "hermeneutics of finitude" and a "hermeneutics of suspicion."[48] Søren Kierkegaard (1813–55) paved the way for the phenomenology and existentialism of the twentieth century by means of his attack on the cold idealism of G. W. F. Hegel (1770–1831) as expressed in the Danish Lutheran Church. His defense of the individual's subjective experience restored the priority of faith as an important category in the philosophy of religion. Building on that legacy, Martin Heidegger (1889–1976) would later develop his contributions to phenomenology and existentialism as a philosophy of "being-in-the-world" that would replace the domineering and abstract rationality of what Kant had called the ontotheological.[49] Heidegger's emphasis on "being-there" finds its fulfillment in the religious phenomenology of Emmanuel Levinas (1906–95) and Jacques Derrida (1930–2004), who summon an ancient ethic of Jewish hospitality "to rethink the religious in terms of our obligation to the other" and envision encounters with God in the face of the stranger.[50] The effects of this interest in the "other" can be seen in a host of disciplines and figures, and as John Caputo explains, it means that, "talk about God and religion in contemporary continental philosophy bears almost no resemblance to what passes for traditional 'philosophy of religion.'"[51] Thus, in order to receive such highly nuanced insights, Christians must be willing to engage in sustained, critical dialogue with postmodern philosophy.

Recently, several important dialogue projects have cultivated the field of Christian wisdom and prompted exploratory forays into philosophy.[52] In many ways, John Caputo has pioneered fruitful modes of exploration in contemporary continental philosophy with his long-standing engagement with Derrida and the school of thought labeled *deconstruction*.[53] In Augustine, they have found a mutual point of interest, but their conversation has grown to include many other philosophical concerns.[54] Along with Caputo and Westphal, successive generations of Christian philosophers and theologians have pursued sustained interaction with representatives of postmodern thought.

Several years ago, a group of theologians in the United Kingdom formed a new school of contemporary theology called Radical Orthodoxy, which endeavors to bypass the influence of post-Enlightenment thought and return to a properly Augustinian and Thomist view of the world.[55] Led by John Milbank, Catherine Pickstock, and Graham Ward, this young movement denies the universal reign of secular reason and has inevitable parallels with prominent thinkers in postmodern theory. Principally, postmodern philosophy becomes a lever for overcoming modernism in this school of thought, and such resonances have cultivated interesting and novel partnerships with Marxist thinkers like Terry Eagleton, Alain Badiou, and Slavoj Žižek. Most significantly, in recent years Milbank and Žižek have begun a debate over who can narrate the significance of the early Christian political moment (Acts 2 and 4).[56] This remarkable conversation between an Anglo-Catholic theologian and a Marxist-Lacanian (and atheist) philosopher has not only demonstrated new possibilities for dialogue but has also sparked a renewed interest in studies of Paul and early Christianity.[57]

Lastly, with his provocative book *Who's Afraid of Postmodernism?* James K. A. Smith has begun a conversation in North America focused on the ways in which Christians and the church might engage with postmodernity and postmodern thought.[58] Intended for broad audience, the "Church and Postmodern Culture" conversation allows Christians of various backgrounds in philosophy at least to consider the most important developments in postmodern critical theory and at best to identify a means of response to these developments. These broad and diverse projects signal multiple ways in which Christian thinkers are finding fascinating ways of enriching Christian wisdom through strategic uses of philosophy, as well as expanding, the horizons of philosophy into nearly every discipline of learning.

A Philosophy of Everything

As a second major opportunity for a faith and learning approach to philosophy, we will consider philosophy's expansion throughout the modern academy. Philosophical engagement with a host of different disciplines has flourished, and it is not uncommon to find academic publications, professional societies, and conferences dedicated to the philosophy of this or the philosophy of that. According to Oxford University philosopher Stephen Mulhall, this development represents a hopeful future for not only the discipline of philosophy but the health of higher education in general.

In a provocative lecture entitled "Why Is There Something Called Philosophy Rather than Nothing?" Mulhall questions the validity of his own discipline in an effort to understand its "inherently parasitic" relationship to the life of the university.[59] Echoing one of philosophy's age-old questions with the title of his lecture, Mulhall proceeds to explain how the discipline of philosophy can be of service throughout the broad landscape of subjects in the university. First, he identifies the natural sympathies that exist between philosophy and any given subject. Each subject within the panoply of human learning can be related to an aspect of philosophy's general questioning of the world and the self. Secondly,

Mulhall stresses the vital link between the future of philosophy and the future of these various subjects and studies.[60]

Mulhall clarifies the unique role that philosophy alone can play in the life of the university. Because philosophy addresses itself to the most general questions of being (e.g., "Why is there something rather than nothing?") and has over time refined its own critical tools, it alone can enable various disciplines to enter into self-evaluation without diverging from their proposed aims. Thus, critical disciplines like philosophy of science emerge to interrogate the purposes, aims, and methods of science without halting the ongoing work of that science. In some cases, philosophy works together with discrete subjects to develop hybrid disciplines that operate in a mediatory space between that subject and philosophy. Interdisciplinary projects such as these indicate that boundless possibilities for philosophy exist today.

Indeed, even as the perennial questions of philosophy are adapted to the purposes of various academic disciplines, philosophy is making a significant impact in society and culture. While philosophy has a valuable place in understanding popular culture, it is the more strategic encounters with contemporary life that will occupy our interests.[61] In the realm of science and technology, studies in bioethics, posthumanism, agrarianism, and design systems such as permaculture or eco-sustainability constitute much more than interesting experiments for our day. These topics designate unique interstices where particular schools of thought are developing critical theories for the implementation of their diverse aims, and the future of topics like these will determine significant aspects of what human civilization looks like in the decades ahead. In this way, philosophy is having a profound impact on the very shape of our lives. In the areas of art and culture, disciplines like media ecology, visual studies, and philosophy of film are analyzing the ways in which the Internet, film, television, fashion, visual arts, and all other forms of media are remaking the life of the mind. A growing literature in philosophy already exists to describe the various ways in which thinking is now being mediated (i.e., transmuted through various media platforms). Many art or media forms construct conceptual scenarios that resemble the philosopher's tool called the "thought experiment." While these options have and will continue to exist in art and culture, we desperately need philosophy to address the ways in which younger generations of digital natives are becoming more and more dependent on thinking *through* media.[62] This kind of study will prove extremely beneficial in the years ahead. In this way, philosophies *of* and *for* everything can ensure that Christians maintain a critical conscience when it comes to the future of higher education in particular and the possibilities for human flourishing in general.

Conclusion

If science and culture are changing the way in which we as humans think, then philosophy will have to adapt to meet these challenges. Perhaps in this cultural moment with conditions of life rapidly changing and the absence of thoughtful reflection, Christians will recognize the stake they have in philosophy's survival. Philosophy calls us to contemplate the world and ourselves in ways that stretch and test us. I would argue that without some of the questioning space that philosophy creates there would be no room for the gospel of Jesus Christ to occupy our lives. Without the critical questioning that philosophy inspires, there would be no place for truth.[63] As Jacques Barzun chides in his book *Begin Here,* "The folly consisted, not in wanting the lofty results, but in thinking that they could be reached directly. I have elsewhere defined this fallacy as 'preposterism'—seeking to obtain straight off what can only be the fruit of some effort, putting the end before the beginning."[64] Philosophy surely represents that hard work, but no toil is too much for making clear the hope of the Christian gospel.

Questions for Further Reflection

1. As we have seen, the core of philosophy as a discipline has been the critical questioning of the world and ourselves. While many of those timeless questions have never left us, we do seem to ask them in new and fresh ways in each generation. What are the big questions of our day? What are the questions that are surfacing throughout society and culture today? How might they intersect with philosophy as seen from a faith and learning perspective?
2. Philosophy has often been associated with a litany of –isms. For instance, we have realism and foundationalism, creationism and Darwinism, capitalism and socialism; on

and on it goes. Many –isms represent schools of thought, specific perspectives on ourselves and the world, or in some cases entrenched forms of ideology. How might philosophy be helpful to extract the basic questions that inhabit or motivate each –ism? For example, what are the common questions that each of these pairs of –isms seeks to answer?

3. While many of the questions posed by philosophers never tire out, we have seen throughout the history of philosophy a process of refinement taking place that seeks to explore all the little questions within each big question. This process can pursue various trajectories, and it often generates additional concepts and methods of argumentation for philosophy. The Christian intellectual tradition attests to many instances of Christian thinkers appropriating or borrowing these developments for the purposes of articulating the timeless Christian faith. What are the lessons we can glean from them so as to articulate the faith without intellectual compromise?
4. Hopefully it is clear at this point that discipleship and evangelism are never done in a vacuum. Each generation of the Church must find strategic ways to communicate the timeless gospel of the Christian faith so that those outside the Church may truly hear it. What are the greatest intellectual challenges to communicating the gospel today? How might Christian philosophers seek to address these and also clear some space for the announcement of our good news?
5. Related to the challenges of gospel proclamation are the issues associated with religious dialogue. How might we utilize certain modern or postmodern critiques of the Church or the Christian faith as resources for understanding ourselves better? Can the philosophical arguments against Christianity so prevalent in modern society actually serve to strengthen our own understanding of the faith? If so, how?

Resources for Further Study

Beaty, Michael D., ed. *Christian Theism and the Problems of Philosophy*. Library of Religious Philosophy 5. Notre Dame, IN: University of Notre Dame Press, 1990.

Brown, Colin. *Philosophy and the Christian Faith: A Historical Sketch from the Middle Ages to the Present Day*. Chicago: InterVarsity Press, 1969.

Brown, Colin, Steve Wilkens, and Alan G. Padgett. *Christianity & Western Thought: A History of Philosophers, Ideas and Movements*. 3 vols. Downers Grove, IL: InterVarsity Press, 1990, 2000, 2009.

Caputo, John D., ed. *The Religious*. Blackwell Readings in Continental Philosophy. Malden, MA: Blackwell, 2002.

Clark, Kelly James, ed. *Philosophers Who Believe: The Spiritual Journeys of 11 Leading Thinkers*. Downers Grove, IL: InterVarsity Press, 1993.

Crisp, Oliver D., ed. *A Reader in Contemporary Philosophical Theology*. New York: T & T Clark, 2009.

Crisp, Oliver D., and Michael C. Rea, eds. *Analytic Theology: New Essays in the Philosophy of Theology*. Oxford; New York: Oxford University Press, 2009.

Dockery, David S., ed. *The Challenge of Postmodernism: An Evangelical Engagement*. 2nd ed. Grand Rapids: Baker Academic, 2001.

Flint, Thomas P., and Michael C. Rea, eds. *The Oxford Handbook of Philosophical Theology*. Oxford Handbooks. New York: Oxford University Press, 2008.

Harris, Harriet A., and Christopher J. Insole, eds. *Faith and Philosophical Analysis: The Impact of Analytical Philosophy on the Philosophy of Religion*. Heythrop Studies in Contemporary Philosophy, Religion and Theology. Burlington, VT: Ashgate, 2005.

Helm, Paul. *Faith with Reason*. Oxford: Oxford University Press, 2000.

———. *Faith and Reason*. Oxford Readers. New York: Oxford University Press, 1999.

McCall, Thomas H., and Michael C. Rea, eds. *Philosophical and Theological Essays on the Trinity*. New York: Oxford University Press, 2009.

Morris, Thomas V. *God and the Philosophers: The Reconciliation of Faith and Reason*. New York: Oxford University Press, 1994.

———. *Making Sense of It All: Pascal and the Meaning of Life*. Grand Rapids: Eerdmans, 1992.

Murray, Michael J., and Michael C. Rea. *An Introduction to the Philosophy of Religion*. Cambridge Introductions to Philosophy. New York: Cambridge University Press, 2008.

Penner, Myron B., ed. *Christianity and the Postmodern Turn: Six Views*. Grand Rapids: Brazos, 2005.

Plantinga, Alvin. *The Analytic Theist: An Alvin Plantinga Reader*. Edited by James F. Sennett. Grand Rapids: Eerdmans, 1998.

Plantinga, Alvin, and Nicholas Wolterstorff, eds. *Faith and Rationality: Reason and Belief in God*. Notre Dame, IN: University of Notre Dame Press, 1983.

Rea, Michael C., ed. *Oxford Readings in Philosophical Theology*. Volume 1: *Trinity, Incarnation, and Atonement*. New York: Oxford University Press, 2009.

———. *Oxford Readings in Philosophical Theology*. Volume 2: *Providence, Scripture, and Resurrection*. New York: Oxford University Press, 2009.

Scruton, Roger. *An Intelligent Person's Guide to Modern Culture*. South Bend, IN: St. Augustine's Press, 1998.

———. *An Intelligent Person's Guide to Philosophy*. New York: Penguin, 1999.

———. *From Descartes to Wittgenstein: A Short History of Modern Philosophy*. New York: Harper & Row, 1982.

Taliaferro, Charles. *Dialogues about God*. New Dialogues in Philosophy. Lanham, MD: Rowman & Littlefield, 2008.

Taliaferro, Charles, Paul Draper, and Philip L. Quinn, ed. *A Companion to Philosophy of Religion*. Blackwell Companions to Philosophy. 2nd ed. Vol. 9. Malden, MA: Wiley-Blackwell, 2010.

Taliaferro, Charles, and Chad V. Meister, ed. *The Cambridge Companion to Christian Philosophical Theology*. Cambridge Companions to Religion. New York: Cambridge University Press, 2010.

Westphal, Merold. *Postmodern Philosophy and Christian Thought*. Indiana Series in the Philosophy of Religion. Bloomington: Indiana University Press, 1999.

———. *Suspicion and Faith: The Religious Uses of Modern Atheism*. New York: Fordham University Press, 1993.

Willard, Dallas, Daniel Cho, and Sarah Park. *A Place for Truth: Leading Thinkers Explore Life's Hardest Questions*. Downers Grove, IL: InterVarsity Press, 2010.

Endnotes

1 Cf. Dave Edmonds and Nigel Warburton, eds., *Philosophy Bites* (New York: Oxford University Press, 2010).

2 Ibid., xiii-xxiii.

3 Jay Allison and Dan Gediman, eds., *This I Believe: The Personal Philosophies of Remarkable Men and Women* (New York: Holt Paperbacks, 2007), xxi.

4 *De Praescriptione Haereticorum* VII.

5 In his work *De Anima* ("On the soul"), he also claimed that pagan philosophies were descended from demons. Cf. *De Anima* I.

6 Colin Brown, *Christianity and Western Thought*, vol. 1 (Downers Grove, IL: InterVarsity, 1990), 91–92.

7 Kelly James Clark, ed., *Philosophers Who Believe* (Downers Grove: InterVarsity, 1993), and Thomas Morris, ed., *God and the Philosophers: The Reconciliation of Faith and Reason* (New York: Oxford University Press, 1994).

8 Augustine, *De Doctrina Christiana* (Book 2.40.60): "Moreover, if those who are called philosophers, and especially the Platonists, have said aught that is true and in harmony with our faith, we are not only not to shrink from it, but

to claim it for our own use from those who have unlawful possession of it. For, as the Egyptians had not only the idols and heavy burdens which the people of Israel hated and fled from, but also vessels and ornaments of gold and silver, and garments, which the same people when going out of Egypt appropriated to themselves, designing them for a better use, not doing this on their own authority, but by the command of God, the Egyptians themselves, in their ignorance, providing them with things which they themselves, were not making a good use of; in the same way all branches of heathen learning have not only false and superstitious fancies and heavy burdens of unnecessary toil, which every one of us, when going out under the leadership of Christ from the fellowship of the heathen, ought to abhor and avoid; but they contain also liberal instruction which is better adapted to the use of the truth, and some most excellent precepts of morality; and some truths in regard even to the worship of the One God are found among them. Now these are, so to speak, their gold and silver, which they did not create themselves, but dug out of the mines of God's providence which are everywhere scattered abroad, and are perversely and unlawfully prostituting to the worship of devils. These, therefore, the Christian, when he separates himself in spirit from the miserable fellowship of these men, ought to take away from them, and to devote to their proper use in preaching the gospel. Their garments, also,—that is, human institutions such as are adapted to that intercourse with men which is indispensable in this life,—we must take and turn to a Christian use."

9 Anselm's motto remains an enduring principle of Christian scholarship. The motto has been adopted to represent the pursuits of such entities as the Evangelical Theological Society and the Christian Theological Research Fellowship.

10 Thomas Williams, "St. Anselm of Canterbury," in *Stanford Encyclopedia of Philosophy* online at www.plato.stanford.edu.

11 Thomas Morris, *God and the Philosophers* (New York: Oxford University Press, 1996), 4.

12 Cf. www.ed.gov. One notable trend in higher education of recent memory is the sudden rise in majors for criminal forensic science programs following the success of Jerry Bruckheimer's television franchise *Crime Scene Investigation.*

13 Cf. a similar warning about false teaching called "knowledge" issued to Timothy in 1 Tim 6:20.

14 The quotes are found in verse 28: from Epimenides of Crete, "In him we live and move and have our being"; and from Aratus, "For we are indeed his offspring."

15 To be sure, this passage remains a hotly contested proof text for various apologetic schools of thought. My goal here is simply to provide a portrait of philosophy based on the apostolic tradition of Scripture and hopefully circumvent the contemporary debates on apologetics as much as possible.

16 By the term *simple* here, I do not mean without complexity or nuance, but rather, in the classic and medieval sense of the term, I mean remarkably consistent and cohesive. In this way, the gospel is akin to the self-justifying and self-affirming character of its author. Because of its divine origins, the gospel can be considered supra-rational just as the Lord of Scripture has no source of validation outside of God's own self. For this reason, God has been described from the time of the ancient church as possessing the quality of divine aseity—the property by

which a being exists *of* and *from* itself only. As the word of Christ, the authority of the gospel functions in much the same way.

[17] Roger Scruton, *An Intelligent Person's Guide to Philosophy* (New York: Penguin, 1999), 8.

[18] Ibid., 7.

[19] Leszek Kołakowski, *Why Is There Something Rather Than Nothing? 23 Questions from Great Philosophers* (New York: Basic Books, 2007).

[20] Scruton explains that it is not enough for philosophy to simply question life, the world and the self; this must be done with a certain criticality. He writes that, "In seeking ultimate explanations, and durable meanings, philosophy is engaged in constructive tasks. It is explaining the world, and telling us how to live in it. But philosophy also has a negative task, which is to analyze and criticize human thinking, to ask awkward questions like 'How do you know?' and 'What do you mean?'" *An Intelligent Person's Guide to Philosophy,* 27.

[21] These include the following works by Plato: *Ion*, *Lysis*, *Euthydemus*, *Meno*, *Menexenus*, *Theaetetus*, *Euthyphro*, the frame of *Symposium*, *Apology*, *Crito*, *Phaedo* and the frame of *Parmenides*.

[22] William J. Abraham, "Faraway Fields Are Green," in Morris, *God and the Philosophers*, 171.

[23] Ibid., 172.

[24] *The Epistle to Diognetus*, in Michael W. Holmes, *The Apostolic Fathers: Greek Texts and English Translations,* 3rd ed. (Grand Rapids: Baker, 2007).

[25] Cf. John 17:14–19.

[26] Section 5–6 in Holmes, *Apostolic Fathers*. Hopefully, the way in which this passage echoes the New Testament witness is clear. I think it parallels much of the encouragement found in the epistle of 1 Peter.

[27] I think we should not take the author's illustration too far here because I do not think it is meant to represent a full picture of a Christian understanding of how the soul and the body together constitute the whole of a human person. Most likely, the author is simply drawing on the familiar associations in Greco-Roman antiquity and the Christian tradition with the soul as the spiritual part of us. A fully formed and Christian understanding of the person is much more complex than that.

[28] What I am here calling "redemptive presence" should be seen as close but not identical to what James Davison Hunter argues for with his term "faithful presence" in his recent book *To Change the World* (New York: Oxford University Press, 2010).

[29] Cf. Eph 5:1–20 and 1 John 4:1–6.

[30] Myron B. Penner, ed., *Christianity and the Postmodern Turn: Six Views* (Grand Rapids: Brazos, 2005), 29.

[31] Cf. Thomas Morris, *God and the Philosophers*, and Kelly James Clark, *Philosophers Who Believe*. Besides the publication of these two helpful volumes, the returning influence of Christians in philosophy can be measured by the formation of a distinctly Christian professional guild for philosophy, the Society of Christian Philosophers, and the organization's journal *Faith and Philosophy.* Cf. www.societyofchristianphilosophers.com.

[32] Oliver D. Crisp, ed., *A Reader in Contemporary Philosophical Theology* (New York: T&T, 2009).

[33] Wolterstorff asserts, "Never since the late Middle Ages has philosophical theology so flourished as it has during the past thirty years." Nicholas Wolterstorff, "How Philosophical Theology Became Possible within the Analytic Tradition," in *Analytic Theology: New Essays in the Philosophy of Theology* ed. Oliver D. Crisp and Michael C. Rea (New York: Oxford University Press, 2009), 155.
[34] Cf. Hent de Vries, *Philosophy and the Turn to Religion* (Baltimore: Johns Hopkins University Press, 1999).
[35] Alasdair MacIntyre and Antony Flew, eds., *New Essays in Philosophical Theology* (New York: Macmillan, 1964).
[36] Charles Taliaferro, *Contemporary Philosophy of Religion* (Malden, MA: Blackwell, 1998), 4.
[37] For example, Alvin Plantinga defines philosophical theology as "a matter of thinking about central doctrines of the Christian faith from a philosophical perspective; it is a matter of employing the resources of philosophy to deepen and expand our grasp of them." Alvin Plantinga, "Christian Philosophy at the End of the Twentieth Century," in *The Analytic Theist: An Alvin Plantinga Reader*, ed. James Sennett (Grand Rapids: Eerdmans, 1998), 340.
[38] Harriet Harris and Christopher Insole, eds. *Faith and Philosophical Analysis* (Burlington, VT: Ashgate, 2005).
[39] One of the most fascinating and important projects at the nexus of philosophy and theology in recent years has to be the work of William Abraham and his Canonical Theism project. This important trajectory seeks to recover a broader place in Christian theology for an ancient and multivalent understanding of canon. Cf. William J. Abraham, *Canon and Criterion in Christian Theology: From the Fathers to Feminism* (New York: Oxford University Press, 1998); William J. Abraham, *Crossing the Threshold of Divine Revelation* (Grand Rapids: Eerdmans, 2006); William J. Abraham, Jason E. Vickers, and Natalie B. Van Kirk, eds., *Canonical Theism: A Proposal for Theology and the Church* (Grand Rapids: Eerdmans, 2008).
[40] Michael C. Rea, ed., *Oxford Readings in Philosophical Theology*, vol. 1: *Trinity, Incarnation, and Atonement*, and vol. 2: *Providence, Scripture, and Resurrection* (New York: Oxford University Press, 2009).
[41] Oliver D. Crisp's recent projects exploring Christology serve as helpful illustrations of the kind of work analytic theology seeks to do. In his two books *Divinity and Humanity* (New York: Cambridge University Press, 2007) and *God Incarnate* (New York: T&T, 2009), Crisp revisits the historical claims of theologians concerning Christ's incarnation and extends the significance of these claims into contemporary life. For instance, with his essay on "Christ and the Embryo" in *God Incarnate* Crisp establishes an ethical foundation for considering current debates on the embryo and the beginnings of human life from sustained reflection on the philosophical implications of the virgin birth.
[42] Westphal describes this shift in terms of "philosophizing about God" to "philosophizing about religion." Merold Westphal, "The Emergence of Modern Philosophy of Religion," in *A Companion to the Philosophy of Religion*, ed. Philip L. Quinn and Charles Taliaferro (Malden, MA: Blackwell, 1997), 111.
[43] Or, "what can philosophy say about the religious dimension of human life now that the metaphysical proofs of God's existence have been taken away?" Merold

Westphal, "The Emergence of Modern Philosophy of Religion," in Quinn and Taliaferro, *Companion to the Philosophy of Religion*, 113.

44 Cf. Nicholas Wolterstorff, "Is It Possible or Desirable for Theologians to Recover from Kant?" *Modern Theology* 14.1 (Jan. 1998): 1–18.

45 Merold Westphal, ed., *Postmodern Philosophy and Christian Thought* (Bloomington: Indiana University Press, 1999), 2. He elaborates on this dialectic: "By appropriation, I mean a certain kind of recontextualization. There is a negative side to this activity, for the need to recontextualize stems from not sharing the same assumptions or the same agenda. Thus, to appropriate is to say, 'No. In this respect and in that respect I do not share your vision and find it necessary to locate myself at a different site from yours.' But appropriation is affirmation and acceptance as well; and it is this which distinguishes it from simple refutation. It says, 'Yes. I think you are right about that, though it will come out a bit differently in the context of my assumptions and agenda.'"

46 Postmodernism can be summarily defined in this way: "That postmodernism is indefinable is a truism. However, it can be described as a set of critical, strategic and rhetorical practices employing concepts such as difference, repetition, the trace, the simulacrum, and hyperreality to destabilize other concepts such as presence, identity, historical progress, epistemic certainty, and the univocity of meaning." Gary Aylesworth, "Postmodernism," in *Stanford Encyclopedia of Philosophy.*

47 Westphal asserts, "Perhaps the peace needs to be disturbed by interpretations and arguments that are not inherently secular but find their motivation outside and even against faith. For the link between pious intentions and genuine insight is not tight in either direction." Westphal, *Postmodern Philosophy and Christian Thought,* 2.

48 Ibid., 3.

49 Cf. Martin Heidegger, "The Onto-theo-logical Constitution of Metaphysics," in John Caputo, ed., *The Religious* (Malden, MA: Blackwell, 2002). Caputo's prefatory statements about Heidegger's religious concerns are very helpful for understanding this turn in his thought. Cf. John Caputo, "Introduction: What Comes After the God of Metaphysics," 4.

50 Ibid., 5.

51 Ibid., 2.

52 The literature demonstrating the intersection of religion and postmodern thought is growing by leaps and bounds. At the center of this growing body of literature are two book series projects. John Caputo edits a series of Perspectives in Continental Philosophy for Fordham University Press, and Merold Westphal edits the Indiana Series in the Philosophy of Religion for Indiana University Press. Along with the University of Chicago Press's series on Religion and Postmodernism, these series boast an ever-growing catalog of fascinating projects.

53 Along with Richard Rorty, John Caputo has been considered the most significant North American commentator and popularizer of Derrida's work. Cf. Caputo's *The Prayers and Tears of Jacques Derrida: Religion without Religion* (Bloomington: Indiana University Press, 1997); *Deconstruction in a Nutshell: A Conversation with Jacques Derrida* (New York: Fordham University Press, 1996); *Augustine and Postmodernism: Confessions and Circumfession*, ed.

John Caputo, Michael J. Scanlon, Indiana Series in the Philosophy of Religion (Bloomington: Indiana University Press, 2005).

[54] In addition to multiple publications between the two, Caputo and Derrida collaborated on several international conferences and public dialogues; most notably the five conferences hosted by Villanova University on Religion and Postmodernism (1997–2006). Cf. *God, the Gift, and Postmodernism*, ed. John Caputo and Michael J. Scanlon, Indiana Series in the Philosophy of Religion (Bloomington: Indiana University Press, 1999); *Questioning God*, ed. John Caputo, Mark Dooley, and Michael J. Scanlon (Bloomington: Indiana University Press, 2001); *Augustine and Postmodernism*, Caputo and Scanlon; *Transcendence and Beyond: A Postmodern Inquiry*, ed. John Caputo, Michael J. Scanlon, Indiana Series in the Philosophy of Religion (Bloomington: Indiana University Press, 2007).

[55] Cf. *Radical Orthodoxy: A New Theology*, ed. John Milbank, Catherine Pickstock, and Graham Ward (London: Routledge, 1999); Graham Ward, *Cities of God* (New York: Routledge, 2000); James K. A. Smith, *Speech and Theology: Language and the Logic of Incarnation* (New York: Routledge, 2002); *The Radical Orthodoxy Reader*, ed. John Milback and Simon Oliver (New York: Routledge, 2009); James K. A. Smith, *Introducing Radical Orthodoxy* (Grand Rapids: Baker, 2004).

[56] Cf. Creston David, John Milbank, and Slavoj Žižek, *The Monstrosity of Christ: Paradox or Dialetic?* (Cambridge, MA: MIT Press, 2009); Slavoj Žižek, *The Puppet and the Dwarf* (Cambridge, MA: MIT Press, 2003); Creston David, John Milbank, and Slavoj Žižek, *Paul's New Moment: Continental Philosophy and the Future of Christian Theology* (Grand Rapids: Brazos Press, 2010).

[57] Cf. *St. Paul among the Philosophers*, ed. John Caputo and Linda Martin Alcoff (Bloomington: Indiana University Press, 2009); Alan Badiou, *Saint Paul: The Foundation of Universalism*, trans. Ray Brassier, Cultural Memory in the Present (Stanford: Stanford University Press, 2003); Giorgio Agamben, *The Time That Remains: A Commentary on the Letter to the Romans*, trans. Patricia Dailey (Stanford: Stanford University Press, 2005); Jacob Taubes, *The Political Theology of Paul*, trans. Dana Hollander (Stanford: Stanford University Press, 2003); Douglas Harink, *Paul, Philosophy, and the Theopolitical Vision: Critical Engagements with Agamben, Badiou, Žižek, and Others* (Eugene, OR: Cascade, 2010).

[58] Smith has primarily provided for this conversation through a weblog entitled *Church and Postmodern Culture* (www.churchandpomo.org) and the Church and Postmodern Culture book series for Brazos Press. Cf. also James K. A. Smith, *The Devil Reads Derrida: And Other Essays on the University, the Church, Politics, and the Arts* (Grand Rapids: Eerdmans, 2009), and James K. A. Smith, ed., *After Modernity? Secularity, Globalization, and the Re-enchantment of the World* (Waco, TX: Baylor University Press, 2008).

[59] Stephen Mulhall, "Why Is There Something Called Philosophy Rather than Nothing?" *Royal Institute of Philosophy Supplement* 65 (2009): 270.

[60] Ibid., 269.

[61] Interestingly, the Open Court Publishing Company lists 59 titles in their Popular Culture and Philosophy series with at least seven more titles expected by Fall 2011. Some of these titles include the following: *Baseball and Philosophy,*

The Beatles and Philosophy, Harry Potter and Philosophy, iPod and Philosophy, and *The Wizard of Oz and Philosophy*. The Wiley publishing group has at least 24 similar and occasionally overlapping titles in their series the Blackwell Philosophy of Pop Culture Series. Though primarily focused on film directors, the University of Kentucky Press offers 20 titles in its Philosophy of Popular Culture Series.

[62] Cf. the work of Marc Prensky (www.marcprensky.com) and the growing body of literature and data on digital natives, digital immigrants, and a digital nation.

[63] The good work of the Veritas Forum organization is seeking to create just such a "place for truth" by creating dialogue opportunities on college campuses around the world where students can hear from Christian thinkers and intellectuals about life's most important questions. Cf. Dallas Willard, Daniel Cho, and Sarah Park. *A Place for Truth: Leading Thinkers Explore Life's Hardest Questions* (Downers Grove: IVP Books, 2010).

[64] Jacques Barzun, *Begin Here: The Forgotten Conditions of Teaching and Learning* (Chicago: University of Chicago Press, 1992).

8

Beauty, Meaning, and Power: Bearing Witness in the Profession of Words

John T. Netland

On the first day of my introductory literature classes, I tell my students that the methodology of a literature class is simple: we read books and then we talk about them. Although there are always those intrepid souls who hope to accomplish the latter without bothering with the former, successful students quickly figure out that classroom activities inevitably coalesce around a primary task: we seek to understand that which we have read. We accomplish this goal by learning how to enter into the kinds of conversations and to ask the sorts of questions that will increase our understanding. The study of literature is thus intensely interpretive. While we may appreciate works of literature or even apply their insights to our own experience, our first obligation is to understand those intricately crafted works of the imagination. To some extent, this purpose may seem self-evident, but it hasn't always been so, and as we survey the development of literary studies, we will note that some of our present practices in literary studies emerged out of distinctively Christian assumptions. Although those Christian underpinnings of the profession have diminished over the past century, Christians can still find ample opportunities for engagement in the field.[1]

Historical Overview

Gerald Graff's lively history identifies the beginnings of the modern, academic profession of literature in the last quarter of the nineteenth century. For many centuries previously, literature was taught in the universities but usually as "ancillary to the study of something else—chiefly to the Greek and Latin languages and to rhetoric, oratory, and forensics."[2] Thus, literature might be used to develop oratorical excellence or to illustrate moral precepts, the idea being that literature would enliven otherwise monotonous lessons. The establishment of modern literature departments offered new rationales for studying literature, first by affirming the validity of contemporary, vernacular literatures in addition to classical literature and second by recognizing that literature could be studied as a discipline in its own right. It need not merely serve as a means to other ends. In the heady excitement that accompanies the creation of a new area of study, however, a crucial question needed an answer: what precisely was the teacher of literature to accomplish in these newly-established literature departments?

Literature had found its way into the modern curriculum because its proponents were persuaded that great poetry, drama, and stories offered something of timeless value to sharpen the mind, refine the heart, and fortify the character of young people. Perhaps nobody had a greater influence on establishing literature in the curriculum than the Victorian poet and literary critic Matthew Arnold (1822–88), who tirelessly promoted culture as the antidote to a host of societal ills. For Arnold, culture was "the pursuit of perfection," a goal characterized by emotional and intellectual refinement or what he referred to as "sweetness and light." Arnold felt that the best way to cultivate this sweetness and light was through the study of "humane letters" through which one comes "to know the best that is known and thought in the world."[3] Later, in his spirited debates with Thomas Henry Huxley over the relative virtues of the humanities and science, Arnold insisted that "if we know the best that has been thought and uttered in the world, . . . we shall find that this art, and poetry, and eloquence, have in fact not only the power of refreshing and delighting us, they have also . . . a fortifying, and elevating, and quickening, and suggestive power, capable of wonderfully helping us to relate the results of modern science to our need for conduct, our need for beauty."[4] This is a rather impressive list of educational outcomes predicted of a literary education: not only to provide personal delight but also to elevate and enliven the mind so as to synthesize knowledge, moral conduct, and aesthetic appreciation.

Judging from the anecdotal data in Graff's history of the profession, there seems to have been a marked gap between this Arnoldian ideal and the actual pedagogical practices of those early literature classrooms. Some professors simply adopted the methods of their predecessors in Classical Languages, inflicting grammatical drills and requiring memorization of their students. Such methods almost inevitably lent themselves to studies of biography or to philology,[5] but were such drills truly the literary education that Arnold had in mind? Other classrooms were characterized by an entirely different spirit of impressionistic conversation, as for instance, were the popular literature courses at Harvard taught by the renowned American writers Henry Wadsworth Longfellow and James Russell Lowell. Lowell's biographer characterized a typical class as one in which the professor was easily diverted into personal reminiscences, leaving students "carelessly amused at the loose scholastic exercise and complacent over the evasion of work [or occasionally] stirred, quickened in their thought."[6] Popular as they may have been, did these classes truly exhibit the professional standards expected of an academic field of inquiry? In order for the academic discipline of English to mature, professional practices would have to develop a common professional vocabulary as well as shared aims and methods.

Arnold's references to "sweetness and light" referred to the aesthetic appreciation and intellectual discernment that he believed the "humane letters" uniquely embodied. Somehow, *through* its appeal to the aesthetic sense, literature could communicate certain truths. While this assumption would be necessary for literature to come into its own as an academic discipline, it has not always been affirmed. Sometimes objections have a clarifying effect, as was the case with two important thinkers who dealt seriously with the objections raised against literature and whose insights into literature have helped define some professional assumptions about literary language.

Christian Engagement in Literature

It should not come as a surprise that Christians have long held ambivalent feelings about literature. While Christians have been amongst the greatest writers of the English language and though the Bible is itself a work of considerable literary complexity and beauty, many Christians have been deeply troubled by literature, among them the great church father Augustine. In his autobiographical *Confessions*, Augustine expressed considerable regret that his youthful studies in literature had fostered sinful attitudes in himself. Not only had he given "pride of place in [his] affection to those empty fables rather than to more useful studies,"[7] he was distressed to discover his emotional investment in fictional characters like Aeneas and Dido while he remained oblivious to his own spiritual condition. He could "weep over the death of a Dido who took her own life from love" while not recognizing that he was "dying by [his] alienation" from God.[8] Augustine's primary concern was the problem of disordered priorities, through which even good things can become corrupted when they displace our primary obligation to love God, but his repeated and dismissive references to "fables" and "superstitions" also indicate an underlying distrust of literature. His criticisms are, as Donald Williams notes, "the familiar ones which would be repeated again and again throughout history. The fictions of the poets are lies; they are a waste of time, distracting us from more profitable pursuits; and they are an enticement to evil."[9]

On the other hand, as Williams adds, "it is evident on every page of his writings that Augustine was impacted for the good by his classical reading." Although his commendations for literature were always carefully qualified, he had "moments in which he recognized something of value even in pagan literature."[10] In *On Christian Teaching,* for instance, Augustine points out that "we should not avoid music because of the associated pagan superstitions if there is a possibility of gleaning from it something of value for understanding holy scripture." Augustine concludes that the Christian should "realize that truth belongs to his Lord, wherever it is found, gathering and acknowledging it even in pagan literature."[11] Drawing from the Exodus story of how the Israelites left Egypt laden with the gold of their erstwhile neighbors, Augustine used this image as a metaphor to authorize the Christian appropriation of secular literature. The analogy works in this way: the "treasures of the ancient Egyptians" contained not only idols to be shunned but also "vessels and ornaments of silver and gold" that the children of Israel could claim "at God's command" in order to make better use of these treasures. Likewise, Augustine argued, "all the branches of pagan learning contain not only false and superstitious fantasies" that Christians "must loathe and avoid," they also offer "studies for liberated minds which are more appropriate to the service of the truth. . . . These treasures—like the silver and gold, which they did not create but dug, as it were, from the mines of providence . . . must be removed by Christians . . . and applied to their true function, that of preaching the gospel."[12] The metaphor of plundering the treasures of the Egyptians still resonates with Christian scholars who seek to engage with an often aggressively secular academy, seeking truth wherever it may be found in order to redeem it for the glory of God.

It would be unfortunate if we concluded from Augustine's discussion that literature is simply a neutral medium that conveys content that might be morally good or bad. What he gives us glimpses of is the internal logic of how literature functions. For example, literature in his experience drew him into emotional identification with characters. That effect is not incidental, for literature is by its nature able to engage the emotions. But it can also communicate something through its use of poetic language. The fact that Augustine made his point about literature through metaphor is significant. The analogy to the children of Israel who left Egypt laden with treasure is not just an illustrative example; rather, it is the means through which Augustine made his point.

Literature and Morality

The most severe critics of literature have not been content to single out topical examples of immorality in literature; rather, such critics argue that literature is *inherently* untrustworthy because it is a species of lying. It relies on the imagination to make up things that are not real, or so the complaint goes. This is an ancient objection, but a sixteenth-century reiteration of the charge roused Sir Philip Sidney to compose one of the most eloquent defenses of poetry (essentially of all forms of imaginative literature). Sidney drew explicitly on Christian theology to make a case both that literary expression is part of the goodness of the created order and that the poet, by creating beautiful things, is acting analogously to God the Creator. This creativity reveals one dimension of what it means to say that humans are created in the image of God. Moreover, Sidney recognized that poetic language and the imagination are not a species of falsehood but operate with a logic and an integrity of their own.

Nearly all students of literature learn Sidney's pithy formulation of poetry as a form of discourse that "teaches" and "delights," but perhaps fewer readers have attended to his subtle explanation of the complex relationship poetry bears toward truth. Sidney defended the integrity of poetry and of the imagination by appealing to the etymological meanings of the poet: the Latin *vates* ("a diviner, foreseer, or prophet"),[13] which he illustrated with the example of David; and the Greek *poiein* (which Sidney translated as "maker"). Many of Sidney's examples of poetry as *poiesis* (as an object of craftsmanship) point to the literary devices that poets employ to create a thing of beauty. The appeal to the poet as *vates* is a bit more cautious, given that Sidney was wary about attributing divine inspiration to all poets. But in addition to the biblical poets (e.g., David, Solomon, Moses, Deborah) mentioned as divinely inspired, Sidney also claimed that poets in general, through the exercise of the imagination, were better suited to modulate between the real and the ideal, between abstract idea and concrete embodiment, than was the philosopher, the historian, and a whole host of other scholars. The poet could see certain things that from Sidney's perspective were less accessible through other ways of knowing. Other disciplines were limited by the constraints of nature, whereas

> . . . the poet, disdaining to be tied to any such subjection, lifted up with the vigor of his own invention, doth grow in effect another nature, in making things either better than nature bringeth forth. . . . Nature never set for the earth in so rich tapestry as divers poets have done; neither with so pleasant rivers, fruitful trees, sweet-smelling flowers, nor whatsoever else may make the too much loved earth more lovely. Her world is brazen, the poets only deliver a golden.[14]

The poet's craft is both imitative and creative, for it takes the given world and imaginatively transforms that reality with such excellence as to inspire delight and insight.

In making a case for the moral worth of literature, Sidney was pointing out that the literary quality of the poem was not incidental to its moral worth. If literature were nothing more than a means of illustrating the virtues, literature would remain merely instrumental, and the significance of its form would be diminished. It is because literature operates by its own rules of discourse that Sidney could defend the poet from the accusation of falsehood without also implying that the poet had nothing of consequence to say. "I will answer paradoxically, but truly, I think truly, that of all writers under the sun the poet is the least liar, and, though he would, as a poet can scarcely be a liar. . . . Now, for the poet, he nothing affirms, and therefore never lieth. For, as I take it, to lie is to affirm that to be true which is false."[15] Far from being evasive, this response is consistent with a truism in language studies: statements can perform a variety of actions in relationship to truth claims. Not every statement represents a propositional claim about the nature of reality nor makes verifiable claims, but that does not mean that such statements are false. This is not to say that poetry has nothing to do with truth whatsoever but, rather, that the kinds of statements that operate in imaginative literature maintain indirect relationships to the truth. Perhaps the best illustration of this point is expressed in Emily Dickinson's aphoristic poem, which—consistent with the logic of literary discourse—makes its case through metaphor and indirection:

> Tell all the Truth but tell it slant
> Success in Circuit lies
> Too bright for our infirm Delight
> The Truth's superb surprise
> As Lightning to the Children eased
> With explanation kind
> The Truth must dazzle gradually
> Or every man be blind.[16]

What precisely does it meant to "tell all the truth but tell it slant"? "Slant" is a spatial image, describing a line that is neither vertical nor horizontal; telling the truth is a verbal activity. Literally, the conjunction of these two terms is nonsense: how can an utterance form a geographical angle between 0 and 90 degrees? Such a statement can only make sense figuratively. A slanted line is made to represent—not falsehood—but a different direction toward the truth, again implying spatial direction as a figure of speech for apprehending truth. Subsequent figurative imagery includes the reference to "circuit" in line two and the doubly embedded analogy in lines 3–8: truth is like a bright light that can blind a person with its dazzling brilliance. Just as we often ease our children into an understanding of what lightning is, lest we frighten them with too much information at once, so too must we ease our way into a full knowledge of the truth. The use of figurative language, then, reinforces the thematic argument of the poem: poetry deals with truth indirectly, through image, analogy, and other "circuitous" ways of using language.

Sidney's defense of the poet should be of particular interest to the Christian, for it offered a robust endorsement of the imagination as a distinctively Christian endeavor. This was no grudging concession that literature might not be impermissible; it was, rather, a rousing endorsement of imaginative creativity as something reflective of God's character. Nor did he believe it to be impious that the poet is in a sense improving Nature; instead, he praised poetic invention as a way to honor God, the source of creativity. "Neither let it be deemed too saucy a comparison to balance the highest point of man's wit with the efficacy of nature; but rather give right honor to the heavenly Maker of that maker, who having made man to His own likeness, set him beyond and over all the works of that second nature: which in nothing he showeth so much as in poetry, when with the force of a divine breath he bringeth things forth surpassing her doings. . . ."[17] Williams praises Sidney's essay as "a profoundly Christian understanding of literature which does not merely salvage it for Christian use but finds the very ground of its being in explicitly Christian doctrine: creation, the *imago Dei*, the 'cultural mandate' to subdue the earth. Christians alone understand why human beings, whether 'literary' types or not, are impelled to make, tell and hear stories. When Christians also do so, they are not so much spoiling the Egyptians as recovering their own patrimony."[18]

Focusing on the Text: Literary Studies in the Twentieth Century

As the profession of literature matured in the twentieth century, critical practices increasingly focused on the text itself, seeking particularly to understand the internal logic of literary language and forms. Such pursuits follow naturally from Sidney's assertion that poetic language operates by a different set of rules than propositional statements do. But what kind of statements does the poet make? In what sense can fiction represent (imitate) the world if in fact the events of the story have not taken place? How should we understand figurative language? How does the arrangement of words and sentences in a literary work shape meaning? Are stanzas, couplets, or sestets merely arbitrary arrangements of words, or do they reorder language into meaningful units? If context affects interpretation, what kinds of contexts are created by genres and other literary conventions? How can one tell if a statement is used ironically? What do we learn by analyzing the sequence of events in a story? Do we approach lyric poetry with a different set of expectations than we do with narrative poetry? To pose such questions of the text is to take a formalist approach to interpretation. Although formalism has fallen out of favor in contemporary literary studies, it was enormously influential in the first half of the twentieth century, and, as Leland Ryken has noted, "its methods still set the agenda for what goes on in the literature classroom."[19] It provided a common vocabulary of critical terminology and a widely shared set of interpretive practices that made it possible to study literature *as literature*. Literature could be understood as particular kinds of art and rhetoric that had their own internal integrity and operating rules, and the task of the critic was to understand how it worked.

David Richter notes that formalism of all varieties "proposed an 'intrinsic' criticism that defined and addressed the specifically literary qualities in the text." Formalism "began in reaction to various forms of 'extrinsic' criticism that viewed the text as either the product of social and historical forces or a document making an ethical statement."[20] Of the three methods that Richter mentions (Russian Formalism, New Criticism, and Structuralism), the New Criticism had the greatest influence on classroom pedagogy and reading practices. Any classroom that has devoted attention to literary genres and devices, the varieties of figurative language and imagery, the consideration of how the parts of a work cohere and fit together, and above all to the particular ways in which imaginative writers exploit the semantic possibilities in language is a classroom that has been shaped by formalistic criticism.

The New Criticism turned its attention almost exclusively on the text itself and the literary devices employed therein. Biographical and historical considerations were deemed unnecessary. In fact, New Critical orthodoxy was marked by a series of prohibitions. The "intentional fallacy" meant that the reader should not seek the intent of the author. The "affective fallacy" indicated that the reader's response was equally irrelevant to the meaning of the text. The greatest offense was to represent the meaning of the poem through paraphrase, for this offense was called the "heresy of paraphrase" (not merely a fallacy). Cleanth Brooks, one of the leading New Critics, conceded that paraphrases might be necessary as a temporary measure to make sense of difficult passages, but insisted that paraphrases "distort the relation of the poem to its 'truth,'" and "split the poem between its 'form' and its 'content.'"[21] Undergirding these prohibitions was the New Critics' belief that literature was the unified embodiment of form and content, the incarnation of what could not be expressed otherwise.

It might seem that New Criticism was nothing more than a set of interpretive techniques that carried no ideological commitments, but as is usually the case, professional practices reveal underlying assumptions and values. The New Critics particularly valued figurative uses of language, especially ones that generated multiple layers of meaning. Ambiguity was viewed as evidence of literary complexity, not confusion, and literature that revealed ironic detachment was particularly valued, not merely for revealing literary cleverness but rather for expressing an attitude toward life. Paradox was especially valued, considered almost as an expression of worldview, for paradox—the conjunction of statements that appear to be contradictory but in fact turn out to make sense on a deeper level—revealed an underlying confidence in the coherence of language and the unity of literary texts. David Richter explains that New Critics "tended to operate by finding within the texture of the poem oppositions and conflicts that were resolved into a harmonious balance. The principal mediator of this resolution was poetic language, specifically the capacity of language to carry multiple meanings that could disclose hidden conflicts and tensions at the outset of the poem and converge into a harmonious balance at the end."[22] Finally, the religious overtones of so much New Critical terminology suggested quasireligious associations with literature. One of the most influential New Critical books was titled *The Verbal Icon*, a term laden with deliberate religious implications. These religious associations could cut both ways. Many Christians were attracted to the idea that the literary symbol had an almost sacramental power to gesture toward transcendent meanings. On the other hand, many readers wondered if this religious language promised too much for literature. If a poem were truly an icon, could the study of literature come uncomfortably close to a pseudo-religion?

Christians and the New Criticism

It is not hard to see why many Christians in the profession found the New Criticism to be a congenial form of literary criticism. For some, the affinities between New Critical reading practices and Biblical exegesis encouraged fruitful interchanges between these two reading practices. In fact, the New Critical attention to literary form had an influence on genre criticism in twentieth-century biblical studies, and literary approaches to the Bible are now widely accepted forms of biblical criticism. For others, the habits of mind that value paradox as the expression of apparently irreconcilable matters fit well with a religious sensibility. Paradox, after all, is pervasive in Scripture: "Blessed are the poor in spirit" (Matt 5:3 NIV). "Love your enemies and pray for those who persecute you" (Matt 5:44 NIV). "Whoever wants to save his life will lose it, but whoever loses his life because of Me will save it" (Luke 9:24 HCSB). "Faith is the assurance of things hoped for, the conviction of things not seen" (Heb 11:1 NRSV). Finally, the attention to allusion and symbolic language allowed many Christian literary critics to track down and explain the innumerable religious motifs and images in literature. In so doing, Christian critics have helped the contemporary academic world maintain a cultural memory of a religious past that is increasingly alien to the modern academy.

Nevertheless, the New Criticism was not without its flaws. It has been accused of a long list of offenses. Formalists ignored history and treated the text as if it existed outside of time or space. They privileged aesthetic categories and minimized the ethical concerns of literature. They exalted certain types of literature—works that demonstrated artistic complexity, layers of irony, complex patterns of imagery and allusion—and often ignored other works of literature that had been highly regarded in their time. They fostered an overconfidence in textual coherence and in the power of the critic to understand the text. While some Christian scholars have defended formalism from these criticisms, others have joined in this critique. The philosopher Nicholas Wolterstorff issued one of the most influential Christian critiques of formalist art (including but not limited to literature) in his 1980 book, *Art in Action*. Wolterstorff questioned why it is that the modern world has typically placed art in contexts (museums) where the expected response is to view it from a disinterested distance and to admire its beauty, a perspective toward art that is very similar to the New Critical tendency to treat the object as an icon for observation and appreciation. In contrast, Wolterstorff was convinced that art was functional and that it has served a broad array of purposes throughout human history, including worship and service to God's kingdom. Reconceptualizing art as an action allowed Wolterstorff to emphasize art's social, ethical, communal, and spiritual functions. As applied to literature, this functional view of art served as a rebuke to formalism and as a signal that ethical and social implications of literature were legitimate.

Other Christian scholars, including Roger Lundin of Wheaton College and John Cox of Hope College, have criticized formalism for its diminishment of history. Lundin has frequently critiqued what he calls "romantic formalism," a term by which he connects the critical practices of twentieth-century formalist critics with Romantic theories of poetic inspiration and human self-sufficiency in nineteenth-century England and America. Lundin rejected the formalist confidence in the motif of the solitary, autonomous, disinterested reader, noting pointedly that contemporary Protestant biblical exegesis often resembled that individualistic, ahistorical mode of reading.[23] Cox has also criticized textual interpretation that ignores history. Among other things, Cox reminds us that history—and an historical sense—is not incidental to Christianity. Noting Christianity's "historical debt to Judaism," Cox writes that both Christianity and Judaism "continued—and continue—to affirm the origin of human history in the uniquely creative power of God, the continuance of God's saving presence in history, and the anticipation of history's fulfillment in a time of God's choosing."[24]

The Rise of Poststructuralism and Deconstruction

With the demise of formalist criticism in the 1960s and '70s, literary study changed dramatically with what has frequently been called the "theoretical turn" to the profession. Theory might be described as a philosophy of criticism; it attempts to explain why we interpret texts in certain ways. This theoretical turn broke the monopoly of formalism and ushered in a sometimes bewildering variety of critical approaches, turning literary studies into one of the most eclectic and methodologically diverse academic fields. While it is impossible to identify a single moment when theory displaced formalist criticism, 1966 may be as good a date as any, for that was the year that a young French philosopher by the name of Jacques Derrida presented a conference paper that announced the inauguration of a "poststructuralist" sensibility. Along with several other French philosophers like Jean-François Lyotard and Michel Foucault, Derrida posed a radical challenge to prevailing assumptions about language and meaning.

"Poststructuralism" implies some relationship to "structuralism," which was a short-lived permutation of formalism. Whereas the New Criticism was almost entirely defined by its attention to *literary* qualities, the structuralists were drawn to linguistics, semiotics (the study of signs), and anthropology in the hopes of discovering a comprehensive theory of communication. Much like the New Critics's confidence in the underlying coherence of the literary text, the structuralists also had confidence in language as a comprehensive and coherent system. Richter describes the optimism pervading structuralist scholarship in the 1960s: "There was a palpable sense at the time that a new method for the synthesis of knowledge was at hand. . . . The notion, barely glimpsed, that by using the tools of semiotics and linguistics, structuralism might manage to reunite the branches of knowledge that post-Renaissance specialization had severed, gave its adherents a messianic sense of mission."[25]

Hence it was all the more ironic, even shocking, that at a conference devoted to structuralism, Derrida proclaimed what would be seen as the death knell of structuralism with his "deconstructive" method of reading texts. Deconstruction, as a theory of interpretation, is highly technical, and I cannot do full justice to it in these pages but will attempt to sketch out some of its salient points. In his lecture, Derrida accepted the premise that language was an all-encompassing system but not structuralism's confidence in the power of linguistic signs to communicate truth claims. According to Derrida's brilliant "deconstruction" of language, signifiers (linguistic signs) are arbitrary, they derive their meaning because of difference, and they can only generate meaning in relationship to other signifiers. The result is that the construal of meaning is always deferred. Derrida created a portmanteau word out of difference and deferral to come up with *différance*, with the implication that meaning is always deferred and differentiated. The task of interpreting leads inevitably to a moment of *aporia*, in which textual meaning breaks down. This is the point, Derrida believed, that the text opens up a "free play" of language, an invitation to the reader to join in the construction of interpretive meaning. Derrida denied what he called metaphysics of presence, claiming that words and signs always indicate an absence—the sign does not refer to some essence in the word but rather indicates an absence. Meaning is conferred not by what is there in the sign but because each signifier is different from other signifiers. He also distrusted the notion of a center to a text, and by center he had in mind "a point of presence, a fixed origin" that would "orient, balance, and organize the structure" of the text.[26]

To the layman's mind, this sounds very much like a form of interpretive relativism—there is no truth or meaning; interpretation is just a language game; the meaning of the text is whatever one wants it to be. Such reactions to Derrida, plentiful as they have been, misrepresent his point, for he was not saying that there is no meaning in the text but rather that meaning is always contingent, always provisional, always constructed. Derrida was not denying the possibility of interpretation as much as he was calling on readers to recognize the inherent instability in language and, as settled interpretations would open up into interpretive free play, to be conscious of how communities of readers construct meanings that themselves must be continually revisited.

The Rejection of "Metanarrative"

Other French poststructuralists such as Jean-François Lyotard and Michel Foucault likewise introduced interpretive practices that challenge authority and power. Both philosophers were particularly skeptical of claims to universal reason, exposing such claims as masks that covered the interests of power. Lyotard is also noted for his skepticism toward "metanarratives," which Kevin Mills explains are

> . . . the old explanatory discourses such as philosophical systems, religious beliefs and political theories, emerging out of the Enlightenment elevation of Reason, and in which Reason is the ultimate test of truth. These "grand narratives," used to underpin and validate the production of knowledge within the limits of learned disciplines (such as the sciences, politics and economics), have broken down under the strain

> of cultural and linguistic change and scientific progress. These have broken down to the point where it is now necessary, Lyotard claims, to have done with any appeal to such *passé* notions as "reason" or "truth," and to look for more localized replacements for those now defunct universal values.[27]

Foucault's main contribution was to expose the relationship between power and reason, more specifically, to follow in the tradition of Nietzsche of seeing "the will-to-power as dominant over any search for truth—as defining, in fact, the meaning and location of truth."[28]

"Textual Indeterminacy"

As an avant-garde literary movement, deconstructionism had a short shelf life. By the middle of the1980s, it had already become dated, and few critics today would claim to be practicing deconstruction. But its influence has been more widespread and lasting in terms of giving legitimacy to the principle of textual indeterminacy. The notion of determinate meaning (a phrase that is preferred by some critics to the term "objective meaning") means that there is a fixed range of meanings possible in a literary text and the range of meaning is determined by the text, not the reader. It does not mean that there is only one single meaning possible, but it does imply that there are acceptable interpretations and unacceptable ones. Textual indeterminacy means that there is no fixed set of meanings to the literary text; there may be an infinite number of interpretations possible, and readers participate in the construction of interpretive meanings. Reader-response theory, which gives priority to the reader to determine the meaning of a text, presumes an indeterminate text. One of the most provocative of reader-response theorists, Stanley Fish, argued that there was potentially no limit to the interpretations possible, the only criteria being an ability to persuade the community of readers that it was a plausible interpretation. He did not deny that we find some interpretations to be utterly unconvincing, but his claim was not that the interpretation was inherently wrong but simply that "there is as yet no elaborated interpretive procedure for producing that text."[29] His example was to take the apparently absurd scenario mentioned by the critic Norman Holland as an example of an obviously wrong interpretation of William Faulkner's "A Rose for Emily": the claim that a scene from the story, which is set in the Reconstruction era American South, could describe an Eskimo. Fish was not willing to say that such a reading was absurd; what he said was that the "Eskimo reading is unacceptable because there is at present no interpretive strategy for producing it."[30] Fish's example is admittedly extreme, but milder forms of textual indeterminacy are widely assumed in literary studies.

The broader influence of poststructuralism can also be seen in literary approaches that challenge political and institutional power structures. Politically engaged forms of criticism, such as postcolonial, Marxist, and feminist criticism, seek to uncover or demystify institutional power structures, ranging from ideologies of empire to patriarchal social structures. Foucault's heirs are those who share his skepticism about taking truth claims at face value, and who believe that power interests more often than not dictate the nature of truth.

Christian Engagement

Christian scholars have responded to poststructuralism in varied ways. It is likely that the predominant view has been critical of poststructuralism and finds it difficult to reconcile poststructuralist assumptions with the confessional statements of the Christian faith. Is Christian doctrine really open to the free play of interpretation, and if so, what is left after the gospel is deconstructed? Lundin spoke for many Christian scholars in cautioning against assuming that the deconstructive critique of Enlightenment modernity would be easily reconcilable with "contemporary Christian critiques of modernity." The fact that Christians have good reason to be critical of many aspects of modernity does not mean, in Lundin's view, that deconstruction will help them make that case. Rather, Lundin concluded that "deconstruction seeks to subvert the various conceptions of truth and transcendence that have grounded Western experience since well before the time of Christ."[31] In the same way, many Christian scholars have found it hard to be reconciled to Lyotard's skepticism about "metanarratives," believing that term to be directed toward Christian belief as well as toward Enlightenment rationality.

On the other hand, some Christian scholars have defended poststructuralism and believe it has much to commend it to the church. Philosopher James Smith recommends that Christians pay attention to the ethical concerns of Derrida and Lyotard:

> Deconstruction's recognition that everything is interpretation opens a space of questioning—a space to call into question the received and dominant interpretations that often claim not to be interpretations at all [but the unquestioned truth]. As such, deconstruction is interested in interpretations that have been marginalized and sidelined, activating voices that have been silenced. This is the constructive, yea prophetic, aspect of Derrida's deconstruction: a concern for justice by being concerned about dominant, status quo interpretations that silence those who see differently. Thus, from its inception, deconstruction has been, at root, ethical—concerned for the paradigmatic marginalized described by the Old Testament as "the widow, the orphan, and the stranger."[32]

Lundin's and Smith's contrasting perspectives on poststructuralism illustrate the difficulty of applying Augustine's permission to "plunder the treasures of the Egyptians," for it is not always clear what one is tacitly accepting when one appropriates a theoretical posture. Is deconstruction nothing more than a technique to challenge unjust power structures? If so, then it may very well be a useful tool to proclaim a message as old as the Old Testament prophets. But does it also mean that one is accepting a view of language that might serve to deconstruct beliefs that are not up for negotiation? Jacobs notes that those who seek to play the deconstructive game on behalf of justice may gain a Pyrrhic victory: "For if all claims, all predicates, can be deconstructed, then how can one say with security that the rich oppress the poor, or that sexism and racism should be resisted? . . . A Deconstructionist who preserves certain claims and predicates from deconstruction is not a deconstructionist at all but merely a critical analyst of other people's ideas."[33] It is not altogether clear why Smith needs to enlist poststructuralism in the pursuit of justice. Smith concludes his treatment of Derrida with these words: "The deconstructive church . . . is deeply prophetic—reflecting the voice not so much of Derrida as of Amos,"[34] to which one might question if Amos needed to deconstruct the word of the Lord in order to proclaim God's judgment and restoration.

One of the significant implications of this turn to theory was a dramatic change in the stance that readers adopted toward the literary text. Traditionally, readers have granted considerable deference to the text. The Arnoldian case for literature, after all, presumed that great literature could teach us or could shape our affections. The critic's or reader's responsibility was to listen to the text on its own terms and whatever critical gymnastics the reader would perform on the text was intended for the purpose of better understanding the text. In the era of theory, however, the critic's relationship to the text changed. In his seminal book, *Freud and Philosophy*, Paul Ricoeur coined a memorable phrase, "the hermeneutics of suspicion," to describe this altered stance toward the text, and he attributed this perspective to the influence of Marx, Freud, and Nietzsche. The hermeneutics of suspicion presumes that the text cannot be trusted on its own terms—that it must be covering something up or must be reflecting a "false consciousness." Ricoeur explained that "this hermeneutics is not an explication of the object, but a tearing off of masks, an interpretation that reduces disguises."[35] One can see this attitude in postcolonial criticism that unmasks ideologies of empire, in feminist criticism that exposes the false consciousness of patriarchy, and in Marxist criticism that exposes the capitalist ideologies of bourgeois culture. One's degree of sympathy to any of these ideologically informed schools of criticism will depend on the degree to which one finds those critiques compelling.

Another consequence of the theoretical turn has been the alterations to the "canon" of great literature. To a great extent, this has been an expansion of the canon, with the inclusion of many more women and minority writers, both North American ethnic writers and writers from the former colonies of Europe. The call to expand the canon was based on claims that the established hierarchy of great writers was not based on "the best that has been known and thought" but rather on other criteria that reflected the privilege of white males. In advocating for the inclusion of other writers, then, categories of gender, race, and ethnicity have been added to other criteria as to what constitutes a writer's importance. Sometimes the inclusion of new voices has meant less attention to established voices, for there is, after all, only a finite number of semester hours that departments can require their students to take in the field. Consequently, many teachers and scholars of a more traditionalist bent have worried that even such luminaries as Chaucer, Shakespeare, and Milton are not read as often in this generation as they were in the past. Leland Ryken has expressed concerns that the altered canon and a pervasive antireligious hostility have made it less likely that students will encounter some of the greatest Christian writers of the English language.[36] Usually, it is not the major writers who get dropped from the curriculum but perhaps the secondary ones. Thus, for instance, fewer readers of American literature will encounter Longfellow, William Cullen Bryant, and William Dean Howells, and the British literature curriculum will be less likely to include Thomas Grey or William Makepeace Thackaray.

While some traditional Christian scholars lament these changes, many others are on the forefront of celebrating these new authors or, in some cases, recovering neglected authors. The case with women writers offers a particularly interesting moment of opportunity for Christian scholars, for many of the women writers from English and American history were devout Christians. In fact, one of the reasons that books like Harriet Beecher Stowe's *Uncle Tom's Cabin* had been neglected for nearly a century—in spite of its enormous popularity in its time—was that the literary tastes of modernist literature and formalist criticism depreciated "sentimental literature." Consequently, writers like Stowe and Elizabeth Barrett Browning were not as frequently read in the first half of the twentieth century, but with the interest in recovering women's voices, there has also been an opportunity to reconsider the overtly religious aesthetic of such writers as Stowe, Browning, Charlotte Brontë, and others. There is considerable work being done in recovering the writings of Renaissance women, who wrote in genres that until recently were not considered sufficiently "literary" to merit inclusion in the older canon of literature.

In a similar vein, the inclusion of writers of color has also provided opportunities for the recovery of Christian writers like Phyllis Wheatley, the African-American poet whose overtly Christian sensibilities sometimes eliminated her from the curriculum. There is even an opportunity for theoretical considerations of race, culture, and religion to open up as we begin to hear more from non-Western theologians and philosophers. Much of the first generation of postcolonial theory has either ignored religious categories or has treated Christianity as part and parcel of empire. Voices of global Christianity like Andrew Walls, Kwame Bediako, Lamin Sanneh, Kazo Kitamori, and Kosuke Koyama have fresh ways of helping us understand the relationship of Christianity to culture, particularly cultures that do not have an extensive history of Christian influence. Although Christian scholars have not been as prominent in postcolonial studies as they have in other aspects of literary theory, there is certainly an opening for Christian theorists and critics to shape the conversation about race, faith, and culture.

Conclusion

The modern profession of literary studies began with the premise that the study of literature could shape one's moral character, but much of twentieth-century literary practice has not quite known what to do with that notion. Formalism tended to ignore the question of literature's ethical and affective power. The recent trend toward politically committed forms of theory tends to assume a moral purpose in those approaches (such as the commitment to justice), though sometimes it seems as if the concern over power trumps ethics, particularly if one subscribes to the notion that all discourses are ultimately about power. Some of the most exciting work being done by Christian literary scholars in recent decades has been to revisit the ethical implications of literature. This essay will close with some reflections on two of those approaches. Alan Jacobs and David Lyle Jeffreys have both explored earlier Christian thinking on hermeneutics. Jacobs has returned to Augustine's reflections on reading and has asked us to rethink what reading and interpretation would look like if we approached our texts from the perspective of love: what would a hermeneutics of charity look like? How can reading help us, as Augustine believed it should, to love God and neighbor? Jeffreys ranges far and wide through the history of English, continental, and American literature to remind us how important the Book of Scripture and books in general have been to the witness of the church. In the process, he asks us to rethink the ways in which we as readers enter into the space created by books. His culminating chapter, "Literary Theory and the Broken-Hearted Reader," asks us to consider if our theories of reading allow for us to experience life-changing responses to literature, responses that might be characterized by a tender, broken heart. In an era in which power seems to dominate all considerations of textual interpretation, Jeffreys and Jacobs remind us that the kingdom of God is based upon a peculiar economy of power in which the weak are made strong, the last are made first, and the greatest of all virtues is love.[37]

Questions for Further Reflection

1. Can you think of ways in which the form of a favorite work of literature affects its meaning?
2. What do you think of the imagination? Do you think it is something frivolous and largely concerned with idle day-dreams? Do you think that the imagination can lead us into truth? Do you agree with Sidney that our exercise of the imagination reflects something of the image of God in humans?
3. Augustine and Plato worried about the moral effects of literature, and many contemporary Christians are concerned with such matters as vulgarity, coarse language, excessive sexuality, and violence in literature. How should Christian writers handle such matters?
4. In what ways can Christian critics and readers find common cause with various forms of literary criticism that do not reflect Christian beliefs?
5. To what extent do current literary studies offer an opportunity for Christians to contribute to the scholarly conversations?

Resources for Further Study

Arnold, Matthew. "The Function of Criticism at the Present Time." In *Poetry and Criticism of Matthew Arnold*, edited by A. Dwight Culler, 237–58. Boston: Houghton Mifflin, 1961.

———. "Literature and Science." In *Prose of the Victorian Period*, edited by William E. Buckler, 486–501. Boston: Houghton Mifflin, 1958.

Augustine. *Confessions*. Translated by Henry Chadwick. Oxford: Oxford University Press, 1998.

———. *On Christian Teaching*. Translated by R. P. H. Green. Oxford: Oxford University Press, 1997.

Brooks, Cleanth. *The Well-Wrought Urn: Studies in the Structure of Poetry*. New York: Harcourt, Brace, 1947.

Cox, John D. "The Turn to History." In *The Discerning Reader: Christian Perspectives on Literature and Theory,* edited by David Barratt, Roger Pooley, and Leland Ryken, 85–102. Leicester, England: Apollos; Grand Rapids: Baker Books, 1995.

Derrida, Jacques. "Structure, Sign, and Play in the Discourse of the Human Sciences." In *The Critical Tradition: Classical Texts and*

Contemporary Trends, edited by David H. Richter, 959–71. Boston: Bedford, 1989.

Dickinson, Emily. *Final Harvest: Emily Dickinson's Poems*. Edited by Thomas H. Johnson. Boston and Toronto: Little, Brown, 1961.

Fish, Stanley. *Is There a Text in this Class? The Authority of Interpretive Communities*. Cambridge: Harvard University Press, 1980.

Graff, Gerald. *Professing Literature: An Institutional History*. Chicago: University of Chicago Press, 1987.

Jacobs, Alan. "Deconstruction." In *Literary Theory: A Christian Appraisal*, edited by Clarence Walhout and Leland Ryken, 172–98. Grand Rapids: Eerdmans, 1991.

Jeffreys, David Lyle. *People of the Book: Christian Identity and Literary Culture*. Grand Rapids: Eerdmans, 1996.

Lundin, Roger. "Our Hermeneutical Inheritance." In *The Responsibility of Hermeneutics*, edited by Roger Lundin, Anthony C. Thiselton, and Clarence Walhout, 1–29. Grand Rapids: Eerdmans, 1985.

———. "Hermeneutics." In *Literary Theory: A Christian Appraisal*, edited by Clarence Walhout and Leland Ryken, 149–71. Grand Rapids: Eerdmans, 1991.

———. *The Culture of Interpretation: Christian Faith and the Postmodern World*. Grand Rapids: Eerdmans, 1993.

Mills, Kevin. "Words and presences: the spiritual imperative." In *The Discerning Reader: Christian Perspectives on Literature and Theory*, edited by David Barratt, Roger Pooley, and Leland Ryken, 121–36. Leicester, England: Apollos; Grand Rapids: Baker Books, 1995.

Richter, David H., ed. *The Critical Tradition: Classic Texts and Contemporary Trends*. Boston: Bedford, 1989.

Ricoeur, Paul. *Freud and Philosophy: An Essay on Interpretation*. Translated by Denis Savage. New Haven: Yale University Press, 1970.

Ryken, Leland. "Formalist and Archetypal Criticism." In *Literary Theory: A Christian Appraisal*, edited by Clarence Walhout and Leland Ryken, 1–23. Grand Rapids: Eerdmans, 1991.

________. "Afterword." In *Literary Theory: A Christian Appraisal*, edited by Clarence Walhout and Leland Ryken, 292–302. Grand Rapids: Eerdmans, 1991.

Sidney, Sir Philip. "Defence of Poetry." *Norton Anthology of English Literature*, edited by M. H. Abrams and Stephen Greenblatt, 1:933–54. 7th ed. New York: Norton, 2000.

Smith, James K. A. *Who's Afraid of Postmodernism*? Grand Rapids: Baker, 2006.

Williams, Donald. "Christian Poets, Past and Present." In *The Discerning Reader: Christian Perspectives on Literature and Theory*, edited by David Barratt, Roger Pooley, and Leland Ryken, 53–68. Leicester, England: Apollos; Grand Rapids: Baker Books, 1995.

Wimsatt, W. K., Jr. *The Verbal Icon: Studies in the Meaning of Poetry.* New York: Noonday Press, 1954.

Wolterstorff, Nicholas. *Art in Action: Toward a Christian Aesthetic.* Grand Rapids: Eerdmans, 1980.

Endnotes

[1] The most coherent and judicious assessment of deconstruction in my judgment is Alan Jacobs's chapter "Deconstruction," in *Literary Theory: A Christian Appraisal*, ed. Clarence Walhout and Leland Ryken (Grand Rapids: Eerdmans, 1991), 172–98.

[2] Gerald Graff, *Professing Literature: An Institutional History* (Chicago: University of Chicago Press, 1987), 19.

[3] Matthew Arnold, "The Function of Criticism at the Present Time," *Poetry and Criticism of Matthew Arnold*, ed. A. Dwight Culler (Boston: Houghton Mifflin, 1961), 243.

[4] Matthew Arnold, "Literature and Science," in *Prose of the Victorian Period*, ed. William E. Buckler (Boston: Houghton Mifflin, 1958), 393.

[5] Graff, *Professing Literature*, 38.

[6] Ibid., 40.

[7] Augustine, *Confessions*, trans. Henry Chadwick (Oxford: Oxford University Press, 1997), 15.

[8] Ibid.

[9] Donald Williams, "Christian Poets, Past and Present," in *The Discerning Reader: Christian Perspectives on Literature and Theory*, ed. David Barratt, Roger Pooley, and Leland Ryken (Grand Rapids: Baker, 1995), 54.

[10] Ibid., 55.

[11] Augustine, *On Christian Teaching*, trans. R. P. H. Green (Oxford: Oxford University Press, 1997), 47.

[12] Ibid., 64–65.

[13] See Sir Philip Sidney, "Defense of Poetry," in *Norton Anthology of English Literature*, ed. M. H. Abrams and Stephen Greenblatt, 7th ed. (New York: Norton, 2000), 1:935.

[14] Ibid., 936–37.

[15] Ibid., 947.

[16] Emily Dickinson, *Final Harvest: Emily Dickinson's Poems*, ed. Thomas H. Johnson (Boston: Little, Brown, 1961), 248–49.

[17] Sidney, "Defense of Poetry," in Abrams and Greenblatt, *Norton Anthology*, 937.

[18] Williams, "Christian Poets," in Barratt et al., *The Discerning Reader*, 60.

[19] Leland Ryken, "Formalist and Archetypal Criticism," in *Literary Theory: A Christian Appraisal*, ed. Clarence Walhout and Leland Ryken (Grand Rapids: Eerdmans, 1991), 1.

[20] David H. Richter, *The Critical Tradition: Classic Texts and Contemporary Trends* (Boston: Bedford, 1989), 721.

[21] Cleanth Brooks, *The Well-Wrought Urn: Studies in the Structure of Poetry* (New York: Harcourt, Brace, 1947), 201.

[22] Richter, *Critical Tradition*, 729.

[23] Roger Lundin, "Our Hermenetical Inheritance," in *The Responsibility of Hermeneutics*, by Roger Lundin, Anthony C. Thiselton, and Clarence Walhout (Grand Rapids: Eerdmans, 1985), 4–23.
[24] John D. Cox, "The Turn to History," in Barratt, Pooley, and Ryken, *Discerning Reader*, 92.
[25] Richter, *Critical Tradition*, 856.
[26] Jacques Derrida, "Structure, Sign, and Play in the Discourse of the Human Sciences," in Richter, *Critical Tradition*, 960.
[27] Kevin Mills, "Words and Presence: The Spiritual Imperative," in Barratt, Pooley, and Ryken, *Discerning Reader*, 124–25.
[28] Richter, *Critical Tradition*, 951.
[29] Stanley Fish, *Is There a Text in This Class? The Authority of Interpretive Communities* (Cambridge: Harvard, 1980), 345.
[30] Ibid., 346.
[31] Roger Lundin, *The Culture of Interpretation Christian Faith and the Postmodern World* (Grand Rapids: Eerdmans, 1993), 203–4.
[32] James K. A. Smith, *Who's Afraid of Postmodernism?* (Grand Rapids: Baker, 2006), 51.
[33] Jacobs, "Deconstruction," in Walhout and Ryken, *Literary Theory*, 190.
[34] Smith, *Postmodernism*, 58.
[35] Paul Ricoeur, *Freud and Philosophy: An Essay on Interpretation*, trans. D. Savage (New Haven: Yale University Press, 1970), 30.
[36] Leland Ryken, "Afterword," in *Literary Theory,* Walhout and Ryken, 295–97.
[37] See Alan Jacobs, *A Theology of Reading: The Hermeneutics of Love* (Boulder, CO: Westview Press, 2001), and David Lyle Jeffreys, *People of the Book: Christian Identity and Literary Culture* (Grand Rapids: Eerdmans, 1996).

9

On Language and Interpretation

Scott Huelin

Christians have often been called a people of the book, and rightly so, for at least three reasons. First, Christians place central importance on the Scriptures as the supreme guide and norm for belief and practice. Consequently, the Bible enjoys an extraordinary place in the individual and corporate lives of Christians.[1] Think of family Bibles, Gideon Bibles, pocket Bibles, pew Bibles, award Bibles, and e-Bibles. Picture the Holy Scriptures held aloft by Catholic priests or Baptist preachers before the watching eyes of worshippers. Recall how presidents, judges, and witnesses all swear oaths by placing a hand on a Bible. Without even detailing the multi-billion-dollar Bible (and Bible paraphernalia) industry in America, it seems apparent that Christians deserve the title, "People of the Book."

Second, Christianity arose in the world at roughly the same historical moment as did the codex.[2] The fortunes of both have been firmly bound together ever since. The spread of apostolic teaching in the early centuries depended heavily on this new communication medium, as the collection of books in our New Testament implies. Centuries later the Reformation succeeded where other late medieval reform movements failed precisely because of its use of the printing press to get the Word out. Furthermore, the spread of Christianity has a strong historical correlation with the founding of book-dependent institutions such as schools and universities and, in the modern era, with rising literacy rates. Conversely, the transformation of oral language into written signs, and therefore the introduction and production of books, remains a central task in missionary work among a variety of preliterate peoples. Wherever the gospel goes, books cannot be far behind, and books, it seems, can help make straight the way of the Lord.

There is yet another sense in which Christians, particularly Protestant Christians, are an especially bookish people. Protestantism was born from a conflict of interpretations: What started as a dispute about the sale of indulgences turned into debate on the proper way to read Scripture. While Rome maintained that the Bible should be interpreted by ecclesial authorities in the light of tradition, Martin Luther asserted that Scripture is and must be its own interpreter because Scripture alone is the only infallible guide of faith and practice (the famous *sola Scriptura* principle). Luther's principle was not accepted by Catholic theologians of the day, but it was eagerly embraced by his fellow Protestants. Yet his fellow reformers found themselves at odds with one another over any number of doctrines they derived from their self-interpreting Bibles: Calvin versus Zwingli on the Lord's Supper; Anabaptists versus Calvin and Luther on baptism; Luther versus Melanchthon on the proper uses of the law, and so on. These interpretive differences, coupled with a strong imperative to purity in doctrine and practice, led directly to the establishment of the first Protestant church bodies. Since the sixteenth century, these have multiplied at an astonishing rate; one current estimate numbers worldwide Protestant denomination around 30,000.[3] If that number is correct, then 61 new Protestant sects have been founded each year, on average, since Luther nailed his Ninety-five Theses to the castle church door in Wittenburg. Whatever else we might say about the fractured nature of the Protestant movement, we can certainly identify in it a painful reminder of the difficulties involved in settling interpretive disputes and the consequences of failing to do so. In other words, we are a bookish people because our many denominational traditions and institutions arose from our profound disagreements over how to read the one Book. We are not only what we read but *how* we read.

Thus we should attend carefully to the "how" of reading. In what follows, I hope to explore some of the basic issues in interpretation theory from a Christian point of view under the rubric of a central question: What is interpretation? Before we can meaningfully address this question, however, we will have to do some thinking about that which serves as both the medium and the object of interpretation: language.[4]

Language

Developments in the philosophy of language over the last century have made it possible for us to rethink interpretation theory in helpful ways. More specifically, the work of philosophers such as Ludwig Wittgenstein and Hans-Georg Gadamer has shown how modern theories of language actually obscure our understanding about the relationship of language and human thought. Heretofore, modern philosophy of language insisted on imagining language as an instrument for the expression of thought. In other words, I think a thought, and then I put that thought into language for the sake of communicating it to others. Granted, this instrumental view of language seems commonsensical to most people today, but we can easily see how our relation to language is far more complex than this view suggests. First, try this little experiment: Think a thought *without using words*. A little effort in this direction reveals the impossibility of the task.[5]

Second, consider a familiar phenomenon: Once we have a word for a certain object or idea, we begin to notice its referent everywhere. This happens in matters sublime and mundane. When my neighbor recently purchased a Nissan Rogue, I had never consciously noticed these vehicles on the road. Now that I have a name for this particular vehicle, I see them everywhere. Clearly west Tennesseans did not begin driving Rogues in huge quantities at that moment; what changed was my ability to perceive the Rogue as a distinct entity among the many vehicles on the streets of my fair city, and this was made possible to a large extent by my acquisition of a word for it. The same dynamic applies equally to nonmaterial objects of perception: When I first began to study theological ethics, I learned words for virtues and vices that had been hitherto indistinct to me, such as envy and jealousy. In common conversation we use these two words as synonyms, but in fact they have distinct meanings: jealousy is the desire to possess something belonging to someone else, while envy is the desire to dispossess someone else of something he rightfully has.[6] The middle-aged man who buys an expensive lawn tractor for his half-acre lot in order to keep up with his neighbor suffers from jealousy; the young woman at the prom who fumes with anger upon seeing another girl wearing the identical dress suffers from envy. Jealousy wants what the other has, whereas envy does not want the other to have what I have or at least desire to have. Once I learned the distinct meanings of these two words, I suddenly found my capacity for moral perception dramatically increased precisely because I had acquired the capacity to name envy and jealousy.

These two observations suggest that the modern view of language as instrumental to thought has the relation precisely backward. In fact, thought arises *from* and *within* language.[7] Because we have the gift of language we have the ability to perceive the world as something more than a jumbled mass of indifferent sense data. We speak, therefore we perceive; we perceive, therefore we think. Language provides the deep structure, the grammar, of thought, such that "*a language-view is a worldview*."[8] Moreover, the means by which we acquire facility with language—the stories, poems, and songs that comprise both a culture and its inheritance—carry forward and hand on to future generations the insights of their forbears. This cultural transmission seems to happen even apart from an individuals' conscious acquaintance with particular texts. For example, most American Christians think that the tempting fruit of which Eve ate in the garden was an apple, though it was John Milton's *Paradise Lost*, rather than Genesis, that so identified the fruit of the tree of the knowledge of good and evil. Yet the power of the written texts to transmit culture resides not just in the propositional statements of moral or theme that can be drawn from them, but also in the very structure of the language in which they are written. The existence of multiple tenses in modern English usage suggests *and perpetuates* a very different experience of time than that of the ancient Hebrews, whose language made no distinction in its grammatical structures between past, present, and future actions.[9] In other words, the world *as we experience it* takes shape in and through the language we learn as children as well as the written texts we internalize in our formal and informal education.

One consequence of this view is the frank admission that a world,[10] that is, any given understanding and experience of all that is, "is always preformed by our cultural inheritance."[11] In the language of Clifford Geertz and Paul Ricoeur, our experience of self and world is always symbolically mediated.[12] That is to say, symbols of all kinds, and especially linguistic ones, fill the gap, as it were, between the knower and that which he wishes to know. Language is the medium of thought. The fact that there are no uninterpreted facts, that there is no view from nowhere, has escaped neither Protestants generally nor evangelicals specifically. In the past 40 years, both groups have found the nineteenth-century concept of *worldview*[13] a useful tool for explaining how all understanding begins from presuppositions. Yet the worldview concept is both too cognitive and too conscious to serve as an equivalent of the linguistic mediation that I have been describing. Language shapes thought first and foremost at the precognitive level, and it certainly shapes our worlds by shaping our feelings about our physical and social environment as much as, if not more than, our ideas about those environments. A worldview, therefore, might best be thought of as the product of the attempt to make explicit the world that is implicit in our manner of speaking, singing, and storytelling. If language construes the world for us, a worldview articulates that construal.

Interpretation

Just as human beings are, by nature, language-users, so we are by nature interpreters. Difficulties in understanding did not first arise with the fall of Adam and Eve; from the beginning, human beings have sought to make sense of the world through language.[14] After all, God brought the animals to Adam "to see what he would call them" (Gen 2:19 ESV).[15] As finite, rational, linguistic creatures, all of our understanding comes by interpretation, and no understanding comes to us that is not already an interpretation. We are born into times, places, and languages not of our choosing, and with them we inherit entire traditions of interpretation, of human world-making.[16] With these traditions come worlds that are ready for our inhabitation, as well as horizons that limit our point of view. So our historicity both locates us, thereby giving us a standpoint from which to perceive, and limits us, with the partiality that necessarily accompanies the very notion of a standpoint. Our finitude thus requires and inspires our interpretive activity. Insofar as human beings are rightly called *Homo sapiens*, it is because we are, far more primordially, *Homo interpretans*.

Interpretation, like breathing, is an activity we constantly perform yet rarely stop to ponder. We typically become aware of our breathing only when it becomes troublesome, when, for example, it becomes too rapid or too shallow, it is obstructed, or it reveals our position in a heated contest of Hide and Seek. So, too, with interpretation: We typically begin thinking about interpretation only when there is a breakdown of interpretation, such as when lawyers debate the meaning of a legal statute, doctors argue over the correct diagnosis in an ambiguous case, or Christians dispute the meaning of "day" in Genesis 1. In such instances, our desire for a simple, obvious, agreed-upon meaning is thwarted, and we find ourselves wondering why one person understood the meaning this way and another that. Ideally, such disruptions force us to look inward and consider our own process of interpretation: Which features of the text give rise to my interpretation? Why do I privilege those features over some others? Which factors outside the text shape what I notice, and what I overlook, within a text? In seeking the answers to such questions, we enter the field of hermeneutics, or the disciplined reflection on the nature and practice of interpretation.

Ironically, the word *interpretation* can have many meanings. In popular usage, "interpretation" often serves as an accusation, as in "That's just your interpretation." When people use "interpretation" in this way, they seem to mean something like this: "That's an unfounded and biased opinion that I need not take very seriously." Such usage is at once insightful and disturbing. On the one hand, this statement grasps something of the necessarily partial character of interpretation; on the other hand, it refuses to apply this insight to the speaker's own interpretation. My position, this statement implies, is certain knowledge, while yours is, by contrast, *mere* interpretation. In other words, such a statement indicates the speaker's refusal to make the leap from interpretation to hermeneutics, from an awareness of a conflict of interpretations to serious reflection (and self-scrutiny) about what separates better from worse interpretations.

A more satisfying meaning for the word *interpretation* harkens back-to-basic practices first learned at a school desk and in the pew: Interpretation is the activity of identifying and articulating the meaning of the written signs (i.e., words) which comprise a text. It is the process of moving from the answer to one question—"What does this say?"—toward the answer to another—"What does this mean?" The pursuit of the answer to the first question is called *textual-sense interpretation*. It involves, at a minimum, basic competence in the language of the text and enough life experience to have some familiarity with the kinds of things described by the text. So, for example, a reader of Genesis 16 (in which Abram tries to fulfill God's promise of a child by sleeping, at his wife Sarai's suggestion, with their servant Hagar) in English translation would need to have a functional command of the English language. But linguistic competence alone proves insufficient when upon arriving at verse 4: "And he went in to Hagar, and she conceived." The ease with which most of us normally read this sentence can obscure what is involved in understanding what it says. The first clause is a circumlocution; without more knowledge than linguistic competence, a reader would have no way of knowing what Abram entered, or what such an entrance had to do with the conception mentioned in the second clause. Moreover, the second clause centers upon a verb with at least two distinct meanings: Does "conceive" here refer to the grasping of an idea or the fertilization of a human egg by a sperm? Clearly something more than a reading knowledge of English is required, namely, a basic familiarity with the way in which humans reproduce and the creative ways that human beings have invented for speaking modestly about sexual acts.

Having grasped the sense of this sentence, an earnest reader would likely find himself beset by an entirely new set of questions: Why were children so important to Abram and Sarai? Why was Sarai so willing to share Abram with another wife? And why was Hagar so contemptuous of Sarai once the servant realized she was pregnant? These questions follow hard on the heels of the establishment of the sense of Genesis 16, and yet they are not addressed directly by the text. Rather, these questions arise from the historical distance between us and this ancient book. Presumably the author did not feel the need to answer these questions because the answers would have been obvious to others who shared his language and his culture. Those of us who read this text in a different language more than two millennia later, however, do not have the same basic assumptions about polygamy and procreation that characterized the ancient Near East in general and the ancient Hebrews in particular. Therefore, in order to go beyond the sense of the words and begin to approach their meaning, we find ourselves in need of some historical and cultural background on ancient beliefs and practices related to marriage and family. Knowing a bit about the shame attached to female infertility in that time and place and about the economic and social importance of descendants in a herding society helps answer the "why?" questions that the text would otherwise leave unanswered. Thus a textual-sense interpretation needs the assistance of historical research when confronted with a text for a distant time or place.

Text and Reader

This combination of interpretive approaches is commonly called *grammatical-historical interpretation.* Its goal is to grasp the author's intention in writing the work or to hear the text as the original audience would have heard it.[17] Evangelical biblical interpretation, on the whole, strongly emphasizes this kind of reading, and with good reason: Close attention to the linguistic features of the text combined with an awareness of cultural difference yield a disciplined effort to take the text seriously, to help prevent an imposition of a totally foreign meaning onto a text. Any tradition—secular or theological, ancient or modern—that regards some text or texts as authoritative will make use of such methods for resisting the all-too-human impulse to read our own ideas into someone else's words. However, this respect for the historical distance between the reader and the text also creates significant interpretive difficulties. While grammatical-historical reading proves helpful in establishing what *was said* in an ancient text, it is not always as helpful determining what that same text *is saying* to us today.[18] Herein lies the source of the painful difficulty, witnessed so often in Bible studies and sermons, of moving from the meaning of a text to its application. Grammatical-historical tools cannot help us bridge the gap between ancient meaning and present application because the tools themselves are sometimes designed to enlarge that gap, not close it.

Fortunately, Scripture itself gives us models of reading Scripture that move us beyond this interpretive impasse. The New Testament is full of examples of early Christians wrestling with the meaning of the Hebrew Scriptures, yet they rarely exhibit the kind of disjunction between meaning and application that is so familiar to us. Take, for example, Paul's interpretation of Genesis 16 in Gal 4:22–5:1. The apostle begins by simply recounting the fact that Abraham had two sons, Ishmael and Isaac, by two different women, Hagar and Sarah. But this reading takes an unexpected turn when Paul effortlessly declares, "Now this may be interpreted allegorically." *Allegory* literally means "to say one thing while saying another," so to interpret allegorically is to find something else which the text is saying *in addition to* or *by way of* its textual sense.[19] For Paul, that "something else" is a meaning that could hardly have been intended by the human author of Genesis 16: "These women are two covenants." Thus Paul, while never denying the grammatical-historical meaning, hears in this ancient text a reference to events in his own day, namely, the establishment of a new covenant in Christ, one that supplants the covenants made with Abraham and Moses. After comparing the old covenant (that is, Judaism and its Scriptures) to Hagar and the new covenant (that is, the church and its gospel) to Sarah, Paul concludes as follows: "Now you, brothers, like Isaac, are children of promise. . . . So, brothers, we are not children of the slave but of the free woman." In other words, Paul sees in Genesis 16 a reference to the two communities of his own day which vied for the right to be called God's covenant people, the people to whom the Old Testament is addressed. This application of Genesis 16 arises naturally out of the text because Paul does not admit a rigid distinction between the original meaning of the text and its contemporary application. Rather, he affirms both the grammatical-historical and a fuller reading as possible meanings. For the apostle, the ancient words of Scripture still speak to us in our present circumstance, and in doing so, the significance of these texts extends well beyond the conscious intentions of their human authors.[20]

Put differently, Paul's example suggests that textual-sense interpretation and grammatical-historical interpretation, for all of their many virtues, ignore altogether the contribution that the interpreter makes to the experience of meaning.[21] A third option, however, promises to take both text and interpreter seriously as cocontributors to the production of meaning. *Performance interpretation*, as in reading a poem or other text aloud with appropriate feeling or playing a musical score on an instrument, requires the existence of a text or score, as well as an instrument with which to bring it to life, whether the voice or the violin. Performance interpretation can be distinguished from other forms of interpretation by its aims. Whereas textual-sense interpretation aims at fixing the propositional meaning of a text, thereby rendering it passive and silent, and grammatical-historical interpretation seeks to recover the meaning intended by the author, thereby amplifying (wittingly or not) the historical chasm between reader and text, performance interpretation seeks to bring a text to life, to restore its voice, to allow it to speak in the present. The practice of oral or dramatic interpretation assumes that human language is meant to be heard rather than read, and such interpretation aims at making the meaning of the text *present* rather than certain or clear. Similarly, musical interpretation is about performance, about taking a script (or, in this case, score) and bringing it to life. By analogy, then, the goal of reading, understood as performance interpretation, is to embody the text and, in so doing, participate in its meaning-making, and therefore in its meaning.[22] While this analogy suggests that texts of all kinds await performers to bring their silent signs to life, it also places a primacy on the authority of the text to direct our performances, particularly when reading the inspired text of Holy Scripture. Orchestras without scores produce little more than noise.

There are least two senses in which the interpretation of Scripture may be thought of as a performance. First, the act of reading, in which all interpretation gets its start, is much more like performance than analysis and explication. This was especially true in the ancient world. In order to demonstrate this point, consider an ancient manuscript of the Bible:

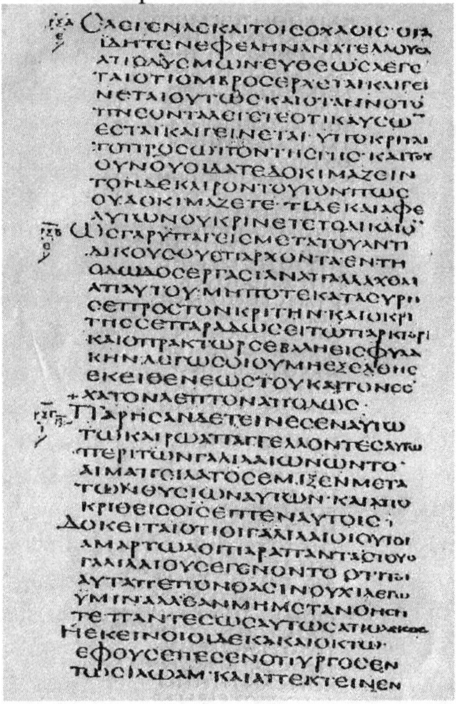

This is a page from one of the oldest and most complete copies of the Bible in existence: the Codex Alexandrinus, now housed in the British Library in London. Notice how different these pages look compared to those of the Bibles with which we are familiar: There are no chapter or verse divisions, no section headings, no paragraph breaks, no punctuation or capitalization, and no spaces between words! This style of writing is called *scriptio continua*, or continuous script. The vellum, or calfskin, on which texts were written in the late ancient and early medieval world was extremely expensive, so *scriptio continua* was a way of fitting as much text as possible onto one page. Moreover, in order to further maximize the use of the page, certain letters have been omitted from the text, and those omissions have been indicated by a system of notation that resembles dots and apostrophes.

What is it like to try to read such a text? Given the lack of visual aids to help the reader organize all of these letters into words, phrases, clauses, sentences, and still larger units of meaning, it made the experience of reading different than what modern readers experience. Unless the reader already was quite familiar with the text, he would have to sound it out, vocalizing small bits at a time until he identified the proper breaks between words and between thoughts. Due in large part to the absence of modern conventions of textual presentation, silent reading was virtually unheard of in the Western world until the eleventh century.[23] In former times reading was, therefore, an audible experience, regardless whether one was reading to himself or being read to by others.

Though the developments in the visual presentation of texts have changed dramatically over the centuries, reading still remains a performance for silent readers today: The text still requires activation by the reader. Its meaning potential depends upon readers who can restore its voice, either mentally and silently or physically and audibly. I have been reminded of this dependence throughout my 20 years of teaching literature in four different academic institutions, especially when I work with students who do not "get" their assigned reading for class. Even though my students all read the same ink spots on the same pages, they have very different reading experiences. Some struggle to follow the plot of Homer's *Odyssey*, while others are swept away not only by its plot but also by its ability to speak profoundly about the glory, the shame, and the fragility of the human condition. Some can explain the sense of a sentence from Augustine's *Confessions* but cannot begin to articulate its meaning, while others wrestle profoundly with not only its meaning but also its implications for their own lives. The range of responses in my classroom says more about my students (and their teacher) than about the works of literature we read; after all, the *Odyssey* and the *Confessions* have been teaching, delighting, and moving readers for centuries. Nonetheless, the impotence of Homer and Augustine before the poorly prepared or stubbornly resistant student demonstrates just how dependent texts are on readers to activate their meaning potential.

At the same time, we must also acknowledge that great works of literature, philosophy, and theology (especially, but not exclusively) have a history of producing extraordinary transformative effects on readers. Augustine's *Confessions* tells the story of the saint's youth and adulthood through his reading: the books he read, how he read them, and what effect they had on him. In narrating his own intellectual and spiritual development, Augustine goes out of his way to consider in some detail how he was shaped by each of the following works, or sets of works: Cicero's *Hortensius*, the Old Testament, Aristotle's *Categories*, Manichaean books, Platonic books, Paul's epistles, and Genesis. I, too, can tell the story of my life with reference to the books that, in addition to the Bible, had a significant impact on me: Heller's *Catch-22* in my youth, Homer's *Odyssey* and Milton's *Paradise Lost* in college, Aristotle's *Ethics* and Augustine's *Confessions* in adulthood. Each of these works played a decisive role in shaping my world, enabling me to perceive and imagine more than I had been able to before. Granted, the power of books to occasion such personal transformation has, at times, been a cause of concern in the Western tradition. This worry surfaces not only among unimaginative defenders of the status quo but even within literature itself, as two famous protagonists of the European novel, Don Quixote and Emma Bovary, testify. Moreover, Jerome and Augustine both worried a good deal over how their pagan literary educations had misshapen their souls. Nonetheless, the power of certain kinds of reading experiences to transform us, whether for good or for ill, is beyond doubt. While texts may be dependent on readers and impotent without them, readers who take their reading seriously make themselves most vulnerable, and willingly so. Perhaps this willingness to be transformed by what we read is a second way in which we might engage in performance interpretation: "The text's reality lies in our keeping it alive, in 'testifying' or 'witnessing' its truth through our own actions. . . . [U]nderstanding means assuming responsibility to make the text speak again with power to affect present action."[24] This participatory understanding of textual meaning should surprise no student of Scripture, since the Epistle of James admonishes us to "be doers of the word, and not hearers only" (1:22).

Conclusion

Paul Ricoeur has helpfully described the task of interpretation as a dynamic interaction between text and reader that oscillates between two poles: explanation and understanding.[25] In explanation, the interpreter seeks to account for the objective facts of the text, both linguistically and historically. Here is where close reading, philological analysis, and historical research play a role. In understanding, the interpreter submits himself to the formative power of the text to shape his world; he begins to entertain not just the question of what *was said* but also what the text *is saying* now about my world. Enriched understanding leads the interpreter deeper into the text, which then results in a newly refreshed understanding of the world, and so on. This is Ricoeur's version of the hermeneutic circle, but it is not a vicious circle. In fact, it is virtuous, for it depends on and encourages the formation of particular intellectual virtues within us. Elsewhere, Ricoeur has memorably remarked that this reciprocal dynamic within the activity of interpretation springs from a "double motivation: willingness to suspect, willingness to listen; vow of rigor, vow of obedience."[26] Interpretation teaches us to take the text seriously and to scrutinize it closely, to test it and allow it to test us.

Insofar as Christians have taken up the calling to read in this manner, it is likely due to a profound awareness of our own need for transformation by the Word. Moreover, we know that in order to read rightly, we have to have eyes to see and ears to hear. The fourth-century church father Athanasius once said that "anyone who wishes to understand the mind of the sacred writers must first cleanse his own life, and approach the saints by copying their deeds."[27] Piety and intellect are mutually supportive endeavors: As Union University's motto would have it, *religio et eruditio*.

Growing in the Christian life aids our understanding, but similarly, the life of the mind feeds the life of Christian discipleship. Our resort to texts of all kinds to aid us in the pursuit of God says much about our confidence that wherever words are spoken, the Word may be found. As Dietrich Bonhoeffer has said, "Because man has a logos, God meets him in the Logos, who speaks and is himself the Word."[28] No wonder, then, that Christians are such bookish people.

Questions for Further Reflection

1. Is it important that Christians remain a "bookish people"? How can Christians remain committed to the Book if it means that interpretive clashes will ensue? Is this a good or bad result? Why or why not?
2. Does the acquisition of new ideas impact the ability of an individual to understand reality at a deeper and more profound level? If so, does this change the way they think about the world? Does it influence their behavior in any way? If so, how?
3. Does language impact experience? If so, how? With an increase of language, does the person change or does the world change? Explain your answer.
4. Is there any scenario where there is such a thing as "an uninterpreted fact"? Is it really possible to have an "original" thought? Why or why not?
5. Are breakdowns in interpretation inevitable? If so, is that a good or bad result? What do interpretive breakdowns signal to the professor/student seeking understanding and unity across academic disciplines?
6. Can one interpretation of any given text be universally regarded as correct? If so, what process is involved to arrive at such a conclusion?
7. How can the university be a place where both explanation and understanding grow even if this means disagreement of interpretations across various areas of academic thought? Is part of the duty of Christian universities to attempt to reconcile differences of interpretation? Why or why not?

Resources for Further Study

Dockery, David S. *Biblical Interpretation Then and Now*. Grand Rapids: Baker, 1992.

Guthrie, George. *Read the Bible for Life*. Nashville: B&H, 2011.

Lundin, Roger, ed. *Hermeneutics: Interpretation in Christian Perspective*. Grand Rapids: Eerdmans, 1997.

Naugle, David. *Worldview: The History of a Concept*. Grand Rapids: Eerdmans, 2002.

Ricoeur, Paul. *Interpretation Theory: Discourse and the Surplus of Meaning*. Fort Worth, TX: Texas Christian University Press, 1976.

Smith, James K. A. *The Fall of Interpretation: Philosophical Foundations for a Creational Hermeneutic*. Downers Grove, IL: InterVarsity, 2000.

Endnotes

[1] The fact that the Bible as *object* is central in the lives of American Christians does not necessarily mean that the Bible's *content* is either well known or well heeded. See George H. Guthrie, *Read the Bible for Life: Your Guide to Understanding and Living God's Word* (Nashville: B&H, 2011), 6–13.

[2] Codex is the technical term for the material form of what we now call books: paper folded, cut, stitched, and bound between two hard covers.

[3] See David B. Barrett, George T. Kurian, and Todd M. Johnson, eds., *World Christian Encyclopedia: A Comparative Survey of Churches and Religions in the Modern World*, 2nd ed. (New York: Oxford University Press, 2001), 1:16–18.

[4] Of course, interpretation can be directed toward nonlinguistic objects, as well, e.g., a strange phenomenon in the sky, a painting, a sequence of events, but in each case, we will have to make use of language to assay and explain the meaning of these things. Thus linguistic texts will be the privileged focus here.

[5] In this exercise, a person might object that wordless images came to mind. But wordless images fall short of thought. Otherwise, why would tyrants in the ancient world value interpreters of dreams like Joseph and Daniel? Or why we would we, in the modern world, pay psychologists to help us decode our dreams?

[6] See, e.g., Thomas Aquinas, *Summa Theologiae* II-II.36.1–4.

[7] A striking corollary to this statement: Our ability to think with subtlety and clarity is determined, in large part, by the richness of our vocabularies. This provides yet another reason why we should lament the demise of reading, especially among young people.

[8] Hans-Georg Gadamer, *Truth and Method*, trans. Joel Weinsheimer and Donald G. Marshall, 2nd rev. ed. (New York: Continuum, 1996), 442 (emphasis his).

[9] Bruce K. Waltke and Michael P. O'Connor, *An Introduction to Biblical Hebrew Syntax* (Winona Lake, IN: Eisenbrauns, 1990), 458–61.

[10] Hereafter, whenever I use the world "world," I will follow the use of Heidegger and Gadamer, for whom *world* means our "being-in-the-world," i.e., our experience of the world within which we already have a place and an orientation as opposed to a world which we find ourselves standing over against. "World," then, stands for the indissoluble combination of the objective universe and our

subjective perception of it. As such, it refuses to think of the world as something merely objective or merely subjective. In this it shares much with the more common notion of "worldview," though it is decidedly and deliberately less cognitive (see below).

[11] John Milbank, *The Word Made Strange: Theology, Language, Culture* (London: Blackwell, 1997), 126.

[12] See, e.g., Paul Ricoeur, *From Text to Action: Essays in Hermeneutics II*, trans. Kathleen Blamey and John B. Thompson (Evanston, IL: Northwestern University Press, 1991), 194ff.

[13] Though this concept has come to be nearly inseparable from evangelical thought, the word was coined by the German philosopher Immanuel Kant and championed early by both Romantics and Marxists in the nineteenth and early twentieth centuries. It shows up in theological discourse relatively late. For a sketch of the origin and development of this term, see David K. Naugle, *Worldview: The History of a Concept* (Grand Rapids: Eerdmans, 2002).

[14] For a sustained theological and philosophical argument that the interpretive character of our knowing is a result of our creaturely finitude and not of our fall into sin, see James K. A. Smith, *The Fall of Interpretation: Philosophical Foundations for a Creational Hermeneutic* (Downers Grove, IL: InterVarsity Press, 2000).

[15] All Scripture references are to the English Standard Version (ESV).

[16] Cf. C. S. Lewis: "Every age has its own outlook. It is specially good at seeing certain truths and specially liable to make certain mistakes. . . . All contemporary writers share to some extent the contemporary outlook—even those, like myself, who seem most opposed to it." From his "Introduction" to St. Athanasius, *On the Incarnation of the Word of God* (Crestwood, NY: St. Vladimir's Seminary Press, 1944), 4–5.

[17] Though the former goal is the most common way, among evangelicals, of describing the aim of grammatical-historical interpretation, it is not free of either conceptual or practical difficulties; see William K. Wimsatt and Monroe C. Beardsley, "The Intentional Fallacy," *Sewanee Review* 54 (1946): 468–88. For a vigorous defense of authorial intention as the goal of interpretation, see E. D. Hirsch, *Validity in Interpretation* (New Haven: Yale University Press, 1967).

[18] See John R. W. Stott, *Between Two Worlds* (Grand Rapids: Eerdmans, 1982); also, Gadamer, *Truth and Method*, 307–11. Also see the helpful discussion in David S. Dockery, *Biblical Interpretation Then and Now* (Grand Rapids: Baker, 1992), 168–83.

[19] For a Protestant defense of the allegorical interpretation of Scripture, see David C. Steinmetz, "The Superiority of Pre-Critical Exegesis," *Theology Today* 37, no. 1 (April 1980): 27–38; also David S. Dockery, "The History of Pre-Critical Biblical Interpretation," *Faith and Mission* 10 (1992): 3–33.

[20] In saying that the meaning of a Scriptural text may exceed the intention of its human author, I am, of course, leaving open the possibility that such meanings may be fully within the intention of Scripture's divine Author. For additional ways of accounting for the possibility of plural meanings in Scripture, see Scott Huelin, "Toward a Theological Ontology of Textual Meaning," *Christian Scholar's Review* 34 (2005): 217–33; also see David S. Dockery, "Author? Reader? Text? Toward a Hermeneutical Synthesis," *Theological Educator* 38

(1988): 7–16; and Dockery, "The Value of Typological Exegesis," in *Restoring the Prophetic Mantle*, ed. George Klein (Nashville: B&H, 1992), 161–78.

[21] See, e.g., Nicholas Wolterstorff, "The Importance of Hermeneutics for a Christian Worldview," in *Disciplining Hermeneutics: Interpretation in Christian Perspective*, ed. Roger Lundin (Grand Rapids: Eerdmans, 1997), 25–47, esp. 42–44. See also Gadamer, *Truth and Method*, 242–64.

[22] For a concise but suggestive exploration of this analogy, see Merold Westphal, "Post-Kantian Reflections on the Importance of Hermeneutics," in Lundin, *Disciplining Hermeneutics*, 57–66, esp. 59–61.

[23] The classic statement of this position comes from Paul Saenger, *The Space between Words: the Origins of Silent Reading* (Stanford: Stanford University Press, 1997). The only extant witnesses to silent reading before the 11th century are found in Euripides's *Hippolytus* (856–65) and Augustine's *Confessions* (6.3.3), and even these are controversial.

[24] Donald Marshall, "Truth, Universality, and Interpretation," in Lundin, *Disciplining Hermeneutics*, 83.

[25] Paul Ricoeur, *Interpretation Theory: Discourse and the Surplus of Meaning* (Fort Worth: Texas Christian University Press, 1976), chap. 4.

[26] Paul Ricoeur, *Freud and Philosophy* (New Haven: Yale University Press, 1970), 27.

[27] Athanasius, *On the Incarnation of the Word of God*, 57.

[28] Dietrich Bonhoeffer, *Christ the Center*, trans. Edwin Robertson (San Francisco: HarperCollins, 1978), 49.

10

The Study of History

James A. Patterson

The Past Is Prologue

As a high school junior, I absolutely dreaded a state-mandated course in American history from the colonial period through the Civil War. While some of my friends ended up with athletic coaches teaching their sections, I faced a year with the notorious "W. W. B."—a.k.a. Walter W. Belfield. So instead of relatively easy tasks like memorizing lists of presidents and the dates of key events, I reluctantly geared myself up for several months of challenging essay tests, research papers, and general emotional and intellectual distress. Several acquaintances who were seniors comforted me with statements that Mr. Belfield, who held a master's in international law and diplomacy from Tufts University, was one of the toughest instructors in our school.

On the very first day of class, W. W. B. distributed a handout entitled "Introduction to intelligent study of history"; we knew immediately that this man meant business and that we could not slide and glide through this course. Furthermore, he was not a sports fan so we could not anticipate wasting time in Monday classes reviewing our weekend high school football game or the previous day's NFL scores. Although I had sat in several social studies courses through eighth grade and a world history class as a high school freshman, I was not prepared for the rigorous approach to historical study that Belfield demanded. In fact, his initial hand-out offered this radical notion: "History and its many scenes fit together like a puzzle if properly studied. Learning to understand it is not easy and requires much practice and constant effort. It is hoped that will be your endeavor throughout this course. So we might grasp the deeper meaning of history, enjoy the rich heritage of the future with pride and intelligence."[1] It was apparent after day one that this bright young teacher was expecting us to work, study, and even think!

Nevertheless, my own professional future was directly affected by what turned out to be two years of study with W. W. B. I enjoyed the junior-year class so much that I signed up to take his honors section of American history from Reconstruction to the 1960s in my senior year. As a result of my courses with Mr. Belfield, I began to grasp that history was much more than simply a factual record of the past; indeed, I gradually sharpened my analytical and critical thinking skills as I realized that the bare data of history needed to be interpreted, explained, and evaluated. Overall, I gained a sensitivity for historical insight, perspective, and context that has served me well to this day.

Although my high school experience profoundly shaped my love and appreciation for the historical enterprise, I was pretty clueless about any possible relationship between it and my then immature Christian faith. As an undergraduate political science major, I did not spend much time agonizing over how to connect faith and history. In addition, some of the other courses of study that I pursued in college did not seem to lend themselves very readily to integration with a Christian worldview (e.g., calculus). It was not until my M.Div. courses and Ph.D. seminars in church history that I came to recognize the close intersections between Christianity and history. Moreover, early in my doctoral studies I joined the Conference on Faith and History, a professional organization founded in 1967 by Christian historians who sought to explore the relationship of their faith to historical studies. CFH meetings and articles in the journal *Fides et Historia* provided much food for thought in matters relating to historiography, pedagogy, and philosophies of history.[2]

In 30-plus years of teaching American, Western, and ecclesiastical history courses in Christian institutions, I have reflected long and hard about both the worth of history as an academic discipline and its correlation with Christian faith and thought. I have had the joy and privilege of sharing my ideas with several generations of students at both the undergraduate and graduate levels.

What follows represents a distillation of my thinking about the fundamental issues that link history and faith.

Why Study History?

A preliminary apologetic for the inherent value of historical study can be constructed on more or less secular grounds. In other words, both believers and nonbelievers can profit from knowledge of the past. Just as in the natural order of things it rains upon the just and the unjust (Matt 5:45), recorded history is accessible to all who are inclined to read and ponder it. Within the realm of God's common grace, special revelation is not essential in order to mine valuable treasures from archives, biographies, chronicles, or other historical resources that typically are featured in the systematic study of the past. As a matter of fact, several benefits of history can be enumerated for students regardless of their religious convictions.

First, exposure to history contributes to the entire process whereby an individual in the modern world becomes educated. It is true that history was not one of the seven traditional liberal arts; it actually matured rather late as a distinct and recognized discipline or profession.[3] Nevertheless, current cultural and societal expectations suggest that a truly educated person will have studied history in some format. Hence, most states require that high school graduates successfully complete some history courses. Likewise, most institutions of higher learning include at least some classes in the history of Western or world civilizations as part of their general core curriculum requirements. Furthermore, many academic departments in colleges and universities offer or even require a course or two in the history of its discipline, such as the history of art or the history of education. It is difficult if not impossible to go through the American educational system without some prescribed study of history. The skeptic, of course, could respond by challenging the legitimacy of cultural and educational norms, but that would ultimately be a useless battle. Additionally, there are other more substantive reasons to study history beyond the reality that "it's required."

Second, history is an undeniably necessary ingredient in the formation of individual and corporate identity. People who ignore their pasts or who suffer from amnesia find it extremely tough to function effectively in part because they do not really know who they are. In a similar manner, institutions and even nations must ascertain their identities through a familiarity with what has unfolded over significant stretches of time. Identity thus leans heavily on memories of past events and experiences, which may help to explain why so many individuals and families in our day are keenly interested in genealogy. An informed historical sense—personal or collective—expands and sharpens memory, which in turn establishes identity on a more reliable and meaningful foundation. So the study of history offers a very practical incentive: it may help people or groups to avoid identity confusion and to cultivate a proper sense of place in our complex modern world.

The history-memory-identity alliance, however, can occasionally reveal some cracks, which imply that caution flags are in order. For instance, human nature is such that our memories are not always trustworthy. A few years ago Joseph Bottum, editor of *First Things*, commented on the pitfalls of utilizing memory for autobiographical purposes: "Memory may be our best tool for self-understanding, but only when we remember how weak a tool it really is: prone to warping under the narrative drive of storytelling, vulnerable to self-interest, susceptible to outside influence."[4] Moreover, simple historical recollections do not automatically guarantee sound explanations or interpretations of the past. On the other hand, faulty and incomplete memories should be a positive spur to deeper and more comprehensive historical explorations.

Third, historical literacy nurtures and reinforces cultural literacy. As social and cultural historians well know, human cultures develop over time; the ideas, values, customs, behavior patterns, social forms, and artistic expressions of a people are, for the most part, historically conditioned. Culture cannot be examined under a microscope or studied in a vacuum. In other words, no society is completely static; historical contexts, therefore, must be taken into account to provide a full picture of cultural activity and change. For this reason, students need historical knowledge to understand their own cultures and other cultures around the globe.

Historical and cultural literacy in due course instill in their possessors the virtues of sympathy and humility. In that regard, historical study functions in many ways like travel. Students who read a good deal of history will inevitably gain new outlooks that will be similar to the ones attained by those who study abroad or participate in an extended overseas mission trip. These kinds of endeavors tend to undermine provincialism and ethnocentrism. Consistent exposure to history and international cultures also help students become more alert to the sometimes myopic suppositions of our own time. It was primarily for this reason that the British apologist and writer C. S. Lewis (1898–1963), in a widely quoted assertion, strongly encouraged the study of history and especially the reading of old books:

> Most of all, perhaps, we need intimate knowledge of the past. Not that the past has any magic about it, but because we cannot study the future, and yet need something to set against the present, to remind us that the basic assumptions have been quite different in different periods and that much which seems certain to the uneducated is merely temporary fashion. A man who has lived in many places is not likely to be deceived by the local errors of his native village; the scholar has lived in many times and is therefore in some degree immune from the great cataract of nonsense that pours from the press and microphone of his own age.[5]

By placing such a high premium on historical perspective, this distinguished literary scholar astutely verified that an earnest study of the past yields dividends for those beyond the guild of professional historians.

Fourth, the track record of history provides a vast quantity of information about human experience that suggests useful applications to the present. To paraphrase the sage words of Western intellectuals like Edmund Burke and George Santayana, those who ignore history are very likely to duplicate its mistakes. While this sentiment can be pushed in fatalistic directions, it still stands as a realistic comment on the human condition. At the same time, history is full of notable achievements that can supply more positive models for decisions and actions today. Overall, perceptive students of the past will learn to cherish a careful scrutiny of both the wisdom and folly that surface in the pages of history.

The historians of ancient Greece and Rome, who shaped the earliest traditions of Western historiography, seemed particularly drawn toward the teaching function of the past. For them, history offered up instruction for moral and professional improvement, chiefly for those in leadership positions.[6] While this lesson-dominated approach to the past has fallen into disfavor with most modern historians, it rightfully seeks to draw attention to the many teachable moments that historical study furnishes.

Fifth, an awareness of history usually makes for better citizens, especially for those who live in countries like the United States with a tradition of representative government. Historically informed voters, for example, will likely be more discerning and less susceptible to overly emotional appeals than those who are ignorant of the past. Likewise, the citizen who knows the historical background of contemporary issues and events should have a better handle on them—and should be in a better position to propose workable solutions. Since responsible and informed citizens, moreover, often assume leadership roles in government or society, the value of historical perspective can thus be magnified. In any field of service, it appears that the best leaders are those who have had some training in the historical enterprise.

Finally, students of history soon discover that the practitioners of the discipline can produce enjoyable literature. Historical scholarship does not have to be dry or boring, and some professional historical scholars have mastered the art of writing colorful narratives in an engaging style. Historian David McCullough's excellent tomes, for example, have drawn a sizable readership from the general public, not just from a narrow circle of specialists.[7] Most people do not take history courses after their formal education is completed; a lifetime of good reading, however, awaits those who pursue less structured historical study.

Christians no doubt can embrace the foregoing rationale for the study of history, even if they might employ a different angle of vision on some of the points. For example, the benefits of history for cultural awareness and sensitivity have special meaning for Christian missionaries ministering in a culture different from their own, or for committed saints trying to understand the proper relationship between the Bible and tradition. For those believers, however, who remain unconvinced about the merits of historical study, they might find motivation in the words of Caleb Evans, an English Baptist pastor and educator from the late eighteenth century:

> The study of history is one of the most improving as well as entertaining studies the human mind can be engaged in. It extends our views, elevates our minds, blots out our narrow prejudices, and from a just and comprehensive view of the past, enables us to improve and enjoy the present moment and prepare for the future. . . . Every Christian ought to be a good historian, and if his knowledge of history be improved by

> him as it ought, the better historian he is, the better Christian he will be.[8]

Whether or not Evans was correct to imply that historical studies aid sanctification, his ringing endorsement of history's usefulness for believers certainly stands in continuity with Christian attitudes and practices through the centuries. The testimonies of both the Scriptures and church history underscore the reality that Christian faith and history share a close bond and an intrinsic compatibility.

History and the Judeo-Christian Tradition

The Old Testament

The Bible consistently incorporates historical accounts into its content and also witnesses to the long-term significance of past events. In the Old Testament, many of the narratives highlight Yahweh, the God of Israel who repeatedly acts within space and time to judge, rescue, or redeem. Hence, modern scholars in the field of Old Testament theology sometimes focus on God's "mighty" or "saving" acts as a central motif in their work.[9] In that framework, it is impressive how frequently the Old Testament calls on the people of God to remember what Yahweh has done for them. Indeed, one of the principal festivals in ancient Israel was the Passover (Exod 12:14–28), which afforded the opportunity to rehearse in vivid ways God's mighty deeds when He judged the Egyptians and delivered His people from bondage.

Furthermore, covenant renewal functions in part as a history lesson for the Jewish people. When Joshua gathers the Israelites at Shechem following their victories in Canaan to remember certain things about the Lord and His past actions (Joshua 24), the elderly leader of the conquest summarizes God's saving exploits by answering questions that modern historians still pose about the past—who, where, what, how, and why. Later, Israel continues to recall the formative stages of her history in both worship and prophecy (e.g., Psalm 78; Isaiah 63). In short, historical memories of God's redemptive work serve a very important purpose in the shaping of Israel's identity.

Israel's continual recollections that God performed specific things at distinct points in time also point to a unique characteristic of Hebrew historiography. Unlike the other cultures of the ancient world, the Israelites viewed history as linear; in other words, events occurred in a meaningful sequence of past-present-future because God ultimately controlled how and where history was going. Therefore, the historical process was not chaotic or cyclical, as the worldview of some other ancient civilizations clearly implied. The genius of the Hebrew philosophy of history was that it combined linear progress with an eschatological expectation—revealed though the prophets—that at some future point God would send His Messiah, and a golden age of peace and blessing would follow. Israel's hope, then, was in the kingdom still to come, not in a lost period of past glory.[10]

At the same time, the Old Testament devotes a hefty amount of space to the historical actions of human beings. Whether in the patriarchal narratives, the extensive material on the Israelite monarchy, or the compelling stories about personalities like Gideon or Ruth, the Old Testament expresses genuine interest in the lives of individuals, as well as the errors or contributions that they made. Thus divine sovereignty and human responsibility work together in the ways that God carries out His purposes. Even the feats of pagan rulers factor into the divine plan; for instance, the Persian Emperor Cyrus the Great is referred to by the prophet Isaiah as the Lord's "anointed" (Isa 45:1) because of his role in freeing the Jews from their captivity in Babylon. Human history, then, figures prominently in the Old Testament, pointing to another reason for Christians today to value knowledge of the past.

The New Testament

In the New Testament, even a cursory reading shows a pervasive interest in history. The New Testament obviously makes no sense at all apart from the birth, life, death, resurrection, and ascension of Jesus Christ. When the Gospel of John proclaims that "the Word became flesh and made his dwelling among us" (1:14 NIV),[11] it implies that God took history seriously enough to enter it—in space and time—in the person of His Son. In fact, church history has demonstrated the vital link between the doctrine of the Incarnation and concern for history. Those like the early church Gnostics who evaded the historical life of Jesus typically did not give much attention, as a rule, to history in general.[12] The pages of New Testament also reveal conscious reflection on historical method, at least by Luke the Evangelist. In the introduction to his Gospel, he notes his (1) use of eyewitnesses in attesting to the events that he recorded; (2) careful investigation of his sources; and (3) desire for an orderly account of "the things that have been fulfilled among us" (Luke 1:1–3). He likewise indicates a concern to root his Gospel story in the appropriate historical contexts, both Jewish and Roman (e.g., Luke 2:1–5). While he is not as explicit about technique at the start of Acts (1:1–3), the sequel to his Gospel reveals a very similar interest in historical detail and accuracy as he describes the broader setting of the early church in the Greco-Roman world.

The New Testament writers, while recognizing that God had done something new and exceptional in Jesus Christ, plainly accept the Old Testament as part of God's revealed truth. They agree with its authors that history is linear, and they also assimilate the eschatology of the prophets under the rubric of promise and fulfillment. While books like Revelation flesh out the ultimate goal of history more thoroughly than the prophetic and apocalyptic literature of the Old Testament, the witness of the New Testament to God's overarching purposes remains marvelously consistent with the messages of Isaiah, Ezekiel, and Daniel. The continuity between the old and new covenants allows the writers of the New Testament to place Jesus, the Jewish Messiah and only-begotten Son of God, at the very center of history.

The essential unity of redemptive history similarly leads authors like the apostle Paul to emphasize the educational value of the past. After discussing the difficult experiences of his Jewish forebears in the wilderness following the exodus, he makes the point that "these things happened to them as examples and were written down as warnings for us, on whom the fulfillment of the ages has come" (1 Cor 10:11). In another context, Paul mentions a more positive motivation for attentiveness to the past: "For everything that was written in the past was written to teach us, so that through endurance and the encouragement of the Scriptures we might have hope" (Rom 15:4). In like manner, the writer of Hebrews cites several personalities from Old Testament history as worthy exemplars of a genuine faith that was "sure of what we hope for and certain of what we do not see" (Heb 11:1). Although this writer understands the incomplete nature of the Old Testament revelation (Heb 11:39–40), like Paul he is an informed student of its history who readily employs it for didactic purposes.[13]

The Scriptures unquestionably contain overwhelming evidence concerning the value and importance of history. Its authors not only record the past in significant detail; they also utilize it for instructive purposes and fit its various pieces into a larger picture of God's design for the human race. Christians, therefore, can build a case for historical study directly from the Bible. Moreover, the serious Bible student recognizes that it is not enough merely to know biblical content. The Scriptures must be interpreted, and evangelical scholars set forth the grammatical-historical method as the most trustworthy.[14] Since this hermeneutic aims to discover authorial intent and meaning within linguistic and historical contexts, it intimates yet another justification for the study of history—historical knowledge may well enhance understanding of the Bible.

The Apostolic Fathers

In light of Scripture's historical orientation and character, it is not surprising that the Christian intellectual tradition reveals a substantial attraction to history. Fourth-century bishop and theologian Eusebius of Caesarea (c. 263–339) saw the need to compile a lengthy account of the history of the church from the apostolic age to his own. In fact, his *Ecclesiastical History* is the main source for that time period. Utilizing materials from the library of Pamphilus in Caesarea and the royal archives of Emperor Constantine, Eusebius covered much ground, including the doctrinal controversies of his own day. Perhaps his most important innovation was his "imperial theology," which glorified Constantine the Great in almost messianic terms and portrayed the Roman Empire in a way that differed starkly from the picture in John's Apocalypse. In addition, Eusebius projected a providential view of history—assured confidence in discovering the direct hand of God behind historical events—beyond the confines of inspired biblical history into his own time. Hence, Constantine's triumphs over his political and military enemies clearly represented the divine plan and resulted from the emperor's purported godliness and love of virtue.[15] Eusebius' uncritical hagiography and his enthusiastic support for the new church-state relationship that emerged during the reign of Constantine offered an optimistic perspective on the notion of a Christian empire that echoed widely throughout the extraordinary political transitions of the fourth century.[16]

Meanwhile, a more nuanced approach to history and the Roman Empire became evident in the late patristic era with Augustine of Hippo's (354–430) magisterial *City of God*. The Eusebian imperial theology, which seemed to gain confirmation during the reign of Emperor Theodosius I (379–95), faced a major crisis in 410 when the city of Rome was sacked by Gothic barbarians. In the aftershock, pagans began to blame Christianity for the weakening of the empire, pointing out that Christians had failed to honor the traditional state gods. Augustine then responded with a long book that initially set forth an apologetic agenda as he argued that the prosperity of the empire had nothing to do with the worship of pagan deities. The North African bishop subsequently interpreted the decline of the Western empire as an inevitable outcome of the prolonged divergence between the temporal city of man and the eternal city of God (a metaphor echoing the book of Revelation's contrast between Babylon the Great and the New Jerusalem). The two cities, in Augustine's analysis, displayed radically different understandings of faith, hope, and—most important—love:

> . . . [T]wo societies have issued from two kinds of love. Worldly society has flowered from a selfish love which dared to despise even God, whereas the communion of saints is rooted in a love of God that is ready to trample on self. . . . In the city of the world both the rulers themselves and the people they dominate are dominated by the lust for domination; whereas in the City of God all citizens serve one another in charity. . . . [E]ven the wise men in the city of man live according to man. . . . [T]hough some of them have reached a knowledge of God, "they did not glorify him as God or give thanks but became vain in their reasonings, and their senseless minds have been darkened. . . ." In the City of God, on the contrary, there is no merely human wisdom, but there is a piety which worships the true God as He should be worshiped and has as its goal that reward of all holiness whether in the society of saints on earth or in that of angels of heaven, which is "that God may be all in all."[17]

Unlike Eusebius, Augustine's view of human history caused him to connect the Roman Empire to the city of man, as well as to map the unmistakable distance between the two cities. In his theological understanding of history, no Christian emperor could inaugurate a golden age from a political base in the earthly city.

Augustine was not and did not intend to be a historian. His handling of history, however, proved to be pivotal in the Christian intellectual tradition for several reasons. First, his realistic assessment of human depravity meshed with both the biblical witness and with the broader history of the human race. His pessimism about realizing the kingdom of God within history served as a healthy antidote to the triumphalist expectations of Eusebius and other fourth-century thinkers. Second, Augustine charted a course for future Christian historiography by working out the implications of the scriptural perspective on history as linear, providential, and purposeful. His *City of God* thus implied a philosophy of history shaped around the biblical narrative of creation, fall, and redemption. Third, Augustine proposed a division of history into seven discrete periods—corresponding to the days of creation—with the first five ages in the past, the sixth epoch as the present church age, and the seventh as the faithful believers' "Sabbath rest."[18] On a related matter, the learned bishop offered a distinct eschatology or theory of the end times, when the goals of Christians in this life would be fully achieved with the return of Christ and the universal establishment of His rule. Hence, the dualism between the two cities that originated from the fall of Adam and Eve would finally disappear at the end of history. While some features of this Augustinian model would eventually be challenged, it dominated Western Christianity for many centuries.

The Medieval Period

In fact, the Western medieval biographers and chroniclers who wrote most of the history during that era largely followed Augustine's theological and philosophical lead in forming their own historical perspectives. For example, the German abbot and bishop Otto of Freising (c. 1112–58) openly evoked the legacy of Augustine with his *Chronicle or History of the Two Cities*, which he compiled in the 1140s. Otto attempted to write a universal history from Adam until 1146 in which his treatment of the biblical era was reminiscent of Augustine; moreover, he shared Augustine's assumptions that history should be recounted as linear, meaningful, and providential. Otto likewise expressed an eschatology, albeit a much more detailed and apocalyptic one than can be found in Augustine's *City of God*. The twelfth-century cleric anticipated the imminent return of Christ and the end of history, which apparently pushed him into speculation about a soon-to-be-revealed Antichrist.[19]

Another medieval figure from the same century who attempted to combine a philosophy of history with eschatology was the Italian Cistercian abbot and biblical commentator, Joachim of Fiore (c. 1132–1202). A church reformer who eventually had a falling out with the Cistercians, Joachim reduced Augustine's seven periods of history to three, and placed them in a Trinitarian framework. The age of the Father ran from Adam to Isaiah; the age of the Son extended from Isaiah's prophecies until the New Testament period; and the age of the Holy Spirit began with the Italian monk Benedict of Nursia and would continue until the consummation of all things, which Joachim fully expected to happen in his own lifetime. Unlike Augustine or Otto of Freising, Joachim entertained millenial views, which meant that he awaited a post-Antichrist time of blessing when Christ ruled on the earth. Historian Bernard McGinn has observed that Joachim connected his millennial views with his hope that the institutional church of his day would be reformed and spiritualized. Joachim, McGinn contends, moved away from the Augustinian tradition "in his conviction that history was not just an inexorable accumulation of ills until the final and worst of all, Antichrist's persecution, but rather that God's plan included a new and better stage of the church on earth before the dawn of eternity."[20] The Calabrian monk thus added a distinct note of optimism to the inherited medieval consensus about the meaning and direction of history. Furthermore, he functioned somewhat like a lightning bolt, striking what had become a lethargic conception of history with new energy. Unfortunately, he also set the stage for more bizarre prophetical speculations that continue to plague the Christian world even today.

The Reformation

The Protestant Reformation, which marked a significant theological renewal led by giants like Martin Luther (1483–1546) and John Calvin (1509–64), bore rather disappointing historical fruit. Augustinian perspectives still held sway for both Roman Catholics and Protestants, but the church histories that were written by each side could best be characterized as polemical propaganda. Rather than focusing on sound historical methods that ensured accuracy, historians of the Reformation era showed more interest in using history to support or justify their partisan causes.

Perhaps the most famous historical work of the period was John Foxe's (1516–87) *Book of Martyrs*, a massive account of the persecution of Christians from the apostolic age to his own day. While a debate has raged about Foxe's overall historical reliability, he demonstrated a concern for truth and was often critical of the sources that he consulted. At the same time, he was an English Protestant who lived in exile on the continent of Europe during the time when Mary Tudor sought to restore Roman Catholicism to the British Isles. Indeed, some of the most gripping passages in the *Book of Martyrs* are Foxe's vivid descriptions of the executions of such English Reformers as Thomas Cranmer, Hugh Latimer, and Nicholas Ridley. Foxe did not write objective history in the modern sense of the term but clearly identified the heroes and villains. Like his medieval predecessors, he also mingled history and eschatology; he certainly provided ammunition for the widely held Protestant conviction that papal Rome was linked to the forces of Antichrist. Keeping alive the memories of those who died for Christ was likely his greatest service to the church.[21]

The Modern Era

In the modern era, Christian historiography has matured and developed into a respected enterprise. Believing historians have given fresh attention to the technical side of their discipline to ensure that the best research methods are utilized. The eschatological orientation of earlier Christian thinkers has been muted, even as some modern Christian scholars have written about the history of Christian ideas about the end times.[22]

Moreover, some Christians have gained respect in the guild of professional historians, such as Herbert Butterfield (1900–1979) in Great Britain and Kenneth Scott Latourette (1884–1968) in the United States. Butterfield, an English Methodist and professor at Cambridge, delivered post-World War II lectures on the BBC that were later published as *Christianity and History*. At a time when providential perspectives on history had declined, Butterfield offered a modified version with his image of God as a composer who makes changes to his work in the middle of a concert, and with his belief in the reality of divine judgments.[23] On this side of the Atlantic, the Baptist Latourette distinguished himself as an authoritative historian of Christian missions and professor at Yale University. In 1948 he was elected president of the prestigious American Historical Association; for his address at the organization's annual meeting, he chose to speak on a Christian understanding of history. Before his peers—many of whom were not believers—Latourette emphasized God's sovereignty, the centrality of Christ's incarnation, human dignity, the ultimate completion of God's purposes for humanity, and the strong probability that the Christian view of history is correct.[24] Butterfield and Latourette both attest to the fact that Christian historians can do their work well and blend a distinctly Christian perspective into their work.

Since the 1970s a generation of American historians has gained recognition for outstanding scholarly achievements that reflect noticeable Christian convictions. Many evangelicals in the United States have at least heard the names of widely published authors like Joel Carpenter, Nathan Hatch, George Marsden, Mark Noll, Harry Stout, and Grant Wacker, all of whom witness to the quality of the research and writing done by Christian historians.[25] These historical scholars generally avoid the overtly providential history that characterized some earlier Christian accounts of the past, preferring "ordinary" history that is done with Christian presuppositions in the framework of a Christian worldview.[26] What that means is that Christian historians will not differ from their secular counterparts in terms of research methods or the nature of the evidence that they cite, but rather in choice of topic, interpretations of evidence, sensitivity toward matters that might be missed by non-Christian scholars, and applications of their research.

George Marsden (b. 1939), now retired from a history chair at Notre Dame and arguably the pioneering dean of evangelical historiography, has aggressively contended for the legitimate place of religious scholarship in the modern university:

> . . . [M]ainstream American higher education should be more open to explicit discussion of the relationship of religious faith to learning. Scholars who have religious faith should be reflecting on the intellectual implications of that faith and bringing those reflections into the mainstream of intellectual life. Although scholars of no faith or of other faiths may strongly disagree on the particular issues involved, all should participate on equal terms in academic dialogue.[27]

By accepting the pluralism of the secular university, Marsden hopes to open the door for those who relate their faith to their scholarship. Just as Marxist and feminist points of view are given their day in the courts of the academy, so should Christian perspectives be entitled to a fair hearing. He thus champions a Christian perspectivalism that offers distinctive angles of scholarly vision, sharp cultural critiques, perceptive moral judgments, and thoughtful theological reflection.[28] Since Marsden gives many illustrations from his own discipline of historical studies, he effectively models what a Christian approach to history would look like. He also upholds much of what previous generations of Christian thinkers have said and practiced.

Concluding Thoughts on a Christian View of History

On the assumptions that historical study is valuable, and that the Christian intellectual tradition offers helpful guidance for integrating history with a Christian worldview, several basic principles can be suggested for viewing the past with Christian lenses. First, history can be classified as a type of general revelation. Whereas special revelation is usually associated with the Bible or the earthly ministry of Jesus, general revelation refers to knowledge that God communicates through more ordinary processes such as the observation of the created order (Rom 1:18–32). While nature primarily instructs us about God as Creator, history supplies significant data about the human race; in fact, history yields valuable insights concerning human nature and its propensity to sin. An honest examination of the historical record confirms what the Scriptures teach about fallen humanity; in other words, the annals of human history illuminate the consequences of the fall. Theologian Reinhold Niebuhr (1892–1971)—the most articulate twentieth-century advocate of Christian Realism—once quoted approvingly a statement in the London *Times Literary Supplement* that "original sin is the only empirically verifiable doctrine of the Christian faith."[29] General revelation through history likewise confirms that humanity has not progressed morally through the centuries; Niebuhr's insights regarding the ambiguities and ironies of history remind us that utopian hopes, which occasionally flare up in good times, are not grounded in an adequate understanding of human nature.[30]

Second, Christians through the ages have consistently declared that history is meaningful, that it ultimately is "His story" or God's grand narrative about His purposes for the world and the people in it. While believers do not always agree on the nature of God's sovereignty or rule—and especially how it relates to human freedom—they typically affirm that God as Creator and Redeemer guides or superintends history, and that history as we know it will one day end with the final judgment and the triumph of God's eternal kingdom. Nevertheless, tracking the hand of God in history—apart from biblical revelation—can be a tricky business. It is as though Christians in this world are looking at a large puzzle that has a Designer, but we are not absolutely certain how all the pieces will eventually fit together. As Paul reminds us, "Now we see but a poor reflection as in a mirror; then we shall see face to face. Now I know in part; then I shall know fully, even as I am fully known" (1 Cor 13:12). God has revealed many things, but He has also kept some things hidden for now, even from the saints. So the Christian avowal that history has meaning and direction cannot be directly proven from the raw data of history; instead, it is rooted in a biblically grounded faith that God will bring history to its intended conclusion.

Christian faith and hope about history's expected outcome means a rejection of secular or cyclical philosophies that deny any definitive purpose or meaning to history or that remain agnostic about such questions. A historian who dismisses entirely any supernatural dimension to history and reflects on the tragic episodes like the Holocaust that dot the historical record might well paraphrase Macbeth's famous complaint as follows: "History is a tale told by an idiot, full of sound and fury, signifying nothing."[31] This counsel of despair, however, is not an option for believers who embrace a conviction that the story makes sense and has an assured ending, even as they recognize their limited abilities to see how everything connects in the plot. A Christian view of history may well be pessimistic about human sinfulness at the same time it is optimistic about the trajectory of God's redemptive plan.

Third, Christian students of history will stress the importance of human agency and personality in the unfolding of historical events. A Christian approach to the past is not compatible with Marxist theories, for example, that tend to explain historical development primarily in terms of impersonal forces such as the inexorable "laws" of economics. Marxist history usually combines a linear perspective with a belief in human and social progress, but minimizes the historical impact of human ideas or actions.[32] The

Christian doctrine of creation, however, brings focus to human agency with its teaching that men and women are made in the image of God, and have been given a degree of dominion in the world that God brought into being (Gen 1:26–28). Thus human beings possess an inherent dignity, even after the Fall, as well as a commission to shape the world in which they live (Ps 8:5–6). In fulfilling the cultural mandate, humans in a sense create history.

As alluded to in the previous section, the Scriptures offer numerous instances of human personalities affecting the course of history. God can basically carry out His purposes in two ways. (1) He can directly intervene in history in a dramatic, miraculous manner such as the parting of the Red Sea (Exod 14:26–31) or the raising of Christ from the grave (Matthew 28 and parallels). (2) He can use human agents, which in the Bible seems to be more common than the overtly supernatural occurrences. These two modes are actually complementary; Moses, for example, was the human agent who had a role in God's deliverance of the Hebrews from Egypt. On biblical grounds, then, there is ample warrant for centering on the human drama of history.

Fourth, Christian historians will insist on truthfulness and honesty in doing their work because the Scriptures uphold these virtues as imperative. A Christian recounting of the past allows no tolerance for deliberate suppression of factual information or calculated distortions of historical records. In the past decade, the historical profession in the United States has been tarnished by plagiarism charges that have been leveled against two popular historians.[33] These cases of scholarly dishonesty, where material allegedly was drawn from sources without proper credit being given, suggest that even prolific historians can be tempted to take shortcuts or compromise their integrity. The relevance of Christian moral standards as a protection against these abuses is obvious; Christian students, in particular, need to apply them in their research and writing.

Finally, as this essay has implied at several points, a Christian worldview provides a grid or a set of lenses through which to approach and analyze the past. Biblical and theological principles function as presuppositions for the Christian student; Christians hold to certain truths about God, humanity, our fallen world, and the future that deeply influence the ways that they read and interpret history. The cynic might respond that believers come to history with evident biases, but in reality humanists, Marxists, and feminists have their own sets of presuppositions that affect their interpretations of the past. The issue is which set offers the most satisfactory and compelling perspective for understanding and explaining history. In this regard, the Christian faith has nothing for which to apologize. At the same time, Christians need to be transparent about the impact of their worldview on what they choose to study, how they interpret evidence, moral judgments that they make about individuals and movements from the past, and their sense of history's direction.

One of the most interesting aspects of the modern historical enterprise is the degree to which it instinctively assumes some broadly Christian ideas in carrying out its work. Christian historian C. John Sommerville lists six "vestiges of Christian thought" that he finds in Western historical scholarship. They are (1) a sense of human sinfulness; (2) a linear view of history; (3) a focus on history as a story with a beginning, middle, and end; (4) skepticism about the notion of progress; (5) belief in human freedom; and (6) and an ironic approach to historiography, which Sommerville claims "makes best sense in a Christian perspective."[34] Christians who study, teach, or write history should be encouraged by these signals of common grace. They suggest that a Christian view of history is not some radically alien concept that is out of place in the academic world. In short, the Christian intellectual tradition continues to influence—even infiltrate—the thought forms of our age, sometimes in the least likely places.

Questions for Further Reflection

1. Why should Christians even bother with history?
2. What does the Bible teach about the importance of history?
3. Were Christian thinkers from the past right to take history seriously?
4. How does a Christian perspective actually change the way that history is done?
5. Why do you think that many modern historians assume certain Christian ideas in their work?

Resources for Further Study

Bauman, Michael, and Martin I. Klauber. *Historians of the Christian Tradition: Their Methodology and Influence on Western Thought*. Nashville: B&H, 1995.

Bebbington, David. *Patterns in History: A Christian Perspective*. Grand Rapids: Baker, 1990.

Cairns, Earle E. *God and Man in Time: A Christian Approach to Historiography*. Grand Rapids: Baker, 1979.

Fides et Historia: Journal of the Conference on Faith and History. Formerly based in the Department of History, Calvin College, Grand Rapids, but now at the Department of History, Eastern Nazarene College, Quincy, MA.

Marsden, George, and Frank Roberts, eds. *A Christian View of History?* Grand Rapids: Eerdmans, 1975.

McIntire, C. T., ed. *God, History, and Historians: Modern Christian Views of History*. New York: Oxford University Press, 1977.

McIntire, C. T., and Ronald A. Wells, eds. *History and Historical Understanding*. Grand Rapids: Eerdmans, 1984.

Swanstrom, Roy. *History in the Making: An Introduction to the Study of the Past*. Downers Grove, IL: InterVarsity, 1978.

Wells, Ronald A. *History through the Eyes of Faith: Western Civilization and the Kingdom of God*. San Francisco: HarperSanFrancisco, 1989.

———, ed. *History and the Christian Historian*. Grand Rapids: Eerdmans, 1998.

Endnotes

[1] After 45 years, I still have the undated, stenciled handout in a file.

[2] *Fides et Historia* is currently published semiannually by the CFH. The CFH website is accessible at http://www.huntington.edu/cfh.

[3] See David L. Wagner, *The Seven Liberal Arts in the Middle Ages* (Bloomington: Indiana University Press, 1983); and Robert Harrison, Aled Jones, and Peter Lambert, "The Institutionalisation and Organisation of History," in *Making History: An Introduction to the History and Practices of a Discipline*, ed. Peter Lambert and Phillip Schofield (London: Routledge, 2004), 9–25.

[4] Joseph Bottum, "The Judgment of Memory," *First Things* 181 (March 2008): 30.

[5] C. S. Lewis, "Learning in War-Time," in *The Weight of Glory and Other Addresses* (Grand Rapids: Eerdmans, 1965), 50–51. For citations of this passage, see Nathan O. Hatch, "Yesterday: The Key That Unlocks Today," *Christianity Today*, August 5, 1983, 18; and George M. Marsden, "A Christian Perspective for the Teaching of History," in *A Christian View of History?* ed. George Marsden and Frank Roberts (Grand Rapids: Eerdmans, 1975), 33.

[6] For a convenient summary of ancient historiography, see Earle E. Cairns, *God and Man in Time: A Christian Approach to Historiography* (Grand Rapids: Baker, 1979), 63–68.

[7] In particular, two of his books have gained wide commendation. See David McCullough, *John Adams* (New York: Simon & Schuster, 2001) and *1776: America and Britain at War* (New York: Simon & Schuster, 2005).
[8] Caleb Evans, "The Remembrance of Former Days" (sermon, Broadmead Church, Bristol, England, November 5, 1778). This message was printed in Bristol by William Pine in the same year.
[9] See, for example, Gerhard von Rad, *Old Testament Theology*, trans. D. M. G. Stalker (New York: Harper & Row, 1962–65), esp. 1:121–28 and 2:106, for a classic treatment of "salvation history." From a more evangelical perspective, the late T. V. Farris agreed that the purpose of OT *narrative* was "to record the unfolding redemptive acts of God in history," but he also countered that Yahweh's salvation *strategy* rather than salvation *history* was the "theological center" of the OT. See his *Mighty to Save: A Study in Old Testament Soteriology* (Nashville: Broadman Press, 1993), 47, 299.
[10] For a helpful discussion of history as linear, see David Bebbington, *Patterns in History: A Christian Perspective in Historical Thought* (Grand Rapids: Baker, 1990), 18–19, 46–49.
[11] Unless otherwise noted, direct biblical quotations are taken from the New International Version.
[12] For a critical discussion of ancient Gnosticism with contemporary applications, see Peter Jones, *The Gnostic Empire Strikes Back: An Old Heresy for the New Age* (Phillipsburg, NJ: P & R, 1992).
[13] For an analogous use of OT history before an obviously different audience, see the sermon of the early martyr Stephen in Acts 7:2–53. History can be dangerous!
[14] For example, see Bill T. Arnold and Bryan E. Beyer, *Encountering the Old Testament*, 2nd ed. (Grand Rapids: Baker, 2008), 28ff.
[15] Eusebius of Caesarea, *Ecclesiastical History* 10.9.
[16] See Lloyd G. Patterson, *God and History in Early Christian Thought: A Study of Themes from Justin Martyr to Gregory the Great*, Studies in Patristic Thought, ed. R. A. Norris Jr. (New York: Seabury Press, 1967), 79–101; and John R. Franke, "Eusebius of Caesarea," in *Historians of the Christian Tradition: Their Methodology and Influence on Western Thought*, ed. Michael Bauman and Martin I. Klauber (Nashville: B&H, 1995), 59–78.
[17] Augustine, *City of God* 14.28.
[18] Ibid., 22.30. For an overview of Augustine's historical divisions and other aspects of his perspectives on history, see Alister E. McGrath, "Augustine of Hippo," in Bauman and Klauber, *Historians of the Christian Tradition*, 79–93.
[19] Otto of Freising, *Chronicle or History of the Two Cities* 6.36 and 8.4–13.
[20] Bernard McGinn, *Antichrist: Two Thousand Years of the Human Fascination with Evil* (San Francisco: HarperSanFrancisco, 1994), 137. I am indebted to McGinn's entire discussion of Joachim, 135–42. See also Bebbington, *Patterns in History*, 58–60.
[21] Foxe's work as a historian is summarized in Donald T. Williams, "John Foxe," in Bauman and Klauber, *Historians of the Christian Tradition*, 117–38.
[22] James A. Patterson, "Clio Encounters Eschatology: Recent Historiographical Interest in Christian Beliefs about the Future," *Journal of the Union University Faculty Forum* 23 (Fall 2003): 38–50.

[23] Herbert Butterfield, *Christianity and History* (New York: Scribner's, 1950), 48–112. For an overview of Butterfield, including a critique of his providentialism, see Robert Clouse, "Herbert Butterfield," in Bauman and Klauber, *Historians of the Christian Tradition*, 519–29. For a recent example of an intriguing providential perspective—more pronounced than Butterfield's—see Steven J. Keillor, *God's Judgments: Interpreting History and the Christian Faith* (Downers Grove, IL: IVP Academic, 2007). The author is the brother of NPR radio personality Garrison Keillor.

[24] Kenneth Scott Latourette, "The Christian Understanding of History," *American Historical Review* 54 (January 1949): 259–76. Perhaps his most important scholarly contribution was *A History of the Expansion of Christianity*, 7 vols. (New York: Harper & Brothers, 1937–45). For an assessment of the Yale historian, see Richard W. Pointer, "Kenneth Scott Latourette," in Bauman and Klauber, *Historians of the Christian Tradition*, 411–30.

[25] Earlier in this period, these scholarly developments were flagged in Leonard I. Sweet, "Wise as Serpents, Innocent as Doves: The New Evangelical Historiography," *Journal of the American Academy of Religion* 56 (Autumn 1988): 397–416. For a more recent discussion, see Tim Stafford, "Whatever Happened to Christian History?" *Christianity Today*, April 2, 2001, 42–49.

[26] See Stafford's summary of his interview with Mark Noll in "Whatever Happened to Christian History?" 45.

[27] George M. Marsden, *The Outrageous Idea of Christian Scholarship* (New York: Oxford University Press, 1997), 3–4. This short book essentially grew out of his earlier *The Soul of the American University: From Protestant Establishment to Established Nonbelief* (New York: Oxford University Press, 1994).

[28] Marsden, *Outrageous Idea*, 59–100. Marsden's perspectivalism has been influenced by the thought of Abraham Kuyper (1837–1920), a Dutch Calvinist politician and theologian.

[29] Reinhold Niebuhr, *Man's Nature and His Communities: Essays on the Dynamics and Enigmas of Man's Personal and Social Existence* (New York: Scribner's, 1965), 24.

[30] Reinhold Niebuhr, *Faith and History: A Comparison of Christian and Modern Views of History* (New York: Scribner's, 1949).

[31] See William Shakespeare, *Macbeth*, 5.5.

[32] There is a debate about just what role Karl Marx himself assigned to human agency. See Bebbington, *Patterns in History*, 117–39. In Marxist nations there has been a pronounced lack of regard for the value of human life, which could be a result of downplaying human agency in history.

[33] Martin Arnold, "Making Books; Writers Beware: History Is an Art, Not a Toaster," *New York Times*, February 28, 2002, E1 and E3.

[34] C. John Sommerville, "Christian Historiography? A Pragmatic Approach," *Fides et Historia* 35 (Winter/Spring 2003): 2–3.

11

The Study of Political Philosophy at the Christian University

Hunter Baker

In our Christian universities, we have retained the idea that students must take courses in areas such as New Testament, Old Testament, and perhaps some other offering in theology or church history. In near lockstep, the same institutions require courses in freshman composition. We insist on composition because writing is the engine of the expression of learning. Students must be able to organize their thoughts and lucidly communicate ideas. By requiring courses like these, we demonstrate that we believe there are some things students truly should learn before leaving our universities. Regrettably, our idea of what is required is far too narrow. The discipline for which I write has been sadly neglected in Christian universities relative to the subjects already mentioned. With this essay, I hope persuasively to endorse the study of political philosophy by every undergraduate. It is a subject properly basic to all of us as *citizens rather than subjects* in a democratic republic. The maintenance of our rights and freedoms depends on understanding how to reason about politics and developing a sense of the sources of our rights and freedoms.

The best way to make the case for the study of political philosophy is to provide a brief summary of some of the thinkers from both the classical and Christian traditions. There are many more I could mention, but these are powerful building blocks of what Robert George has called "the central tradition" in Western political thought and will serve to highlight the importance of the topic.[1] One of the reasons why it is important to understand something of political thought (which could also be characterized as the *old* political science) is to avoid the reductionistic tendencies of newer versions of political science that would leave us with a plethora of descriptions of political behavior and theories for manipulating it without a strong examination of values.

The Greeks: Plato and Aristotle

While none of us are able to get into a time machine and see exactly how political communities were formed, Aristotle offered a convincing account of politics. He said the family is the beginning of political society. The man is the father and the provider, while the woman is the mother and caregiver. Together, they produce children. Without children, there is no lasting society. Thus, children are essential to a political community. (The novelist P. D. James brilliantly demonstrated what the world would be like if we lost the ability to reproduce in her futuristic book *The Children of Men*.) The family develops into multiple families. Families broaden into a village. The village was likely ruled by the patriarch, the oldest and most central ancestral male. Think about the similarity in the words "kin" and "king" and perhaps you have a sense of the development of monarchies. Villages coalesce into cities. Cities, according to Aristotle, are special. They are the political association for which human beings were made.[2]

Here we have a potent assertion. Human beings were made to live together in political association. Why is that? Aristotle reasoned from facts he observed in nature. Looking at human beings, he saw that they differed from animals in a such a striking way as to make them *sui generis* (unique). The difference is language and how it is used. Animals are capable of expressing pain or pleasure. They may even be able to communicate the existence of danger or closeness of a food source. Unlike animals, though, humans can discuss things like good and evil. Human beings talk about justice. And that is why human beings should live together in political associations. They should pursue the good life, a life characterized by justice, in civic friendship designed to spur each other on to excellence.

In offering this idealistic view of political life together, Aristotle knew that he was ambitious. The alternative models are ready made. Some argue that the strongest should rule, whether that be a tyrant or a mob, and that when either the empowered minority or majority confiscate goods and rule in their own interest it is just, because they are doing so as a sovereign government. That point of view is acted out spectacularly and to some humorous effect in Plato's *Republic* by Thrasymachus, a young man with no time for justice as a lofty ideal who insists that justice is nothing more than the interest of the stronger.[3]

On the other hand, there are those who endorse government in a stripped down form. It will exist merely to protect from external threats and to enforce contracts. (See, the libertarian impulse has been around for a long time!) But Aristotle believed his insight of man as a political animal, one interested in justice, led logically to the idea of a just society, a moral society with greater hopes than providing for mere noninterference between human beings.

As the situation currently stands in American higher education and in Christian colleges and universities, the great majority of students will not come across Aristotle's work in *The Politics*. In fact, the majority of political science majors in the United States will probably not read Aristotle. They will focus on American government, Congress, the courts, the executive branch, political polling, campaigns, and other seemingly more relevant subjects. But they will not learn the most important thing, which is to think at a basic level about the phenomenon of political life. *What is politics for?* Why do we do it? And if we do engage in politics, what vision should be guiding our participation? How will citizens have the critical faculties necessary to evaluate political campaigns and their proposals without falling prey to tactics of stage management and focus-group crafted rhetoric if our educational offerings fail to equip them? The deep questions don't get asked.

Plato, in criticizing the sophists (cynical users of rhetoric), related a parable about a terrible monster.[4] The monster's handler learns its likes and dislikes, its habits and how to soothe its temper. The handler and those who depend on him learn to call the handling, the manipulation, of the monster "good." But this is a very poor understanding of good. The monster is public opinion. The manipulation of opinion is what the handler learns to achieve. Plato's metaphor is as good as any I've ever read for modern politics. The smooth, secular political operator strives to be a manipulator of the monster and would laugh at anyone who insisted that his understanding of the good is shallow and insufficient.

What we really need is for the both the public and the political class to return to the Aristotelian insight about human beings. We are not here simply to satisfy our wants. We are not here, as Aristotle wrote, for *mere* life which is basically the meeting of biological needs. We have an obligation (given to us by Nature, Aristotle would say; given to us by God, Christians would say) to pursue the *good* life. We care about justice. We naturally discuss good and evil. We are susceptible to giving in to the less noble side of our nature such as selfishness and acquisitiveness, but there is the nagging sense that there is something more about which we should be concerned.

Both Plato and Aristotle insisted on rising beyond the idea of politics as the satisfaction of interests or the successful manipulation of crowds. They were interested in justice. What is it? How do we obtain it? Plato believed it was possible to train young philosophers to contemplate the unchanging realities that undergird the world as we perceive it and thus to understand what is true rather than merely perceiving a constant flux of relativities. Aristotle paid attention to the inability of persons to make good judgments in regard to themselves and their corresponding tendency to make unjust arguments favoring their own cause. Just as one outfitting an orchestra would decide who should have the best flutes on the basis of merit in music rather than on the basis of wealth or status of birth, we should decide political rights (and especially leadership) on the basis on goodness and civic excellence.

Out of this great tradition also comes an admirably sober and dignified view of the human soul. We have reason, will, and appetite. Plato thought this arrangement was so fundamental he tried to arrange an ideal society around it. The good man will successfully govern himself by aligning his will with his reason to triumph over his appetite. The appetite is necessary. It keeps us alive. It is a force to keep us moving, to overcome inertia, but it cannot be allowed to rule. The man who is guided by the unchecked power of appetite is likely to be an unjust man, a disaster both for himself and for his community. The animals are almost completely will and appetite. We are something more. We are called to be more.

One of the things lacking in the classical tradition of political philosophy is a sufficient appreciation of *all* human beings. Plato's vision of justice includes locking some persons in a position on the social hierarchy based on a centralized view of their attributes. For him, some human beings are the soul of the society while others are merely the appetite. Aristotle defended the idea of slavery on the basis that some are simply fitted by nature for that task. I raise these points without intending to indict either man or hold them up for some retroactive censure; there is something ugly about a critic self-righteously doing that from a comfortable spot in the modern world. Indeed, the debt we owe to these two philosophers is gigantic. Alfred North Whitehead once claimed that the entire European philosophical tradition is a series of footnotes to Plato.[5] However, I mention these things to set the stage for the first major Christian political thinker and to help show why it is important for Christian colleges and universities to revive the study of political philosophy on their campuses and in their curricula.

Augustine

After I've taken students through Plato and Aristotle, they sometimes wonder how we got from there to where we are now. Specifically, how do you reach a point where something like slavery becomes almost unthinkable? That is when I point them to Augustine, easily one of the great Christian political minds and a star in the constellation of Western thinkers. Augustine holds the distinction of having authored two works that are fixtures in the great literature of the world. The adult convert to Christianity is perhaps best known for his *Confessions*, which continues to be one of the most insightful works of self-disclosure ever written. He is very nearly as well known for his epic defense of the Christian faith which he wrote in the face of the imminent decline of the Roman Empire, *The City of God*. No great compilation of Western political thought is complete without a meaty excerpt from that text. What is especially notable, for our purposes, is his emphasis on the rights and value of all persons. He does not divide the human race into high and low so much as he sees all men beneath the loving and righteous fatherhood of God.

Augustine, while still a believer in good order and legitimate authority, insisted that the situation in which one man rules over another man as though his superior is a consequence of sin, specifically the sin of pride. Before the fall, Augustine wrote in *The City of God*, man was made to be a shepherd rather than a king. He was designed to rule over the animals (irrational creatures) rather than to rule over his fellow men (rational creatures made in God's image). Prior to the awful moment of the first sin, Adam did not even rule over Eve. She was simply his companion. Servitude, both for Eve and for the human race, is a judgment for transgression against God. The servitude is double. Men suffer not only as slaves to other men but also as slaves to sin. In their original condition, neither of these things were true. Now, after the fall, even the masters are slaves to their own unrighteousness. Nevertheless, God will bring satisfaction. The slave can gain some degree of freedom by resisting sin in his own life. He can serve his master with faithful love, knowing that God will bring an end to all unrighteousness and will put all authorities and powers down before His own perfectly just and loving rule.[6] Better to be a slave to a man than to be a slave to sin. There is a message implicit in what Augustine wrote. Those who rule over men with arbitrary force as masters need not examine it for long in order to comprehend it. The unrighteous rule *will be put down*. The fear of God might cause a man to think twice before treating another man as a chattel possession.

The City of God remains one of the most profound reflections on political theory ever offered. One of the outstanding features of Augustine's work is that when he thought about justice, he didn't look at it only from the horizontal perspective of person to person. He was concerned with God's priority as our creator.

As a consequence, he was not impressed with the state merely because it is official. To him, even an empire could be nothing more than a giant band of robbers wearing the uniforms of the state. He memorably related a story about a pirate who was captured by Alexander the Great. Alexander asked the pirate who he thought he was infesting the sea. The pirate responded with equal indignance asking Alexander who he thought he was infesting the whole earth![7]

Augustine's sense of God's priority as our Creator has some very interesting implications. For example, his indictment of slavery and unjust rule speaks powerfully against the petty totalitarianism of human dictatorships. Pride is what causes the wicked to want to rule. Pride hates the equality that comes from fellowship with God. Therefore, the prideful will disrupt the just peace of God and try to impose their own dominion, which can be mistaken for peace. Dominion and peace, however, are not equitable or compatible.

In order to get this point across to students, I give them an example of two families. In the first family, a harsh and unloving father imposes his will on his wife and children through the use of fear and violence. There is no conflict because the bad father has precluded it. There is no peace, either. Peace includes justice. In the second family the father leads with love, temperance, openness, communication, and justice. This second family has peace.

True peace is the relationship of equals in harmony before God. All persons have their proper place not because they are higher or lower, but because they have gifts to do particular things. Consider how different that is from a network of servile relationships going from top to bottom. If a person has the gift of leadership that does not mean that person is superior or has rule over others.

Augustine shared Plato and Aristotle's preoccupation with justice, and he conceived of justice as an ideal rather than a sorry reflection of a strongman's will to power. He insisted that a commonwealth cannot be maintained without justice. No one has the right to act unjustly, and an unjust law is no law at all. It is utterly untrue that justice is merely the interest of the strong in society because justice is what makes a people. An agreement about justice is what makes a people.

Aquinas

Several centuries later, Thomas Aquinas emerged as the great master of the concept of natural law. He recognized that awareness of the natural moral law, which he described as being just as true as the fact that the three angles of a triangle add up to 180 degrees, makes human beings special in the whole of creation.[8] In this sense, he elaborated upon the ideas of the man he respected so greatly as to refer to him simply as "the philosopher." He was referring to Aristotle. Aquinas noted that human beings have some share of the eternal reason and this reason working in them is the natural law. The natural law is "nothing else than an imprint on us of the divine light."[9]

Many evangelical Christians are aware of the idea of natural law through the work of C. S. Lewis, especially in his *Mere Christianity* and *The Abolition of Man*. To put the matter in modern terms, I often tell students that natural law is in them like preloaded software in a computer. (My description is in danger of being dated. Perhaps I could take a page from the iPhone and say that there's a preloaded, nonoptional "app" for natural law.) Aquinas observed, as have others, that across cultures, there are some things we all seem to know are right and others we all seem to know are wrong. A man in North America and a man in Africa will possess the same basic ideas about morality. Even when there are exceptions, like Julius Caesar's observation that Germanic tribes seemed to approve of stealing, there is a justification to explain it.[10] The Germanic tribes didn't think it was right to steal from others in the same tribe, only from those outside. The reason was that they saw those outside the tribe as somehow less human. We still have that problem today. Those we dehumanize, like the unborn child, enjoy less extensive rights and protections. Indeed, this was a pathology of the old Greco-Roman world.

Working from this idea of natural law, Aquinas built out the plan of a society. The natural law provides the broad principles or speculative reason, as he called it.[11] In many cases natural law is enough, because the law was promulgated by God who has written it on our heart. But there are a number of more specific cases in which the natural law will be too general to provide a solution. Those cases make it clear where human law is needed. These more specific rules, based on our practical reason, must be rooted in the natural law. And the reason to have laws rather than merely judges is to make sure that we set rules while removed from a particular situation and we can more effectively rein in our passions. This last idea flowed beautifully from Aristotle to Aquinas, as Aristotle noted that men are bad judges in their own case. In other words, rules of decision should be made as much as possible in abstraction from an actual dispute in motion. Imagine a football game where the rules can be changed in the fourth quarter. Changes in the heat of the moment are too likely to be designed to favor some interest.

Like Augustine, Aquinas insisted that the proper object of law is justice. Without justice, there is no law, but rather an arbitrary assertion of some fallible human being. All laws must derive from the just natural law. If not, it is no law at all. Human laws only bind the conscience if they are just. We know they are just if they are truly aimed at the common good and lay burdens on subjects with equality of proportion.

Summary of Aristotle to Aquinas

What I have done so far is survey some of the great political thought of the West. I have discussed political and legal thought which seriously considers the unique nature of man relative to other living things; the possibility of the afterlife and of true justice that follows you there; the existence of God; and our need to conform ourselves to some kind of objective moral standard that is not set by unrooted human preference. This sampling of political thought also shows an awareness of the imperfectibility of human beings and their sinful nature. Unfettered and invisible to God, we all are capable of becoming self-serving monsters. Plato told the unforgettable story of a man who found a ring to make him invisible, perhaps even to God. The man, a shepherd, promptly used his power to seduce the queen and assassinate the king![12] Aristotle wrote that when men are not governed by justice, they become the frightening bearers of armed injustice, the worst and most dangerous creatures in the world.[13]

This kind of political thought sets out a basis for human rights and a hedge against totalitarianism. Augustine's thought regarding human servitude and God's priority as our Creator is especially effective in that regard. The flowing mixture of Christian and classical sources embraces dispassionate constitutionalism (a regime of preset laws setting out limits to power) as an answer to the sinful nature of human beings and their ability to be overwhelmed by their appetites. As will be evident, the political thought from Aristotle to Aquinas is strikingly unmodern.

The Emergence of Value-Free Politics

The Prince

Machiavelli's *The Prince* marked the emergence of a different kind of political thought. Some would say that he is the father of *true* political science. In my book, *The End of Secularism*, I identified *The Prince* as a watershed event in the development of secularism. And the reason I say that is that his advice to the prince is not based on any absolute standard of right and wrong. It is based on effectiveness, or we might even say "winning."[14] Machiavelli advises the prince to *appear* humane, truthful, religious, charitable, and so on. But he also tells him he should be ready to abandon any of those virtues as soon as it proves beneficial. The prince should not worry about losing the trust of the people with his deceptions because ordinary people are always willing to be deceived. And the world, according to Machiavelli, is full of ordinary people.[15]

Machiavelli's advice in *The Prince* is a transition point. Rather than focusing on questions of God and man, the emphasis shifts to politics as a means of fulfilling personal aims and desires. This point of view is sometimes praised as *realpolitik* or political realism. The guiding principle of political realism is simple pragmatism, rather than vague notions of duty to the natural law. A true prince will always do what is in his best interest.

Machiavelli is truly a grand figure. He has acquired a reputation as a stylish villain as much to be admired as to be criticized. This is not the place to explore his larger body of work, but an examination of all his writings reveals a more complex figure with redeeming qualities. The point here is less to hold him up as a negative example than to show the influence of his most famous work.

Holmes and Legal Positivism

Proceed down the road a bit further to Oliver Wendell Holmes Jr. This Supreme Court Justice with his fantastic moustache (matched only by the one worn by actor Sam Elliott in the film *Tombstone*) is one of the iconic American figures. He is, for many, the Platonic ideal of the wise old jurist. But Holmes was a man without a great deal of time for the type of political thought with which I began this chapter. He rejected Aquinas's framework of natural law affecting human law in the pursuit of justice. For him the law was not, as he said, "some brooding omnipresence in the sky," but was instead simply the voice of a sovereign.[16] Philip Johnson, in his marvelous and underappreciated book *Reason in the Balance*, characterized Holmes's view of the law as "the science of state coercion." He expressed his desire to see every word of moral significance banished from the law. The supreme law for him was the law of the nation that could "lick all the rest."[17] In Holmes's highly capable hands, Thrasymachus, Plato's character who insisted justice is merely the interest of the stronger, comes roaring back to life.

Certainly, Oliver Wendell Holmes was one of the major legal minds of the American jurisprudential tradition. He was bright and bold. But I would submit that his blindness in seeing the moral importance of the law and his lack of appreciation for the need of the law to connect with the unique nature of human beings left him lacking as a jurist. In particular, I think about his opinion in the Virginia sterilization statute case *Buck v. Bell*:

> It is better for all the world, if instead of waiting to execute degenerate offspring for crime or to let them starve for their imbecility, society can prevent those who are manifestly unfit from continuing their kind . . .
> Three generations of imbeciles are enough.[18]

So, anyone considered unfit, and at the time that meant retarded, sexually promiscuous, or a number of other things, could be legally sterilized against their will for the good of the state. This is an example of jurisprudence left poorer for its lack of consideration of the moral law and of the law of God prevalent in so much of Western civilization.

But still, what if Holmes was right and there is no natural law and no ultimate moral code written in our hearts by God or revealed by revelation? It is always possible that he is correct, but in comparison to Aristotle, Holmes's view of the facts does not comport as well with reality. Recall that Aristotle did not formulate his priority for justice by pulling it out of thin air or remembering it from a dream. He developed it by observing the speech and behavior of human beings. It cannot be dismissed as mere mysticism the way Holmes seemed to think it could. We expect and insist on justice, especially for ourselves but also for others.

As an example, whenever I've had the occasion to talk with peers or students willing to argue fiercely against the existence of the natural law, I always ask the following question: So, what exactly was it that we did at Nuremberg?

At the conclusion of World War II, the triumphant Allied powers faced the question of what to do with the Nazis who had committed spectacular atrocities in the course of the war, the most notable of which was the genocidal holocaust of the Jews.

Here is the problem. Everything the Nazis did was 100-percent, undeniably, unquestionably, according to the laws of the nation at the time, legal. It was authorized by the person and the regime that Oliver Wendell Holmes would have to agree was, in fact, the sovereign. If law is nothing more than the voice of the sovereign and you want to hold these fellows to account, well, you've got a problem.

On the other hand, if you stand with Augustine, Aquinas, and traditional political thought in the insistence that an unjust law is no law at all, no matter who made it, then you are standing on a pretty firm foundation. Men cannot cloak their unjust acts in the guise of positive law approved by a sovereign and make the offense against right and wrong go away.

The history has been written. We tried the Nazis. We did not allow their obedience to the law of Germany to prevent us from putting them on trial. We convicted them of crimes against humanity. If those trials were not a dramatic repudiation of a Holmesian secular-atomistic view of law by the West, I don't know what it would take to establish one. Holmes's view, essentially legal positivism, has failed. Men are not like atoms to be manipulated and arranged by whomever has power enough to do it.

The Western Political Tradition and a Birmingham Jail

I mentioned that Holmes was an iconic American figure who exerted considerable influence on the direction of our laws. He is not, however, nearly as good an exemplar of American political thought as another more famous and influential American icon. The man of whom I speak is the Reverend Dr. Martin Luther King Jr. King's name included that of the great reformer, Martin Luther, who was a major political thinker in his own right. The original Luther was the great proponent of distinguishing the functions of church and state, thus urging them to persist in their proper roles. Thus, the church must focus on persuasion and care of souls and the state must justly excel in the protection of life and limb. He simultaneously urged Christians to see service in the area of law as equal to the ministry of providing food and water, because people need order and protection just as much as they need other necessaries of existence. His namesake, Dr. King, merits recognition here not only because he was the single greatest force for racial equality in America through his use of prophetic oration, organization, and creative nonviolence, but also because he wrote the *Letter from Birmingham Jail*[19] (his own version of the 95 Theses in terms of listing grievances), which sits now like a cherry on top of the great tradition of Western and Christian political thought.

The occasion for the letter was King's imprisonment as a consequence for launching a massive social protest against rampant segregation in Birmingham, Alabama. He wrote specifically to his fellow clergymen (white clergymen) who questioned his motives in bringing the protest and wondered why he couldn't just wait for conditions to improve. King is impressive in his answer. The section where he described what it was like to be a black man, woman, or child in the South is heart-rending. But what is even more powerful is his discourse on social and political thought justifying his course of action.

He began with the matter of choosing to break laws. His fellow clergymen were surprised at his willingness to disobey democratically established statutes. He made the obvious point that blacks, in many cases, had been unable to vote, but went much deeper in his analysis and defense. First, he considered the nature of law. He acknowledged that he had been an advocate for the obedience of law and that he urged states to follow the Supreme Court's ruling in *Brown v. Board of Education*, which outlawed school segregation. King traced the distinction between breaking some laws and following others to Augustine who argued that "an unjust law is no law at all." Just laws make a right demand upon the citizen to follow, while unjust statutes create a responsibility to resist.

Dr. King's mixture of Christian and classical social and political thought was especially evident in the way he added scripture and church history into his indictment of those who would counsel him simply to wait. He traced civil disobedience to Shadrach, Meschach, and Abednego willingly accepting the punishment of death in a fiery furnace in consequence of choosing God over the earthly sovereign Nebuchadnezzar. King also called attention to the martyrs of the early church who submitted to death at the jaws of hungry lions and on chopping blocks rather than submit to unjust laws that would claim a higher loyalty to that which we owe to our Creator.

The civil rights pioneer built his case out further by looking to Thomas Aquinas. Just laws are those which correspond to the "moral law or the law of God." Segregation is an expression of sinfulness. It is a denial of the image of God imprinted in men and women of all races. It creates a barrier that the natural law would not recognize. Statutes enforcing segregation thus created an unjust sense of superiority in one race and similarly instilled inferiority in their peers of another race. King also made the important point—easily buttressed by Aquinas's definition of law as being oriented to the common good—that segregation imposes burdens on a minority that the majority chooses not to take upon itself.

King held up the dual examples of Socrates and Jesus Christ. Both men successfully created incredible tension within the minds of elites in their respective societies. Socrates, the teacher of Plato (from whom we know about Socrates) and the man who has sometimes been viewed as a sort of proto-Christian, pushed his commitment to truth so far that he was forced to drink hemlock. Christ offered such a radical challenge to the religious authorities of His day (and indirectly to the empire) that He, too, suffered a death sentence. Both men maintained their innocence, but accepted their sentences despite the injustice involved.[22] In setting up this example, King could not have more beautifully and succinctly tied together the two strands of political thought that have formed the tradition in which we live today.

As we know, King's case against institutionalized racism and segregation eventually prevailed in the United States. He left Birmingham Jail and was later assassinated, but his political ideals gained firm purchase in our constitutional regime. Our human laws thus moved into closer alignment with the justice we believe God would have us observe. King's language, as I have demonstrated here, was unapologetically Christian. In the *Letter from Birmingham Jail*, he wrote forcefully as a pastor, modern-day prophet, Christian scholar, and friend of the Western humanist tradition.

King's choice of language is very disappointing to those who embrace him as a progressive political figure, but would much prefer he had confined himself to more secular language. In *The End of Secularism*, I recalled the story of a colleague who assured me King would have employed a Marxian critique instead of Christian rhetoric had he at the time possessed adequate sophistication.[23] His reaction reminds me of an old Jerry Clower story in which a rural churchwoman, upon hearing of Jesus turning water into wine at the wedding ceremony, ruefully explained that she'd have thought a lot more of Him if He hadn't done that! Secular progressives would greatly prefer that King had not used Scripture and church fathers to such great effect. They appreciate the result, but not the philosophical and spiritual path King set out in his highly convincing argument.

A Tradition that Reformed Itself

To this point, I have tried to demonstrate the indispensability of the tradition of Christian political philosophy that mixed with the older classical (Greco-Roman) tradition to form the basis of our rights, freedoms, and responsibilities in public life today. Surely, there are some who have read this far who have thought, "What about the negative record of Christianity and politics? What about the Crusades or the Inquisition?"

I have several responses with regard to these questions. The first and most obvious is to ask how it was that the church became such a powerful political player, not merely in terms of influencing values or priorities, but in terms of raw institutional power. There is a one-sentence answer to that question. *The Roman Empire fell, but the Christian church did not.* One of the few things for which the church actually gets credit is that it survived the fall the Rome to become a preserver of civilization in Europe. The church was a teacher and a living archive for a great deal of valuable knowledge. In such circumstances, it would almost be surprising had the church not gained substantial political power. However, once in power, it is clear that the church had a mixed record. One should not be surprised that Machiavelli was cynical toward the church of his time. It was a prime player in power politics and not necessarily the good example one might expect.

With regard to the Crusades, the answer is not difficult. The Crusades were an answer to aggressive warfare in the Holy Land carried out by the Muslims. The Pope rallied troops in response to a direct plea for help by the Byzantine Empire. Contrary to popular belief, crusading was not a lucrative way for landless second sons to gain their fortune. Instead, it was extraordinarily costly in terms of both blood and treasure. Crimes committed by some crusaders are not excusable, but the endeavor at large can clearly be justified as a kind of rescue mission.

The things that are harder to deal with, such as the Inquisition or some of the church's economic practices such as selling indulgences, are the focus of this section. If the church's historico-political record is to be sullied by these misdeeds, then it must likewise receive the credit for the reforms that emerged from within the church's own ranks. Martin Luther, a monk, was under the authority of the Catholic hierarchy when he first issued his

95 Theses in challenge to practices and doctrines he identified as variances to Scripture.

Luther is too rarely acknowledged for his political thought. His writings on the proper relationship of church and state endeavored to set each entity to its proper task. No longer should souls be ruled with steel. The state must take as its task the restraint of evil men. It must provide the peace and order that people need as much as they need food and water. Christians, all Christians, should stand ready to participate in God's ministry of justice and order. The church, on the other hand, does not wield the sword. It has the responsibility to persuade the people through the ministry of the Word and to care for their souls.

John Locke, also a Christian, later offered a very similar understanding of the roles of church and state in his *Letter Concerning Toleration*. His influence on the American founding is well documented. Locke built his case on the person of Jesus Christ and His actions as seen in the New Testament. Christ was the king of kings, but did He force right belief with a foot on the neck of His adversaries? He issued a call and those who would, answered. If Christ would not coerce men to believe during His time on earth, then how can it be that His church would wield torture or death as implements of ministry?

What becomes clear, looking at Luther, Locke, and many others, including the modern Catholic Church, is that the Christian tradition has successfully recovered from its unhappy entanglement with empire through engagement with its own primary sources. The successful reform of the church has not been imposed from without but has instead bubbled up from within. By the time of the twentieth century, the church was able to serve as one of the prime obstacles to totalitarianism and abuses of human rights committed by socialist, communist, and corporatist states all believing they acted in accord with some scientific construction of man and history. Indeed, the Christian church is today arguably the single strongest advocate for freedom, democracy, and human rights on the globe.

Conclusion

Perhaps in all of this, the thing about which I've said the least is the Bible itself. The Bible's importance as God's revelation to us is obviously surpassingly large. But the Bible is also important in a different, but connected, way as a political phenomenon. With the widespread publication of the Bible in popular languages as a consequence of the Reformation, it began to serve as the constitution above all constitutions in the same way it tells us Jesus Christ is the ruler of all the kings in the earth. With the Bible as a ready reference for the people, the scene was set for people to hold kings to account. At one time it was said that the ploughboy with Scripture on his side stood on better ground than a king.[24] The implications for politics were staggering. The Bible made possible the kind of political accountability for which the old partisans of justice could only dream.

Thanks to the prior existence of the Bible and the corpus of political thought that has included men like Augustine, Aquinas, and Luther, Martin Luther King Jr. was able to draw upon a formidable armamentarium of justifications in his resolute argument for freedom and equality before the law for an oppressed and despised minority. We cultivate this great tradition by studying it and employing it as we participate in the civic process. Our attempt at engaging in civic friendship with one another is destined to fail should we ignore this rewarding responsibility.

Questions for Further Reflection

1. Why is the study of political philosophy important? Should it be part of the core of knowledge needed in order to be an educated person?
2. Has empirical political science made political philosophy irrelevant?
3. What is the difference in responsibility for a free citizen with a role in the governing process versus the responsibility of an unfree subject of a king or a dictator?
4. Why are constitutions important?
5. What is the relationship between human sinfulness and constitutions? What is the relationship between human sinfulness and limited government?
6. Do you think there is such a thing as natural law? Why or why not?
7. Are current efforts at political advocacy by Christians suitably well-informed by political philosophy?

8. Based on this essay, do you think it is fair to say that Christianity has a contribution to make with regard to politics?

Resources for Further Study

Aquinas, Thomas. *Summa Theologiae*. New York: Benzing, 1948.

Aristotle. *The Politics*. Translated by H. Racham. Cambridge, MA: Harvard University Press, 1932.

Augustine. *The City of God*. Edited by R. W. Dyson. Cambridge: University of Cambridge Press, 1998.

The Birth of Freedom. DVD film. Acton Institute (www.acton.org).

Budziszewski, J. *Written on the Heart: The Case for Natural Law*. Downers Grove, IL: InterVarsity, 1992.

Locke, John. *Letter Concerning Toleration*. Maestro Reprints, 2011.

Luther, Martin. *On Secular Authority*. Cambridge: Cambridge University Press, 1991.

King, Martin Luther, Jr. *Letter from Birmingham Jail*. New York: Harper Collins, 1994.

Kirk, Russell. *The Roots of American Order*. Wilmington, DE: ISI, 2003.

Plato. *The Republic*. Edited by R. F. Ferrar and Tom Griffin. Cambridge: Cambridge University Press, 2000.

Stark, Rodney. *The Victory of Reason*. New York: Random House, 2005.

Endnotes

[1] Robert P. George, *Making Men Moral: Civil Liberties and Public Morality* (Oxford: Oxford University Press, 1993), 18.

[2] Aristotle, *Politics*, Book I, chap. 2. (I will follow this format for classic sources long in the public domain and thus available in many editions.)

[3] Plato, *Republic*, Book I, 338c.

[4] Ibid., Book VI, 493.

[5] Alfred North Whitehead and David Ray Griffin, *Process and Reality* (New York: Simon & Schuster, 1979), 39.

[6] Augustine, *The City of God*, Book XIV, chap. 15.

[7] Ibid., Book IV, chap. 4.

[8] Thomas Aquinas, *Summa Theologiae*, Question 94, Fourth Article.

[9] Ibid., Question 91, Second Article.

[10] Ibid., Question 94, Fourth Article.

[11] Ibid.

[12] Plato, *Republic*, Book II, 359c–360b.

[13] Aristotle, *Politics*, Book I, chap. 2.

[14] Hunter Baker, *The End of Secularism* (Wheaton, IL: Crossway Books, 2009), 44–46.

[15] Niccolo Machiavelli, *The Prince*, chap. XVIII.

[16] The famous and much-repeated statement comes from Holmes's dissenting opinion in *Southern Pacific Co. v. Jensen*, 244 U.S. 205 (1917).

[17] Phillip Johnson crystallized this way of thinking about Holmes for me in *Reason in the Balance* (Downers Grove, IL: InterVarsity Press, 1995), 139–43. Throughout, he is referring to Holmes's famous lecture, "The Path of the Law," which was given at Boston University in 1897 and published as "The Path of the Law," *Harvard Law Review* 10 (1897).

[18] *Buck v. Bell*, 274 U.S. 200 (1927).

[19] Throughout this section I will refer to the text of King's much-anthologized open letter. The 1963 letter can be read in full and easily searched at the King Institute's website at http://mlk-kpp01.stanford.edu/index.php/encyclopedia/encyclopedia/enc_letter_from_birmingham_jail_1963.

[20] Ibid.

[21] Ibid.

[22] Ibid.

[23] Baker, *The End of Secularism*, 179.

[24] David Ginsberg, "Ploughboys versus Prelates: Tyndale and More and the Politics of Biblical Translation," *The Sixteenth Century Journal* 19, no. 1 (Spring 1988): 49.

12

An Invitation to Sociology

Roman R. Williams

> Keep pressing home on him the ordinariness of things. Above all, do not attempt to use science (I mean, the real sciences) as a defense against Christianity. They will positively encourage him to think about realities he can't touch and see. . . . If he must dabble in science, keep him on economics and sociology; don't let him get away from that invaluable "real life."
>
> —Screwtape to Wormwood,
> in *The Screwtape Letters*[1]

Sociology is among the most important fields of study—perhaps *the most important* field of study—for living, working, and ministering in the twenty-first century. It offers a robust intellectual toolkit of concepts, skills, and insights, which are, in turn, useful for analyzing, understanding, and transforming the contemporary world in which we live. Yet, for one reason or another, sociology is also among the least understood—perhaps *the least understood*—fields of study. Too few college or college-bound students, by no fault of their own, have ever been properly introduced to this academic discipline. When they finally stumble upon it, they often ask a straightforward question, "What is sociology?" Students considering sociology as a major also have questions about the prospects of pursuing the discipline. They may be unsure about employment prospects or anxious about how long sociology graduates work at Starbucks and live in their parents' basement before finding a job in their field. They wonder (along with their parents), "What does one do with a degree in sociology?"

Others are burdened with a different set of concerns. For them the sentiments expressed by C. S. Lewis through Screwtape have the ring of truth. The relevant question among these Christians is, "Why bother?" After all, following Screwtape's line of reasoning, sociology is not a "real science." These pragmatists question the value of studying something that seems to be nothing more than common sense adorned in academic jargon. Likewise, the more theologically minded among them take the implications of Screwtape's advice seriously—perhaps a little too seriously; it is fiction, after all—and object to going down an intellectual path that potentially leads to the gates of hell.

Perhaps you have similar questions. This chapter intends to address the concerns raised above. As such, it is an invitation to sociology, an appeal to you to consider the possibilities and importance of sociology. Before proceeding, it should be noted that the notion of an invitation to sociology is not entirely my own; I take my inspiration from an influential book written in 1963 by Peter Berger with the same title.[2] Here I extend the invitation to sociology to a new generation, in my own words, and to a decidedly Christian audience. I do so by organizing my thoughts around the three questions posed above: What is sociology? What does one do with a degree in sociology? And why should Christians study sociology?

What Is Sociology?

Sociology is an invitation to engage one's intellectual imagination about social relationships, social action, and culture. Sociology invites us to explore a world that we take for granted, to peel away its many layers of meaning, and to consider how the "discovery of each new layer changes the perception of the whole."[3] It is easier—and much more interesting as far as I am concerned—to show you what I mean by all of this than to offer a more technical discourse on all matters sociological. To do so, I will briefly consider coffee.[4]

Coffee is a powerful beverage. It is able to energize our bodies, enliven conversations, increase productivity, and stimulate the economy. For many people, coffee is a necessity. My day begins with coffee—more accurately, my day does not begin without coffee. It keeps me going throughout the day. When I am on the go, a stainless steel travel mug keeps me company. A vanilla latte is usually sufficient to ease me through the postprandial doldrums. I also like coffee shops and enjoy meeting students, colleagues, and friends for coffee. Sometimes visiting a coffee shop provides an escape from my office; it offers a change of pace, a different place to read, write, or think. When I go out for coffee, frequently I am reminded of the many interesting things coffee reveals about society and culture.

Thanks to the coffee revolution started by Starbucks, specialty coffeehouses have become a feature of everyday life. In 1990 there were approximately 200 free-standing coffee shops in America.[5] By 1997, according to the US Census Bureau, their numbers grew to over 3,100 establishments and by 2007 there were 19,045 (factfinder.census.gov). These coffee retailers serve a variety of hot, blended, and iced coffee and espresso drinks in hip, relaxed atmospheres carefully engineered to create a calm and inviting ambiance. Paradoxical, yet practical, this juxtaposition of a powerful stimulant and a calm environment prevents over-caffeinated consumers from bouncing off the walls while encouraging them to linger, relax, make themselves at home, and purchase additional expensive caffeinated drinks.

There is more going on in a coffee shop, however, than selling coffee. Beyond feeding an addiction to caffeine, specialty coffee shops also fulfill a craving for a place for people to hang out. Like the sentiment expressed in the lyrics of the title song of the popular 1980s television sitcom *Cheers*, for some people coffeehouses become places where "everyone knows [their] name." When a barista knows a patron's name and the particular (or peculiar) way that person prefers her drink to be prepared, not only does she feel special; she is also likely to become a loyal customer. As fellow customers become known to one another, coffee shops create a feeling of community, establish a sense of belonging, and shape a person's identity. Locations such as coffee shops, pubs, bookstores, and cafés that fill the gap between home and work are referred to as "third places" by sociologists. These places fulfill important social functions by bringing a diverse range of people together (young and old, working and retired, singles and families, etc.), creating interpersonal connections, and providing a location where a sense of community may be cultivated.[6]

Because specialty coffee shops bring different kinds of people together in one place, they are wonderful venues for people-watching. One might observe helicopter parents hovering over hyperactive four-year-olds fueling up on hot chocolate and whipped cream, stressed-out college students cramming for midterm exams, retirees discussing the news, a pastor conducting a Bible study for busy executives, and perhaps a traveling pharmaceutical salesperson who breaks from his loud cell phone conversation only long enough to place an order for a double-cupped-venti-soy-extra-sweet-hazelnut-cappuccino-to-go. Given enough time, identifiable patterns would begin to emerge: the strategies parents deploy to manage their children's behavior in public, the concerns of the retired, the ways executives express their faith in public (or not), the unwritten rules of cellphone etiquette, and the cultural lexicon of caffeinated beverages. These observations, in turn, may generate a curiosity to find out what happens at similar coffee shops and how these patterns vary across the range of consumers (e.g., consumption patterns by age, gender, social class, or race) or coffee retailers (e.g., comparing Starbucks, a local independent coffeehouse, and a Dunkin' Donuts). These patterns and comparisons would give us insight into coffee culture and the society in which coffee shops and their patrons are situated.

Coffee shops, however, are not for everyone. In fact their share of total coffee sales in the United States is only 17 percent.[7] Brewed and specialty coffee drinks are expensive. Depending on the retailer, the same $2.00 cup of coffee could be brewed at home for 25 cents or less. As such, those who purchase beverages there are saying something about themselves—especially for the few who make a coffee shop their home away from home. Coffee shop regulars may be saying they have ample money or time, that they may want to be identified with a place that others regard as cool, or that they simply (or sadly) may not have anywhere else to go. Many Americans, however, do not visit coffeehouses on a regular basis. Not only are they constrained by economic considerations, the realities of home and work leave little or no room for lingering in a coffee shop with regularity. Constrained by what Hochschild refers to as the time bind, Americans spend so much time at work that it begins to feel like home, and when they finally get home at the end of a long workday, the legion of responsibilities (preparing meals, cleaning, laundry, helping children with homework, etc.) make home feel more like working a second job.[8] Perhaps the demands of contemporary life in America help to explain the popularity of coffee: an estimated 85 percent of American adults consume a significant amount of caffeine on a daily basis, with 56 percent of Americans drinking at least one cup of coffee a day.[9]

When people drink coffee—whether in a chic coffeehouse, out of a vending machine in a break room, or from a favorite mug at home—they are unwittingly participating in a complex arrangement of social, political, and economic relationships, called a commodity chain, that stretches around the world. Coffee passes through a global system of cultivation, transportation, preparation (roasting), distribution, and consumption that pours the fruit of more than 25 million coffee farmers' labor into approximately 1.5 billion coffee cups around the world each day.[10] Money flows back along this chain with each link receiving a portion of the money spent by consumers.

The coffee revenue stream is important to the less-developed countries in which it is grown. For some of these countries, coffee accounts for more than 20 percent of their exports: Guatemala (21 percent), El Salvador (26), Nicaragua (30), Rwanda (43), Uganda (55), Ethiopia (67), and Burundi (80).[11] Unfortunately, the flow of coffee dollars to these and other coffee-producing countries slowed to a trickle in recent years. The share of every dollar spent on coffee in America that makes it back to coffee-producing countries dropped from 37 cents in 1986 to 12 cents in 2001, a 70-percent decline. Yet, during the same 15-year period, the price of coffee in the United States rose by 40 percent.[12] This is good news for corporate profits but bad news for the many coffee farmers who, because of market forces, are compelled to sell their coffee for less than it costs to cultivate it. Under these conditions, workers on plantations are paid the equivalent of sweatshop wages: they earn approximately $3.00 per day, about the cost of a cappuccino in an American coffeehouse. Not only are their wages low, many workers "live in poverty without plumbing, electricity, medical care, or nutritious foods."[13] While one may believe in a free-market economy or the benefits of globalization, it is important not to ignore the consequences for those people who find themselves economically vulnerable.

Fair-trade coffee represents one way in which these and other inequities are being addressed. In 1998, coffee became the first certified fair-trade product, and by 2009 fair-trade coffee sales in the United States returned an estimated $220 million dollars to coffee producers. Fair-trade certification assists farmers by creating new business opportunities for coffee growers and by cutting unnecessary and exploitative intermediaries out of the commodity chain. In addition, a premium of 10 cents per pound is added to fair-trade-certified coffee in the United States. Money generated through this premium is placed under the control of locally managed community development cooperatives that use the funds for "social and environmental projects within [their] community" such as improving productive capacity, investing in the local infrastructure, supporting environmental sustainability initiatives, and building schools and health clinics.[14]

America—indeed, the world—is awash with coffee, so much so that we take it for granted. Usually, we overlook the irony of drinking a stimulant in the calm atmosphere of a coffee shop. We miss the ways in which social interactions in coffeehouses build relationships and community. We are blind to what drinking coffee (or not) says about who we are individually or as a society. And typically we are oblivious to the social, political, and economic forces that shape the global coffee industry, much less the many ethical issues associated with it. Sociology, however, helps us to see these nuances. It invites us to view the world from a new perspective. It offers an opportunity to examine our taken-for-granted social world as an outsider might and to peel away its many layers of meaning. It equips us with the tools necessary to think about the ways people, events, and society shape our sense of identity and inform the way we interact in everyday life. It focuses our attention on people, their patterns of interaction, and the powerful social forces they create; and it reveals how these social forces, in turn, act back on the same people who created them in ways that shape social interactions and individual life-worlds. And sociology empowers us to think critically about society and culture, brings social issues and problems into sharper focus, and offers insights for those interested in transforming the world in which we live.

What Does One Do with a Degree in Sociology?

Working in a coffee shop to help make ends meet while in college is an economic reality for many. Serving lattes for a living after college, as rewarding as that may be, is not the kind of career to which college graduates typically aspire. Faced with a difficult job market, one characterized by an unemployment rate that hovered around 10 percent in 2010, the prospect of not finding a job in one's field is a very real worry for many. In these uncertain times, it is especially important to choose a major that broadens one's employment opportunities. Unfortunately, many underestimate the market value of a sociology degree and therefore miss out on its potential. It seems that part of this miscalculation has to do with a lack of familiarity with sociology and the range of employment possibilities it generates.

Many degrees have a recognizable employment outcome. It is taken for granted, for example, that those who major in business, nursing, journalism, and engineering step into predictable careers as managers, nurses, journalists, and civil engineers. When it comes to sociology, however, the college-to-career connection is not as obvious. Intuitively, many will suppose that those who major in sociology go on to become sociologists (e.g., professors, demographers, social researchers) or perhaps social workers. While this instinct is correct, these professions only represent one-third of the overall range of possibilities. What careers, then, does a degree in sociology anticipate?

According to the American Sociological Association's national survey of sociology majors who graduated in 2005, 5.7 percent of graduates were employed full time as professional sociologists and 26.5 percent worked in social service careers in 2007.[15] The rest go on to work in a variety of other vocations, which fall into broad categories including administrative support, management, sales and marketing, the public and private service sector, and education (table 12.1). This research also revealed that two years after graduation, 60.3 percent of people with sociology degrees were employed, 13.1 percent were pursuing graduate degrees, and 22 percent were both employed and in graduate programs.[16]

Not only does a degree in sociology prepare people for a variety of professional pursuits, it also establishes a solid foundation for graduate school. By 2009 about half of the 2005 graduates in sociology pursued advanced degrees (i.e., master's or doctoral degrees) in fields of study including sociology, social work, education, law, psychology, engineering, business, and public policy.[17] It is interesting to note that many sociology majors also go on to seminary. According to the Association of Theological Schools' annual survey of incoming students, approximately 23 percent of seminarians held undergraduate degrees in the social sciences in 2010.

Thanks to sociology's robust toolkit of concepts, skills, and insights, students are prepared for a wide range of professions. While some will pursue careers as sociologists and social workers, the majority of sociology graduates will find great utility in a degree that keeps their employment options open in a time of uncertainty in the marketplace. Likewise, the strength of a sociology degree is not lost on employers interested in someone who is able to ask and answer difficult questions, use computer-based technology to analyze and solve problems, make sense of information and data, and communicate ideas using evidence in cogent and compelling ways. Finally, because sociology seeks to understand human life in all its complexity and diversity, students are prepared to work with people from backgrounds different than their own.

Table 12.1 Types of Occupations Held by People with Sociology Degrees

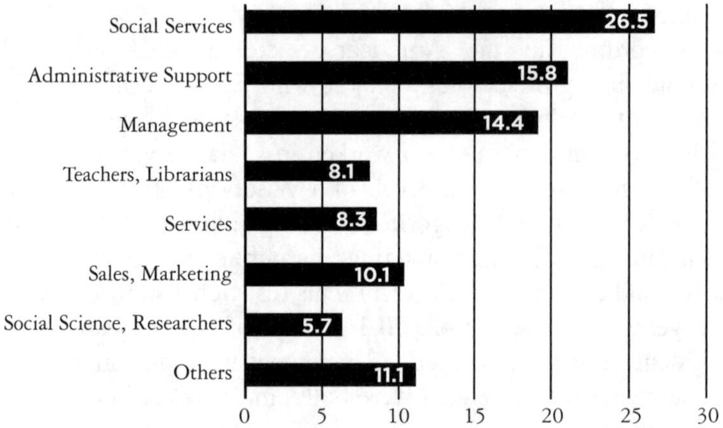

Why Should Christians Study Sociology?

Christians hold a curious variety of perspectives on sociology. Some may have been bedeviled by a college professor—or the legend thereof—who seemed to have gone out of his or her way to disabuse Christians of their "unfounded" faith. Others may have had a tamer experience with a stodgy professor who, for want of imagination and enthusiasm, made the subject interminably boring. In other cases, certain Christian leaders have dismissed sociology, among other academic disciplines, as only good for this-worldly pursuits and therefore not pertinent to the work of spreading the gospel. In contrast, other believers—ones no less committed to the mission of the church—regard sociology as offering invaluable insights for the ministry of the church in the world. These compelling accounts and conflicting views obscure the value of sociology from Christians who are determined to have a redemptive impact through their lives, work, and service. Therefore, I offer the following arguments for why a Christian should study sociology.

A Different Way of Seeing the World

First, sociology invites Christians to see the social world from a new perspective, one that peers beyond the surface of everyday life to reveal the rich textures, nuances, and complexity of society and culture. Most people, many of whom are thoughtful Christians, take their social, cultural, and historical context for granted. Few ever ponder, for example, the irony of sipping a stimulant-fortified beverage in the calm environment of a coffee shop. The rapid growth of coffee shops in the United States over the past 20 years from 200 to more than 20,000 does not typically enter into casual conversation, even though it is latent in the gratitude that a decent coffee shop is going in down the street from one's office. Coffee's power to shape identities, build relationships, and create community usually goes unnoticed. People tend not to notice the global economic and political forces that structure the coffee industry from its cultivation to its consumption, yet these very real, very powerful forces shape our everyday lives. And the idea that there may be ethical questions associated with coffee is not on the typical American's moral radar.

Life is much more than coffee. Very few people, however, stop to think even about coffee, much less the rest of social life. We fail to see the powerful ways in which social, cultural, and historical forces shape everyday life. Factors such as race, social class, and gender are off the proverbial radar screen, not to mention the moral questions raised by these features of daily life. Few consider the complex ways in which life is structured by social forces, how they shape our sense of who we are (or not), and help determine what we are capable of doing (or not) in the world. Sociology, however, makes visible the unseen features of everyday life. As such, it is an opportunity to see one's own society and culture as an outsider might: with wonder, curiosity, and a healthy dose of criticism.

The ability to perceive in these ways requires a sociological imagination. Sociologist C. Wright Mills developed the notion of the sociological imagination, which "enables us to grasp history and biography and the relations between the two within society."[18] Americans are often characterized by their tendency toward individualism, a focus on the capacity and responsibility of the individual to direct his own affairs. With this focus comes a propensity to think in individualistic, or strictly autobiographical, terms about oneself and others. For example, what comes to mind when you encounter a homeless person on the street? Perhaps you, like many Americans, would wonder what that individual did to end up in such dire straits. While individual decisions and issues may play a role in a homeless person's life, broader social forces are also at work. Certainly the fact that Americans are in the midst of an economic recession, for example, with high rates of unemployment across the board and certain sectors of the economy being hit harder, has something to do with unemployment and homelessness. Thus, for a homeless man in Detroit, his circumstances may have something to do with the collapse of the American car manufacturing industry. He may have built the car you drive but is now unemployed and homeless due to factors beyond his control.

Sociology invites a more complex and nuanced view of the world, one that involves the capacity to understand individual experience within the broad patterns of society in specific places and at specific times in history. This is what Mills means by grasping history and biography and the relationship between the two in society. Once the relationships of people and society over time become apparent, sociology offers concepts, skills, and insights that allow people to peer beneath the surface, to see the invisible forces that shape our everyday lives. Consider, for example, my experience as a recent immigrant to the South from an idyllic seaside village on the New England coast near Boston. When people ranging from my dental hygienist to the salesperson at a furniture store realized that I was new to Tennessee, I was surprised that their first question was not "What brings you to Jackson?" Instead, they were more likely to ask, “What church do you attend?” or “Where do your children go to school?” within the opening minutes of a conversation with a complete stranger.

Back in Massachusetts, one’s religious commitment is not a topic for polite conversation with a new acquaintance. And while there is nothing terribly intrusive about asking where someone’s children go to school, it is not a typical conversation starter with your dental hygienist or a furniture salesperson. Why, then, were so many people in Jackson interested in the church I attend and the school to which I send my children? The answer, as you might expect, is a social one. It turns out that, in my new context, these two questions help to locate an individual’s social position. While a complete stranger may be genuinely interested in my spiritual condition, when she asks what church I attend, she really wants to know where to locate me on her cultural map. By knowing the church I attend she gains insight into my beliefs, values, and practices. Church membership signals the kind of person I am. Because Christianity in Jackson includes a broad range of denominations—51 percent of adults in Tennessee are evangelicals who belong to scores of denominations, for example (see chart 12.1; Pew Forum)—knowing where I go to church adds a level of certainty to the kind of person I am. These distinctions were less relevant in Massachusetts, where the notion of being a Christian carries a different set of meanings.

Where I send my children to school reveals another important detail about my identity, one that gives clues about my socioeconomic status. Attending a public school places a household on a map in a school district, which is a defined geographic region that draws children from particular kinds of neighborhoods. These neighborhoods, in turn, suggest something about one’s income level. On the other hand, enrolling children in a private school signals another set of resources, commitments, and statuses. Likewise, the kind of private school makes a difference. After all, enrolling one’s children in a private Christian school says something different than sending them to a college prep school, which of course is very different than homeschooling one’s children. Private school represents a commitment to a particular kind and quality of education. Having one’s children in private school also indicates the ability to pay the $6,000 (or more) annual tuition rate for each child. In each case, where one’s children attend school has much to say about a family's socioeconomic status. Thus, when people ask me where my children attend school, I decode their question as a polite way to inquire about my standard of living, the kind of company I keep, and my priorities.

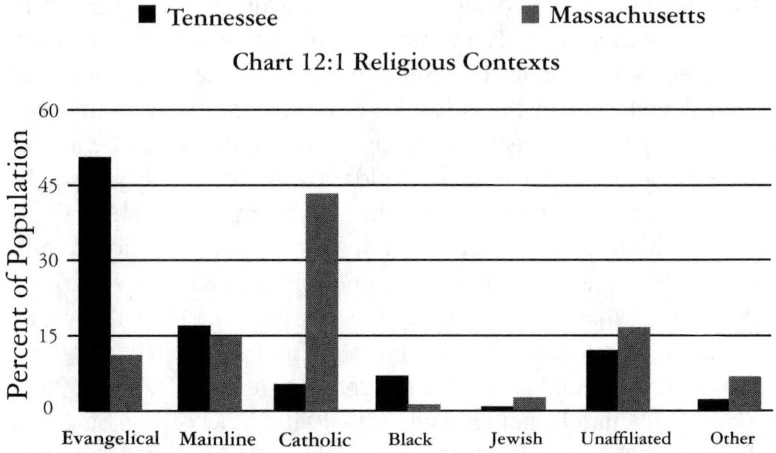

A third question about my place in society goes unasked but is always answered in any initial face-to-face interaction: "What is your race?" When someone meets me for the first time, there is little questioning that I am a white male. Being white in Jackson, Tennessee, is different than being white in Manchester, Massachusetts. Jackson is a small city of over 60,000 residents with a population that is 55 percent white and 42 percent black (quickfacts.census.gov). Manchester is a small town with a population of 5,500 that is 98.9 percent white (Department of Housing and Community Development). In Jackson, race is a salient feature of everyday life, one that structures the ways in which people live. Like much of America—indeed, the world—Jackson is racialized; that is, it is a place where "*race matters profoundly for differences in life experiences, life opportunities, and social relationships.*"[19] Race is more than the color of one's skin. Race tells you where to live. Race decides whether and where you go to school. Race helps determine your salary. Race informs where you worship. Race influences friendships. In short, race structures society. This structuring is more apparent to me in Jackson than it was in Manchester, a fact that may be attributed to demographic differences of place.

Race, social class, and religion are not alone in their ability to structure social life. They just happen to be the social forces that are most apparent to me in my new social setting. While I may experience these and other forces in unique ways, I am not alone. Everyone experiences social structures. Few, however, are aware of their presence. In their study of evangelical Christianity and race in America, Michael Emerson and Christian Smith point out that evangelicals are especially blind to social structures. The cause of this myopia, they argue persuasively, is wrapped up in evangelical culture, which precludes an ability "to perceive or unwillingness to accept social structural influences."[20] As a result, many of the most important social issues of the day are obscured from view and misunderstood.

The ability to see the social and cultural forces that, for better or worse, shape everyday life is one reason for Christians to study sociology. Like a good student of the Bible, one who reads Scripture within its biblical, historical, and theological contexts, sociology helps Christians situate their individual experiences within the broader contexts of history and society. Sociology broadens one's ability to understand how the world works, offers a more informed perspective on society and culture, and helps people to interpret the many meanings present in the layers of everyday life.

Seeing the world from the sociological perspective also invites an evaluation of the complex layers of culture and the unseen social structures that shape everyday life. Sociology is known for—or perhaps notorious for—its critical-thinking approach to the social world in which we live. Unfortunately, critical thinking is often misunderstood as an inherently negative enterprise; in reality, however, critical thinking is a constructive and necessary practice that entails the careful evaluation of assumptions, ideas, and knowledge based on evidence. From a sociological perspective, a critical approach involves "engaging in systematic doubt about accounts of the social world, proceeding with skepticism about the claim of any statement to be a valid account of a particular matter, and then narrowing down the range of doubt as much as possible."[21] Thinking critically about something as mundane as coffee uncovers the moral consequences of modern life in a global economy. A critical perspective on whether, where, and under what circumstances a child goes to school raises important questions about the educational system, social classes, and future of America. An evaluation of assumptions about homelessness uncovers the roots of the problem. And through the critical lens, the power of race is brought into sharper focus and identifies a blind spot for many conservative Christians. In short, by thinking critically about the social world, the sociological perspective helps to "uncover and expose the ambiguities, misrepresentations, distortions, and even falsehoods in competing explanations for particular social phenomena."[22]

Changing the World around Us

The concepts, skills, and insights of sociology are not only useful in explaining and evaluating the contemporary world in which we live, but these tools are foundational to transforming society and culture. It would be unsatisfying to identify a misrepresentation, distortion, falsehood, or problem in society and do nothing. Seeing a social problem and doing nothing may be likened to the priest and Levite in the parable of the Good Samaritan who avoided helping a person who was obviously in need (Luke 10:25–37). Instead, Christians are called to act like the Good Samaritan who, despite the social structures that would normally prevent him from interacting with a Jew and in contrast to the religious leaders who passed by a man in need, went out of his way to respond to a stranger who had been beaten by robbers and left for dead.

In a similar way, sociology compels people to go out of their way to make a difference in someone's life. In contrast to the individual action of the Good Samaritan, sociology invites Christians to challenge, confront, and transform the social structures that ignore those who are mistreated, passed by, and left for dead. The Good Samaritan in Jesus' parable was commended for loving his neighbor as he loved himself. He fulfilled and epitomized the Great Commandment. While his act may have impacted Jewish–Samaritan relations, directly addressed a symptom of crime, or exemplified what it means to love one's neighbor, this kind of action is individual, localized, and not likely to affect significant societal change.

Generally speaking, changing society requires a group of people pooling their resources—for example, people, money, tools, technology, and organizational knowhow—and putting those resources into action. If the Good Samaritan had been inspired by this encounter to transform society, it would have required something more than his individual efforts. The issues at stake—crime, unwillingness to help those in critical need, and ethnic tensions between Jews and Samaritans—are simply too big for one person's efforts to overcome.

However, if the Good Samaritan had organized a group of citizens for safe roadways or a neighborhood watch to deter criminal activity, it might have been possible not just to help a victim of a mugging but to address the root causes of crime. While his heroic effort to help a person in need is to be commended, working together with other people to address widely held cultural distortions of what it means to love one's neighbor is an entirely different project, one that requires putting resources into action collectively. Likewise, even though the Good Samaritan's care for someone who came from a culture that regarded Samaritans as inferior may have changed a small number of people's minds, only an organized and widespread campaign of random acts of kindness by Samaritans, on the other hand, might have been sufficient to transform Jewish prejudices toward Samaritans. If this individual was commended by Jesus for loving his neighbor, one wonders what Jesus might have said of those who would work together to transform society for the good of those who are mistreated, ignored, and left for dead.

Sociology's interest in transforming society and culture goes hand in hand with the Great Commandment of loving one's neighbor. By providing an understanding of how the social world works and offering tools with which to evaluate society and culture, sociology identifies ways in which Christians might play a role in changing society. Likewise, sociology's perspective on how social change takes place offers insights useful for transforming the world. Christians should study sociology, then, because sociology offers tools for changing society in ways that fulfill the Great Commandment.

Fresh Approaches for Gospel Witness

Not only does sociology equip Christians to be more effective in living out the Great Commandment, it also invites greater effectiveness in pursuing the Great Commission. For quite some time now, missionaries preparing for and participating in cross-cultural ministry have appropriated the insights of anthropology to great effect.[23] What anthropology is to traditional missionary work, sociology is to the contemporary global mission of the church. So whether it means loving one's neighbor across the street or taking the message and ministry of the gospel around the world, sociology offers helpful tools for ministering in the twenty-first century.

Perceiving the many layers of meaning present in the social world allows for more authentic and effective strategies for outreach. The ability to utilize demographic information, for example, to analyze and describe the community in which a church is situated opens up new strategies for serving the people to whom a congregation is called. Sociological insights on culture and society equip pastors to communicate the Christian message in more creative and compelling ways. Through sociology, church leaders are able to make more informed and more strategic decisions. And the insights of sociology assist everyday Christians in their efforts to serve others and share the gospel message winsomely.

Relating to Culture and Society

Finally, sociology is an important field of study because it offers Christians a new vocabulary with which to express ideas, one that is more commonly shared by the rest of society. While sound theological ideas may undergird one's critique of culture or efforts to transform society, those who live outside the Christian community do not share the same sources of authority, morality, or power. Sociology provides rational explanations, critiques, and strategies of change that are legitimate for everyone. If Christians are to contend in the public square, it is essential to become fluent in the same logic, rhetoric, and standards of veracity as their fellow, non-Christian citizens. Doing so adds up to a more informed, strategic, creative, and winsome Christianity. Likewise, it strengthens the reputation of Christians and places new resources within reach.

An Invitation to Sociology

Sociology offers a robust intellectual toolkit of concepts, skills, and insights useful for understanding, assessing, and transforming the contemporary world in which we live. It invites people to explore their taken-for-granted social world from a new perspective, one that involves the ability to "grasp history and biography and the relations between the two within society."[24] Engaging the sociological imagination in this way helps people to see the invisible yet palpable social structures and forces that shape everyday life. People begin to see, for example, the social function of coffee, the roots of poverty, and the power of race. Once visible, sociology invites a critical assessment of these (among other) features of society and culture. And sociology equips Christians with the tools necessary for effecting significant change in society by fulfilling the great commandment and pursuing the Great Commission.

Because sociology prepares college students for a wide variety of career paths, it offers students great latitude in pursuing employment. Likewise, the concepts and critical thinking skills of sociology constitute a solid foundation for graduate school and seminary. For these reasons, I contend that sociology is among the most important fields of study for living, working, and serving in the twenty-first century.

Questions for Further Reflection

1. After reading this chapter how would you respond to the assertion made by Screwtape in C. S. Lewis's *The Screwtape Letters* that sociology is an intellectual path that potentially leads to the gates of hell?
2. Coffee and coffee shops are a taken-for-granted feature of everyday life. Through the sociological imagination, however, new layers of meaning and significance emerge along with important moral questions. What aspect of your own life do you wonder about? What do you imagine sociology reveals about it? What, if any, moral questions does it evoke? And what changes (if any) does the sociological perspective inspire?
3. What kind(s) of change (e.g., individual, social, cultural, or spiritual) are legitimate for Christians to pursue?
4. In your perspective, what is the relationship between the great commandment and the Great Commission? Is one more important than the other? How might sociology inform, sustain, or challenge your views?
5. On what basis do you accept or reject the claim that sociology is *the most important* field of study for living, working, and ministering in the twenty-first century?

Resources for Further Study

A comprehensive list of resources for further study is available on the Association for Christians Teaching Sociology website at http://www.actsoc.org/biblio.htm. As a sociologist of religion, I also recommend the following as interesting and accessible texts.

Ammerman, Nancy. *Bible Believers: Fundamentalists in the Modern World.* New Brunswick, NJ: Rutgers University Press. 1987.

Bellah, Robert N., Richard Madsen, William M. Sullivan, Ann Swidler, and Steven M. Tipton. *Habits of the Heart: Individualism and Commitment in American Life.* Berkeley and Los Angeles: University of California Press, 1985.

Emerson, Michael O., and Christian Smith. *Divided by Faith: Evangelical Religion and the Problem of Race in America.* New York: Oxford University Press, 2000.

Finke, Roger, and Rodney Stark. *The Churching of America, 1776–2005: Winners and Losers in Our Religious Economy.* New Brunswick, NJ: Rutgers University Press, 2005.

Fraser, David, and Tony Campolo. *Sociology through the Eyes of Faith.* New York: Harper One, 1992.

Smith, Christian, with Melinda Lindquist Denton. *Soul Searching: The Religious Lives and Spiritual Lives of American Teenagers.* New York: Oxford University Press, 2005.

Wright, Bradley R. E. *Christians Are Hate-Filled Hypocrites . . . and Other Lies You've Been Told.* Minneapolis, MN: Bethany House, 2010.

Wuthnow, Robert. *Boundless Faith: The Global Outreach of American Churches.* Berkeley and Los Angeles, CA: University of California Press, 2009.

Endnotes

1 C. S. Lewis, *The Screwtape Letters* (London: G. Bles, 1943), 14.

2 Peter L. Berger, *An Invitation to Sociology* (Garden City, NY: Anchor, 1963).

3 Ibid., 23.

4 See Anthony Giddens, Mitchell Duneier, Richard P. Applebaum, and Deboreh Carr, *Essentials of Sociology* (New York: Norton, 2011), 6–9.

5 Craig J. Thompson and Zeynap Arsel, "The Starbucks Brandscape and Consumers' (Anticorporate) Experiences of Glocalization," *The Journal of Consumer Research* 31 (2004): 631.

6 See Ray Oldenburg, *The Great Good Place: Cafés, Coffee Shops, Bookstores, Bars, Hair Salons and Other Hangouts at the Heart of a Community* (New York: MarLowe, 1999).

7 Nina Luttinger and Gregory Dicum, *The Coffee Book: Anatomy of an Industry from Crop to Last Drop* (New York: New Press, 2006), 154.

[8] See Arlie Russell Hochschild, *The Time Bind: When Work Becomes Home and Home Becomes Work* (New York: Metropolitan, 1997).
[9] See Bennett Alan Weinberg and Bonnie K. Bealer, *The World of Caffeine: The Science and Culture of the World's Most Popular Drug* (New York: Routledge, 2001); and "Coffee Consumption Remains Stable, Says Survey," *Tea & Coffee Trade Journal* 182, no. 4 (April 2010): 20.
[10] See Luttinger and Dicum, *Coffee Book.*
[11] Daniel Jaffee, *Brewing Justice: Fair Trade Coffee, Sustainability, and Survival* (Berkeley: University of California Press, 2007), 47.
[12] Luttinger and Dicum, *Coffee Book*, 115.
[13] Mark Pendergrast, *Uncommon Grounds: The History of Coffee and How it Transformed the World* (New York: Basic, 2010), xvi.
[14] See "Fair Trade Certified Coffee," *TransFair USA* (Oakland: TransFair, 2010), 8–9.
[15] Roberta Spalter-Roth, Mary S. Senter, and Nicole Van Vooren, *Launching Majors into Satisfying Careers* (Washington, DC: American Sociological Association, 2010), 16.
[16] Ibid., 1.
[17] Ibid., 47; see Stephen E. Lambert, *Great Jobs for Sociology Majors* (New York: McGraw-Hill, 2009).
[18] C. Wright Mills, *The Sociological Imagination* (New York: Oxford, 1959), 6.
[19] Michael O. Emerson and Christian Smith, *Divided by Faith* (New York: Oxford, 2000), 76, emphasis in original.
[20] Ibid.
[21] Evan Willis, *The Sociological Quest: An Introduction to the Study of Sociology* (New Brunswick, NJ: Rutgers University Press, 1996), 83.
[22] Ibid.
[23] See Paul G. Hiebert, *Anthropological Insights for Missionaries* (Grand Rapids: Baker, 1985), and Charles H. Kraft, *Anthropology for Christian Witness* (Maryknoll, NY: Orbis, 1996).
[24] Mills, *The Sociological Imagination*, 6.

13

CHRISTIANITY AND THE ARTS

Steve Halla

The visual arts, literature, music, and the performing arts have played an important role throughout Christian history. This is true of Catholicism, Protestantism, and the Orthodox tradition, though to varying degrees in each. From the days of the early church to the present, the arts have served as an effective means of stirring the soul, engaging the intellect, arresting the emotions, enlivening the imagination, and motivating the will. Many Christian theologians and intellectuals from John of Damascus and Thomas Aquinas to John Calvin and C. S. Lewis have reflected on the nature and value of the arts. What we think about the arts has a direct impact on what we think about other important biblical and theological issues such as the nature of God, the Bible, Christian education, and vice versa. The arts, by virtue of their biblical, theological, and philosophical roots and historical use within the church form a vital part of Christian life and education.

Since the late nineteenth century, the arts in general have undergone a tremendous amount of cultural, stylistic, technological, and philosophical change. Unfortunately, the Christian community has not always maintained an active artistic presence in and through these times of change, despite the laudable efforts of individuals such as Gerardus van der Leeuw, Marie-Alain Couturier, C. S. Lewis, Francis Schaeffer, Hans Rookmaaker, Dorothy Sayers, Calvin Seerveld, Nicholas Wolterstorff, Leland Ryken, and, more recently, William Dyrness, Gregory Wolfe, and Daniel Siedell. The result, in many instances, has been a sense of disconnect not only between Christianity and various facets of the arts, but also between Christianity and elements of its own rich artistic tradition, which, in today's aesthetically charged cultural environment, is no slight matter. All too often it seems many Christians nowadays assume the role of armchair cultural critics, espousing endless personal opinions *about* the arts while seldom making significant contributions *to* the arts. Transformative artistic engagement, however, requires both word *and* deed. Thus there is an ongoing need to cultivate and maintain meaningful Christian dialogues with the arts that encourage artistic activity and innovation as well as biblical, theological, and philosophical artistic reflection.

The following chapter is designed to provide some general thoughts and observations on the subject of Christianity and the arts as a way of stimulating reflection. First, we will begin by sketching out a biblical perspective of the arts. Second, we will consider the role of the arts in Christian history with an emphasis on the pedagogical value of the arts. Finally, we will reflect on several guiding principles for the Christian artist. Through this brief study, my hope is that we might be reminded that today we stand as heirs of a rich Christian arts tradition.

The Arts and the Bible

The Bible is the divinely inspired and inerrant Word of God. It is central to the Christian life and sheds light on all areas of human activity, including the arts. Although the Bible does not directly address the arts, it does contain various principles, patterns, examples, and doctrines that faithfully govern how God's people are to approach, think about, and engage the arts. In his book, *The Christian, the Arts, and Truth*, Frank E. Gaebelein writes that in the Bible "we find no ambivalence to the arts in themselves. Instead we find deep implications regarding them, for the Bible speaks to us about who we are and about our aesthetic responsibility under God."[1] Throughout Christian history, theologians and other intellectuals have generally grounded their discussions of the arts in Genesis 1–3, and for good reason. The opening three chapters of the book of Genesis not only introduces us to God the Creator but also provides invaluable insights into the nature of human artistry, creativity, and imagination.

The Creation Account

The book of Genesis opens with the iconic words, "In the beginning God created the heavens and the earth" (Gen 1:1 HCSB). The very first thing we learn about God in the Bible is that He is *the* divine Creator, the Artisan of all creation. Before we learn that God is righteous, for example, we learn that He is creative; before we learn that He is compassionate, we learn that He is imaginative; before we learn that He is love, we learn that He is artistic. Although we need to be careful not to make too much of these opening words, we must also not make the opposite mistake of treating them too lightly. Millard Erickson reminds us that God "thought the fact of creation significant enough to put it first."[2] The importance of God's creative, imaginative, and artistic nature is reflected elsewhere in the Bible where it speaks about God in decidedly artisan terms, particularly as a potter. For example, the prophet Jeremiah declares, "Just like clay in the potter's hand, so are you in My hand, house of Israel" (Jer 18:6 HCSB), while the apostle Paul writes, "But who are you, a mere man, to talk back to God? Will what is formed say to the one who formed it, 'Why did you make me like this?' Or has the potter no right over the clay, to make from the same lump one piece of pottery for honor and another for dishonor?" (Rom 9:20–21 HCSB). Such artisan language has been used by Christian artists and intellectuals throughout the centuries to craft fresh ways for us to think about God and our relationship to Him. The early church father and apologist Irenaeus, for example, in his treatise *Against Heresies,* writes (as translated by Thomas Merton), "If you are the work of God wait patiently for the hand of your artist who makes all things at an opportune time. . . . Give to Him a pure and supple heart and watch over the form which the artist shapes in you . . . lest, in hardness, you lose the traces of His fingers. . . . If, therefore, you hand over to Him what is yours, namely, faith in Him and submission, you will see his skill and be a perfect work of God."[3] In the same spirit, the Scottish poet Horatius Bonar paints a moving portrait of God as the master sculptor of our lives in his poem "The Master's Touch":

> In the still air the music lies unheard;
>   In the rough marble beauty hides unseen;
> To wake the music and the beauty needs
>   The master's touch, the sculptor's chisel keen.

Great Master, touch us with thy skillful hand;
 Let not the music that is in us die!
Great Sculptor, hew and polish us; nor let,
 Hidden and lost, thy form within us lie!

Spare not the stroke! Do with us as thou wilt!
 Let there be naught unfinished, broken, marred;
Complete thy purpose, that we may become
 Thy perfect image, O our God and Lord![4]

The artistic, creative, and imaginative nature of God as inferred in Gen 1:1 is *the* starting point for thinking Christianly about the arts.

Continuing in Genesis 1, the Bible records that on the sixth day of creation, God made man "in his own image" (cf. Gen 1:26–27). Historically, Christians have affirmed the belief that human artistry, creativity, and imagination is ultimately rooted in the *imago Dei*. In 1999, Pope John Paul II delivered an address to artists wherein he affirmed this belief saying, "through his 'artistic creativity' man appears more than ever 'in the image of God,' and he accomplishes this task above all in shaping the wondrous 'material' of his own humanity and then exercising creative dominion over the universe which surrounds him."[5] God, in His infinite wisdom, chose to create human beings as spiritual *and* physical beings with the ability to think as well as the aptitude to create. Francis Schaeffer, in his essay "Art and the Bible," notes that "an art work has value as a creation because man is made in the image of God, and therefore man not only can love and think and feel emotion, but also has the capacity to create."[6] We are artistic, creative, and imaginative, i.e., "aesthetic," because God Himself is artistic, creative, and imaginative. We take pleasure in the arts because God Himself takes pleasure in the arts. We are all, having been made in God's image, aesthetic beings. Consequently, everything we do in life has, to some degree, an aesthetic dimension.

In Gen 1:28, God continues by revealing His plan of how His image bearers are to function within His creation: "Be fruitful, multiply, fill the earth, and subdue it. Rule the fish of the sea, the birds of the sky, and every creature that crawls on the earth." At the heart of God's plan is the task of stewardship. Central to this task of stewardship is the activity of subduing, or bringing further order to, God's creation. Every activity we do in life is, in essence, an act of subjugation. The same is true of the arts. All art is an act of subjugation; poets bring order to words, potters bring order to clay, musicians bring order to sounds, conceptual artists bring order to ideas, and so on. Without the act of subjugation, the arts simply would not exist. The poet T. S. Eliot reminds us of this when he writes that "it is a function of all art to give us some perception of an order in life, by imposing an order upon it."[7] From this perspective, I personally define the arts, generally speaking, as the *aesthetic*, i.e., artistic, creative, and imaginative, subjugation of creation. An important aspect of our role as God's image bearers is the aesthetic stewardship of His creation.

When we faithfully exercise our aesthetic stewardship, we not only bring glory to God through our actions, but we also testify to the reality of God's existence. While postulating on the nature of icons, Pavel Florensky writes, "Of all the philosophical proofs of the existence of God, that which carries the most conviction is not mentioned in any textbook. It may be summarized as follows: 'Rublev's Holy Trinity icon exists, therefore God exists.'"[8] When we act aesthetically we reflect, through the very nature of our actions, the aesthetic nature of our Creator. No artwork has ever come into existence apart from an artist, i.e., an aesthetic being, who made it. For this reason, I believe art museums, for example, are among the most theologically rich environments in all of society. Every work of art displayed therein, by virtue of its existence, provides me with an opportunity to reflect on the glorious truth of the *imago Dei* and its source *Deus omnipotens*. The arts, when viewed from this particular theological perspective, are ever-present cultural fingerprints of God's existence.

The Wilderness Tabernacle

Following God's miraculous delivery of the sons of Israel out of bondage in Egypt, He led them safely to Mount Sinai. There, He gave Moses the Law, which included specific instructions for the construction of a sacred tent of meeting, the tabernacle. The instructions included, among other things, the use of a wide range of artistic mediums and techniques as well as representational and nonrepresentational forms of visual art. To commence the project, God filled and empowered Bezalel, son of Uri, with great artistic skill, intelligence, and craftsmanship and blessed a whole host of skilled artisans, including Oholiab, son of Ahisamach. To complete the project, God called upon all the sons of Israel to contribute the necessary materials, of which they did willingly and generously. Upon completion, the cloud of the Lord "covered the tent of meeting, and the glory of the LORD filled the tabernacle" (Exod 40:34 HCSB).

Though much could be said about the wilderness tabernacle and its relationship to the arts, there are two observations in particular worth noting. The first observation is that it was God Himself who supplied the tabernacle's designs. Nowhere else in the Bible are we given a more intimate glimpse into how God Himself conceives of earthly sacred space than here in tabernacle account. The second observation is that the designs provided by God were acutely creative, wildly imaginative, and intensely artistic. From the gold-covered ark of the covenant to the colorful priestly garments, the designs called for the making of beautiful objects of exquisite artisanship that appealed directly to the senses. In other words, God provided His people with designs that were consistent with how He had created them as aesthetic beings. Artistry, creativity, and imagination were central features of the tabernacle worship environment.

The Nature of the Bible

While the Bible is the divinely inspired and inerrant Word of God, at the same time it is also a compilation of literary works of art. All literature, including the Bible, is an artistic expression that simultaneously engages the intellect and imagination. Literary critic and theorist Northrop Frye once referred to literature as the "language of the imagination."[9] Although the Bible is much more than literature, it is also no less. The literary nature of the Bible, like the tabernacle, reminds us, once again, of God's desire to engage us as aesthetic beings. For rather than providing us with a formal treatise or encyclopedic-type document, He chose instead a literary form that, by its very nature, requires the active use of the imagination. An important observation about the imagination is that it requires healthy exercise if it is to grow and develop properly. The Bible, by virtue of its literary nature, addresses this need every time we read it. For when we read the Bible, we instinctively make use of our intellect *and* imagination.

Structurally speaking, the Bible is a composite work consisting of 66 interdependent books representing a wide variety of literary genres including poetry, narrative, apocalyptic, and many more. It has recently been estimated that the Bible may contain more than 100 different literary genres.[10] One of the Bible's most artistic genres is the parable, i.e., a dramatic story that paints vivid word-pictures designed to engage the intellect through the imagination in order to elicit a response. Leland Ryken, in his book *How to Read the Bible as Literature*, writes that "the parables represent the beauty of simplicity, and they can be enjoyed first of all as examples of narrative art."[11] Throughout His teaching ministry, Jesus made great use of parables, which make up approximately one-third of His total recorded teachings. Such usage suggests Jesus' confidence not only in the use of an artistic form to communicate truth, but also in the ability of the imagination to receive truth. Jesus placed no less faith in parables than He did other forms of communication, such as sermons, to advance the kingdom of God on earth. Here again, we find an example of God engaging people as aesthetic beings.

It is often said that a leading characteristic of an artistic "masterpiece" is its ability to inspire the creation of other artworks. If this is true, then Jesus' parables, from a purely artistic perspective, are bona fide masterpieces. Throughout history, Jesus' parables have inspired the creation of countless artworks, many of which are masterpieces in their own right. One such work is Rembrandt van Rijn's *Return of the Prodigal Son* (c. 1662), which shows the prodigal son ragged and on his knees resting in the warm embrace of his loving father. In 1983, Henry H. M. Nouwen encountered a reproduction of Rembrandt's *Return of the Prodigal Son* that forever changed his life. A few years later in 1992, he published an account of his transformative experiences with this artwork: "A seemingly insignificant encounter with a poster presenting a detail of Rembrandt's *The Return of the Prodigal Son* set in motion a long spiritual adventure that brought me to a new understanding of my vocation and offered me new strength to live it. At the heart of this adventure is a seventeenth-century painting and its artist, a first century-parable and its author, and a twentieth-century person in search of life's meaning."[12] Nouwen's book remains a stirring example of the value of the arts in theological reflection and the ongoing transformative power of Jesus' parabolic teachings.

Enjoying the Arts

Based on even the little that we have discussed thus far, we can confidently say that the Bible presents a positive view of the arts. At the same time, however, the Bible warns repeatedly against the misuse of the arts, which leads to idolatry. The arts, like everything else in creation, have the potential to be used inappropriately and lead us away from God rather than draw us closer to Him. Whenever we engage the arts there will always be a tension between rightfully enjoying the arts and wrongfully loving the arts. Let us therefore be careful to employ the arts with all humility, wisdom, and prayer. Augustine said it best when he wrote, "If the things of this world delight you, praise God for them but turn your love away from them and give it to their Maker, so that in the things that please you, you may not displease him. . . . The good things which you love are all from God, but they are good and sweet only as long as they are used to do his will. They will rightly turn bitter if God is spurned and the things that come from him are wrongly loved."[13]

The Arts and Christian History

In much the same way that the Bible presents a positive view of the arts, the arts have played a positive role throughout Christian history. Generally speaking, the arts have been used by the church to aid in the presentation, promotion, and preservation of biblical and theological truths and ideas. More specifically, the arts have been used for such things as to inspire and motivate toward godly behavior, aid in personal and corporate prayer and worship, illustrate and beautify the biblical text, adorn sacred space, combat heresy, wage propaganda wars, and assist in evangelism, just to name a few. As a leading purveyor of Western culture for much of its history, the church has functioned as an important patron of the arts not only by commissioning works of art, but also by encouraging artistic production and providing a biblical and theological lens through which to envision the arts.

At the same time, the arts have always been a source of controversy in the church. In fact, there has never been a time in Christian history when the arts, especially the visual arts,[14] have not been a source of concern. Twice, such concern reached a breaking point, once during the Byzantine iconoclastic controversy (eighth and ninth centuries) and the other during the iconoclastic controversy of the Protestant Reformation (sixteenth century). In each event, issues involving the arts were woven into a larger complex and disputed cultural and theological context. While not all Christian theologians and intellectuals have agreed on the precise nature of the relationship between Christianity and the arts, few have ever denied that such a relationship exists. We will examine the relationship between Christian history and the arts more in depth by reflecting on two topics that make up part of the life-blood that flows through the veins of the Christian arts tradition: the artistic spirit of the medieval cathedral and Martin Luther's engagement with the arts.

The Artistic Spirit of the Medieval Cathedral

The period of history commonly known as the Middle Ages (c. 600–1400) represents a high point in the history of the integration of Christianity and the arts. In 600, Pope Gregory the Great wrote a letter to Serenius, the bishop of Marseilles, admonishing him for his recent iconoclastic actions: "It is one thing to worship a painting, and quite another to learn from a scene represented in a painting what ought to be worshipped. For what writing provides for people who read, paintings provide for the illiterate (*idiotis*) who look at them, since these unlearned people see what they must imitate; paintings are books for those who do not know their letters, so that they take the place of books, especially among pagans."[15] Although not all of Gregory's contemporaries agreed with his pedagogical assessment of the visual arts, others heartily approved and actively followed suit. Through the use of symbolism, in particular, medieval Christianity developed a vibrant iconographic language that became central to its didactic ministry. From a rose among thorns to a human skull, all of God's creation became a storehouse of spiritual truth mediated by the arts. The poet Alan of Lille, expounding on this belief, wrote:

> Every creature of this earth
> is like a picture or a book:
> it is a mirror of ourselves.
> It is a faithful mark
> of our life and of our death,
> of our state and of our fate.
> The rose is a picture,
> a fitting image of our state,
> a lesson on our life;
> for it flowers in early morning,
> and the fading flower flowers
> in the evening of age.[16]

While viewing life through a fourfold hermeneutical lens of literal, allegorical, moral, and anagogical senses, artisans and theologians worked together to create sacred environments that were as pedagogically rich as they were arrestingly beautiful. The arts as *biblia pauperum* (*Bible of the poor*), provided access to biblical and theological truths and ideas otherwise inaccessible except to the learned few. In no other place was such access more palpable than the great medieval cathedrals.

The magnificent cathedrals of the late medieval period, e.g., Chartes, Soissons, Reims, Amiens, Bourges, and Beauvais, represent the height of medieval art and applied theology. Even now, these "doorways to heaven" stand as enduring monuments of the aesthetic Christian faith that once blanketed much of Europe. From delicately carved pulpits to color-saturated stained-glass windows, nearly every square inch of the cathedral was designed to beautify and illuminate, to arrest the senses as well as to redirect one's thoughts. Every cathedral, in its own unique way, stood as an embodiment of the full breadth of Christian knowledge and was constructed in a manner fitting the God it sought to magnify. The cathedrals represent the epitome of ecclesiastical form and function.

Today, the artistic spirit of the great medieval cathedrals lives on in a variety of creative and innovative ecclesiastical structures. One such structure is the Chapelle du Rosaire (Chapel of the Rosary) in Vence, France, designed by the celebrated French artist Henry Matisse. The story behind the chapel's inception is just as engaging as the chapel itself. In 1942, Matisse, while recovering from cancer surgery, placed an ad at a local nursing school seeking "a young and pretty nurse." The ad was soon answered by first-year student Monique Bourgeois. Shortly after Matisse's recovery, Monique changed her life's direction and entered a Dominican convent in Vence and took the name Sister Jacques-Marie. In response to a letter written by Sister Marie inquiring as to the nature of Matisse's religious beliefs, Matisse candidly replied, "Thank you for your prayers. Ask God to give me in my last years the spiritual life to keep me in touch with him and permit me to end my long and laborious career as I've always sought so that the earthly nourishment of my art may reveal his manifest glory to those who are blind to it. This for you, J. M., is my profession of faith that comes in response to your letter. I am grateful to you for having stilled this in me. The need to answer your letter forced me to find deep within myself things I have never before expressed in words, because until now I've never felt a need to say them to anyone."[17] Over time, their friendship prompted the building of the Chapelle du Rosaire, which was consecrated on June 25, 1951. For Matisse, the chapel represented the culmination of his life's work. "This work has taken me four years of exclusive and assiduous work and it represents the result of my entire active life. I consider it, in spite of its imperfections, to be my masterpiece."[18] The platonic relationship between Matisse and Sister Marie remains one of the great love stories in the history of art.

The Chapelle du Rosaire embodies a masterful blend of traditional ecclesiastical features and modern aesthetic sensibilities. Every inch of the chapel, down to the anemone-inspired candelabra, bears the unique stamp of Matisse's artistic genius and late signature style. Traditional ecclesiastical features include, for example, the colorful stained-glass windows; the main altar, which Matisse made from stone resembling brown bread; and the monumental line drawings of St. Dominic and the Virgin and Christ Child, which help to create a heightened sense of vertically in an otherwise limited space. On one occasion, Sister Marie questioned Matisse about the highly transparent nature of the stained glass windows, to which he wittingly replied, "Of course, you have to pray for the people outside too."[19] One of the most controversial features of the chapel has been its representation of the Stations of the Cross. Upon first seeing the Stations, Sister Marie recalled: "I felt like I'd been kicked in the stomach. I stared at what I was tempted to call 'scribble.' I looked at these drawings and thought, 'How am I going to get my sisters to accept this?'"[20] Somewhat anticipating such a response, Matisse, in a letter to the Dominican friar Marie-Alain Couturier, mused, "The drawing is rough, very rough, in fact it will dismay most people who see it. God held my hand. What could I do but obey?"[21] In his unwavering defense of the Stations, Marie-Alain Couturier, who also posed for the initial drawings of the St. Dominic design, wrote, "I want to try to say, as simply as I can, what I think of this work: I think it is the most important and most beautiful thing in the chapel. I also think that it is what will most deeply disturb the public of our time. I say 'of our time' because I already see the youngest among us, the twenty-year olds, accepting and living it readily. It belongs to their world. It speaks a language they understand."[22]

Matisse's Stations of the Cross, much like the chapel itself, is a *biblia pauperum* for the modern age. Through the inclusion of both traditional ecclesiastical features and modern aesthetic sensibilities, the chapel, much like the cathedrals of old, is a triumph of form and function. It is a provocative example of how to engage the Christian arts tradition without becoming enslaved to it. Matisse's stylized design anchors the chapel firmly in the present while, at the same time, its traditional features roots it securely in the past. Even today, the chapel exemplifies the importance of architectural design and iconography in the life and worship of the local church, regardless of denomination or affiliation. Matisse's Chapel of the Rosary is a beautiful reminder of the ongoing need to engage the aesthetic sensibilities of our own age while, at the same time, to foster a greater understanding of and appreciation for the larger Christian arts tradition. As Richard Kieckhefer writes, "A church is a work of art meant not only for the benefit of those who worship in it but for the sake of the environment in which it is planted."[23]

Martin Luther and the Visual Arts

By the early sixteenth century in Europe, images, along with relics and indulgences, had become central features of Christian worship. Unfortunately, they had also become leading instruments of ecclesiastical corruption and abuse. In 1521, artist Michael Ostendorfer captured the cultish devotion to images in his "tabloidish" woodcut illustration *Pilgrimage to the Church of the Beautiful Virgin in Regensburg*, which shows crowds of pilgrims clamoring to catch a glimpse of the miraculous image of the "Schöne Maria." In view of such displays, an important question that faced the Protestant reformers was what to do about images. Their varied responses not only further widened the gap between themselves and their Catholic rivals but also sparked a variety of internal skirmishes as well. For while some reformers such as Andreas Karlstadt, Ludwig Hätzer, Ulrich Zwingli, and John Calvin advocated largely iconoclastic views, Martin Luther, comparatively speaking, espoused a much more moderate[24] and, in the words of Carl Christensen, "utilitarian"[25] perspective. Luther's primary response to images came in the form of several Lenten sermons delivered March 11–12, 1522, and a treatise titled *Against the Heavenly Prophets in the Matters of Images and Sacraments* (1525). Two important and timely principles that emerge from Luther's ideas, among others, include (1) the importance of maintaining a proper distinction between the nature and abuse of images and (2) the pedagogical value of the arts.

Because the Bible neither explicitly condemns nor condones the use of images, Luther argued that they ultimately belong in the realm of Christian liberty or freedom. Christians are free either to use images or not. Where images are being abused, however, their removal may be necessary for a time until such idolatry has been rooted out of the heart through the teaching of God's Word. A right understanding of God's Word, Luther argued, paves the way for a right relationship with images: "I approached the task of destroying images by first tearing them out of the heart through God's Word and making them worthless and despised. This indeed took place before Dr. Karlstadt ever dreamed of destroying images. For when they are no longer in the heart, they can do no harm when seen with the eyes."[26] Luther reminded his audience that the physical nature of an image is neither inherently evil nor malicious. Yet like all physical things, images can be used either appropriately or inappropriately depending, in large measure, on the spiritual disposition of the viewer. This same idea was expressed by the Northern Renaissance artist and Luther advocate, Albrecht Dürer, who, while discussing the nature of art, wrote, "A sword is a sword, which may be used either for murder or justice. What God hath formed, that is good, misuse it how ye will."[27] In his fourth Lenten sermon, Luther declared:

> Now, although it is true and no one can deny that the images are evil because they are abused, nevertheless we must not on that account reject them, nor condemn anything because it is abused. This would result in utter confusion. God has commanded us in Deut. 4 [:19] not to lift up our eyes to the sun [and the moon and the stars], etc., that we may not worship them, for they are created to serve all nations. But there are many people who worship the sun and stars. Therefore we propose to rush in and pull the sun and stars from the skies. No, we had better let it be. Again, wine and women bring many a man to misery and make a fool of him [Ecclus. 19:2; 31:30]; so we kill all the women and pour out all the wine. Again, gold and silver cause much evil, so we condemn them. Indeed, if we want to drive away our worst enemy, the one who does us the most harm, we shall have to kill ourselves, for we have no greater enemy than our own heart, as the prophet,

Jer. 17 [:9], says, "The heart of man is crooked," or as I take the meaning, "always twisting to one side." And so on—what would we not do? [28]

For Luther, it seems that the abuse of images was never a legitimate reason for the complete rejection of images. As followers of the Lord Jesus Christ, we too should never simply reject or devalue the arts simply on account of their broader cultural or ecclesiastical abuse or misuse. Rather, through prayerful engagement with the arts we have the unique opportunity to demonstrate the value and beauty of the arts as embodied in the lives of men and women governed by God's Word and guided by His Spirit. The ability to cultivate and maintain an informed and balanced perspective on issues not explicitly addressed in Scripture is the unsung "art" of the Christian life.

Luther, like many theologians before him, e.g., Basil of Caesarea, Bonaventure, and Thomas Aquinas, also advocated a positive view of the pedagogical value of the arts:

> I thought it expedient to add to the Personal Prayer Book the old "Book of the Passion," especially for the sake of children and simple people who are more apt to retain the divine stories when taught by pictures and parables than merely by words of instruction. As St. Mark testifies, Christ also preached in ordinary parables for the sake of simple-minded folk [Mark 4:11]. . . . I do not think it wrong to paint such stories along with the verses on the walls of rooms and chambers so that one might have God's words and deeds constantly in view and thus encourage fear and faith toward God. And what harm would there be if someone were to illustrate the important stories of the entire Bible in their proper order for a small book which might become known as a layman's Bible? Indeed, one cannot bring God's words and deed too often to the attention of the common man.
>
> Even if God's word is sung and said, preached and proclaimed, written and read, illustrated and pictured, Satan and his cohorts are always strong and alert for hindering and suppressing God's word. Hence our project and concern is not only useful, but necessary-in fact, very badly needed.[29]

Likewise, in his treatise *Against the Heavenly Prophets* Luther wrote, "Pictures contained in these books we would paint on walls for the sake of remembrance and better understanding, since they do no more harm on walls than in books. It is to be sure better to paint pictures on walls of how God created the world, how Noah built the ark, and whatever other good stories there may be, than to paint shameless worldly things. Yes, would to God that I could persuade the rich and the mighty that they would permit the whole Bible to be painted on houses, on the inside and outside, so that all can see it. That would be a Christian work."[30] Luther's high view of *sola scriptura* did not result in an inferior view of the arts. Rather, he envisioned the Bible and the arts as enjoying a complementary, not contradictory, relationship. The arts are good gifts from God, he argued, and should be used accordingly for the advancement of the Gospel and Christian teaching. "I am not of the opinion that because of the Gospel all arts should be rejected violently and vanish, as is desired by the heterodox, but I desire that all arts, particularly music, be employed in the service of Him who has given and created them."[31]

In addition to discussing the arts, Luther was intimately involved with the production of the arts, including images. One of Luther's closest confidants was the celebrated German artist Lucas Cranach the Elder, who helped develop a uniquely Protestant interpretation of traditional Christian iconography.[31] Perhaps the greatest example of this can be found in Cranach's "law and gospel" themed works, which, according to John Dillenberger, represents "the fullest expression of Reformation art."[33] According to Luther, knowing the difference between the law and the gospel was of utmost importance for the believer: "This difference between the Law and the Gospel is the height of knowledge in Christendom. Every person and all persons who assume or glory in the name of Christian should know and be able to state this difference. If this ability is lacking, one cannot tell a Christian from a heathen or a Jew; of such supreme importance is this differentiation."[34] To aid in this endeavor, Cranach and his workshop produced a host of "law and gospel"-themed works ranging from black and white woodcut prints to colorful panel paintings. Generally speaking, the images were arranged horizontally and divided into two distinct halves with the left half representing the Law and the right half the gospel. Typically included on the left were representations of Christ seated enthroned in the heavens as divine ruler and judge; the fall of Adam and Eve; death and the devil chasing a naked sinner into the flames of hell; and Moses holding the two tablets of the law amid a group of Old Testament prophets. In contrast, representations typically included on the right were the Annunciation; the paschal lamb holding a banner of victory; the resurrected Christ standing victorious atop a defeated death and the devil; John the Baptist pointing a repentant sinner to the crucified Christ; and the brazen serpent (which sometimes appears on the left). Though few "law and gospel"-themed works were ever exactly alike, they all sought to convey Luther's basic theology of the law and the gospel. In an age of rampant illiteracy, they served as indispensable didactic tools designed to help meet the pedagogical needs of Luther's audience. They were theology made visible.

Cranach's "law and gospel"-themed works are but one example of the way in which Luther envisioned the arts playing a positive pedagogical role in Christian education. By creating such works, Cranach appealed not only to the aesthetic sensibilities of his own age but also aided in the reinterpretation of traditional iconography for a uniquely Protestant audience. By acting resolutely on his theological *and* aesthetic beliefs, Luther left behind a rich and diverse arts legacy that continues to minister, even to a twenty-first-century audience. May we too, by God's grace, leave behind such a fruitful arts legacy, knowing that such a legacy isn't simply a record of our aesthetic sensibilities but also a measure of the resoluteness of our theological convictions and beliefs.

The Contemporary Artist

With the steady rise of a post-Christian culture and prodigious advancements in technology, the arts of the twenty-first century are undergoing a period of monumental change. Technology, in particular, is not only radically changing the way art is produced, distributed, marketed, accessed, purchased, analyzed, researched, and enjoyed, but it is also a leading impetus driving the development of new and exciting art forms such as interactive digital art and techno music. Along with these changes in the arts have come changes in our thinking about the arts. Today, perhaps more than ever, we are seeking answers to even the most basic art questions such as: What is art? What is the value of art? What is the function of art? Nowhere is this search more copious, perhaps, than in the visual arts. Thankfully, for the Christian, the Bible is not silent on these issues. Rather, as we have seen, it contains truths and principles that can help us think through these tough and complex questions.

In particular, I would like to speak more specifically here to Christian artists. While the functions of art are as numerous as the intentions of the human heart, the goal of art, in every instance, is *always* the same: the glory of God. The apostle Paul writes: "Therefore, whether you eat or drink, or whatever you do, do everything for God's glory" (1 Cor 10:31 HCSB). But what does it mean to make art that glorifies God? Jesus sheds light on this question when he states, "'Listen, Israel! The Lord our God, the Lord is One. Love the Lord your God with all your heart, with all your soul, with all your mind, and with all your strength.' The second is: Love your neighbor as yourself. There is no other command greater than these" (Mark 12:29–31 HCSB). One way, then, that we can glorify God as artists is to love God, ourselves, and others in and through our artwork. But what does this look like practically speaking?

We can love God as artists by striving for artistic excellence in all that we produce. We should never settle for anything less than the absolute best that we can give. Honesty and quality should characterize every stage of our artistic process from the formulation of our ideas to the execution of those ideas. In his essay "Art and Love," the British artist Eric Gill argued that "only from the point of view of God is it worth to make a thing as well as it can be made."[35] Inspired by the artists and artisans who built the great cathedrals, the quality of our art should also be a direct reflection of the love we have for our Creator. In a contemporary arts culture that all too often celebrates artistic mediocrity and panders to the lowest common aesthetic denominator, Christians, on the other hand, should be known for their artistic excellence and moral integrity. Let us love God in both word *and* artistic deed.

We can love ourselves as artists by simply being artists. If God created you with a desire and aptitude to paint, then paint; with a desire and aptitude to dance, then dance; with a desire and aptitude to write, then write; with a desire and aptitude to sing, then sing; with a desire and aptitude to film direct, then film direct. When we work hard to develop our God-given artistic gifts and abilities, we become active apologists to the creative power of God in us, but *only* if we act. The inactive artistic life is a wasted artistic life. The vocation of an artist is a divine calling that, like all divine callings, requires discipline, devotion, and self-sacrifice. In 1952, the artist and Quaker Fritz Eichenberg wrote, "Art is a magnificent obsession. It requires tenacity, an almost monastic devotion that keeps you engaged on all levels of your existence, day in and day out."[36] To love ourselves as artists means being true to ourselves as God created us. For the devout Christian artist, the daily activity of refining artistic skill is itself an act of worship and the studio, for that matter, a sanctuary.

Finally, we can love others as artists by making art that is others-minded. This does not mean that we become slaves to our audience and mortify all traces of our own personal artistic vision, but rather that we keep our audience's best interests always in mind. The apostle Paul exhorts the believers of Philippi, "Everyone should look out not only for his own interests, but also for the interests of others" (Phil 2:4). For artists this means, in part, making art that is sensitive to the spirit of the age in which we live. In the early 1950s, Thomas Merton, in his essay "Sacred Art and the Spiritual Life," recognized the need for such sensitivity in the wake of the horrors of World War II:

> But in an age of concentration camps and atomic bombs, religious and artistic sincerity will certainly exclude all "prettiness" or shallow sentimentality. Beauty, for us, cannot be a mere appeal to conventional pleasures of the imagination and senses. Nor can it be found in cold, academic perfectionism. The art of our time, sacred art included, will necessarily be characterized by a certain poverty, grimness and roughness which correspond to the violent realities of a cruel age. Sacred art cannot be cruel, but must know how to be compassionate with the victims of cruelty: and one does not offer lollipops to a starving man in a totalitarian death-camp. Nor does one offer him the message of a pitifully inadequate optimism. Our Christian hope is the purest of all lights that shines in darkness, but it shines in darkness, and one must enter into darkness to see it shining.[37]

Our art, like our lives, should be substantive, authentic, and always seeking to move people forward and upward in their pilgrimage through life. Our art should be not like a mirror but like a window, which not only reflects something of our audience in it but also provides them with a vision to see beyond it. Goodness, truth, and beauty should characterize all that we make, regardless of artistic medium.

Summary Thoughts

Artistry, creativity, and the imagination are good gifts from God and fundamental aspects of what it means to be human. As G. K. Chesterton famously wrote, "Art is the signature of man."[38] Whenever we encounter the arts in the Bible, they are never treated as something distinct or separate from life but rather as an integral and inseparable part of life, especially the spiritual life. As aesthetic beings made in the image of God, it is only natural for us to respond aesthetically to God's creation. To respond in any other way would be, quite frankly, unnatural. All human beings long for meaningful aesthetic experiences and will seize upon whatever is made available to them, good or bad.

Throughout history, Christianity and the arts have enjoyed a rich and meaningful relationship, despite its share of controversies. The arts have not only given voice and vision to the church's teachings and beliefs, but they have also provided all of humanity with wondrous glimpses of the glory and majesty of Almighty God as evidenced in and through artistic activity. Today, there is great need of men and women who, like Luther, are willing to wrestle deeply with ongoing issues of theology and the arts and who, like Cranach and Matisse, can craft artistic visions that are as aesthetically relevant as they are historically rooted and qualitatively excellent. As followers of the Lord Jesus Christ, our reputation as Christians should be defined, in part, by our zealous enthusiasm for the arts. T. S. Eliot, in one of the choruses from his drama "The Rock" (1934), writes:

> Lord, shall we not bring these gifts to Your service?
> Shall we not bring to Your service all our powers
> For life, for dignity, grace and order,
> And intellectual pleasures of the senses?
> The Lord who created must wish us to create
> And employ our creation again in His service
> Which is already His service in creating.
> For Man is joined spirit and body,
> And therefore must serve as spirit and body.[39]

One of the leading characteristics of the arts in the twenty-first century is freedom—freedom to explore, innovate, and think outside the box. As disciples of the one, true, and living God, we must never grow content simply to lag behind and "baptize" the scraps of popular culture. Rather, we must actively forge ahead and be a Christ-centered voice providing Bible-based artistic leadership and vision. "The hearing ear and the seeing eye—the Lord made them both" (Prov 20:12 HCSB). Let us, then, by God's grace, fly like birds with two wings soaring to ever higher artistic, creative, and imaginative heights. *O great God of all creation—Father, Son, and Holy Spirit—open our eyes that we might see the arts anew and renew our minds that we might engage the arts afresh, soli Deo gloria. Amen.*

Questions for Further Reflection

1. How do the incarnation, death, and resurrection of the Lord Jesus Christ further influence our thinking about the arts?
2. What are some practical ways that we can encourage and support Christian artists even today?
3. What role should Christian tradition play in our thinking about the arts?
4. Should we be concerned about leaving behind a rich Christian arts legacy for future generations? If so, what are we doing about it?
5. How might we cultivate and maintain meaningful Christian dialogues with the arts that encourage artistic activity and innovation as well as biblical, theological, and philosophical artistic reflection?

Resources for Further Study

Brown, Michelle P., ed. *The Lion Companion to Christian Art*. Oxford: Lion Hudson, 2008.

Dyrness, William A. *Reformed Theology and Visual Culture*. Cambridge: Cambridge University Press,2004.

Evdokimov, Paul. *The Art of the Icon: A Theology of Beauty*. Redondo Beach, CA: Oakwood Publications, 1990.

Gaebelein, Frank E. *The Christian, the Arts, and Truth: Regaining the Vision of Greatness*. Portland, OR: Multnomah, 1985.

Hart, David Bentley. *The Beauty of the Infinite*. Grand Rapids: Eerdmans, 2003.

Husbands, Mark, and Roger Lundin, eds. *The Beauty of God: Theology and the Arts*. Downers Grove, IL: InterVarsity Press, 2007.

Loverance, Rowena. *Christian Art*. Cambridge, MA: Harvard University Press, 2007.

Ryken, Leland. *Windows to the World: Literature in Christian Perspective*. Eugene, OR: Wipf and Stock, 2000.

Thiessen, Gesa Elsbeth, ed. *Theological Aesthetics: A Reader*. Grand Rapids: Eerdmans, 2004.

van der Leeuw, Gerardus. *Sacred and Profane Beauty*. Oxford: Oxford University Press, 2006.

Viladesau, Richard. *Theology and the Arts*. New York/Mahwah, NJ: Paulist Press, 2000.
Wolterstorff, Nicholas. *Art in Action*. Grand Rapids: Eerdmans, 1980.

Endnotes

1 Frank E. Gaebelein, *The Christian, the Arts, and Truth: Regaining the Vision of Greatness* (Portland, OR: Multnomah, 1985), 70.
2 Millard J. Erickson, *Christian Theology* (Grand Rapids: Baker Book House, 1991), 366.
3 Thomas Merton, *Dancing in the Water of Life: Seeking Peace in the Hermitage*, Journals of Thomas Merton 5, ed. Robert E. Daggy (San Francisco: HarperSanFrancisco, 1997), 285, citing Irenaeus, *Against Heresies* 4.39.2.
4 Harold Vincent Milligan, ed., *The Best Loved Hymns and Prayers of the American People* (New York: Halcyon House, 1942), 406.
5 Pope John Paul II, *Letter of His Holiness Pope John Paul II to Artists*, 1999; available accessed 26 May 2006 from http://www. vatican.va/holy_father/john _paul_ii/letters/documents/hf_jp-ii_let_23041999_artists_en.html.
6 Francis A. Schaeffer, *Art and the Bible* (Downers Grove, IL: InterVarsity Press, 1973), 34.
7 T. S. Eliot, *Poetry and Drama* (London: Faber & Faber, 1950), 33–34.
8 Pavel Florensky, *Iconostasis*, trans. Donald Sheehan and Olga Andrejev (Crestwood, NY: St. Vladimir's Seminary Press, 1996), 68.
9 Northrop Frye, *The Educated Imagination* (Bloomington: Indiana University Press, 1964), 134.
10 Leland Ryken and Philip Graham Ryken, introduction to *The Literary Study Bible* (Wheaton, IL: Crossway Bibles, 2007), x.
11 Leland Ryken, *How to Read the Bible as Literature* (Grand Rapids: Zondervan, 1984), 144.
12 Henry H. M. Nouwen, *The Return of the Prodigal Son* (New York: Image Books, 1992), 3.
13 Saint Augustine, *Confessions*, trans. R. S. Pine-Coffin (London: Penguin Books, 1961), 82.
14 Sergiusz Michalski, in his book *The Reformation of the Visual Arts* (New York: Routledge, 1993), reminds us of this when he writes: ". . . in the two millennia of Christianity there have been few periods of unquestioning acceptance of religious imagery. Even in periods of an almost exuberant flowering of religious art—as in the late Gothic or the Baroque period—the feeling persisted in quite a few theological and intellectual circles that the religious image as a medium for transmitting religious truth was replete with inner contradictions" (x).
15 Quoted in Alain Besançon, *The Forbidden Image: An Intellectual History of Iconoclasm,* trans. Jane Marie Todd (Chicago: The University of Chicago Press, 2000), 149.
16 Quoted in Umberto Eco, *Art and Beauty in the Middle Ages*, trans. by Hugh Bredin (New Haven, CT: Yale University Press, 1986), 59.
17 Barbara F. Freed, *A Model for Matisse* (First Run Features, 2003), DVD.
18 Ibid.
19 Ibid.

[20] Ibid.

[21] Marcel Billot, ed., *The Vence Chapel: The Archive of a Creation* (New York: Abbeville Press, 1999), 303.

[22] M.-A. Couturier, *Sacred Art* (Austin, TX: The University of Texas Press, 1989), 96.

[23] Richard Kieckhefer, *Theology in Stone* (New York: Oxford University Press, 2004), 100.

[24] Between 1520 and 1530, Luther's view of images seems to have evolved from a position of relative indifference to that of positive affirmation.

[25] Carl C. Christensen, "Luther's Theology and the Use of Religious Art," *Lutheran Quarterly* 22 (1976): 147.

[26] Martin Luther, *Luther's Works,* vol. 40, *Church and Ministry II*, ed. Conrad Bergendoff (Philadelphia, PA: Muhlenberg Press, 1958), 85.

[27] Albrecht Dürer, *The Writings of Albrecht Dürer*, trans. and ed. William Martin Conway (New York: Philosophical Library, 1958), 176.

[28] Martin Luther, *Luther's Works,* vol. 51, *Sermons I*, ed. John W. Doberstein (Philadelphia, PA: Muhlenberg Press, 1959), 85.

[29] Martin Luther, *Luther's Works*, vol. 43, *Devotional Writings II*, ed. Gustav K. Wiencke (Philadelphia, PA: Muhlenberg Press, 1968), 42–43.

[30] *Luther's Works,* 40:99.

[31] Quoted in Christensen, "Luther's Theology and the Uses of Religious Art," 148.

[32] See Jane Dillenberger, *Image and Spirit in Sacred and Secular Art* (New York: Crossroad, 1990), 132–50.

[33] John Dillenberger, *Images and Relics* (Oxford: Oxford University Press, 1999), 29.

[34] Quoted in Carl C. Christensen, *Art and the Reformation in Germany* (Ohio: Ohio University Press, 1979), 129.

[35] Eric Gill, "Art and Love," in *Art Nonsense and Other Essays* (London: Cassell & Company, 1934), 197.

[36] Fritz Eichenberg, *Artist on the Witness Stand*, Pendle Hill Pamphlet #257 (Wallingford, PA: Pendle Hill Publications, 1984), 12.

[37] Thomas Merton, *Disputed Questions* (New York: Harcourt Brace, 1985), 164.

[38] G. K. Chesterton, *The Everlasting Man* (1925; repr., Westport, CT: Greenwood Press, 1974), 16.

[39] T. S. Eliot, *The Complete Poems and Plays: 1909–1950* (New York: Harcourt, Brace, 1962), 111.

14

Music Education from a Christian Perspective

Christopher W. Mathews

A Historical Overview

It does not take a great deal of imagination to envision the first man, enjoying a cool afternoon in the garden, singing a tune to his beloved. In fact, it seems impossible to consider any civilization at any time in any land without music at its very core. Surely since the dawn of our existence, music has embraced us, inspired us, and empowered us to gather our people, tell our stories, share our passions, and engage our purposes.

In the Beginning

While imagination must tell the story of music in the initial chapters of humanity, it is merely eight generations into the creation account that we read the first specific record of musicians. According to Gen 4:21, Jubal was "the father of all who play the lyre and the flute" (HCSB). At that point until the final prophetic proclamation of the Revelation, God's written word is resplendent with musical references. The final exhortation of the Psalms to "let everything that breathes praise the Lord" (Ps 150:6) is not only stated, but also modeled liberally, consistently, and passionately throughout the Bible. From songs chronicling the exodus to the lamentations of God's messengers, from the resounding trumpets dedicating the temple to the sorrowful tones of the Psalms of penitence, from the heralding of the incarnation of Christ to the declaration of the lordship of Christ, music is woven into the very fabric of the Holy Narrative.

Since the time man first began to contemplate music, we have been fascinated by its inexplicable, mystical power. What is it about sounds ordered in certain ways, rendered by particular performers, and heard at a given moment, that seem to affect, even *infect*, us? According to the Bible, it was music that soothed the soul of Saul, a fact we believe even without knowing the sounds themselves because we, too, have known the consolation of music. It was music that enflamed fear in the Ammonite and Moabite forces and confidence in the armies of Judah when the appointed singers led the march with praise. Though we do not know the tune, the scene nonetheless resonates with us as we recall our own courage and pride quickened through music and the tension we experience when a particular type of music is heard in the suspenseful moments of a movie. The Bible further gives insight into the power of music to unite us with both those around us and those in our past, as was surely the case when Jesus sang a hymn with His disciples following the Passover meal. Have we not known and experienced community and tradition when singing together familiar hymns and carols at poignant moments in our lives?

The great Greek philosophers also considered the powerful attributes of music and advocated the inclusion of music in any type of educational system. In *The Republic*, written four centuries before the birth of Christ, Plato's fictitious dialogue between Socrates and Glaucon focuses on the role of education in the development of young men so that, through "works of beauty," they may experience "health" and grow "to likeness, to friendship, to harmony with beautiful reason." What is it that best leads a young person to such growth? Music.

> And is it not for this reason, Glaucon, that education in music is most sovereign, because more than anything else rhythm and harmony find their way to the inmost soul and take strongest hold upon it, bringing with them and imparting grace, if one is rightly trained, and otherwise the contrary? And further, because omissions and the failure of beauty in things badly made or grown would be most quickly perceived by one who was properly educated in music, and so, feeling distaste rightly, he would praise beautiful things and take delight in them and receive them into his soul to foster its growth and become himself beautiful and good. The ugly he would rightly disapprove of and hate while still young and yet unable to apprehend the reason, but when reasons come

> the man thus nurtured would be the first to give her welcome, for by this affinity he would know her.[1]

Likewise, Aristotle in *The Politics* writes, "it is plain that music has the power of producing a certain effect on the moral character of the soul, and if it has the power to do this, it is clear that the young must be directed to music and must be educated in it."[2]

While there was agreement that proper training in music was essential because of its unparalleled power over man, the manner in which music affected the listener was not as clear or unquestioned. Plato, for example, believed that the Ionian and Lydian modes were inappropriate because they created in the listener a sense of laziness and fear. Yet Aristotle held that these collections of pitches could be used without such ill effects. Regardless of the particular mode, however, the common belief remained that music pointed to some yet unknown force in the universe that was to be explored, discovered, and wisely employed.

The Middle Ages

The same belief formed the foundation of study and writing for the early Christian thinkers, though, to them, the unknown force was a knowable God who manifested Himself in Jesus Christ. For this reason, the quest to know the unknown was ultimately a Spirit-led desire to know God and His truth more fully and to glorify Him in each endeavor. The study of music provided a primary vehicle to understand the Creator and His universe. It was not, however, the performance of music but rather the study of music and its mathematical relationships that guided the pursuits. As author Jeremy Begbie notes, "in Augustine's world, *musica* was first of all understood not in terms of something you would compose, play, or perform, but as a technical subject, a mathematical discipline, and a discipline concerned with numbers (*numerus*)."[3]

Writing in the early sixth century, the Christian philosopher Boethius divided the seven liberal arts of Augustine into two categories: the *quadrivium*, composed of geometry, arithmetic, astronomy, and music, and the *trivium*, including grammar, rhetoric, and dialectic. Of the *quadrivium*, Boethius writes, "since there happen to be four mathematical disciplines, the other three share with music the task of searching for truth; but music is associated not only with speculation but with morality as well."[4]

The mathematics of music dates back at least to the time of Pythagoras who, according to tradition, identified those harmonies with the simplest ratios as resonating most closely with our inner being. According to Boethius, Pythagoras "put no credence in human ears, which are subject to change," but rather was the first to determine "by what ratio the concord of sounds was joined together."[5] Through careful observation at a blacksmith's workshop, Pythagoras realized that pleasing harmonies occurred with the simultaneous sounding of hammers weighted at ratios of 2:1, 3:2, and 4:3, resulting in what we know today to be the octave, perfect fifth, and perfect fourth. He confirmed his research by studying the ratio of various lengths of strings and was thus able to derive the mathematical proportions of all tones used in a scale.

The belief that beauty in music could be discovered through numeric ratios and that mathematical proportions unify the cosmos at every level of existence meant that music could provide an accessible, audible portal through which the intellect could travel between worlds of the known and unknown. Cassiodorus, a contemporary of Boethius, declared, "The heavens and the earth, indeed all things in them which are directed by a higher power, share in this discipline of music, for Pythagoras attests that this universe was founded by and can be governed by music."[6] In *De institutione musica*, Boethius recognized three categories of music as it exists in the universe: *musica mundana*, including the orbits of the planets and the regulation of the seasons; *musica humana*, the harmony of body and soul; and *musica instrumentalis*, that which is heard. He goes on to write, "from all these accounts it appears beyond doubt that music is so naturally united with us that we cannot be free from it even if we so desired. For this reason the power of the intellect ought to be summoned, so that this art, innate through nature, may also be mastered, comprehended through knowledge."[7]

As monastic life continued through the Middle Ages, liturgical practices became increasingly formalized and music played an essential role. Unaccompanied melodies were crafted through which words of Scripture could be proclaimed and pondered and by which the congregants could corporately praise God. As these chants grew in number and complexity, they were grouped according to their modes, and a system of notation was necessary to insure accurate rendering of the sacred tunes.

Guido of Arezzo, an Italian monk, is credited with developing the first accurate system of musical notation, employing a collection of horizontal lines and notes known as "neumes" to indicate both pitch and rhythm. In addition, Guido developed a method of learning to sing the notation whereby different syllables correspond to given pitches. With the exception of the first and last syllables of the scale, we use the same syllables to teach sight singing today: *do-re-mi-fa-sol-la-ti*.

The work and writings of Guido demonstrate a shift in the focus of musical training from the rational to the experienced, from the philosophical to the performed. Nonetheless, Guido draws a clear connection between the two in his conclusion to *Micrologus*, a book intended to train others in the singing of chant. "Up to this day our science has gradually increased and grown in strength, with that same Teacher bringing light to the darkness of human affairs whose supreme wisdom flourishes through all the ages."[8] Cleary, Guido viewed music as a revelation of God, previous discoveries as a pursuit of God, and his task of teaching others to sing rightly as a divine calling of God.

The Renaissance and Reformation

For centuries to follow, the development of music and the life of Christian worship were inextricably tied. As chant continued to form the basis of liturgical song, complementary melodic lines were added, resulting in the first polyphonic compositions. Principal among these early works were the writings of Notre Dame musicians Leonin and Perotin, collected in the twelfth-century *Magnus liber organi* and consisting of music written for the Mass and divine offices. Through the remainder of the Middle Ages, composers experimented with and debated over new means of coupling melodic lines, new patterns of rhythmic motion, and new methods for notating these concepts. By the beginning of the Renaissance, vocal polyphony had pervaded every avenue of musical life from the chapel to the court, and composers became directly associated with their works, much of which was dedicated to the life of the church. Perhaps most popular and influential among the early Renaissance composers was Josquin des Prez, remembered particularly for his careful attention to the meaning and emotional content of the text. Of his compositions, Martin Luther wrote, "God has preached through music, as may be seen in Josquin, all of whose compositions flow freely, gently, and cheerfully, are not forced or cramped by rules, and are like the song of the finch."[9]

Although there was a general consensus in the early sixteenth century regarding the quality and esteem of Josquin's work, there was little agreement among the Reformers pertaining to the role of music in the newly formed churches. Regarding the use of music in worship, Luther was the most liberal among them, stating, "next to the Word of God, music deserves the highest praise."[10] He advocated the incorporation of music in schools, vocal training for all men entering the ministry, the prominence of congregational song, and the inclusion of the highest form of art music in the worship service, including vocal polyphony. On the other end of the spectrum was Swiss reformer Huldrych Zwingli. While a trained and accomplished musician himself, he was wary of the public spectacle of performance and recommended the prohibition of all music in worship. Concerning music, the most moderate of the three magisterial Reformers was John Calvin, who embraced music as a gift from God but allowed only single-line, unaccompanied renderings of biblical texts during worship. Instrumental music and polyphony were encouraged for home and school but, according to Calvin, were not referenced in the New Testament and were thus disallowed in the liturgy.

In reaction to the theological upheaval of the Reformation, the Catholic Church met at the Council of Trent and included among their principal topics the appropriate inclusion of music within the liturgy. Clearly, the primary thinkers of music during this period, as in ages past, belonged to the church, both Protestant and Catholic, and firmly grounded their thoughts concerning music in Scripture. Albeit the results were quite diverse interpretations, they nonetheless agreed that music belonged to God's kingdom and had a powerful effect on its people. Furthermore, their doctrines concerning music had a significant impact on musical thought, composition, and performance far beyond their own time and location.

Perhaps the greatest impact of Reformation thinking on the musical development of the Western world came, not surprisingly, through those associated with the Lutheran movement in Germany. Prominent among these is perhaps the most widely esteemed composer of all, Johann Sebastian Bach. Not only did Bach craft works that represented the apex of musical development in nearly all major genres of his time, but each endeavor was endowed with a deep, personal theology that continues to speak 300 years after his works were crafted. As Begbie notes of Bach, "the fact remains that he was well informed biblically and theologically, and his musical output shows he could penetrate the most demanding theological issues with a remarkable acuity, so much so that a growing number of Bach scholars are prepared to recognize that any serious treatment of this composer cannot avoid engaging theological issues."[11]

In America

More directly associated with the musical thinking of the Reformers, particularly John Calvin, was the musical development occurring on the other side of the ocean. With their arrival in 1620, the Pilgrims brought the Sternhold and Hopkins Psalter with them to the new land, a book of metrical settings of the Psalm texts to be sung to commonly known tunes. By 1640, the colonies were developed enough to begin their own publications, the first of which was *The Whole Book of Psalms Faithfully Translated in English Metre*, referred to as the Bay Psalm Book. In 1698, the Bay Psalm Book entered its ninth edition, adding for the first time printed music, consisting of 13 two-voice tunes printed in the back without text. For the first century of their existence, churches gathered in the New England colonies sang biblical texts in the Calvinist tradition. In most cases, these were performed *a cappella* and by "lining-out," when a cantor would sing a line of the Psalm, often very slowly, repeated by the congregation, even more slowly and with many embellishments performed by individuals extemporaneously and uninvited.

This practice led to the demise and even disdain of congregational songs in the colonial churches as fewer and fewer people could understand musical notation or sing properly. In 1720, Harvard-trained preacher Thomas Symmes delivered a memorable sermon to his Boston congregation entitled "The Reasonableness of Regular Singing," in which he argued that all people in the congregation be trained to sing well from a musical score to glorify God and edify His church.[12] Many regard this sermon as the catalyst for the rise of itinerate singing schools and, consequently, church music education and even music education in public schools in the United States.

Just one year after Symmes's impassioned message, John Tufts published his tune book *Introduction to the Singing of Psalm Tunes* for the express purpose of training congregations to sing from printed notation. In this book, Tufts outlined an ingeniously simply method of sight singing with its heritage embedded in the medieval solfege system of Guido. Tufts assigned one of the four syllables Fa, Sol, La, and Mi to every note of the scale, and rather than the common note-head and stem, he placed the first letter of each syllable at its corresponding location on a musical staff, notating rhythms with a system of dots following each letter. While the specific system had a relatively short life, his concept of four syllables became associated with early American singing schools and grew roots that continue to bear fruit in the shape-note traditions of the *Southern Harmony* and *Sacred Harp*.

In 1798, William Little and William Smith built on Tufts's concepts of musical training and designated shaped note-heads for each of the four syllables, and as Tufts did with his letters placed them on the appropriate location of a musical staff. From their early tune book publication, *The Easy Instructor*, until the time of the Civil War, a large number of four-shape tune books were published in America, particularly in the South. The music of these tune books was closely associated with the revivalist songs of the camp meeting movement, although they also included many of the traditional hymns of England and even some of the mature anthems from the late eighteenth century. Hundreds of thousands of copies were sold as part of the increasingly popular singing-school movement, and scores of Americans learned basic music-reading skills through their dissemination.

About the same time, Lowell Mason, considered to be the father of music education in America, returned to his home state of Massachusetts and would eventually teach the first music classes as part of the public school curriculum in Boston. Having served as a church musician in Savannah and Boston, and convinced that the revivalist movement had failed to produce the best in church music, Mason began the Boston Academy of Music in 1833 established with the purpose of training teachers. In its second year, the academy grew to 3,000 students and Mason became an outspoken advocate for musical training. In 1837, under the guidance of Horace Mann, Massachusetts formed the first State Board of Education and in 1838 the School Board of Boston made music a regular part of the curriculum. Lowell Mason volunteered to teach the first year without pay and, just prior to his start, wrote to a friend, "I am fully convinced that we need a reformation in the music of the Church. . . . But how shall this reformation be brought about? Musical knowledge must be extended, and attention of the people must be called to the subject. . . . If we could have a man well qualified who would . . . do something practical in the way of enlightening and leading taste, great good might be expected to result."[13]

Modern Times

The tradition of music education in the schools of our nation has remained intact for nearly two centuries. According to the 2001 edition of *Teaching Music in the Twenty-first Century*, "music education is alive and well in North America. In spite of periodic economic setbacks, shifts in educational focus, and 'back to the basics' movements, more children are receiving more music lessons in more schools than ever before in the history of the North American school music movement."[14] A 2009 Chorus America report, *The Chorus Impact Study*, estimates that there are more than 41,000 K–12 grade choirs with over 10 million children in the United States singing in a chorus. In a recent address to the National Association of Schools of Music, Dr. Daniel Sher cited a 2006 Gallup poll commissioned by the National Association of Music Marketers that indicated 41 percent of students are engaged in an instrumental music program, a percentage that has increased steadily over the past decade.

Across the country and around the world, school and civic music programs are routinely performing past and contemporary musical works of the highest quality while successfully recruiting participants and engaging audiences. Particularly in choral settings, religious texts set by masters such as Tallis, Palestrina, Vivaldi, Bach, Handel, Mozart, Haydn, Beethoven, Schubert, Mendelssohn, Brahms, Bruckner, Poulenc, Stravinsky, Copland, and Barber are performed with great frequency. In addition, publishers are selling large quantities of serious sacred works by modern composers, such as Morten Lauridsen, David Dickau, Randall Stroope, and Vytautas Miškinis. Yet, these works are frequently performed without a deep understanding of the texts or a connection to the Christian heritage from which they were derived. At the same time, these very pieces are ignored or intentionally omitted from the worship practices of most evangelical churches today, inaccessible to untrained musicians and perceived as irrelevant to uneducated ears.

Those who profess the name of Christ must understand the paramount importance of reclaiming the wonderful traditions of music and music education that have pervaded our collective journey since creation. While none can deny that a myriad of unbelievers have contributed greatly to our musical heritage, music and in particular the great music of the Western tradition has at its very core the Christian intellectual tradition. Contemplation of the power and appropriate utilization of music, the creation of music notation, the development of polyphony and resultant compositional techniques, and the regular implementation of music education all have at their foundations Christian people and Christian perspectives. We must realize our vast opportunities to utilize the vehicle of music to reach people with the sacred, expressing through music what words alone cannot. We must take advantage of every opportunity to compose, perform, and promote music that expresses our Christian heritage in its word and its construction in order to engage our culture and to exalt our Creator. We must train ourselves along with those around us to recognize, appreciate, and enjoy what is beautiful in music and to honor it above the commercial music that fills every crevice of our space and time.

Evaluating the Options

In the book *The Four Loves*, C. S. Lewis separates companionship from friendship and, while identifying our need for both, proclaims the rarity and beauty of the latter. In doing so, he recognized that "we do not disparage silver by distinguishing it from gold."[15]

In similar fashion, we do not necessarily disparage popular forms of music by distinguishing them from genuine art music. To say vegetables are necessary for a healthy diet does not suggest that all chocolate be discouraged or rejected. "There *is* harm, however," as Chuck Colson notes, "in making a steady diet of pop culture, because it encourages an unreflective, emotional response to life instead of disciplined thought and analysis—which can lead, in turn, to a simplistic spiritual life."[16]

Engaging a process of learning whereby we can distinguish between various types of music while avoiding an esoteric air is essential. As believers, it is possible, beneficial, even necessary that we regularly, thoughtfully, and prayerfully examine the music we perform and hear so that we may choose wisely how we allow it to influence our personal lives, our educational systems, and our corporate gatherings. Granted, such a task is precarious for at least three reasons: (1) It is impossible to create categories small enough in number and clear enough in attributes to neatly discuss all music. (2) Almost every composition and musical performance has overlapping features. (3) No single person or earthly entity can rightly claim sole authority to manufacture categories or objectively deposit music into them.

Three questions, however, may assist in beginning the process of reasonably sifting through the seemingly infinite musical possibilities. First, does the composition of this music appropriately reflect our understanding of God? This is not limited solely or even primarily to texts but to the very nature of the musical composition. For example, our God is a God of order, of both predictable patterns and infinite variety, of the intellect and emotion. In this regard, the music we perform should also be ordered, should have patterns that are understandable (though perhaps not immediately accessible), should be creative in the incorporation of variety, and should be disciplined in the mind as well as endearing to the heart.

Second, how does interaction with the music affect the performer and the listener? This is not a matter of manipulation but of wisely and intentionally selecting the influences we allow into our minds, our homes, our schools, and our churches; not a matter of immediate, superficial response but of genuine, disciplined formation of the mind, the will, the character, and the spirit. In many cases, this may mean not choosing music based on natural tastes but rather working to acquire a taste for music that is virtuous. As Lewis points out in *The Abolition of Man*, "St. Augustine defines virtue as *ordo amoris*, the ordinate condition of the affections in which every object is accorded that kind of degree of love which is appropriate to it. Aristotle says the aim of education is to make the pupil like and dislike what he ought."[17]

A third question to guide us in thinking about music may be the easiest to answer: what was the primary catalyst for its composition or presentation? Much of the music we encounter today is intended solely for the commercial market, quickly composed and quickly consumed. Here, however, we must use caution in making comparisons, for a large portion of what may be termed "classical music" was also written for a specific instance, for example, the Coronation Anthems of Handel, or solely for profit, such as most great operas and oratorios. Yet the enduring nature of these works along with their connection to great musicians and musical traditions of the past certainly place them in a category separate from modern commercial music.

The reality that music is not easily categorized remains obvious, frustrating, and even overwhelming. However, it is precisely for this reason that Christ's followers must avoid blithely acquiescing to whatever music wafts our way. We must continuously and enthusiastically engage the discussion regarding the quality, suitability, and aesthetic of the music we espouse. With caution and compassion, we should assess music not only for ourselves but also for our children, our congregations, and our culture. We must be active in offering formal and informal educational opportunities to foster understanding of and appreciation for excellence in music past and present. Further, we should commit to composing and performing the best of music, that which is full of truth and beauty. As Colson states, "we must encourage Christians to go beyond being critical and start being creative."[18]

At a Unique Junction

Christian colleges and universities stand at a unique junction, the point of convergence of religious life and affiliations, academic pursuits and relationships, and cultural influences and impact. This is particularly true of the musical endeavors of these schools, which, during any routine semester, include presenting multiple concerts to local audiences, assisting with or leading worship services in local church settings, engaging in outreach through community music endeavors and performance tours, and interacting with other musical and artistic entities from K–12 education to professional guilds and associations. Additionally, music units of colleges and universities typically connect with a cross-section of the student population, appealing to the musical novice as well as the career-bound professional through course offerings, private lessons, and ensemble opportunities. This confluence of people, organizations, ideas, and aesthetic experiences provide a potent epicenter from which significant influence can radiate to impact individuals, the church, and society through the avenue of music.

Therefore, faculty and administration of Christian colleges and universities must be clear in their understanding of the Christian heritage and perspectives that shaped musical thought for centuries, committed in their support and promotion of music and music education, and strategic in the development of music curriculum and use of resources. We should always exhibit patience, persistence, wisdom, and intentionality as we engage those around us. We must avoid any tone of condescension toward popular music or music of other cultures, instead finding genuine joy in a wide variety of styles and genres. At the same time, we should uphold the best of our musical past, embrace the best of our musical present, and consistently follow the most effective means of infusing our musical future with God's truth and beauty. The following are some suggestions for the manner in which this may be accomplished.

Music Appreciation and a Philosophy of Music

At least one course designed to develop appreciation for music from a historical perspective should be an essential part of all liberal arts education, especially for those schools upholding the Christian intellectual tradition. Students should be exposed to great musical works of the Middle Ages, Renaissance, Baroque, Classic, Romantic, and Contemporary idioms. These should include not only sacred selections but also secular works, as the latter frequently played an integral role in the development of the former, especially from the Classical era until now. Students enrolled in a music appreciation class should learn to identify principle composers and their works by name as well as to recognize more generally compositional styles and time periods that marked historical processes in the development of music. Time should be allocated to explore music outside the Western tradition as well as commercial idioms so prevalent in the world of modern students. It should be understood in this process that none of the representative examples was composed in isolation, but rather that all music has similar essential elements of pitch and rhythm and similar religious, civic, or entertainment purposes.

A mere knowledge of historical facts, however, should not comprise the ultimate goal of such a class, nor is it by itself a validation to continue the course offering. Instead, such knowledge forms the foundation to enjoy genuinely and to discuss clearly and intelligently a variety of compositions, styles, and performances. The primary objective of such a curriculum, then, is a philosophy or *understanding* of music: how music both reflects and affects society; how we not only communicate but also understand ourselves through our own musical experiences, creations, and tastes; and how we might more accurately assess the construction, utility, and quality of music we hear and perform. Of the latter, Thomas Symmes noted in his sermon "The Reasonableness of Regular Singing,"

> It does not make a tune to be truly melodious because it pleases your ear; the very same may be unpleasant in another's ear. And who made your ear a judge of the controversy? Why may not another's ear determine when there is true melody as well as yours? He only is a proper judge in a case who understands it; it is merely accidental if any other passes a right sentiment.

Therefore, dialogue should be liberally woven throughout this course, or perhaps multiple courses, with intentionality and focus given to the refinement of a well-informed, Christ-centered understanding of music. The questions posed at the end of this chapter are intended to provide a good resource for the initiation of these conversations and the development of a sound philosophy of music.

Performance Opportunities

Music appreciation and understanding without musical experience is inadequate, if not impossible. As Begbie observes, music is not principally an object to be studied but rather something to do. He writes, "I would suggest it makes more sense to view music as first and foremost a set of *practices* or *activities* from which works may or may not emerge."[19] Therefore, whether through curricular offerings or through the promotion by student life administrators, musical performance should be an essential part of any student's university experience.

Choirs and instrumental ensembles on college campuses remain a strong tool for recruitment, retention, and the building of social networks, and they provide students the opportunity to participate in musical performance. Students of a wide array of musical backgrounds and skill levels can find an ensemble through which to engage in successful music making. Within the appropriate rehearsal, participants learn not only facts about compositional periods, musical construction, performance technique, and skill development, but they also become integral participants in these endeavors, quickening the composer's notation, interpreting the musical nuisances, and crafting their own vocal and instrumental skills for a lifetime of musical enjoyment. These organizations should be applauded and highlighted with enthusiasm not only for their benefits to campus life, but also for the educational rewards offered to students through them.

Ideally, in a liberal arts-based curriculum, participation in a musical ensemble will be credited toward an educational core, at the very least as an elective. Adequate space, resources, and faculty load will be allotted to encourage the success of the ensemble. Additionally, performance opportunities should abound, including opportunities such as playing the national anthem at sporting events, singing at graduation, or presenting multiple concerts both on and off of the campus. Singing or playing in an ensemble should not be viewed as an isolated student activity but valued as a characteristic part of campus life.

Community Music Programs

While the educational activities of the university are most directly focused on enrolled students, they should also take the form of community involvement and nondegree-granting programs. These aspects of university life play an important role in fulfilling the mission of a university and should be viewed as prominent means to foster music appreciation and skills in society at large.

No one can deny that economic limitations, time constraints, and increased standardization are depleting time and resources dedicated to music education in many public school systems. Additionally, congregations have frequently decreased or ended programs geared toward quality musical training. As these programs diminish in our communities, who will carry the responsibility? Should it not be the Christian university that advocates for the availability of music education for all and fills in the gap in its absence?

A thriving music program in an institution of higher education should be intentional about connecting with the community at large through a myriad of performance and educational offerings. Concerts featuring student ensembles, faculty members, and guest artists should be regularly sponsored by the university and promoted to the community. Schools may also want to consider lecture series, summer programs, private and group lessons, and community choirs as means of connecting with people in the region, developing their musical understanding, and advocating music of the highest quality and beauty. Further, existing programs in public and private schools as well as through other organizations should be supported whenever possible through the sharing of faculty, students, and physical resources.

Professional Preparation

In addition to those activities afforded the more general population and in order to continue great traditions of music making that benefit participants, build society, edify the church, and honor God, there must be programs offered in higher education specifically for the development of highly skilled professional musicians. It is of utmost importance that schools offer at least one well-crafted degree program that will prepare students for a musical vocation, either as a composer, performer, musicologist, or educator. Because of the necessity of close mentorship, specialized courses, and quality equipment, such programs will be expensive and will not frequently see a large margin of profit, if any at all. Yet their importance must not be measured by financial merit alone but by the long-term, positive impact on humanity and civilization.

An individual in this type of degree program, shaped by his professors and musical experiences, will view music creation and performance through biblical lenses, understanding the Christian intellectual tradition that surrounds music and embracing the call to utilize his talent to inspire others and exalt God. He will be able to enter the professional world of music with confidence, having been trained to compete with the best of musicians in a spirit of humility and a genuine attitude of love. He will write music that will not only provide a wage for living but that will properly reflect beauty that emanates from the Creator. He will study music of the past and present with integrity and diligence, convinced that all beauty is God's beauty. And he will be well suited to teach others to do the same, able to work with individuals and ensembles to create compelling performances and deeper understandings of music.

The music student will then be sent out, commissioned to bear the Christian message in the pervasive field of music. He will be a penetrating influence embraced for his musical understanding, respected for his musical prowess, and heard for the role he has played in the lives of others. He will rightly question music that is birthed solely for commercial gain yet will astutely employ the music of his surroundings to encourage and educate others. Through all, he will serve as salt and light in the world of music, seasoning it with the sovereignty of God and shining the light of God's love on every corner of his influence.

As a professional musician, the alumnus can be a jewel in the crown of any Christian college or university through the degree program that influenced him. Therefore, a potential music student should be pursued with the understanding that he has spent years and much of his parents' money for the early development of his craft. He should be provided professors who are accomplished musicians and able pedagogues who will firmly guide him through the hours of monotonous practice and tedious study necessary to the refinement of musical arts. And he should know the support of his peers, faculty, and community expressed through strong attendance at his concerts, consistently encouraging words, and genuinely enthusiastic applause.

A Wise Investment

For the School

The rewards of music education for students and the university are apparent and numerous. Multiple research results have drawn clear connections between musical involvement and successes in other academic areas. Music naturally lends itself to cross-disciplinary thinking and can create unity between such divergent fields as physics and English, mathematics and history, and anatomy and theology. Further, students involved in ensembles tend to form strong social connections within the group, augmenting their student life experiences and presumably the school's retention rates. In addition, the visibility of an excellent music program enhances the reputation of the university as a whole and, particularly for most Christian schools, is a primary means of maintaining strong relationships with local churches and denominational entities.

For the Church

The church, too, benefits greatly from Christian colleges and universities committed to the highest standards of music education, performance, and creativity. If the church is to continue to have a voice with which to sing God's praise and proclaim His deeds, it must have leaders capable of making appropriate selections, leading effective rehearsals, and crafting new works.

Lowell Mason expressed this longing:

> May the future progress of music in this land be so directed and controlled as to insure its important aid to the highest degree of human culture, and thus to the attainment of a higher and more enduring happiness than that of the mere sensuous gratification which its performance does not fail immediately to afford. May its refining and elevating influence be experienced in private, in the family, in school, in social life, and *may the house of worship be made to resound with the chorus of universal praise*.[20]

This is possible only as the academy prepares church leaders, musicians, pastors, and laity who understand music's power, appreciate our musical heritage, and are capable of quality performances, whether in a concert hall or a congregation.

For the World

The greatest advantage of a strong music program rooted in the Christian intellectual tradition is the access such a program gains to impact the world with the gospel of Christ, especially in geographic and cultural areas that may not be receptive otherwise. This is not suggesting explicit evangelism through the performance of Christian lyrics, but rather that music remains a place for the sacred in a world that has rejected the sacred in almost every other realm.

Institutions of Christian higher education seek to train students in specific disciplines to be competent and successful in their career fields, displaying the faithfulness of God through their work. In this manner, schools "salt the earth" with professionals who work quietly and effectively, spreading the good news indirectly through their quality service, excellent products, earned respect, and loyal dedication. The ideal is a society that is full of attorneys who practice law with a Christian perspective, landscape artists who shape the scenery with a Christian view of creation, nurses who treat patients with Christian compassion, teachers who mentor students with Christian wisdom, and the like.

In the same manner, these schools shape Christian musicians to compose, perform, research, and teach music with the mind of Christ, doing all with the highest degree of artistic sensitivity and technical excellence. Yet the access these students are afforded through the discipline of music provides an even more direct route of exposing listeners to the message of the Bible. Audiences that will not tolerate the direct preaching of the gospel message will listen intently to the performance of a sacred Bach cantata by an ensemble of noted achievement. Ensembles that would never read Scripture in a rehearsal will spend countless hours learning a poignant setting of a sacred text by a believer. Parents who will not open their door to an evangelist will knock on the door of a respected music teacher, who will then spend years lovingly molding the character of her student, preparing the soil of his heart for the word of Christ. The gift of music abounds with opportunities to take God's Word to all people, to explore with them God's self-revelation expressed through beauty, to guide them into a life that honors Jesus, and together to influence the culture by His Spirit.

Questions for Further Reflection

1. What is music?
2. What Christian values guided early musicians as they contemplated and developed musical systems, notations, and styles?
3. What makes music "good" or "bad," "beautiful" or "ugly"?
4. How does music most accurately reflect the attributes of God?
5. In what ways can we measure the success of a composition or performance?
6. In what ways has sinful man corrupted music?

7. Will any of the compositions we know today be heard in eternity? If so, which ones?
8. How can Christian schools and churches most effectively reclaim our musical heritage while genuinely connecting with the present-day culture?

Resources for Further Study

Begbie, Jeremy. *Resounding Truth: Christian Wisdom in the World of Music*. Grand Rapids: Baker Academic, 2007.

Boethius. *Fundamentals of Music*. Translated by Calvin M. Bower; edited by Claude Palisca. New Haven: Yale University Press, 1989.

Cassiodorus—Institutiones, II.5; Isidore of Seville—Etymologie, III.15–23. Translated by Helen Dill Goode and Gertrude C. Drake. Colorado Springs: Colorado College Music Press, 1980.

Choksy, Lois. *Teaching Music in the Twenty-first Century*. 2nd ed. Upper Saddle River, NJ: Prentice Hall, 2001.

Colson, Charles, and Nancy Pearcey. *How Now Shall We Live?* Wheaton, IL: Tyndale House, 1999.

Hucbald, Guido, and Johannes. *Hucbald, Guido, and John on Music: Three Medieval Treatises*. Translated by Warren Babb and Claude Palisca. New Haven: Yale University Press, 1978.

Lewis, C. S. *The Abolition of Man*. New York: HarperCollins, 1974.

———. *The Four Loves*. New York: Harcourt Brace, 1988.

Pemberton, Carol A. *Lowell Mason: A Bio-Bibliography*. New York: Greenwood Press, 1988.

Strunk, W. Oliver. *Source Readings in Music History from Classical Antiquity through the Romantic Era*. New York: Norton, 1950.

Endnotes

[1] W. Oliver Strunk, *Source Readings in Music History from Classical Antiquity through the Romantic Era* (New York: Norton, 1950), 8.

[2] Ibid., 19.

[3] Jeremy Begbie, *Resounding Truth: Christian Wisdom in the World of Music* (Grand Rapids: Baker Academic, 2007), 84.

[4] Boethius, *Fundamentals of Music*, trans. Calvin Bower, ed. Claude V. Palisca (New Haven: Yale University Press, 1989), 2.

[5] Ibid., 17, 19.

[6] *Cassiodorus—Institutiones, II.5; Isidore of Seville—Etymologie, III.15–23*, trans. Helen Dill Goode and Gertrude C. Drake (Colorado Springs: Colorado College Music Press, 1980).

[7] Boethius, *Fundamentals of Music*, 8.

[8] Hucbald, Guido, and Johannes, *Hucbald, Guido and John on Music: Three Medieval Treatises*, trans. Warren Babb and Claude Palisca (New Haven: Yale, 1978), 83.

[9] Begbie, *Resounding Truth*, 101–2.
[10] Ibid., 98.
[11] Ibid., 112.
[12] Thomas Symmes, *The Reasonableness of Regular Singing* (Boston: B. Green for Samuel Gerrish, 1720).
[13] Lowell Mason, letter to Austin Willey, June 27, 1838, quoted in Carol A. Pemberton, *Lowell Mason: A Bio-Bibliography* (New York: Greenwood, 1988), 15.
[14] Lois Choksy, *Teaching Music in the Twenty-first Century,* 2nd ed. (Upper Saddle River, NJ: Prentice Hall, 2001), 1.
[15] C. S. Lewis, *The Four Loves* (New York: Harcourt Brace and Company, 1988), 65.
[16] Charles Colson and Nancy Pearcey, *How Now Shall We Live?* (Wheaton: Tyndale, 1999), 468.
[17] C. S. Lewis, *The Abolition of Man* (New York: Harper Collins, 1974), 16.
[18] Colson, *How Now Shall We Live?* 474.
[19] Begbie, *Resounding Truth*, 40.
[20] Lowell Mason, "Closing Remarks" of draft of his proposed harmony textbook (italics added), quoted in Pemberton, *Lowell Mason*, 35.

15

A Christian Perspective on Communication and Media

Kevin S. Trowbridge

A YouTube video of twin baby boys gibbering with one another became another viral sensation early in 2011, gaining more than 5.6 million views in just over a month.[1] And while home videos of babies are a recurring and popular trend in online media-sharing, this two-minute clip drew attention to and generated grand questions about the development of language and human communication abilities. The home video, which garnered widespread media attention for both the parents and the children, is further evidence that we are created as relational beings with an innate longing to communicate with one another—even before we acquire language to facilitate more efficient exchanges. In fact, our sophisticated ability to communicate differentiates humankind from the rest of creation.

Communication permeates every facet of who we are and what we do. Through it we define, shape, redefine, and even reflect the realities of our surrounding cultures. Whether we are scanning the day's headlines, collaborating with colleagues on a project, interacting with friends over dinner, or relaxing with a book or movie, our lives are infused with activities that allow us to express ourselves to one another while at the same time having potential to transform ourselves as well as those around us. Myriad activities such as these have become the foci of study for communication students and scholars. Though each of us acquires and begins to practice basic communication functions as early as infancy, our broader understanding of communication, its multitudinous functions and its powerful potential, continues to develop through childhood, adolescence and into adulthood. Without careful examination, the ubiquitous nature of communication can result in a naive understanding of communication's practices, professions, and potency.

Though most students begin their study of communication with a public speaking class or even a media criticism class as early as high school, undergraduate and graduate students of communication are challenged to think creatively and more critically about the functions of communication in society. While they develop their abilities to analyze and assess communication events (e.g., interpersonal interactions, group dynamics, oral and written presentations, as well as other creative productions utilizing electronic or digital media), students are challenged to hone their skills to become more effective communicators. This is at the heart of communication study in public, private, secular, and religiously-affiliated institutions across the world. However, it is through heightened awareness, skill development, and a commitment to communication excellence that each of us can more effectively and efficiently fulfill our divine calling as Christians, which becomes the distinctive of a Christ-centered approach to the field.

This chapter seeks to define communication and media through an examination of their biblical foundations. Then after surveying relevant developments in the field from ancient times to the present, we will consider how communication and media have found a home in the academy. Finally, this chapter will conclude with a discussion of the communication and media challenges to the Christian faith and how Christian higher education is poised to play a pivotal role in reclaiming this field for God's glory.

Defining Communication and Media

Soon after I went to college where I was majoring in communication arts, I overheard my grandmother try to explain to one of her elderly friends what I was studying. After several attempts to summarize my academic pursuits, she concluded, "He's just learning how to be a better speaker and writer." As a college freshman I chuckled at the overly simplistic explanation but never seriously pursued a more substantial definition until I was challenged to do so in graduate school. When I was asked, I resorted to sharing my vocational aspiration of "working in the media."

My grandmother wasn't alone in her struggles to define communication. In fact, communication scholars have grappled with definitions for decades.[2] With more than 120 definitions documented by Frank E. X. Dance and C. E. Larson as well as the steady proliferation of refined definitions posited by scholars in the field over the past four decades, still no single definition has surfaced as an accepted standard by which we define the academic or professional field of communication.[3] Stephen W. Littlejohn and Karen A. Foss concluded, "Different definitions have different functions and enable the theorist to do different things." They went on to suggest that "a definition should be evaluated on the basis of how well it helps a scholar to accomplish the purpose of an investigation."[4] Thus, I offer the following definitions for the purposes of this chapter.

Generally, *communication* is the relational process of creating meaning while *media*, more specifically, refers to the channels through which messages pass from one communicator to another. While others have offered definitions accompanied by much more thorough exegeses of the linguistic origins and evolution of the terms, I will only highlight here those that are most germane to our understanding of communication and media from a Christian worldview. Before proceeding, it is essential to acknowledge that communication consists of the motivation and meaning while the medium involves the means, so that it would be negligent to separate one from the other.

Communication is similar to several terms in the Christian vernacular (e.g., "communion" and "community"), all of which have origins in the Latin as explained by John Durham Peters:

> From the Latin *communicare*, meaning to impart, share, or make common, it [the word "communication"] entered the English language in the fourteenth and fifteenth centuries. The key root is *mun-* (not *uni-*), related to such words as "munificent," "community," "meaning," and *Gemeinschaft*. The Latin *munus* has to do with gifts or duties offered publicly . . . In Latin, *communicatio* did not signify the general arts of human connection via symbols, nor did it suggest the hope for some kind of mutual recognition. Its sense was not in the least mentalistic: *communicatio* generally involved tangibles.[5]

With an emphasis on sharing or making common, one must consider what is actually being shared. For at the heart of communication is the creation of meaning, or significance, purpose, or understanding.

Understanding communication as the relational process of creating meaning is rooted in Scripture and begins with the story of creation and continues throughout the Holy Bible. God created man and woman in his own image (Gen 1:27), and throughout Scripture God reveals Himself to us as a creator and as a communicator. Scripture tells us that, "In the beginning God created the heavens and the earth" (Gen 1:1 HCSB). Within His perfect creation—all of which was *spoken* into existence—was humankind. Further, it is significant to point out that Jesus is referred to as the "Word":

> In the beginning was the Word,
> and the Word was with God,
> and the Word was God.
> He was with God in the beginning.
> All things were created through Him,
> and apart from Him not one thing was created
> that has been created.
> (John 1:1–3 HCSB)

The creation accounts in Genesis 1–2 lay the foundation for understanding communication as a relational process of creating meaning. The Lord God declared, "It is not good for the man to be alone" (Gen 2:18 HCSB). So after man gave names to the living creatures of the earth and when no suitable companion was found that was like him, God created woman and ordained the first human relationship.

Created in God's image, man and woman were capable of perfect communion and communication with God and with each other. It is worth noting that Gen 2:25 describes the purest form of relational communication: "Both the man and his wife were naked, yet felt no shame" (HCSB). This ideal state of communication can be understood as perfectly shared meaning, significance, purpose, or understanding. However, the man and woman were tempted and willfully chose to disobey God, thus destroying the perfect communion that existed in the garden of Eden. Experiencing one of the consequences of sin, humankind has been unable to return to that optimal condition of communion despite its countless efforts. These efforts to attain the original intimacy and fellowship can be observed in our often inadequate and even futile attempts to communicate, an ability that still separates humankind from the rest of God's earthly creation.

In addition to revealing God's nature as a creator, throughout Scripture we see evidence of God as a communicator in His enduring pursuit of humankind. God presented Noah with a sign of the rainbow to represent His covenant with humanity (Gen 9:12–17). Despite habitual disobedience, the children of Israel experienced abiding protection throughout the Old Testament. The revelation of God as communicator culminates with the birth of Jesus Christ, Immanuel (Matt 1:23). These acts of communication epitomize the relational process of God's responsiveness to humankind and our situations. The idea of God as communicator is not new. In fact, Knud Jorgensen expressed it clearly: "The basic theme in all of Scripture: God is continually seeking man out to talk with him, from the story of Eden until the proclamation of the new heavens and the new earth. In the same way, the concept of covenant is based on two-way communication."[6]

Meaning is created through a relational process that involves the interaction of communicators, messages, and channels on any of the following five levels: (1) *Intrapersonal* communication encompasses the meaning-making process at the deepest and most individual level where a communicator utilizes language or internal thought to foster understanding. Examples of intrapersonal communication include journaling, quiet times of private devotion, and prayer. (2) *Interpersonal* communication occurs when there are two communicators who, through the exchange of verbal and/or nonverbal messages, create new meaning. Interpersonal communication can be observed in any dyadic interaction (e.g., a conversation between a professor and student about a class project, a boy and a girl defining their relationship status, or even two colleagues preparing for an upcoming presentation). (3) *Group* communication describes the interactions among at least three individuals with a shared purpose. The size of the group may be as many as 12 or 13, but to constitute a group each member must be able to communicate with all other members of the group. (4) *Public* communication occurs in a setting larger than a group and is characterized by predominantly one-way communication (i.e., a speaker delivering a message to an audience). At the public communication level, immediate interaction is generally limited to nonverbal feedback. (5) Finally, *mass* communication describes the transmission of messages from a communicator to very large audiences and typically using mass media technologies (e.g., newspapers, radio, television, the Internet, etc.).

At the beginning of my teaching career, in an effort to integrate my faith with my subject matter, I described Jesus Christ as the master communicator from whom we can learn much about effective communication. Then during the following class meeting, I described the levels of communication and challenged the students to think of examples and role models for each level. As a class, we began to discuss examples from the New Testament where we saw Jesus pull away from the crowds to pray (i.e., intrapersonal), share with the woman at the well (i.e., interpersonal), share experiences with His inner circle of disciples (i.e., group), and teach in the Sermon on the Mount (i.e., public). When we reached the mass communication level, the entire class seemed to be confounded to find an example. Finally one student suggested that an example of mass communication could be seen in the Holy Bible itself. The master communicator used and continues to use the inspired and inerrant Word of God to facilitate the relational process for creating meaning. Gene Fant expounded on how God "reveals Himself in ways that comprise His Story, that communicate His point to His intended audience, humankind, through special revelation."[7] Indubitably, God has revealed Himself to us as a communicator, and this revelation should become the underpinning for the study of communication and media in Christian higher education.

In addition to face-to-face communication at the interpersonal, group, and public levels of communication, channels include an array of media through which messages are shared between communicators. As mentioned earlier, we should not analyze the medium and neglect the communication or vice versa. Canadian scholar and media theorist Marshall McLuhan first suggested the symbiotic relationship whereby media influence how messages are interpreted with the phrase, "The medium is the message." McLuhan wrote:

> The message, it seemed, was the content, as people used to ask what a painting was *about*. Yet they never thought to ask what a melody was about, nor what a house or a dress was about. In such matters, people retained some sense of the whole pattern, of form and function as a unity. But in the electric age this integral idea of structure

> and configuration has become so prevalent that educational theory has taken up the matter.[8]

McLuhan's commentary on media has become increasingly relevant nearly half a century later as new digital technologies have further expedited the transmission of communication messages between communicators and facilitated a heightened sense of connection across time and space.

Communication Revolutions and Society

As we have observed thus far, communication is ubiquitous from the beginning of creation to the present day, but for the purposes of this chapter we will narrow our focus to some of the specific communication revolutions as observed through the functions, technologies, and media that have manifested through the ages. There are five general eras in which communication can be categorized: (1) oral, (2) literary, (3) print, (4) electronic/broadcast, and (5) digital/interactive. Each is characterized by the role that communication and media played in society during the particular era. Further, the study and practice of communication and media are rooted in each of these areas and around the general purposes of communication (i.e., to inform, to entertain, and to persuade). From the oral and the early written eras of communication we have rhetoric, public discourse, and the performing arts such as theatre. The print revolution gave way to the capabilities for mass communication of the written word and images (e.g., photographs and illustrations). The electronic age saw the introduction of technologies such as the telegraph, telephone, radio, motion pictures, and television. And, finally, computer technology facilitated the advent of the digital age while the Internet and World Wide Web were the impetus for the age now known for its interactivity (e.g., Web 2.0).

Historians David Crowley and Paul Heyer, in *Communication in History: Technology, Culture, Society*, traced the development of communication beginning with the media of early civilizations, which were exclusively oral societies, to the origins of writing and the development of literary cultures. However, like most accounts of communication history, their treatment focuses significantly more on the development of mass media beginning with print and continuing to telegraphy and telephony before examining photographs, motion pictures, radio and television broadcasting, and the most recent introduction of computers and the Internet. With essays written by vanguards of each media sector, Crowley and Heyer's anthology provides an insightful look at the ways in which each new communication medium came into existence, how the medium influenced the culture into which it was introduced, and how the use of the medium shaped and, inversely, was shaped by society.[9]

Orality and Ancient Civilization

Before focusing on mass communication media, we must consider how oral communication dominated much of early civilizations. With the exception of rudimentary art and symbols, most ancient societies communicated through oral traditions in face-to-face settings. It was through verbally shared stories passed from one generation to the next within societal groups that people were able to communicate, teach, and reinforce timeless traditions and truths. Walter Ong, in his magnum opus *Orality and Literacy: Technologizing the Word*, first published in 1982, characterized this prehistoric era of communication as "primary orality" and pointed out that these early cultures were "totally untouched by any knowledge of writing or print."[10] "In a primarily oral culture," Ong wrote, "where the word has its existence only in sound, with no reference whatsoever to any visually perceptible text, and no awareness of even the possibility of such a text, the phenomenology of sound enters deeply into human beings' feel for existence, as processed by the spoken word."[11] Orality limited modes of expression as well as the complexity of thought, Ong asserted. Further, oral societies had no efficient ways of documenting their stories or transactions, which pushed societies toward innovative techniques that gave rise to the development of alphabetic characters and the technologies (paper, ink, etc.) that enabled writing. With the necessary tools for writing, civilization entered the literary age.

The Rise of the Literary Age

The literary age spans from approximately 4000 BC to the fifteenth century AD and, most ironically, is characterized by the little amount of reading materials available and the fact that only a select few were able to read written texts. This is evident in church history where monastic communities and bishops controlled much of the world because of the broader society's illiteracy, which only began to improve with the advent of movable type and the printing press by German Johannes Gutenberg in the 1400s. The social, cultural, and political impact of the printing press and more widely distributed print media on the course of history is incalculable. Ong aptly noted humankind's desires to create and communicate as the driving force behind the shift from a primarily oral society to a literate one: "Without writing, human consciousness cannot achieve its fuller potential, cannot produce other beautiful and powerful creations."[12]

With the exponential advancements toward a literate society and the increased availability of educational institutions and libraries, written information was no longer the sole domain of the few literate elite. One of the most significant consequences of the printing era was its influence on the Protestant Reformation, since printing enabled swift dissemination of Martin Luther's ideas that challenged and condemned the practices of the Roman Catholic Church. Although the medium (i.e., print) did not cause the Reformation, it did facilitate the social change. Sterin even suggested that the printing of the Bible by Gutenberg was the beginning of the dissolution of the Latin-trained, Catholic clerical elite. "The ability to reproduce the 'word of God' through a mechanism outside the privileged elite and Church allowed more individuals to read the Bible on their own and thus develop their own ideas, interpretations and opinions about it."[13] The print era noted for increased literacy as well as an abundance of printed materials in the forms of books, pamphlets, and newspapers opened new doors for communicators to disseminate messages to the masses. In the previous era, those who could read held power; the power soon shifted with the printing revolution beyond those who were literate to those who owned or controlled the tools for mass distribution of messages—for example, publishers and printing press owners.

The Electronic Age

Following the era of print came the electric revolution, which introduced societies to communication technologies that expedited the transmission of messages between communicators. For example, the electric telegraph enabled written messages to be sent and received quickly across large expanses—crossing the spatial and temporal boundaries that had previously restrained human communication. James Carey, in *Communication as Culture: Essays on Media and Society*, called the telegraph a watershed in communication history: "The innovation of the telegraph can stand metaphorically for all the innovations that ushered in the modern phase of history and determined, even to this day, the major lines of development of American communications. The most important fact about the telegraph is at once the most obvious and innocent: It permitted for the first time the effective separation of communication from transportation."[14]

The telegraph was a precursor to the invention of radio, moving pictures, and eventually television. Each expanded the sensory connections beyond mere printed words that were read.

Ong explained how the emergence of this electronic media brought about an age he called "secondary orality." He articulated the similarities and dissimilarities between primary and secondary orality, which are in contrast to the literary age:

> Like primary orality, secondary orality has generated a strong group sense, for listening to spoken words forms hearers into a group, a true audience, just as reading written or printed texts turns individuals in on themselves. But secondary orality generates a sense for groups immeasurably larger than those of primary oral culture—McLuhan's "global village." Moreover, before writing, oral folk were group-minded because no feasible alternative had presented itself. In our age of secondary orality, we are group-minded self-consciously and programmatically. The individual feels that he or she, as an individual, must be socially sensitive. Unlike members of a primary oral culture, who are turned outward because they have had little occasion to turn inward, we are turned outward because we have turned inward.[15]

Ong specifically outlined four parallels between the two oral cultures: participatory mystique, fostering of a sense of community, concentration on the present moment, and use of formulas. However, the key difference he stressed was that secondary orality is more deliberate and members are more self-conscious of their participation in and use of the communication media. An even more obvious difference is secondary orality's dependence upon technology for the transmission and reception of messages.[16]

The electronic age introduced new media devices such as telephone, radio, television, and even computers into society that quickly became a springboard for the rise of the digital and interactive era. Killingsworth extended Ong's typology by introducing the concept of "secondary literacy" to explain the process for encoding messages to be exchanged using the technology of secondary orality. Though personal computers were regularly being used for educational and business tasks in the 1980s and early 1990s, their use for computer-mediated personal communication remained extremely limited. Thus, the perspectives offered by Ong and Killingsworth provided embryonic explanations for the communication dynamics that would evolve throughout the 1990s and into the twenty-first century with the advent of the World Wide Web as a public and private communication platform.[17]

Radios and televisions found their place in homes across the world almost as soon as they were introduced. From the huddles of families around the radio to listen to news of the world wars to the neighborhood gatherings to watch early quiz show broadcasts, these electronic boxes have transported listeners and viewers to places they never dreamed of going. The advent of the computer was no exception, and it has transformed the way people interact. Since the Internet became accessible for the common computer user in the late twentieth century, people across the globe have taken hold of the new technology and its seemingly endless capacities for their own egocentric purposes. As all humans are innately created to communicate, Internet users of all sorts have transformed the global network of computers into a megamedium that annihilates the boundaries that had so distinctly separated interpersonal communication from mass media in the prior millennium.

Modern Technological Communication

From the first cryptic text message that was transmitted between two computers in the twentieth century to the modern-day use of Internet technology for surfing the Web, e-mailing, finding new information, getting news, shopping, or playing games, the Internet and its resulting components have revolutionized the way individuals interact and create meaning. Fox observed that "one of the most crucial aspects of humans' growing use of the Internet is how they have embraced it as a community-forming device—a space where they may meet and interact with one another and, in many cases, develop what has become commonly referred to as virtual community."[18] Tim Berners-Lee, inventor of the World Wide Web, even acknowledges the communication potential of his creation: "The Web is more a social creation than a technical one. I designed it for a social effect—to help people work together—and not as a technical toy."[19]

Today, communication media are dominated by personal technologies that are mobile, scalable, and accessible. Despite the widespread use of these technological devices, it is imperative that the media channels be examined critically and liberally. This can happen most effectively in a Christian liberal arts university. As Dockery pointed out, "a technological society needs the broad understanding and wisdom of the liberal arts and the Christian Scriptures because they are essential for the thinking and decision making a technological society needs, as well as for giving substance to a Christian worldview."[20]

Communication, the divinely ordained, relational process of creating meaning, and the increasing channels (or media) through which it occurs are innately neither good nor bad. They are merely powerful tools for creation. Peters takes a somber approach to the subject to his historical examination of communication through the ages and predicates his commentary on the problems of communication. The problem is centered on society's unattainable dream and even obsession with the concept of communication as evidenced by the abundance of how-to books, workshops, and even technologies to help us traverse the chasms that have separated each of us from one another. Peters explained that "communication, in the deeper sense of establishing ways to share one's hours meaningfully with others, is sooner a matter of faith and risk than of technique and method."[21] He went on to compare and contrast various perspectives of communication that have emerged in different fields and historical eras, all pointing to his notion that these perspectives have been too narrow and geared toward finding cure-alls to the problem of human communication. This, according to Peters, merely leads to frustration and actually inhibits our growth in understanding and practicing communication. He asserted that the process of discovery, even though we may not find all the answers, is fine and it even opens each of us up to the spiritual dimensions of communication.

Communication and the Christian Liberal Arts Academy

A department of communication and media is uniquely situated among its counterparts within the academy, particularly at a liberal arts university. Though some may categorize the study of communication and media as solely professional, I contend that an intentionally Christ-centered approach to the field should possess a distinct blend of the liberal arts as well as professional education. Clearly the field is most recognized because of the observable media channels that are used to inform, entertain, and persuade (e.g., plays, newspapers, magazines, films, television, radio, websites, and other oral or written communications). While many facets of communication could be reduced unwittingly to mere technical training (e.g., operating a camera, building a set, writing a news story, taking a photograph or designing an advertisement), it is essential for practitioners and scholars to understand the grander scope and potential for effective communication across all of its platforms.

The study of communication dates back to early Greek and Roman civilizations. In fact, Aristotle's (384–322 BC) *Rhetoric* might be considered the first communication textbook. The teachings of this Greek philosopher-teacher in the academy, as documented in his prolific writings, are the foundation for classical communication models that center on the use of oral communication for persuasive purposes. Roman educator Quintilian (c. AD 35–95) advanced Aristotle's methods for persuasive speaking in *Institutio Oratoria* where he provided instruction for becoming a good speaker-statesman. Like rhetoric, debate, and public discourse, we can also trace the development of theatre as an art of communication to early Greek and Roman societies.

Modern communication studies, driven by curiosities about the effects of mass communication, did not find their home in the academy of higher education until much later. During the Rockefeller Foundation Seminar on Mass Communication in 1939–40, Harold Lasswell, a Ph.D. in political science from the University of Chicago, captured the basic elements of communication when he described communication with this question: "Who says what to whom via what channels with what effect?" Everett Rogers, who provided an extensive biographical account of the history of communication study, included Lasswell among the forerunners who made contributions to the study of communication though they did not consider themselves to be communication scholars.[22]

Illustrations of the communication process began with Claude E. Shannon's information theory, which depicted a transmission model of communication where the process was simplified to the most basic elements of one-way communication. Over the years scholars have advanced the original model of communication to describe further dimensions of the communication process. Wilbur Schramm, later credited as the founder of communication study by Rogers, was one of the first to modify the original mathematical model to illustrate a two-way interchange of messages. While there have been other illustrations that sought to capture the essence of communication across its many forms, Schramm's model remains at the core of communication and media studies. With only slight enhancements to Schramm's illustration, the relational model of communication (see fig. 1) may be used to extrapolate the multiple dimensions of communication as the relational process of creating meaning.[23]

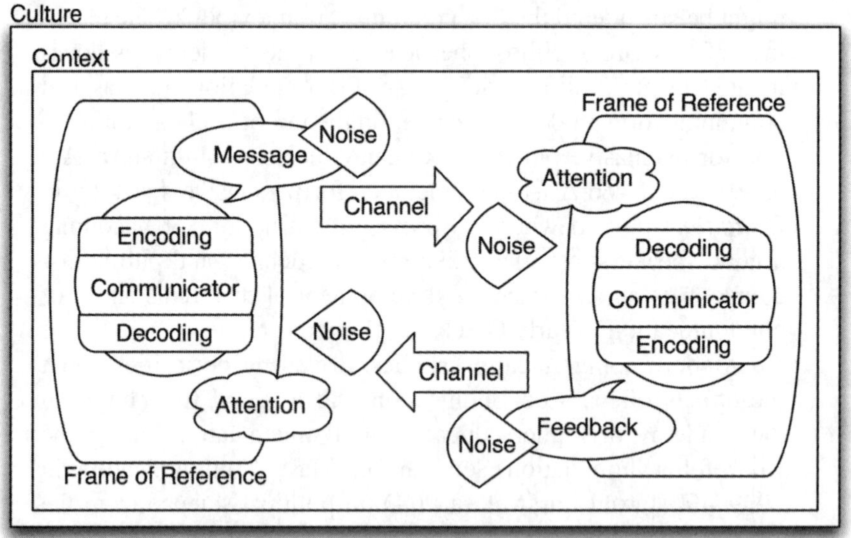

Figure 1. Relational Model of Communication

These definitions, drawn from the phenomenological, sociopsychological, and sociocultural traditions of communication theory as explained by Craig, serve as a framework for examining a field that emerged as a subject for formal academic study primarily in the twentieth century. As we have observed, the study and practice of communication and media are extensive and the academic label of their study is inconsistent from one institution to the next.[24] While some larger, public institution might fragment the studies of communication and media into separate departments or schools (e.g., theater, speech, journalism, advertising, public relations, media, etc.), it is unrealistic and unnecessary to detach the various functions of communication study with such divisions. Instead, to solidify their place within the academy of Christian higher education, I offer the following typology for a liberal arts-based approach to communication and media.

Theatre Arts	**Communication Studies**	**Media Studies**	**Strategic Communications**
Performance	Rhetoric	Mass Communication	Journalism
Production	Public Speaking	Film	Public Relations
Studies	Interpersonal	Broadcasting	Advertising
	Small Group	Digital Media	Visual
	Intercultural		
	Organizational		

Figure 2. Christian Liberal Arts Approach to Communication and Media

Alongside traditional communication studies from ancient Greece and Rome were the theater arts. Similarly, they continue to hold a place in higher education. Theater arts include both literary and production studies as well as performance and technical aspects (costuming, lighting, set design, etc.). Communication studies encompass the classical art of rhetoric as applied in public speaking, public discourse, and debate contexts. Additionally, other facets of human communication (interpersonal, small group, intercultural, etc.) fall under the category of communication studies. Media studies focus primarily on the mediated channels through which communication occurs, including the broader subject of mass communication as well as the more specific media of film, broadcasting, and digital media. Digital media embodies the newest forms of communication (e.g., Internet-based programming and content design). Finally, strategic communications describe the communication functions by purpose. Journalism is the craft of storytelling for the purpose of information sharing, while public relations is the communication management function through which organizations build and maintain relationships with the public on whom the organization's success or failure depends. Similarly, advertising focuses on the creative process of selling products and services, while visual communication represents the arts of photography and design for communication purposes.

Today, communication and media can find their way into other academic disciplines. Conversely, the academic study of communication draws upon the scholarship of other disciplines, including education, sociology, psychology, and other social sciences. Recognizing that academic disciplines are artificial creations that provide institutional structure, scholars and practitioners must be able to answer the question of what is the communication phenomenon being studied. The methodological frameworks used in communication studies (i.e., historical/critical, quantitative, and qualitative) are similar to a tool shed with instruments of varying degrees of complexity and application for the study of the phenomenon in various contexts.

Communication and the Christian Faith

Throughout this chapter, we have observed the breadth and depth of communication from oral and face-to-face to written and mediated. Believing that communication is a gift from God, it is essential for believers to consider how their own communication and their use (consumption and production) of mediated communication fulfill their callings as Christians. Christian higher education is the consummate setting for such discovery and analysis.

All of us are participants in communication and, to varying extents, consumers of media. Thus, we should evaluate how such consumptions influence who we are. Research and theory, originating from communication and media scholars, provide us with a framework for assessing the results of media on intrapersonal, interpersonal, group, public, and mass levels of communication. Shane Hipps, in *Flickering Pixels*, made an astute observation when he challenged readers to consider how the screens with which we surround ourselves (theater, television, computers, mobile devices, etc.) influence our faith:

> Christianity is fundamentally a communication event. The religion is predicated on God revealing himself to humanity. God has a habit of

> letting his people know something about his thoughts, feelings, and intentions. God wants to communicate with us, and his media are many: angels, burning bushes, stone tablets, scrolls, donkeys, prophets, mighty voices, still whispers, and shapes traced in the dirt. Any serious study of God is a study of communication, and any effort to understand God is shaped by our understanding—or misunderstanding—of the media and technology we use to communicate.[25]

Assessing communication and media from a Christian worldview must extend beyond analysis and criticism from a consumer's perspective. By applying one's understanding of the communication process to the production techniques of various channels—whether on a stage, in print, on a big screen, or on a small screen—the student of communication and media should gain a paramount realization of the potential for the Christian faith and beyond. Avery Dulles, a Jesuit priest, theologian, and cardinal of the Roman Catholic Church, insisted that the church "cannot wall itself up in a cultural ghetto at a time when humanity as a whole is passing into the electronic age."[26] In response to Dulles's call for Christian engagement with their culture, a significant observation must be raised about the role communication and media play in shaping and reflecting culture. Kurt Fredrickson posited that "culture is what humans do with creation. In this sense we are co-creators, taking the raw materials that God has placed in the world and in humanity. From these materials we craft human cultures full of artifacts reflecting our creativity."[27]Andy Crouch, in *Culture Making: Recovering Our Creative Calling*, provided countless examples of how the co-creation of culture is reflected in our communication and media.[28] This advances the ideas espoused by Quentin Schultze in *Communicating for Life: Christian Stewardship in Community and Media.* By co-creating culture, we reach out to our immediate community through communication and, with increasing frequency, through media. The culture that is created results from our relationship with God and others as well as the products of those relationships. Schultze insisted that we become symbolic stewards of God's creation as we embark on a journey to make meaning of the world.[29]

As beings created in God's image, we are communicators and have a high calling and responsibility for how we use the abilities that we have been given. As such, a worthy question centers on the difference between Christian communicators and communicators who are Christian. This regularly becomes a topic for considerable dialogue when I teach an introductory journalism course. Specifically, what is a Christian journalist? The religious adjective may be interpreted as describing the subjects that the journalist covers (i.e., stories of the Christian faith) or as a modifier of the journalist (i.e., a Christian who reports and writes stories about any number of subjects). This question can be extended to any form of communication, such as a Christian filmmaker, a Christian public relations practitioner, or a Christian actor. Bruce Demarest exhorted the believer and follower of Christ to "nurture and develop to the best of our abilities all our God-created capacities: our minds, our wills, our emotions, our moral discrimination (conscience), and our relationships/relational capacities."[30] To it we can add our capacities as communicators. "Recognizing our likeness to God, we should be eager to develop our full potential as good stewards—in particular those qualities that God shares with his creatures: kindness, compassion, mercy, etc. As thinking, willing, feeling, and relational beings we have been created for fellowship with, and service to, God for both time and eternity."[31] The study and practice of communication and media has tremendous potential for enabling the Christian to fulfill the two Great Commandments as well as the Great Commission. In response to the question about which is the greatest commandment, Jesus responded: "Love the Lord your God with all your heart, with all your soul, and with all your mind. This is the greatest and most important command. The second is like it: Love your neighbor as yourself" (Matt 22:37–39 HCSB). With an understanding of the principles and process of communication, we have the ability to gain a new understanding of our Creator as He has revealed Himself to us. Further, it is through the obedient acts of communication that we can also love Him with all that we are. As Paul explained to the Romans, we must not be conformed to this world, but we must be transformed by the renewing of our minds (Rom 12:2). In the same way that the world cultivates our values, the Christian church and community of believers has the power to cultivate beliefs and values. This renewal of the mind occurs in the context of community—through our interactions with other people. As a part of the church of Jesus Christ, each believer also has a responsibility for helping to transform one another (i.e., loving our neighbor) through our face-to-face communication as well as our use of media.

In the Sermon on the Mount, Jesus reminded His followers of their responsibilities to the world. He said, "You are the salt of the earth. . . . You are the light of the world. A city situated on a hill cannot be hidden. No one lights a lamp and puts it under a basket, but rather on a lampstand, and it gives light for all who are in the house. In the same way, let your light shine before men, so that they may see your good works and give glory to your Father in heaven" (Matt 5:13a,14–16 HCSB). In his epic book *Roaring Lambs*, Bob Briner called for a radically different way for individual Christians to embrace their God-given capacities and engage with the world and its culture—to fulfill our calling to be salt and light by seizing the fields and professions that had previously been vacated by the church. "If a religion is really vital, meaningful, relevant, and important, it will make a difference not only in the lives of individuals but also in society itself," Briner wrote. "Evangelical Christians in America must face up to this challenge."[32] In the age of digital and interactive media, the stakes have never been higher and the potential has never been greater for excellence-driven communicators who can engage with their communities and shape their cultures for the kingdom of God.

Questions for Further Reflection

1. What are your definitions of communication and media? How are they shaped by your faith and understanding of Scripture?
2. What is the difference between a Christian communicator and a communicator who is a Christian? How can one differentiate Christian communication and media from that which is produced and/or consumed by a Christian?
3. Why is shaping culture through communication and media such an important part of being salt and light in today's world? What are some practical ways you can be salt and light through your engagement with communication and media?
4. If you are considering a career in communication or media, what are the specific beliefs, principles, and practices on which you will not negotiate or compromise?

5. What can you do to commit to excellent communication that will reflect the *Imago Dei*?

Resources for Additional Study

Communication History, Theory, and Culture

Briggs, Asa, and Peter Burke. *A Social History of the Media: From Gutenberg to the Internet*. 3rd ed. Malden, MA: Polity Press, 2009.

Carey, James W. *Communication as Culture: Essays on Media and Society*. London: Routledge, 1988; rev. ed., 1992.

Crouch, Andy. *Culture Making: Recovering Our Creative Calling*. Downers Grove, IL: InterVarsity Press, 2008.

Griffin, Emory A. *A First Look at Communication Theory*. 8th ed. New York: McGraw Hill, 2012.

Rogers, Everett M. *A History of Communication Study: A Biographical Approach*. New York: Free Press, 1994.

Theater Arts

Johnson, Todd E., and Dale Savidge. *Performing the Sacred: Theology and Theatre in Dialogue*. Grand Rapids: Baker Academic, 2009.

Taylor, W. David O. *For the Beauty of the Church: Casting a Vision for the Arts*. Grand Rapids: Baker Books, 2010.

Communication Studies

Chapel, William Blakeslee. *Communication: God's Design*. Pittsburgh: Red Lead Press, 2007.

Holladay, Tom. *The Relationship Principles of Jesus*. Grand Rapids: Zondervan, 2008.

Maxwell, John C. *Everyone Communicates, Few Connect: What the Most Effective People Do Differently*. Nashville: Thomas Nelson, 2010.

Muehlhoff, Tim, and Todd V. Lewis. *Authentic Communication: Christian Speech Engaging Culture*. Downers Grove, IL: InterVarsity, 2010.

Schultze, Quentin J. *Communicating for Life: Christian Stewardship in Community and Media*. Grand Rapids: Baker Academic, 2000.

Media Studies

Briner, Bob. *Roaring Lambs: A Gentle Plan to Radically Change Your World.* Grand Rapids: Zondervan, 1993.

———. *Final Roar*. Nashville: B&H, 2000.

Hipps, S. *Flickering Pixels: How Technology Shapes Your Faith.* Grand Rapids: Zondervan, 2009.

Rice, Jesse. *The Church of Facebook: How the Hyperconnected Are Redefining Community.* Colorado Springs: David C. Cook, 2009.

Schultze, Quentin J., and Robert H. Woods Jr., eds. *Understanding Evangelical Media: The Changing Face of Christian Communication.* Downers Grove, IL: InterVarsity, 2008.

Woods, Robert H., Jr., and Paul D. Patton. *Prophetically Incorrect: A Christian Introduction to Media Criticism.* Grand Rapids: Brazos Press, 2010.

Strategic Communications

Olasky, Marvin N. *Telling the Truth: How to Revitalize Christian Journalism.* Wheaton: Crossway Books, 1996.

Willis, Jim. T*he Mind of a Journalist: How Reporters View Themselves, Their World, and Their Craft*. Los Angeles: Sage, 2010.

Endnotes

[1] Jayrandall22011. "Twin Baby Boys Have a Conversation—part 2." Retrieved from http://www.youtube.com/watch?v=_JmAZCIUUY (February 14, 2001).

[2] See Frank E. X. Dance, "The Concept of Communication," *Journal of Communication* 20 (1970): 201–10; Alex Gode, "What Is Communication?" *Journal of Communication* 9 (1959): 5; Gerald R. Miller, "On Defining Communication: Another Stab," *Journal of Communication* 16 (1966): 92; and W. Barnett Pearce, *Communication and the Human Condition* (Carbondale, IL: Southern Illinois University Press, 1989).

[3] Frank E. X. Dance and Carl E. Larson, *The Function of Human Communication: A Theoretical Approach* (New York: Holt, Rinehart, and Winston, 1976).

[4] Stephen W. Littlejohn and Karen A. Foss, *Theories of Human Communication*, 8th ed. (Belmont, CA: Thomason Wadsworth, 2005), 13.

[5] John Durham Peters, *Speaking into the Air: A History of the Idea of Communication* (Chicago: University of Chicago, 1999), 7.

[6] Knud Jorgensen, "Christian Communication: Remote Control or Incarnation?" *World Evangelization* 5 (1996/1997): 5.

[7] Gene C. Fant, *God as Author: A Biblical Approach to Narrative* (Nashville: B&H, 2010), 67.

[8] Marshall McLuhan, *Understanding Media: The Extensions of Man* (Cambridge, MA: MIT Press, 1964), 13.

[9] See David Crowley and Paul Heyer, eds., *Communication in History: Technology, Culture, Society*, 5th ed. (Boston: Pearson, 2007).

[10] Walter Ong, *Orality and Literacy: The Technologizing of the Word* (New York: Routledge, 2002), 11.

[11] Walter Ong, "Orality, Literacy, and Modern Media," in Crowley and Heyer, *Communication in History*, 71.

[12] Ong, *Orality and Literacy*, 15.

[13] J. Charles Sterin, *Mass Media Revolution* (Boston: Pearson, 2011), 40.

[14] James W. Carey, *Communication as Culture: Essays on Media and Society* (New York: Routledge, 1989), 203.

[15] Ong, "Orality, Literacy, and Modern Media," in Crowley and Heyer, *Communication in History*, 69.
[16] See Ong, *Orality and Literacy*.
[17] See M. Jimmie Killingsworth, "Product and Process, Literacy and Orality: An Essay on Composition and Culture," *College Composition and Communication* 44:1 (1993): 26–39.
[18] Steve Fox, "The New Imagined Community: Identifying and Exploring a Bidirectional Continuum Integrating Virtual and Physical Communities through the Community Embodiment Model (CEM)," *Journal of Communication Inquiry* 28:1 (2004): 48.
[19] Tim Berners-Lee, *Weaving the Web: The Original Design of the World Wide Web by Its Inventor* (New York: Harper Collins, 2000), 173.
[20] David S. Dockery, *Renewing Minds* (Nashville: B&H, 2007), 27.
[21] Peters, *Speaking into the Air*, 30.
[22] See Everett M. Rogers, *A History of Communication Study: A Biographical Approach* (New York: Free Press, 1994).
[23] See Claude E. Shannon, "A Mathematical Theory of Communication," *Bell System Technical Journal* 27 (1948): 379–423, 623–56; Rogers, *History of Communication Study*; Wilbur Schramm, ed., *The Process and Effects of Communication* (Urbana, IL: University of Illinois Press, 1954), 3–26.
[24] Robert T. Craig, "Communication Theory as a Field," *Communication Theory* 9:2 (1999): 99–161.
[25] Shane Hipps, *Flickering Pixels: How Technology Shapes Your Faith* (Grand Rapids: Zondervan, 2009), 13.
[26] Avery Dulles, "The Church and the Media," *The Catholic Mind*, October 1971, 6.
[27] Kurt Fredrickson, "Creation," in *Dictionary of Everyday Theology and Culture*, ed. Bruce Demarest and Keith J. Matthews (Colorado Springs: NavPress, 2010), 92–93.
[28] Andy Crouch, *Culture Making: Recovering Our Creative Call* (Downers Grove, IL: InterVarsity, 2008).
[29] Quentin J. Schultze, *Communicating for Life: Christian Stewardship in Community and Media* (Grand Rapids: Baker, 2000).
[30] Bruce Demarest, "Image of God," in Demarest and Matthews, *Dictionary of Everyday Theology and Culture*, 231–32.
[31] Ibid.
[32] Bob Briner, *Roaring Lambs* (Grand Rapids: Zondervan, 1993), 56.

16

A CHRISTIAN IN THE SCIENCES

Mark Bolyard

I have given much thought to what it means to be a Christian in the sciences. Several years ago I became the Chair of the Biology Department at Union University. Prior to that, I served on the faculty of Southern Illinois University Edwardsville. There have been many positive benefits resulting from the move to Union. I can talk about issues in biology from a Christian perspective. I can pray before my classes. The faculty in my department and the administration are great to work with, and we approach our careers from a similar worldview. But is that really all that it means to be part of Christian higher education? Is that what it means to be a scientist in a Christian context?

As a biologist, I will address these questions in the context of the life sciences, the primary arena of controversy between faith and science. First, I will touch on some key points in the development of science and natural philosophy, as well as identify key figures in the Christian intellectual tradition in the life sciences. Second, I will consider how scientists within the Christian intellectual tradition have approached the relationship between faith and science.

Third, I will discuss evolution and the origin of life as an example of one of the more challenging issues for Christians in the life sciences. Fourth, I will examine some additional issues in the life sciences and how a Christian worldview impacts what one concludes about those issues. Finally, I will explore some personal questions that I have wrestled with regarding how being a Christian impacts my role in higher education.

A Brief History of Modern Science

Modern science is a product of the development of Western civilization but traces its roots back much farther than that. The ancient Greeks, particularly Socrates, Plato, and Aristotle (roughly 430–330 BC), developed ideas about all areas of life, including what we now think of as areas of science (biology, astronomy and physics) as well as the nature of God. They saw a single God, contrary to many of their countrymen who worshipped many gods.[1] They understood the universe as ordered and comprehensible. This idea is also found in the Old and New Testaments. This connection between an orderly God and an ability to make sense of the natural world was known in the Middle Ages as "natural philosophy." Until the modern era, there wasn't the divide between science and other disciplines that we see today. The modern word "science" comes from the Latin *scientia*, which simply means "knowledge."

Important figures in natural philosophy and its transition to modern science (what is sometimes called the "scientific revolution") were Thomas Aquinas (1225–74), William of Ockham (1288–1348), and Rene Descartes (1596–1650), all of whom were Christians. However, Francis Bacon (1561–1626), also a Christian, was a central figure in making this transition. His major contribution was in emphasizing inductive reasoning, which "makes generalizations based on a number of specific instances," over the prevailing idea of deductive reasoning, in which "general principles are applied to specific instances,"[2] although both are important. "Without deductive logic science would be entirely useless. It is merely a barren game to ascend from the particular to the general, unless afterwards we can reverse the process and descend from the general to the particular, ascending and descending like angels on Jacob's ladder."[3] While Bacon's intent was to use these new scientific principles from a Christian perspective to solve real-world problems, more modern uses of what we now know as the "scientific method" are used to focus purely on the material world without looking at its underlying meaning. So, while Christians sometimes blame those outside of Christianity for the rise of science over and against theology, it was Christians that were heavily involved with the development of science.

This rise of modern science during the late sixteenth and early seventeenth centuries involved figures like Bacon, Galileo, and

Descartes and was pivotal in the history of natural philosophy. This period of time represented the overthrow of an entire system of thinking or worldview, namely, the ancient Greek paradigm that dominated the Middle Ages. Initially, this paradigm shift was motivated by observations of the universe that did not mesh with previously established ideas. Later, Darwin's publication of *On the Origin of Species* (1859) had a similar effect. Darwin provided a framework within which one could, in principle, have an account of the origin of life that did not depend upon supernatural intervention. Thus, Darwin effectively created the intellectual space for a fully naturalistic account of the universe, a universe without a God.

This view of the natural world was not widely shared beyond the West, although significant contributions to science have been made by scientists from across the globe. For example, the "Chinese in the eighteenth century" believed that "the idea that the universe could be governed by simple laws which human beings could and had discovered was foolish in the extreme. Their culture simply was not receptive to such notions."[4] However, Middle Eastern scholars contributed quite a bit to natural philosophy,[5] including the translation of writings important to the foundations of modern science.

On the other hand, scientists who were Christians, such as Kepler, Newton, Pascal, Boyle, Faraday, Mendel, Pasteur, and Kelvin [along with those mentioned above], made remarkable contributions to their scientific disciplines. "Most of the great scientific figures who contributed to the meteoric rise of science at the time [sixteenth–eighteenth centuries] found belief in a Creator God . . . positively stimulating; indeed, for many of them, it was their prime motivation for scientific investigation."[6]

The intersection of a Christian worldview and an interest in the natural world, what Kepler called "thinking God's thoughts after Him," required some kind of structure. The advent of scientific inquiry required the same things that it does today: good ideas, time, and money. Looking at the biographies of the early scientists indicates that many of them were either from wealthy families, supported by a benefactor, or, as with Gregor Mendel (an Austrian monk who studied inheritance in peas), in the business of dealing with living things as part of their everyday lives. In addition to the "scientific method" that arose out of the work of Bacon and Descartes, another major advancement was the development of scientific societies in the mid-1600s.[7] These societies enabled scientists to share their findings with each other and quickly led to the publication of journals, so those not able to attend the meetings could learn about discoveries. Many scientific societies continue to carry out similar functions today.

Within these structures emerged the "Christian intellectual tradition" in the sciences, which involved many of the scientists and philosophers we have already noted, as well as many others. This tradition traces its history back much earlier in other disciplines. It is noteworthy that the list of prominent scientists who are Christians begins to decline in the second half of the nineteenth century, corresponding with, but not necessarily caused by, battles involving evolution, materialism, and scientific reductionism (the idea that everything, most specifically living things, can be described simply as a collection of their most basic components). Scientists, such as George Washington Carver, who dared to acknowledge God in public, were ridiculed.[8] The scientific societies began to move away from their original harmonization of Scripture and nature,[9] gradually squeezing theological elements from their documents and doctrines. For example, the National Academy of Sciences (U.S.) has position papers on evolution, indicating that the advent of life is a purely "naturalistic" phenomenon (meaning that it can be explained entirely on the basis of natural causes). In addition to these written statements, 87 percent of scientists in the U.S. support the idea that humans and other living things on earth evolved over time due to naturalistic causes.[10] Students under their instruction are taught that reductionism is the only "scientific" approach to these issues, and that they should self-censor any thoughts they have about a supernatural being at work in the universe.[11] This is ironic, since authoritarianism was one of Descartes's motivations for developing his systematic approach to science.

Combining Faith and Practice

The foundation of the Christian intellectual tradition in the sciences involves an effort on the part of the scientist to think actively about the faith/science relationship. There are several ways that Christians who are scientists can carry this out. First, they can separate faith and science into separate spheres, each intentionally ignoring the other. While Christianity is fundamentally about the nature of God, and the relationship between God and man, it also informs us how to live.[12] Many scientists will use their Christianity as a moral compass but will draw a clear line with regard to how it impacts their work on a daily basis. This was described by the late Stephen Jay Gould as "nonoverlapping magisteria," or NOMA. Accordingly, faith and science each have their space, with each serving as authorities within their domain.[13]

Alternatively, scientists can separate faith and science into separate spheres, each informing the other. This division will frequently result in the establishment of a hierarchy between the two spheres. We'll see examples of how this plays out in the next section.

Still other scientists work hard at integrating their science and their faith, which in some areas is a difficult task. For example, these scientists may try to reconnect science to the rest of the disciplines as a way of reconstituting "natural philosophy." One key way that some scientists who are Christians approach science is to integrate science with the other areas of knowledge. Since the dawn of the modern era, areas of knowledge have become increasingly disconnected from each other. But Christians should view truth as one integrated whole. There are efforts underway at some Christian universities to have cross-disciplinary discussions that emerge from this holistic view of knowledge. David Dockery, president of Union University, in his book *Renewing Minds*, describes the need for such conversations.[14]

Christians make contributions to science all the time, but it is hard to say that their being Christian has much to do with it. It may provide motivation in some cases, but the things that Christians (or other theists) know that atheists do not are by definition excluded from contemporary science. However, being Christian does impact the relationship between the way a scientist functions on a daily basis and the framework within which science operates. It is certainly possible to be a Christian and a practicing scientist without thinking about the value of the current paradigm (the way science currently works) within which one's science proceeds. Most scientists in the history of science, Christians included, have in fact practiced science in this way. Indeed, many Christians have been engaged in science over the past century under the current scientific paradigms and have produced many valuable results for humanity. This is a good that should be acknowledged.

When, however, we ask what difference being a Christian "should" make in the practice of science, a Christian should be open to the real possibility that the paradigms within which science operates, within his or her own specialty, might be rooted in assumptions that are contrary to a Christian understanding of the world. So, while Christians should be scientific practitioners, they should also be philosophers of science. Therefore, science curricula at Christian universities should make students aware not only of the practice of science within a given paradigm, but they should also teach students about the very nature of the paradigms themselves. Christian universities should produce scientists who can "think Christianly" about the very nature of science, to reflect on the degree to which current scientific paradigms are consistent with a Christian outlook on reality.

Approaches to Evolution and the Origin of Life

Now that we have an idea of how scientists who are Christians view relationships between science and faith, let us explore how this might apply to a long-standing controversy in the life sciences. How do Christians approach the questions of evolution and the origin of life? How important are our answers to these questions? This section will provide us with an opportunity to apply the Christian intellectual tradition to the key questions of evolution and the origin of life.

First, let's look at an overview regarding the history of the questions of origins as it relates to the Christian faith. As mentioned above, the number of scientists who "thought God's thoughts after Him," studied science because "all truth was God's truth," and pursued an understanding of the natural world to understand more about the nature of God began to decline in the last half of the nineteenth century. Two significant things took place around 1860—one that had an immediate impact and one that would lie dormant for about 50 years. The first was the publication of Charles Darwin's book, *On the Origin of Species by Means of Natural Selection, or the Preservation of Favoured Races in the Struggle for Life*, in 1859. The second event was the publication of Gregor Mendel's work on patterns of inheritance in peas, "Experiments on Plant Hybridization," in 1865.

Darwin's work provided scientists with a framework for thinking about the origins of life that did not require a deity.

Scientists did not have to think God's thoughts after Him after all. Universities and scientific societies transitioned from places where God was honored to places where He was, at best, ignored. But the picture was very muddy for those next hundred years. There were still numerous questions for which "God did it" was still a good answer. The nature of cells, chromosomes, and DNA were still a mystery. There was no good explanation for the origin of the "stuff" of the universe. While God was on the hot seat during those times, He was still in the room. However, the Christian intellectual tradition during this window of time began to grow silent; fewer scientists were motivated by understanding the works of the Creator God, as institutions that generate scientists, the universities, began to dispense with Him.

By 1960, the value of Mendel's work describing the physical nature of inheritance had been fully appreciated, and the fusion of work started by Mendel, on the nature of chromosomes, DNA, and genes, with Darwin's work on evolution, had greatly matured into what we now call the "neo-Darwinian synthesis."[15] For scientists who could see the explanatory power of molecular evolution, there were fewer questions requiring a "God" answer. In addition, around this time the "Big Bang" theory of the origin of matter in the universe, and the formation of stars and planets and other stellar bodies, was coalescing.[16] So, from a scientific perspective, God was no longer required to explain the origin of life or the origin of matter.

Before continuing, it is important to identify what we mean by evolution. According to Ernst Mayr, evolution is "the gradual process by which the living world has been developing following the origin of life." Current evolutionary models attempt to do at least two things: explain the differences we see among individuals in a population (microevolution, "evolution at or below the species level") and provide a mechanism to explain how all life on earth came into existence over very long periods of time (macroevolution, "evolution above the species level").[17] Evolutionary biologists see these as largely the same process, just viewed at different points in time. Because parts of evolutionary theory require inferences and extrapolations beyond the laboratory, scientists interpret the phenomena in a variety of ways, particularly regarding the extent to which God might be involved in the process (chart A). We will explore this further below.

Chart A	*God's role in initiating life*	*God's sustaining role*	*Mechanism by which life arose*
Naturalistic Evolution	None	None	Processes which are determined by natural laws of physics and chemistry
Deistic Evolution	Set process in motion	None	Processes which are determined by natural laws of physics and chemistry
Theistic Evolution	Set process in motion	Wide array of views, but involved macroevolution and long periods of time	God used same natural laws of physics and chemistry to direct the formation of life
Intelligent Design	Designer was involved from the beginning; complexity of first cells points to designer	Not clear; no alternative mechanism proposed. Design points to designer	Designed through unknown mechanisms
Creationism	Brought all things into being by His Word	God sustains all things	God produced organisms in His timing according to their "kinds" (young and old earth creation)

Four qualifications should be made before going forward in our discussion of how scientists who profess to be Christians approach the subject of evolution. First, unless otherwise indicated, these are my thoughts and observations, and should not necessarily reflect upon anyone else associated with this chapter or with the book as a whole. I recognize that it is dangerous to generalize, so I realize that some people in the groups that I am outlining will likely disagree with some of my specifics. Second, it is important to mention that the topics about to be discussed encompass, for some people, their life's work, which should give a sense of the scope of the topic. Third, I have no intention of calling into question anyone's "faith." Unfortunately, that is sometimes the outcome of these conversations. Finally, all of the groups that I am going to describe have the same goal, to understand how nature and Scripture inform each other. Each group may be approaching this task with different assumptions and experiences, using different tools and methodologies, but each is starting from the foundation that, because God is the author of both, there can ultimately be no conflict between the two.

Creation Science

Creation science is an approach to the relationship between faith and science that involves using Scripture as a means for interpreting science. This approach to origins was popularized by Henry Morris, co-author of *The Genesis Flood* (1961) and founder of the Institute for Creation Research (ICR). The original mission of the ICR was simply to provide answers to scientific questions based on particular interpretations of the events in Genesis, using scientific data as an apologetic for Scripture. This organization, however, has come a long way since its inception. It is now involved in the analysis of current scientific findings from a Christian worldview and appears to be more involved in compiling alternate explanations to various scientific findings. Ken Ham's organization Answers in Genesis, the Creation Museum near Cincinnati, and Kent Hovind's ministry Creation Science Evangelism (among others) seek to interpret contemporary scientific explanations through a particular Christian lens, and, along with ICR, have employed people with more substantial scientific backgrounds to provide commentary on issues particularly relevant to evolution and cosmology. They seek to interpret the data, distinct from mainstream scientific thought, starting from a biblical perspective. In an effort to be faithful, these investigators have subjected themselves to ridicule from the greater scientific community, as well as the general public (including other Christians).

The challenge for creation scientists within the Christian intellectual tradition is that they are not often taken seriously by mainstream scientists or even at times by mainline Protestants. Nor do they really conduct scientific experiments. Their work, however, positions them to ask questions that few others are asking, such as "are these fossils really as old as claimed?" and "is evolutionary theory really a cohesive explanation of life as we see it?"

So, how do they deal with all of the scientific evidence that supports evolutionary theory and the Big Bang, including DNA evidence and molecular systematics, radioactive decay and fossil evidence, and background microwaves? At this point, they suggest that much ongoing analysis of this type of data may someday point us in a different direction. As Thomas Kuhn has reminded all in the scientific community, science sometimes involves paradigm shifts and revolution.[18] However, I wonder if taking the two data sets (science and Scripture) and simply merging them is the best answer. It is helpful to recognize that in the practice of science, scientists make a distinction between data and the meaning of the data. We can make an observation that DNA sequences are more similar between humans and gorillas than between humans and corn (at least for most genes), but that is different than saying that this *definitively proves* that we are more closely related to gorillas than to corn. In fact, if God made each "kind" unique, then we are related to gorillas and corn in the same way; we are all made by the same Creator.

Intelligent Design

Intelligent design (ID) is an attempt to integrate the spheres of science and faith and involves the cataloging of design in the universe, providing counterweight to those elements of evolution that suggest pervasive randomness. William Paley originally pointed to evidence for design and, using the analogy of a watch and a watchmaker, pointed to a Designer in his book *Natural Theology* (1803). ID has been critiqued many times over the past 200 years, most recently and most vehemently by Richard Dawkins.[19] While Paley provided an apologetic for the Christian God, intelligent design proponents today are pointing to the intelligence behind the design, without necessarily identifying the designer. Some do identify the Designer as the God of the Bible, and it is these individuals who are part of the Christian intellectual tradition. This approach has involved more credible science and scientists over time, although some of the best known advocates for intelligent design, such as Phillip Johnson, are not scientists. Yet, Michael Behe (Lehigh University) and others hold significant positions in the scientific community. ID proponents approach questions of evolution and design from a different perspective than that proposed by the creation scientists. In the public square, intelligent design advocates have been attempting to integrate alternate texts into the science curricula of public schools. The legal response has been for intelligent design to be labeled as "pseudoscience," thus limiting its ability to influence perspectives on origins relative to the secular scientific establishment. The rebuttal from the intelligent design community is that the legal system is confusing "the evidence of design with the implications of design" in assigning ID the creationism label.

There are two elements of intelligent design that need to be taken into account. The first is the idea that a Creator has injected order in nature that cannot be explained any other way. This is a proposition that cannot be tested scientifically, leading many scientists to claim that ID is not "science." However, ID also contains the proposal that this order led to the development of structures and systems that could not have evolved through a series of small, incremental changes. This includes the idea of irreducible complexity, which can be, and has been, tested scientifically, at least for several systems. Irreducible complexity, one of the hallmark concepts of ID proposed by Behe, uses the argument that there are some systems in nature that cannot function if all of the parts are not present, such as the human eye or the bacterial flagellum. Many within the scientific community, including some Christians, have rejected ID, particularly the concept of irreducible complexity, as scientific evidence is mounting to demonstrate that some of these systems can in fact evolve in incremental steps.[20]

The work of intelligent design proponents points to intelligence in the universe, but does not suggest scientific alternatives to naturalistic evolution. However, indicating that something does not explain an observation does not mean that an alternative explanation is required. In contrast to creation scientists, intelligent design advocates are not necessarily Christian, although some intelligent design adherents can be found at Christian universities.

Theistic Evolution

Many scientists who are Christians prioritize the science/faith relationship by placing science over theological systems while still holding Scripture as sacred. This section is organized to: (1) describe some of the various approaches to evolution based on the extent of God's involvement in the process; (2) describe theological challenges for Christians who adopt an evolutionary framework to explain life on earth; and then (3) provide an introduction to how some Christian evolutionists deal with these challenges.

There are several positions that scientists take regarding God's role in creation. First, naturalistic evolution is based on the idea that all of life arose by a process dependent only on the laws of physics and chemistry without any divine influence. Second, deistic evolution asserts that God set the whole process in motion, perhaps through the Big Bang, but that naturalistic processes continued, and God was not involved after that. Third, theistic evolution affirms that, while evolutionary mechanisms were required, God was involved in some way (see chart B).

Those who hold to a position of naturalistic evolution are convinced that only natural phenomena, independent of God, drive the mechanisms of evolution. The overall evolutionary story currently contains a number of "chapters." These include the "RNA world" (the origins of biological molecules such as nucleic acids and proteins), the development of the first cell from nonliving components, the "endosymbiont theory" (describing the way our cells obtained some of their specialized compartments), macroevolution (the idea that changes in DNA followed by natural selection over time account for the diversity of all life), and human evolution (that humans arose from the same natural processes as all other life). On the other hand, Christians who adhere to an evolutionary model retain the flexibility to accept or reject various aspects of this model in coherence with their understanding of the genesis of living things as laid out in the Bible. However, Christians who engage evolutionary ideas must address particular theological concerns related to the Scriptures involving the

Chart B: Physical/Biological theories (Nontheist view)	*Young Earth Creationism*	*Theistic Evolution*	*Gradual or Progressive Creationism*
Origin of Matter: Big Bang: universe came into existence through the explosion of a "singularity"; a particle of infinite density	God created everything out of nothing	The Big Bang was God's creative act but still requires pre-existing matter/energy	God creates without pre-existing matter/energy.
Origin of Life: RNA World (evolution of precellular macromolecules) leads to the first cell; multicellular organisms; death	God created life in abundance according to "kinds" by the power of His Word, not by undirected processes by which collections of molecules lead to living organisms	God used the evolutionary processes as scientists describe them (and keeping with current findings); not clear whether or not evolutionary mechanisms are random, as definitions of evolution demand	God directs every atomic and subatomic action, and so there is no randomness. Scientists observe changes that God has directed. Actual mechanisms unclear, but RNA world leading to the first cell (among other theories) are too tenuous a foundation for theology or worldview.
Origin of Man: "Descended" as any other animal through evolutionary process; no "fall," no "sin"	Man is created specially with a unique relationship to God; man fell and damaged not only his relationship to God but that of all of nature	Man the animal evolved from other animals, but at a particular point in time, once men evolved the particular capacities, God reached down to establish a relationship with their race, not necessarily with a particular person. The "fall" was simply a result of the evolution of self- and God-awareness and the rejection of God's sovereignty (Lewis)	At a particular point in time, God created mankind through a unique man and woman, and established a special relationship with them. God was "proactive" in forming the man and woman. They were created with self- and God-awareness, and through their specific act of disobedience ("the fall") they served as representatives for all of their offspring.

creation of matter and living things, including, but not limited to, the first three chapters of Genesis.

First, a Christian evolutionary framework should account for the special relationship between God and humanity that is distinct from all other creatures (Gen 1:26 through chap. 2), and so the first man, but not his father, must be sinless. Everyone in an evolutionary model has a father. Thus there cannot be the sudden appearance of man on the earth, as there appears to be in the Genesis narrative. Second, this first sinless man and his wife displease God in some way so that there is separation and disruption of that initial special relationship (theologians refer to this as "the fall"), and an evolutionary model should allow for this. Third, an evolutionary model allows for the extinction of each organism (as many have) and so a Christian evolutionary model would have to anticipate the possibility of humans becoming extinct or evolving into something else. Different theological requirements (or none at all) could be placed on a Christian evolutionary model, but I believe these are the most pertinent.

I have invested more time in this section than the previous two because many Christians have adopted a general evolutionary model into their worldview including Catholics (58%), mainstream Protestants (51%), and some Evangelicals (24%), as compared to 48 percent of the general population.[21] When it comes to the application of evolutionary principles to the development of man, theistic evolution is held by a smaller number of Americans (36% in 2008) than creation (44%) and higher than a naturalistic evolution position (14%),[22] whereas scientists believe that naturalistic evolution is the best explanation for the origins of man (55% in 1997), followed by theistic evolution (40%) and special creation (5%).[23]

At this point the leading public proponent of theistic evolution is Francis Collins, a scientist of the highest caliber, former leader of the Human Genome Project, and current Director of the National Institutes of Health. Collins has made his views known through a number of presentations, including his 2006 book *The Language of God*, and through his online resource "BioLogos." Collins' ideas are finding inroads within Christian universities in the United States.[24] BioLogos also provides some answers to the questions posed above, particularly the question of original humans and the fall.[25] Based on the words of C. S. Lewis in *The Problem of Pain* (1962), the Biologos site states:

> at a certain point in history, it is possible that God bestowed special spiritual gifts on those who had developed the necessary characteristics. This historical event would endow the recipients with what the Bible calls the "image of God." We can say that *Homo divinus* was therefore created from *Homo sapiens*. With these spiritual gifts came the ability to know and experience evil—an opportunity that was grasped with tragic consequences that have carried through the history of *Homo divinus*.[26]

Part of my struggle with theistic evolution is with the philosophical connections between evolution and naturalism/atheism (although these are not necessarily required). Having spent more than 15 years at a state university and having heard negative comments about Christians who believe that God has played a significant (ultimate) role in everything that exists, it is hard for me to admit that perhaps the secular evolutionary models were right all along, particularly since my objections are not just philosophical but scientific as well. I am, however, also intrigued by Christians (and even non-Christians) who have adopted an evolutionary model but have decided that there are portions of the model that they do not like. They are fine with microevolution, and an extraordinarily old age of the universe, and maybe some elements of shared ancestry with other animals, but they really struggle with the origin of life, human evolution, the application of natural selection to human societies, and the possibility of humans directing human evolution through eugenics and genetic engineering. This selectivity may undermine the integrity of the theistic evolutionary model and leads to what is sometimes called a "God of the gaps," or a God who accounts for what science has not yet adequately explained.

Within the theistic evolution model, God uses the random events of evolution to determine His plan. I find it difficult to determine whether according to this model He is reacting to the work of physical forces or is in fact sovereign over them. Was the formation of humans from these chance events a surprise for Him, or did He simply see beyond the time horizon and know that we were coming but had to wait for the physical forces to do their work before He could interact with us? What some Christians may mean when they talk about "theistic evolution" is perhaps "gradual or progressive creationism," in which the creative process is in fact not random, but that every change in DNA, protein structure, and physiological adaptation of every organism for all time is directed by God. In this sense, there is no evolution as scientists understand it, but there is instead a series of unbroken providential atomic and subatomic events. Because we see a pattern, we attribute them to physical laws, but this may be simply following God's breadcrumbs.

Several prominent thinkers with various perspectives see the two ideas (evolution and the Christian faith) as irreconcilable.[27] There is no doubt, however, that ongoing debate and discussion will continue.

Current Issues in the Life Sciences

So, how does one's position on creation and evolution influence the way one views other issues in the life sciences? How we view ourselves and others is going to be one of the key indicators as to how we deal with controversial topics. For instance, if we see ourselves as uniquely and specially created by God, that His intimate knowledge of us in the womb (Psalm 139) is real, then we will have a special concern for people at all stages of life, even from conception. If, on the other hand, we are advanced animals, products of naturalistic evolution, then we may treat people the way we treat other animals, perhaps worse. This leads us to consider how Christians might view some other current issues:

Human Cloning, Stem Cells, and Genetic Engineering

If humans are not of value as individuals, then we will be tempted to see humans as commodities, sources of cells, expendable for experimentation in cloning, and malleable to human-directed evolution. These processes are already underway through embryo selection, which involves choosing from among a set of embryos produced through in vitro fertilization the one with the most desirable traits. We also see this in a form of cloning known as somatic cell nuclear transfer (SCNT). This is used to make genetically matching embryonic stem cells and is the same process that would be used to begin reproductive cloning. However, if one does not consider embryos to be human beings, then SCNT is in fact not a form of human cloning. One's positions on each of these issues will be predominantly determined by what you think of human life and when you think human personhood, which some see as distinct from human life, which we know scientifically begins at life. This opens the door for human genetic engineering, as some embrace evolutionary ideas of eugenics and the genetic justification of a racial hierarchy that has existed for millennia.[28]

Climate Change, Carbon Footprint, and Endangered Species

These "green" issues stem from our view of humanity in relation to the environment. Is there really a cultural mandate ("Be fruitful, multiply, fill the earth, and subdue it. Rule the fish of the sea, the birds of the sky, and every creature that crawls on the earth," Gen 1:28 HCSB), or does this simply point to some vague relationship that humans have with nature? Or are humans, evolutionarily speaking, organisms that have dominated the earth for too long and which must be self-contained, leading to such things as the regulation of our overproduction of carbon? Certainly there are important things that humans can do to be better stewards of the earth, which is the essence of this "cultural mandate," and because we are stewards, Christians should be at the forefront of caring for the environment. However, we are to balance this stewardship with a worship of the Creator, rather than the creature or the creation (Rom 1:20–25); we also need to balance our own needs with the needs of other organisms that live on earth with us. The challenge here for Christians is to do what is right for the planet that is the handiwork of the One who made us, without being dragged into the worldview of the earth-worshippers. It is similar to gaining the health benefits of karate without being impacted by the underlying spirituality commonly associated with it.

Health Care, Pharmacogenomics, and Euthanasia

No topic is "hotter" right now than how to deal with the health care system in the United States, and nowhere is the connection between how human personhood is defined and public policy more acute than in deciding how to provide health care for all. A utilitarian ethic of the collective good seems to have supplanted the previous Judeo-Christian ethic, as the relationship of people to their Creator and each other has changed. This utilitarian ethic sees people as data points on actuarial tables, as parts of the gross domestic product, rather than as uniquely created beings. They are disposable. They are casualties of statistical analyses. These ethical approaches will not only play out in how health care is distributed but in "end-of-life" issues as well. As of this writing, physician-assisted suicide is legal in Montana, Oregon, and Washington. Scientists are sometimes finding that quality of life questions have different answers than they expected, as in the case of a man who was diagnosed as comatose for 23 years but was apparently conscious much of that time.[29]

Pharmacogenomics is another exciting area that builds on information from the human genomic project and is designed to enable doctors to prescribe types and dosages of particular medications based on individual genetic information. This may be beneficial, but there is a possibility that this information could be used in other ways. One concern is the use of this information by insurance companies to deny coverage, although this fear has been allayed somewhat by the Genetic Information Nondiscrimination Act, passed in 2008 in response to the human genome project.[30]

Nanotechnology, Artificial Intelligence

If humans are nothing more than a cosmic accident, a thinking machine, then other thinking machines should be possible, with "consciousness," perhaps achieving similar moral status to humans. Reductionists (those who see humans, and in fact all living things, as nothing more than a collection of atoms functioning within the laws of nature) who follow a logical extension of evolutionary thought from the nonliving to the living and back again, will see humans as one of many options of sentient beings, some of which we can create. Films like *I, Robot*; *Surrogates*; *Bicentennial Man*; *The Matrix* series; and *Bladerunner* have imagined worlds populated by man-made beings that assume their place in human society. As machines ourselves, why should we choose the company and community of organic over inorganic machines?

Again, how we view ourselves will impact our interest in community with others. What does it really mean to be human? To what extent will humans, and human parts, become commodities? What will be the fate of the hybridization of humans with other animals or with machines, such as the development of the first human "cyborg"?[31] Will we move toward the ideals of Joseph Fletcher, where we will engineer "parahumans" for particular tasks, such as those adapted to low-gravity conditions for space travel and those who are small and designed to pick strawberries?[32] It will be interesting to see.

Bioethics

Bioethicists study what has been and should be done in cases involving difficult decision-making, particularly in the area of medical ethics. Bioethicists are playing increasingly prominent roles in a variety of areas, including public policy and health care, as described above. The challenge for the public with regard to bioethics is to decipher *whose* ethics are being asserted. There can be Christian bioethics, Communist bioethics, Muslim bioethics, etc., but the public seems only to hear from what are portrayed as "generic" bioethicists. I would argue that there is no such thing, as all ethics are grounded in some worldview. There are a few excellent Christian bioethicists at work today, including C. Ben Mitchell, Gilbert Meilaender, Edmund Pellegrino, Nigel M. de S. Cameron, Scott Rae, and John Kilner. Publications such as *Journal for Christian Bioethics* and *Ethics and Medicine*, as well as the Center for Bioethics and Human Dignity, engage in Christian intellectual discourse in the field of bioethics. These practitioners ask "why" and "should" questions, as well as analyze how groups have made moral decisions about science in the past, and assess the outcomes of those decisions.

Personal Approach to Being a Christian and a Scientist

What does it mean for me to be a Christian and do science? Does it make any difference at all? We can start by looking at two different parts of my job: mentor/researcher (in working with students on research projects) and instructor (teaching several different courses). Most scientists wear a number of different hats, and their worldview impacts the way they do each. Let us look at how my worldview as a Christian impacts each of these roles.

Mentor/Researcher

There are two elements of my role here. The first is in leading students to first become "question askers," and then "question answerers." I enjoy working with students as colleagues in the discovery process, leading them to the point where they are working independently and really don't need my help. In this aspect I see students as fellow creations, and I work to treat them with respect. The second is as a discoverer of new knowledge, of one who asks and answers my own questions, "thinking God's thoughts after Him," as Kepler said. My interest in discovery follows the pattern of so many other Christians, like Francis Bacon, using new knowledge to solve "real world" problems. It motivates me that my work could be of some value to someone somewhere. I am particularly interested in solving problems that affect "the least of these," but those problems can be hard to identify, and even harder to address.

Course Instructor

As a professor, one of the most important things that I do is teach. I have the privilege of teaching both biology majors and nonmajors. Through teaching I try to emphasize God's role as Creator of the universe, to connect biology to the everyday lives of my students, and to treat them with respect. I also try to ask questions that will force students to examine the information that I present from a Christian context. There are many ways that instructors at Christian universities approach the science and faith issue, which may depend to some extent on their role models in graduate school. In this area of training, I did not have any Christian role models. I went to a private, secular college and a large public state university, and did not knowingly run into Christian faculty in either place. I am still learning this part of the job, and it is a very personal process for each of us. However, the Christian university environment encourages us to wrestle with these issues, both with each other and, when appropriate, with our students.

I pray this chapter has provided some helpful things for you to consider as you explore the world of Christian higher education, particularly in the areas of the sciences. There are great challenges, and even greater opportunities. None of these are beyond the sovereignty of the Creator God of the universe.[33]

For Further Reading

Achinstein, P. *Science Rules: A Historical Introduction to Scientific Methods*. Baltimore: John Hopkins, 2004.

Anderson, P. M. *Professors Who Believe*. Downers Grove: InterVarsity, 1998.

Behe, M. *Darwin's Black Box*. New York: Free Press, 1996.

Collins, F. *The Language of God*. New York: Free Press, 2006.

Coyne, Jerry. http://www.usatoday.com/news/opinion/forum/2010–10–11-column11_ST_N.htm, "Science and Religion aren't Friends," USA Today.

Dawkins, R. *The Selfish Gene*. Oxford: Oxford University Press, 1976.

———. *The Blind Watchmaker*. New York: W. W. Norton & Company, 1986.

———. *The God Delusion*. Boston: Houghton Mifflin, 2006.

Dembski, W. A., and M. Ruse. *Debating Design: From Darwin to DNA*. Cambridge: Cambridge University Press, 2006.

Dockery, D. S. *Renewing Minds*. 2nd ed. Nashville: B&H, 2008.

———, and G. A. Thornbury. *Shaping a Christian Worldview: The Foundations of Christian Higher Education*. Nashville: B&H, 2002.

Gould, S. J. "Nonoverlapping Magisteria" *Natural History* 106 (1997): 16–22, http://www.stephenjaygould.org/library/gould_noma.html.

Hadot, Pierre. *What Is Ancient Philosophy?* Cambridge, MA: Harvard University Press, 2002.

Harlan, D. M. *The Big Bang: A View from the 21st Century*. London: Springer-Praxis, 2004.

Hawking, S. W. *A Brief History of Time: From the Big Bang to Black Holes*. Toronto: Bantam, 1988.

Irwin, Terence. *Classical Thought*. New York: Oxford University Press, 1989.

Kuhn, T. *The Structure of Scientific Revolutions*. Chicago: University of Chicago Press, 1962.

Lennox, J. C. *God's Undertaker: Has Science Buried God?* Oxford: Lion, 2009.

Lewis, C. S. *The Problem of Pain*. New York: Macmillan, 1962.

Mayr, Ernst. *What Evolution Is*. New York: Basic Books, 2001.

"Men of science never talk that way," *The New York Times*, November 20, 1924.

Mohler, R. A., Jr.: http://www.christianpost.com/article/20101013/science-and-religion-arent-friends/pageall.html, "Science and Religion aren't Friends?" Christian Post.

National Academy of Sciences. Science and Creationism: A View from the National Academy of Sciences, Washington, DC: National Academies Press, 1999. Available at: http://www.nap.edu/catalog/6024.html.

Olasky, Marvin. *The Tragedy of American Compassion*. Wheaton: Crossway, 1998.

Paley, W. *Natural Theology. Or, Evidences of the Existence and Attributes of the Deity*, collected from the Appearances of Nature; Bridgewater Treatises, Faulder, 1803 (repr., Cambridge University Press, 2009).

Schaeffer, Francis. *How Should We Then Live? The Rise and Decline of Western Thought and Culture* (25th anniversary edition). Wheaton: Crossway, 2005.

Strobel, L. *The Case for a Creator*. Grand Rapids: Zondervan, 2004.

Walton, J. *The Lost World of Genesis One: Ancient Cosmology and the Origins Debate*. Downers Grove: InterVarsity, 2009.

Whitehead, A. N. *The Aims of Education and Other Essays*, New York: Free Press, 1967.

Additional information on the history of science, and the integration of faith and science, can be found at:

http://www.godandscience.org/apologetics/sciencefaith.html#gfeEELNFm26T;

http://www.johnny-lin.com/presn/faithsci.html;

http://www-personal.ksu.edu/~kbmill/scifaith.html;

http://biology.georgefox.edu/~jduerr/Faith_Science.html;

http://www.christianity.co.nz/science4.htm; "Beginnings of Modern Science"; Exploring Christianity;

http://www.religioustolerance.org/ev_publi.htm; "Results of public opinion polls on evolution and creation science," Ontario Consultants on Religious Tolerance.

Endnotes

[1] For more information, see Pierre Hadot, *What Is Ancient Philosophy?* (Cambridge, MA: Harvard University Press, 2002); Terrence Irwin, *Classical Thought* (New York: Oxford University Press, 1989); http://webspace.ship.edu/cgboer/athenians.html.

[2] http://www.thefreedictionary.com/deduction; for a more detailed discussion see P. Achinstein, *Science Rules: Historical Introduction to Scientific Methods* (Baltimore: Johns Hopkins, 2004).

[3] Alfred North Whitehead, *The Aims of Education and Other Essays* (1929; repr., New York: Free Press, 1967), 52.

[4] J. C. Lennox, *God's Undertaker: Has Science Buried God?* (Oxford: Lion, 2009), 20.

[5] http://www.csa.com/discoveryguides/medieval/review3.php.

[6] Lennox, *God's Undertaker*, 10.

[7] http://www.lib.uwaterloo.ca/society/history/Ornstein.html.

[8] "Men of Science Never Talk That Way," *New York Times*, Nov. 20, 1924.

[9] http://www.christianity.com/ChurchHistory/11630137.

[10] http://people-press.org/2009/07/09/Section-5-evolution-climate-change-and-other-issues.

[11] http://www.religioustolerance.org/ev_publi.htm.

[12] See Francis Schaeffer, *How Should We Then Live? The Rise and Decline of Western Thought and Culture, 25th Anniversary Edition* (Wheaton: Crossway, 2005).

[13] See S. J. Gould, "Nonoverlapping Magisteria," *Natural History* 106 (1997): 16–22.

[14] David S. Dockery, *Renewing Minds: Serving Church and Society through Christian Higher Education* (Nashville: B&H Academic, 2008).

[15] See W. B. Mayr and E. Provine, *The Evolutionary Synthesis: Perspectives on the Unification of Biology* (Cambridge, MA: Harvard, 1980).
[16] http://www.umich.edu/~gs265/bigbang.htm. See Stephen Hawking, *A Brief History of Time* (New York: Bantam, 2004); David M. Harlan, *The Big Bang: A View from the 21st Century* (London: Springer-Praxis, 2004).
[17] Ernst Mayr, *What Evolution Is* (New York: Basic Books, 2001), 286–87.
[18] See Thomas Kuhn, *The Structure of Scientific Revolution* (Chicago: University of Chicago Press, 1962).
[19] See Richard Dawkins, *The Selfish Gene* (Oxford: Oxford University Press, 1976); idem, *The Blind Watchmaker* (New York: Norton, 1986); idem, *The God Delusion* (Boston: Houghton Mifflin, 2006).
[20] See the discussions in Michael Behe, *Darwin's Black Box* (New York: Free Press, 1996); William Dembski and M. Ruse, *Debating Design: From Darwin to DNA* (Cambridge: Cambridge University Press, 2006).
[21] http://pewforum.org/Science-and-Bioethics/Religious-Differences-on-the-Question-of-Evolution.aspx.
[22] http://www.gallup.com/poll/21814/evolution-creationism-intelligent-design.aspx.
[23] http://www.religioustolerance.org/ev_publi.htm.
[24] http://www.gordon.edu/article.cfm?iArticleID=961&iReferrerPageID=5&iPrevCatID=30&bLive=1.
[25] "How does the Fall fit into evolutionary history? Were Adam and Eve historical figures?" http://biologos.org/questions/evolution-and-the-fall.
[26] Ibid.
[27] See the responses of Jerry Coyne (http://www.usatoday.com/news/opinion/forum/2010–10–11-column11_ST_N.htm) and R. Albert Mohler Jr. (http://www.christianpost.com/article/20101013/science-and-religion-arent-friends/pageall.html).
[28] www.cnn.com/2007/TECH/science/10/18/science.race/index.html.
[29] http://www.timesonline.co.uk/tol/life_and_style/health/article6930589.ece.
[30] http://www.genome.gov/24519851.
[31] http://www.kevinwarwick.com.
[32] http://www.christianliferesources.com/?library/view.php&articleid=392.
[33] The author would like to give special thanks to Justin Barnard (Associate Professor of Philosophy, Union University) and Jennifer Gruenke (Associate Professor of Biology and Director of the Hammons Center for Scientific Studies, Union University) for their contributions to, and conversations regarding, this manuscript. Without them this document would never have come to fruition. I would also like to thank C. Ben Mitchell for his contributions and discussions, particularly on the segment on bioethics, Gene Fant for his suggestions and advice, and Michael McMahan, for his comments on the sections addressing evolution. I'd like to thank Kevin Chiarot, Patrick McGill, Jeremy Sink, Curtis Cook, Mark Slater, Daneen DeMaagd, and my wife, Susan Bolyard, for their reading of the manuscript and their helpful comments. Finally, I'd like to thank Greg Thornbury for his comments and his guidance on how to approach this work.

17

Science, Theology, and the Search for the Historical Adam

Jimmy H. Davis

The historicity of Adam has become a subject of significant controversy among evangelicals. The September 2010 issue of *Perspectives on Science and Christian Faith* from the American Scientific Association bore the theme, "Reading Genesis: The Historicity of Adam and Eve, Genomics, and Evolutionary Science."[1] The *Christianity Today* cover article for June 2011 was "The Search for the Historical Adam."[2] On August 9, 2011, National Public Radio broadcast the story, "Evangelicals Question the Existence of Adam and Eve."[3] These examples, which present an overview of scientific and theological thinking on the origin of humanity, reveal an opening divide among evangelicals over the relative value of current scientific findings and historic Christian doctrines.

Evangelical scholars, such as biochemist Fazale Rana of Reasons to Believe, Albert Mohler, president of The Southern Baptist Theological Seminary, Old Testament scholar C. John Collins, pastor Tim Keller, and pastor Richard Phillips present an orthodox view. They state that Adam and Eve are historical individuals made in the image of God; that their disobedience brought sin into the world; and that the obedience of the second Adam (Christ) brought redemption into the world. As Mohler states, "Without Adam, the work of Christ makes no sense whatsoever in Paul's description of the gospel, which is the classic description of the gospel we have in the New Testament."[4]

On the other hand, theologian John Schneider, biologist Dennis R. Venema, and director of the National Institute of Health Francis S. Collins wish to reformulate previous views in light of the findings of science. Collins founded the BioLogos Foundation to present a reconciliation between his Christian faith and science. BioLogos argues that since the latest genetic data implies that modern humans came from a genetic bottleneck of several thousand individuals and since the genomes of humans and chimps are 95–99 percent the same, a historical Adam and Eve did not exist. As evolved creatures, humans already had behaviors associated with the fall.

How does one reconcile the two books of God (as Francis Bacon called them: the book of God's word and the book of God's works)[5] regarding the question of the historical Adam? Philosopher William Hasker offers one way in his *Christian Scholar's Review* article, "Faith-Learning Integration: An Overview."[6] Hasker presents his model of faith-discipline integration as a

> systematic mapping . . . of the general ways in which the worldview issues connect with the particular concerns of various disciplines . . . Integration is concerned with *integral* relationships between faith and knowledge, the relationships which *inherently exist* between the content of the faith and the subject-matter of this or that discipline; such connections do not have to be invented or manufactured.[7]

I will present Hasker's main points and apply his model to the question of the historical Adam.

For a theoretical discipline like biology, Hasker lists four major dimensions of integration:

1. Worldview Foundations

"Here the question to be asked is, What fundamental insights and convictions, derivable from the Christian world-view, are relevant to the discipline?"[8] In the current discussion of the historical Adam, a fundamental conviction would be the doctrine of creation—all things (earth, heaven, living beings, and mankind) were created by God and pronounced good. Other important doctrines are of the creation of man in God's image, the fall, and redemption through Christ's sacrifice. The *Christianity Today* International Statement of Faith summarizes these doctrines: "God created Adam and Eve in his own image. By disobedience, they fell from their sinless state through the temptation by Satan. This fall plunged humanity into a state of sin and spiritual death, and brought upon the entire race the sentence of eternal death. From this condition we can be saved only by the grace of God, through faith, on the basis of the work of Christ, and by the agency of the Holy Spirit."[9]

2. Disciplinary Foundations

"Here the scholar considers the foundational assumptions—methodological, epistemological, and ontological—which are stated or presumed as the basis of the discipline, and asks whether any of them are particularly significant or problematic from the standpoint of the Christian faith."[10] Foundational to biology/anthropology are the assumptions that the universe is orderly and understandable, that methodological naturalism is the way to understand nature, that the universe is very old, and that all life has a common ancestor related by evolution through natural selection.

Modern science explains natural phenomena in terms of natural events and does not invoke supernatural intervention. In 1983 the ethicist Paul de Vries coined the term "methodological naturalism" to describe how science functions in the modern world.[11] De Vries states that "the goal of inquiry in the natural sciences is to establish explanations of contingent natural phenomena strictly in terms of other contingent natural things—laws, fields, probabilities. . . . A 'God hypothesis' is both unnecessary and out of place within natural scientific explanations."[12] How did the formulation of methodological naturalism come about? The fundamental question of causation and our ability to identify it accurately is one that Christian theologians and natural philosophers have dealt with since the beginning of Christianity.

In the patristic period, Augustine of Hippo (354–430) affirmed the view that "all truth is God's truth": "Let every good and true Christian understand that wherever truth may be found, it belongs to his Master."[13] Although he believed ultimate reality is spiritual, Augustine used natural knowledge to interpret Scripture. The regularity of the natural order causes some to cease to wonder and miss that God is the primary cause. Augustine writes,

> But there is one kind of natural order in the conversion and changeableness of bodies, which, although itself also serves the bidding of

> God, yet by reason of its unbroken continuity has ceased to cause wonder. . . . And so the vanity of philosophers has found license to assign these things also to other causes, true causes perhaps, but proximate ones, while they are not able to see at all the cause that is higher than all others, that is, the will of God.[14]

During the Middle Ages, Christian theologians and philosophers, considered the extent of God's activity in nature and contributed to the development of modern thought. They saw God almost always acting in nature through secondary causes. Why? Although they believed that God could do anything he wished, they believed that God almost always restricts Himself with the *cursus communis naturae* (the common course of nature). This restriction assures the validity of investigations into an almost constant world. Because of this belief that God acts through secondary causes, natural philosophers promoted the use of observation and experiment in addition to reason when studying the *cursus communis naturae* through the work of theologians and philosophers, such as Robert Grosseteste (1168–1253), Albert the Great (1193–1280), Roger Bacon (1214–94), and William of Ockham (1285–1350).

A second effect of this emphasis on the *cursus communis naturae* was that it put the visible activity of God outside the common course of nature. Of course to the medieval philosophers, God was the primary cause behind the secondary causes and, thus, involved in everything. The Dominican priest and theologian Thomas Aquinas (1225–74), in his great work, *Summa Theologiae*, reaffirmed that secondary causes can be used to study nature but that all events are directed by God. During the Protestant Reformation, John Calvin (1509–64) reaffirmed Augustine's idea that all truth is God's truth. English philosopher and pioneer in the scientific revolution, Francis Bacon (1561–1626), urged study and proficiency in "the two books of God."[15] The American Presbyterian theologian B. B. Warfield (1851–1921), who served as professor of didactic and polemic theology at Princeton Seminary for 34 years, reaffirmed the thoughts of Aquinas by insisting that God is the ultimate governor of His creation. Yet, God chooses to govern the cosmos by regular cause and effect relations that can be understood as we observe the world.

But the emphasis on the *cursus communis naturae* and on the regularity of the laws of nature put Western scientific thought on a path that led some thinkers to position God as an absentee first cause (deism), to have no need for God in explanation (methodological naturalism), and finally to conclude that there is no God (ontological naturalism). In his essay "When Faith and Reason Clash: Evolution and the Bible," philosopher Alvin Plantinga expresses concern over this progression.[16] Regarding how scientific metanarratives are developed, Plantinga states,

> Judgments here, of course, may differ widely between believers in God and non-believers in God. What for the former is at best methodological restriction is for the latter the sober metaphysical truth; her naturalism is not merely provisional and methodological, but, as she sees it settled and fundamental. But believers in God can see the matter differently. The believer in God, unlike her naturalistic counterpart, is free to look at the evidence . . . and follow it where it leads, rejecting the scheme if the evidence is insufficient. She has a freedom not available to the naturalist. . . . What we need here, of course, is not natural science, but a broader inquiry that can include all that we know, including truths that God has created life on earth and could have done it in many different ways.[17]

Both de Vries and Plantinga have hit upon a truth as to how science functions. As de Vries points out, on a daily basis methodological naturalism or *cursus communis naturae* is how scientists answer their questions about how plants adapt or chemicals react, and they do this without thinking out the philosophical methods. As Plantinga points out, when it comes to the metanarratives (the history of the universe, the history of life), methodological naturalism restricts the findings of science. This is an old problem; Aquinas had to confront the eternal universe of Aristotle in light of God as Creator.

3. Disciplinary Practice

"Here we are concerned with issues that arise in the day-to-day practice of one's discipline—of 'doing one's job.'"[18] For the biologist/anthropologist, this could involve reflection on how the theory of evolution and methodological naturalism relates to the Christian doctrine of creation and man. Following the work of David L. Wolfe and Ronald R. Nelson, Hasker presents three strategies for relating one faith to a particular discipline: compatibilist, transformationist, and reconstructionist.[19]

Compatibilist

The compatibilist "does not recognize any deep, fundamental tension between the assumptions and procedures of her discipline and the Christian faith. She feels comfortable and 'at home' both in her faith and in her discipline; her aim is to demonstrate and exhibit the unity between them which already exist, at least potentially."[20] One compatibilist approach is commonly called theistic evolution, but many Christians and scientists who hold this view do not like that label, since evolution is the noun and theism is the adjective. This is one of the reasons the physicist Howard J. Van Till coined the phrase *fully gifted creation*,[21] the biologist/theologian Denis O. Lamoureux uses the phrase *evolutionary creation*,[22] and the geneticist Francis S. Collins uses the label *BioLogos*.[23] This compatibilist position can be summarized by the following statement from Lamoureux:

> Evolutionary creation asserts that God created the universe and life through an ordained, sustained, and design-reflecting evolutionary process. This position fully embraces both the religious beliefs of biblical Christianity and the scientific theories of cosmological, geological, and biological evolution. It contends that the Creator established and maintains the laws of nature, including the mechanisms of a teleological evolution. Notably, this view of origins argues that humanity evolved from pre-humans ancestors, and through this process the Image of God and human sin were gradually and mysteriously manifested. Evolutionary creationists experience God's love and presence in their lives, and they enjoy a personal relationship with the Lord Jesus that includes miraculous signs and wonders.[24]

When both the Bible and science address the same question (the origin of humanity), many compatibilists seem to adopt a zero-sum game regarding the relationship between the biblical and scientific insights. To them a 100-percent natural explanation seems to mean a 0-percent divine involvement. Do the following relationships hold? If there is a process for which we do not have a physical explanation, can we say that this process involves 100 percent divine involvement? As we gain physical understanding, does the divine involvement now become less than 100 percent? And finally, does a full physical understanding equal 0-percent divine involvement? This thinking relating the percent divine and percent physical explanation is sometimes labeled "God of the Gaps" thinking.

One can admire the scientific work that Francis Collins has done with the human genome and be encouraged by his public faith statements. However, his assumptions raise concerns for the orthodox believer. He appears to be presenting a mutually exclusive argument, joining those who say a natural explanation means there is no room for God. Collins seems to promote the idea that scientific data is all there is and that one should ignore biblical texts indicating that the creation of man and woman was a combination of a physical body and a special divine action (God "breathed the breath of life into his nostrils, and the man became a living being," Gen 2:7 HCSB).

Transformationist

"The scholar who follows the transformationist strategy finds the relationship between his faith and his discipline to be somewhat more problematic than does the compatibilist."[25] Building on legitimate discipline insights, the transformationist will try to transform his discipline by adding a Christian orientation.

The transformationist accepts the findings of astronomy and geology in terms of the age of the universe. This view is sometimes called *old-earth creationism.* The transforming occurs in the area of the story of life; the transformationist does not view the story of evolution as a continuous narrative but believes God has intervened at different times to cause a higher level of life to occur. For this reason, this view is sometimes called *episodic or special creationism.* The late nineteenth- and early twentieth-century theologian B. B. Warfield held this view when he proposed mediate creation to explain the origin of life, the origin of mankind, and miracles.[26] The astronomer Hugh Ross and astronomer and theologian Robert C. Newman prefer the label *progressive creationism.* They "think that God's activity in creation occurred in a progression—a number of steps over a long period of time in which God established and perfected each level of the environment before he added a higher level that rests (so to speak) upon the preceding levels."[27]

Some Christians use "intelligent design" concepts in their transformational thinking, even though it is a scientific technique rather than a way to integrate faith and science. *Intelligent design* (ID) "holds that certain features of the universe and of living things are best explained by an intelligent cause" rather than continuous, nondirected processes.[28] Phillip Johnson, author of the 1992 work *Darwin on Trial*, is considered the father of the intelligent design movement. With the publication of *Darwin's Black Box* (1996), biochemist Michael Behe defined intelligent design in terms of irreducible complexity. As Behe states,

> By *irreducibly complex* I mean a single system composed of several well-matched, interacting parts that contribute to the basic function, wherein the removal of one of the parts causes the system to effectively cease functioning. An irreducibly complex system cannot be produced directly (that is, by continuously improving the initial function, which continues to work by the same mechanism) by slight, successive modifications of a precursor system, because any precursor to an irreducibly complex system that is missing a part is by definition nonfunctional. An irreducibly complex biological system, if there is such a thing, would be a powerful challenge to Darwinian evolution. Since natural selection can only choose systems that are already working, then if a biological system cannot be produced gradually it would have to arise as an integrated unit, in one fell swoop, for natural selection to have anything to work on.[29]

Behe presents the bacterial flagellum as an example of a biological irreducibly complex object. The flagellum is composed of 30 proteins that provide propulsion for some bacteria. According to Behe, it is too complex to function if one protein is removed and therefore is "irreducibly complex." At first it seemed that the intelligent design concepts might be incorporated into science experiments. Scientists responded to Behe's challenge to prove that subsets of his examples of irreducible complex molecular systems could function and, thus, be steps in the evolution of the final product. Soon many examples of functional subsets were found, such as the type III secretory system (TTSS) used by gram-negative bacteria for ejecting toxins into the cells of their hosts. The TTSS proteins are a subset of the flagellum proteins and are fully functional even though it is missing many of the flagellum parts. Another blow to intelligent design proponents occurred when their nonscientific supporters began trying to require that intelligent design be taught in public K-12 schools. In Dover, Pennsylvania, opponents of teaching intelligent design sued in federal court to stop the process. In *Kitzmiller vs. Dover Area School District*, the judge ruled that ID is not science, since it is not testable and does not use natural explanations.[30] Both of these events have caused intelligent design to fade as a possible paradigm for how to do science. It is important to remember that design in nature is a very broad topic with the ID movement being just one facet of the many approaches to design.

Reconstructionist

The reconstructionist "finds that the existing disciplines are so deeply permeated with anti-Christian assumptions of secularism, rationalism, and naturalism he has no choice but to reject" the assumptions of the disciplines and start over by reconstructing the disciplines on a biblical foundation.[31] One version of reconstructionism is young-earth creationism (also called creation science). *Young earth creationism* rejects many of the tenets of modern science as either a reflection of naturalism or as a conflict with an interpretation of the Bible. Young-earth creationists deny that methodological naturalism is the way to understand nature, that the universe is very old, and that all life has a common ancestor that is related by evolution through natural selection. In place of these claims, they propose a methodological theism that posits a young universe, six literal days of creation, a physical creation of Adam and Eve, the fall as the origin not only of sin but also of death and distortion to nature, a global flood as the primary source of ancient geological and fossil records, and no common ancestry to life but instead each kind being created separately. Young-earth creationists have truly started over by reconstructing science on their biblical foundation. With the publication of *The Genesis Flood* (1961), Henry Morris, one of the founders of the Creation Research Society and of the Institute for Creation Research, is considered the modern father of creation science. Today one of the leading voices of creation science is the applied scientist Ken Ham, founder of Answers in Genesis. Although creation science has had almost no impact on how science is practiced, it has had a great impact on how science is taught in homeschool and Christian high school environments.

4. Worldview Contribution

"In this dimension of integration we ask, what specific contribution does this discipline make to the Christian vision of reality? . . . In short, what difference does the discipline make for Christians who are not its students and practitioners? . . . This last dimension, world-view contribution, is the one which has been least emphasized in the literature on faith-learning integration."[32] Some contributions that science makes to the Christian vision of reality include the age of the universe, the nonstatic view of history of the earth and life, and the relationship of humans to the rest of life. How one answers the extent of this contribution to theology depends upon whether one is a compatibilist, transformationist, or reconstructionist.

Following the thoughts of B. B. Warfield and C. S. Lewis, a transformationist would argue that the universe is very old, that both the earth and life have changed greatly during this long time period, that the physical bodies of humans are related to the physical bodies of the rest of life, and that God directly acted to impart His image upon the first humans. Combining traditional Christian orthodoxy and the findings of science, Lewis's thoughts in *The Problem of Pain* (1940) present a reasonable integration of faith and biology regarding the validity of the historic Adam:

> For long centuries God perfected the animal form which was to become the vehicle of humanity and the image of Himself. He gave it hands whose thumb could be applied to each of the fingers, and jaws and teeth and throat capable of articulation, and a brain sufficiently complex to execute all the material motions whereby rational thought is incarnated. The creature may have existed for ages in this state before it became man: it may even have been clever enough to make things which a modern archaeologist would accept as proof of its humanity. But it was only an animal because all its physical and psychical processes were directed to purely material and natural ends. Then, in the fullness of time, God caused to descend upon this organism, both on its psychology and physiology, a new kind of consciousness which could say "I" and "me," which could look upon itself as an object, which knew God, which could make judgments of truth, beauty, and goodness, and which was so far above time that it could perceive time flowing past. . . . We do not know how many of these creatures God made, nor how long they continued in the Paradisal state. But sooner or later they fell. Someone or something whispered that they could become gods—that they could cease directing their lives to their Creator.[33]

As C. John Collins states, "When you start talking about what it means to be human, much more than molecular biology is involved."[34] For example, John R. Schneider questions the doctrine of the fall: "Vices we associate with consequences of the Fall and original sin, such as self-serving behavior, exist in lower primates and would have been passed on via evolution to humans."[35] In *The Problem of Pain*, Lewis also addresses this issue. As Lewis states, "No animal has moral virtue."[36] Because of the fall and the knowledge of good and evil, Lewis concludes that a particular behavior is wicked only when it is practiced by man. Although evolutionists like to emphasize the 95–99 percent match between the genome of the chimp and mankind, they never have a good explanation for the massive gap between the abilities of chimps and humans.

Conclusion

The article by Hasker has helped organize the conflicting claims regarding the faith-discipline integration issue of the historic Adam. It also helps to consider the compatibilist, transformationist, and reconstructionist positions in terms of primary, secondary, and tertiary issues in Christian theology. Primary issues are the bedrock doctrines of the faith as found in the historic creeds and confessionals; secondary and tertiary issues are disagreements that can split Christians into different denominations or congregations.[37] Regarding primary theological issues—the fall of the first Adam and redemption through Christ, the second Adam—transformationists and reconstructionist are in agreement.[38] It is only compatibilists who raise questions about the historicity of Adam and the validity of Paul's statements about the second Adam (e.g., Rom 5:12–21).

We need humility as much as technical expertise as we continue to explore this important issue. As an editorial in the *Christianity Today* issue states, "No Adam, No Eve, No Gospel."[39] The story of the gospel begins with the disobedience of the first Adam and concludes with the obedience of the second Adam. This primary issue must not get lost in all these discussions.

Questions for Further Reflection

1. What do you envision as the next steps in the science and faith conversation? How can you prepare for these challenges?
2. How should an unchanging gospel influence the way Christ-followers respond to the ongoing changes in the world of science?
3. How does the Christian intellectual tradition inform and shape our understanding of key issues related to such important questions as the "search for the historical Adam"?

For Further Study

Collins, Francis. *The Language of God*. New York: Free Press, 2006.

Davis, Jimmy, and Harry L. Poe. *Science and Faith*. Nashville: B&H, 2000.

Heie, Harold, and David Wolfe, eds. *The Reality of Christian Learning*. Grand Rapids: Christian University Press. 1987.

King, Don, ed. *Taking Every Thought Captive: Forty Years of the Christian Scholar's Review*. Abilene, TX: Abilene Christian University Press, 2011.

Moreland, J. P., and John Mark Reynolds, eds. *Three Views of Creation and Evolution*. Grand Rapids: Zondervan, 1999.

Noll, Mark A. *Jesus Christ and the Life of the Mind*. Grand Rapids: Eerdmans, 2011.

Warfield, B. B. *Evolution, Science, and Scripture*. Edited by Mark A. Noll and David N. Livingstone. Grand Rapids: Baker, 2000.

Endnotes

[1] *Perspectives on Science and Christian Faith* 62, no. 3 (September 2010).

[2] Richard N. Ostling, "The Search for the Historical Adam," *Christianity Today*, June 2011, 23–27.

[3] Barbara Bardley Hagerty, "Evangelicals Question the Existence of Adam and Eve," NPR Morning Edition (Aug. 9, 2011). See also http://www.npr.org/2011/08/09/138957812/evangelicals-question-the-existence-of-adam-and-eve.

[4] Ibid.

[5] Francis Bacon, *Advancement of Learning*, chap. 1, The Project Gutenberg EBook of *The Advancement of Learning*, by Francis Bacon, transcribed from the 1893 Cassell & Company edited by David Price: accessed Aug. 20, 2010 http://www.gutenberg.org/dirs/etext04/adlr10.txt.

[6] William Hasker, "Faith-Learning Integration: An Overview," in *Taking Every Thought Captive: Forty Years of the Christian Scholar's Review*, ed. Don King (Abilene: Abilene Christian University Press, 2011), 109–21.

[7] Ibid., 109.

[8] Ibid., 116.

[9] "What We Believe: Christianity Today International Statement of Faith," item C; *Christianity Today*, accessed Aug. 30, 2011, http://www.christianitytoday.com/help/features/faith.html.

[10] Hasker, "Faith-Learning Integration," 117.

[11] Paul de Vries, "Naturalism in the Natural Sciences," in *Taking Every Thought Captive*, ed. King, 187–95. He seemed to have coined the phrase "methodological naturalism" at a 1983 conference at Wheaton College.

[12] Ibid.

[13] Augustine, *On Christian Doctrine*, J. F. Shaw translation, II.18 (28), accessed Aug. 20, 2010, http://www9.georgetown.edu/faculty/jod/augustine/ddc.html.

[14] Augustine, *On the Trinity* III.2 (7), accessed Aug. 20, 2010, http://www.newadvent.org/fathers/130103.htm.
[15] Bacon, *Advancement of Learning*, chap. 1.
[16] Alvin Plantinga, "When Faith and Reason Clash: Evolution and the Bible," in King, *Taking Every Thought Captive*, 87–108.
[17] Ibid, 105–6.
[18] Hasker, "Faith-Learning Integration," King, *Taking Every Thought Captive,* 117.
[19] David L. Wolfe, "The Line of Demarcation between Integration and Pseudo-Integration," and Ronald R. Nelson, "Faith-Discipline Integration: Compatibilist, Reconstructionist, and Transformationalist Strategies," both in *The Reality of Christian Learning: Strategies for Faith-Discipline Integration*, ed. Harold Heie and David L. Wolfe (Grand Rapids: Christian University Press, 1987).
[20] Hasker, "Faith-Learning Integration," King, *Taking Every Thought Captive,* 113.
[21] Howard J. Van Till, "The Fully Gifted Creation," in *Three Views of Creation and Evolution*, ed. J. P. Moreland and John Mark Reynolds (Grand Rapids: Zondervan, 1999).
[22] Denis O. Lamoureux, *I Love Jesus and I Accept Evolution* (Eugene, OR: Wipf & Stock, 2009).
[23] Francis S. Collins, *The Language of God: A Scientist Presents Evidence for Belief* (New York: Free Press, 2006).
[24] Lamoureux, *I Love Jesus and I Accept Evolution*, 26–27.
[25] Hasker, "Faith-Learning Integration," in King, *Taking Every Thought Captive*, 113.
[26] B. B. Warfield, *Evolution, Science, and Scripture: Selected Writings*, ed. Mark A. Noll and David N. Livingstone (Grand Rapids: Baker Books, 2000).
[27] Robert C. Newman, "Progressive Creationism," in Moreland and Reynolds, *Three Views of Creation and Evolution*, 103–33.
[28] Center for Science and Culture, "Questions about Intelligent Design," accessed Aug. 30, 2011 at http://www.discovery.org/csc/topQuestions.php#questionsAboutIntelligentDesign.
[29] Michael J. Behe, *Darwin's Black Box: The Biochemical Challenge to Evolution* (New York: Free Press, 1996), 39.
[30] John E. Jones III, "United States District Court Opinion, *Kitzmiller vs. Dover Area School District.*"
[31] Hasker, "Faith-Learning Integration," in King, *Taking Every Thought Captive,* 113.
[32] Ibid., 117.
[33] C. S. Lewis, *The Problem of Pain* (New York: HaperSanFrancisco, 1940), 72, 75.
[34] John Collins, quoted in Richard N. Ostling, "The Search for the Historical Adam," *Christianity Today*, June 2011, 23–27.
[35] Ibid., 26.
[36] Lewis, *Problem of Pain*, 67.
[37] David S. Dockery, *Renewing Minds: Serving Church and Society through Christian Higher Education* (Nashville: B&H Academic, 2008), 126.

[38] The transformationists and reconstructionists would disagree over many secondary and tertiary aspects of Adam's life.
[39] "No Adam, No Eve, No Gospel," *Christianity Today*, June 2011, 61.

18

Christian Scholarship in Math, Physics, and Engineering

Jeannette Russ

The sum of two and two is four, regardless of worldview, and a non-Christian mathematician can successfully take the Fourier transform of a function as well as a Christian. Similarly, Earth remains in its orbit around the sun without regard to worldview, and gravity equally anchors people of all faiths—or no faith—to the planet. The expectation that cars will run and telephones will ring is based on faith in the technological competence of an engineering design team rather than the hope that those engineers have any kind of personal Christian faith. Is there any advantage, then, to bringing a Christian worldview to the study of math, physics, and engineering? Indeed, is worldview even relevant in these areas?

Aristotle said that "it is not the facts which divide men but the interpretation of the facts."[1] Most people would agree that the *facts* of undergraduate-level math, physics, and engineering are accessible to anyone who has an interest in and an aptitude for these subjects. It is an observable and undeniable reality that many students learn math, physics, and engineering on the factual level without delving into the philosophical foundation upon which mathematical and physical truths are built. Unfortunately, these students miss the opportunity to find rich meaning in the *interpretation* of facts—to go beyond knowing *how* to make calculations and advance into pondering *why* certain calculations work as they do and what the results imply. It is in this interpretation of facts that worldview becomes critically important.

In physics and math, a conflict has raged for several centuries regarding how certain facts should be interpreted, and as the body of knowledge increases, the interpretations become more divergent. There are now and have historically been both Christians and unbelievers with deeply held convictions about the philosophical implications of a wide variety of facts. In order to continue the dialogue in a meaningful way, one goal of Christian education in the areas of math, physics, and engineering should be to instill a strong curiosity in students to go beyond the mechanics and to be prepared to engage the culture with a thoughtful and reasonable Christian response. This chapter is intended to provide a starting point for forming and articulating such a response.

The Birth of Modern Science

Interest in math, physics, and engineering is as old as civilization. Early civilizations quickly realized the need for at least counting and perhaps some simple arithmetic, introducing basic math into the world. Curiosity regarding the world in which we live has been an ever-present part of the human psyche, leading to ancient observations and speculations regarding what we now call physics. If engineering is taken to mean the building of simple devices to improve the quality of life, it is as old as the first structure erected to provide shelter or the first tool devised to help carry a load.

Such early interest shows the tremendous importance of these fields to humanity, but advanced mathematics and a reasonably correct view of physics did not arise until the scientific revolution, generally agreed to have begun with the work of Copernicus, Galileo, and others in the sixteenth and seventeenth centuries.[2] Engineering as a profession had an even later genesis, with the systematic application of advanced math and science to engineering problems proliferating in the middle of the nineteenth century, although some schools dedicated to early engineering principles arose in the mid-eighteenth century.[3] The scientific revolution coincides to a time of great Christian influence in the world at large, and indeed many of the outstanding early mathematicians and physicists had a strong faith in Christ. Selected examples follow, although space does not permit more than a brief and decidedly incomplete sampling of Christians who made crucial contributions.

Copernicus

Nicholas Copernicus (1473–1543) is credited with devising the first comprehensive heliocentric model of the universe. Copernicus believed that the universe was "wrought for us by a supremely good and orderly Creator," a conviction that led him to seek consistency in the behavior of the universe.[4] Although he understood that his proposal was going to be difficult for people to accept, he saw it less as a theological threat than a threat to common sense; after all, simple observation suggests it is the *sun* that moves! He was also concerned about angering the many loyal followers of Aristotle and Ptolemy among his contemporaries. For these reasons and because of some concerns with his mathematical models (which were indeed incorrect), he delayed publication of his major work, *On the Revolutions of the Heavenly Spheres*, for many years. It was finally published near the end of his life and was edited by Andreas Osiander, a Lutheran clergyman who was also knowledgeable in astronomy and math. Interestingly, Osiander suggested the addition of a preface to explain that the contents of the book should be taken as useful hypotheses rather than actual truths. Even though Copernicus rejected the advice, Osiander inserted the preface anyway and thereby invited charges of suppression of scientific truth. For his part, Copernicus maintained his Christian commitment throughout his life and did not see any conflict between his faith and his pursuit of scientific truth.[5]

Galileo

The conflict between science and faith—or at least the official Church—famously arose with the work of Galileo Galilei (1564–1642), although some historians have suggested that the conflict was more complex than a simple rejection of scientific reasoning by the Catholic Church.[6] Using his excellent mathematical skills along with his improved version of the telescope to study the heavens, Galileo provided strong support for the Copernican model by both theory and observation. (Incidentally, Galileo designed, manufactured, and sold high-quality telescopes in addition to pursuing his scientific studies,[7] making him at least a precursor to an engineer.) Like Copernicus, Galileo was a devout Christian who did not feel that his scientific discoveries were in conflict with his faith. He believed that there is only one truth, but that it can be found through both science and religion; any conflict between the two is due to a misinterpretation in one area or the other. As a scientist, he trusted his interpretation of physical observations but clearly mistrusted certain biblical interpretations, as established by a letter to one of his students in which he said that "though Holy Scripture cannot err, nevertheless some of its interpreters and expositors can sometimes err in various ways."[8] While Galileo is best known for seeking to advance science by disseminating truth about the heliocentric model, he also attempted to advance theology by protecting it from the mistake of turning a scientific dispute regarding the accuracy of new discoveries into a question of faith.[9] Looking back after the passage of several centuries filled with surprising scientific discoveries, Galileo's advice to the church seems both wise and prescient. In spite of Galileo's genuine devotion to the church, he was ultimately brought to trial and agreed to confess to errors and heresy. Even though the trial was motivated partly by interests outside of the Catholic Church and was the result of a complex response to both the Renaissance and the Reformation, the episode unfortunately continues to be used as a prime example of the hostility of Christianity to science.[10]

Kepler

Johannes Kepler (1571–1630) was another early advocate of the Copernican model, but he was a Protestant and thus escaped Galileo's fate of being accused of heresy.[11] Kepler considered his study of the universe to be an obligation through which he could learn more about the Creator.[12] Based on copious amounts of data and lengthy computations, Kepler realized that the planetary orbits are elliptical rather than circular. This discovery had spiritual significance for him, since the circle had been considered a symbol of perfection for several centuries; in fact, it is said that he "apologized for introducing the inexplicably eccentric ellipse into God's perfect creation."[13] He ultimately rationalized that the ellipse is a combination of the perfect circle, representing heavenly perfection, and a straight line, representing the material world.[14] This rationalization is typical of Kepler, who sought spiritual meaning in everything. However, his willingness to accept the observed truth of elliptical orbits was in fact a means of submitting to the pre-eminence of the Creator by accepting that man's preference for circles did not have to be shared by Almighty God.[15] Ultimately,

Kepler believed that "our piety is the deeper, the greater is our awareness of creation and its grandeur."[16]

Pascal

The idea of deep piety brings to mind Blaise Pascal (1623–62), a child prodigy who published an original work on conic sections when he was only 16. Pascal made valuable contributions in several areas, including probability theory, projective geometry, and fluid mechanics. He was also an inventor who designed a mechanical calculator and built about 50 models to sell. Even though the machine worked, it was a commercial disappointment due to its requirement of great mechanical precision and its subsequently high cost of manufacturing. Undeterred, Pascal proposed additional machinery, including a modern-style wheelbarrow and a hydraulic press.[17] In spite of his many accomplishments in math, science, and early forms of engineering, Pascal is perhaps best known for a dramatic conversion experience when he was about 30 years old. This conversion, considered by some to be a second conversion as he was already a practicing Roman Catholic, led him to renounce all worldly pursuits, including his scientific studies. He spent the remaining few years of his life studying and writing about theology, leaving an unfinished defense of Christianity, the *Pensées*, in which he contests the idea that one cannot be both intellectual and spiritual.[18] He defended the truth of reason and observation with statements like "indeed, faith tells us what the senses cannot, but it is not contrary to their findings. It simply transcends, without contradicting them."[19] In spite of his support for a complementary relationship between faith and reason, he is sometimes inaccurately accused of fideism, with critics of his own time and ours failing to understand his complete devotion to theology at the expense of his brilliant potential in the sciences.[20]

Newton

Many people do not realize that the renowned Isaac Newton (1643–1727) devoted more of his time to theology than he did to science.[21] Like Pascal, he was criticized by some of his contemporaries;[22] unlike Pascal, he lived a long life and made such vast contributions to math and physics that his reputation as one of the most brilliant scientists of all time is secure. It is well known that Newton discovered calculus (although Gottfried Leibniz is credited with an independent discovery) and determined many important laws of physics, perhaps most notably the law of universal gravitation. It is less well known that he had a great aptitude for the design and construction of complex mechanical toys and other mechanisms.[23] Newton believed strongly in a *designed* universe, noting that the designer was "not blind or fortuitous but very well skilled in mechanics and geometry."[24] In addition to being specifically designed by a knowledgeable Creator, Newton believed that the universe must also be constantly sustained, and this belief contributed to his remarkable insight into forces such as gravity, magnetism, and fermentation. Newton's writings are estimated to comprise several million words, and they cover an immense array of topics including alchemy, church history and chronology, eschatology, optics, physics, and math—all of which he claimed were consistent with one another. Although Newton was officially an Anglican, some have described him as an Arian due to his questions about the Trinity.[25] Even so, he is an excellent example of a scientist who relied upon his faith to help him search out scientific truth.

Euler

Leonhard Euler (1707–83) was a devout Protestant who also found inspiration for his work in his Christian faith. He was a brilliant and incredibly prolific mathematician who generated over 500 publications during his lifetime, contributing approximately one-third of European publications in the fields of math, theoretical physics, and engineering mechanics between 1726 and 1800.[26] His publications were of high quality, too; for example, Euler's identity ($e^{i\pi} + 1 = 0$) was voted the "Most Beautiful Mathematical Equation Ever" by readers of the *Mathematical Intelligencer* in 1988, and three of the top five "beautiful" formulae in the polling results were developed by Euler.[27] His work with exponents, logarithms, and complex numbers continues to find practical use in many fields of engineering. Throughout his lifetime, he maintained an appreciation for Christianity not only as a source of order in the work that he performed so effectively, but also as a source of consolation and hope. According to Euler, "the idea of the Supreme Being, as exalted as it is consolatory, ought to replenish our hearts with virtue the most sublime, and effectually prepare us for the enjoyment of life eternal."[28]

These men of the sixteenth, seventeenth, and eighteenth centuries shared many characteristics: a strong Christian faith, a belief in a created and orderly world, and broad interests that spanned not only math, physics, and engineering (or at least its predecessors of inventiveness and craftsmanship) but also philosophy and theology. They shared a strong conviction regarding the inerrancy of the Bible as well as the unassailable truth of scientific observations and mathematical proofs. Was their Christianity a coincidence, or did it contribute to their success? More generally, was the scientific revolution nurtured by the generally Christian culture of its time and place in history? Although it is impossible to answer these questions definitively, they are interesting matters to ponder and will be explored in the following section.

The Unique Association with Christianity

Christian scientists often speak of their appreciation for an orderly God who does things in a logical and systematic way. Consequently, the universe exhibits consistent behavior and can therefore be studied and understood. This argument, while certainly true, does not provide convincing evidence that Christianity is *uniquely* able to assist in the development of scientific reasoning. It might give Christianity an edge over polytheistic religious traditions, since they tend to view the world as unpredictable and chaotic due to the intervention of often capricious gods. However, it does not necessarily confer any inherent advantages to Christianity over other monotheistic religions like Judaism or Islam.

Foundation for Science

One critical distinction proposed by Dinesh D'Souza is that Christianity is a religion based on reason, a fact that implicitly encourages its adherents to search out the rationale behind things we can observe. The foundation of reason is easily advantageous in the pursuit of rigorous science when compared to polytheistic traditions with their failure to expect consistency in the natural world. However, D'Souza makes the more subtle point that reason is also superior to law, which is the basis of the major non-Christian monotheistic religions. Following dictated laws does not produce the same curiosity as following a God of reason who invites people to consider His purposes and even to enter into a relationship with Him.[29]

Stanley Jaki (1924–2009), a priest and physics professor with doctorates in both theology and physics, supports the importance of reason when he says that "non-Christians usually find it difficult if not impossible to sense the impact of that confidence which credited the universe with full rationality long before its details were traced out by exact science."[30] Jaki goes even farther to propose that perhaps the Trinitarian nature of the Christian God was ultimately necessary for the advancement of physics. Acceptance of Jesus Christ as the only-begotten of the Father allowed Christian scientists to discard the ancient view of ascribing divinity to the heavenly bodies. By demoting the universe to its proper place as a created entity, they were able to study and understand it more effectively.[31]

Nancy Pearcey and Charles Thaxton agree that the demotion of the universe to a material entity was a critical ingredient for the scientific revolution, but they attribute its demotion in part to the rise of voluntarism in the thirteen century. With its focus on the free will of God, voluntarism argues against the Aristotelian thought that the universe is driven by internal laws which demand certain behavior, such as circular planetary motion being absolutely necessary due to the supposedly inherent perfection of the circle. Carrying this assertion of God's freedom from theology into science results in a proper view of the universe as being subject to God's sovereignty rather than being somehow intrinsically or even divinely complete in itself. Pearcey and Thaxton also note that Christianity teaches that the world is both real and good. The fact that the world is real gives Christian scientists an advantage over adherents to religions like Hinduism, since there would be a decided lack of motivation to study and understand something illusory. The goodness of the world gives Christian scientists an advantage over cultures like the ancient Greeks, who are famous for rejecting empirical science or any type of manual labor in favor of "thought experiments"—a rejection that many historians believe is based partly on their view of the material world as evil and disorderly.[32]

These assertions regarding the superiority of Christianity as a foundational worldview for the development of science can certainly be disputed by non-Christians. However, it is more difficult to dispute the historically observable correlation between Christian influence and scientific progress. D'Souza writes that "an unbiased look at the history of science shows that modern science is an invention of medieval Christianity, and that the greatest breakthroughs in scientific reason have largely been the work of Christians."[33] Lest one think that D'Souza has overstated the fact due to his personal opinions, consider the following words penned by science writer Loren Eiseley, certainly not known for having a Christian bias.

> In one of those strange permutations of which history yields occasional rare examples, it is the Christian world which finally gave birth in a clear, articulate fashion to the experimental method of science itself.[34]

Note his lack of enthusiasm in giving credit to Christianity! Nevertheless, he does admit the importance of Christianity to the development of science. Indeed, modern scholarship is increasingly finding evidence to help dispel the myth that Christianity is hostile to science—a myth that was popularized during the latter part of the nineteenth century by people who wanted to replace the Christian worldview with secularism.[35] Unfortunately, popular opinion often lags behind current research, and the myth remains prevalent among the general public.

While an accurate reading of history shows that Christianity has provided a nurturing environment for the growth of scientific knowledge, certainly no scholar would suggest that an *individual* must have a Christian worldview in order to make valuable contributions to math, physics, and engineering.[36] Although many key figures of the scientific revolution and its aftermath were indeed Christians, some were not. For example, Pierre-Simon Laplace (1749–1827), a physicist and mathematician perhaps best remembered today for the incredibly useful transform that bears his name, was asked by Napoleon Bonaparte why he did not mention God in one of his major works. Laplace famously replied, "I have no need of that hypothesis."[37] It may be that Laplace needed the "hypothesis" after all, in the sense that the overall environment of Christianity during the scientific revolution provided an intellectual framework within which science could thrive.[38] According to D'Souza, "even atheist scientists work with Christian assumptions that, due to their ignorance of theology and history, are invisible to them."[39]

Mathematics

What about mathematics? It is more difficult to find evidence that Christianity could be a uniquely necessary worldview for the development of math. Indeed, great contributions to math have been made through the ages from pagan antiquity to medieval Islam and beyond. For example, Pythagorean's theorem remains a staple of geometry, and over a thousand editions of Euclid's *Elements of Geometry* have been published; only the Bible has surpassed that number.[40] The development of algebra during the ninth century is credited to the Arabic world,[41] and the use of positional notation—a crucial factor in simplifying arithmetic—was introduced by Indian mathematicians around the same time.[42] Perhaps it would be helpful to ask a different question regarding math: Instead of pondering whether Christianity is uniquely qualified to provide a foundation for math, one should seek to understand the nature and origin of math itself. In other words, can mathematics reveal the Christian God? As an interesting historical note, René Descartes tried to prove the existence of God using math, but his proofs were not convincing.[43] Since the Bible teaches the necessity of faith, one would not expect to find a mathematical proof for God! However, there are some intriguing facts about math that might hint at certain characteristics of God.

Once a mathematical truth is discovered, whether a geometrical theorem or an algebraic manipulation or some other finding, it is generally never proven incorrect. It may be subsumed into a more complete truth, but it typically stands as something true and useful from its initial discovery forward. In this regard, math is quite different from physics, in which theories are regularly presented, tested, discarded, and replaced as new observations are made.[44] Much has been made of this idea of *truth* as a seemingly fundamental characteristic of mathematics, and the theme of God as a mathematician has been present through the ages. The author of *Is God a Mathematician?* (a book whose very title hints at the transcendental nature of math) asserts that this concept originates with the work of Archimedes, the great Greek mathematician who departed from the more typical theoretical math of his day to examine connections between abstract objects and physical reality. In doing so, "he provided the first empirical . . . evidence for an apparent mathematical design of the universe."[45] From this early foundation, many have pondered the undeniably mathematical nature of our world. One author describes "just six numbers" that provide mathematical guidelines for the entire universe; if any of these numbers were even slightly different, life could not be sustained.[46] Another notes that the "Great Architect of the Universe now begins to appear as a pure mathematician."[47]

The truths (more properly called theorems) of mathematics are often explored via rigorous proofs, which are instructive not only for building mathematical understanding but also for developing philosophical insight. Consider the fact that proofs are performed by correctly applying a previously proven theorem or a postulate at each step. Now recall from junior high math that postulates are merely assumptions: They are not proven and in fact cannot be proven. Since the truths of math rest upon assumptions, one could correctly surmise that different assumptions would lead to different math.[48] The rise of non-Euclidean geometries in the nineteenth century is a well-known example of this fact: By replacing Euclid's fifth postulate, geometries of curved spaces and multiple dimensions can be created. These new geometries do not invalidate Euclidean geometry; they simply provide alternate representations of physical space.[49] Obviously, the initial selection of assumptions is therefore very important in gaining the correct result. To illustrate with a very practical example, many people wonder why long airline flights bear so far north. The explanation is that they are following the rules of elliptic geometry (in which the shortest distance between two points is the arc of a great circle) rather than Euclidean geometry (in which the shortest distance between two points is a straight line). Since the earth is spherical, elliptic geometry is the proper choice.[50]

Since a variety of mathematical systems can be generated by selecting different initial postulates, it is possible to explore abstract mathematical concepts that have little to do with physical reality, and indeed, mathematicians have done so. However, another fascinating aspect of math is that in many cases these abstract pursuits are found to have physical meaning after all. A prime example is knot theory, an esoteric field within mathematics that has surprisingly turned out to be applicable to the disentangling of DNA. These unexpected linkages between theoretical math and the physical world are often discussed as the "unreasonable effectiveness" of mathematics and are cited as evidence that there is something mysterious and inexplicably powerful about math.[51]

Another mystifying area of math that has been well publicized has to do with numbers like pi and phi. Pi, the ratio of the circumference of a circle to its diameter, has been calculated to over 51 billion decimal places with no appearance of any sort of pattern.[52] For centuries, people have pondered the random nature of pi compared to the absolute simplicity of the circle. Phi, the so-called "golden ratio," occurs in a variety of unrelated places in nature from the florets of a sunflower to the shape of the Milky Way.[53]

Recall the initial question that led to this discussion of the characteristics of math: Can mathematics reveal the Christian God? We have noted that there are inherent truths within math, and certainly God is truth. Rigorous proof of mathematical truths requires initial assumptions that are unproven. Similarly, Christian apologists make convincing arguments for the truth of Christianity, but the arguments invariably include some elements that must be accepted on faith. There is often an "unreasonable effectiveness" associated with even very abstract branches of math, just as God is completely coherent in all His ways. Finally, certain very common numbers have inexplicable properties, and the ways of God are ultimately far beyond human understanding. A non-Christian could easily dismiss these comparisons as contrived or irrelevant, preferring to see the nature of math as merely an astonishing coincidence. For Christians, however, the internal consistency of math is beautiful evidence of the presence of God in the world. In other words, starting with the "hypothesis" of the Christian God can lead one to a great appreciation of both mathematics and God.

Valuable Insights for Christian Students

The relationship between Christianity and math, physics, and engineering is a two-way street. Not only has Christianity historically contributed to the development of these subjects both factually and philosophically, but studying these subjects can provide worthwhile insights about God to the perceptive Christian student.

Facts and concepts in math, physics, and engineering can potentially bring the thoughtful student to a richer appreciation for some of the attributes of God. To provide some general examples, both calculus and physics focus on the infinitesimally small and the extremely large, a vast range that hints at the unlimited nature of God. Engineering encourages creativity with its emphasis on innovative design, providing a glimpse of our being made in the image of (a very creative) God. More specific examples abound. Georg Cantor's theory of the infinite, which he believed was given to him by God, has made substantial contributions to math, but it has also provided philosophers and theologians with fascinating questions regarding the nature of infinity.[54] One way to state Einstein's theory of relativity is that when traveling at the speed of light, there is no passage of time—an interpretation that arguably connects the biblical description of God as light with the knowledge that He exists outside of time. Heisenberg's uncertainty principle, which states that the exact position and velocity of a particle cannot be simultaneously known due to interference of the measurement process, has great philosophical significance and was thus initially difficult for many scientists to accept. Not only does the principle undermine scientific determinism, thereby providing greater freedom for God to intervene in the world,[55] but it also gives humankind a more important role in "the cosmic drama."[56] Admittedly, it is difficult to fully appreciate the significance of these comments without understanding the underlying principles more completely, which is the point. The study of math, physics, and engineering can give the student fresh thoughts to contemplate regarding the magnificent glory of God and His actions in our world.

In addition to pondering individual concepts, the diligent student of these subjects can benefit by discovering how seemingly diverse principles have been unified as new discoveries have been made. In math, René Descartes combined the previously separate fields of geometry and algebra through his development of the Cartesian coordinate system and the subsequent introduction of mathematical functions—a huge breakthrough.[57] In physics, James Clerk Maxwell devised four equations relating electricity to magnetism,[58] an early success in the on-going search for a "theory of everything." The concept of unification is important to scholarship in general, since it mitigates the often-lamented problem of fragmentation of knowledge in today's universities; it is important to Christian scholarship specifically, since it highlights the fact that all truth is God's truth.

Challenges in Contemporary Society

Since the early days of the scientific revolution, when irrefutable observations began to topple long-held ideas about the universe, there has been an often fierce debate about the relative positions of scientific truths and theological truths. (While this section will use the term "science" in keeping with much of the literature in this area, the discussion will focus on physics and particularly theoretical physics, which has an indispensable mathematical component.) William Dembski labels four commonly discussed models for the relationship between science and faith as compartmentalization, complementarity, conflict, and mutual support.[59] From the labels, it is easy to surmise that "mutual support" would be the preferred view, but all four views are present in scientific circles and thus merit discussion. The first two actually have some level of official support, with the National Academy of Sciences advocating compartmentalization and the American Scientific Affiliation promoting complementarity.[60] Thus, it is a worthwhile exercise to briefly consider some significant challenges facing Christian scholars in the context of each model.

Compartmentalization

In the compartmentalization model, science and theology are completely unrelated, with science dedicated to the study of the natural world and theology dedicated to matters of morality and faith.[61] This view presents an obvious and potentially pernicious difficulty for Christians who choose to work in the sciences, suggesting that convictions arising from personal faith should be completely ignored when focusing on professional pursuits. In the broader view, compartmentalization gives rise to the possibility of disengagement by the Christian community from the sciences, and so a challenge under this model is to stay engaged and to resist efforts to consign Christianity to a position of irrelevance.

Complementarity

The complementary view acknowledges that both science and theology are required for a complete understanding of reality, but they deal with the same issues "in languages so different that no translation between the two, not even a partial translation, is possible."[62] There is some validity to this view: The methods of discovering scientific and Christian truths are indeed quite different, as are their goals, and one can successfully argue that each should be allowed to speak to reality in its own way. However, allowing both faith and science to address reality but not each other can be a complicated position to maintain over time. In spite of the best efforts of all involved, issues of science might eventually have unavoidable implications for faith and vice versa.

Some of the great figures of the scientific revolution seem to have taken the complementary view, and in many cases they were able successfully to maintain their beliefs without compromise. Nonetheless, there were some notable exceptions that could be interpreted as a harbinger of things to come. The Galileo trial is an obvious example, and the ensuing showdown between science and religion continues to reverberate to this day. Regardless of the nuanced motivations for the trial that may have been incorrectly portrayed in historical accounts, the fact remains that when Galileo's scientific observations clashed with established theological views, conflict arose in spite of Galileo's personal complementarity. Thus, while this view is appealing in that it allows science and faith to exist in relative harmony, it may be impossible to avoid conflict indefinitely. Under this model, Christians should guard against slipping into compartmentalization while also being prepared for the very real possibility of conflict.

Conflict

The conflict model needs little explanation: If there appears to be any disagreement between science and faith, one of them must be incorrect.[63] This model arguably gets the most attention, since many prominent contemporary scientists are quite vocal in their nonbelief. For example, Albert Einstein often invoked God in his writings but was a self-declared "deeply religious nonbeliever,"[64] and Stephen Hawking is probably best described as an agnostic or perhaps a deist.[65] In fact, the author of *The Faith of Scientists* divides the book into two sections: "Founders of Modern Science" and "Scientists of Our Time." Five out of eight scientists profiled in the first group are Christians, and the three non-Christians lived in the nineteenth century and beyond. By contrast, out of the 13 profiles in the second group, only one is a Christian. Even though one could question the choice of scientists to be profiled, this rather dramatic difference raises some interesting questions.

Has the conflict between faith and science intensified over the centuries, or is it simply better publicized? Are these prominent spokesmen for science representative of all scientists in terms of faith? Most pertinent for the present discussion, how can Christians most effectively participate in the dialogue?

While there have been acrimonious exchanges between believing and unbelieving scientists for centuries, the present conflict does seem to be more intense in light of the increased secularization of society at large combined with the previously described difficulty of indefinitely maintaining a complementary view of science and faith. However, the loudest voices certainly do not speak for everyone, as there are many devout Christians who do excellent work in the sciences, including some Nobel prizewinners who are professing Christians.[66] The presence of Christians working successfully in math, physics, and engineering is an important foundation for meaningful dialogue, and indeed the conversation has been taking place for decades. Still, challenges remain.

A key challenge for Christians under the conflict model is that science is often considered the obvious "winner." With its reliance on empirical evidence, science is accepted by many as being undeniably true even though scientific theories are regularly discarded and replaced as new data are collected. Moreover, in society at large, science is generally accorded a much higher status than faith. Consider, for example, the following statement made by a Christian physicist.

> An expression like "Jesus is at the same time truly God and truly man" is irritably brushed aside as nonsense, as something people cannot cope with. A completely analogous statement like "An electron is at the same time a particle and a wave" is listened to with reverence and awe.[67]

Most people do not fully understand either the faith statement or the scientific one, but anyone outside the Christian community is much more likely to "believe" the scientific one. The continual fight for respect is wearying, especially when the other side has already declared victory in the conflict.

Another significant challenge in the conflict between science and faith is that complicated scientific principles are often oversimplified and misunderstood, resulting in confusion about their implications for the Christian faith. A prime example is the big bang theory, which is greeted with suspicion by many Christians. However, because the theory describes the *aftermath* of the big bang without pinpointing its *cause*,[68] its theological implications are actually quite positive for Christianity or at least for the existence of God.[69] No less a physicist than Stephen Hawking says that "it smacks of divine intervention."[70] In fact, after discussing some specific details about the initial condition of the universe in his influential book *A Brief History of Time*, Hawking makes the following comment.

> This means that the initial state of the universe must have been very carefully chosen indeed if the hot big bang model was correct right back to the beginning of time. It would be very difficult to explain why the universe should have begun in just this way, except as the act of a God who intended to create beings like us.[71]

In fairness to Hawking's views, he goes on to explain other ideas and does not generally support the idea of a Creator. In fact, although the work of Hawking was instrumental in cementing widespread acceptance of the big bang theory, he is now investigating other ideas![72] So, the challenges are compounded: The theories that cause conflict are complex and virtually impossible for the nonspecialist to understand; consequently, some degree of interpretation is required, making oversimplification an almost intrinsically necessary part of communication and putting the nonspecialist at the mercy of the interpreter's worldview.[73] To make matters worse, the theories are constantly being revised and updated, making it even more difficult to avoid misunderstanding or a too-facile interpretation.

Conflict does not always stop with a mere lack of understanding; it sometimes progresses to condescension and dismissal or even outright hostility. The intelligent design movement illustrates this point particularly well, since it has drawn negative reactions from both the scientific and faith communities. Theologians accuse the movement of misunderstanding the actions of God, and scientists accuse it of being "just creationism in disguise."[74] For examples of hostility, one needs only to read the work of Richard Dawkins, a prominent atheist and vocal opponent of the intelligent design movement. In a single article, he calls proponents of intelligent design IDiots, scientific ignoramuses, and creation wingnuts.[75]

This type of name-calling and the disdain behind it are hardly conducive to discussing points of conflict in a reasonable way, much less resolving them. However, the challenge for Christians is to respond in kindness and grace; after all, we are not simply defending our own ideas, but we are representing Christ in the world.[76] If Christians can help set a tone of reason and cooperation, there might be hope of at least occasionally moving beyond conflict into the mutual support model.

Mutual Support

The mutual support model proposes that science and faith overlap and can provide support (although not proof) for each other, but they are not coextensive. In other words, according to Dembski, "theology can lend credence, increase the conditional probability of, or render plausible certain scientific claims and not others. Likewise, science can do the same for theology." [77] This model is undoubtedly appealing but potentially difficult to put into practice. Consider the following statement made by a physicist after a discussion of the inflation theory, which postulates how the universe could have arisen from an infinitesimally small seed.

> Cosmologists sometimes claim that the universe can arise "from nothing." But they should watch their language, especially when addressing philosophers.[78]

It is clear that the author does not want the inflationary theory to be used to offer credibility to the theological doctrine of *ex nihilo* creation. What may appear to be an obvious implication to someone who already accepts a particular doctrine is considerably less obvious to someone who does not. This observation recalls to mind once again the Aristotelian proposition that the interpretation is divisive, not the facts (or in this case, the theoretical suppositions).

The desire to have a meaningful dialogue between theology and science in which each discipline can contribute to the other requires adherents on both sides to invest time and energy. Once the discussion has begun, continuing commitment is required to keep an open mind to accept new ideas and perhaps even to discard long-cherished beliefs in the face of compelling evidence. This type of dialogue should not threaten Christianity: If our faith is true, there will never be any evidence compelling enough to abandon the tenets of the faith. However, there may be evidence enough to abandon peripheral ideas that do not have any bearing on salvation, with a classic example once again being the conflict between the geocentric and heliocentric models.

The mutual support model, however difficult to achieve and maintain, has experienced some success. One of the more interesting examples of reasonable dialogue leading to reconsideration of long-held beliefs is the story of Antony Flew, a well-known atheist who became a deist through his careful consideration of scientific and mathematical evidence.[79] His compelling story is encouraging in light of the very real challenges discussed in this section.

Opportunities for Cultural Engagement

Previous sections have largely neglected engineering, not because of a lack of pertinent information but simply due to space limitations. This section will focus solely on engineering, since its applied nature makes it an excellent bridge between math and physics and the culture at large.

Engineering is sometimes considered to be a sterile discipline, one that is more focused on objects than on people and one that is therefore an unlikely candidate for cultural engagement. The actual history of engineering suggests otherwise, though, with modern-day engineers all the way back to their primitive technological forebears sharing the goal of designing solutions to address human needs.[80] In addition to the basic focus of improving life for humankind, a strong emphasis on morality and social responsibility has been a part of the engineering profession since its inception.[81] Toward these ends, engineers have designed artificial hearts and advanced prosthetics, highways and bridges, smart phones and laptops, faster snow skis and better golf balls, and an innumerable host of other products. While some of these items make a more obvious contribution to humankind than others, all of them confer some benefit to the user; additionally, they are representative of the many engineered "artifacts" that "make culture" in the sense recently popularized by Andy Crouch.[82]

The act of building things for public use provides multiple opportunities for directly engaging the culture. Ethical issues are a critical consideration, since an engineer cannot always foresee how a particular design will be used or even all of the unintended consequences of its expected use. Technology is often said to be morally neutral, but this assertion may be overly simplistic. In many cases, specific technologies are designed for specific uses and are therefore biased toward certain values.[83] For example, the developers of technological weaponry generally understand the end use of their designs. Even seemingly benign technologies can have negative consequences, including the most humanitarian item mentioned previously: The development of advanced medical devices is sometimes cited as a factor in skyrocketing health costs. Engineers of all faiths take these types of issues seriously, and most branches of engineering have codes of ethics that provide guidelines for ethical behavior. Even so, Christian engineers can add value by bringing the additional constraints of biblical ethics into the discussion.

In politics, important policy decisions increasingly have a technological component.[84] The need for alternative energy sources is always in the news, but it is difficult to sort through all of the information and truly understand the issues that accompany generating and paying for alternative fuels. Water is an even more fundamental need than energy and is in short supply in some areas, but many people do not realize that water and energy are competing needs in the sense that water is required to produce energy in most types of power plants. In fact, a *lot* of water is required: One writer estimates that about 150,000 liters of water are required just to power the 300 million Google searches done in a single day.[85] The global warming debate is complex and hotly debated. In all of these areas and many others, engineers have an opportunity to join the conversation and contribute to an improved understanding of complex issues. Perhaps some Christian engineers will find that they even have a calling to engage culture in this vital way.

Technology truly is ubiquitous, and so it has implications that reverberate throughout society, including marketing, economics, labor relations, the environment, child and elder care, transportation, and communication, just to name a few. Technology is viewed with a certain degree of mistrust by many in today's society due to its pervasiveness as well as its potential for harm,[86] and yet it is a wonderful gift to humankind in most of its manifestations. A Christian engineer is in a unique position to appreciate the benefits of technology while also understanding that our fallen world makes it prone to abuse. Because of this added insight into the dichotomous nature of technology, Christians can offer a perspective that enlightens and advances public discourse.

Conclusion

There is a rich history of Christian scholarship in the fields of math, physics, and engineering, with many historians acknowledging that Christianity was crucial to the successful birth of modern science. All students could benefit from a more vigorous study of these subjects than is dictated by the typical core curriculum, and Christian students who have sufficient interest and aptitude should seriously consider pursuing a major or minor in one or more of these areas. Having knowledgeable Christian scholars is imperative if we are to address in a meaningful and effective way the very real challenges that exist within the fields themselves and at the interface between these fields and society at large. Students who take on this challenge will be blessed through the study of the mysterious order and logic of mathematics that teaches us something about the attributes of God, the awe-inspiring universe created by our loving God, and the joy of creating and building something as a means of emulating our creative and active God. It could, in fact, be argued that one does not simply bring a Christian perspective to the study of these fields, but rather one actually studies the Christian perspective by investigating the works of God.

Johannes Kepler, one of the great men of the scientific revolution, wrote a letter to a former teacher in 1595 stating, "I had the intention of being a theologian. For a long time I was restless: but now see how God is, by my endeavors, also glorified in astronomy."[87] Study math! Study physics! Study engineering! And learn of God. *Soli Deo Gloria.*

Questions for Further Reflection

1. If Christianity historically provided the necessary conditions for the birth of modern science, what is its contribution now? Are there ways in which math, physics, and engineering might fail to thrive if all Christian influence were removed?
2. What attributes of God might be illuminated through the study of math, physics, and engineering? For example,

how can awareness of the "unreasonable effectiveness" of mathematics refine the Christian's understanding of God?

3. How can Christians avoid drawing theological boundaries too narrowly—in a way that might erroneously exclude new scientific discoveries? What are some differences between how science relates to Christianity and how it relates to specific theological principles as articulated by fallen humanity?
4. When conflicts arise between science and Christianity, how should Christians respond? What types of responses are most likely to lead to compartmentalization or complementarity or mutual support?
5. In what ways are Christians *uniquely* equipped to address questions at the intersection of technology, ethics, and public policy? What might be some societal ramifications if Christians fail to engage in these areas?

Resources for Further Study

The books listed below span a wide variety of approaches, ranging from explicitly addressing the contributions of Christianity to introducing aspects of math, physics, and engineering that lead the thoughtful reader to ponder God. Not all of the books are written from a Christian perspective, but one can sometimes find surprising support for the truth claims of Christianity even when the author intends a different purpose.

Chappell, Dorothy F., and E. David Cook, eds. *Not Just Science.* Grand Rapids: Zondervan, 2005.

Dembski, William A. *Intelligent Design.* Downers Grove, IL: InterVarsity, 1999.

Florman, Samuel C. *The Existential Pleasures of Engineering.* New York: St. Martin's Griffin, 1994.

Frankenberry, Nancy K., ed. *The Faith of Scientists.* Princeton, NJ: Princeton University Press, 2008.

Hawking, Stephen. *A Brief History of Time.* New York: Bantam, 1988.

Hummel, Charles E. *The Galileo Connection.* Downers Grove, IL: InterVarsity Press, 1986.

Livio, Mario. *Is God a Mathematician?* New York: Simon & Schuster, 2009.

Pearcey, Nancy R., and Charles B. Thaxton. *The Soul of Science: Christian Faith and Natural Philosophy.* Wheaton, IL: Crossway, 1994.

Rees, Martin. *Just Six Numbers.* New York: Basic Books, 2000.
Stewart, Ian. *Why Beauty Is Truth.* New York: Basic Books, 2007.

Endnotes

[1] Charles E. Hummel, *The Galileo Connection* (Downers Grove, IL: InterVarsity, 1986), 23.
[2] Ibid., 16–17.
[3] Samuel C. Florman, *The Existential Pleasures of Engineering* (New York: St. Martin's Griffin, 1994), x; Daniel E. Williams, "Morrill Act's Contribution to Engineering's Foundation," in *The Bent of Tau Beta Pi* (Spring 2009): 15.
[4] Nancy R. Pearcey and Charles B. Thaxton, *The Soul of Science: Christian Faith and Natural Philosophy* (Wheaton, IL: Crossway, 1994), 25.
[5] Hummel, *Galileo Connection*, 47–56.
[6] Nancy K. Frankenberry, ed., *The Faith of Scientists* (Princeton, NJ: Princeton University Press, 2008), 5–6.
[7] Hummel, *Galileo Connection*, 88–89.
[8] Frankenberry, *Faith of Scientists*, 4.
[9] Hummel, *Galileo Connection*, 109.
[10] Ibid., 81, 118–23.
[11] Frankenberry, *Faith of Scientists*, 6.
[12] Mario Livio, *The Golden Ratio* (New York: Broadway, 2002), 153.
[13] Leonard Shlain, *Art and Physics* (North Yorkshire, UK: Quill, 1991), 67.
[14] Frankenberry, *Faith of Scientists*, 37.
[15] Stanley L. Jaki, *The Savior of Science* (Grand Rapids: Eerdmans, 2000), 97.
[16] Frankenberry, *Faith of Scientists*, 39.
[17] Hans Camenzind, *Much Ado about* Almost *Nothing* (BookLocker.com, 2007), 169–70.
[18] Frankenberry, *Faith of Scientists*, 80–81; James M. Houston, ed., *Mind on Fire* (Minneapolis: Bethany House, 1997), 19–20.
[19] Houston, *Mind on Fire*, 136.
[20] Frankenberry, *Faith of Scientists*, 83; Houston, *Mind on Fire*, 32.
[21] Hummel, *Galileo Connection*, 142.
[22] Houston, *Mind on Fire*, 32.
[23] Frankenberry, *Faith of Scientists*, 107; Hummel, *Galileo Connection*, 127.
[24] Frankenberry, *Faith of Scientists*, 104.
[25] Ibid., 102–5.
[26] Paul J. Nahin, *Dr. Euler's Fabulous Formula* (Princeton, NJ: Princeton University Press, 2006), 324.
[27] Accessed July 19, 2010, http://en.wikipedia.org/wiki/Euler#cite_ref-MathInt_25–0.
[28] Nahin, *Dr. Euler's Fabulous Formula*, 345.
[29] Dinesh D'Souza, *What's So Great about Christianity* (Washington, DC: Regnery, 2007), 84–85.
[30] Jaki, *Savior of Science*, 96.
[31] Stanley L. Jaki, *The Origin of Science and the Science of Its Origin* (South Bend, IN: Regnery/Gateway, 1979), 69–70; Jaki, *Savior of Science*, 79–80.
[32] Pearcey and Thaxton, *Soul of Science*, 21–33.

[33] D'Souza, *What's So Great about Christianity*, 84.
[34] Quoted in Pearcey and Thaxton, *Soul of Science*, 18.
[35] Ibid., 19–20.
[36] Ibid., 21.
[37] William A. Dembski, *Intelligent Design* (Downers Grove, IL: InterVarsity, 1999), 98.
[38] Pearcey and Thaxton, *Soul of Science*, 21.
[39] D'Souza, *What's So Great about Christianity*, 84.
[40] Ian Stewart, *Why Beauty Is Truth* (New York: Basic Books, 2007), 19.
[41] Ibid., 36–37.
[42] Accessed July 20, 2010, http://en.wikipedia.org/wiki/Positional_notation.
[43] Mario Livio, *Is God a Mathematician?* (New York: Simon & Schuster, 2009), 114–17.
[44] Anthony Van den Beukel, *The Physicists and God* (North Andover, MA: Genesis Publishing, 1995), 118–23.
[45] Livio, *Is God a Mathematician?* 58–59.
[46] Martin Rees, *Just Six Numbers* (New York: Basic Books, 2000).
[47] Eric Temple Bell, *Men of Mathematics* (New York: Simon & Schuster, 1937), xvii.
[48] Stewart, *Why Beauty Is Truth*, 24.
[49] Livio, *Is God a Mathematician?* 150–62.
[50] Ibid., 160–61.
[51] Ibid., 203–24.
[52] David Blatner, *The Joy of* π (New York: Walker and Company, 1997), 2, 72–73.
[53] Livio, *Golden Ratio*, 114–20.
[54] Robert L. Brabenec, "Cantor's Theory of the Infinite," presented at Union University's Mathematics Lecture Series, November 13, 2009.
[55] Stephen Hawking, *A Brief History of Time* (New York: Bantam, 1988), 55.
[56] Van den Beukel, *The Physicists and God*, 48–55.
[57] Livio, *Is God a Mathematician?* 93–97.
[58] Van den Beukel, *The Physicists and God*, 25–26.
[59] Dembski, *Intelligent Design*, 187–92.
[60] Ibid., 189.
[61] Ibid., 188–89.
[62] Ibid., 189.
[63] Ibid.
[64] Frankenberry, *Faith of Scientists*, 148.
[65] Henry F. Schaefer III, *Science and Christianity: Conflict or Coherence?* (Watkinsville, GA: Apollos Trust, 2003), 61.
[66] Ibid., 26–31.
[67] Van den Beukel, *The Physicists and God*, 127.
[68] Rees, *Just Six Numbers*, 137–39.
[69] Dembski, *Intelligent Design*, 204.
[70] Hawking, *Brief History of Time*, 46.
[71] Ibid., 126–27.
[72] Ibid., 50–51.

[73] Dorothy F. Chappell and E. David Cook, "How Does Society Interact with Science?" in *Not Just Science*, ed. Dorothy F. Chappell and E. David Cook (Grand Rapids: Zondervan, 2005), 89.
[74] Dembski, *Intelligent Design*, 13.
[75] Accessed July 23, 2010, http://richarddawkins.net/articles/2394.
[76] Tim Morris and Don Petcher, *Science and Grace* (Wheaton, IL: Crossway, 2006), 302.
[77] Dembski, *Intelligent Design*, 191–92.
[78] Rees, *Just Six Numbers*, 137–45.
[79] Antony Flew, *There Is a God* (New York: HarperOne, 2007).
[80] Florman, *Existential Pleasures of Engineering*, 113.
[81] Ibid., 19.
[82] Andy Crouch, *Culture Making* (Downers Grove, IL: InterVarsity, 2008), 27–36.
[83] Stewart M. DeSoto and Gayle E. Ermer, "Does Engineering Contribute to a Better Future?" in Chappell and Cook, *Not Just Science*, 251–52.
[84] Richard A. Muller, *Physics for Future Presidents* (New York: Norton, 2008), 14.
[85] IEEE Spectrum Staff, "IEEE Spectrum Special Report: Water vs. Energy" in *IEEE Spectrum*, June 2010, 26.
[86] Florman, *Existential Pleasures of Engineering*, 99.
[87] Frankenberry, *Faith of Scientists*, 38–39.

19

The Study of Health Care at the Christian University

E. Blake Watkins

When questioned by the Pharisees as to the greatest commandment found in the law, Jesus responded, "Love the Lord your God with all your heart, with all your soul, and with all your mind" (Matt 22:37 HCSB). His answer was hardly a surprise to the teachers of the law. Yet, Jesus did not stop with this statement. He continued, "Love your neighbor as yourself. All the Law and the Prophets depend on these two commands" (Matt 22:39–40 HCSB). Love and service to God and to man form the foundational mission of the church and its members, the body of Christ. Our threefold devotion of heart, soul, and mind to God, which flows out of hearts of gratitude and thanksgiving, informs our response to and care for our neighbor as the Holy Spirit infuses the love of God into our souls. We are able to show true compassion because God has shown absolute compassion toward us through His Son Jesus Christ. It is within this framework that we will examine the structure and purpose of health care programs within the Christian university.

The study of any of the various fields of health care at the Christian university ultimately has its origins in the ministry and work of Jesus Christ. A brief examination of the four Gospels quickly reveals an overarching concern for those who were sick and in need of healing, whether spiritual or physical. Jesus instructed and enabled His disciples to "heal the sick, raise the dead, cleanse those with skin diseases, drive out demons" (Matt 10:8 HCSB). In fact, Jesus often addressed the physical needs of those who came to Him before He addressed their spiritual needs.

In modern language we would say that Jesus used a holistic approach to healing. Only recently has the modern medical community begun to appreciate this approach to health care. A distinct advantage that health care programs on Christian university campuses have over secular universities is the ability to apply a truly holistic approach to patient care, not in a coercive but rather a grace-filled manner, utilizing all of the tools of modern medicine and the best evidence-based practice methods. The holistic approach mentioned here must be understood within a Christian framework or Christian worldview. Holistic medicine, in the traditional sense, is antithetical in many ways to modern medicine and seeks to provide physical, spiritual, and emotional healing using a variety of methods, typically devoid of conventional medical techniques or pharmaceutical agents. Many of these practices have their origins in ancient Eastern medical practices or religions.[1] While not completely misdirected in their approaches, adherents to traditional holistic methods fall short of a truly holistic approach to healing and health care.

A Christian holistic approach, on the other hand, recognizes the nature of mankind as created yet fallen and the impact this fallenness has on health in general. Thus, the Christian health care program must teach and train future practitioners to address the physical, spiritual, and emotional health of their patients using a model of creation, fall, redemption, and consummation. Not since the creation of Adam and Eve in the garden has mankind experienced perfect health. As sin entered the world, so did sickness and death. For thousands of years since, mankind has searched endlessly to find natural or supernatural methods of healing. A proper approach to health care must start with a mindset of the sin-origin of sickness and the consequent need for redemption and work on that basis toward a goal of restoration and healing.

Since the fall of man, God has been actively working to redeem His creation, ultimately culminating in the creation of a new heaven and a new earth. Our role in this plan, as health care educators and health care providers, is to seek to redeem our present time in history and to work to provide the means for future generations to do the same. This can be accomplished through caring for the sick, healing the sick, developing new methods to ease or minimize the suffering associated with a fallen world, exploring both cause and progression of disease, expanding our options for eliminating these diseases or for managing their symptoms, and addressing the full spectrum of the physical, spiritual, and emotional needs of our patients. Christian universities are in a unique position to address each of these critical areas.

Characteristics of a Christian Health Care Program

A cursory examination of health care programs around the country will likely reveal only subtle differences between secular and Christian universities, as all of them have similar goals—caring for and restoring health to the sick. Upon scrutiny, however, one significant difference becomes quite evident, that of purpose. *Why* do we care for the sick and the weak? The answer is quite complex and must consist of more than the simplistic reply "to make people well again." There are various economic reasons for providing health care. Citizens who are healthy and strong are more likely to be productive members of society and, hence, not a burden to others or to the government. Other reasons may include the financial benefit to the practitioner or the job security provided by such a position. While neither of these reasons for providing care to the sick is necessarily erroneous, each of them is completely inadequate and runs the risk of producing a health care system whose central focus is not the overall welfare of the patient. As such, Christian universities must be foundationally Christ-centered in order to provide a meaningful base from which to build a proper health care program of study. Moreover, the individual program must be designed to ensure that its curriculum is rigorous, providing students with more than just a foundational knowledge of their area of interest (academic excellence). It should emphasize, teach, and model compassion in practice on a daily basis (compassionate care) and the servant leadership displayed by Christ (servant leadership). It should also ensure that research is a critical component (innovation and scholarship), allowing our Christian universities to contribute significantly to the development and discovery of knowledge in the areas of disease etiology and treatment.

Christ-Centered

The term "Christ-centered" is commonly used by Christian institutions of higher learning, but what, if anything, does it actually mean? The answer to this important question is vital specifically for health care programs at these institutions, as it is the driving force behind their very mission. Improperly understood, the term can result in programs that resemble anything but Christ, being characterized by legalistic tendencies on the one hand and antinomianism on the other. A Christ-centered health care program is not defined by how many Bible classes are included in the curriculum or how many Bible studies are available to students and faculty. Rather, a Christ-centered program is characterized by a strong commitment to excellence in academics and practice grounded on the foundational principles of our faith laid down in Scripture. We must continually strive to work out the implications of our faith generally within the field of health care and more specifically within our own particular area of study.

Is Scripture still relevant in today's society? Does the Bible have anything useful to say about the challenges we face and the problems we encounter? Has science become the be-all and end-all? Science has certainly progressed tremendously over the past 200 years, providing us with answers to complex questions about disease and treatment. The technological explosion of the past 20 years is evidence of the value and impact that science and scientific inquiry can have on a civilization. But science alone is not enough. It is unable to explain the greater questions that plague us or to give us a complete framework or worldview that addresses these questions. Within Christian institutions, we believe that Scripture is very much still relevant and absolutely necessary to fully understand the world in which we live and to understand the patients we treat. We must be diligent to work out how Scripture informs what we do on a daily basis and how our faith impacts our practice and our work. Later in this chapter we will examine some contemporary health-related issues and possible approaches to them within this framework.

Academic Excellence

We often hear the term *academic excellence* tossed about in reference to postsecondary institutions, primarily as a means of attracting the top academic students to these programs. Unfortunately, unbridled use has resulted in a term devoid of meaning and significance. Nevertheless, health care programs at Christian universities must stand as the epitome of excellence. We must be willing and able to teach our students and to train our students at the highest academic levels to prepare them to impact health care practice upon graduation. If the primary purpose of our programs is to emulate Christ and to obey His command to care "for the least of these," then our obligation as educators is to ensure that our students are properly equipped to carry out the ministry to which they have been called.

Academic excellence is multifaceted and begins with a rigorous curriculum that contains the individual components required within a given field of study to ensure adequate preparation of graduates for the practice setting. A well-designed curriculum does not guarantee academic excellence. Rather, excellence comes through a highly qualified faculty that is committed not only to the idea of excellence but to the reality of excellence as well. Health care programs require that faculty be familiar with or competent in current practice methods and philosophy. As such, faculty must be committed to their own academic development through rigorous study, discipline-specific conferences, and the scientific/clinical literature, rather than simply relying on outdated textbooks for information, to help ensure that the content of their teaching matches with current knowledge and understanding of disease or treatment options and guidelines. Furthermore, as Augustine argued, all truth is God's truth; therefore, faculty must also be students of a broad variety of areas including philosophy, ethics, history, sociology, and so on, in order to gain a more thorough understanding of the times in which we live and to help them prepare students for the times to come.

Concurrent with an exceptional didactic component must reside an equally exceptional clinical component. Foundational knowledge and understanding is readily provided in a classroom setting, but true learning and application occurs best in actual practice. Thus, health care programs must be diligent to establish clinical sites in partnership with professionals who are equally committed to the development of excellent practitioners that embody the ministry of Christ and have the knowledge and understanding to practice competently and proficiently, helping to ensure that all patients are given the best care possible regardless of person.

Compassionate Care

One characteristic that marked the ministry of Jesus was that of compassion. Jesus was truly compassionate with those He encountered, especially those who were in need. A foundational quality of our students and our graduates should be compassion; they must be compassionate practitioners, recognizing that they are ministers to patients who are made in the very image of God and are, therefore, worthy of the care they receive, regardless of person. God displayed great compassion toward us by sending His Son as the atonement for our sinfulness, condescending to take on human flesh while retaining His divinity. The church historian Eusebius puts it this way:

> For he alone, as the only all-gracious Son of an all-gracious Father, in accordance with the purpose of His Father's benevolence, has willingly put on the nature of us who lay prostrate in corruption, and like some excellent physician, who for the sake of saving them that are ill, examines their sufferings, handles their foul sores, and reaps pain for himself from the miseries of another, so us who were not only diseased and afflicted with terrible ulcers and wounds already mortified, but were even lying among the dead, he hath saved for himself from the very jaws of death. . . . But he alone having suffered the punishments due for our impieties, having recovered us who were not half dead merely, but were already in tombs and sepulchers, and altogether foul and offensive, saves us, both anciently and now, by His beneficent zeal, beyond the expectation of any one, even of ourselves, and imparts liberally of the Father's benefits,—he who is the giver of life and light, our great Physician and King and Lord, the Christ of God.[2]

Gary Ferngren in his excellent book, *Medicine and Health Care in Early Christianity*, argues that the Hebrew concept of man created in the image of God (Gen 1:26–27) and the incarnation of Christ together had a tremendous impact on the development of health care in early Christianity in four distinct ways.[3] The first was that these doctrines provided a foundation on which Christian charity could be based. "We love because He first loved us" (1 John 4:19 HCSB). Caring for and compassion toward the sick, weak, and poor were divine imperatives. God had displayed His love for mankind in the sending of His Son for the redemption of sinners. Jesus displayed both His identity as the Christ and His love for mankind by healing the sick and the lame and through giving His life sacrificially to bridge the gap between God and man;

therefore, this same love was expected to mark the lives of the followers of Christ. Similarly, Christians recognized the inherent worth of others as image bearers of God. Christ had shown compassion on others during His ministry; therefore, the followers of Christ were to show compassion for those in need as well. We see this, for example, in the Acts of the Apostles. As the early church began to grow and flourish, its members sold their possessions and used the proceeds to help other members of the church who were in need. There is no indication that this was a requirement or even that it was an expectation, but as the new converts heard the teachings of the apostles regarding God's actions toward them and the redemption available through Christ, their hearts were moved to give freely of what they had received.

This idea is further elucidated in the writings of the apostle Paul as he urges unity within the developing church through the metaphorical use of the body. Jesus Christ is the head, while His followers constitute the remainder of the body. The body is made up of multiple parts, each one equally important. All must work together to allow the body to function efficiently. "If one member suffers, all the members suffer with it; if one member is honored, all the members rejoice with it" (1 Cor 12:26). Paul saw no room for division within the body of Christ; rather, the chief characteristic that described the body should be love for one another and for those outside of the church.

Furthermore, early Christians strongly opposed the pagan practices of abortion, infanticide, and suicide because each took the life of one who bore the image of God. An early record of this is found in the *Didachē*, likely written at the end of the first century: "And this is the second commandment of the teaching. Thou shalt do no murder, thou shalt not commit adultery. . . . thou shalt not murder a child by abortion nor kill them when born" (2.1–2).[4] Furthermore,Tertullian writes at the end of the second century:

> In our case, a murder being once for all forbidden, we may not destroy even the foetus in the womb, while as yet the human being derives blood from the other parts of the body for its sustenance. To hinder a birth is merely a speedier man-killing; nor does it matter whether you take away a life that is born, or destroy one that is coming to the birth. That is a man which is going to be one; you have the fruit already in its seed.[5]

The incarnation also debunked the Platonic and Greek idea that the physical was evil and should be separated from the soul. The Christian idea of God taking on human flesh provided the basis for the care, restoration, and concern for the physical body. Irenaeus writes in *Against Heresies*, "for if the flesh were not in a position to be saved, the Word of God would in no wise have become flesh."[6] Likewise, Tertullian argues in *On the Flesh of Christ* that Christ came to abolish "sin in the flesh" (*peccatum carnis*) not "sinful flesh" (*carnem peccati*);[7] that is, Christ came to redeem the flesh, not to separate it from the soul. Christians had a foundation for strengthening the spiritual body as well as the physical body, rather than trying to escape the physical. The apostle Paul writes, "I beseech you therefore, brethren, by the mercies of God, that you present *your bodies* a living sacrifice, holy, acceptable to God, which is your reasonable service. And do not be conformed to this world, but be transformed by the renewing of your mind, that you may prove what is that good and acceptable and perfect will of God" (Rom 12:1–2 NKJV). Furthermore, Gedaliahu G. Stroumsa argues in an excellent article, "*Caro salutis cardo* [the flesh is the axis of salvation]: Shaping the Person in Early Christian Thought," that Christianity created and sustained the image of a "person as a unified composite of soul and body,"[8] for whom Christ was born and died in the flesh, a concept completely foreign to the philosophical mindset of the Greeks of that day.

The fourth and final impact of *imago Dei* and the incarnation was a change in the individual and corporate approach to the poor. Jesus said in Luke 14:13–14, "On the contrary, when you host a banquet, invite those who are poor, maimed, lame, or blind. And you will be blessed, because they cannot repay you; for you will be repaid at the resurrection of the righteous" (HCSB). No longer were the poor ignored or simply cast away; Christ had shined a light upon them, and they were to be cared for because they too bore the image of God.

The word *compassion* literally means "to suffer together." *Imago Dei* and the incarnation provided the basis for one person to suffer with or alongside another. These doctrines forcefully displayed the divine view of the physical. In a sense, a person's physical condition mirrored the spiritual condition of all humans in general. Each person is in need of the Great Physician, not necessarily in a physical sense but rather in a spiritual sense. During

Jesus' ministry He often dealt with a person's spiritual needs by first addressing their physical needs. Likewise, as we minister to a person's physical needs in a tangible way, we provide opportunities for their spiritual health to be restored as well.

Possibly the greatest catalyst to the care of the sick and compassion toward them was the parable of the Good Samaritan (Luke 10:25–37) that Jesus shared with His disciples and the teachers of the Law. One of the teachers of the Law in discussions regarding obtaining eternal life inquired of Jesus the definition of "my neighbor." Jesus answered the man's question with a parable, a story of a Jew who was traveling from Jerusalem to Jericho when he was viciously attacked, robbed, beaten, and left to die. As he lay dying, a priest and a Levite saw him, but rather than stop to care for the man, they passed by, not wanting to get involved. The third traveler was a Samaritan man, a member of a race of people thoroughly despised by the Jews. All expectations were that he would likewise pass by as well. Surprisingly, the Bible says that the Samaritan had *compassion* on the wounded, bleeding man, and rather than pass by, he stopped, treated the man's injuries, bandaged him, and took him to a nearby inn for care and rest. The story does not end here, however. Jesus said that the Samaritan paid the innkeeper two denarii to continue to care for the injured Jew until he had recovered, promising to pay any additional costs associated with his care if warranted. Ferngren says that it was this parable which "furnished the pattern for the Christians' care of the sick: every stranger in need was a neighbor who bore the image of God and to whom the love of God ought to be demonstrated," irrespective of person.[9]

Servant Leadership

The servant leadership that was evident in the ministry of Jesus Christ must be an additional key characteristic of a health care program at a Christian university. In talking with His disciples, Jesus said, "the Son of Man did not come to be served, but to serve, and to give His life—a ransom for many" (Matt 20:28 HCSB). Jesus' life was marked by selfless devotion to His Father and to those He came to serve and redeem, ultimately resulting in His death on a cross at the hands of the Romans.

While most of us will unlikely be called to such a level of service to others, our lives should be marked by the same sacrificial love that Jesus demonstrated. Within a Christian university, this should be true of our faculty and their relationships with colleagues, students, and patients; this certainly must describe the attitude of our students and graduates toward their peers, faculty, and patients. Faculty, students, and healthcare providers who demonstrate the servant leadership of Christ are characterized by the same qualities that described Jesus. These include humility, patience, empathy, integrity, influence, and many others. Our programs should be centers of professionalism, not based on some ever-changing, worldly standard but rather based on the immutable standard set by Christ Himself. Our duty is to educate our students to be the best at their specific calling, while at the same time teaching them to emulate Christ in all that they say and do. In health care practice, a servant attitude toward patients affords those patients the dignity and respect deserving of those created in the image of God. The same may be said of the relationship with colleagues and other healthcare practitioners in a practice setting.

Innovation and Scholarship

A final key component should be scholarship and research. Christians have historically been a part of discovery and innovation. Only in the nineteenth century did interest in science and scientific inquiry begin to wane as Christians fell victim to the scientific revolution. Nancy Pearcey and Charles Thaxton in their book, *The Soul of Science: Christian Faith and Natural Philosophy*, point out that until this time, Christians had sought to determine the implications of their faith in all areas of inquiry. Christian faith only recently became a private matter, as though it had nothing to say about science and the workplace.[10] Names like Francis Bacon, Johannes Kepler, Blaise Pascal, Robert Boyle, Isaac Newton, and Michael Faraday, among many others, continue to grace the pages of science books today because of the great contributions they made to our present-day understanding of a variety of topics including mathematics, astronomy, physics, and chemistry. Kepler regarded his discoveries as simply him "thinking God's thoughts after Him." The inherent motivation was to uncover what God had hidden in creation in order to further understand how God had created originally. This, in turn, would provide us with the understanding needed to repair certain aspects of the created order that had been damaged as a result of the fall.

In health care today, this remains true; we are primarily concerned, however, with disease etiology, pathophysiology, and treatment. As Christians in the health care field, we are charged with using the talents God has given us to continue the earthly ministry of Jesus Christ. Part of this ministry was the physical healing of the sick and caring for the poor. Within our Christian universities is a tremendous concentration of knowledge, experience, and expertise that should be properly focused and utilized as one of the many means of continuing this ministry to the sick.

Christians have done a tremendous job historically of caring and providing for the sick and the poor. Since the first century, Christians have gained the reputation for being selfless in their devotion to victims of plagues and natural disasters, to the point of risking their safety as well as that of their own families.[11] While such loving devotion to our neighbors is precisely the response that should characterize true followers of Christ, such love can also be expressed through making contributions to the science that can provide lasting benefits to neighbors throughout our society. Faculty, students, and graduates of Christian university health care programs must be committed to expanding our knowledge base and understanding of a myriad of health-related topics and their applications to the greater ministry to which we are all called.

Within a health care curriculum, scholarship may take various forms. Students and faculty may be involved in laboratory-based discovery research, or they may be engaged in clinical or pedagogical/educational research. The means is less important than the end. Our energies must be focused on providing new and innovative ideas and opportunities that may find application within the field of health care to help alleviate the pain and suffering often associated with sickness. Regardless of the specific area of inquiry, students should be trained and given the opportunity to analyze and think scientifically. With the skills acquired within such an academic program, they will be more likely to enter their specific field of practice with the observational ability and knowledge to identify areas of need and to be innovators, problem solvers, and leaders required to meet the need.

Historic Christianity and Health Care

A brief look at the approach Christians and great Christian thinkers have historically taken to health care may provide a better understanding of a truly biblical approach to caring for the sick.[12] A philanthropic spirit arose quickly within the early church. As mentioned previously, the first noted occurrence of mutual concern for the poor, sick, and needy is found in the book of Acts. Luke, the physician, relates the corporate response to the teachings of the apostles following the day of Pentecost. Immediately upon hearing of what Christ had done for them, they sold their possessions and gave their earnings to the apostles to be distributed to the poor and those in need. With the sudden exponential growth of the church, the need soon arose for a more systematic and organized means to minister to the less fortunate. The apostles selected seven men—Stephen, Philip, Prochorus, Nicanor, Timon, Parmenas, and Nicolas—and gave them the responsibility of overseeing the ministry to the poor and needy. With this separation of duties, the church and its newly established philanthropic ministry flourished. Later, the ministry began to expand beyond Jerusalem, with the local church sending relief supplies to neighboring Judea as a means of providing support during an anticipated famine. It was these early movements in the infant church that resulted in the development and systemization of health care and care for the poor.

Over the next two centuries, although Christians remained the targets of attacks and unfettered persecution, their care for the sick continued nevertheless. As plagues caused widespread death and sickness throughout Northern Africa, Europe, and the Middle East, Christians gained reputations of caring for and ministering to the sick and infirm. They were often called *Parabolani* or reckless ones because of their fervent dedication to those stricken with the plague and often abandoned by their families.[13] Their devotion and service to the sick were the direct result of their calling in Christ and their loose hold on this world. Because of their faith in Jesus Christ, they were certain that death had no grasp on them. Death was simply a means of gaining their salvation in Christ. Dionysius the Great wrote of their commitment to care for the sick and dying.

> Certainly very many of our brethren, while, in their exceeding love and brotherly-kindness, they did not spare themselves, but kept by each other, and visited the sick without thought of their own peril, and ministered to them assiduously, and treated them for their healing in Christ, died from time to time most joyfully along with them, lading

> themselves with pains derived from others, and drawing upon themselves their neighbors' diseases, and willingly taking over to their own persons the burden of the sufferings of those around them. And many who had thus cured others of their sicknesses, and restored them to strength, died themselves, having transferred to their own bodies the death that lay upon these.[14]

The apostle Paul had written earlier that salvation meant eventually to be absent from the body (dead) and present with the Lord (2 Cor 5:8). Cyprian, Bishop of Carthage, addressed a letter to fellow believers who were troubled by the number of Christians being killed by the disease. He argued that the disease was a plague to the enemies of Christ, but to the followers of Christ it was a means unto salvation. It was a vehicle that took them to a place of eternal rest and refreshment while simultaneously taking the unrighteous to punishment.[15] For the follower of Christ, death was not to be feared because Jesus had defeated it through His resurrection from the dead. Paul wrote that victory over death had been granted by God through Jesus Christ (1 Cor 15:54–57). It was the church, the body of Christ, that provided the necessary care to the victims of the plagues throughout the first three centuries and beyond. Ferngren concludes, "No charitable care of any kind, public or private, existed apart from Christian diaconal care because there was no religious, philosophical, or social basis for it."[16]

The commitment to care for the sick and poor and the organizational structure to do so in the first century provided a firm foundation for organized care over the next two centuries. Local churches and monasteries continued to provide care to those in need. In AD 313 Emperor Constantine issued the Edict of Milan, which legalized Christianity throughout the Roman Empire. This proclamation afforded Christians the protection they had yet to experience and provided an unparalleled opportunity for the growth of the church and, likewise, its ministry to the sick. In the short years immediately following the edict, a number of small ministries arose to care for travelers, orphans, the elderly, and the poor. In the latter half of the fourth century, Basil the Great of Caesarea, who was widely known for his philanthropic spirit, opened the Basiliad in Caesarea, arguably the first hospital in the Roman Empire. While significantly different than a modern hospital, the Basiliad was a massive complex with facilities devoted to the care of the poor, orphans, elderly, travelers, homeless, lepers, and sick. Although Christians had been providing for these groups since the first century, the Basiliad represented the first time that care was provided to all at a central location. Gregory of Nazianzen, in his funeral oration of Basil (*Oration XLIII*), described the Basiliad as a "new city" where the sick and dying were treated with respect and dignity due them because of Christ. "Basil's care was for the sick, and the relief of their wounds, and the imitation of Christ, by cleansing leprosy, not by a word, but in deed."[17]

Early ministries of the church to the sick focused primarily on meeting the basic needs of the patient, providing them with shelter, food, clean water, and a place to rest. Medical care, in the tradition of the Greeks, was not available in many cases, especially outside of the larger metropolitan areas. Nevertheless, what care could be provided was supplied to those in need. With the opening of the Basiliad in Caesarea, Basil was able to assemble a trained medical staff capable of providing comfort and healing to the sick. While most Christians were supportive of human healing, there were a few who showed disdain for medicine as it supplanted the opportunity for divine healing. Basil countered that healing, regardless of the mechanism, was in fact divine in origin. In his *Ascetical Works*, he argued that the medical arts were a gift from God to man, just as agriculture was, to counteract the effects of the fall. God had granted to man the knowledge and understanding to facilitate healing in the sick. Furthermore, pharmaceutical care through the use of herbs, leaves, and fruits was a means of God's provision. He cautioned, however, that care for the physical body must be provided in concert with care for the soul.[18]

The church had historically viewed sickness as having spiritual cleansing power, capable of driving the afflicted to repentance. Paul wrote, "This is why many are sick and ill among you, and many have fallen asleep. If we were properly evaluating ourselves, we would not be judged, but when we are judged, we are disciplined by the Lord, so that we may not be condemned with the world" (1 Cor 11:30–32 HCSB). Proper care for the sick must, therefore, involve physical as well as spiritual treatment, providing healing for the whole person, not simply of the flesh. Early Christians well understood that man's primary sickness was spiritual in nature and required restoration and healing by the Great Physician through His forgiving and atoning work of redemption.

Physical sickness was temporal, while spiritual sickness was eternal.

With the protection afforded by the Roman government, Christianity flourished and expanded throughout the Roman Empire. With this expansion came the spread of hospitals and other institutions capable of caring for large numbers of sick, with the Basiliad as a model. John Chrysostom was responsible for the construction of a number of hospitals during the latter half of the fourth century. As the church grew, so did its ability to care for greater numbers of people, especially those outside the church. Chrysostom writes that help to the sick and the needy should be provided regardless of person because all people are created by and belong to God.[19] Monasteries became places of refuge and rest for weary travelers and the sick alike. This model continued until well into the eighteenth century, when privately funded hospitals began to emerge in Europe and England, complete with full medical staffs for the care of the physically ill.

Contemporary Health Issues

The disciples of Jesus Christ witnessed countless miraculous healings and physical restorations of the sick and lame both during the ministry of Jesus and at their very own hands in the early days of the church. The practice of medical healing was, at best, in its infancy. Limited understanding of human anatomy, physiology, pathophysiology, and disease etiology allowed physicians to practice the art of healing with some success. As Hector Avalos points out in his book, *Health Care and the Rise of Christianity*, it was the idea of caring versus curing that helped to distinguish early Christianity from the philosophies and competing religions of the Greco-Roman era in the treatment of members of society afflicted with chronic illnesses.[20]

Chronically ill people imposed a tremendous burden on society, on their families, and on the government. They were often considered "unproductive members of society" because they were shunned or unable to work. They were taxing on their families who were charged with their care. In many cases, efforts were undertaken to completely rid society of these burdensome and fruitless members, especially when their numbers became unmanageable. It was into this Greco-Roman mindset that Christianity was born. In Jewish law, lepers were considered unclean and ordered to live apart from other members of society until they had been healed and deemed clean by the priest. Yet, during the ministry of Jesus, a common theme was His association with lepers, even to the point of eating with them and physically touching them to restore their health. This ushered in a completely new mindset toward those with chronic physical diseases or disorders.

Because of the divine imperative to care for the sick, the church took upon itself the business of providing basic care and provision for those with a multitude of ailments. Ultimately the goal was physical healing, but the early church recognized that this was not always possible for a variety of reasons. As such the penultimate goal became one of relief and compassion. Whether the patient was sick, terminally ill, or chronically ill was immaterial. Because each one was created in the image of God and because God through Christ had shown compassion on His people, they in turn would use the resources at their disposal and the limited skills afforded to them to care for and show compassion toward those who were sick or poor.

Many of the same issues faced by early Christians still exist today. Although our understanding of disease and the disease process has grown exponentially over the past 2,000 years, our world is still plagued by chronic disease, chronic disorders, and a myriad of other health-related concerns. Our contemporary society continues to wrestle with related issues such as euthanasia; the chronically ill; unwanted pregnancies and abortion; and care for the elderly, handicapped, and the poor. Each of these specific matters and other related ones represent multifaceted, complex subjects for which society has worked for millennia to uncover how best to address them. While the answers to each one are certainly not trivial or even absolutely clear in every case, a great deal can be gained by examining how the church has historically related to these matters. As has been mentioned, the dominant view of man held by the early church originated not from human philosophical reasoning or through evolution of thought, but rather from the life and teachings of Jesus Christ and through God working in His creation. The Hebrew concept of *imago Dei* and the incarnation form the foundation on which human dignity, care, and compassion are built. Furthermore, the completely Christian idea of *agape* permeates the Christian's role, response, and responsibility to society and to the issues facing society today.

The Greek word *agapē* is used throughout the New Testament to describe God's love for man and man's love, in turn, toward his neighbor. Anders Nygren, in his seminal work *Agape and Eros*, formulates four main characteristics of "Divine Agape" as the basis for man's love for his neighbor. Though distinctions in the meaning of *agape* should not be overemphasized, Nygren's study still provides categories that can be applied to health care. (1) "Agape is spontaneous and unmotivated."[21] God's love toward man, displayed in both creation and in His Son Jesus Christ, is based solely on His own character and not on the qualities or qualifications of the object of His love. God is lacking in nothing and, therefore, does not seek love to fulfill a longing within Him. Rather, God loves because He is love. (2) "Agape is indifferent to value."[22] God's love is not extended to man because of any inherent value or worth. Instead He poured out His love in spite of who man was. "But God proves His own love for us in that while we were still sinners, Christ died for us!" (Rom 5:8 HCSB). (3) "Agape is creative."[23] Man has inherent value because God loves him. Objects that have no value in and of themselves become priceless when God's love is extended to them. (4) "Agape is the initiator of fellowship with God."[24] Man is powerless to establish fellowship with God apart from God acting initially. Man's inward desire, apart from the influence and work of the Holy Spirit, is to run from God rather than toward Him. These four key characteristics of "Divine Agape" provide a means to address the complex issues faced in health care today.

Health care is a field of service to one's neighbor. The "Divine Agape" informs the practice of health care and our approach to the complex issues faced by Christian health care providers and the church in general. As God has demonstrated His agape toward us, in spite of ourselves, we must in turn display agape to those whom we serve out of the abundance of love that God has infused into us. Our love toward others stems not from any qualities inherent within us. On the contrary, the love we show our neighbors flows from hearts of gratitude and thanksgiving to God for the value He assigned to us and for the worth He assigns to mankind in general, created in His image and the recipients of His divine grace. Martin Luther called this *quellende Liebe*, an overflowing love.[25] Likewise our love toward our neighbor is "unmotivated," in that devotion and compassion extended to them is irrespective of any qualities either inherent or absent within them. We love them because God loves them.

It is on these simple principles that we can base our approach to the issues facing health care today. Man has value because God has ascribed him value. As Adolf Harnack points out, the church took strong stands against abortion and other issues related to the "value and dignity of human life, refusing to allow it to be destroyed or dishonored at any stage of its development."[26] Likewise Ferngren contrasts the early church's view on abortion, exposure (abandonment), and suicide with those of the pagan culture of the day.[27] To the early church, the body and human life were to be protected and tended. The value of a person, regardless of age or stage of development, was not measured by their contributions to society or their tax revenue-generating ability. Instead value was of divine origin. Man was in no place to devalue or determine the value of another. His response was simply to love those whom God loved and to care for those in need, regardless of their ability to repay him or to contribute in any way. With regard to human life today, our approach should be similar. We are to show compassion to those who are in need of it, at any and all stages of life, with no thought of their inherent value or lack thereof to society.

Conclusion

Within the Christian university, we have the unique opportunity to impact the present as well as the future as we prepare students today for practice tomorrow. Properly done, our students will be situated and equipped not only to care for the sick but also to impact global health care in general as they influence and inform and become the decision makers of the future. Health care from a Christian standpoint is far more than simply caring for those in need. It is about working out the implications of the Christian faith as laid out in Scripture in each area related to patient care. We must view our patients, not as diabetics or cancer patients but as people created in the very image of God, placed before us, and in need of our compassion and skills, regardless of who they are. We must be diligent to seek God and to love God with all of our heart, soul, and mind continually. Out of this overwhelming desire for God will flow a desire to serve and care for those in need. As a result we will have spent our lives focused on and devoted to the two greatest commandments.

Questions for Further Reflection

1. The New Testament uses the Greek word *agape* to describe the love of God toward man and the love of man toward his neighbor rather than the Greek word, *eros*. In general, what characteristics of each of these words are found within our modern health care system? Is our current model based on *agape* or *eros*?
2. In what ways are the sin nature of man and sickness related? What were some of the ways in which the early church fathers viewed sickness?
3. What characteristics should be evident in a health care program at a Christian university that may or may not be present in a similar program at a secular university?
4. In what specific ways does the Christian faith inform the practice of health care?
5. How do the goals of our current health care system compare with the goals established in the early church?
6. How can Christian health care programs and institutions influence present and future practice?

Resources for Further Study

Avalos, Hector. *Health Care and the Rise of Christianity*. Peabody, MA: Hendrickson, 1999.

Crislip, Andrew T. *From Monastery to Hospital: Christian Monasticism and the Transformation of Health Care in Late Antiquity*. Ann Arbor: University of Michigan Press, 2005.

Dockery, David S. *Renewing Minds: Serving Church and Society through Christian Higher Education*. Nashville: B&H, 2007.

Ferngren, Gary B. *Medicine and Health Care in Early Christianity*. Baltimore: Johns Hopkins University Press, 2009.

Jonsen, Albert R. *A Short History of Medical Ethics*. New York: Oxford University Press, 2000.

Nygren, Anders. *Agape and Eros*. London: SPCK, 1953.

Pearcey, Nancy R., and Charles B. Thaxton. *The Soul of Science: Christian Faith and Natural Philosophy*. Wheaton, IL: Crossway, 1994.

Endnotes

[1] Richard Grossinger, *Planet Medicine: Origins*, 7th ed. (Berkeley, CA: North Atlantic Books, 2000), 295–303.

[2] Eusebius, *Church History*, X.IV.11–12, in Philip Schaff, ed., *Nicene and Post-Nicene Fathers*, second series (Peabody: Hendrickson, 1999), 1:371–72.

[3] Gary B. Ferngren, *Medicine and Health Care in Early Christianity* (Baltimore: Johns Hopkins University Press, 2009), 98–104.

[4] Kurt Niederwimmer, *The Didache: A Commentary*, trans. Linda M. Maloney (Minneapolis: Fortress, 1988), 88. *Ancient Christian Writers: The Works of the Fathers*, ed. Johannes Quasten and Joseph C. Plumpe, trans. James A. Kleist (New York: Paulist), 1948.

[5] Tertullian, *Apology*, IX, in Alexander Roberts and James Donaldson, eds., *Ante-Nicene Fathers*, first series (Peabody: Hendrickson, 1999), 3:25.

[6] Irenæus, *Against Heresies*, V.XIV.I, in Alexander Roberts and James Donaldson, eds., *Ante-Nicene Fathers*, first series (Peabody: Hendrickson, 1999), 1:541.

[7] Tertullian, *On the Flesh of Christ*, XVI, Ibid., 3:535.

[8] Gedaliahu G. Stroumsa, "*Caro salutis cardo:* Shaping the Person in Early Christian Thought," *History of Religions* 30:1 (1990): 44.

[9] Ferngren, *Medicine and Health Care in Early Christianity*, 144–45.

[10] Nancy R. Pearcey and Charles B. Thaxton, *The Soul of Science: Christian Faith and Natural Philosophy* (Wheaton: Crossway, 1994), xii.

[11] Rodney Stark, "Epidemics, Networks, and Conversion," in *The Rise of Christianity: A Sociologist Reconsiders History* (Princeton: Princeton University Press, 1996), 73–94.

[12] More detailed and systematic examinations of this topic can be found in Ferngren, *Medicine and Health Care in Early Christianity,* and Albert R. Jonsen, *A Short History of Medical Ethics* (New York: Oxford University Press, 2000).

[13] Jonsen, *A Short History of Medical Ethics,* 14.

[14] Dionysius, *Epistle XII to the Alexandrians*, in Roberts and Donaldson, *Ante-Nicene Fathers*, 6:108–9.

[15] Cyprian, *Treatise VII: On the Morality*, in Roberts and Donaldson, *Ante-Nicene Fathers*, 5:469–75.

[16] Ferngren, *Medicine and Health Care in Early Christianity*, 121.

[17] Gregory Nazianzen, *Oration XLIII.63: The Panegyric on Saint Basil*, in Schaff, *Nicene and Post-Nicene Fathers*, 7:416.

[18] Saint Basil, *Ascetical Works* in *The Fathers of the Church, a New Translation*, trans. M. Monica Wagner (Washington: Catholic University of America, 1962), 330–37.

[19] St. John Chrysostom, *Homily X.7–9 on Hebrews 6:7–8,* in Schaff, *Nicene and Post-Nicene Fathers*, first series, 14:416–17.

[20] Hector Avalos, *Health Care and the Rise of Christianity* (Peabody: Hendrickson, 1999), 66–71. Note: Avalos's book is an examination of the role that health care played in the growth and popularity of early Christianity. He does this by comparing the practices of early Christians with their non-Christian counterparts (Greco-Roman and Jewish traditions). Admittedly, Avalos does not hold necessarily to the truth of miracles in the New Testament. Rather, the rise

of Christianity was due in great part to the socioeconomic advantage it offered to those in need (95).

[21] Anders Nygren, *Agape and Eros*, trans. Philip S. Watson (London: The Society for Promoting Christian Knowledge, 1953), 75.

[22] Ibid., 77.

[23] Ibid., 78

[24] Ibid., 80.

[25] Ibid., 729–30.

[26] Adolf Harnack, *The Mission and Expansion of Christianity in the First Three Centuries,* trans. James Moffatt (New York: G. P. Putnam, 1908), 123.

[27] Ferngren, *Medicine and Health Care in Early Christianity,* 100–101.

20

Social Work and Counseling in the Christian Intellectual Tradition

Mary Anne Poe

A professional social worker or a counselor on any given day might encounter social problems that include poverty, mental illness, caregiving for elderly parents, lack of access to health care, juvenile crime and justice, child abuse, domestic violence, immigration, substance abuse, and myriad other causes of human distress. Social work and counseling are professions about helping people as well as the greater society muddle through these issues. How did a fundamental human impulse—helping—become professionalized? What are motivations for helping? What underlying values inform various approaches? What challenges do social workers and counselors have in the world of the twenty-first century? How can Christian professionals engage the culture and the academy effectively? This chapter will address these foundational questions as they shape the professional and academic landscape for social work and counseling.

The Nature of Helping

Part of what it means to be human is to be interdependent. We need each other. Helping is simply human action in response to need. We all help one another on a regular basis. No special academic preparation is required and good manners with basic social interaction skills suffice. Young children, for example, can be excellent helpers. Human relationships are constantly dependent on helping exchanges between people—the helper and the one being helped. Not all attempts to help do, in fact, help. *What* is given in help and *how* it is given can be more important in evaluating effectiveness of the help than merely the act of helping itself. Though usually help is given with the best of intentions, great harm can be done.[1] How to help effectively in a specific situation is much more complicated than many people suspect.

Alan Keith-Lucas, perhaps the most significant Christian thinker and social work practitioner of the twentieth century, published what has become a classic in social work literature on helping relationships, *Giving and Taking Help*.[2] He asserted that most people resist taking help that will significantly change their life. Keith-Lucas suggests that taking help requires four things: one must recognize a problem that cannot be solved alone, tell someone else about the problem, submit to their knowledge or expertise, and finally do what the helper suggests.[3] A skilled helper understands the challenges inherent in this process and why it is often resisted. People do not relish being in need, much less confessing it. Furthermore, submission is not the natural human impulse. The helper brings to those being helped the sense of reality of their situation—the fact of their need. This is not often a welcome truth. The effective helper offers an empathetic presence or what Keith-Lucas called "an act of loving imagination"[4] and finally the helper gives assurance of support in the relationship. The helping process as Keith-Lucas described it applies to any helping relationship whether professional or not and whether motivated by religious faith or not. But for the Christian, this description of the helping process coincides with a Christian view of the human need to be helped and the offering of God's help. Keith-Lucas relates the helper's roles to the functions of the Trinity. In God the Father, people are confronted with the reality or fact of their need. Jesus is the model of empathetic presence with His people, and the Holy Spirit offers the ongoing support.[5] The Scriptures tell the story of God's help resisted and rejected repeatedly by the ones He created as they are faced with the reality of their dire situation.

Christian believers have Jesus as a model for knowing how to be a helper and have instructions in Scripture about receiving help. Helpers, professional or not, are often surprised by the lack of receptivity to help and the apparent lack of gratitude for the help they have offered. This unresponsiveness can lead to discouragement and professional burn-out for the helper. The willingness and eagerness of the helper may or may not succeed in convincing those needing help. Parents of a child with a terminal illness may welcome the comforting presence and support of the hospice social worker and a woman fleeing a violent husband may experience extraordinary relief upon arriving at the safe shelter provided by the worker. Conversely, another couple may not welcome a relative stranger into their grievous ordeal and the vulnerable woman in her terror may be untrusting of anyone. The nature of the *relationship* between the helper and one in need is at least as important as *what* is offered in help. For this reason, all professional helpers focus on the helping relationship in order to do their work effectively. Persons in a relationship bring their particular worldviews to the relationship and that makes a difference.

Worldviews Make a Difference

David Sherwood, another well-known Christian thinker and social worker, articulates the importance of underlying philosophical presuppositions to how people behave. Helping professions, like all human endeavors, have foundational beliefs that shape action. Sherwood says that "values, practice, theories, assessments, intervention decisions, and action strategies are all shaped by our worldview assumptions and beliefs."[6] What is moral or intrinsically valuable to one may not be to another. He asserts that secular philosophies may claim to be defenders of the value of the individual, but that belief is not automatic or natural to humans. For this reason, Sherwood notes the importance of understanding where "values come from and what gives them moral authority and obligation."[7] Our faith or beliefs have an impact on what we do.

All human societies throughout history have developed strategies for helping those who are in need. Humans live within families and communities that offer support and care for the members. Life begins and often approaches the end with utter dependency and vulnerability. Not all societies have the same values that shape specific practices, but all societies organize systems designed to sustain the community. Societies can value life and aim to care for others at great cost to the whole of society or they can embrace values that measure the worth of life based on that life's contribution to the whole. Thus, extraordinary care can be given in one society to babies who are born with physical or mental disabilities while in other societies such babies are deemed cursed or useless and left to die. Some societies extend care for its aged members at great cost while other societies spare the community the hard work and cost of care by various methods of ending the lives of those aged members.

Social welfare history reveals the tension between valuing and care for life in all its circumstances and the need to manage the cost of such care to those without such need. How families and communities structure their responses to human dependency and vulnerability—or need—is fundamentally ordered by the values and worldview of those families and communities.

The Church and State in Social Welfare History

The Hebrew law and traditions that were precursors to the life of the church stood in stark contrast to the prevailing norms of surrounding cultures. God's law was concerned with family and community relationships. It emphasized truthfulness, justice, compassion, and faithfulness. Special care was expected for vulnerable and dependent populations—widows, orphans, foreigners, and the poor—in order that all could participate fully in the *shalom* of God. The Hebrew prophets continually warned of God's judgment when these laws were violated or when Israel simply fell into the worldly patterns of their surrounding cultures.

The ministry of Jesus began when He declared His purpose in the synagogue with a reading from the prophet Isaiah:

> The Spirit of the Lord is on Me,
> because he has anointed Me
> to preach good news to the poor.
> He has sent me to proclaim freedom to the captives
> and recovery of sight to the blind,
> to set free the oppressed,
> to proclaim the year of the Lord's favor. (Luke 4:18–19 HCSB)

His life and ministry model compassionate care for vulnerable and disadvantaged people and rebuke to those who claimed religious piety but did not demonstrate a love for God through love for others. Jesus affirmed the Great Commandment that the Hebrew people had been taught to love God with all their heart, soul, mind, and strength, and also that they were to love their neighbor as they loved themselves (Matt 22:37–39). And just before His death,

Jesus taught the disciples that when He returns and the nations are gathered before Him, He will distinguish between true and false followers by pointing to the way they treated others. His true followers will be those who have loved those considered the least in the eyes of the world, the hungry, sick, imprisoned, and strangers, because the way a nation or people treats the most vulnerable reflects the attitude and treatment toward Jesus Himself (Matt 25:31–46).

The early church continued to follow Jesus and the Hebrew law in concern for the poor and needy. Acts 4:35 declares that those in the earliest church shared what they had so that none had need. The church became a "haven of vital mutual aid within the pagan environment."[8] It was centered in the midst of the powerful Roman Empire and had no overt political power, but its practices of care for all had dramatic influence over time. Jesus had told His disciples that the world would know Him by the way they loved one another (John 13:35). This would perhaps be one of the most critical ways that the faith would spread around the world. In the first three centuries the church accomplished its mission of care in spite of government oppression. By the fourth century, society had been Christianized through Constantine's conversion and leadership. Church leaders during the patristic period addressed the abuses of wealth and power and instituted the beginnings of organized philanthropy. Basil of Caesarea (330–79), Gregory of Nazianzus (330–90), and John Chrysostom of Antioch (349–407) are well-known for their attention to mercy in their preaching and work.[9] No structured assistance existed for those in need until these early Christian bishops developed the first system of social services to care for the sick and the poor.[10]

Until the fifteenth and sixteenth centuries in the West, the church was the delivery system for social services.[11] In 1349, Parliament in England had passed the Statute of Labourers, which was the first time that government assumed responsibility for the poor legislatively. The law was primarily a means for managing the poor and controlling employment practices rather than extending charity.[12] The Elizabethan Poor Laws beginning in 1601 and amended regularly through the years were pivotal in shifting responsibility to the state in England while clergy and congregations continued to give leadership to the actual delivery of services. The Reformation of the church contributed to dividing and thus weakening Christendom's unified efforts toward helping the poor, resulting in a decentralization of the systems of organized aid. Government involvement grew through legislation and organization, and the role of the institutional church dimmed.[13] On the European continent, the Christian tradition also continued to inspire leadership in the delivery of social services. Both the Protestant sects as well as the Catholic Church understood that God required attention to human needs, even though the systems of care did not always reflect the compassion and grace of God.[14]

In the eighteenth and nineteenth centuries, the Christian church in Europe and the United States continued its provision of social services. William Wilberforce, inspired by Christian faith, worked through the Parliamentary process over many years to abolish slavery; George Whitefield and George Muller established orphanages; Jonathan Edwards advocated for just treatment of American Indians; church schools became stations on the Underground Railroad; Christians promoted reforms of prisons, the justice system, and labor practices.[15] This period fostered the beginnings of the modern social sciences of psychology and sociology as well.

Beginnings of Professional Social Work and Counseling

The late nineteenth century is generally considered the beginning of professional social work. Three distinct approaches to providing services emerged in social work—the Charity Organization Societies, the Social Settlement Movement, and establishment of large institutions to house vulnerable populations. These three approaches each developed out of ministries of the faith community.[16] The contribution of Christian faith to the origins of social work, however, has generally been neglected in histories of the profession.

The shift away from religious affiliation was gradual. Institutions of care for the poor, the aged, or the mentally ill developed originally under the auspices of Catholic or Protestant groups. The state began assuming responsibility for these institutions through boards of charity with "professionals" emerging as experts on administration and care. Such large institutions were the standard of care late into the twentieth century. As medical doctors and social scientists studied human behavior in these facilities, they began to formulate theories about human need and how to help. Sigmund Freud's characterization of religion as "infantile neurosis" is an example of the theories formulated during this time. Orthodox Christian thought and new Enlightenment thinking struggled with each other for authority to provide meaning to the outcomes of these studies. Scientific theories of human behavior and social problems were beginning to supplant the theological and moral explanations that had been accepted for centuries.[17]

Charity Organization Societies (COS) began in England in the mid-nineteenth century and delivered systematic care according to a "scientific" approach. The aim was to eliminate poverty by use of volunteers, "friendly visitors," who worked to reform the poor, teach life skills, and reduce dependency. The intent was well-meaning, but the often paternalistic and judgmental approach was demoralizing and insufficient. Mary Richmond, the administrator of the COS in Baltimore and Philadelphia, founded the first training schools. In 1904, the first school of social work in the United States was founded, the New York School of Philanthropy, what is now Columbia University School of Social Work. Richmond authored in 1917 what is generally considered the first social work textbook, *Social Diagnosis*.[18] Her work had begun in church activities and had impetus from her faith. What is now called "clinical social work" can be traced to the work of Mary Richmond. During the same period, analytic psychology was developing its clinical basis for counseling.[19]

The Social Settlement Movement, often associated with Jane Addams and Hull House in Chicago, was the third approach to practice in social work's history. It focused on the environmental and structural factors that cause poverty and other social problems. Where "friendly visitors" or early caseworkers had sought to reform the poor, social settlements organized communities, labor unions, sought government reform, and engaged in economic development and reform. They conducted their own scientific research to identify causation of problems and plan interventions related to unjust conditions. Jane Addams's social settlements eliminated direct religious teaching from their programs giving rise to the secularization of those services in contrast to the settlements which maintained a religious emphasis.[20]

Although the stated values of the social work profession reflected the prevailing values of the Judeo-Christian tradition, it was growing away from the rich Judeo-Christian tradition of service. The practice models and knowledge base reflected the views of the prevailing culture of scientific materialism. The three major approaches to social work practice merged in the early twentieth century to formalize the structure, purpose, and standards for the profession. People were typically motivated to action by religious faith, but the dominant cultural philosophical stance of scientific materialism shaped the practice. In some respects the desire to claim professional legitimacy by attaining a seat in the academy led away from the faith that had spawned the work.

In the twentieth century, meeting human needs through helping relationships spurred numerous subcategories of professions. Each of these professions has its own code of ethics, theoretical presuppositions, professional associations, processes, literature, and following. These professions found a way into university settings, gained credibility as professions, articulated clear purpose and values, and standardized practices. Some developed a distinctive professional identity relatively early, such as social work and psychology. While social work began with both an emphasis on practice with individuals as well as social change efforts through community organizing and advocacy, it trended toward a microfocus in practice. This was largely due to the rise of psychoanalytic theories, a medical or disease model of helping, funding focused on individuals and families rather than communities, and a Western focus on rugged individualism. Other professions developed to accommodate particular contexts or theoretical orientations, such as pastoral counseling or marriage and family therapy. Each is focused, though, on the helping relationship and the processes or transactions of helping. Each recognizes the necessity and relevance of values and ethics in practice and the power of values and ethics to shape helping relationships. Professionalization coincided with secularization. Philosophical traditions such as naturalism and materialism competed with the Christian and biblical perspectives that had undergirded social welfare practices for centuries.

An Example of Values that Shape One Helping Profession—Social Work

A set of six core values, as articulated by the National Association of Social Workers (NASW), gives direction to the profession of social work. They are (1) service, (2) social justice, (3) worth and dignity of persons, (4) importance of human relationships, (5) integrity, and (6) competence.[21] Any person familiar with values that define Christianity can see the correlation of the values of the social work profession and Christian faith and practice. An examination of each of these core values will demonstrate the congruence of Christian faith and practice with the profession of social work.

Service

Social work's first core value states, "The social workers' primary goal is to help people in need and to address social problems."[22] Social workers embrace the notion that the role of the professional is one of supporting and empowering the client, whether an individual, family, or whole community, to access available resources in order to sustain overall well-being. Social work professionals draw "on their knowledge, values, and skills to help people in need,"[23] but these are not to be used as agents of control or domination or coercion. Rather, social workers acknowledge the right and responsibility the client has to be free to make their own choices—self-determination. Jesus modeled this approach of service in numerous encounters with people along the way. When the rich young ruler asked for help, Jesus offered guidance and the man refused the help, going away sorrowfully. Jesus served those who were blind, lame, or sick by asking what they wanted or needed. The stories of the Good Samaritan and the Prodigal Son also illuminate helping another as an act of service, not control. Jesus said in Matt 20:26, "Whoever wants to be great among you must be your servant" (HCSB).

Social Justice

The NASW Code of Ethics states as a second core principle that "social workers challenge injustice."[24] They advocate for social change on behalf of vulnerable groups. Because professionals understand the power of oppression to dehumanize, they work to ensure access to resources and information and to advocate for meaningful participation in decision-making that has an impact on communities. The prophet Micah asserts that God has shown people what is required, "to act justly, to love faithfulness, and to walk humbly with your God" (Mic 6:8 HCSB). The prophet Isaiah stated that God's plan was for a world where "they will rebuild the ancient ruins; they will restore the former devastations; they will renew the ruined cities . . . for I the LORD love justice" (Isa 61:4,8a HCSB). Jesus defined His mission in the inaugural sermon in the synagogue after reading from this same passage in the book of Isaiah. And Jesus says in His Sermon on the Mount, "But seek first the kingdom of God and His righteousness [justice]" (Matt 6:33). Bringing justice, the opportunity and challenge to restore right relationships,[25] was Jesus' purpose and that which He commissions His followers to undertake.

Dignity and Worth of the Person

The NASW Code of Ethics states that social workers "respect the inherent dignity and worth of the person."[26] People should be treated with respect and compassion. Those whom social workers serve should be empowered and encouraged to be socially responsible as respect for persons suggests both a responsibility to the individual and also to the broader society. People should not be allowed to harm others or the general well-being of a community. It is a dual responsibility. Conflict resolution and mediation are roles for social workers in pursuit of a culture that respects the value of life. The Scriptures teach that humans are "remarkably and wonderfully made" (Ps 139:14 HCSB) and that Jesus came that we "may have life and have it in abundance" (John 10:10 HCSB). The gospel story proclaims the value of each person as Christ died for all that all might be reconciled to God (John 3:16; 2 Cor 5:18–19; Col 1:20–22).

The Importance of Human Relationships

The profession of social work in its Code of Ethics says that professionals "recognize the central importance of human relationships."[27] Healthy relationships between and among people promote the overall well-being of individuals, families, groups, organizations, and communities. Strengthening relationships is a key to whatever kind of social work practice one conducts. Jesus said that the most important thing that people can do is to love one another, even their enemies (Matt 5:44; 22:39; John 13:35; 15:13). People demonstrate love for God by love for others, even love for those with whom there is disagreement.

Integrity

"Social workers behave in a trustworthy manner"[28] is the fifth core principle. Integrity is the quality of behaving according to the standards of the profession so that trust and respect can be established. Acting with honesty and responsibly ensures ethical practice that does no harm to those served by the professional. Certainly the Scriptures teach as a principle that Christians should live with integrity—not presenting ourselves as something we are not and being truthful and trustworthy (Phil 2:14–18; 4:8–9).

Competence

The profession requires that social workers "practice within their areas of competence and develop and enhance their professional expertise."[29] The Scriptures teach that whatever is done should be done with enthusiasm, as though it was being done for the Lord (Col 3:17). While the Bible says that we can do all things through Christ who gives us strength (Phil 4:13), it also affirms difference in gifts and abilities and assignments. Part of practicing within one's area of competence is representing oneself honestly to those who might be served and doing the hard work of intellectual development to gain the knowledge needed to be effective.

Human Service Professions: Both Art and Science

A complex and sometimes confusing assortment of separate professions are providers of help to meet social and emotional needs in the modern world. Psychiatry and psychiatric nursing grew out of the medical arena. Educational systems developed school counseling. Religious systems cultivated pastoral counseling and clinical pastoral education. And social work has both a clinical practice focus as well as community development and organizing in order to address social welfare needs. One can use the Internet browser and search for "counselors" or "counseling services" and become overwhelmed by the options. These various helping professions have essentially the same purpose or goal, use similar techniques and activities, rely on the same research and interdisciplinary knowledge about human behavior, and strive for the same legitimacy as professions. The nuances that distinguish these groups are often not understood by the general public and may seem unimportant or irrelevant.

The historical relationship among all of these human service professions and the underlying philosophical assumptions about human nature and the world that created them can be characterized as a dynamic and complex dialectic between the worlds of science and that of the arts. The scientific world in which we live uses sophisticated research methodologies in an attempt to eliminate subjective bias in understanding human well-being. Science aims to drill down to the most basic facts. We might ask the question, "What triggers a seemingly irrational violent act and how can we predict which person will be the one to commit that act?" The scientific mind tries to simplify and quantify and predict behavior by systematically identifying and eliminating the factors that are undesirable. Thus, the counselor can assess behavior in a client and reduce the presenting problem to a diagnosis located in the latest *Diagnostic and Statistical Manual of Mental Disorders* (DSM) published by the American Psychiatric Association.[30] Treatment approaches correspond to the diagnosis.

Scientific methods are important tools for practice but leave gaping holes in regard to the relational and personal aspect of work. Science cannot account for all the factors that influence behavior. Helping relationships, thus, are often more art than science. Humans are complicated and multifaceted. Behavioral patterns are unpredictable. The innumerable factors that influence behavior cannot be tracked and measured in the same way that a mathematician or physicist can solve their problems. Each person is unique. The life experiences, family and friend connections, biological, spiritual and psychological makeup resemble a character in a novel with layers of subjectivity and creativity and unpredictability waiting to unfold. Each person presents as a painted work of art, a musical composition, or literary masterpiece unfinished and perhaps stuck or damaged in production. The scientific method cannot account for or quantify these more subjective aspects of behavior.

Naturalism, socialism, humanism, and capitalism have been dominant philosophies of the past century. These philosophies value personhood in a distinctly different way than Christian faith.

No real basis exists for valuing life apart from the contribution that life can make to society if the material world is the extent of reality and if production and profit are the primary goals of society. Vulnerable and dependent populations serve no purpose; they drain resources and pose an onerous burden. Christian orthodoxy, though, stands in stark contrast to these philosophies and maintains that each person has intrinsic worth as a child of God and with a destiny to fulfill.

The same century that banished the "story" from literature, the rhymes from poetry, and the forms from art had also banished the human story and its art and meaning from the social sciences. The person whose life painted delusions or splattered bouts of depression was reduced to a DSM diagnosis. The mechanics of help often became automated and impersonal.

The twenty-first century is beginning to recover from the long artless century and is recapturing the power of history and story and context. In recent decades, some of the allure of naturalism and scientific materialism has given way to what is called post-modernity. This shift in culture opened the way for spirituality and subjectivity of personal experience to re-establish its place in the academy and society. Psychology, social work, and counseling professions have shifted toward a new attentiveness to personhood and the spiritual and subjective influences on behavior. Narrative therapy is now popular with the emphasis on the meaning attached to one's "story." This culture shift has not meant adherence to the tenets of biblical Christianity, but it does allow space for spiritual life to be recognized as legitimate and credible.

Professional disciplines, by their nature, are interdisciplinary. One needs to understand scientific reasoning and methodologies both to uncover new knowledge and to use what research knowledge has already been developed by the professions. The humanities assist in grasping the quality of human behavior in history, politics, economics, music, and art. Literature, perhaps the most revealing of human behavior among all disciplines, exposes mystifying characteristics of human relationships and how they can go wrong. A novelist can plumb the depths of human pain, grief, and suffering as well as human motivations such as greed and envy and love that drive to action. The art and science of professional life confirms the value of broad liberal arts education for the professional. Often, the challenge for Christians in helping professions is to keep both the science and the art in the helping process.

Engaging the Culture

Human service professionals daily encounter the complex realities of human life and relationships. They must make decisions and interact on the basis of their best judgment and knowledge about the issues presented to them. Our own worldview, faith, and personal experiences of life are constant companions in our work along with our professional education. In the course of just one day, a professional social worker or counselor might face several diverse client situations that manifest deep moral ambiguities. How does the Christian professional engage these? How do professional role and personal values and beliefs intersect in practice? And how can Christian core beliefs be a filter through which we practice?[31] The Bible is a helpful guide in all situations, but it does not sort out the complicated twists and turns in all human relationships and it does not provide a script for the counselor. The answers for the helping professional are not to be found in simple legalism. Moral relativism does not resolve the above issues either.[32]

On a daily basis, helping professionals do their work focused on particular problems with varying degrees of moral clarity. It is always right to protect a child from vicious abuse, but what if, in your assessment, the parent-child relationship can be made healthy through supportive services, counseling, and supervision? Should the child be removed from the home and placed into a stranger's care? Practice experiences and solid knowledge based on scientific research serve to inform the professional's judgment in such cases, and whether or not the professional is a Christian may not really matter. Social workers with no Christian faith can make excellent clinical assessments and decisions on behalf of a vulnerable child. So what does Christian faith bring to the helping relationship? What would a Christian do or think differently than the non-Christian in any of these examples? The context out of which a professional works is one important factor that shapes practice.

Contexts for Practice

Social services in congregational settings or in faith-based organizations continue to serve the broader community in extraordinary and diverse ways. Most congregations work to improve the well-being of their communities and encourage members to be fully engaged in service in their own individual lives. Cnaan and Boddie concluded that people in need most often seek help from the multitude of faith-based groups supplying aid.[33] "Compassionate conservatism," part of George W. Bush's campaign platform for his presidency, indicates a public perception of and attraction to the idea that aid is often best left to the religious or private sector. Clearly, social welfare in the modern world is still dependent on religious groups offering support to the efforts so opportunities for professional helping in religious contexts exist.

The growth of Christian counseling in the twentieth century is to some extent a result of the recognition that the faith and worldview orientation of the helper are important to those being helped. Its rise can be attributed both to the fear that vulnerable people seeking help may be led astray toward secular thought, moral relativism, or pop psychology and a desire to seek biblical insight for the problem at hand. Seward Hiltner's book *Pastoral Counseling,* published in 1949, was perhaps the first in a series of defining texts for a specifically Christian approach to counseling as a profession. Wayne Oates's *An Introduction to Pastoral Counseling*, Jay Adams's *Competent to Counsel*, Larry Crabb's *Basic Principles of Biblical Counseling*, and Gary Collins's *Christian Counseling* each offered in their time a counter-voice to the prevailing secular psychologies guiding most professional counseling.[34] Christian schools and training programs and specifically Christian counseling agencies proliferated in the past half-century.

Christian professionals also practice in a multitude of secular environments and have opportunity for significant influence in these settings. Christians filled with the Holy Spirit bring that reality into every relationship whether God is mentioned or not. This is not inconsequential. Spiritual help is sometimes merely presence and quiet prayer. Professionals of faith can draw on the personal resources that come from their faith to practice with confidence and compassion and can be invigorated to work toward justice as the Bible directs. Christians who work in secular contexts also have opportunity to influence and help colleagues, to advance knowledge and research in the field, and to challenge beliefs about human behavior and culture that may conflict with Christian faith. Some research has been done about the relationship of spirituality and well-being, but this is a field ripe for Christians to pursue. When conclusive evidence resulting from rigorous scientific research methodology is presented that supports the effectiveness of spiritual intervention, Christians can advocate for more societal support for such interventions. In secular arenas, Christians can also be translators and mediators of spiritual and biblical models of helping with other approaches. If all Christians abandon the secular helping professions, Christian faith loses a voice and opportunity for influence in the world. Jesus prays for His disciples as they are in the world that they would be protected from the evil one but His intention for believers is that they be light to the world (Matt 5:14–16; John 17:15).

How Faith Informs Practice

Fundamental core beliefs of the Christian faith furnish an orientation for one's character and actions. They are a lens through which we make decisions in practice. We need not apologize for relying on core beliefs as all people rely on worldview assumptions. Indeed, Christians can be people of integrity and authenticity by understanding and grappling with their core beliefs and the complexities encountered in human relationships.

Opportunities for Christians in human services to engage their professional culture and the academy arise in at least three arenas. The most basic and important for the Christian is to be knowledgeable and conversant with one's own core beliefs and worldview and that of the broader culture in which one lives. Many professionals, Christian or not, do not do the hard work of drilling down with intellectual rigor to their core to address foundational questions. Why should I care? Why do I care? What kind of world do I live in? Why is every person of infinite value? Why be truthful, a person of integrity? It is actually very difficult to have this discourse with oneself. Having conversation with those around us and especially those of differing views can be the most effective means of sharpening one's insight into foundational belief systems. Different starting points result in different outcomes, and the journey along the way matters as well as the destination.

A second arena of opportunity for Christians to engage their academic and professional culture concerns how we think about social issues in a particular time and place. What should be the norms for society? What are the moral and relational demands of Christian faith? Christians have struggled through the centuries with how freedom in Christ is operationalized in the particulars of our lives. The apostle Paul addresses issues about dietary norms and gender roles that perplexed the early Christians. His New Testament epistles reflect different cultural issues in different cities of the time. Cultural norms about many things have changed through the centuries and vary from one place to another. Some examples of how behavioral norms in human relationships have changed are instructive here. For much of Christian history, slavery was considered a normal type of human relationship. It took centuries for Christians to determine that the very idea of "ownership" of persons violated the fundamental premise of what God intended in human relationships. The Old Testament law had provided for a Sabbath every seven years in which all Hebrew slaves would be set free.[35] The necessity for some to sell themselves to more prosperous neighbors because of poverty did not mean they should lose forever access to their own productive resources and be prohibited from free participation in the community. The fact that the Hebrew people did not generally follow this law does not negate its legitimacy. In fact, the Babylonian captivity may have resulted at least in part from Israel's disobedience to God's instructions about the Sabbath years.[36] Modern-day slavery, called human trafficking, continues to be a focus of work for human service professionals. They advocate for policies that constrain trafficking, work to rescue victims, and provide after-care in the form of counseling.

Another transformation in cultural ideas about human relationships concerns marriage and the role and status of women. Historically, women have been considered "property" of their fathers and then husbands. Women in the West are now equal in relationship to men in regard to property ownership, employment, voting rights, opportunity to serve in elected public office, and many other ways. American Christians would not ever choose to return to an earlier normative cultural pattern for women and marriage relationships, but exactly what God intends for women in relation to men is still contested in many Christian circles. The broader Enlightenment culture has equalized the roles of men and women more thoroughly than many conservative, evangelical churches that assert that men should be the leaders in home and church and maintain restrictions on what women are allowed to do. Human service professionals navigate the cultural ambiguity about gender roles around myriad issues such as domestic violence, crisis pregnancy, and when conducting marriage and family therapy.

Societal norms cannot be reduced to simplistic categories of one philosophical system versus another or Christian faith versus nonfaith. They do, however, illustrate how social issues such as these create challenges to Christians in these professions. Is one's allegiance primarily to one's faith or to the norms of one's professional affiliation? And does Christian faith lead everyone to exactly the same conclusions about what should be "normal" or "accepted"?

A third arena of opportunity for engaging culture, especially academic and professional culture, concerns the methodologies or techniques of practice. Two people might agree at a core belief level that every citizen should have access to basic health care. These two people may develop strikingly different approaches, though, about how a society should organize for this goal. Whose responsibility is it? Should the government assert its place in this social welfare arena by legislating that all citizens have health care access, or should individuals be responsible to purchase insurance and allow free markets to run their course? Current dialogue about the role of government in the provision of services offers a way to be engaged in solving social problems. On a clinical level, multiple counseling methods and theories can be congruent with Christian faith, but practitioners can use these methods with very different philosophical presuppositions about them. Whether a practitioner chooses to use cognitive behavioral therapy, narrative therapy, or psychodynamic techniques may not matter as much as the nature of the helping relationship itself that is formed in a therapeutic environment. Christian faith does not necessarily dictate that one therapeutic approach exists that is "right."[37] Both Christian and non-Christian professionals can use multiple strategies for how to accomplish goals.

Conclusion

The relationship of helping professions, such as social work and counseling, with Christian faith and practice can be compared to a tug of war between the truth claims of Christian orthodoxy and the claims of secular philosophy. Jesus described this tug of war in the prayer for His followers, "I am not praying that You take them out of the world but that You protect them from the evil one. They are not of the world, as I am not of the world" (John 17:15–16 HCSB). We have to know how to negotiate the push and pull of competing truth claims and practices. Options for those interested in a professional career of helping are numerous and this tug of war can be part of the experience for the professional. One can choose to work in a secular context where Christian faith and practice will necessarily be more implicit, or one can work in a faith-based context in which religious symbols and language can be openly and freely expressed. Both kinds of contexts need the presence of people of faith who have grappled with their worldview assumptions and can think critically about how to help effectively. Christian history is replete with examples of well-intentioned efforts to help that resulted in great harm. The context by itself does not make helping effective or ensure sound practice. The willingness of the helper to be reflective, knowledgeable, compassionate, faithful, and engaged in a responsible way in the helping relationship will be what makes the difference.

Questions for Further Reflection

1. Reflect on your own experiences of helping and being helped through the years. Have you been eager to help others? Is it easy for you to accept or ask for help? Is Christian help any different from other help? If so, how?
2. How and why do the beliefs we have motivate or direct us toward helping? If anyone can be a helper, whether Christian or not, what is the motivation beyond a particular faith?
3. If Christianity historically has provided reason and motivation toward providing social welfare services, what are the challenges for Christian faith and helping in today's world?

4. What are some of the contemporary truth claims or helping methods that you might find most challenging in a helping profession? What are the tensions and difficulties often present between religious orientations toward helping and secular orientations?
5. Who is responsible for the poor and vulnerable in society? Is it the church's responsibility alone or primarily? What is the responsibility of "civil society" for social welfare? What theological, political, economic, or social arguments might support your views?
6. How have the political, economic, religious, cultural, and social contexts through history shaped social welfare practices? What do you think the future holds if these contexts make a difference?

Resources for Further Study

Books

Cheydleur, John R. *Called to Counsel: A Counseling Skills Handbook.* Wheaton, IL: Tyndale House, 1999.

Clinton, Timothy, and George Ohlschlager. *Competent Christian Counseling.* Vol. 1. Colorado Springs: Waterbrook, 2002.

Clinton, Timothy, Archibald Hart, and George Ohlschlager, eds. *Caring for People God's Way: Personal and Emotional Issues, Addictions, Grief, and Trauma.* Nashville: Thomas Nelson, 2005.

Garland, Diana S. Richmond, ed. *Church Social Work: Helping the Whole Person in the Context of the Church.* Botsford, CT: North American Association of Christians in Social Work, 1992.

Hodge, David. *Spiritual Assessment: Helping Handbook for Helping Professionals.* Botsford, CT: North American Association of Christians in Social Work, 2003.

Hugen, Beryl, and T. Laine Scales, eds. *Christianity and Social Work: Readings on the Integration of Christian Faith and Social Work Practice.* 3rd ed. Botsford, CT; North American Association of Christians in Social Work, 2008.

Keith-Lucas, Alan. *Giving and Taking Help.* Rev. ed. Botsford, CT: North American Association of Christians in Social Work, 1994.

———. *The Poor You Have with You Always: Concepts of Aid to the Poor in the Western World from Biblical Times to the Present.* Botsford, CT: North American Association of Christians in Social Work, 1989.

———. *So You Want to Be a Social Worker: A Primer for the Christian Student*. Botsford, CT: North American Association of Christians in Social Work, 1985.

Sherwood, David, ed. *Charitable Choice: The Challenge and Opportunities for Faith-Based Community Service*. Botsford, CT: North American Association of Christians in Social Work, 2000.

Unruh, Heidi, and Ronald J. Sider. *Saving Souls, Serving Society: Understanding the Faith Factor in Church-Based Social Ministry*. New York: Oxford University Press, 2005.

Journals

International Journal of Practical Theology
Journal of Pastoral Care
The Journal of Social Work Values and Ethics; website, http://www.socialworker.com/jswve/.
Journal of Psychology and Christianity
Pastoral Psychology
Prism, Journal of Evangelicals for Social Action
Social Work and Christianity, Journal of the North American Association of Christians in Social Work
Sojourners

Websites and Associations

American Association of Christian Counselors: www.aacc.net
National Association of Social Workers: www.naswdc.org
North American Association of Christians in Social Work: www.nacsw.org
Society for Christian Psychology: http://www.christianpsych.org

Endnotes

[1] See Steve Corbett and Brian Fikkert, *When Helping Hurts: How to Alleviate Poverty without Hurting the Poor and Yourself* (Chicago: Moody, 2009), for a fuller exploration of how harm can be done in the helping relationship, even when motivated by Christian faith.

[2] Alan Keith-Lucas, *Giving and Taking Help* (Chapel Hill, NC: University of North Carolina Press, 1972). Keith-Lucas, perhaps more than any other individual, published books and articles about how Christian faith informs social work practice. His life was celebrated in fall 2010 upon the anniversary of the North American Association of Christians in Social Work, which he helped to found.

[3] Alan Keith-Lucas, *So You Want to Be a Social Worker: A Primer for the Christian Student* (St. David's, PA: North American Association of Christians in Social Work, 1985), 14. Also, see *Giving and Taking Help* by Keith-Lucas for a more thorough discussion of this.

[4] Keith-Lucas, *So You Want to Be a Social Worker*, 15.

[5] Ibid., 15.

[6] David Sherwood, "The Relationship between Beliefs and Values in Social Work Practice: Worldviews Make a Difference," in *Christianity and Social Work: Readings in the Integration of Christian Faith and Social Work Practice*, ed. Beryl Hugen and T. Laine Scales, 3rd ed. (Botsford, CT: North American Association of Christians in Social Work, 2008), 9.
[7] Ibid., 15.
[8] Ernst Troeltsch, *The Social Teaching of the Christian Churches* (Chicago: University of Chicago Press, 1960), 134.
[9] Susan R. Holman, ed., *Wealth and Poverty in Early Church and Society* (Grand Rapids: Baker, 2008). Also see Peter Brown, *Poverty and Leadership in the Later Roman Empire* (Hanover, NH: University Press of New England, 2002); D. J. Constantelos, *Byzantine Philanthropy and Social Welfare*, 2nd ed. (New Rochelle, NY: Aristide D. Caratzas, 1991), and Rodney Stark, *The Rise of Christianity: A Sociologist Reconsiders History* (Princeton, NJ: Princeton University Press, 1996).
[10] Cheryl Brandsen and Paul Vliem, "Justice and Human Rights in Fourth Century Cappadocia" in Hugen and Scales, *Christianity and Social Work*, 60.
[11] Philip R. Popple and Leslie Leighninger, *Social Work, Social Welfare, and American Society*, 2nd ed. (Boston: Allyn and Bacon, 1993), 5.
[12] R. Dolgoff and D. Feldstein, *Understanding Social Welfare: A Search for Social Justice*, 7th ed. (Boston: Allyn and Bacon, 2007). Also see Mary Anne Poe, "Good News for the Poor: Christian Influences on Social Welfare," in Hugen and Scales, *Christianity and Social Work*, 105–18.
[13] Popple and Leighninger, *Social Work, Social Welfare and American Society*.
[14] Poe, "Good News for the Poor," in Hugen and Scales, *Christianity and Social Work*.
[15] Ibid.
[16] Popple and Leighninger, *Social Work, Social Welfare, and American Society*, 98.
[17] Todd Stanfield, *Causes, Cures, and Compliance*. For more reading on the relationship of social science/medicine and religion issues see Dan Blazer, *Freud vs. God* (Downers Grove, IL: InterVarsity, 1998), and Armand Nicholi, *The Question of God: C. S. Lewis and Sigmund Freud Debate God, Love, Sex, and the Meaning of Life* (New York: Free Press, 2002).
[18] Popple and Leighninger, *Social Work, Social Welfare, and American Society*.
[19] Keith-Lucas, *Giving and Taking Help*, 165.
[20] Sarah S. Kreutziger, "Social Work's Legacy: The Methodist Settlement Movement," in Hugen and Scales, *Christianity and Social Work*, 87.
[21] The National Association of Social Workers (NASW) developed a Code of Ethics to provide standards of practice for its members. The entire Code of Ethics can be found at http://www.naswdc.org/pubs/code/default.asp.
[22] Ibid.
[23] Ibid.
[24] Ibid.
[25] Mary Anne Poe, "Fairness Is Not Enough: Social Justice as Restoration of Right Relationships," in Hugen and Scales, *Christianity and Social Work*, 161–78.
[26] NASW Code of Ethics.

[27] Ibid.

[28] Ibid.

[29] Ibid.

[30] The American Psychiatric Association updates regularly the *Diagnostic and Statistical Manual of Mental Disorders*. It was first published in 1952 and is currently revising for the fifth edition. It identifies or classifies each mental health disorder and its presenting symptoms that can be used for diagnosis and treatment.

[31] Rick Chamiec-Case, "Exploring the Filtering Role of Christian Beliefs and Values in the Integration of Christian Faith and Social Work Practice," in Hugen and Scales, *Christianity and Social Work*, 93–104.

[32] David Sherwood, "Doing the Right Thing: A Christian Perspective on Ethical Decision-Making in Social Work Practice," in Hugen and Scales, *Christianity and Social Work*, 333–50.

[33] Ram Cnaan and Stephanie C. Boddie, "Philadelphia Census of Congregations and Their Involvement in Social Service Delivery," *Social Service Review* 75 (2001): 559–80.

[34] Timothy Clinton and George Ohlschlager, eds., *Competent Christian Counseling, Volume One* (Colorado Springs: Waterbrook Press, 2002), xiii.

[35] See Leviticus 25 and Deuteronomy 15.

[36] Ronald J. Sider, *Just Generosity: A New Vision for Overcoming Poverty in America* (Grand Rapids: Baker Books, 2007), 79. Also see Leviticus 26 and 2 Chronicles 36.

[37] See Stanton Jones, *Modern Psychotherapies: A Comprehensive Christian Appraisal* (Downers Grove, IL: Intervarsity Press, 1991), for a comparison of practice models and theories in relation to a Christian worldview.

21

The Study of Business at the Christian University

Emily Lean

It seems that the media headlines of today are continually filled with the harmful results of unethical business practices. The poor decisions made by a few have had a large, negative impact on the masses not only in our own economy but in marketplaces all over the world. If we identify ourselves as a Christian nation, how then can we explain the situation in which we currently find ourselves? As Christians, we are called to be salt and light to the world (Matt 5:13–16). That is to say, we are not to be separate from society but rather we have the responsibility to influence society for the good. With regard to an undergraduate education, this responsibility goes beyond simply offering one or two ethics courses within our schools of business; it extends to developing an atmosphere of learning in which a Christian perspective is integrated into all classes—yes, even online classes. It is only by teaching Christian values in each and every business class that students may eventually understand how to incorporate these values into all aspects of their own business life.

The business department has a unique place among its peers within the liberal arts. The various subdivisions of business such as management, marketing, accounting, and finance may be viewed as direct applications of psychology, sociology, philosophy, mathematics, communications, and the like.[1] At some point, all professions overlap with business: artists need someone to market their music; hospitals have directors to set budgets; social workers must understand how changes in the economy impact clients; developers seek financing for construction projects; church leaders need to manage the people who support them; and even museums require human resource directors. Christian universities might take advantage of this overlap between business and the professions and begin to reinterpret the business department as a sort of nontraditional missionary training ground. Combine the fact that business administration is one of the most popular undergraduate degrees among both public and private universities along with the perception of the world of business as an opportunity for ministry and we see an entire marketplace of evangelistic opportunities open before us.[2]

As a basis for understanding the importance of being a Christian in the business arena, we must first understand the Bible's view of work. Following an explanation of the biblical perspective on work, I will describe the influence of the Protestant Reformation on the development of commerce in North America. After reviewing the work of Christian business leaders who may be more widely recognized among this current generation of students, I conclude this chapter with a discussion of the contemporary and future challenges to the Christian faith in business.

What Does the Bible Say about Work?

Too often, self-professing Christians reach the conclusion that the Scriptures have no bearing on their work life. In an interview, for example, the chairman of the board of one of America's largest dry goods corporations, known for having read the Bible through at least 70 times stated that, "I never mix the Bible with business. Good business is good business. There's no Christian way of doing business."[3] Some have even suggested that the stories told in the Bible are simply not relevant to the economic realities of this day and age.[4] When you consider that the average Christian spends much more time at work than at church or in prayer, this incorrect perception of the need for separate lives is sad indeed. Contrary to such analyses of the Scriptures and business, however, the Bible does in fact take a firm stance on work and the Christian's role within a place of business. Furthermore, there are definite consequences for those who choose not to work.

Chewning, Eby, and Roels construe the business world to be an "institutionalization of God's intention for us to work and to serve each other."[5] In fact, aside from creating man, one of the first things God does for man is give him a job. He places Adam in the garden of Eden in order "to work it and watch over it" (Gen 2:15 HCSB). Another way to understand the importance God places on work is to recognize that work existed before sin was first introduced to the world. Moreover, one of the most widely memorized Bible verses, and one often cited as a call to work hard in one's chosen career, states, "Whatever you do, do it enthusiastically, as something done for the Lord and not for men" (Col 3:23 HCSB). Likewise, Eccl 5:18–19 tells us that work is an expression of God's grace, not his anger, as Solomon proclaims, "It is appropriate to eat, drink, and experience good in all the labor one does under the sun during the few days of his life God has given him, because that is his reward. God has also given riches and wealth to every man, and He has allowed him to enjoy them, take his reward, and rejoice in his labor. This is a gift of God." Our Heavenly Father meant for us to enjoy our work! We are also taught to work hard in good times and bad. In Genesis, we see Joseph laboring so diligently to store grain in a time of great prosperity that eventually "he stopped measuring it because it was beyond measure" (Gen 41:49 HCSB). God even meant for us to work hard in a hostile environment: "Seek the welfare of the city I have deported you to. Pray to the LORD on its behalf, for when it has prosperity, you will prosper" (Jer 29:7 HCSB). The vast majority of non-Christians are familiar with Jesus' command, drawn from the Old Testament, to "love your neighbor as yourself" (Matt 22:39; see Lev 19:18). This commandment may be readily applied to both an individual's personal and business relationship with others.

The Bible gives at least two reasons for going to work: it is commanded by God, and it is where the believer is placed to represent Christ to the world. There are also negative repercussions for those individuals who either refuse to work or choose not to work hard enough. For instance, Paul reminds the Thessalonians:

> We did not eat anyone's food free of charge; instead, we labored and struggled, working night and day, so that we would not be a burden to any of you. It is not that we don't have the right to support, but we did it to make ourselves an example to you so that you would imitate us. In fact, when we were with you, this is what we commanded you: "If anyone isn't willing to work, he should not eat." (2 Thess 3:8–10 HCSB)

It is through strong statements such as this that we clearly see the Scripture's view of work.

The Creation and Development of the Protestant Work Ethic

While most people are familiar with the Protestant Reformation, either through church services or a high school history class, few realize the lasting impact that this religious movement would later have on the development of commerce in the United States.

The Protestant Reformation began in the early sixteenth century, lasted well over a century, and eventually led to the formation of many of today's Christian denominations. The Puritans, a group of English Protestants, began an extensive emigration to New England during the seventeenth century, and historians estimate that by 1640 over 20,000 Puritans had settled in the new colonies. This resettlement, stemming primarily from the religious persecution they were facing in England, led to an enormous shift in financial resources throughout the civilized world and eventually provided the religious, cultural, and economic foundations of modern-day North America.

In 1905, Max Weber, a well-known German philosopher, was the first to link the economic success of the United States to the religious background of its early settlers in his combined series of essays entitled *The Protestant Ethic and the Spirit of Capitalism.* In this seminal work, Weber shows his admiration for countries such as America and idealizes the toughness and strong personality of the peoples such cultures produce. He identifies the differences between the United States and certain European nations as a difference based on religious tradition. Whereas the rigorous Protestant foundation in America instilled a notion of self-discipline among its citizens, other European denominations were prone to "instill a discipline of authoritarian submissiveness."[6]

There are several hypotheses as to why the Protestant Reformation created such a disparity in the economic development between North America and continental Europe. At least four primary changes brought about by the Reformation have been suggested as creating the conditions favorable to the financial growth and innovation witnessed in the New World:

> (1) by stimulating religiously based persecution and migration, the Protestant Reformation redistributed human capital and rearticulated commercial networks; (2) by decreasing the number of

> religious holidays and lengthening the average work day, the Protestant Reformation increased the effective supply of labor; (3) by dissolving monastic properties and abolishing monastic orders, the Protestant Reformation changed the structure of landholding and avenues of social mobility; and (4) by [stimulating bureaucratic] reforms, the Protestant Reformation contributed to the formation of less predatory and more predictable forms of government.[7]

Often considered one of the most widespread effects of the Protestant Reformation on development of commerce in North America was the considerable increase in the supply of labor. One explanation for the unprecedented boost in productivity has been attributed to the substantial reduction in the number of religious holidays. An English observer, writing in 1624, estimated that the saints' days in combination with various other nonworking holidays consumed no less than five months of the annual calendar in Spain.[8] In addition to the increase in work days, there was a shift in the manner with which work was performed. English Puritans, for example, not only worked more hours per day, but also tended to labor harder during those hours than their European counterparts.[9]

This industriousness on the part of the Puritan citizenry was due in part to the belief that economic success in one's work was an indication of God's blessing and thus one's predestined status as a rightful member of the church. Since attending church services and taking the sacraments could not establish one's salvation, some members of Puritan churches were left with the personal responsibility of discovering for themselves the signs of their preordained status. If financial success through hard work and perseverance were achieved, for example, these believers could then interpret their wealth as a sign that they were favored by the almighty God. They held that nothing occurred simply by chance and because God would only help those whom He had predetermined should receive His salvation and therefore His blessing, they were extraordinarily motivated toward hard work and its resulting wealth. An individual's work was no longer just a job to be done but rather a personal calling to be fulfilled. When viewed in this light, Protestant workers did not toil because they felt that they had to but because they wanted to. They worked to please God, not themselves.

The work ethic forged by the Protestants also had an impact on individuals outside of the New England area congregations. As

Kaelber interprets Weber's work below, he points out that the trust and goodwill engendered among the Puritan business community eventually became a principal component of early American commercial relations.

> Ascetic Protestant congregations in colonial America and the early United States called into being and cultivated candor and trust among persons unrelated by blood. Sect and church members understood their activity as involving a great mission to create communities of believers in which all would be brothers. New family relationships of trust, helpfulness, allegiance, and ethical conduct under the watchful eyes of God were born among "the brethren." A quite practical mechanism ensured the purity of this ethical community: Owing to rigid investigative procedures, only persons of "good moral character" could enter the devout community. Thus, membership implied a seal of righteous behavior as well as the member's commitment to treat God's children in strict accordance with an ethos of equality and fair play. Good will and openness, rather than fear, threat, insecurity, manipulation, and the sheer calculation of interests, prevailed in the congregation. Indeed, sect and church membership established so secure a reputation for honesty and candor in business that nonbelievers preferred to conduct commercial dealings with the devout; fair treatment, they were convinced, would be their reward. In this way, carried by ascetic Protestant congregations, trust, ethical conduct, and good will broke through their original locus in the particularistic ties of the family and clan and became awarded to "unknown others"—as long as they were members of an ascetic Protestant sect or church. Trust now became, Weber argues, understood as an impersonal and binding principle—a firm ideal even for commercial relationships—rather than as constituted from strong personal relationships alone. This transformation proved to be a crucial step toward the formation of a delimited civic sphere characterized by an ideal of trust.[10]

Although it eventually lost its religious underpinning, this Protestant philosophy toward work eventually shaped a sense of responsibility for financially productivity that became the norm in America.[11] A routine of hard work became institutionalized within the culture. Such an attitude toward achieving success in one's business life, Weber argues, is not "something which occurs naturally. It cannot be directly produced either by high wages or by low wages, but has to be the product of a long, slow 'process of education.'"[12] The Protestant Work Ethic, or PWE as it is commonly referred to among academics, is inherent within many a North American psyche and has been studied to such an extent that managerial scholars now relate it to a kind of personality trait or belief system that an individual might possess. Although there is no specific, agreed upon definition of the term, the broader meaning of PWE generally refers to a person's attitude regarding the moral value of work, self-discipline, individual responsibility over one's economic well-being. There is also a corresponding negative attitude toward leisure activities, emphasis on productivity, belief in hard work as an almost religious duty, desire for punctuality, honesty, viewing idleness and wasting money as sin, willingness to forgo immediate pleasure to reach long-term goals, and an internal locus of control (denying that other people or outside forces are to be blamed for one's personal faults or misfortunes). Various scales have been created to measure this trait. Many of today's large organizations actually screen prospective employees for PWE because it is generally viewed as a favorable characteristic to possess and can thus improve the overall efficiency and effectiveness of the organization.

Modern-Day Christian Business Men and Women

Maintaining and promoting a Christian worldview in business is more than just practicing ethics at work and, as we have already discussed, the Bible has a distinct opinion on the need for and value of work. By understanding the impact of our religious history, it is not surprising that many of the world's great Christian business leaders have risen out of North American marketplaces. The prominence of such Christian business leaders is not atypical, and it is important to note that even in a world of condemning media headlines, "a strong Christian culture, supported by a guiding mission statement and nurtured by the founder and current leaders, is possible."[13] Moreover, it is not unexpected to see a pattern of hard work reflected among each of the success stories outlined below, another manifestation perhaps of our austere Protestant beginnings. The business men and women described herein embody what the Scriptures have commanded us to do with regard to our work. While this is by no means an exhaustive list, I have chosen instead to identify a few of those Christian leaders who I thought might be most recognizable to the current generation of college students.

John Beckett, CEO of R. W. Beckett Corporation

John Beckett is the son of founder Reginald W. Beckett. The R. W. Beckett Corporation is the world's largest producer of oil burners for residential heating. Biblical principles serve as the organization's foundation for customer relationships, and among its corporate values the company "endeavors to apply a biblically-based philosophy throughout every phase of its operations, providing a corporate atmosphere that promotes individuals health, advancement in learning and strong families."[14] John Beckett identifies the Bible as a sort of "corporate compass" for his business activities, adding, "The more time I spend with it, the more I am instructed, challenged, and encouraged by timeless truths that reach into every area of my life—including day to day aspects of my work."[15] Despite the success the organization has had under his management, Beckett is quick to point out that business is about more than financial profit. "It's about treating everyone with integrity, whether customers or employees, and making sure Jesus is always number one. Focus on these things," he says, "and the bottom line will take care of itself."[16]

S. Truett Cathy, Founder and CEO of Chick-fil-A

Originally founded in Georgia in 1946, Chick-fil-A has spread to nearly 1,500 locations across 38 states and grossed more than $3.2 billion in 2009 alone. Truett, like so many other Christian business leaders, attributes his accomplishments to operating his business based on biblical principles. In 1982, the corporate purpose was established, "To glorify God by being a faithful steward of all that is entrusted to us. To have a positive influence on all who come in contact with Chick-fil-A."[17] One way in which the organization directly exhibits its biblical foundation is by closing on Sundays. This includes all locations whether they are in a mall, hospital, university, or free-standing. Cathy's decision to close on Sunday was his "way of honoring God and directing our attention to things more important than our business. If it took seven days to make a living with a restaurant, then we needed to be in some other line of work. Through the years, I have never wavered from that position."[18] Chick-fil-A also promotes Christian initiatives through the toys and accessories included in its children's meals. The success of his business has allowed Cathy the opportunity to pursue his interest in the development of young people. In 1984,

Cathy created the WinShape Foundation, a youth support program designed to shape winners by helping young people through summer camps, retreats, foster care, and other services. In addition, to date, Chick-fil-A has awarded more than $25 million in college scholarships, with nearly $2 million annually set aside for its restaurant employees. Jimmy Carter, former United States President, once said this of Cathy, "I hope that people will learn from Truett Cathy the virtues that have brought him remarkable success in life. He has dedicated himself to service in the broadest sense, following Christian principles, not only in his personal life, but in his relations with his customers and employees."[19]

David Green, Founder and CEO of Hobby Lobby

Owning more than 450 stores across 39 states, David Green was included by *Forbes* magazine among the 400 wealthiest American citizens in 2009. Green created Hobby Lobby in 1972 based on biblical principles and attributes his success to his faith in God. The organization's inclusive statement of purpose exemplifies Green's Christian perspective:

> In order to effectively serve our owners, employees, and customers the Board of Directors is committed to:
>
> Honoring the Lord in all we do by operating the company in a manner consistent with Biblical principles.
>
> Offering our customers an exceptional selection and value.
>
> Serving our employees and their families by establishing a work environment and company policies that build character, strengthen individuals, and nurture families.
>
> Providing a return on the owners' investment, sharing the Lord's blessings with our employees, and investing in our community.
>
> We believe that it is by God's grace and provision that Hobby Lobby has endured. He has been faithful in the past, we trust Him for our future.[20]

Unlike the majority of large commercial retailers, Hobby Lobby's stores are closed on Sunday. In addition to playing acoustical versions of classic Christian hymns over the in-store sound systems, Christian references are frequently made in both the store and its advertising, and Hobby Lobby often partners with Christian-affiliated organizations to spread the good news around the world.

Harry and Esther Snyder, founders of In-N-Out Burger

Among original developers of the drive-thru restaurant, Harry and Esther Snyder founded the California-based In-N-Out Burger in 1948. Since that time, the organization has grown to over 250 locations across five states. While this growth is slow when compared to other fast food chains, the family maintains private control over the organization and does not allow franchising. The menu is very basic and everything is made fresh; there are no heat lamps, microwaves, or freezers within the restaurants. The organization has been recognized for paying and treating their employees respectfully with a starting wage well over minimum wage, benefits included. In addition, managers on average make over $80,000 annually. While the Snyders did profess Christian values, they took a more subtle approach in sharing their faith with the public. Beginning in the 1980s, Bible references such as Rev 3:20 and John 3:16 were discreetly printed on the bottoms of cups or sandwich wrappers. The couple also created the In-N-Out Burger Foundation in 1984 as a way to help abused and neglected children.

Stanley Tam, Founder and President of United States Plastic Corporation

Upon visiting the home of United States Plastic Corporation, the parent company of Rubbermaid, one can't help but notice the giant stainless steel words along the side of the building proudly announcing that "Christ is the Answer." Tam built his organization on the promise in Matt 6:33 (HCSB), "But seek first the kingdom of God and His righteousness, and all these things will be provided for you." Even among its Christian peers, however, US Plastic is unique. Following a conviction he felt during an altar call in Medellin, Columbia, in 1955, Tam and his wife Juanita went home and, in effect, turned the business over to God by legally making God the literal owner of the business. One hundred percent of the ownership of US Plastic Corporation was placed in a foundation whose sole purpose is to establish churches in third-world countries. Tam made a promise to God more than 60 years ago that if He would prosper the business, he would honor God in any way he could. The result of this promise has been a debt-free $30 million business with over 100,000 customers.

Marion Wade, founder of ServiceMaster

Marion Wade founded ServiceMaster, a privately held Fortune 500 company, in 1947. The organization's brands include TruGreen, Terminix, American Home Shield, Furniture Medic, AmeriSpec, ServiceMaster Clean, and Merry Maids. The name ServiceMaster represents Wade's commitment to service to the Master. He had a strong personal faith and respected all employees and customers, believing that all were made in the image of God. ServiceMaster's "foundational commitment" is "to honor God in all we do."[21] While it is not company policy that the CEO of the organization be a Christian, they "hold to the formula that pay is based on performance and promotion is based on potential. But, [they] trust in God's sovereignty and believe He has a strong voice in determining who leads."[22]

Sam Walton, Founder of Wal-Mart and Sam's Club

Born during the Great Depression and having served in World War II, Sam Walton went on to found the world's largest public corporation, Wal-Mart. His goal in creating Wal-Mart was to offer the American public products at affordable prices. This dream has since expanded to include nearly 10,000 stores across no less than 28 countries. Although he is most famous for founding Wal-Mart and Sam's Club retail warehouse, Walton was also known for his strong commitment to his Christian faith and showed that faith through his various charitable organizations and donations. In addition to his donations to local church and civic organizations in Northwest Arkansas, in 1991, through a $6 million contribution, the Sam and Helen R. Walton Award was created to provide annual awards to new church developments working in creative ways to share the Christian faith in local communities. In an effort to stop the spread of communism in Central America, he created the Walton International Scholarship Program in 1985 to make scholarships to American universities available to students from these countries. Students attend one of three Christian universities: John Brown University, University of the Ozarks, or Harding University. Of the more than 800 Central American students who have graduated thanks to the Walton International Scholars program, nearly 700 have returned to work in their home countries, fulfilling Sam Walton's vision.[23]

His family has continued Walton's legacy since his death. Helen, his wife, was president of the Walton Family Foundation when it donated $300 million to the University of Arkansas and later followed that contribution with another for $50 million to the university's Sam Walton School of Business. John Brown University, the nearest Christian university to Wal-Mart's headquarters, has likewise received multiple donations and has become a major training ground for Wal-Mart's Christian managers.[24] Following the devastation of Hurricane Katrina in 2005, $20 million in cash and merchandise were set aside to aid storm victims.

Contemporary and Future Challenges to the Christian Faith in Business

We see from the deeds of the various modern-day Christian business leaders discussed above that how persons incorporate the Christian worldview into their workplace is as different as each individual. Some people, like Harry and Ester Snyder, take a more subtle approach to sharing their values while others like Stanley Tam literally shout it from the rooftop, or the side of a building in his case. But in the end, what matters is that each person uses the economic success of their business to glorify our Lord. While we are all created in His image, God did not make us alike and therefore does not expect each of us to interpret His call to give to the church and those in need in the same way. Paul reminds us, "Each person should do as he has decided in his heart—not reluctantly or out of necessity, for God loves a cheerful giver" (2 Cor 9:7 HCSB). Having said that, we should also keep in mind that "if the eagerness is there, it is acceptable according to what one has, not according to what he does not have" (2 Cor 8:12 HCSB). Very few business leaders will have the resources such as those achieved by Sam Walton through Wal-Mart and Sam's Club to set aside hundreds of millions of dollars for charitable expenditures. This does not mean, however, that God is dissatisfied with the $50 check a small business person is able to give to fund scholarships to a local Christian university each year. Quite the contrary! He is just as pleased with this $50 as He is with Chick-fil-A's $2 million contribution toward scholarships because of the honest and praiseworthy intent behind each gift.

Questions and Concerns

This may undoubtedly raise a few questions. What about someone who is not successful in their work? Did the Puritans have it right in their notion that the Lord only blesses those He considers deserving? The simple answer of course is that being a Christian in business does not necessarily guarantee success. Just as Christ never said following Him would be easy—actually, he made it pretty clear that it would be difficult—neither did He say that those who did follow Him would achieve financial prosperity in their business life. This line of discussion always creates an interesting dynamic in the classroom when business-minded men and women are asked to consider whether financial success can be equated with God's blessing and, likewise, whether financial failure may be construed as God's displeasure.

Another challenge I like to pose, and one that is always guaranteed to create a fiery discourse among even the most stoic of classrooms, is whether Christian business leaders should donate a portion of their organization's profit? Making charitable gifts with excess money is not as easy a decision as some might think. Business leaders have a responsibility not only to the church but also to the employees who work for their company and the families who depend upon them. As Chewning, Eby, and Roels argue:

> Moral choices do not always involve choices between one thing that is wrong and another that is right. Often choices are between two or more "rights." Let's examine business decisions relating to the use of profits. Should they be used to increase wages, cut prices, reinvest in capital equipment, or increase the owner's dividends? The morally superior alternative is not completely clear, since any of the choices will benefit some stakeholder group.[25]

These are difficult choices for an experienced business owner to make, much less a young man or woman fresh out of college. What is hard for many to understand is that there is no one right answer. Any of these decisions may rightfully serve others, and it is only through thoughtful prayer that business leaders are able to determine where and how the Lord wishes the prosperity to be passed on. This provides yet another reason that Christian values need to be incorporated into all aspects of the learning process.

A very serious concern quietly looming on the horizon of many Christian business managers is the matter of social responsibility.

One such issue of social responsibility is environmental sustainability. Regardless of an individual's personal stance on issues such as the global warming debate, the Bible makes it clear that man was put on earth to tend it and care for it (Gen 2:15). As with any of His commands, the failure to take care of God's creation as He required does not come without ramifications. "The time has come for the dead to be judged and to give the reward to Your servants the prophets, to the saints, and to those who fear Your name, both small and great, and the time has come to destroy those who destroy the earth" (Rev 11:18 HCSB). This generates yet another stakeholder to consider, the Earth itself, as Christian organizations try to determine how to best spread their wealth.

A second issue is the growing social needs many communities require that their governments either will not or cannot afford to meet. John Langan, a Jesuit priest, made this prediction:

> In societies as different as the United States and Poland, the United Kingdom and Mexico, greater reliance is steadily being put on the private sector to meet a wider variety of personal and social needs. This ensures that even more of the vexing problems of contemporary societies will come to be ethical problems for business. But business itself is constantly being subjected to new strains and new pressures for change as markets and production processes become global, as technology makes vast quantities of information more readily available, and as demands for rapid decisions are intensified.[26]

These strains and pressures that Langan says private organizations will soon face may create an entirely new dimension for the Christian business leader to consider. Changes we cannot even begin to imagine may one day come our way. Regardless of what new or unpredictable difficulties are thrown before us, our duty is to ensure that we tackle these problems in such a way that others may see Christ in us. By understanding our history, looking to our peers as examples, knowing what the Bible says about our condition, and incorporating as much of this wisdom as possible into every aspect of our learning, we as Christian business men and women will be better prepared to meet whatever challenges and needs the ever-changing marketplace may lay before us.

Questions for Further Reflection

1. How has the Christian foundation of Western culture influenced the development of its business community?
2. Why do you think some Christians feel the need to separate their religious identity from their business identity? How can this be confusing for those around them?
3. How do you feel about the idea that economic prosperity is a sign of God's blessing? What might this theory say about Christians who are forced to file bankruptcy or are unsuccessful in their workplace?
4. Think of a few Christian business leaders in your community. How do they differ in the way in which they let the world see Christ in them? How does this influence the way they conduct their business?
5. Why do business leaders have a responsibility to the environmental sustainability of their community? Is there a biblical precedence for this?

Resources for Further Study

Anderson, Dave. *How to Run Your Business by the Book: A Biblical Blueprint to Bless Your Business*. Hoboken, NJ: John Wiley & Sons, 2009.

Baer, Michael R. *Business as Mission: The Power of Business in the Kingdom of God*. Seattle, WA: YWAM Publishing, 2006.

Downey, Deane E. D., and Stanley E. Porter. *Christian Worldview and the Academic Disciplines: Crossing the Academy*. Eugene, OR: Pickwick Publications, 2009.

Grudem, Wayne. *Business for the Glory of God: The Bible's Teaching on the Moral Goodness of Business*. Wheaton, IL: Good News Publishers, 2003.

Meaux, Reneé. *God's Hands in My Business: Will He Let My Business Fail?* Mustang, OK: Tate Publishing & Enterprises, 2009.

Sherman, Doug, and William Hendricks. *Your Work Matters to God*. Colorado Springs: NavPress, 1987.

Tam, Stanley. *God Owns My Business*. Camp Hill, PA: Horizon House, 1989; Camp Hill, PA: Wingspread Publishers, 2008.

Endnotes

[1] See Samuel L. Dunn, "The Strategic Importance of the Christian College Business Department," *Faculty Dialogue* 13 (1990): 105–18.

[2] See Patrick Erwin, "Ten Most Popular Majors and What They Pay," retrieved from http://articles.cnn.com/2008–10–27/living/cb.what.majors.pays_1_graduate-degree-biology-degree-computer-science?_s=PM:LIVING (November 19, 2010); Gordon Adams, "Do You Like Your Job?" in *The Complete Christian Businessman*, ed. Robert J. Tamasy (Brentwood, TN: Wolgemuth & Hyatt, 1991).

[3] William J. Krutzka, "The Nearsighted Ethics of Christian Businessmen," *Eternity*, September 1976, 15.

[4] See J. Dalla Costa, *Magnificence at Work: Living Faith in Business* (Toronto: Novalis, 2005).

[5] Richard C. Chewning, John W. Eby, and Shirley J. Roels, *Business through the Eyes of Faith* (San Francisco: Harper Collins, 1990), 7.

[6] Martin Riesebrodt, "Dimensions of the Protestant Ethic," *The Protestant Ethic Turns 100*, ed. William H. Swatos and Lutz Kaelber (London: Paradigm, 2005), 41.

[7] Philip S. Gorski, "The Little Divergence: The Protestant Reformation and Economic Hegemony in Early Modern Europe," in Swatos and Kaelber, *The Protestant Ethic Turns 100*, 168.

[8] Christopher Hill, *Society and Puritanism in Pre-Revolutionary England* (New York: Schocken, 1967).

[9] Gorski, "The Little Divergence," in Swatos and Kaelber, *The Protestant Ethic Turns 100*, 168.

[10] Lutz Kaelber, "Utilizing Max Weber's 'Iron Cage' to Define the Past, Present, and Future of the American Political Culture," in Swatos and Kaelber, *The Protestant Ethic Turns 100*, Swatos and Kaelber, 199–200.

[11] See Riesebrodt, "Dimensions of the Protestant Ethic" in Swatos and Kaelbrer, *The Protestant Ethic Turns 100*.

[12] Max Weber, *The Protestant Ethic and the "Spirit" of Capitalism: And Other Writings*, ed. and trans. Peter Baeh and Gordon C. Wells (New York: Penguin, 2002), 17.

[13] Donald Lester and Walton Padelford, "Christian Worldview and the World of Business," in *Shaping a Christian Worldview: The Foundation of Christian Higher Education*, ed. David S. Dockery and Gregory A. Thornbury (Nashville: Broadman & Holman, 2002), 342.

[14] Beckett Corporation, "Corporate Values," accessed November 27, 2011, http://www.beckettcorp.com/Company2/corporatevalues.asp.

[15] John D. Beckett, *Loving Monday: Succeeding in Business without Selling Your Soul* (Downers Grove, IL: InterVarsity, 1998), 79–80.

[16] See K. Miller and J. Beckett, "Following the Golden Rule," accessed November 29, 2010, http://powertochange.com/discover/faith/beckett.

[17] Chick-fil-A, "Corporate Information," November 27, 2011, http://www.chick-fil-a.com/FAQ#?category=12.

[18] Quoted in Jordan Vivian, "Conservative Fried Chicken?" *Human Events*, 11/3/2009, accessed November 27, 2011, http://www.humanevents.com/article.php?id=34404.

[19] "Quotations from and about S. Truett Cathy," on "About Truett," accessed November 27, 2011 http://www.truettcathy.com/about.asp, .

[20] Hobby Lobby, "Statement of Purpose," accessed November 27, 2011, http://www.hobbylobby.com/our_company/purpose.cfm, .

[21] ServiceMaster, "About Us," accessed November 27, 2011, http://www.service-master.com/about-us.
[22] Tamasy, *Complete Christian Businessman*, 26–27.
[23] See John Brown University, "International Programs," November 27, 2011, http://www.jbu.edu/international/walton/.
[24] Bethany Moreton, *To Serve God and Wal-Mart: The Making of Christian Free Enterprise* (Cambridge, MA: Harvard University Press, 2009), 33.
[25] Chewning, Eby, and Roels, *Business through the Eyes of Faith*, 240.
[26] John Langan, "The Ethics of Business," *Theological Studies* 51 (1990): 81–82.

Concluding Applications

22

FAITH AND TRANSFORMATIONAL TEACHING[1]

Thomas Rosebrough and Ralph Leverett

Integrating a concern for spiritual outcomes along with academic and social goals in teaching is an audacious quest. Most in the secular realms of teaching do not consider taking even the first step in such a journey. Indeed, many in Christian higher education fear an integrative approach. Ironically, the trend currently in public education is to focus on academic goals alone, with standardized testing to demonstrate that the goals are met. We call this concept "informational teaching." Surely we are meant to aim higher.

Great teachers are few. Study of what makes for great teaching reveals that it is much more complex than we realize. All who serve in higher education have had numerous experiences in classrooms, and such familiarity can breed simplicity of thinking, as though anyone with deep knowledge of a subject can teach. (Mark Twain offered that "if teaching were the same as telling we would all be geniuses.") The act of teaching is a complex, not simple, dynamic between a teacher and a student. The discipline of education is devoted to the analysis of teaching and learning.

The identity of the field of education within the academic community seems vague and undervalued. It is rarely seen as a discipline equal to classical fields. Although emerging from respected academic domains, it is often separated from its philosophical underpinnings. Typically, it is seen as a professional tool—the means of informing students of the arts and sciences. The discipline of education is generally classified as a professional area, but its relationship to the liberal arts is indisputable. It provides a home to mathematics, languages, natural science, the social sciences, music, art, and kinesiology in the elementary grades. During the middle and high school years, all that is preparatory to success at the college level depends on skilled classroom instruction across the range of the content areas.

While education today may often exist to serve other content areas, it has its own history, philosophy, psychology, and practical value. At the core of education is pedagogy, the art and science of teaching and learning. Pedagogy owes much to psychology and philosophy as a field of study. At times the discipline of education could be described as the ignored guest at the party, so much a part of the creation and growth of other fields that it is overlooked as having a right to exist independently. Education is the study and practice of the most effective means to "transfer" the concepts and utilization of classical and practical academics to new and future generations. At its best, education describes how we can transform the novice student to a mature and expert learner. Effective teacher education can change the naïve and passionate student from observer and listener to the competent and effective practitioner.

Let's compare education with selected and respected Christian college major subjects. The study of art and sculpture include instruction in form, color, texture, techniques, the use of space, the orientation of a completed work to highlight the purposes of the artist, and a thorough grounding in art history. A performance degree in music will require music history, technique, at least one foreign language, music theory, and requirements to perform in a variety of venues. A student majoring in Christian studies who is preparing for the ministry will typically learn the history of Christianity and, perhaps, world religions. Courses such as hermeneutics, apologetics, and homiletics provide necessary background in the "what," "why," and "how" of a sermon. The listener will learn biblical terms, the "defense of our faith," and, hopefully, will increase in spiritual maturity through the delivery of a well-crafted sermon. The training of a good teacher has much in common with these other fields.

We should bear in mind that two of the most transformational figures in the Scriptures were teachers—Jesus and St. Paul. The quality and integrity of their teaching have endured the attacks of critics throughout the centuries. They transformed the complex concepts of salvation and grace-filled living into practical everyday language through metaphors. At times, their teaching was pointed, unsettling, and revolutionary. They connected the "heavenly" to the earthly realm, the sacred to the secular. Their teaching has eternal value. Over the centuries, these teachers transformed their times and ours.

From Informational to Transformational Teaching

We have the wrong idea about this concept called teaching. Most of us approach the classroom by thinking first about what we will teach. Being deeply and richly prepared in our subject is our passion for succeeding as teachers. While such motivation is worthy and essential, it should not be our highest priority. Both from pedagogical and spiritual perspectives our highest priority must be the learner in our classrooms. This is the difference between merely *informational teaching* and *transformational teaching.* Robert Sternberg from his study of the psychology of intelligence reminds us that "if we teach only for facts, rather than for how to go beyond facts, we teach students how to get out of date."[2] Transformational teaching as a concept subsumes the more limited imparting-of-information conception of teaching. Transformational pedagogy is holistic and richer because it includes academic, social, and spiritual goals for the students.

To have spiritual goals in our teaching means that we connect to the spiritual in our students. Willard tells us that spiritual is who we already are, not something we become.[3] Galatians 5 can remind teachers that we are called to model the spiritual qualities of joy, peace, patience, kindness, goodness, faithfulness, gentleness, and self-control. Character dispositions, indeed universal values, that students would want to see in their teachers, are embedded here. Students are looking for teachers who model such. The connection between teacher and students is their relationship. While our students are looking at and judging their teachers, the question might be how do teachers perceive students? Where do we "place" our students? The list below offers five teaching attitudes[4] often displayed in classrooms:

1. *Condescension*: a top-down, "I've got it and you don't" attitude, which originates in arrogance. Arrogance is

selfish because it inhibits development of a teacher-learner relationship. In contrast, the act of teaching should teach us a humility that the more we learn the more we realize how much we do not know.

2. *Analysis*: "I will focus on the parts but not worry about the learning potential of my students." This view blossoms in outcomes-obsessed curricula. Analysis quickly loses track of the learner because of a desire to isolate an objective, teach to the objective, and assess the objective. Though contemporary standards are formulated to move learners forward, they can accomplish just the opposite: Students are lost in the effort to fulfill accountability standards. Analysis is a perception of students as consumers rather than the human resources they can be.
3. *Entitlement*: "I want to find the smoothest route to accomplishing this job and being liked as well." This viewpoint flows from social goals being allowed to trump academic goals instead of *synergizing* with them. The greatest risk taken by transformational teachers is to trust and respect learners because, like love, it makes teachers vulnerable to their students' wants and wishes and manipulations. Entitlement plays into students' worst attitudes—that they deserve an easy class, grading system, and path in life.
4. *Compassion*: "I sincerely want to help you by displaying kindness and love even if it costs me." This perspective seems strongly spiritual—and it is. Compassion is displayed by teachers committed to holistic goals, and it doesn't come easily, usually growing in teachers bit by bit. It is a love tempered by disciplined focus on the real needs of students.
5. *Synthesis*: "I see learners as more than the sum of some parts. I view them as needing a multifaceted approach to meet their needs." This teaching perception demands the greatest work in knowledge, attitude, and in effort. Love is demanded, but understanding and empathy are also essential for synthesis. Its context is not only holistic but long-term.

Teachers may possess a combination of teaching attitudes, and, indeed, attitudes can shape what we teach and how we teach it. Readers will notice in the teaching attitudes listed above that they move from subject-centered or teacher-dominated (condescension, analysis, entitlement) to learner-centered (compassion, synthesis). A caveat: While we advocate learner-centered classrooms, teachers must not compromise high expectations. Placing students at the center of pedagogy does not preclude devotion to and enthusiasm for a scholar's subject. Teachers as *scholars* have reason to be confident in their knowledge of subject. But teacher-scholars at their best care about students first. Student-centered teaching includes a deep commitment to the rigor needed for students to reach their potential as learners.

In order to prioritize the learner in our classrooms, we have to understand at least two salient principles in transformational teaching:

1. Teachers have to reflect upon *why* they teach. We believe that *why* we teach equals *who* we teach. And,
2. Teachers have to know *how* students learn before they can teach. How our students learn should dictate how we teach.

In a recent book, we assert that teachers can change lives through inspiration and attention to process skills in learning, that higher achievement is a by-product of focusing first on the learner and demanding depth of understanding. We propose the "Transformational Pedagogy Model" as a construct for understanding the holism of the goals and roles of teaching. Figure 22.1 (p. 480) expresses the basis for our thinking about transformational teaching.

Notice first that the learner is at the center of our model.[5] As we said above, teachers must consider students their priority both in regard to how they learn and who they really are. They are spiritual beings, people who hold what poet Stanley Kunitz termed an "indestructible essence." This belief takes us to a holism of goals and roles in the model. Holism of goals means that we teach not just for academic reasons but also for social and spiritual reasons. Holism of roles means that teachers must be multifaceted in their roles: Scholars, Practitioners, and Relaters. The model draws us into examining our primary reason for teaching.

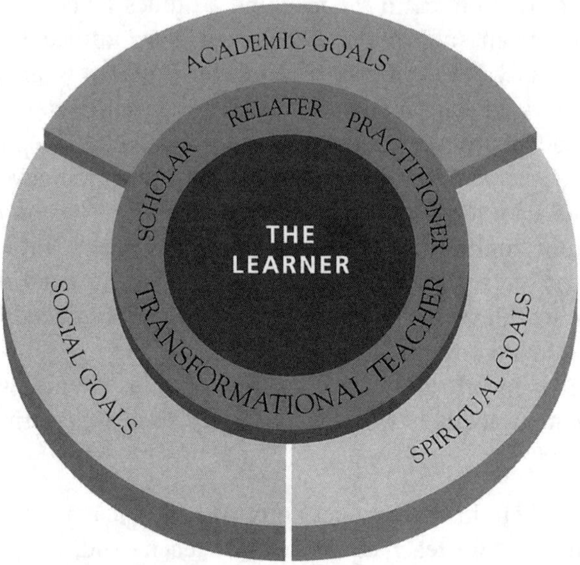

TRANSFORMATIONAL PEDAGOGY MODEL

Figure 22.1

Why We Teach

To teach well we must first examine our motivation, our rationale, for teaching. The world of the classroom is like every other human endeavor in at least one way: In the classroom we encounter our own crises of spirit on account of our humanity. The relationship formed between teacher and student is a holy one because we are seeking not just to inform a mind but more importantly to transform a soul. Teaching, we contend, is like no other profession in its intensity, breadth, depth, and absolute importance and impact on the future. Our students need the assistance of transformational teachers to reach their God-given potential.

An integral part of the model is the presence of spiritual goals in the classroom. Spiritual goals can be met in any discipline and in both public and private educational settings by teachers who recognize the transcendent qualities of their students. Believing in our students does not necessarily require a religious persuasion, but it does mean that teachers view their students as timeless, transcendent treasures. Plato in *The Republic* recognized this truth thousands of years ago, "The soul of man is immortal and imperishable."[6] We teach not just a learner but a human spirit, an "indestructible essence."

To explore the spiritual in transformational teaching, we have found it useful to contrast the dynamic tension between the secular and sacred in education. Barry Harvey formed a significant conclusion while studying the Latin root *saeculum* of the word *secular*. He found its meaning to be centered more on *time* rather than on a worldly or evil dimension. If we contrast secular with sacred, its root has more to do with the material versus the transcendent, or especially, with time versus the timelessness of the sacred.[7]

We like to conceive the two concepts as overlapping in a Venn diagram with two clearly different ways of viewing the world of people we serve. Those who advocate sacred or spiritual goals focus on transcendent values, a sense of timelessness in an approach toward life. Secularists, by contrast, are very much rooted in this world of space, time, and matter. The Venn overlap of sacred with secular is significant for teachers. This zone can be thought of as life's calling because it is where we find purpose and passion to serve.

The greatest transformational teachers in the Christian intellectual tradition were in the "zone" so strongly that the circles became one. Augustine, Aquinas, Erasmus, Melanchthon, Comenius, Pestalozzi, Booker T. Washington, Mary Bethune, and others were teachers in the world of time but transcended their worlds. They served higher purposes while toiling in secular societies. The greatest teachers recognize that the sacred can illuminate the secular darkness.

Clearly, however, belief in the eternal transcendence of our students is a worldview choice that has intellectual and theological implications. Many scholars in the secular realm are unwillingly to take the risk. Howard Gardner termed the human sense of the spiritual as *existentialist* intelligence in his theory of multiple intelligences. He found it less controversial as he applied the science of psychology. He refers to this intelligence "with respect to such existential features of the human condition as the significance of life, the meaning of death, the ultimate fate of the physical and the psychological worlds, and such profound experiences as love of another person or total immersion in a work of art."[8] This definition of spirituality is broad and safe. We certainly admire the emphasis on the relational aspects of spirituality; indeed, many Christians are still learning that their faith is relational in its essence. Teachers who work in a Christian environment need to embrace with passion spiritual and social goals for their students.

We use the term *Relaters* in our model because we wish to emphasize the pedagogical relationship between teachers and students. Relaters meet both social and spiritual goals in teaching. To believe in our students is to believe they can succeed, that they can be nurtured to achieve their potential holistically. Learners can be encouraged to develop deeper social and spiritual values like cooperation, empathy, self-sacrifice, and hopefulness through study of a subject and through interaction with peers, teachers, and the community.

We accept academic goals readily in higher education. Our hope is to clarify further why belief in the indestructible spirits of learners is also vital. Serving something or someone beyond themselves is more than a desire for students; it is a belief and a need for action and commitment in their lives. Transformational teachers can nurture the concept that service above self ultimately frees students to understand themselves and other people. By looking outward to serve, learners can go inward and deeper into their education.

Antidote for Twenty-first-Century Education[9]

Valuing the holistic potential of learners can lead to other compelling conceptions of schooling. Education perceived as transformational was hardly an invention of a group of first-century religious thinkers. Dallas Willard asserts that the goal of the teacher in Jesus' time was not to impart information but *to make a significant change in the lives of the hearers.* Willard notes that it is a modern notion to bring people to know things that may not have an effect on their lives:

> In our day learners usually think of themselves as containers of some sort, with a purely passive space to be filled by the information the teacher possesses and wishes to transfer—the "from jug to mug model." The teacher is to fill in empty parts of the receptacle with the "truth" that may or may not later make some difference to the life of the one who has it. The teacher must get the information *into* them. We then "test" the patients to see if they "got it" by checking whether they can *reproduce* it in language rather than watching how they live.[10]

Transformational teaching in contrast to informational teaching might thus be seen as an antidote to modern education. Despite all research evidence to the contrary over the last century, modern education persists in its paradigm of traditional pedagogy. We seem to have taken the wrong concept from nature, choosing amoeba assimilation of food over the more complex and profound concept of the transformation of the caterpillar into the beautiful butterfly. Learning is complex and profoundly beautiful.

Teachers can inspire students to succeed. William Butler Yeats said that "education is not the filling of a pail, but the lighting of a fire." Paradoxically one of the afflictions in our educational systems is the intentional removal of information that is relevant to the real needs of learners. Essentialists may do it in the name of "back to basics" as they excise the humanities; politically correct educators may do it in the name of removing confrontational ideas that would "offend" a minority or interest group; and progressives may do it by removing language that would shed light on the truth of traditional values.

Knowledge is remembered when it is personal, and knowledge is personal when holistic goals are met by teachers who inspire their students. Without a sense of the sacred, all knowledge remains abstract. We live in an increasingly abstract educational world, where social and spiritual development is often not a part of students' learning experience. The twenty-first century is fast—faster than we often realize. Perhaps we all should hit the pause button and reflect on what really matters in learning. A teacher's heart and soul need not be left at the school house door.

Why do we teach? This question is, among other things, a question that relates to cultivating richness in education. Knowing why we teach is only relevant if we also know how our students learn.

How Our Students Learn[11]

In Charles Dickens's *Hard Times*, Mr. Gradgrind was a model of the worst sort of teacher, exemplifying the force-feeding of information into his students' heads. Our lexicon indeed reflects the word *grind* to describe a bad or laborious school (or work) experience. Mr. Gradgrind condemned a student for not knowing the dictionary definition of a horse, despite having knowledge of the child's extensive home experience with horses. In the teaching profession, we spend most of our time putting the cart (of teaching) before the horse (learning). As teachers, we must know how our students learn before we can teach well.

Teachers as *practitioners* are experts on how people learn and on how to choose a variety of teaching methods to meet learning needs. We have a growing problem this century: Informational teaching and learning seems to be dulling many students' perceptions and understandings of their world. Informational teaching occurs when teachers adopt the mindset of presentation of facts and ideas to their students as though learners are there simply to assimilate the information presented. Teachers of students are not found exclusively in classrooms and schools. Informational teaching and "learning" are part of the fabric of contemporary culture. Nicholas Carr addresses an underlying philosophic issue of the Information Age by asking, "Is Google making us stupid?" The concern is that digital natives are creating a blurred distinction between the surface nature of information and the deep understanding required for knowledge.[12]

Mark Bauerlein expresses the worry of many teachers that the digital culture has altered the way students learn at the expense of literacy and cultural awareness. He relates his thesis that the Internet crowds out critical thinking and values of citizenship as young learners immerse themselves in video games, cellphones, laptops, and blogs. The angst of teachers is not that we should forsake the remarkable research tools of the Information Age, but that students are too self-absorbed in the digital culture. This self-absorption has critical educational implications.[13] The digital culture offers to many learners a temptation that is not only addictive but rather irresistible: to plug in and tune out. While it is certainly true that many digital learners are quite tuned in, it is highly ironic that the most connected generation in history also demonstrates tendencies to be the most disconnected learners educationally and culturally. Don Campbell writes that "the Internet has moved knowledge from the brain to the fingertips: Who needs to know about Impressionism or Charles Dickens or George Washington Carver or . . . even George Washington? Why carry such information around in your head when Google will deliver it in seconds?"[14]

And, coincidentally, this disconnection seems to be occurring as many students are lagging in school achievement. Higher education is beginning to feel the impact. Wilson writes in *The*

Washington Post that in her many years of experience interviewing Rhodes Scholar candidates, current high-performing students seem less able to confront issues that require critical thinking and cross-disciplinary reflection.[15] Students in this century are quite vulnerable to a shallow, fingertip understanding of knowledge and culture—a perspective of which learners are often unaware until challenged. Students need, as we shall see, the profound social support of adults who are expert learners in the learning environment in order to "put it all together." We must focus on the unique being who is the learner. We turn to three brief explanations of how humans learn by regarding the work of Jean Piaget, Lev Vygotsky, and brain-based learning theorists.

Informational to Transformational Learning

For learning to be transformational, students must go beyond merely adding and assimilating new information into an existing schema. The process that renowned Swiss learning theorist and epistemologist Jean Piaget described as accommodation involves changing an existing schema or adding new ones. For example, a child has an "established" schema for horses until one day she sees a Great Dane. An adult or more experienced learner says, "No, that Great Dane is a very big dog, not a horse. Dogs bark and horses neigh." The child now has to modify or change her horse schema and add a new dog schema (if she did not already have one). Such change is what we call learning.[16]

This description of learning is informational in its essence. It is based on learners encountering and reacting to discrepancies (sometimes called dissonance) in their objective learning environment. The work of Piaget is still very popular today because it is the single most global theory of intellectual development of how students learn, thus deserving some extended discussion of learning theory and pedagogy. Piagetian theory is quite relevant to transformational teaching and learning.[17]

When teachers recall the theoretical ideas of Jean Piaget, most think of his stages of cognitive development, each with its own unique characteristics. But Piaget also established *constructivism,* the notion that new ideas and ways of thinking emerge from old ones (diSessa, 2006). We learn by building meaning upon prior experiences. David Ausubel, one of the first cognitive educational psychologists, in his 1968 textbook, *Educational Psychology: A*

Cognitive View, wrote: "If I had to reduce all of educational psychology to just one principle, I would say this: The most important single factor influencing learning is what the learner already knows. Ascertain this and teach him accordingly."[18]

Although some research suggests Piaget may have underestimated children's cognition and overestimated adolescents' or adults' cognitive sophistication, his learning ideas still seem quite valid.[19] Piaget found that learning ability develops in a progressive, orderly, but uneven fashion. Lack of understanding of the Piagetian theory is most unfortunate because it causes us to miss the optimism of his findings about learning. Maturation of the central nervous system (ages and stages) controls the rate of cognitive development to some extent. But, there is so much more: Teachers can intervene in the learning environment and make a difference! Here are some *theory-into-practice* parts of his learning theory:

- People are active processors of information. This concept is perhaps the most critical one for teachers to embrace. Unlike his behaviorist contemporaries, Piaget portrayed human beings as individually *engaged* in interpreting and learning from people and from the physical environment, from *others* and *objects.* Professors who complain about ill-prepared students entering their classes might need to reflect upon Piaget's interventionist and engagement concepts. The learner is capable of adaptation and should be at in the center of the learning model. Knowledge is stored in a "schema," a mental unit that can *change* with development. This idea is one of the most optimistic in all of learning theory: The goal of teaching is to affect change in the learner, and what the novice learner lacks is experience in an appropriate learning environment. Literally, all students can learn if we tailor classroom learning *to start where learners are.*
- Learners have a God-given gift to try to make sense of the world. A state of *equilibrium* is the zone of comfort for a learner to explain new events in terms of existing schemata. Inexplicable or confounding events/information can cause *disequilibrium,* a mental discomfort sometimes called *cognitive dissonance*. The movement back and forth between mental comfort and discomfort enables

increasingly complex levels of thought and knowledge. Jerome Bruner gave great assistance in understanding this process in learners in his discussion of learning modes: (a) *concrete* or three-dimensional representations of the social and physical world, (b) *iconic* or pictorial visuals, and (c) *symbolic* or abstract/theoretical ideas. College professors need this understanding as they present lessons and activities to 18-year-olds. Typically, only about half of college freshmen are developmentally ready for abstract concepts and ideas. An old *Peanuts* cartoon pictures Snoopy and his little friend, Woodstock, sitting across a chess board, with Snoopy intoning, "It is hard to play chess with a checkers mentality."[20]

Vygotsky's Theory as Transformational

Another cognitive theorist, Len Vygotsky, focused not on stages but on what he termed the *zone of proximal development,* a bandwidth of competence that learners use within a supportive context. On the bandwidth we find the distance between actual developmental level (independent) and the level of potential development (with adult or peer aid). The teacher is the vital force in closing the gap. To find out where the learner is on this developmental continuum, a teacher utilizes trial and error. When the instruction is appropriate, learning occurs more quickly.[21]

A second aspect of Vygotsky's theory is that learning has a social and, we contend, even spiritual quality where the learner interacts and internalizes ideas. In contrast to Piaget's developmental stages, the Russian psychologist portrayed growth as more seamless and gave greater weight to social context as a stimulator. Student's abilities change through social interaction provided by more capable peers and adults. Teaching methods that prize social interaction or goal structures that encourage cooperative learning are obvious applications of sociocultural learning theory. Vygotsky saw the teacher-student dynamic as having greater potential for cognitive change in the learner, but perhaps this potential is even more expansive.

The relationship between teacher and student is the basis for social constructivist theory which includes sociocultural belief in transformational learning. The belief has spiritual dimensions if the teacher allows for a relationship of commitment, trust, and respect. A mutual commitment to hard work and reasonable expectations, a trust in the teacher's evaluative judgments and the student's clear purpose in doing the work, and a mutual respect for academic classroom contributions are all spiritual in dimension. The dynamic between teacher and learner can be a covenant where the classroom environment is tuned to the potential of the whole learner where students (and teachers) can embrace the joy and hope of learning. As Price states it, "Classroom social systems are organic structures and processes rooted and grounded in an 'invisible/unspoken' sphere of influence and person power initiated by the classroom teacher."[22]

Vygotsky's learning concepts demand all three of the teacher-transformer roles of scholar, practitioner, and relater. Teachers who encourage their students with reflective questions, analysis of concepts into smaller ideas and tasks, demonstration of how real things work, formative feedback on how they are doing, and assisting learners to meet challenges are helping to close the gap between actual and potential development. Most of us would admit that we routinely seek the easiest or smoothest path in learning and in life. But, with experience we would also confess that it is the challenges that promote our growth. And, so it is with Vygotsky's theory: Teachers with intentionality do best when they challenge students in an environment of support. While not as comprehensive a theorist as Piaget, Vygotsky added important social and cultural understandings to developmental theory. Both Piaget and Vygotsky assist teachers in understanding how the human mind responds to its environment.

Learning and the Brain

Piaget's and Vygotsky's conceptions of how people learn coincide closely with findings in neuroscience over the past two decades especially. Knowledge of these findings forms an extremely useful foundation for the work of the teacher-practitioner. The brain learns from one neuron "talking" to another, forming communities or columns of neurons around significant concepts. Such brain cell chatter cannot occur smoothly until a body of experiences has been built up. Dendrites connect to axons via synapses stimulated by our sensory experiences.

The brain seems to learn best when the following factors can be found in the learning environment:

- *Challenge*: A discrepancy is placed before the learner that is, at least in some respect, outside the mind's understanding or experience.
- *Novelty*: Something new or different stimulates curiosity.
- *Meaning*: The brain perceives the knowledge as having coherence.
- *Feedback*: The learner must have timely reinforcement of new knowledge.
- *Repetition*: Memory is influenced strongly by repetition of experiences.
- *Emotion*: Knowledge with emotional import will be remembered.

The teacher's role as a sensitive practitioner is critical in the dimension of challenging students with appropriate curriculum. *Challenge* to one learner can be frustration or threat to another; and, it takes sensitive teachers who are attuned to their students to perceive the difference. Asking great questions is a simple but profound way of creating a challenging environment. The process of finding answers seems more essential to brain growth than the answers themselves. In *Transformational Teaching* we write about "strategic learning qualities" that teachers can assist students in developing: openness, skepticism, civility, persistence, imagination, curiosity. The goal is to use inquiry-pedagogy that promotes a critical thinking process that creates more self-directed learning and learners.[23]

Classrooms with more self-directed learners can be anxious classrooms. Patricia Cranton (2002) writes of an environment of challenge in transformative learning that strikes a balance between support and challenge. Students with lower levels of anxiety can be expected to perform more effectively, but it is vital also to understand that challenge is integral to problem solving in order for learners to generate new ideas.

In classic studies on rats conducted by William Greenough and his colleagues, the animals that had grown up in the complex environment that included problem-solving learned more quickly, made fewer errors, and had thicker synapses than rats from standard cages.[24] The Piagetian learning theory has provided an explanation for this in its assimilation-accommodation biological model.

The old adage that variety is the spice of life seems to have never been truer than in relation to brain learning. The brain seems to crave *novelty*, that is, all things new. But, new must connect to "old." New sensory data are critical to the stimulation of new learning.[25] Other studies of animals show changes in the brain through learning. Rats which were exposed to new opportunities for learning and in a social context (with other rats) demonstrated altered gross structure in the cerebral cortex. The combination of "others and objects" produced better performing animals.[26]

So what about people-studies? People who have learned to read and write (an incredibly significant experience that many of us take for granted) have thicker fibers in their corpus callosums (the nerve fibers that divide the right and left hemispheres of the brain).[27] People who learn to play a musical instrument show different organizational patterns in the brain than nonmusicians (Elbert et al., 1995). The term *plasticity* is used to describe the brain's adaptability to new and different circumstances and experiences. Plasticity in the brain is a concept of tremendous optimism for learners if we think about the continuing debate of "nature vs. nurture." The human brain literally can adapt and change as it is presented with new and different experiences. There are no limitations to what teachers can do in providing nurturing experiences for students. Only our attitudes can hold us back.

Varieties of new data alone are not enough, however. The learner must perceive *meaning* or relevancy in the new information in order for long-term memory to be a reality. Memory formation takes time for "consolidation" where the hippocampus plays a key role. Nonsense data or information perceived to be unrelated to the learner's experience is resisted or rejected by the brain. Ormrod concludes from her research-synthesis that "meaningful learning promotes better transfer than rote learning,"[28] an important insight that should challenge some contemporary classroom practices. This research underlines how important a role teachers play in placing their subject in a meaningful context.

Indeed, the combination of novelty and meaning seems to be at the crux of cognitive process itself. Learning is the interaction between persons and situations—cognitive process is not just what goes on in our minds. Students need teachers who continually provide new, meaningful experiences.[29]

Teachers also play a critical role in the area of *feedback*. Studies confirm that human beings need reinforcement, especially timely reinforcement for maximum learning to occur. It is not enough for the learner to encounter meaningful, new information in a challenging context. Nature's stamp of approval, timely feedback, is necessary for the information to transform into knowledge. It can be human feedback or nonhuman like a computer. Simply telling students that their answer is right or wrong (without explanation) has a negative effect on achievement.[30] After analyzing almost 8,000 studies on the effects of feedback on achievement, Hattie concluded, "The most powerful single modification that enhances achievement is feedback. The simplest prescription for improving education must be 'dollops of feedback.'"[31] We learn by being corrected by caring teachers.

The fifth factor in brain-learning is similar to feedback at least in terms of the value of reinforcing elements in the learning environment. *Repetition* of individual experience (sometimes called "rehearsal" by educational psychologists) is a key to memory and learning. Memory can be seen as the "displacement of knowledge a little bit into the future."[32] Neurons must acquire the potential for being able to fire, and their sensitivity is tied to how often they have fired before. Old-fashioned practice after the initial introduction of a concept is part of good teaching, but it must include relevancy, not just rote-repetition. Deliberate practice which takes into account learner characteristics seems to be a key factor.[33] This can mean that some students need more repetition than others. Unfortunately, we are quick to label them as "slow learners." We often miss the most glaring variable: Students are novice learners to varying degrees and simply lack experience.

The final vital factor in learning is for some the most unlikely: *emotion*. Our brains are hardwired with the emotions of fear, joy, anger, and sorrow. The *amygdala* is a small structure located inside and below the brain cortex that works extensively with the negative emotions. The amygdala helps us associate particular emotions (like fear and anger) with particular memories.[34]

The importance of emotions in education is underestimated, but knowledge of the connection between education and emotions is not new. Aristotle valued the stimulation of change in knowledge by touching the learner's mind, emotions, and attitude. Recent researchers no longer discount emotional influences on motivation and change.[35] The emotional nature of a memory may assist us in our ability to retrieve it—high emotional content is more easily recalled. It has been suggested that the brain's hippocampus tells us who someone is while the amygdala tells us whether we like them or not. Indeed, Ormrod and Schunk write that when information is emotionally-laden it directs our attention, helps us to think about it over a period of time, and to repeatedly elaborate on it.[36] The subjective and personal can provide the context needed for learning.

Rachael Kessler recommends that teachers "invite joy into their classrooms."[37] Emotion is a key that unlocks learning in the brain. Teachers can look for ways for their students to express themselves out of body if you will. By employing humor, celebrations, physical movement, and enjoyment of nature in various ways, teachers will find that three things happen. (1) Learners will for a few ecstatic moments move away from their egos and self-absorption. (2) They will see their teachers in a new light, respecting them as real people who share the same emotions as their students. (3) Students will remember what was taught. An inspirational movie, a nature walk, or a simple classroom celebration of a completed assignment can trigger sensations of joy that nurture the human mind and spirit.

Consider the learning power of a good story—it always has an emotional element. It explains why we remember certain movies so easily. Great teachers tap into this flow, this synergy of emotion and cognition. Contrary to what many educators have been led to believe, emotion (when used with intentionality and judiciousness) not only does not inhibit learning, it actually facilitates learning. Emotions with all their corollary feelings of satisfaction, disdain, nostalgia, hate, love, suspicion, surprise, and more are a vital part of who we are. To suggest that a spiritual element in our learning is irrelevant as a goal seems ill-advised in the face of the role emotions and feelings play in our lives.

A sentence-mnemonic device might be helpful here. If we scramble the order of the six brain-based facets to **R**epetition, **C**hallenge, **N**ovelty, **M**eaning, **F**eedback, and **E**motion, perhaps we can remember them by *Resilient Chaps Need More Fun Everyday.* These elements of brain learning are certainly worth remembering, in that they are such a vital part of a knowing how our students learn.

How students learn is as complex as the brain, but it is also as profoundly simple as a transformational teacher who knows (scholar), does (practitioner), and cares (relater). Transformational teaching changes what students know and how they feel. It also changes how they apply these elements of thinking and feeling to the world in which we live, recognizing that learning is both a part of us and beyond us.

Conclusion

Another generation of college students, what some have called the "iGeneration," is flowing into our classrooms. For this generation, it is *all* about technology constantly connecting them to the world. The same desire for individualized immediacy existed for their predecessors, the Millennials, only now the conditioned experience is supersized. How do we cope with students who prefer texting over talking, digital screens over books, and indeed answers over questions?[38]

Our response as educators has been twofold in dimension: Teachers have to know why they are teaching, and we believe that an understanding of how our students learn must precede how we think about teaching. How we teach should be dictated by such knowledge, and it is our conviction that our intentions are for naught if we do not teach to the potential of the human spirit, focus more on the pedagogy of process, and use the power of great questions in the classroom.

Great teachers strike a livable balance between recognizing the needs of contemporary culture and attention to the whole person's deep need for synergy in academic, social, and spiritual illumination. Connecting these needs creates a vital force both in education and in life. We must be careful to avoid the divisive word *or* and to embrace balance through the connecting conjunction *and*. The past is important to understanding the future. Educators through the ages made the following connections with the divine *and*:[39]

- Plato: matter *and* ideas
- Aristotle: reason *and* virtue
- Aquinas: spiritual *and* rational thought
- Erasmus: knowledge of words *and* knowledge of truth
- Dewey: school *and* society

- Piaget: physical *and* social environment
- Bruner: process *and* product
- Gardner: thinking *and* feeling
- Jobs and Gates: immediacy *and* customization

Transformational teaching embraces holism, saying that we do not always have to choose. We can have it all in education. As we teach our students to adapt and compete in the global marketplace, we can also seek our spiritual summons. Christian higher education can be a place where transformation is a daily reality.

Questions for Further Reflection

1. Is education a legitimate academic discipline to be studied in the university setting? Why or why not?
2. Is there a particular attitude of teaching that is the most helpful for teachers to employ in the classroom? If so, what is it, and why is it important?
3. Should the process of teaching change according to the needs and/or aptitudes of the student? Why or why not?
4. In the interplay between the roles of scholar, practitioner, and relater, how can a teacher help begin the process of transformation in a student's thought and life? Is there a proper path for all students to follow to which teachers must direct, or are there multiple paths toward acquisition of knowledge and transformation of thought? Explain.
5. Is there a difference between secular and spiritual teaching and learning? If so, what is it? Is it proper or even possible to unite the two spheres of understanding into a holistic worldview? If so, how?

Resources for Further Study

Adolphs, Ralph, and Antonio R. Damasio. "The Interaction of Affect and Cognition: A Neurobiological Perspective." In *Handbook of Affect and Social Cognition*, ed. Joseph P. Forgas, 27–49. Mahwah, NJ: Lawrence Erlbaum, 2001.

Alexander, Patricia A. *Psychology in Learning and Instruction*. Upper Saddle River, NJ: Prentice-Hall, 2005.

Bauerlein, Mark. *The Dumbest Generation: How the Digital Age Stupefies Young Americans and Jeopardizes Our Future*. New York: Penguin, 2008.

Bruner, Jerome S. *Relevance of Education.* New York: Penguin, 1974.

Byrnes, James P. *Minds, Brains, and Learning: Understanding the Psychological and Education Relevance of Neuroscientific Research.* New York: Guilford, 2001.

Carr, Nicholas. "Is Google Making Us Stupid? What the Internet Is Doing to Our Brains." *The Atlantic*, July/August 2008.

Castro-Caldas, A., P. Cavaleiro Miranda, I. Carmo, A. Reis, F. Leote, C. Ribeiro, and E. Ducla-Soares. "Influence of Learning to Read and Write on the Morphology of the Corpus Callosum." *European Journal of Neurology* 6 (1999): 23–28.

Cobb, P., and J. Bowers. "Cognitive and Situated Learning Perspectives in Theory and Practice." *Educational Researcher* 28:2 (1999): 4–15.

Dockery, David S. *Renewing Minds: Serving Church and Society through Christian Higher Education.* Nashville: B&H, 2008.

Elbert, T., C. Pantev, and E. Taub. "Increased Cortical Representation of the Fingers of the Left Hand in String Players." *Science* 270 (1995): 305–7.

Gardner, Howard. *Intelligence Reframed: Multiple Intelligences for the 21st Century.* New York: Basic Books, 1999.

Gordon, Gary, and Steve Crabtree. *Building Engaged Schools: Getting the Most out of America's Classrooms.* Princeton, NJ: Gallup Press, 2006.

Hattie, John. "Measuring the Effects of Schooling." *Australian Journal of Education* 36:1 (1992): 5–13.

Jayson, Sharon. "iGeneration Has No Off Switch." *USA Today*, February 10, 2010.

Kessler, Rachael. *The Soul of Education: Helping Students Find Connection, Compassion, and Character at School.* Alexandria, VA: Association for Supervision and Curriculum Development, 2000.

Marzano, Robert, Deborah Pickering, and Jane Pollock. *Classroom Instruction that Works: Research-Based Strategies for Increasing Student Achievement.* Alexandria, VA: ASCD, 2001.

Ormrod, Jeanne Ellis. *Human Learning.* 5th ed. Columbus, OH: Pearson/Prentice Hall, 2007.

Piaget, Jean. *Psychologie et Pedogogie.* Paris: Denoel/Garnier, 1969.

Reisberg, Daniel. *Cognition: Exploring the Science of the Mind.* 4th ed. New York: Norton, 2009.

Rosebrough, Thomas R., and Ralph G. Leverett. *Transformational Teaching in the Information Age: Making Why and How We Teach Relevant to Students.* Alexandria, VA: ASCD, 2011.

Schunk, Dale H. *Learning Theories: An Educational Perspective.* 6th ed. Columbus, OH: PearsonPrentice-Hall, 2008.

Shayer, Michael, and Philip Adey. *Towards a Science of Science Teaching: Cognitive Development and Curriculum Demand.* London: Heinemann Educational, 2002.

Shulman, Lee. "Taking Learning Seriously." In *Learning from Change: Landmarks in Teaching and Learning in Higher Education from Change Magazine, 1969–1999*, ed. D. DeZure. Sterling, VA: AAHE and Stylus, 1999.

Siegler, Robert S., and Martha Wagner Alibali. *Children's Thinking*. 4th ed. Upper Saddle River, NJ: Prentice-Hall, 2004.

Singley, Mark K., and John R. Anderson. *The Transfer of Cognitive Skill*. Cognitive Science Series 9. Cambridge, MA: Harvard University Press, 1989.

Sternberg, Robert J. "Assessing What Matters." *Educational Leadership* 65:4 (December 2007–January 2008): 20–26.

Trueblood, D. Elton. *A Life of Search.* Richmond, IN: Friends United Press, 2009.

Vygotsky, Lev S. *Mind in Society: The Development of Higher Psychological Processes.* Cambridge: Harvard University Press, 1978.

Willard, Dallas. *The Divine Conspiracy: Rediscovering Our Hidden Life in God*. San Francisco: HarperCollins, 1998.

Wilson, Heather. "Our Superficial Scholars." *Washington Post*, January 23, 2011. Retrieved at http://www.washingtonpost.com/wp-dyn/content/article/2011/01/21/AR2011012103554.pf.html.

Endnotes

[1] Adapted from Thomas R. Rosebrough and Ralph G. Leverett, *Transformational Teaching in the Information Age: Making Why and How We Teach Relevant to Students* (Alexandria, VA: ASCD, 2011), 16, 44–47, 56, 68–69, 99–105, 142–43. Reprinted and adapted with permission.

[2] Robert J. Sternberg, "Assessing What Matters," *Educational Leadership* 65:4 (December 2007–January 2008): 21.

[3] See Dallas Willard, *The Divine Conspiracy: Rediscovering Our Hidden Life in God* (San Francisco: Harper Collins, 1998).

[4] Rosebrough and Leverett, *Transformational Teaching in the Information Age*, 68–69.

[5] Ibid., 16.

[6] Plato, *The Republic* 8.608-D.

[7] See Barry A. Harvey, *Another City: An Ecclesiological Primer for a Post-Christian World, Christian Mission and Modern Culture* (Philadelphia: Trinity Press International, 1999), 69–70.

[8] Howard Gardner, *Intelligence Reframed: Multiple Intelligences for the 21st Century* (London: Heinemann, 1999), 60.

[9] Rosebrough and Leverett, *Transformational Teaching in the Information Age*, 44–47.

[10] Willard, *Divine Conspiracy*, 112–13.

[11] Rosebrough and Leverett, *Transformational Teaching in the Information Age*, 99–105.

[12] See Nicholas Carr, "Is Google Making Us Stupid?" *The Atlantic* (July/August 2008): 58.
[13] See Mark Bauerlein, *The Dumbest Generation: How the Digital Age Stupefies Young Americans and Jeopardizes Our Future* (London: Penguin, 2008).
[14] Don Campbell, "Plugging In, Tuning Out," *USA Today* (September 10, 2008): 8–11A.
[15] Heather Wilson, "Our Superficial Scholars," *Washington Post*, January 23, 2011, retrieved at http://www.washingtonpost.com/wp-dyn/content/article/2011/01/21/AR2011012103554.pf.html.
[16] Jean Piaget, *Psychologie et Pedagogie* (Paris: Denoel/Garnier, 1969).
[17] See Jeanne Ellis Ormrod, *Human Learning*, 4th ed. (Columbus, OH: Pearson Merrill—Prentice Hall, 2004).
[18] Cited by Lee Shulman, "Taking Learning Seriously," in *Learning from Change: Landmarks in Teaching and Learning in Higher Education from Change Magazine, 1969–1999*, ed. D. DeZure (Sterling, VA: AAHE and Stylus, 1999), 39–41.
[19] See Robert S. Siegler, *Children's Thinking*, 3rd ed. (Upper Saddle River, NJ: Prentice Hall, 1998).
[20] Jerome Bruner, *Relevance of Education* (New York: Penguin, 1974).
[21] See Lev Vygotsky, *Mind in Society* (Cambridge: Harvard University Press, 1978).
[22] V. C. Price, "I Don't Understand Why My African-American Students Are Not Achieving: An Exploration of the Connection among Personal Power, Teacher's Perceptions, and the Academic Engagement of African-American Students," in *White Teachers/Diverse Classrooms*, ed. J. Landsman and C. W. Lewis (Sterling, VA: Stylus, 2006), 127.
[23] Rosebrough and Leverett, *Transformational Teaching in the Information Age*, 56.
[24] William Greenough and F. Volkmar, "Maze Training Effects on Dendritic Branching in Occipital Cortex of Adult Rats," *Behavioral and Neural Biology* 26 (1979): 287–97.
[25] See Dale H. Schunk, *Learning Theories: An Educational Perspective.* 6th ed. (Columbus, OH: PearsonPrentice-Hall, 2008).
[26] See M. Rosenzweig and E. Bennett, "Experiential Influences on Brain Anatomy and Brain Chemistry in Rodents," in *Studies on the Development of Behavior and the Nervous System,* vol. 4: *Early Influences*, ed. G. Gottlieb (New York: Academic Press, 1978), 289–330.
[27] See A. Castro-Caldas et al., "Influence of Learning to Read and Write on the Morphology of the Corpus Callasum," *European Journal of Neurology* 6 (1999): 23–28.
[28] See Ormrod, *Human Learning*, 367.
[29] See P. Cobb and J. Bowers, "Cognitive and Situated Learning Perspectives in Theory and Practice," *Educational Researcher* 28:2 (1999): 4–15.
[30] See Robert Marzano et al., *Classroom Instruction that Works* (Alexandria, VA: ASCS, 2001).
[31] John Hattie, "Measuring the Effects of Schooling," *Australian Journal of Education* 36:1 (1992): 5–13.

[32] See Gary Gordon and Steve Crabtree, *Building Engaged Schools* (Princeton: Gallup Press, 2006).
[33] See Schunk, *Learning Theories.*
[34] See R. Adolphs and A. Damasio, "The Interaction of Affect and Cognition: A Neurobiological Perspective," *Handbook of Affect and Social Cognition*, ed. J. P. Forgas (Mahwah, NJ: Lawrence Erlbaum, 2001).
[35] See Patricia A. Alexander, *Psychology in Learning and Instruction* (Upper Saddle River, NJ: Pearson/Merrill Prentice Hall, 2006).
[36] See Ormrod, *Human Learning*; Schunk, *Learning Theories.*
[37] Rachael Kessler, *The Soul of Education* (Alexandria, VA: Association for Supervision and Curriculum Development, 2000), 76.
[38] See S. Jayson, "iGeneration Has No Off Switch," *USA Today* (February 10, 2010): 1D–2D.
[39] Rosebrough and Leverett, *Transformational Teaching in the Information Age*, 142–43.

23

STUDENT LIFE: THINKING BIBLICALLY ABOUT *VOCATIO* AND COMMUNITY

Kimberly C. Thornbury

When one thinks about campus life on a college or university campus in the United States, a number of competing images come to mind. Some may envision preppy young scholars strolling across the quad with their favorite absent-minded professor. Others imagine the kinds of academic debates that go on inside the classroom, some of which tend toward the esoteric and deep. This scholarly aspect of "high culture," as the philosopher Roger Scruton lovingly refers to university life, still remains an important part of the ethos of Western society. When Woody Allen cracks, "I was thrown out of college for cheating on the metaphysics exam; I looked into the soul of the boy next to me," he knows that educated people will get the joke.

Others maintain a less savory view of campus life. They may have read an article in the news about the binge drinking culture at American universities or have heard Bill O'Reilly skewer some campus radical for his unpatriotic propaganda. Still others might subconsciously think that *Animal House* was actually a documentary. The caricature wouldn't be so far from the truth after reports emerged in February 2011 of a professor at Northwestern University whose sexuality class featured actual demonstrations of lewd and immoral acts. Parents, students, alumni, and friends of the university were rightly outraged.[1]

A Non-compartmentalized View of the Christian Intellectual Tradition

As this volume has beautifully demonstrated, however, there is a remarkable phenomenon in American campus culture that defies the stereotypes of the university being either an out-of-touch island of ivory tower academics or a debauched citadel of malcontents. It is called Christian higher education. In the halls of schools that have Christ-centered mission statements, students are invited back into the heart of what a college education should be: a place to think great thoughts and prepare for a life and career marked by good works. This sort of environment is the salutary result of a glorious past, a past informed by the great Christian intellectual tradition. Throughout this volume, my colleagues in Christian higher education have dedicated their chapters to helping the next generation of students, parents, and church leaders understand current issues in the academic disciplines, and set forth the men and women who have and continue to reclaim these age-old subjects for the glory of God.

The amazing thing about the Christian intellectual tradition as an educational framework, however, lies in the fact that the tradition knows no boundaries. It affects not only the academic disciplines, but it encompasses the whole of the university, including student life. Stated differently, Christian higher education cares just as much about how you pursue life together on campus as it does what happens in the classroom. This is because throughout its entire history, Christianity opposed the notion that head knowledge trumps practical living in the real world. Quite to the contrary, the gospel demands a certain kind of life out of Christ-followers. And those of us on campuses that recognize our society's roots in biblical values and norms know that the four years an undergraduate spends with us are the perfect training ground for exhibiting the fruits of the Spirit. Will you leave the university having studied chemistry and public speaking? Yes. Will you be further along in your quest to become a teacher, artist, or entrepreneur because of the material taught? Absolutely. But will we have failed if a student has not been taught how to live in a "holy, self-controlled" life, as the apostle Paul put it (Titus 1:8 HCSB)? To that question, we respond with a sobering "yes." So in this chapter, we will examine the kinds of learning that happen outside formal classroom walls, and a distinctive Christian approach to faith and living as well as faith and learning.

The 90 Percent of Time Spent Outside the Classroom

One of the most dramatic features of college will be your new physical residence. You will also face the new freedom to choose how your day is shaped. In high school, a traditional teen lives with his parents and visits his friends. In college, the majority of students will now live with friends and visit their parents. Mom and Dad now experience a sudden and dramatic reduction in control and knowledge of their child's movements, and the student experiences unprecedented choices even at colleges with the most well-intentioned and (clearest of) boundaries. Unless these freedoms are coupled with an increasing demonstration of responsibility, an environment can arise that can head off course very quickly.

Despite the common image of university life being students in a lab or listening to a professor lecture, the truth of the matter is that 90 percent of college time is spent outside the classroom, and the ability to master those other 153 hours a week with limited parental control can be challenging. (The figure of 153 hours of "discretionary time" assumes that a student is spending 15 hours a week actually showing up for class!)

In other words, your university years set you to sail on a sea of choices. Some of those choices will make you feel wonderful, like you are competing in the Americas Cup. Other choices will make you feel like a castaway on an ocean without food or water to drink. When it comes to your college experience, if you choose the wrong thing, choose too many things, or choose to do the wrong things with the wrong people, your life will suffer. And poor choices can potentially affect your life for a very, very long time.

The abundance of choices is undoubtedly why the ages of 18–21 is listed as one of the three major key times of moral decision making. The first is ages 6–14 months, when a child is strapped in her highchair and learning to resist throwing peas to the dog, and learning not to resist trying lima beans for the first time. The second key period of moral decision making comes at ages 10–12 (or 4th–7th grade), when a student's peer group reaches a new level. Friendships solidify during this time in life, and students are beginning intentionally to choose their friends. When I look back on that period in my life, I remember how much I learned at sleepovers, even with the "godliest" of girlfriends. This awkward time in life sets a tone for the future because influential peer groups are formed. The third pivotal period comes at age 18, when a teen often leaves home and heads to college. Even if that college is down the street, college provides the space for an 18-year-old to begin thinking about the values and principles that will be internalized. Psychologist James W. Fowler designated this time in life as the "synthetic-conventional" season of faith in a young person's life—a time in which people are mostly likely to adopt the belief systems of those closest to them without too much struggle.[2] Adopting a tried-and-true pattern can, of course, be a good thing. But this stage in life is crucial because it is a time when young people are examining the values of their parents (whether good and bad) and comparing them with the worldviews of friends and other mentors. Eventually, as adults they decide which of them they will adopt and personally own. These decisions are made when "no one is looking," so to speak—or at least when Mom and Dad are not "looking" (even if they ARE checking your Facebook page).

While this volume has rightly stressed the importance that the various academic disciplines play in faith formation, I can confidently say after spending almost 15 years in the field, student life is the acid test for seeing how undergraduates are going to live out their faith. As the old British expression puts it, "The proof of the pudding is in the eating." It is certainly wonderful to espouse what you think and belief verbally, but the real measure of a person's faith is found in residence life halls, weekend trips, and extracurricular activities. These commonplaces of life are not abstract. Rather they test the mettle of everyone who says in theory "I honor my father and my mother" or "Jesus is Lord." And make no mistake about it. Thinking Christianly about student life is rare. Once upon a time, universities thought that moral knowledge was not only real, but that it could be taught, acquired, and transmitted, but no more. Speaking to this point Dallas Willard writes, "In their effort to be in control of knowledge," colleges and universities "*have redefined knowledge*, through 'specialization' and 'professionalization,' *in such a way that it cannot deal with those questions*. So real life—which must assume answers—is, as a matter of fact, abandoned by our 'knowledge institutions' to feeling, force, politics, and 'traditions.'"[3]

In an age that is fleeing from the answers required by the demand of "real life," the challenge of those who serve students through a university's residence life, programming, and leadership development opportunities becomes clear: offer the tools that build the habits for the best practices in life. By teaching students how to live virtuously in the midst of day-to-day hard decisions, we are helping to reaffirm and strengthen the faith taught to them by their parents. Anything less than such resolve gives aid and comfort to poor moral decision-making. And as ethicist James Spiegel has demonstrated, immorality eventually leads to unbelief.[4]

Calling and Community

Vocatio

Student life at all colleges and universities involves, but is not limited to, issues of residence life, personal health and wellness, counseling, career services, and decisions about choosing one's major and discovering gifts. It addresses dealing with time management and study habits. In addition to this, student life also evokes images of involvement and engagement in areas spanning Greek life, student organizations and leadership development, internships, external study, campus ministries, a local church, and probably a part-time job.

Faith challenges arise in each of these many areas of student life. During their time at college, students will make long-term decisions about important social and cultural issues such as civility, sexuality, racism, academic and financial integrity, and entertainment choices. These commitments take shape within their very first semester. Faith will be tested, and one hopes that faculty, staff, and older students with biblical counsel are layering solid advice to students. It is important to have a university where issues of faith and real life questions can be explored and addressed safely. As Boston University professor Donna Freitas has recently pointed out, evangelical Christian colleges perform in precisely this way by, for example, inculcating a "purity culture" versus the "hook-up culture" that prevails at secular universities.[5]

Of all of the many important issues to discuss regarding the practical issues of life on campus, however, there are no more important issues than these: exploring one's giftings and finding one's calling (*vocatio*) and how to find, develop, and sustain community. In the former, there is proper biblical approach to academic preparation as a part of determining one's calling which usually has the attending benefit of helping a student find a major. With respect to the latter, the Christian university can help students learn what makes a gospel-centered community flourish, and how those skills can transform campuses, families, churches, and nations. Thinking Christianly about these matters allows us to approach these two areas in unique ways.

One of the central convictions that distinguish Christian higher education from its secular counterparts is the concept of *vocatio*—that the Creator of the universe gives to each one of his children a special role in helping develop His kingdom. The notion that God Himself not only has given individuals special giftings but also seeks for them to direct these talents toward a clear focus and direction in life stands in stark contrast to the secular view that if God exists at all, He is not involved in our personal lives or futures. But knowing that God has a plan is only the first step of recognition. The real work for the Christian university is to work with students to help them understand both the *what* and the *how* of vocation.

Becoming literate on the subject of vocation is the first step. By far the most helpful volume on the subject of *vocatio* is Os Guinness's *The Call*. In this book Guinness makes an important distinction between career and calling. Although the two might overlap, and certainly all of us hope this happens for us individually, we need to realize that there may be times in life where our particular job-of-the-moment may not be of our deepest calling. Building on this distinction, Guinness prophetically exhorts American society that we are not "what we do," but rather we are who God wants us to be in Him and for Him. Finally, he takes the narcissism right out of our pretensions about a subject such as "giftings" when he writes, "*God normally calls us along the line of our giftedness, but the purpose of giftedness is stewardship and service, not selfishness*."[6] This is a much-needed corrective to the primary concern about choosing a major or thinking after graduation about how lucrative your job will be, how much stuff you can accumulate, and how ostentatious your lifestyle can become. After the economic meltdown of the past few years, perhaps we are starting to learn to dream God's dreams rather than those of self-indulgent capitalism.

Another recommended resource is Chip Anderson's Strengthsfinder approach, which is used on Christian and secular campuses alike. Anderson's central insight is that you really cannot be anything that you want to be. Now while this may sound like a negative assessment at first, consider its inverse: you were created for a specific and unique purpose. God has created you to feel most alive when you are doing what you are called to do. As an illustration of this, I am thinking right now about our Provost at Union University, Carla Sanderson. Her training initially was as a trauma nurse, and for this reason, she can jump into action at the sight of blood. By way of contrast, I can't even hold a pencil in my shaking fingers when someone is describing any medical issue they are having if their condition is any worse than a headache! The agrarian poet and philosopher Wendell Berry underscored this truth when he wrote:

> Young people are being told, "You can be anything you want to be." Every student is given to understand that he or she is being prepared for "leadership." All of this is a lie. Original discovery is not everything. You don't, for instance, have to be an original discoverer in order to be a good science teacher. A high professional salary is not everything. You can't be everything you want to be; nobody can. Everybody can't be a leader; not everybody even wants to be. And these lies are not innocent. They lead to disappointment. They lead good young people to think that if they have an ordinary job, if they work with their hands, if they are farmers or housewives or mechanics or carpenters, they are no good.[7]

The slow process of discovering one's gifts is well worth the investment of your time and university experience. It provides a motivating factor to pursuing school. It will assist you in staying motivated to persist and graduate, even when you are asking yourself the dreaded question, "Why do I have to take this class again?" You will even find that getting in touch with your calling will help you to deal effectively with distractions and discouragements, such as an eating disorder or damaged relationships. Further, I am of the settled opinion that the best place to think about your calling is in the context of a traditional liberal arts college. The liberal arts are those subjects that help free societies from various sorts of tyranny, those perspectives born of "smallness of mind, tightness of heart, banality of spirit, frenzy masquerading as efficiency, myopic views of reality, faddish techno-babble, obsession with the bottom line, or the fear that is masked by arrogance in too many intellectuals' lives."[8] And certainly there is no tyranny like self-imposed or even parent-imposed tyranny about asking a question like, "What are you going to do for the rest of your life?" without giving due diligence to the weighty matters of calling.

In summary, while colleges certainly want you to declare a major and prepare you for future employment, Christians working in the field of student development have a perspective that includes a God who creates every aspect of a person, including their talents, gifts, passions, and motivations. A student's vocation is not a random choice, but rather an understanding of specific gifts and unique talents bestowed by the Creator God. In addition to this God-given gift, Christian student development seeks to connect those gifts with a need in this world. Talents are not given simply for personal gain or pleasure but for a God-given purpose. As Cornelius Plantinga so beautifully puts it, "The point of all of this learning is to prepare to add one's own contribution to the supreme reformation project, which is God's restoration of all things that have been corrupted by evil."[9] Student development professionals take time to reinforce the holistic nature of God's work. Students shouldn't be pressured to be a traditional missionary, a worker in a nonprofit evangelical setting, or even a pastor, although we trust and hope some will do so. Student development professionals from the career counselor to the residence director to the leadership development director layer the truth that God's kingdom can be seen in the marketplace, classroom, courtroom, and laboratory. In this sense, then, they are the faculty and administration's best friends on the front lines of helping students "connect the dots" about their future place of service in Christ's kingdom.

Community

Here is a fact that most university academics will not readily admit to you: students looking at schools are just as (if not more) concerned about community and having a place of belonging as they are about their major and the level of academic preparation the school can offer. Questions such as "Who will I room with?" "Who will I eat with?" and "What will I do on the weekends?"

occupy as privileged a place in most students minds as does "Where does this college fall in the *U.S. News and World Report* rankings?" Students crave community—that coterie of friends who will share life together, take time to get to know them, and remain loyal when challenges arise. As sociologist Ray Oldenburg explains, "For most students today, college life is probably the closest thing to community they'll ever experience and college is the place to sell them on the idea."[10]

What kind of community exists in this post-*in loco parentis* ("in place of parents") age? A Christian university that looks for ways to create intentional community from the very beginning of the freshman experience sustains that focus in residence halls, makes connections with an academic major and its sponsoring department, and facilitates introductions to the right campus organizations for the specific student interest. But experiencing community entails not only positive enterprises but warning against certain dangers. Such challenges include "hooking up" before marriage, alcohol abuse, the improper use of technology (e.g., pornography, inappropriate behavior on Facebook or other social media), and getting involved with outside organizations that militate against the successful completions of one's academic responsibilities. Indeed, as Donna Freitas argues,

> I agree that there is evidence that opportunities to explore and practice religion and spirituality on campus abound—and many students take advantage of these. However, I am interested here in whether that interest and even experimentation among nonevangelical college students "grip" them in ways that affect their decision making and behavior among peers, and most especially, in how they interact with the social/party scene on campus, which is also tied to hookup culture and the dominant peer ethic about sex. . . . at least when it comes to sex, religion and spirituality are rather ineffective within this realm in any meaningful way (short of some guilt) unless one attends an evangelical college.[11]

We would respond to Freitas that a Christian academic community engages students at every level on these matters: in the classroom, in the student government, and even on the intramural field. If you really want to see where the challenges arise in compartmentalizing faith and life, go to the flag football intramural championships or participate in the conversations about what images are appropriate for a poster promoting a campus party or what choreography is appropriate for the annual variety show. These moments take faith and learning out of the realm of the abstract and into the world of real daily choices. Community is where the theories learned in your ethics seminar and lessons learned from history class meet the test of lived experience an hour later in the residence complex. Confirming this analysis, Freitas, referencing the work of Sharon Daloz Parks, says that she:

> makes a profound case for meaningful mentorship and attention to college students' spiritual longing on campus at every level, most especially in relationships between faculty and students both within and outside of the classroom—but the evidence from the young women and men with whom I spoke at Catholic, nonreligious private and public institutions shows that college students are overwhelmingly adrift when it comes to spiritual seeking. Most specifically, this covering hampers their ability to use religious resources to say no to unhealthy cultural norms about sex or, for that matter, to use religious resources to foster commitment to any moral norms whatsoever.[12]

In other words, the things that we may not think about as much when it comes to the experience of university life turn out to be perhaps some of the most important. As sociologist Ray Oldenburg explains, "Stories, twinkling eyes, back-slapping, and an ability to laugh and express compassion for troubles are essential, not university degrees or majors."[13] He goes on to say,

> Great hangouts also allow college students to try out new personalities and they teach manners of a democratic kind. In the classroom, at campus meetings, or at home, students need to assume an expected role. But hangouts provide freedom from social roles and expected demeanors. Hangouts enforce a democratic etiquette too. One cannot be a bore, an insulter of others (except in jest), an egotist or braggart, or a monopolizer of talk. Whatever interrupts conversation's lively flow is ruinous, be it a horde or barbaric fellow students, angry outbursts, or music turned up too loud (even Bach or Mozart), making talk inaudible. Fellowship has its rules.[14]

Such thinking is counterintuitive for many of the people who run higher educational institutions. After all, why invest in building coffee shops, student lounges, and performance spaces when there are always so many needs elsewhere—equipment for the engineers, materials for the chemistry program, and books for the library. The reason for such a focus and investment is actually quite simple. Building a healthy community, let alone a Christian one that honors Christ and His gospel, is not automatic. It must be intentionally shaped by faculty and staff personalities, campus architecture, gathering spaces, and above all, shared experiences and campus traditions. It is a matter of contextualization to the needs of the students who, after all, pay the bills, graduate into the alumni organization, and preserve the heritage of an institution for years to come. The simultaneously frightening and exciting realization is this: every single activity on a college campus needs careful attention. The neglect of the common everyday life of the student body will inevitably result in declining retention rates, low student morale, and missed opportunities to shape undergraduates into the kind of academically, socially, spiritually, and organizationally prepared adults that the workforce needs and that a world without Christ needs to encounter.

Conclusion

The professionals who give their careers to student life understand that what they are doing is a tremendous calling from God. Student life is perhaps the greatest undiscovered mission field in society today. The residence hall directors and student life personnel are there at odd hours giving wisdom and counsel during a young woman's moments of deep depression or in the midst of a guy's crossroads in a relationship. Although it is the newest discipline represented in this book, student development is a profession with a bevy of skills, best practices, and real-world scholarship all its own. They are the staff that works tirelessly to come alongside faculty and administration to assist with the development of the whole person, physically, socially, emotionally, spiritually, and intellectually. They are often the ones to whom students will turn first if they are having struggles with their faith, doubts about their future, or sexual temptations at this vulnerable point in life.

Some students who have seen the good work of the staff in these areas may actually want to consider student life as a profession. The Association of Christians in Student Development publishes the helpful resource *Growth*, which is a worthy read for faculty, staff, and administrators alike. I think I can speak for my colleagues in the field when I say that few professions have greater one-on-one practical implications for gospel witness than being a student life professional at a Christian college or university.

Thinking about *vocatio* and community—the foundational concepts behind student life—reminds us that education is not a subject just for the elite, not just for a select few, but it is a deeply important topic for every person who cares about the future and direction of our society. In his regular BBC radio broadcast Jonathan Sacks, the Chief Rabbi of Great Britain, addressed the crisis of discipline in the schools:

> [I]f discipline is a problem in our schools it isn't only because of the schools. Teachers are just one of the many influences to which our children are exposed. There are parents, neighbors, culture and society and if discipline isn't a value there, then schools can't create it alone. There's a moment in the Bible that's long fascinated me. When Moses addressed the Israelites as they were about to leave Egypt after two centuries of exile and slavery, he didn't speak about freedom, or about the land flowing with milk and honey. Instead he spoke about the duty of parents to educate their children. Why? Because to defend a country you need an army; but to defend a civilization, you need education.[15]

We cannot do without excellence in education. We are all in this together. But unlike our postmodern culture that struggles to rally around any set of norms or axioms, Christian higher education is a wonderful exception to the rule, with its Christ-centered mission, hope in the gospel, and common aims to see the kingdom of God flourish in the lives of our graduates and the communities we reach. Our hope is that anyone reading this book who is thinking about joining such an evangelical academic community will finish these pages with no doubt that Christian higher education is important, that in our secular society it is rare, and that the minds of prospective students and parents will be convinced that it is worth the investment.

Questions for Further Reflection

1. Does a Christian college or university possess an advantage in its own community and in its ability to educate and produce a graduate of exceptional character and quality? If so, what advantages are present in the Christian university that are absent in more secular institutions?
2. Should the Christian university limit or broaden the number of choices of a student? How should students' newfound

freedom in the college community impact their ability to make good choices for their lives?

3. Should student activities and opportunities outside the classroom be an intentional supplement to what takes place in the classroom? If so, how? Are there certain aspects of student life that should be maximized in a Christian university? Should some be minimized? Why?
4. How can student life in an academic community aid in the development of "exploring one's gifts and finding one's calling"?
5. Is it proper to tell a student they can be anything they want to be? Why or why not? Does this statement impact their spiritual growth? How?
6. What specific activities should be offered (in a cocurricular sense) that might reinforce and "test the mettle" of the student's worldview outside the classroom? Should these activities reinforce instruction? If so, how?
7. Does the Christian university offer an alternative to the modern "hook-up" culture present in many other academic communities? If so, what is it? How is it nurtured and advanced?

Resources for Further Study

Gilligan, Carol. *In a Different Voice: Psychological Theory and Women's Development*. Cambridge, MA: Harvard University Press, 2002.

Marsden, George. *The Soul of the American University: From Protestant Establishment to Established Nonbelief.* New York: Oxford University Press, 1996.

McDonald, William M., et al. *Creating Campus Community: In Search of Ernest Boyer's Legacy.* New York: Jossey-Bass, 2002.

Oldenburg, Ray. "Making College a Great Place to Talk." In *The Best of Planning for Higher Education*, ed. George Keller, 99–103. Ann Arbor, MI: Society for College and University Planning, 1997.

Opitz, Donald, and Derek Melleby. *The Outrageous Idea of Academic Faithfulness: A Guide for Students*. Grand Rapids: Brazos Press, 2007.

Parks, Sharon Daloz. *Big Questions, Worthy Dreams: Mentoring Young Adults in Their Search for Meaning, Purpose, and Faith.* San Fransisco, CA: Jossey-Bass, 2000.

Plantinga, Cornelius. *Engaging God's World: A Christian Vision of Faith, Learning, and Living*. Grand Rapids: Eerdmans, 2002.

Ream, Todd C., and Perry L. Glanzer. "The Moral Idea of a University: A Case Study." *Growth* 8 (2009): 2–14.

Riley, Naomi Schaeffer. *God on the Quad: How Religious Colleges and the Missionary Generation Are Changing America.* New York: St. Martin's, 2005.

Santasiero, Ellen. "The 'Third Place': Essential for Campuses and for Communities" (interview, Ray Oldenburg). *The Lawlor Review* (Fall 2002): 10–13.

Smith, Christian. *Soul Searching: The Religious and Spiritual Lives of American Teenagers.* New York: Oxford University Press, 2005.

Winner, Lauren. *Real Sex: The Naked Truth about Chastity*. Grand Rapids: Brazos, 2005.

Endnotes

[1] Mary Schmich, "At the Center of NU's Sex Storm," *Chicago Tribune*, March 3, 2011; available at: http://articles.chicagotribune.com/2011–03–03/news/chi-0304-schmich-column-story_1_research-lab-professor-j-michael-bailey-poor-judgment.

[2] James W. Fowler, *Stage of Faith* (New York: Harper Collins, 1981), 301ff.

[3] Dallas Willard, *Knowing Christ Today: Why We Can Trust Spiritual Knowledge* (New York: Harper One, 2009), 57.

[4] James Spiegel, *The Making of an Atheist: How Immorality Leads to Unbelief* (Chicago: Moody, 2010).

[5] Donna Freitas, *Sex and the Soul* (New York: Oxford University Press, 2008).

[6] Os Guinness, *The Call: Finding and Fulfilling the Central Purpose of Your Life* (Nashville: Thomas Nelson, 1998; reprint, 2003), 45.

[7] Wendell Berry, *Life Is a Miracle* (New York: Counterpoint, 2000), 58.

[8] Parker J. Palmer, "Foreword," in William M. McDonald and associates, *Creating Campus Community: In Search of Ernest Boyer's Legacy* (San Francisco: Jossey-Bass, 2002), xiii.

[9] Cornelius Plantinga, *Engaging God's World: A Christian Vision of Faith, Learning and Living* (Grand Rapids: Eerdmans, 2002), xii.

[10] Ray Oldenburg, in Ellen Santasiero, "The 'Third Place' Essential for Campuses and for Communities" [interview], *The Lawlor Review* (Fall 2002): 11.

[11] Freitas, *Sex and the Soul*, 265.

[12] Ibid., 269.

[13] Ray Oldenburg, "Making College a Great Place to Talk," in *The Best of Planning for Higher Education*, ed. George Keller (Ann Arbor, MI: Society for College and University Planning, 1997), 101.

[14] Ibid.

[15] Jonathan Sacks, *Thought for the Day*, BBC Radio 4, February 4, 2005, http://www.bbc.co.uk/ religion/programmes/thought/documents/t20050204.shtml.

24

Engaging the Culture and the Academy

C. Ben Mitchell

Culture is everywhere, all around us. We are part of it, shaped by it, and contribute to it. But what is it? English anthropologist, Sir E. B. Tylor (1832–1917)—one of the first to offer a formal definition of culture—said, "Culture is that complex whole which includes knowledge, belief, act, morals, laws, customs, and other capabilities and habits acquired by man as a member of society."[1] More recently, Princeton professor Clifford Geertz (1926–2006) said culture is "the ensemble of stories we tell about ourselves."[2] I like the way the distinguished missionary-theologian Lesslie Newbigin put it: "By the word *culture* we have to understand the sum total of ways of living developed by a group of human beings and handed on from generation to generation."[3] Finally, contemporary theologian Kathryn Tanner insists that "culture is not primarily located in the intellectual or spiritual achievements of the community—its great works of art, philosophy, or literature. Instead, culture refers to the whole social practice of meaningful action, and more specifically to the meaning dimension of such action—the beliefs, values, and orienting symbols that suffuse a whole way of life."[4]

So, our culture is the air we breathe, the water in which we swim, the things we make, the stories that inform our way of living, the art we create, the objects of our devotion, the meaning we attach to life, and the social atmosphere we inhabit. We cannot escape culture. We can move from one culture to another. We can participate in "high culture," "low culture," or "pop culture." We can sink deeper into one subculture or another. But we cannot live a cultureless existence.

Those who call themselves the people of God and followers of Jesus Christ cannot abandon culture but are called to make, understand, interpret, and engage culture, both within the larger culture and, where appropriate, within the academy. In this chapter, after a brief discussion of understanding and interpreting the culture, I will describe in more detail some tools for and examples of cultural engagement.

Cultural Exegesis

Our English word "exegesis" comes from the Greek word *hegeisthai*, which means "to lead or to guide," preceded by the prefix *ex*, which means "out." And it is a word that is typically used of the analysis of written texts. To exegete a text is to analyze the words. The text itself, with its background and context, guides our understanding of what the writer meant by the words he or she chose. In this sense, exegesis is a descriptive task, simply trying to understand what the words of a given text mean. So when we read the words, "the car is blue," we understand that there is a subject called a car that is blue. Although we may never have seen a car or know what one is, we know that whatever it is, it is blue. And, although we may not know whether blue is a color or an emotion, we know just by exegeting the sentence that whatever a car is, and whatever blue is, the car is blue. That is pure exegesis, letting the words guide our understanding of the sentence.

Just as we exegete texts, we can exegete culture. We can analyze a culture by parsing the artifacts, language, symbols, rituals, art, music, and practices that shape a given culture. For instance, we could exegete one aspect of a culture by exegeting a shopping mall. What could we learn about a culture by walking through the mall with eyes wide open to the language of the culture? First, we might notice the vast size of the mall and its surrounding parking lot. That would tell us that malls are meant for people and people get to the mall via automobiles. Second, once inside the mall we would find a huge variety of stores, from the department stores which anchor the typical mall to the specialty shops scattered throughout the mall to the single-item kiosks that pepper the interior of the mall space. In many malls we would also find entertainment and food: movie theaters, restaurants, and food courts.

So what would we learn? These observations would tell us that whoever it is who frequents the mall is a consumer of goods and services. Moreover, this consumer likes variety and convenience. The mall is a one-stop-shop.

In a similar way, we can exegete a community, a city, or a nation. I often ask my students to pretend they had been dropped off in our city by an alien spacecraft. I ask them to tell me what they would observe. Invariably, if they are from a smaller community, they talk about how large Jackson is. If they are from a large city, they talk about how small Jackson is. They talk about some of the unusual traffic patterns in Jackson and the even more unusual driving habits. They observe that Jackson seems to have one example of every restaurant chain in America. Likewise, Jackson is full of big-box hardware, electronics, and sporting goods stores. And on it goes. They are exegeting a city like one would exegete a text.

We actually have a very clear example of cultural exegesis in the apostle Paul's famous encounter at Mars Hill in the Greek city of Athens. Doubtless, as Paul walked around that city, he would have observed some of the wonders of the ancient world. Commenting on Paul's trip to Athens, John Stott suggests:

> Of course he could have walked around Athens as a tourist, as we would probably have done, in order to see the sights of the town. He could have been determined, now that at last he had the opportunity, to "do" Athens thoroughly and tick its spectacles one by one. For the buildings and monuments of Athens were unrivalled. The acropolis, the town's ancient citadel, has been described as "one vast composition of architecture and sculpture dedicated to the national glory and to the worship of the gods." Even today, although now a partial ruin, the Parthenon has a unique grandeur. Or Paul could have lingered in the *agora*, with its many porticoes painted by famous artists, in order to listen to the debates of its contemporary statesmen and philosophers, for Athens was well known for its democracy. And Paul was no uncultured philistine. In our terms he was a graduate of the universities of Tarsus and Jerusalem, and God had endowed him with a massive intellect. So he might have been spellbound by the sheer splendor of the city's architecture, history, and wisdom.[5]

Yet physician-historian Luke tells us that when Paul came to Athens he "saw that the city was full of idols" (Acts 17:16 HCSB), or as he put it to the Athenians, "I see that you are extremely religious in every respect" (v. 22 HCSB).

> Xenophon referred to Athens as "one great altar, one great sacrifice." In consequence, "there were more gods in Athens than in all the rest of the country, and the Roman satirist hardly exaggerates when he says that it was easier to find a god there than a man." There were innumerable temples, shrines, statues and altars. In the Parthenon stood a huge gold and ivory statue of Athena, "whose gleaming spear-point was visible forty miles away." Elsewhere there were images of Apollo, the city's patron, of Jupiter, Venus, Mercury, Bacchus, Neptune, Diana and Aesculapius. The whole Greek pantheon was there, all the gods of Olympus. And they were beautiful. They were made not only of stone and brass, but of gold, silver, ivory and marble, and they had been elegantly fashioned by the finest Greek sculptors.[6]

In an analogous way, our American mall culture resembles ancient Athens. Instead of the Parthenon, there is the mega-mall. Instead of the image of Jupiter we have a variety of marts and arches. These icons are symbols of our own pantheon: money, stuff, brand identity, and fad. Any disinterested observer of North American culture would have to agree that ours is a consumerist culture, as these authors and titles make clear: *Consumed: How Markets Corrupt Children, Infantilize Adults, and Swallow Citizens Whole* by Benjamin R. Barber; *I Want That! How We All Became Shoppers* by Thomas Hine; and *Affluenza: The All-Consuming Epidemic* by John De Graaf, David Wann, and Thomas H. Naylor.

One of the tools we need for cultural exegesis is the discipline of sociology. As Roman Williams says in chapter 12 of this volume, "Sociology invites us to explore a world that we take for granted, to peel away its many layers of meaning, and to consider how 'the discovery of each new layer changes the perception of the whole.'"[7] Other disciplines that are helpful in exegeting a culture include economics, anthropology, geography, linguistics, psychology, history, religion, folklore, and even ethnomusicology, the study of how music shapes and reveals information about a culture.

Cultural Hermeneutics

Hermes was the Greek god of science, invention, speech, art, writing, and eloquence. Thus, hermeneutics came to mean the art and science of interpreting texts. If we intend to understand an author, it's not sufficient to know what her words say; we need to know what she means by her choice of words. That is, we have to interpret their meaning. So, when someone says "the car is blue," we pay attention to the context of the person who utters those words. Is he pointing to a paved road? Then that might lead us to believe that the car is an automobile instead of a railroad car. Is he contrasting one color of car with another? Then we can take "blue" to refer not to an emotional state of the automobile but to its color. Thus, on the basis of those interpretive clues we believe we know what the author means when he says "the car is blue."

In the same way, cultural hermeneutics should follow cultural exegesis. When we observe the phenomena of the culture—what T. M. Moore calls, "the artifacts, institutions, and conventions with which we surround ourselves"[8]—we must ask, "what do they mean?" How do we make sense of what we see?

In his very helpful volume, *Culture Making: Recovering Our Creative Calling*, cultural analyst Andy Crouch offers five important questions for evaluating every cultural artifact:

- What does this cultural artifact assume about the way the world is?
- What does this cultural artifact assume about the way the world should be?
- What does this cultural artifact make possible?
- What does this cultural artifact make impossible?
- What new forms of culture are created in response to this artifact?[9]

What interpretive tools are we going to use to understand the meaning of our exegetical observations of culture? With respect to biblical hermeneutics, the interpretation of the Bible, several tools are necessary. First, one must have a text to interpret. Therefore, an interpreter would need the latest critical editions of the texts of the Old and New Testaments. Lexicons, grammars, and concordances of the Hebrew and Greek languages are important tools for understanding word meaning and usage. Commentaries on the texts written by learned scholars help interpreters get at the original meaning of the biblical witness. Bible dictionaries, encyclopedias, atlases, and histories help interpreters understand the context, geography, and practices of the ancient world.

When it comes to culture, similarly, some interpretive tools are helpful in understanding the meaning the exegesis may be revealing. While certain aspects of the exegetical disciplines of economics, anthropology, geography, linguistics, psychology, history, etc., will be helpful hermeneutically, the principal tools of culture are philosophy, theology, and ethics. These are tools that help one focus on value, virtue, and vice.

As Harry Lee Poe argues in this volume, the gospel of Jesus of Nazareth with its philosophical, theological, and moral entailments is the interpretive lens through which Christians understand our current milieu. In other words, we interpret our story through the Jesus story. "A culture's worldview," maintains Poe, "involves commonly held core beliefs and values about religion, philosophy, science, government, economics, human relationships, and anything else of concern to culture."[10] Although historically speaking the gospel has had a profound influence on the development of Western culture, by almost any method of reckoning that culture is in the process of imploding. Nearly all of the cultural indicators show that Americans, and most other Westerners, are becoming more violent and less tolerant. Drug and alcohol abuse continue to skyrocket along with their sequelae: spouse abuse, suicide, unemployment, and divorce. Nearly 1 in 100 American adults is in jail or prison! Traditional marriage is being eroded by cohabitation on the one side and homosexual civil unions on the other. Although abortion rates have dropped recently, over 53 million babies have been aborted in the U. S. since 1973, and we now have three states in the union where physician-assisted suicide is legal: Oregon, Washington, and Montana. On and on we could go. It is, as philosopher Roger Scruton has put it, "a world besieged."[11] But, as Poe observes, "The gospel has not merely survived the collapse of Western culture twice before; it has provided the spiritual and intellectual basis for the renewal of Western culture twice before."[12] That brings us to cultural engagement.

Cultural Engagement

Since this is not the first time the people of God have found themselves living in a decaying culture, what might we learn from their history that might inform our future? We should return to the beginning to discover afresh what God's plan was for His people.

Be Culture Makers

God did not make humankind merely to experience or absorb culture; instead He created us to make culture. Consider the teaching of the first and second chapters of Genesis concerning God's creation of human beings:

> Then God said, "Let Us make man in Our image, according to Our likeness. They will rule the fish of the sea, the birds of the sky, the livestock, all the earth, and the creatures that crawl on the earth." So God created man in His own image; He created him in the image of God; He created them male and female. God blessed them, and God said to them, "Be fruitful, multiply, fill the earth, and subdue it. Rule the fish of the sea, the birds of the sky, and every creature that crawls on the earth." God also said, "Look, I have given you every seed-bearing plant on the surface of the entire earth, and every tree whose fruit contains seed. This food will be for you, for all the wildlife of the earth, for every bird of the sky, and for every creature that crawls on the earth—everything having the breath of life in it. I have given every green plant for food." And it was so. God saw all that He had made, and it was very good. Evening came and then morning: the sixth day.
>
> So the heavens and the earth and everything in them were completed. By the seventh day God completed His work that He had done, and He rested on the seventh day from all His work that He had done. God blessed the seventh day and declared it holy, for on it He rested from His work of creation.
>
> These are the records of the heavens and the earth, concerning their creation at the time that the LORD God made the earth and the heavens. No shrub of the field had yet grown on the land, and no plant of the field had yet sprouted, for the LORD God had not made it rain on the land, and there was no man to work the ground. But water would come out of the ground and water the entire surface of the land. Then the LORD God formed the man out of the dust from the ground and breathed the breath of life into his nostrils, and the man became a living being. The LORD God planted a garden in Eden, in the east, and there He placed the man He had formed. The LORD God caused to grow out of the ground every tree pleasing in appearance and good for food, including the tree of life in the middle of the garden, as well as the tree of the knowledge of good and evil. A river went out from Eden to water the garden. From there it divided and became the source of four rivers. The name of the first is Pishon, which flows through the entire land of Havilah, where there is gold. Gold from that land is pure; bdellium and onyx are also there. The name of the second river is Gihon, which flows through the entire land of Cush. The name of the third river is the Tigris, which runs east of Assyria. And the fourth river is the Euphrates.
>
> The LORD God took the man and placed him in the garden of Eden to work it and watch over it. And the LORD God commanded the man, "You are free to eat from any tree of the garden, but you must not eat from the tree of the knowledge of good and evil, for on the day you

> eat from it, you will certainly die." Then the LORD God said, "It is not good for the man to be alone. I will make a helper as his complement." So the LORD God formed out of the ground every wild animal and every bird of the sky, and brought each to the man to see what he would call it. And whatever the man called a living creature, that was its name. The man gave names to all the livestock, to the birds of the sky, and to every wild animal; but for the man no helper was found as his complement. So the LORD God caused a deep sleep to come over the man, and he slept. God took one of his ribs and closed the flesh at that place. Then the LORD God made the rib He had taken from the man into a woman and brought her to the man. And the man said:
>
> This one, at last, is bone of my bone
> and flesh of my flesh;
> this one will be called "woman,"
> for she was taken from man.
>
> This is why a man leaves his father and mother and bonds with his wife, and they become one flesh. Both the man and his wife were naked, yet felt no shame. (Gen 1:26–2:25 HCSB)

Several observations from this lengthy passage of Genesis are in order here. In his intriguing volume *Genesis: The Movie*, Robert Farrar Capon likens the book of Genesis to a film in which God the Father is the producer, His Eternal Word is the star, and the director is the Holy Spirit. It is a Trinity Film.[13] Capon is not being cavalier or sacrilegious in the least by suggesting this way of thinking about Genesis. Rather, he is attempting to capture the fact that we should read Genesis as a story. Although it is historical, it is "not just a sequential narration of occurrences. That would be only a *chronicle*."[14] This narrative has a setting, characters, mystery, intrigue, heroes, villains, and a moral to the story.

The tale is pregnant with meaning. Notice, first, that God created humankind in His own image and likeness to be fruitful and increase in number, to be dominion-stewards over all he had made (Gen 1:26–28). As the psalmist exclaims, "You have made him [humankind] lord over the works of Your hands; you put everything under his feet" (Ps 8:6 HCSB).

We are also told something about the character of this dominion-stewardship: "The LORD God took the man and placed him in the garden of Eden to work it and watch over it" (Gen 2:15). The Hebrew word translated "work" here is easy enough to understand; it is sometimes translated "to till" (Gen 3:23; 4:2,12 NKJV). When a farmer tills the ground, he is working it. "Watch over" describes the nature of Adam's labor. Interestingly, the word is used of the vocation of Abel (Gen 4:9), who *cared for* the land and his flocks. The word is also used of *protecting* persons (Gen 28:15,20). When God appeared in Jacob's dream He said He would "keep him" wherever he went. Finally, the word is used of the priests who "served" God, faithfully carrying out His instructions (Lev 8:35; Num 1:53; 18:5). Thus, humanity's accountability to the Creator to exercise stewardship over the creation restrains against both extremes of worshipping the creation and abusing the creation. Both extreme treatments of creation are to be avoided. Stewardship sees to it that they are.

This text also implies that some form of technology was meant to be a feature of human stewardship. Working and tilling the garden required tools. Tool-making was recognized as a vocation, for Zillah "made all kinds of bronze and iron tools" (Gen 4:22 HCSB). Not only were tools a feature of early human life but procedures of classification were also developed. Adam *named* all the animals, a process that can be taken to be a form of taxonomic classification (Gen 2:20). Adam was, as it were, the first natural scientist.

Alas, as the film continues, the created order did not remain a paradise. Adam and Eve acted irresponsibly by disobeying God's command. Thus a divine curse on the entire order followed human sin. God declared to Adam: "The ground is cursed because of you. You will eat from it by means of painful labor all the days of your life. It will produce thorns and thistles for you, and you will eat the plants of the field" (Gen 3:17b–18). In eschatological hope, the apostle Paul adds: "For we know that the whole creation has been groaning together with labor pains until now" (Rom 8:22). Human sin and its curse wreaked havoc in the universe. Creation is not pristine, therefore. Entropy prevails for now. Because of the fallenness of the world, we should not assume its indestructibility, and because of the eschatological hope we should not pander to its fragility.

Nevertheless, the children of Adam and Eve built boats (Gen 6:14–16), made weapons (Gen 10:9), and planned and built cities (Gen 10:20). These are examples of a dominion kind of stewardship. *Homo sapiens* (human knowers) were also meant to be *Homo faber* (human makers). As Henry Petroski expresses it, "to engineer is human."[15] From this perspective, as Union University professor Jeanette Russ says in this volume, "A Christian engineer is in a unique position to appreciate the benefits of technology while also understanding that our fallen world makes it prone to abuse."[16]

The creation mandate not only obliged humanity to make artifacts but to make music, art, science, literature, and more. This has led cultural analysts Ken Myers and Andy Crouch to say: "Culture is what we make of the world."[17] Or, on a societal level, noted sociologist Peter Berger suggests that, "Every human society is an enterprise of world-building."[18] Culture is, in this sense, what human beings cultivate.

Two additional observations leap out from this passage that should inform our thinking about making culture. First, God made humanity for vocation. Work is not, as some people seem to suspect, a result of the curse for Adam's sin. The drudgery of work—"by the sweat of your brow" (Gen 3:19 HCSB)—is an aspect of the fall, but work itself is not. The work of our hands is an honorable aspect of the creation mandate. As with Adam and Eve before their sin, "working" and "tilling" are ways of exercising creativity, innovation, and of bringing everything under proper dominion. Christians, of all people, should celebrate, reward, and encourage hard work.

Just after World War II had ended, Dorothy L. Sayers (1893–1957), the Christian writer and apologist wrote:

> It is the business of the Church to recognize that the secular vocation, as such, is sacred. Christian people, and particularly perhaps the Christian clergy, must get it firmly into their heads that when a man or woman is called to a particular job of secular work, that is as true a vocation as though he or she were called to specifically religious work. The Church must concern herself not only with such questions as the just price and proper working conditions: she must concern herself with seeing that the work itself is such as a human being can perform without degradation—that no one is required by economic or any other considerations to devote himself to work that is contemptible, soul-destroying, or harmful. It is not right for her to acquiesce in the notion that a man's life is divided into the time he spends on his work and the time he spends in serving God. He must be able to serve God in his work, and the work itself must be accepted and respected as the medium of divine creation.
>
> In nothing has the Church so lost her hold on reality as in her failure to understand and respect the secular vocation. She has allowed work and religion to become separate departments, and is astonished to find that, as a result, the secular work of the world is turned to purely selfish and destructive ends, and that the greater part of the world's intelligent

> workers have become irreligious, or at least, uninterested in religion.
>
> But is it astonishing? How can anyone remain interested in a religion which seems to have no concern with nine-tenths of his life? The Church's approach to an intelligent carpenter is usually confined to exhorting him not to be drunk and disorderly in his leisure hours, and to come to church on Sundays. What the Church should be telling him is this: that the very first demand that his religion makes on him is that he should make good tables.
>
> Church by all means, and decent forms of amusement, certainly—but what use is all that if in . . . his life and occupation he is insulting God with bad carpentry? No crooked table legs or ill-fitting drawers ever, I dare swear, came out of the carpenter's shop at Nazareth. Nor, if they did, could anyone believe that they were made by the same hand that made heaven and earth. No piety in the work will compensate for work that is not true to itself; for any work that is untrue to its own technique is a living lie.[19]

Second, we observe from this text that work is not all that people are for. Just as God rested, so we must rest from our labors. Echoing Genesis, Jewish theologian Abraham Joshua Heschel said, "The Sabbath is a day for the sake of life. . . . The Sabbath is not for the sake of the weekdays; the weekdays are for the sake of the Sabbath. It is not an interlude but the climax of living. . . . Labor is a craft, but perfect rest is an art."[20] Indeed, if all we do is work, other facets of culture suffer. Where is the time for music, art, conversation, and worship? Without attending to a Sabbath rest, there is little place for contemplation, prayer, and even physical refreshment. In fact, leisure is, in a real sense, as Josef Pieper has written, "the basis of culture."[21] Without it, culture is slavish. We are not made to work all the time, grinding out our days in endless toil. Life has a rhythm set by God Himself, who rested on the seventh day. And although what has become known as the Protestant work ethic is rooted in Christian theology, it is not all there is to the story. My wise friend and former colleague, theologian Graham Cole, often reminds me that we are creatures before we are Christians.

Seek the Welfare of the City

Alas, we no longer live in an Edenic paradise. The world is tragically fallen. Christians are exiles in a foreign land. How are we to live as strangers and pilgrims? Throughout most of their history the people of God have known what it meant to exist as a minority culture. Even today, most Christians live in cultures that either tolerate them or are hostile toward them. Only in American and a few other Western countries do Christians enjoy majority status. Even where we are a numerical majority, we often still occupy cultural minority status. The legacy of Christianity in the West is slowly sinking, and rising in its place is either a virulent religious pluralism calling on all religions to "coexist" as if there were no meaningful differences between Christianity and the other religions, or an increasingly robust and sometimes hostile Islamic culture, taking the world by procreation as much as evangelization.

So, how are Christians to live as exiles? Let's examine four historical examples: two from the Old and New Testaments and two from more recent history.

Jeremiah 29. In Jeremiah 29, we have a letter, probably written in 597 BC, by the "weeping prophet" to the people of God who were taken captive under King Nebuchadnezzar and deported to Babylon. The city of Babylon was a very different culture from what the Jews had known in Jerusalem. There was no temple to the one true and living God. God's law was not observed by the state. False prophets and diviners sought to deceive the people, especially Shemaiah, who is rebuked by name.

Nevertheless, despite the fact that His people were in a foreign land, God tells them through Jeremiah to settle down and get to the business of life.

> This is what the LORD of hosts, the God of Israel, says to all the exiles I deported from Jerusalem to Babylon: Build houses and live in them. Plant gardens and eat their produce. Take wives and have sons and daughters. Take wives for your sons and give your daughters to men in marriage so that they may bear sons and daughters. Multiply there; do not decrease. Seek the welfare of the city I have deported you to. Pray to the LORD on its behalf, for when it has prosperity, you will prosper. (Jer 29:4–7 HCSB)

In a time of exile, God's people were to work and build, marry and have children, and seek the welfare of the city of Babylon. They were even instructed to pray to God on behalf of the city. This is extraordinary! Instead of praying for its overthrow and working clandestinely for its destruction, the people of God were actually to pray, work, and live for the good of Babylon. What God said was that "when it has prosperity, you will prosper" (v. 7). I take that to mean that when God's people work for the common good not only do others benefit, but they benefit too. Conversely, when

God's people selfishly pursue their own good, they end up not only alienating others, but making things worse for themselves.

Were they to forget God, His promises, their land, and their families in other places? Of course not. As a matter of fact, Jeremiah's letter is followed close on its heels by a word of promise for the restoration of Israel and Judah, the turning of their mourning into joy, and a firm hope grounded in a new covenant (Jeremiah 30–31). They were doubtless to live in anticipation of the fulfillment of God's good and gracious promises. In the meantime, however, they were to seek the good of the city and its inhabitants. There is a powerful lesson here about living in exile. One important strategy for cultural engagement, therefore, requires contributing to the common good, seeking the welfare of the city.

1 Peter 1–3. In his rich exploration of the role of first-century Christians in the Greco-Roman world, biblical scholar Bruce Winter argues that the public life of the early Christians was to be characterized by a civic consciousness in which Christians, like the people of God in Jeremiah's day, sought the welfare of the city. "To stand in 'the true grace of God' demanded a deep commitment to the welfare of the city within the framework of a living eschatological hope. That enabled the Christian to place personal concerns second to the needs of others in the city," says Winter in his book *Seek the Welfare of the City: Christians as Benefactors and Citizens*.[22]

As the apostle Peter writes to Christians who were "temporary residents dispersed" in various lands (1 Pet 1:1 HCSB), he calls them to live lives worthy of the people of God. Because their salvation and inheritance were secure and they were being preserved until the day when they would receive what God had stored up for them with Christ in heaven (1:3–10), they could focus on being "obedient children" (1:14 HCSB) and rid themselves "of all malice, all deceit, hypocrisy, envy, and all slander" (2:1 HCSB).

Winter points out first that "the fundamental purpose of the elect race, the royal priesthood, the holy nation . . . was to declare the virtues or characteristics of the One who called them out of darkness into his marvelous light (2:9–10)."[23] In other words, their good works were meant to point to the greatness of the God who not only had called them to Himself, but who had drawn them together for this common purpose. This is very reminiscent of the words of Jesus in the Sermon on the Mount when He said: ". . . let your light shine before men, so that they may see your good works and give glory to your Father in heaven" (Matt 5:16).

Those good works were to be observed in honorable conduct so that when opponents of Christ and His gospel speak evil of those who bear His name, the detractors must do so in the face of the good deeds of God's people who are "strangers and temporary residents" (1 Pet 2:11–12 HCSB). "God does good, because good needs to be done. His pilgrim people must do the same."[24]

Furthermore, argues Winter, "The Christian citizen's duties were discharged in part by obedience to civic ordinances."[25] So Peter says that the dispersed Christians, even though dwelling in a foreign land, were to "submit to every human authority because of the Lord, whether to the Emperor as the supreme authority or to governors as those sent out by him to punish those who do what is evil and to praise those who do what is good" (1 Pet 2:13). He goes on to give specific instructions to household servants and to husbands and wives (2:18–3:7). Even if called upon to suffer unjustly, the Christians were not to repay evil with evil (3:8), but with gentleness, respect, and a good conscience (3:16) to bless those around them, following the example of their Lord Jesus Christ who "suffered for sins once for all, the righteous for the unrighteous, that He might bring us to God" (3:18 HCSB).

Athenagoras. We see this pattern lived out among the early Christians. During the second century, Christians faced increasing persecution at the hands of the Roman Empire—an unjust oppression that resulted in the torture of Christians in the Coliseum and a great deal of suffering elsewhere. Christians endured this persecution due to a host of false rumors and trumped-up charges, including that they were atheists, incestuous, and cannibalistic. The charge of atheism came from the fact that they would not recognize the emperor as divine. Because they called one another "brother" and "sister" and then married, the charge of incest was leveled against them. They were called cannibals because they ate the flesh and drank the blood of Christ in their celebration of the Eucharist. Of course these are profound misunderstandings of the early Christians' doctrine and practice.

In the face of these misrepresentations, Athenagoras, a pagan philosopher turned Christian apologist, wrote his moving treatise, *A Plea for the Christians*, as an open letter to the emperors Aurelius and Commodus around AD 177. He implored his secular superiors to examine the lives of Christians, for their conduct was open for audit. First, he maintained that "we commit no wrong" but "are of all men most piously and righteously disposed towards the Deity and towards your government."[26] Contrary to the accusation that Christianity foments civil disobedience and discord, the philosopher reported that Christians "pray for your government, that you may, as is most equitable, receive the kingdom, son from father, and that your empire may receive increase and addition, all men becoming subject to your sway."[27] The point was clear: Christians can be at the same time followers of Jesus and contribute to the common good, obedient to both divine and civil law. Second, he argued that sexual promiscuity could not be named among them, for they believe "it is not lawful among us to indulge even a lustful look."[28] Moreover, he contended, believers do not engage in adultery or countenance divorce. Finally, Christians demonstrated such respect for the sanctity of human life that they said "that those women who use drugs to bring on abortion commit murder, and will have to give an account to God." In fact, they regarded "the very foetus in the womb as a created being, and therefore the object of God's care."[29] So they could not be guilty of cannibalism.

This is a remarkable story not least because Athenagoras was willing to put the morality of these Christians on the line without fear of being embarrassed. Sadly, Athenagoras could not write a similar letter today. But when Christians most faithfully follow the Lord Jesus, they most transparently reveal His glory before the eyes of a watching world.

The Clapham Group. A final historical example of a cadre of Christians who were committed to seeking the welfare of the city is John Venn, William Wilberforce, and the other members of the so-called Clapham Sect. William Wilberforce (1759–1833) is perhaps most famously remembered as the member of British parliament who was responsible for the abolition of the slave trade in England. He did not act alone, however, and the exploits of the group went far beyond ending slavery.

When, as a young elected official, Wilberforce became a Christian he recorded in his personal journal: "God Almighty has set before me two great objects, the suppression of the slave trade and the reformation of manners."[30] And fully 46 years after his first attempt, and only three days before his death in 1823, the bill to abolish slavery in the British Empire passed its second reading in the House of Commons.

Among Wilberforce's coconspirators were the pastor of Clapham Church, John Venn; an educator and child advocate, Hannah More; the economist and banker, Henry Thornton; civil servant and biblical scholar Granville Sharp; and John Shore, who in 1792 was appointed governor-general of India and was the first president of the British and Foreign Bible Society. Probably one of the best-known members of the company was John Newton, the former slave trader and author of the hymn *Amazing Grace*.

This was a very close-knit group of Christians who made it their aim to develop relationships with politicians and others of influence. They were committed to God, to their families, and to one another. They were also dedicated to the well-being of their community and the world. As Michael Hennell chronicles in his excellent volume, *John Venn and the Clapham Sect*,[31] this little fraternity was remarkable in their achievements, many of which are still with us. Together, they:

- Formed the Clapham Armed Association to protect the neighborhood
- Helped found the *Christian Observer* magazine
- Established the Church Missionary Society
- Worked to abolish the African slave trade
- Called for reform of child labor laws
- Helped establish Foundling Hospital for children
- Built a hostel for former prostitutes with job training
- Promoted vaccination of children
- Founded the Society for the Betterment of the Poor

In language mirrored from 1 Peter, John Venn declared in a sermon at Clapham Church:

> Religion is not merely an act of homage paid upon our bended knees to God; it is not confined to the closet and the church, nor is it restrained to the hours of the sabbath; it is a general principle extending to a man's whole conduct in every transaction and in every place. I know no mistake which is more dangerous than that which lays down devotional feelings alone as the test of true religion. . . . Let us be convinced that all prayer, all preaching, all knowledge, are but means to attain a superior end; and that end the sanctification of the heart and of all the principles on which we are daily acting. Till our Christianity appears in our conversation, in our business, in our pleasures, in the aims and

> objects of our life, we have not attained a conformity to the image of our Saviour, nor have we learned His Gospel aright.[32]

By no means does living as exiles mean passivity. Jeremiah did not endorse passivity, Peter did not encourage passivity, the early Christian did not exemplify passivity, and the Clapham group was anything but passive. Living as exiles means actively living as those who are faithful to God through the risen Christ in the power of the Holy Spirit. It means seeking the welfare of others above one's own welfare. And it means investing one's life and energies in doing so for the glory of our great God and King in the realization that we have an inheritance stored up for us and we are being preserved by God until the day when it will be revealed to us in heaven. In the words of the old spiritual, "This world is not our own; we're just a passin' through." But rather than leading us to indolence, that reality gives us the courage to engage the culture for the common good and the glory of Christ.

Engaging the Academy

In a book on faith and learning, we undoubtedly need to deal, at least briefly, with engagement with culture of the academy itself. Just as in the larger culture, we are to be culture makers in the academy. My colleagues have been exploring what that means in each of the chapters preceding this one. Whether in philosophy, theology, or history; whether in biology, chemistry, or political science; and whether in engineering, computer science, pharmacy, or nursing, we should be "working" and "tilling" the academic soil and cultivating the life of the mind.

An Incarnational Community

In every important way a community of scholarship, which is what a university is, should be a community. And a Christian university is a learning community and a liturgical community. But even prior to that, we are an incarnational community.

One definition of a community is a group of people living in the same locality under the same government. Or as the farmer-philosopher-poet Wendell Berry has put it, a community "'has to do first of all with belonging': 'It is a group of people who belong to one another and to their place.'"[33] That is true of a Christian academic community like Union University. We share a common commitment to a body of authoritative truth revealed in the Old and New Testaments and most compellingly in the person of Jesus of Nazareth, the Son of the living God, through His Spirit. If this is not true, we might remain a university, but we could not be identified as Christian. Thus, we are a community of like-minded persons who love, worship, and serve the personal trinitarian God.

This emphasis on persons should, in my view, characterize a Christian university education. We are, in that sense, an incarnational university. In their volume, *The Passionate Intellect: Incarnational Humanism and the Future of University Education*, Norman Klassen and Jens Zimmerman helpfully put some flesh (pun intended) on this idea. For too long, they argue, we have been dualistic about Christian education, separating essential elements of our humanity. "For the Christian," they submit, "all spheres of human existence and creation are united in Christ."[34]

In God's becoming human, He "affirms the intrinsic worth of human existence." God not only made us in His image and after His likeness, but, God in human flesh has sacralized our humanity. The worth of every individual is affirmed in Christ. It seems to me that this requires that we understand the Christian university as a distinctly human community. Faculty, students, administration, and other staff are imagers of God whose lives matter to God and ought to matter to us. This is not merely an appeal to be "nice," although there is much to be said for being decent human beings. Rather, the incarnation calls on us to recognize the priority of persons. The Christian university is not to serve itself or exist for itself; it is to exist to serve the personal God and those made in God's image. We therefore belong to God, and we belong to one another.

Furthermore, implicit in this understanding of the university as an incarnational community is the reality that, of all people, humility should mark our lives. The knowledge we gain, the information we receive, the ideas we employ are gifts—donations of the self-revealing God and bequests of those who have gone before us. "Knowledge inflates with pride, but love builds up," says the apostle Paul (1 Cor 8:1 HCSB). Therefore, as members of an incarnational community, we offer ourselves as "living sacrifices" both to God and to others, whether it is to our students, our faculty, our staff, or to the world. Because we are a Christian community, we too seek the welfare of the city.

Finally, the incarnational nature of the Christian university carries implications for the so-called delivery of education. Although educational technologies can be helpfully employed in Christian education, at the heart, ours is an embodied, personal, flesh-and-blood enterprise. In this case our Christology informs our anthropology which in turn informs our educational methodology. Christian higher education is incarnational and personal, or it is not Christian in my view. This is so, not least because from the Christian worldview knowledge does not serve knowledge. We know in order to worship the one who is Truth, and we learn in order to love our neighbor as ourselves.

Secondly, say Klassen and Zimmerman, "God's affirmation of human nature in the incarnation also points to the intrinsic worth of creation."[35] Because this is so, we find warrant for all of the natural sciences, among other things.

> Creation and matter are themselves worthy of investigation because, by paying attention to them, we honor the Creator who is at work in them. Even though the actual design of the universe has turned out much more complex than science had imagined, science continues to operate on the basic assumption that the universe is somehow rationally designed in patterns that yield explanations for the empirical observations we make. If we abandon this notion, science itself becomes futile. If we embrace it, however, we have good grounds for interdisciplinary work.[36]

And by its very nature, the Christian university should be interdisciplinary, seeking to discern the unity of truth. Some time ago, Columbia University professor Mark C. Taylor called for "The End of the University as We Know It."[37] He advocated the restructuring of the curriculum, the abolition of departments, increased collaboration among institutions, transformation of the dissertation system, expansion of the range of professional options for graduate students, and mandatory retirement and the abolition of tenure for professors. Although his prescription for university education is too radical to be imaginable, it reveals a keen diagnosis of some of the problems facing contemporary higher education.

Among the formidable problems we encounter in the university are the knowledge silos. Despite the fact that our very name—university—is meant to signal the unity of knowledge and truth, because of the ways most of us have been formed academically and the ways we are promoted professionally, we tend more often than not to operate within the narrow confines of our own disciplines, subdisciplines, concentrations, and specialties. We have to make a concerted effort to think holistically and interdisciplinarily. Often, our efforts to convene discussions across disciplines are plagued with misunderstandings because the vocabularies of our disciplines are so disparate and we lack a university Esperanto. Academic culture suffers when we work in silos.

Admittedly, we live in a world where there is increasingly specialized information. If there was a period when a university professor could be a generalist who knew most of what there was to know about most things, those days are long gone. Christian universities, therefore, must redouble their efforts to build interdisciplinary conversations among faculty members and students. Our daily schedules and our semester calendars reflect what we value, and if we value interdisciplinarity as a crucial facet of incarnational community, we will make time for it.

Third, "the incarnation demonstrates that truth is always interpretation," maintain Klassen and Zimmerman.[38] This is not a denial of the reality or accessibility of truth but a recognition that truth is always mediated. Knowing God and knowing His world is hard work, requiring the best of our critical tools. The personal God speaks to us through the means of human language and a human person. His revelation of Himself in creation comes mediated through rocks, trees, and animals. So whether we study texts or historical records or stars or DNA, there is no direct and immediate knowledge of God. "For now we see in a mirror, dimly," says Paul, "but then we will see face to face. Now I know only in part; then I will know fully, even as I have been fully known" (1 Cor 13:12 NRSV). What this means, among other things, is that we must continue to learn, clarify, study, examine, revise, and reform until the consummation of all things. The university is needed as long as Jesus tarries.

A Liturgical Community

The incarnational nature of the university also means that we are a liturgical community. We do not learn and transmit learning only through information transfer. We also learn through desiring and doing, through ritual and liturgy. "Because our hearts are oriented primarily by desire, by what we love," says Jamie Smith at Calvin College, "and because those desires are shaped and molded by the habit-forming practices in which we participate, it is the rituals and practices . . . that shape our imaginations and how we orient ourselves to the world."[39]

Although Smith develops at length the relationship between liturgies, practices, and rituals, his central task is to "argue for a more affective picture of the human person that situates and relativizes the importance of the intellect and instead places (renewed) emphasis on the 'heart' as the affective, embodied, pre-conscious core of the human person that drives and shapes our action and behavior."[40] He offers a counterbalance to what he perceives to be an overly rationalistic, intellectualized orientation to evangelical Christian worldview thinking. He argues that practices, ritualized behavior, and community expectations have a much greater impact on worldview than most have acknowledged. What we think with our minds informs what we do with our bodies, and what we do with our bodies informs how we think. Orthopraxy contributes to orthodoxy.

Another way to make the case for a more holistic, incarnational anthropology and, therefore, a more holistic view of thinking about the university, is to examine the roles of focal things and focal practices. Building on the work of philosopher Albert Borgmann, theologian Brent Waters distinguishes between focal things and focal practices. A focal thing is "an objective reality that shapes the values and behavior of those whose attention is seized by its presence. A focal practice consists of acts that express and perform the convictions and behavior that are formed by those devoted to the focal thing."[41]

According to Borgmann and Waters, a family meal is an example of a focal thing, a reality that shapes the behavior of those who participate in it. Family meals are not merely about the consumption of calories but about gathering as family, sharing a common history, traditions, and conversation. The meal unites individual members to a larger network of social relationships. The family meal has a temporal beginning and end; it is a focal thing in that sense. Focal practices are those behaviors that underwrite, facilitate, and inform a focal thing. Careful preparation of the meal, proper setting of the table, the giving of thanks for the bounty, and convivial conversation are examples of those practices. Moreover, the family meal is (or was) the place where the story of the family is told, where the moral and religious values of the family are expressed and where the expectations of the family are shaped in embodied relationships.

Just as with Jamie Smith's liturgies, focal things and practices do not so much pick out specific intellectual affirmations as they shape human behaviors, activities and rituals. Children, for instance, do not learn first about the philosophical facts of the family as an institution; they first enjoy the experience of the family. They are not first taught an abstract definition of "family" as a social institution; they themselves and their ideas of family are formed primarily by the experience of living in a family.

Similarly, the incarnational nature of the Christian university will be recognized by its ritual and liturgy. Are our community values revealed in community liturgies? Do we take seriously the gathering of the university for governance (in faculty meetings), worship (in chapel), and celebration (in commencement)? Do we create informal opportunities for faculty and students to shape one another? Do we share meals together? Is the unity of the university revealed in a common life?

The answers to these questions are important markers of the kind of culture we value in an incarnational university community. One of the clearest indicators of what we value is how we construct our calendars and carve up our days. Thus, there is even a way of thinking Christianly about class schedules and semester calendars, about class size and syllabus construction. The liturgies of a university-based community development project or international mission trip are not extraneous activities, but vitally important focal practices that underscore our affirmation of the incarnation. In an incarnational university the cocurriculum is as important as the curriculum.

Creating a Great Commandment and Great Commission Culture

I have tried to argue that cultural engagement in both the wider and narrower senses of that term involves the prerequisites of cultural exegesis and cultural hermeneutics. In reality, the exegesis and hermeneutics of culture, like engaging culture, are ongoing projects. Culture is not static, especially in a hypertechnological, consumerist, sexualized, and global culture like that of the West. So, cultural exegesis, hermeneutics, and engagement require dexterity, suppleness, and wisdom.

Our engagement with culture should reflect the Great Commandment to love God with all our hearts, souls, minds, and strength, and our neighbor as ourselves. I maintain that to do so we must be faithful to the creation mandate or so-called cultural mandate. We are culture makers, and we should employ our very best efforts to make culture well. But in another sense we also inhabit culture—sometimes a culture that, as exiles, we did not create. Neighbor love requires, therefore, that we seek the welfare of those with whom we dwell. This requires also taking seriously the Great Commission. We are to make disciples of Jesus of all the nations, baptizing them in His name and teaching them to follow His will. This is not always easy and will require enormous grace, perseverance, and courage. We are not called to be passive, however, but actively engaged for the glory of our God.

Likewise, we should employ the same tools of exegesis, hermeneutics, and engagement in the university community. Here, however, we share a common set of core affirmations. Incarnating those commitments in ways that reflect and respect our common humanity is the challenge. But because the Christian university is an incarnational community, we are called to love the personal trinitarian God, those who are made in His image, and the world He has created. We are a Great Commandment institution. Furthermore, since our liturgies matter, we also send those who are shaped and formed by the university to fulfill the Great Commission.

Creating an environment where Great Commandment and Commission are part of the culture is not for the faint of heart, but it is also required for faithful, Spirit-filled followers of the incarnate God in Jesus Christ.

Questions for Further Reflection

1. How have Christians as culture makers shaped the Western world of science, technology, education, innovation, philanthropy, and service to meet human needs?
2. What is the difference between a utilitarian emphasis on the "greatest good for the greatest number" and Christian attention to the common good?
3. Suggest additional strategies for serving the common good.

4. In what ways might university focal practices more consistently reflect the values and focal things of the university?

Resources for Further Study

Carson, D. A. *Christ and Culture Revisited.* Grand Rapids: Eerdmans, 2008.

Eberly, Don, and Sam Brownback. *Building a Healthy Culture: Strategies for an American Renaissance*. New York: Hudson Institute, 2001.

Elliott, Barbara J. *Street Saints: Renewing America's Cities*. Philadelphia: Templeton Foundation Press, 2004.

Henry, Douglas, and Michael Beaty, eds. *Christianity and the Soul of the University: Faith as a Foundation for Intellectual Community.* Grand Rapids: Baker Academic, 2006.

Hunter, James Davison. *To Change the World: The Irony, Tragedy, and Possibility of Christianity in the Late Modern World.* New York: Oxford University Press, 2010.

Long, D. Stephen. *Theology and Culture: A Guide to the Discussion.* Eugene, OR: Cascade Books, 2008.

McGrath, Alister. *The Passionate Intellect: Christian Faith and the Discipleship of the Mind.* Downers Grove: InterVarsity, 2010.

Moore, T. M., and Richard John Neuhaus. *Culture Matters: A Call for Consensus on Christian Cultural Engagement.* Grand Rapids: Brazos, 2007.

Endnotes

[1] Edward Burnett Tylor, *Primitive Culture: Researches into the Development of Mythology, Philosophy, Religion, Language, Art, and Custom* (New York: H. Holt, 1871).

[2] Clifford Geertz, *The Interpretation of Cultures* (New York: Basic Books, 1973), 448.

[3] Lesslie Newbigin, *Foolishness to the Greeks: The Gospel and Western Culture* (Grand Rapids: Eerdmans, 1986), 3.

[4] Kathryn Tanner, *Theories of Culture: A New Agenda for Theology* (Minneapolis: Fortress Press, 1997), 70.

[5] John Stott, *The Spirit, the Church, and the World: The Message of Acts* (Downers Grove: InterVarsity Press), 277.

[6] Ibid.

[7] Roman R. Williams, "An Invitation to Sociology," in this volume.

[8] T. M. Moore, *Culture Matters: A Call for Christian Consensus on Christian Cultural Engagement* (Grand Rapids: Brazos, 2007), 11.

[9] Andy Crouch, *Culture Making: Recovering Our Creative Calling* (Downers Grove: InterVarsity, 2008), 29–30.

[10] Harry Lee Poe, "The Gospel, Worldview, and Christian Higher Education," in this volume.

[11] Roger Scruton, *Culture Counts: Faith and Feeling in a World Besieged* (New York: Encounter, 2007).
[11] Poe, "The Gospel, Worldview, and Christian Higher Education."
[13] Robert Farrar Capon, *Genesis: The Movie* (Grand Rapids: Eerdmans, 2003), 3.
[14] Ibid., xiii.
[15] Henry Petroski, *To Engineer Is Human: The Role of Failure in Successful Design* (New York: Vintage, 1992).
[16] Jeanette Russ, "Christian Scholarship in Math, Physics, and Engineering," in this volume.
[17] See Kenneth Myers, *All God's Children and Blue Suede Shoes: Christians and Popular Culture* (Wheaton: Crossway, 1989); Crouch, *Culture Making*.
[18] Peter Berger, *The Sacred Canopy: Elements of a Sociological Theory of Religion* (Garden City, NY: Anchor, 1990), 3.
[19] Dorothy L. Sayers, "Why Work?" in *Creed or Chaos?* (New York: Harcourt, Brace, 1949), 56–57.
[20] Abraham Joshua Heschel, *The Sabbath* (Boston: Shambhala Publications, 2003), 2–3.
[21] Josef Pieper, *Leisure, The Basis of Culture* (South Bend: St. Augustine's Press, 1998).
[22] Bruce W. Winter, *Seek the Welfare of the City: Christians as Benefactors and Citizens* (Grand Rapids: Eerdmans, 1994), 19.
[23] Ibid., 20.
[24] Ibid., 23.
[25] Ibid., 21.
[26] Athenagoras, *A Plea for the Christians* 1, in *The Ante-Nicene Fathers*, ed. Alexander Roberts and James Donaldson (New York: Charles Scriber's Sons, 1905).
[27] Ibid., 32.
[28] Ibid., 37.
[29] Ibid., 35.
[30] Kevin Belmonte, *Hero for Humanity: A Biography of William Wilberforce* (Colorado Springs, CO: NavPress, 2002), 102.
[31] Michael Hennell, *John Venn and the Clapham Sect* (London: Lutterworth Press, 1958).
[32] John Venn, *Sermons*, vol. 2: 238–39, quoted in Hennell, *John Venn and the Clapham Sect*, 205.
[33] Wendell Berry, "Sex, Economy, Freedom, and Community," in *Sex, Economy, Freedom, and Community: Eight Essays* (New York: Pantheon, 1992), 23, cited in Stanley Hauerwas, "What Would a Christian University Look Like? Some Tentative Answers Inspired by Wendell Berry," in *Wendell Berry and Religion: Heaven's Earthly Life*, ed. Joel James Shuman and L. Roger Owens (Lexington: University Press of Kentucky, 2009), 22.
[34] Norman Klassen and Jens Zimmerman, *The Passionate Intellect: Incarnational Humanism and the Future of University Education* (Grand Rapids: Baker Academic, 2006), 149.
[35] Ibid., 152.
[36] Ibid.

[37] Mark C. Taylor, "The End of the University as We Know It," *The New York Times*, April 26, 2009, A23.
[38] Klassen and Zimmerman, *The Passionate Intellect*, 153.
[39] James K. A. Smith, *Desiring the Kingdom: Worship, Worldview, and Cultural Formation* (Grand Rapids: Baker Academic, 2009), 25.
[40] James K. A. Smith, "From Christian Scholarship to Christian Education," *Christian Scholar's Review* 39 (2010): 230.
[41] Brent Waters, *This Mortal Flesh: Incarnation and Bioethics* (Grand Rapids: Brazos, 2009), 43–44.

Name Index

C

D

E

F

G

H

Q

R

S

T

Subject Index